Visual C++™ 1.5

By EXAMPLE

que

Greg Perry

Jim Ross

Visual C++ 1.5 By Example

© 1994 by Que

Library of Congress Catalog Card Number: 94-65330

ISBN: 1-56529-687-7

98 97 96 95 94   9 8 7 6 5 4 3 2 1

Interpretation of the printing code: the rightmost double-digit number is the year of the book's printing; the rightmost single-digit number, the number of the book's printing. For example, a printing code of 94-1 shows that the first printing of the book occurred in 1994.

The examples in this book should work with Visual C++ versions 1.0 and 1.5.

Publisher: *David P. Ewing*

Director of Publishing: *Michael Miller*

Publishing Director: *Joseph B. Wikert*

Managing Editor: *Michael Cunningham*

Marketing Manager: *Ray Robinson*

Publishing Manager
Brad Koch

Product Development Specialist
Bryan Gambrel

Production Editor
Colleen Rainsberger

Technical Editor
Ed Toupin

Book Designer
Amy Peppler-Adams

Indexer
C. Small

Production
*Angela Bannan, Cameron Booker
Anne Dickerson, Karen Dodson,
Denny Hager, Carla Hall,
Bob LaRoche, Joy Dean Lee,
Beth Lewis, Aren Munk,
Wendy Ott, Alan Palmore,
Linda Quigley, Nanci Sears Perry,
Caroline Roop, Susan Shepard,
Becky Tapley, Michael Thomas,
Tina Trettin, Donna Winter,
Lillian Yates*

Composed in *Palatino* and *MCPdigital* by Prentice Hall Computer Publishing.
Screen reproductions were created by using Collage Complete.

Acknowledgments

The C++ programming language continues to grow stronger daily. I have taught hundreds of students the C++ programming language, and I grow fonder of the language with each course. The C++ programming language is now the main-stream computer course in colleges and a much-needed language for use in the computer industry. I hope that this book helps fill a niche not found in the vast number of C++ books currently in print—that niche being a straightforward, friendly, and comfortable feel that provides a stepping-stone style for beginners to C++.

I appreciate Stacy Hiquet and Joseph Wikert at Prentice Hall for trusting me completely with the direction and style of this book.

G. M. P.

I could not have completed this without the loving support of my wife, Brenda, and Candy, our ward. They have been helpful, supportive, and above all, loving, during this project. I thank them from the bottom of my heart for just being there.

I wish to express deepest gratitude to Joseph Wikert at Prentice Hall for giving me the opportunity to do this book, to Bryan Gambrel and Colleen Rainsberger for their help and guidance, and to Ed Toupin for his assistance.

J. R.

About the Authors

Greg Perry has been a programmer and trainer for the past 14 years. He received his first degree in computer science and then a Masters in corporate finance. He is currently a professor of computer science at Tulsa Junior College, as well as a computer consultant and lecturer. Greg Perry is the author of 10 other computer books. In addition, he has written articles for several publications, including *PC World*, *Data Training*, and *Inside First Publisher*. He has traveled in several countries, attending computer conferences and trade shows, and is fluent in nine computer languages.

Jim Ross has been a programmer for the past 24 years, the past nine of which have been spent with microcomputers. He currently maintains and writes network utilities for Nations Bank in Dallas, Texas, where he has also been an internal instructor in beginning dBASE and microcomputer basics.

Trademark Acknowledgments

Overview

Contents

Contents

Contents

Contents

Part VII Data Structures

Contents

Introduction

Visual C++ By Example is one of several books in Que's line of *By Example* titles. The philosophy of these books is a simple one: computer programming concepts are best taught with multiple examples. Command descriptions, format syntax, and language references are not enough for a newcomer to learn a programming language. Only by looking at many examples, where new commands are used immediately, and by running sample programs can programming students get more than just a "feel" for the language.

Who Should Use This Book?

This book teaches on three levels of examples: beginning, intermediate, and advanced. Text accompanies the many examples at each level. If you are new to C++, and even if you are new to computers, this book attempts to put you at ease and gradually builds your C++ programming skills. If you are an expert at C++, this book tries to provide a few extras for you along the way.

The Book's Philosophy

This book focuses on programming *correctly* in C++ by teaching structured programming techniques and proper program design. Emphasis is always placed on a program's readability instead of "tricks of the trade" code examples. In this changing world, programs should be clear, properly structured, and well documented, and this book does not waver from the importance of this philosophy.

The book teaches you C++ by using a holistic approach; you learn the mechanics of the language, tips and warnings, how to use C++ for different types of applications, as well as a little of the history and interesting "sidebars" of the computing industry.

Although many other books build single applications, adding to them a little at a time with each chapter, the chapters of this book are stand-alone chapters showing you complete programs that fully illustrate the commands discussed. There is a program for every level of reader, from beginning to advanced.

Over 200 sample program listings are provided. These programs show ways that C++ can be used for personal finance, school and business record keeping, math and science, and general-purpose applications that almost everybody with a computer can use. This wide variety of programs shows you that C++ is a very powerful language which is easy to learn and use.

Overview of This Book

Visual C++ By Example is divided into 10 parts. Part I introduces you to the C++ environment and introductory programming concepts. Starting with Part II, the book presents the C++ programming language commands and library functions. After mastering the language, you can then use the book as a handy reference. When you need help with a specific C++ programming problem, turn to the appropriate area which describes that part of the language to see various examples of code.

The following sections describe the parts of this book.

Part I: Introduction to C++

Part I explains what C++ is by describing a brief history of the C++ programming language and then presenting an overview of C++'s advantages over other languages. This part of the book describes your computer's hardware, how you develop C++ programs, and the steps you follow to enter and run programs. You will write your first C++ program in the fourth chapter.

Part II: Using C++ Operators

Part II covers the entire set of C++ operators. The rich assortment of operators (more than in any other programming language except APL) makes up for the fact that the C++ programming language is very small. The operators and their order of precedence are more important to C++ than to most programming languages.

Part III: C++ Constructs

C++ data processing is most powerful because of the looping, comparison, and selection constructs that C++ offers. This part of the book shows you how to write programs that correctly flow with control computations to produce accurate and readable code.

Part IV: Variable Scope and Modular Programming

To support true structured programming techniques, C++ must allow for local and global variables, as well as offer several ways to pass and return variables between functions. These subjects are the focus of Part IV. C++ is a very strong, structured language that attempts, if the programmer is willing to "listen to the language," to protect local variables by making them visible only to the parts of the program that need those variables.

Part V: Character, Input, Output, and String Functions

C++ contains no commands that perform input or output. To make up for this omission, C++ compiler writers supply several useful input and output functions, described in this part of the book. By separating input and output functions from the language, C++ achieves better portability between computers; if your program runs on one computer, it should work on any other.

In addition, Part V describes several of the math, character, and string library functions available with C++. These functions keep you from having to write your own routines to perform common tasks.

Part VI: Arrays and Pointers

C++ offers single-dimensional arrays and multidimensional arrays—the subjects of Part VI. A multidimensional array holds multiple occurrences of repeating data but does not require lots of effort on your part to process.

Unlike many other programming languages, C++ uses pointer variables a great deal. Pointer variables and arrays work together to give you flexible data storage, allowing for easy sorting and searching of data.

Part VII: Data Structures

Variables, arrays, and pointers are not enough to hold the types of data your programs will require. Structures and classes, discussed in Part VII, allow for more powerful grouping of many different kinds of data into manageable units.

Your computer would be too limiting if you could not store data to disk and retrieve that data back into your programs. Disk files are required by most "real world" applications. This part of the book describes how C++ processes sequential and random access files, as well as teaches the fundamental principles needed to save data to the disk effectively.

Part VIII: Object-Oriented Programming

The whole purpose of C++ is to implement object-oriented programming, but so far everything you have learned is basically related to procedural programming. Classes, inheritance, polymorphism, and class hierarchies are the C++ tools by which you write object-oriented programs.

You will learn how to apply the basics of object-oriented programming to examples like the ones you will have already written in the earlier chapters. As you become familiar with object-oriented programming, you also begin to fully appreciate the power of the programming method that is being touted as "the method of the 90s."

Part IX: The Microsoft Foundation Classes

The Microsoft Foundation Classes are a set of C++ classes that greatly simplify the task of writing Microsoft Windows programs. MFC, as Microsoft Foundation Classes are called, is more than just a library of classes and functions. Several Visual C++ utilities are available that make it easy to create a fully working Windows program using MFC.

In this final section of the book you will create a working Windows program, complete with print and print preview capabilities, working menus, and a toolbar. You will also add a fully functional dialog box to the program.

Part X: Appendixes

The appendixes provide support information for the rest of the book. You will find a review of binary and hexadecimal numbers, answers to the Review Questions for each chapter, a comprehensive ASCII table, and a C++ precedence table.

Conventions Used in This Book

The following typographic conventions are used in this book:

- ♦ Program code lines, variable names, and any text that you see on the screen are in monospace.

- ♦ Placeholders on program code lines are in *italic monospace*.

- ♦ User input following a prompt is in **bold monospace**.

- ♦ File names are in regular text.

- ♦ Optional parameters on program code lines are enclosed in flat brackets ([ ]). You do not type the brackets when you include these parameters.

- ♦ New terms are in *italic*. Most of the italicized terms are also listed in the glossary.

Index to the Icons

The following icons appear throughout this book:

 Level 1

 Level 2

 Level 3

 Tip

 Caution

 Note

Part I

Introduction to C++

CHAPTER 1

Welcome to Visual C++

This book teaches you how to write programs with Visual C++. In this chapter, you learn about the history of Visual C++ and of C and C++. You review the PC system, and you learn how Visual C++ supports programming for IBM PC systems. Although the book uses Visual C++ Version 1.5, all of the examples work with Visual C++ Version 1.0 as well.

What Is Visual C++?

Visual C++ is Microsoft Corporation's implementation of a compiler for the C and C++ computer languages, designed to execute on MS-DOS-based systems utilizing the Microsoft Windows environment. It can create programs that will execute under either MS-DOS or Windows. If you are already familiar with C or C++, you may want to skip this section.

What Is a Computer Language?

Remember that a computer, for all its ever-increasing speed and power, is only a device that manipulates numbers. Some of the numbers are interpreted by the computer as instructions; other numbers are interpreted as data. A *program* is a set of instructions that causes the computer to manipulate data. A *programming language* is a means for you, a human, to generate those instructions so that the computer can manipulate the data in the way you want it manipulated. Programming languages must be translated into the set of instructions, this is usually done by another program called a *compiler*, such as Visual C++.

Low-Level Languages

Computer languages are sometimes categorized as either low level or high level. Low-level languages work closely with the computer's native set of instructions; the computer is viewed as being at a lower level than a human, and rightly so. Because such languages are so close to the computer's native set of instructions, a program written in a low-level language can achieve a high degree of efficiency. The program can be written to minimize the amount of time it needs to manipulate data, or to minimize the number of instructions required. The trade-off is that a program written in a low-level language is very difficult to read and write; the program may use several lines of code to do something as simple as "print a character," and it is not at all obvious that that's what is being done.

Furthermore, low-level languages are tailored to the computer. A program written in a low-level language for a Motorola 68000 would have to be completely rewritten in a low-level language for an Intel 80386. The ability to take a program written on one computer and make it run, as written, on a completely different computer is called *portability*. Low-level languages offer no portability. Because of the bond between a low-level language and its computer, there are no formal standards a low-level language may be expected to meet. Thus, there are usually subtle barriers to portability even between similar low-level languages implemented on a given computer. Assembly language and machine language are examples of low-level languages.

High-Level Languages

High-level languages work more closely with the human programmer and often attempt to emulate human language or activity. Programs written in high-level languages are not generally as efficient as programs written in low-level languages but are often more readable and easier to write. High-level languages are usually hardware-independent; a program written in a high-level language on one hardware platform will generally run, as written, on another hardware platform. High-level languages also have a high degree of portability. Many high-level languages have been standardized by organizations such as ANSI (American National Standards Institute) or industry organizations, and this standardization aids in writing portable programs. Examples of high-level languages are FORTRAN, COBOL, and Pascal.

What Is C?

C is a programming language that falls somewhere between a low-level language and a high-level language. Programs written in C are not glorified lists of machine instructions; C is a block-structured, procedural language. A well-written program in C can be very readable, and writing programs in C is easy. The authors of the first C implementation, Brian W. Kernighan and Dennis M. Ritchie, wrote C to exploit the native capabilities of the computer they were working on, and further specified that C should always exploit the native capabilities of the computer on which it is implemented. Thus, C can be used to write very efficient programs—although not quite as efficient as programs written in a low-level language (but sometimes very close), and usually more efficient than programs written in a classical high-level language. An ANSI standard for the C language now exists, and writing portable programs in C is not too difficult.

What Is C++?

In the last few years, a new method of programming came into existence: *object-oriented programming*. Instead of manipulating numbers, programs manipulate data objects. The basic idea is that when a new data object is to be manipulated, the new object will share some characteristics with an existing object, and a program that manipulates the existing object can be used as the basis of a program that manipulates the new, similar object.

C++, as an extension of C, implements object-oriented programming practices. The first C++ implementation was developed by Bjarne Stroustrup of AT&T Laboratories. C++ allows C programmers a migration path into object-oriented programming; programs written in C should compile correctly under a C++ compiler. C++ inherits much of the efficiency of its parent, as well as the readability and ease of writing programs. Although no standard exists for C++ yet, a de facto standard does exist, and the industry is generally tracking the AT&T specifications because that is the implementation that was designed by the originator of C++. Consequently, programs written in C++ may not be quite as portable, but generally the differences between implementations are minor, and porting a program from one implementation to another requires little effort.

The History of Visual C++

Microsoft has been supplying language products for programmers on MS-DOS-based PCs since IBM introduced the IBM PC in 1981. Microsoft provided both the operating system (MS-DOS), and a language (BASIC) for the then new IBM PC, and has been a leading supplier of language products, including C and C++ compilers, for PC programmers since then.

Visual C++ Version 1.0 was released in February 1993. It represented a major improvement in state-of-the-art Windows-based C++ language products. The most dramatic change in Version 1.0 of Visual C++ was the degree of integration among all of its components.

Visual C++ provides excellent integration of traditional programming tools such as an editor, compiler, debugger, and source code profiler. It also includes integration of Windows specific tools such as the Microsoft Foundation Classes and Windows resource editor (called App Studio). Finally, it adds several new tools such as a skeleton application generator (App Wizard), a C++ Class Manager (Class Wizard), and a Class Browser. Each tool was carefully optimized to work in cooperation with the other tools, all within the Windows 3.1 operating environment.

Visual C++ Version 1.0 shipped in two versions: Standard and Professional. The Standard version was able to build and debug Microsoft Windows programs utilizing either traditional methods or the Microsoft Foundation Classes application framework. The Professional edition added the capability to create traditional MS-DOS programs, an improved debugger, a compiler capable of creating highly optimized code, and a source profiler to help locate performance bottlenecks.

Visual C++ Version 1.0 was followed in July 1993 by Visual C++ 32-Bit Edition. The 32-Bit Edition will produce applications for Microsoft Windows NT, and 32-Bit applications for the Win32s interface. Win32s is a set of libraries that allows a 32-bit application to run under Windows 3.1.

Microsoft shipped Visual C++ Version 1.5 in December 1993. The major changes in Version 1.5 are support for ODBC and OLE2. ODBC stands for Open DataBase Connectivity, a set of libraries and specifications that allows an ODBC application to utilize data from most of the popular database formats. OLE2 is Object Linking and Embedding Version 2.0. OLE2 is a greatly enhanced method of communication between applications.

All of the examples in this book were developed and tested using Visual C++ Version 1.5. None of the code examples utilize any of the new features of Version 1.5, so owners of Version 1.0, either the Standard or Professional edition, will be able to use this book, as will owners of Visual C++ 32-Bit Edition. However, all of the discussions of the Visual C++ environment are based on Version 1.5 and its enhanced tools. This will be especially apparent in the last section of the book where extensive use is made of the new versions of App Wizard and Class Wizard.

A Review of the PC System

Now take a look at what a C compiler has to support in the PC environment. If you are already familiar with the PC's programming, you may want to skip this section.

Operating Systems

Today, several operating systems are supported on PCs, including MS-DOS, Windows, OS/2, DR DOS, and Deskview. These operating systems provide a means of controlling the PC hardware; programming the PC through the operating system's function calls is the most reliable way to control the PC hardware.

The BIOS

Generally, the operating systems, which are programs themselves, don't control the hardware directly. They usually operate through the BIOS (*Basic Input and Output System*), which is another program that does interface directly to the hardware. Programming the PC through BIOS calls is slightly less reliable than through operating system calls, but the resulting program is usually much faster.

The Hardware

Finally, you can manipulate the hardware directly. This is the riskiest way to control the PC, however, because the program is at the mercy of variations in behavior from one vendor's hardware to another's. The payoff is that manipulating the hardware directly is faster than through the BIOS and much faster than through the operating system.

Visual C++ and the PC System

In addition to offering compliance with the ANSI C standard, Visual C++ enables the programmer to control the PC through its three interfaces: the operating system, the BIOS, and the hardware.

Operating system support is through library calls to support the MS-DOS and Windows operating systems. A full software developer's kit is offered for Windows, and many of the common MS-DOS system calls are supported directly through library calls. Some MS-DOS system calls must be performed through the mechanism of setting up a list of registers and executing a software interrupt. Library calls are provided for this as well. BIOS calls also are supported through setting up register lists and executing software interrupts.

Accessing the hardware directly is accomplished through a set of library functions that allows the C code to interface with the PC's input/output (I/O) ports. Although it is generally best to use assembly language to write portions of the program that must interface directly with the PC's hardware, you *can* write the program in C if you prefer.

Another feature of the PC is its segmented memory architecture. The PC's internal computer, a member of Intel's 80x86 family of CPU chips, accesses memory in 64K sections, called *segments*. Program code can be in one memory segment, and data in another. If two subroutines are in the same segment, a function call from one to the other needs to specify only the offset of the called routine within the segment. Similarly, if data is in the same segment as the instructions manipulating it, the instructions can manipulate the data by its offset within the segment. This method is faster and produces smaller code than if the function calls are in separate segments, or if the function and data are in separate segments. Memory access must include a segment as well as an offset, making the code larger and slower.

Visual C++ supports the PC's segmented memory architecture through several program models. These models let the programmer make decisions, such as whether all the code can fit in one segment, but the data can't. Moreover, by using the keywords near and far, the programmer can dictate whether an access requires a segment as part of its address.

Summary

In this chapter, you learned about the history of Visual C++ and of C and C++. You reviewed the PC system, and you saw how Visual C++ supports programming for IBM PC systems.

Review Questions

Answers to Review Questions are in Appendix B.

1. Describe the differences between low-level languages and high-level languages.

2. Is C a low-level language or a high-level language?

3. How is C++ different from C?

4. How does Visual C++ stand apart from the other C++ compilers?

5. What operating systems does Visual C++ support?

6. What are the advantages and disadvantages of programming the PC through BIOS calls rather than through operating system calls?

CHAPTER 2

The Visual C++ Environment

Microsoft Visual C++ for Windows is designed to be a complete development environment for both Windows and DOS programs. Visual C++ supports all phases of the application development cycle from within a single, central workbench. There is a program editor with color syntax highlighting, one of the industry's best C++ compilers, debuggers for both DOS and Windows programs, a Windows Resource Editor, an application generator, a source code browser, and a class library that greatly simplifies the development of Windows programs. These tools are all very tightly integrated so that each part works well with each other part.

The heart of Visual C++ is called *Visual Workbench*. Visual Workbench provides the framework from which you choose the tool or tools for whatever job you are about to do.

This chapter introduces the following topics:

◆ Starting Visual C++

◆ Understanding Visual Workbench's screen

◆ Using Visual Workbench's menus

◆ Getting help in Visual C++

◆ Leaving Visual C++

The chapter provides the necessary tools for you to begin entering Visual C++ programs.

Starting Visual C++

To begin using Visual C++, power up your computer and start Windows. When you installed Visual C++, the installation program should have created a Windows group named Microsoft Visual C++. Locate this group and choose the Visual C++ icon. Figure 2.1 shows the Microsoft Visual C++ group with the Visual C++ icon selected.

Figure 2.1

The Microsoft Visual C++ group.

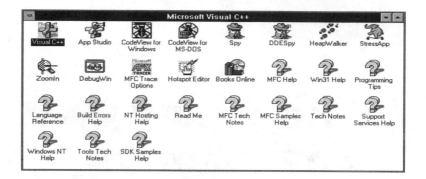

Tip: If your Microsoft Visual C++ group becomes damaged, or is accidentally deleted, you can easily rebuild it by using the Visual C++ Setup program with a special switch, /F, on the command line. To run Setup with this switch, insert the Visual C++ CD into your CD drive, (or, if your Visual C++ came on floppy disks, insert Disk 1 in your floppy disk drive). In Program Manager, click the **F**ile menu, and then click the **R**un command. This will bring up the Run dialog. Type the following line into the Command line in the Run dialog:

```
d:\msvc\setup.exe /F /O
```

Or, if you are running from a floppy disk, type the following:

```
a:\setup.exe /F /O
```

The /F and /O must be in uppercase. Setup will only install the Microsoft Visual C++ group. (/F tells Setup not to copy any **F**iles. /O tells Setup not to change any of your Windows c**O**nfiguration.)

Power Up Properly

There is a proper sequence to follow when you turn on your computer. The sequence is easy to remember with the following rule: *The boss always comes to work last and is the first to go home.*

Have you had bosses like that? Your computer's power-up sequence should follow a similar rule: *The system unit (the "boss" that holds the CPU) should come to work last.*

In other words, turn on everything else first, including the printer, monitor, and modem. Only then should you turn on the system unit. This keeps system-unit power surges to a minimum and protects the circuits inside the unit.

When you are ready to turn off the computer, turn off the system unit first (the boss goes home first). Then turn off the rest of the equipment in whatever order is most convenient.

Tip: If your computer equipment is plugged into a switched surge protector, it is fine to use the single switch for all your equipment, including the system unit. The surge protector ensures that power gets to the system unit as evenly as possible.

The Visual Workbench Screen

Figure 2.2 shows the parts of the Visual C++ screen. From this screen, you create, modify, build, and execute Visual C++ programs. Start the Visual C++ program, and you see the Visual Workbench screen. If you have a mouse, move it around on your desk so that you can see the mouse pointer.

The most important part of the screen is the *program-editing window*, where you work with Visual C++ programs. The window acts like a word processor's document-editing area. You can move the cursor with the arrow keys or mouse and make any necessary changes to the text. The number of windows that can be open is limited by available memory, but only one window is active at a time.

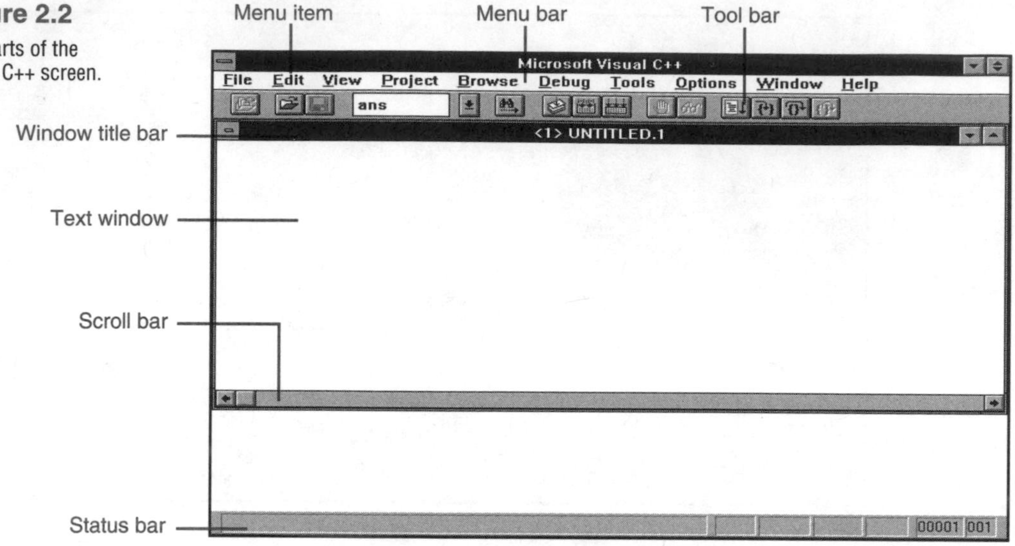
Menu item
Menu bar
Tool bar
Microsoft Visual C++
File Edit View Project Browse Debug Tools Options Window Help
ans
<1> UNTITLED.1
Window title bar
Text window
Scroll bar
Status bar
00001 001

Figure 2.2
The parts of the Visual C++ screen.

Using the Mouse

You use the mouse to move the cursor around on the screen quickly. Before mouse devices became common, users had to press the arrow keys continually to move the cursor from one location to another. Now you can move the cursor by moving the mouse across the desk and clicking the mouse when the cursor is at the desired position.

To *click* the mouse, press and immediately release the left mouse button. Clicking the mouse selects an item from a menu or moves the text cursor around the screen. Sometimes you click the mouse after moving the mouse cursor over a **Y**es or **N**o answer in response to a question.

To *double-click* the mouse, press the left mouse button twice in rapid succession. You sometimes need to double-click the mouse to execute a menu command.

To *drag* the mouse, press and hold down the left mouse button and then move the mouse cursor across the screen. Usually, the area you drag the mouse across is highlighted on-screen so that you can see the path the mouse leaves. When you are finished marking the path, release the mouse button. This is one way to select several lines from a Visual C++ program, so that you can move or erase them.

Selecting from Visual C++'s Menus

How do you know what to order when you go to a new restaurant? You choose from a menu. Restaurant owners know that people who eat in their restaurants have not memorized everything the restaurant serves. Likewise, the authors of Visual C++ understood that users would not want to memorize the commands that control Visual C++. They would rather look at a list of possible commands and select the ones they want. The *menu bar* at the top of the screen makes using Visual C++ easy.

Just below the menu bar is another area called the *tool bar*. The toolbar contains buttons that you can click with the mouse to invoke many menu options without going through the menus.

The Visual C++ menu bar displays the words File, Edit, View, Project, Browse, Debug, Tools, Options, Window, and Help. You can select these items from the Visual C++ screen. They are not commands but are headings for additional menus. These menus are called *pull-down menus* because selecting them resembles pulling down a window shade. For example, figure 2.3 shows what happens if you select the File pull-down menu.

Figure 2.3

Viewing the File pull-down menu.

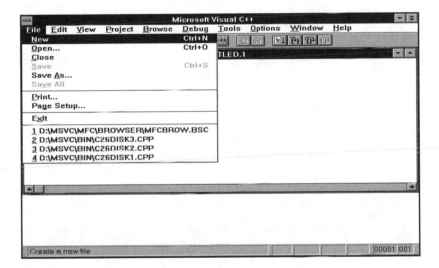

When you want to look at any of the pull-down menus, you can use either the mouse or the keyboard. To display a pull-down menu with the mouse, move the mouse pointer over a menu bar item and click (see the previous sidebar, "Using the Mouse"). You can click the rest of the items on the menu bar to view the other pull-down menus in succession.

Displaying a pull-down menu from the keyboard is just as easy as displaying the menu with the mouse. Press the Alt key and the highlighted letter of the menu you want to see. For example, to display the Edit pull-down menu, press Alt+E. You pull down the system menu (the Command menu) by pressing Alt+space bar.

If you change your mind, you can press Esc to remove a displayed menu. You are, in effect, escaping from the option you selected.

> **Tip:** To display a menu, mouse users sometimes prefer the keyboard's Alt+key combination to clicking the mouse. Because your hands are already on the keyboard, pressing Alt+E for **E**dit might be faster than pointing with the mouse and clicking.

Choosing an Option

When you display a pull-down menu, you must tell Visual C++ which command on the menu to perform. For example, the File pull-down menu lists several commands. You can request a command in one of three ways:

♦ Click the command with the mouse.

♦ Highlight the command with the up- and down-arrow keys and then press Enter.

♦ Press the command's highlighted letter.

For example, to request the New command, mouse users move the mouse cursor until it rests anywhere on the word New. One click of the mouse chooses the New command. Keyboard users press the down-arrow key until the New command is highlighted and then press the Enter key to carry out the command. Keyboard users also have a shortcut: simply typing the highlighted letter of the command. By typing N or n, the keyboard user can execute the New command. Note that you can use an uppercase letter or a lowercase letter to select any command or option.

If you begin to select from a menu but then change your mind, press Esc to close the menu and return to the program-editing window. Mouse users just click the mouse outside the pull-down menu area to close the menu.

> **Tip:** The best way to learn how to choose from Visual C++'s pull-down menus is to experiment. As long as you don't save anything to disk, you don't harm existing Visual C++ program files or data.

Sometimes commands appear in gray and are not as readable as others. For example, notice in figure 2.4 that most of the options on the Edit pull-down menu are in gray and have no highlighted letter. You cannot choose any of these commands. Visual C++ displays the unavailable commands so that you will remember where they are when you need them. These commands return to their normal colors when they make more sense in the context of your Visual C++ session.

Figure 2.4

Viewing the **Edit**
pull-down menu.

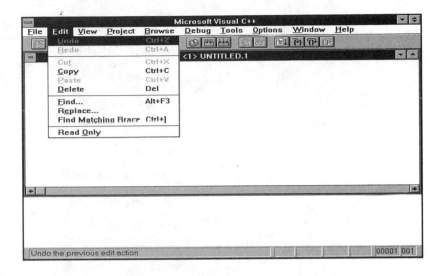

The Menu Accelerator Keys

After using Visual C++ for a while, you will become familiar with the commands on the pull-down menus. Despite the ease of using Visual C++ menus, there is a faster way to select some of the commands. Visual C++'s *accelerator keys* are faster to use than the menus, whether you use a mouse or the keyboard.

Notice in figure 2.4 that several of the options on the pull-down menu show key combinations on the right side of the menu, opposite the command name. These represent *accelerator keys* that can be used to access the menu commands directly. Table 2.2 lists some of these shortcuts. For example, to choose Execute (execute a Visual C++ program you are writing), you could display the Project pull-down menu and then select Execute. The Project Execute menu option, however, has Ctrl-F5 listed to the right of it. The key or key combination listed beside the menu option is the *accelerator key* for that option. Instead of going through the menu steps, you can press Ctrl-F5 and immediately run the Project Execute command. You will understand the function of each of these shortcut keys as you learn more about Visual C++.

Table 2.2. Some Visual C++ menu accelerator keys.

Key(s)	Menu Command
F1	Help
F2	Find next bookmark
Shift+F2	Find previous bookmark

continues

Table 2.2. Continued

Key(s)	Menu Command
F3	Repeat the last find
Alt+F3	Open the Find dialog box
Ctrl+F3	Find the selected text
Shift+F3	Search backward
F4	Find the next error (After Build or Compile)
Shift+F4	Find the previous error (After Build or Compile)
F5	Run current program
Ctrl+F6	Switch to the next document window
F6	Switch to the next window (includes all windows)
Shift+F6	Switch to the previous window (includes all windows)
Ctrl+F4	Close the active window
Alt+F8	Rebuild all files
Ctrl+F8	Compile current file
Shift+F8	Build only changed files
Ctrl+Tab	Switch to the previously active window
Ctrl+]	Find matching brace

Using Dialog Boxes

Not all menu commands execute when you select them. Some are followed by an ellipsis (…), such as the File Open... command. If you choose one of these commands, a *dialog box* opens on-screen. You must type more information before Visual C++ can carry out the command. This extra information might be a number, a word, a file name, or the selection of an option from several that are offered. Sometimes a dialog requires several actions from you.

Figure 2.5 shows the Project Options dialog box. This is a good time to practice using a dialog box. Select the Options menu and then choose Project. Notice that the label on each of the three buttons in the box labeled Customize Build Options (Compiler, Linker, and Resources) is followed by another ellipsis. Each of these buttons opens, in its turn, another dialog box. Notice in the other box, labeled Build Mode, the small circles, one with a black dot in the middle. These circles are called *radio buttons*. You can select only one radio button from a group of buttons; when you select a button, the previously selected button's dot is cleared. You select a radio button by using the arrow keys, by pressing Alt plus the selection's highlighted letter, or by clicking the radio button or its text.

Another option in this dialog box is preceded by a square box. This box is called a *check box*. If there is more than one check box, you may select any or all of the check boxes, or none of them. A selected check box is indicated by an x in the box. You select check boxes in the same way you select radio buttons.

Finally, on the right-hand side of the dialog box is another set of push buttons labeled OK, Cancel, and Help. When you are finished choosing options from the dialog box, click the OK button to signal to Visual C++ that you are finished making selections and want to use the selections you have made. If you want Visual C++ to ignore any actions you have taken in the dialog, click the Cancel button. Finally, if you need more information about the current dialog box, click the Help button. Visual C++ will respond with a help screen that explains the options in the current dialog box.

Figure 2.5

The **P**roject **O**ptions dialog box.

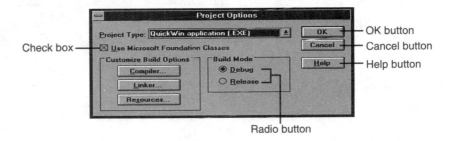

Getting Help

Getting Help

When using Visual C++, you can get help at any time by using the on-line Help feature. Help is available for virtually every aspect of Visual C++. The Visual C++ Help system gives several kinds of help. You already have seen how help is available in dialog boxes by clicking a button labeled Help. Depending on your request, Visual C++ helps you with whatever you need and even offers sample programs that you can merge into your own programs.

The Help Menu

Use the mouse to point at the Help item in the main menu and click. You will see the menu shown in figure 2.6. You can always use this menu to get help from anywhere in Visual C++ except some dialogs which provide their own help button. As you can see, help is broken down into several broad areas. The **V**isual Workbench option provides help on all aspects of using Visual Workbench itself. **B**uild Tools provides help on the compiler and linker. Choose **C**/C++ Language for help on any question about the C and C++ languages themselves, or any of the library functions provided with Visual C++. Foundation Classes is the Microsoft Foundation Classes, a large, complex library for developing Windows programs. Windows 3.1 SDK (Software Development Kit) is the specifications for working with Windows as a programmer. If you know a word or concept, but are not sure which help item under which it might be found, use Search for Help On. Finally, if you need to contact Microsoft Technical Support for help, Obtaining Technical Support describes the various support options available from Microsoft and explains how to use each one. The last item,

bout Visual C++, displays a dialog that tells you the version number of Visual C++ you are using and some information about your computer's resources.

Figure 2.6

The Help menu.

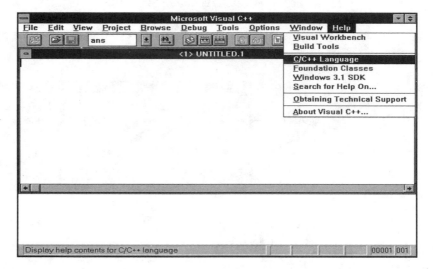

Context-Sensitive Help

Most of the time when you need help, you will be working on a program or using one of the menu items. Whenever a menu is active, or the cursor is positioned on a word in the editor, you can press F1 and Visual C++ will locate and display help for that menu option or word. The word can be any legal C or C++ word, or any function or class in the libraries provided with Visual C++. Suppose that you are working on a program that uses a function named cout. (You will be working with this function a lot all throughout this book. Imagine that you have typed the word cout, but can't remember what comes next to use it properly. If you press F1 with the cursor in or adjacent to the word cout, Visual C++ will "look" at what you are doing (working with cout) and search the help files for that topic. Figure 2.7 shows part of the help information that Visual C++ will display for cout. If no help is found, Visual C++ will tell you that it can't find any help for the specified word. Even that message can be a help—it might help you see that you just misspelled the word.

Figure 2.7

A typical Visual
C++ Help Screen.

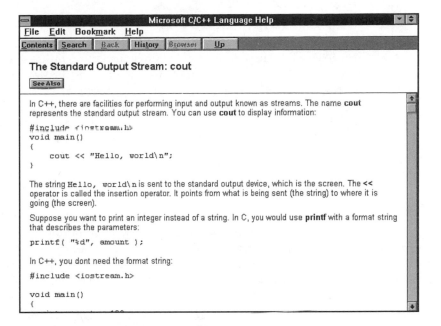

Searching Help

There are two ways you can search for help in Visual C++. The first way is through the Search for Help On option on the main Help menu. When you choose this option from the main Help menu, a dialog box appears to prompt you for a help topic. Type the word you are interested in locating in the area labeled Help Keyword and press Enter. Now a list of main help topics that contain your keyword will appear in the box below the Help Keyword area. Choose one of the main topics by pointing at it with the mouse and double-clicking, then click the OK button. Figure 2.8 shows the Search dialog ready to request help for Quickwin from the Visual Workbench help file.

Figure 2.8

The Search for
Help On dialog.

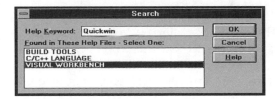

The second way way to search for help in Visual C++ is within a specific help file while you are viewing it. Figure 2.7 shows a typical help screen. Just beneath the menu bar there are several buttons, one of which is labeled Search. When you click this button, another search dialog is shown, one that shows you all the available help topics in the current file. Although slightly more complex, this second search dialog is very similar in operation to the one shown in figure 2.8.

Other Help Features

The Visual C++ Help system has many other features to help you find what you want. These include tables of contents, hypertext links, sample code that can be pasted directly into your program, a class hierarchy browser when you are working with a Microsoft furnished class library, bookmarks, and printing. The system literally provides so much rapidly accessable information that you will find you hardly ever need to use a manual. Take some time to explore the Help system, and you may find that Visual C++'s help is one of your most useful tools.

Quitting Visual C++

When you finish your Visual C++ session, you can exit Visual C++ and return to DOS by choosing File Exit, or by pressing Alt-F4. It is important to properly end Visual C++ so that changes to your files will be saved. If you made changes to a Visual C++ program and you try to exit the program without saving the changes to disk, Visual C++ displays the warning message in the dialog box shown in figure 2.9.

Figure 2.9

The Visual C++ warning message to save a file.

If you choose **Yes**, Visual C++ prompts you for a file name under which to save the file (if you haven't named it previously). Choosing **No** instructs Visual C++ that you want to exit the program without saving the file, although the latest changes are not recorded. Cancel instructs Visual C++ to return to the program-editing window.

Summary

This chapter familiarized you with the Visual C++ environment. The major advantages of Visual C++ over its predecessors are the tight integration of all components of the development environment and the on-line Help system. You learned how to start Visual C++, use the menus, request online help, and exit the program. With its intuitive interface, Visual C++ makes working easy, whether you use a mouse or the keyboard.

Review Questions

Answers to Review Questions are in Appendix B.

1. True or false: You can find Visual C++ in your \DOS subdirectory.

2. Which part of the Visual C++ screen retains the program as you type it?

3. What are the differences in clicking, double-clicking, and dragging a mouse?

4. Do you need to remember command names so that Visual C++ can execute them? Why or why not?

5. How do you display the Help menu?

6. What does *context-sensitive help* mean?

7. What are two ways to get help in Visual C++?

8. For what are the keyboard shortcut keys used?

CHAPTER 3

What Is a Program?

This chapter introduces you to fundamental programming concepts. The task of programming computers has been described as rewarding, challenging, easy, difficult, fast, and slow. It is all of these, and more. Programming your computer takes some time to do well, but you will have fun along the way, especially with the rich assortment of features offered by C++. Writing complex programs to solve advanced problems takes time and can be frustrating, but once you get a complex program working, the feeling is gratifying.

In this chapter, you learn about the concept of programming, from a program's design to its execution on your computer. The most difficult part of programming is to break up the problem into logical steps that the computer can carry out. Before you finish the chapter, you will have typed and executed a simple C++ program.

This chapter covers the following topics:

♦ Programming concepts

♦ Running C++ programs

♦ The program's output

♦ Program design

♦ Using the Visual C++ editor

♦ Using the Visual C++ compiler

♦ Microsoft QuickWin programs

After completing this chapter, you will be ready for the remaining chapters, which explain in detail the elements of the C++ programming language.

Computer Programs

Before you can make C++ work for you, you must write a C++ program. As you learned in Chapter 1, a program is a set of instructions that causes the computer to manipulate data.

Keep in mind that computers are just machines. They are not smart—quite the opposite! They will not do anything until they are given very detailed instructions. If you use your computer for word processing, the word processor is actually a program that someone wrote (in a language such as C++) that tells the computer exactly how to behave when you type words into it.

You are familiar with the concept of programming if you have ever followed a recipe. A recipe is just a program (a set of instructions) that tells the cook how to make a certain dish. A good recipe gives the instructions in the proper order and provides a complete description so that the cook can make everything successfully and with no assumptions.

If you want your computer to help with your budget, keep track of names and addresses, or compute gas mileage for your car travel, the computer needs a program that tells it how to do those things. There are two ways to supply that program for your computer:

♦ Buy a program written by somebody else that does the job you want.

♦ Write the program yourself.

Writing the program yourself has a big advantage for many applications: the program will do exactly what you want it to do. If you buy one that is already written, you will have to adapt your needs to those of the designers of the program. That is where C++ comes into the picture. With the C++ programming language (and a little study), you can make your computer perform any task needed.

To create a C++ program for your computer, you must have an *editor* and a C++ *compiler*. Similar to a word processor, an editor is a program that lets you type a C++ program into memory, make changes (such as moving, copying, inserting, and deleting text), and save that program more permanently in a disk file.

After you type the program by using the editor, you must compile the program before you run it. C++ is usually implemented as a *compiled* language. You usually cannot write a C++ program and run it on your computer unless you have a C++ compiler. A C++ compiler translates the C++ instructions into a form executable by your computer. The Visual C++ compiler comes with its own built-in editor.

The process of compiling a program before running it may seem like an added and meaningless step to beginning programmers. If you know the BASIC programming language, you may not have heard of a compiler, or understand the need for one. That is because BASIC (as well as APL and some versions of other computer languages) is not a compiled language but an *interpreted* language. Instead of translating the entire program into machine-executable form (as a compiler does), an interpreter translates each program instruction and then executes it before translating the next one. The difference between a compiler and an interpreter is subtle, but the bottom line is not: Compilers produce *much* more efficient and faster-running programs than interpreters do. In addition, the program you've written does not require that the user have a copy of the interpreter in order to run the program; the compiler will produce an independently executable program. The seemingly extra step of compiling is worth the effort (and with today's compilers, there is not much extra effort needed).

Because computers are machines that do not think, the instructions you write in C++ must be very detailed. You cannot assume that the computer understands what to do if the instruction is not in your program, or if you give an instruction that does not conform to the C++ language requirements.

After you write and compile a C++ program, you then must *run*, or *execute*, it. Otherwise, your computer will not know that you want it to follow the instructions in the program. Just as a cook must follow a recipe's instructions before the dish is made, your computer must execute the program instructions before it can accomplish what you want it to do. When you run a program, you instruct the computer to start performing the instructions in the program.

The Program and Its Output

While programming, remember the difference between the program and its output. Your program contains the instructions you write by using C++. Only after you run the program does the computer actually follow your instructions.

Throughout this book, you often will see a program listing (the C++ instructions in the program) followed by the program's results (what occurs when you run it). The results, which are the output of the program, go to an output device, such as the screen, the printer, or a disk file.

Program Design

Design your programs before typing them at the computer.

You must plan your programs before typing them in your C++ editor. When a carpenter builds a house, he or she does not get a hammer and nails and start building! The carpenter first finds out what the owner of the house wants, draws up the plans, orders the materials, gathers the workers, and *then* starts hammering the nails.

The hardest part of writing a program is to break it into logical steps the computer can follow. Learning the C++ language is a requirement, but that is not the only thing to consider. There is a method of writing programs, a formal procedure you should learn, that makes your programming job easier. To write a program, you should follow these steps:

1. Define the problem to solve with the computer.

2. Design the output of the program (what the user sees).

3. Break the program into logical steps to achieve the program's output.

4. Write the program (this is where the editor is useful).

5. Compile the program.

6. Test the program to make sure that it performs as expected.

As you can see, the actual typing of the program occurs toward the end of programming. The order of these steps is important; you must plan how to tell a computer the way to perform a certain task.

Your computer only can perform instructions step-by-step. You must assume that the computer has no previous knowledge of the problem, and it is up to you to supply it with that knowledge. That is what good recipes do. It would be foolish if a recipe for baking a cake simply said, "Bake the cake." Why? Because it assumes way too much on the part of the cook. Even if the recipe is written out step-by-step, care must be taken (through advance planning) that the steps are in the proper sequence. Putting the ingredients in the oven *before* stirring them would not be prudent!

Throughout this book, as programs are presented, this programming process is adhered to. Before seeing a program, you will read about its design. The goals of the program will be presented, those goals will be broken down into logical steps, and then the program will be written.

Designing the program in advance makes the entire program structure more accurate and keeps you from having to make many changes. A builder knows that a room is much harder to add after the house is built. If you do not properly plan and think out every aspect of your program's steps, it will take you longer to create the final, working program. Making major changes to programs is more difficult after they are written.

Using the previous six steps to develop programs will become more important to you as you write longer and more complicated programs. Throughout this book, you will see tips for program design. Now is the time to launch into C++ so that you can see what it's like to type your own program and watch it run.

Using the Visual C++ Editor

The instructions in your C++ program are called the *source code*. You type source code into your computer's memory with your editor. Once you type the C++ source code (your program), you should save it to a disk file before compiling and running the program. Most C++ compilers expect C++ source programs to be stored in files with names ending in CPP. For example, all the following are valid file names for most C++ compilers:

MYPROG.CPP SALESACT.CPP EMPLYEE.CPP ACCREC.CPP

Figure 3.1 shows a Visual C++ screen. Across the top of the screen is a menu bar that offers pull-down menus for editing, compiling, and running options. The middle of the screen is the body of the program editor; the program goes in this area. From this screen, you type, edit, compile, and run your C++ source programs. Without Visual C++'s integrated environment, you would have to start an editor, type your program, save the program to disk, exit the editor, run the compiler, and only then run the compiled program from the operating system. With this integrated environment, you just type the program into the editor, and then select the proper menu option that compiles the program. When the compile is finished, another simple menu choice will run the program.

Figure 3.1

Visual C++'s integrated environment.

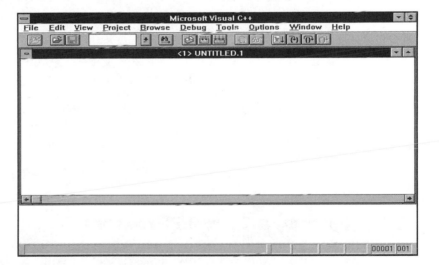

Using the Visual C++ Compiler

Once you type and edit your C++ program's source code, you must compile the program. All you do is select the Project menu, highlight the option labeled Build C3SAPMPLE.CPP and press Enter to compile the program. (Or, just press Shift-F8.) When you compile the program on your PC, the compiler will eventually produce an executable file whose name begins with the same name as the source code but ends in an EXE file extension. For example, if your source program is named GRADEAVG.CPP, you will wind up with a compiled file called GRADEAVG.EXE, which you could run from the Windows Program Manager by choosing the **File Run** menu option, and typing **GRADEAVG**. You also can run the program directly from within Visual C++ by pressing Ctrl-F5.

> **Note:** Each program in this book contains a comment that specifies a recommended file name for the source program. You do not have to follow the file-naming conventions used in this book. The file names in the program listings are only suggestions for you. If you decide to obtain the sample diskette that contains a listing of each program in this book, however, the file names of the program listings will match those on the diskette you receive. Visual C++ will require you to provide a name for each program before you compile it.

Unlike many other programming languages, your C++ program is normally routed through a *preprocessor* before it is compiled. C++ source code can contain *preprocessor directives*, which control the way your programs compile. The preprocessor step is performed automatically by Visual C++, so it requires no additional effort or commands to learn on your part.

There is actually one additional step your program must go through after compiling and before running. This step is called the *linking* stage. When your program is linked, needed runtime information (which is not always available to the compiler) is supplied to your program. You also can take several compiled programs and combine them into one executable program by linking them together. Visual C++ initiates the linking stage automatically; you do not have to worry about the process.

Figure 3.2 shows the steps that Visual C++ performs to produce an executable program.

Running a Sample Program

Before delving into the specifics of the C++ language, you should take a few moments to become familiar with the Visual C++ editor and compiler. Beginning in the next chapter, "Your First C++ Program," you should concentrate all your efforts on the C++ programming language.

Start Visual C++ by double-clicking (pressing the left mouse button twice rapidly) on the Visual C++ icon, and then type the following program into your computer. Be as accurate as possible; a single typing error can cause the C++ compiler to generate a series of errors. You do not have to understand the program's content at this point; its purpose is simply to give you practice using the Visual C++ editor and compiler.

Comment your program with the program name.
Include the header file iostream.h.
Define the variable GOODBYE to begin with 2 newline commands (\n), followed
by the goodbye message
Start of the main() function.
    Initialize the integer variable ctr to a zero.
    Define the character array fname to hold 20 elements.
    Print to the screen What is your first name?
    Accept a string from the keyboard.
    Process a loop while the variable ctr is less than 5.
        Print the string accepted from the keyboard.
        Increment the variable ctr by one.
    Skip 2 lines and print out the phrase "Goodbye, now."
    Return out of the main() function.

Note: The preceding description is the design of the C3SAMPLE.CPP
program. This is called *pseudocode*. Pseudocode is one of several design
methods you might use; it is particularly good for writing code in C++.

```
// Filename: C3SAMPLE.CPP
// Requests a name, prints the name 5 times,
// and skips 2 lines before printing a goodbye message.

#include  <iostream.h>

#define   GOODBYE "\n\nGoodbye, now."

main()
{
    int  ctr = 0;          // Integer variable to count
                           // through loop
    char fname[ 20 ];      // Define character array to hold
                           // name

    cout << "What is your first name? "; // Prompt the user
    cin >> fname;                        // Get the name from
                                         // the keyboard
    while (ctr < 5)                      // Loop to print the
        {                                // name exactly 5 times
        cout << fname << "\n";
```

```
        ctr++;
      }
    cout << GOODBYE;              // Print out goodbye phrase
    return 0;                     // Return status
  }
```

Figure 3.2

Compiling C++
source code into
an executable
program.

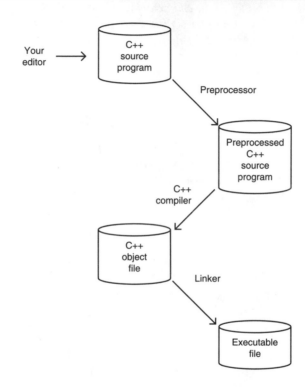

Again, be as accurate as possible. In most programming languages, and especially in C++, the characters you type in a program must be accurate. In this sample C++ program, there are parentheses (()), brackets ([]), and braces ({}), and none of them can be used interchangeably.

Although the comments to the right of some of the lines (the words after //) do not have to end in the same columns as shown in this listing, if you enter the program exactly as shown, you will familiarize yourself with the editor and learn to be accurate with the characters you type.

Compile the program by selecting Project from the Visual C++ main menu, highlighting Build C3SAMPLE.EXE from the Project menu, and pressing Enter (or by holding down the Shift key and pressing F8). When the compile is finished (Visual C++ will tell you when it is finished), execute the program by selecting Project from the main menu, choosing Execute C3SAMPLE.EXE, and pressing Enter (or pressing Ctrl-F5.)

If There Are Errors

You are typing instructions for a machine, so you must be very accurate. If you misspell a word, leave out a quotation mark, or make another mistake, your C++ compiler will inform you with an error message. The error will appear in a separate message window, as shown in figure 3.3. The most common error is a *syntax error*, which usually implies a misspelled word.

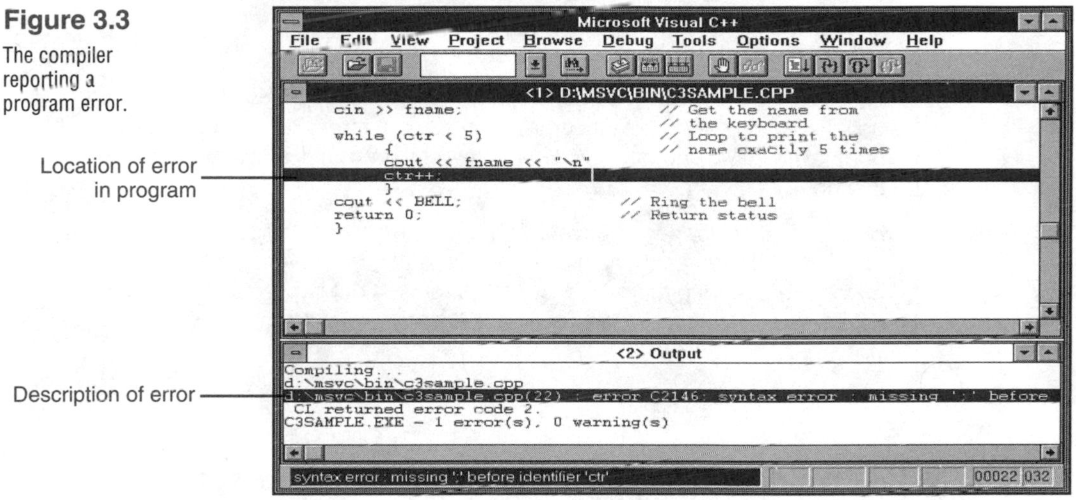

Figure 3.3

The compiler reporting a program error.

Location of error in program

Description of error

When you get an error message (or more than one), you should return to the editor window and fix the problem. The error message usually will tell you what line contains the error, and clicking the mouse on the error will put the cursor on the offending line in the editor window. If you don't understand the error, you may have to check your reference manual or simply scour your program's source code until you find the offending problem.

Once you have typed your program correctly and you get no compile errors, it will run properly by asking for your first name and then printing it five times on-screen. After the fifth name is printed, the program will skip two lines and print out a farewell message.

This sample program helps illustrate the difference between the program and its output. You must type the program (or load it from disk) and then run the program to see its output.

Getting the Bugs Out

One of the first computers, owned by the military, refused to print some important data one day. After programmers tried for many hours to find the solution within the program, a lady named Grace Hopper decided to check out the printer.

She found a small moth lodged between two important wires. When she removed the moth, the printer started working perfectly (although the moth did not have as much luck).

Grace Hopper is now a retired Admiral, and although she is responsible for developing many important computer concepts (she was the author of the original COBOL language), she may be best known for discovering the very first computer bug.

Since Admiral Hopper discovered the bug, errors in computer programs have been known as computer bugs. When you test your programs, you may have to debug them—get the bugs (errors) out by fixing your typing errors and changing the logic so that the computer does exactly what you want.

Microsoft QuickWin Applications

Until you get to the final part of this book, all of the programs you write will be compiled and executed as QuickWin programs. QuickWin is a special type of Windows program you can compile in Visual C++ that allows to you create simple DOS Text programs that will run as Windows-hosted programs.

Figure 3.4 shows the C3SAMPLE program running as a QuickWin program. The *title bar* (the dark bar across the top of the window) shows the name of the program—C3SAMPLE. Immediately below the title bar is a typical Windows menu bar, which contains options to control the execution and appearance of the program. If you choose the File option from the menu bar, for example, you will then see an option to exit the program. Whenever you execute one of the example programs in the exercises, you will need to choose this option when the program is finished.

Below the menu is another, smaller window with the title Stdin/Stdout/Stderr. The title means that this window is accepting input from the standard input stream (Stdin), displaying output for the standard output stream (Stdout), and displaying error messages for the standard error output stream (Stderr). This is where you will type all input for your programs, and where all output will appear. Figure 3.4

Figure 3.4

Sample program
running as a
QuickWin
program.

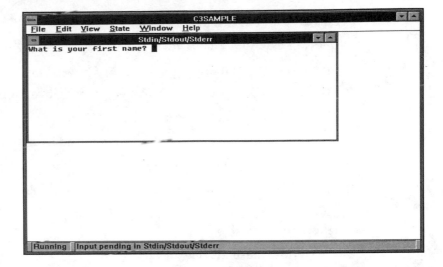

shows the example program waiting for you to type your first name.

QuickWin provides a very easy way to write a true Windows-hosted program, as you can see from the sample you just completed. The QuickWin environment has some limitations, however, that make it unsuitable for major Windows programs. The QuickWin menu cannot be customized, for example, and a QuickWin application cannot display dialog boxes or other custom Windows controls.

QuickWin offers an excellent way for a beginning C++ programmer to write and test programs within the Visual C++ and Windows environments. You can focus on the basics of the C++ language without getting involved in the complexities of a Windows program. In the last part of this book, you will write some true Windows programs.

Summary

After reading this chapter, you should understand the steps necessary to write a C++ program with Visual C++. You know that advanced planning makes the program writing much easier and that the program's instructions produce the output only after you run the program.

You also saw how to use Visual C++'s editor and compiler. Now that you know how to run a C++ program, it is time to start learning the actual C++ programming language.

Review Questions

Answers to Review Questions are in Appendix B.

1. What is a program?

2. What are the two ways to obtain a program that you want?

3. True or false: Computers can think.

4. What is the difference between a program and its resulting output?

5. What do you use to type C++ programs into the computer?

6. What file-name extension do C++ programs typically have?

7. Why is typing the program one of the *last* steps in the programming process?

8. What does the term *debug* mean?

9. True or false: You must link a program before compiling it.

10. What are two limitations of QuickWin programs?

CHAPTER 4

Your First C++ Program

Before looking at the specifics of the C++ language, many people like to walk through a few simple programs to get a feel for what a C++ program is like. This chapter introduces you to a few C++ language commands and elements.

The following topics are covered:

♦ An overview of C++ programs and their structure

♦ C++ comments (the /*...*/ and // language symbols)

♦ Variables and constants: what they are and their types

♦ Simple math operators

♦ Screen output

The rest of the book covers more formally some of the commands mentioned in this chapter.

Looking at a C++ Program

Figure 4.1 shows the outline of a typical small C++ program. No C++ commands are shown in the figure. Although there is much more to a program than the outline suggests, this is the general format of the early programs in this book.

Figure 4.1

A skeleton outline
for a simple C++
program.

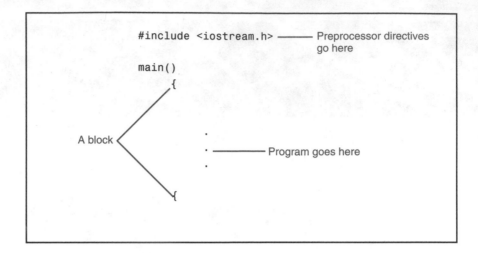

To get acquainted with C++ programs as quickly as possible, you should look at a C++ program in its entirety. Following is a listing of a very simple C++ program. It does not do much, but it lets you see the general format of the C++ language. The next few sections discuss elements from this program. You may not understand everything in the program, even after finishing this chapter, but it is a good place to start. If there is something specific that you do not understand, that is okay for now.

```
// Filename: C4FIRST.CPP
// Initial C++ program that demonstrates the C++ comments
// and shows a few variables and their declarations

#include      <iostream.h>

main()
{
    int      i;   // These 4 lines declare 4 variables
    int      j;
    char     c;
    float    x;

    i = 4;         // i and j are assigned integer constants

    j = i + 7;
```

```
    c = 'A';       // All character constants are enclosed in
                   // single quotes

    x = 9.087;     // x requires a floating-point value
                   // since it was declared as a
                   // floating-point variable

    x = x * 4.5;   // Change what was in x with a formula

    // Send the values of the variables to the screen
    cout << i << j << c << x;

    return 0;      // ALWAYS end programs and functions with
                   // return
}
```

For now, just familiarize yourself with the overall program. Look through it to see whether you can understand part or all of it. The computer will look at each line of the program, starting with the first line and working its way down, until all the instructions given in the program have been performed. (Of course, the program first has to be compiled, as described in the preceding chapter.)

The output of this program is minimal; it simply displays four values on-screen after performing some assignments and calculations of arbitrary values. Just concentrate on the general format at this point.

The Format of C++ Programs

C++ is a free-form language.

Unlike some other programming languages, such as COBOL, C++ is a *free-form* programming language. This means that programming statements can start in any column of any line. You can insert blank lines in a program if you want. This sample program, called C4FIRST.CPP, contains several blank lines. (You can find the name of each program in this book in the first line of each listing.) These blank lines help separate parts of the program. In a simple program such as this, the separation is not as critical as it might be in a longer, more complex program.

Generally, spaces within C++ programs are free-form as well. Your goal should not be to make your programs as compact as possible but as readable as possible. For example, the C4FIRST.CPP program *could* be rewritten as the following:

```
// Filename: C4FIRST.CPP Initial C++ program that
// demonstrates the C++ comments and shows a few variables
// and their declarations
#include <iostream.h> main() {int i;
// These 4 lines declare 4 variables
```

```
int j;char c;float x;i=4;//i and j are assigned integer
// constants
j=i+7;c='A';// All character constants are enclosed in single
// quotes
x=9.087;// x requires a floating-point value since
// it was declared as a floating-point variable
x=x*4.5;// Change what was in x with a formula
cout<<i<<j<<c<<x; // Send the values of the variables
// to the screen
return 0;}// ALWAYS end programs and functions with return
```

To your C++ compiler, these two programs are exactly the same and will produce the same results. However, to people who must read the program, the first style is *much* more readable. Granted, this is an extreme example.

Readability Is the Key

As long as programs do their job and produce correct output, who cares how well they are written? In today's world of fast computers, abundant memory, and disk space, you should care. Even if nobody else will ever look at your C++ program, you might need to make a change to it at a later date. The more readable you make it, the faster you will be able to find what needs changing and make those changes.

One technique you can use to make your programs more readable is to put lots of *white space* in your programs. As noted, white space consists of the separating lines and spaces throughout a program. Notice that the first few lines in C4FIRST.CPP start in the first column, but the body of the program is indented a few spaces. This helps programmers "zero in" on the important code. When you write programs that contain several sections (called *blocks*), white space helps the programmer's eye drop down more easily to the next indented block.

If you work as a programmer for a company, you will almost certainly be expected to modify someone else's source code, and others will modify your programs. In programming departments, it is said that long-term employees write readable programs. Given this new global economy, and all the changes that face businesses in the years ahead, companies are seeking programmers who write for the future; that is, their programs are straightforward, readable, contain lots of white space (separating lines and spaces), and don't include hard-to-read programming tricks that make for messy programs.

Using Uppercase and Lowercase

Use lowercase abundantly in C++!

Your uppercase and lowercase letters are much more significant in C++ than in most other programming languages. You will find that most of C4FIRST.CPP is in lowercase letters. The entire C++ language is in lowercase. For example, you must type the keywords int, char, and return in lowercase characters. If you used uppercase, your C++ compiler would produce many errors and refuse to compile the program until you fixed them.

Most C++ programmers reserve uppercase characters for some of the words and messages sent to the screen, printer, and disk files, and use lowercase, or mixed case letters for almost everything else. One exception is discussed in Chapter 7, "Preprocessor Directives," covering the #define preprocessor directive.

Braces and *main()*

All C++ programs require the following line:

```
main()
{
```

A C++ block is enclosed between a pair of braces.

The statements following main() will be the first statements executed. The section of a C++ program that begins with main(), followed by an opening brace, {, is called the *main function*. A C++ program is often composed of many functions (small sections of code), and the function called main() is required and is always the first function executed.

All executable C++ statements must end with a semicolon (;).

In the sample program shown here, almost the entire program is main() because the closing brace, }, that follows the opening brace in main(), is at the end of the program. Everything between the two braces is called a *block*. You will read more about blocks later. For now, you should realize that this sample program contains only a single function, main(), and that the entire function is a single block because there is only one pair of braces.

In addition, you should realize that many statements have a semicolon (;) after them. Every executable C++ statement must be followed by a semicolon so that C++ will know where the statements end. The computer ignores all comments, so you don't need to put semicolons after comments. The lines with main() and braces do not end with semicolons either; these lines simply define the beginning and ending of the function and do not actually execute.

As you become better acquainted with C++, you will learn when to include the semicolon and when to leave it off. Many beginning C++ programmers learn quickly when semicolons are required. Your compiler will certainly let you know if you forget to include a semicolon where one is needed.

Figure 4.2 repeats the sample program and contains additional markings to help acquaint you with these new terms. Also included are a few other items that are described later in the chapter.

Figure 4.2

The parts of the
sample program.

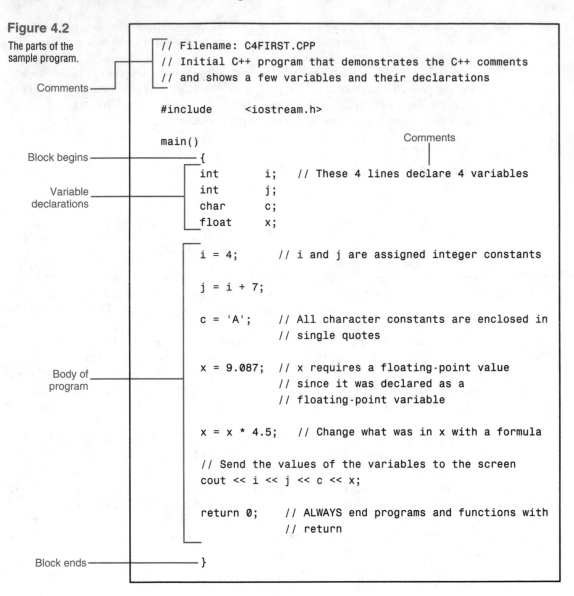

Comments

Block begins

Variable
declarations

Body of
program

Block ends

```
// Filename: C4FIRST.CPP
// Initial C++ program that demonstrates the C++ comments
// and shows a few variables and their declarations

#include      <iostream.h>

main()
{
   int      i;    // These 4 lines declare 4 variables
   int      j;
   char     c;
   float    x;

   i = 4;         // i and j are assigned integer constants

   j = i + 7;

   c = 'A';       // All character constants are enclosed in
                  // single quotes

   x = 9.087;     // x requires a floating-point value
                  // since it was declared as a
                  // floating-point variable

   x = x * 4.5;   // Change what was in x with a formula

   // Send the values of the variables to the screen
   cout << i << j << c << x;

   return 0;      // ALWAYS end programs and functions with
                  // return
}
```

Comments

Comments in C++

In Chapter 3, you learned the difference between a program and its output. Most users of a program do not see the program itself; they see the output from the execution of the program's instructions. Programmers, however, look at the program listings, add new routines, change old ones, and update for new advancements in computer equipment.

As explained earlier, the readability of a program is important so that you and other programmers can look through it without a lot of effort. Nevertheless, no matter how clearly you write C++ programs, you can always improve readability by putting *comments* throughout the program listings.

A comment is a message that explains what is going on at that point in the program. If you wrote a payroll program, for example, you would put a comment before the check-printing routine to describe what was about to happen. You do not put C++ language statements inside a comment—a comment is a message to people looking at your programs, not a message to the computer. Your C++ compiler ignores all comments in a program.

Comments can span more than one line. Notice in the sample program, C4FIRST.CPP, that the first three lines are actually a single comment. This comment explains the filename and a little about the program.

Comments can also share lines with C++ commands. There are several comments out to the right of much of the C4FIRST.CPP program. These comments explain what the individual lines do. Use abundant comments but remember who they are for: *people, not computers.* Use comments if they help explain the code but do not *over*comment. For example, even though you may not be familiar with C++ yet, the following statement is easy; it prints Visual C++ By Example on-screen:

> Comments describe to people what the program is doing.

```
cout << "Visual C++ By Example"; // Print Visual C++ By
                                 // Example on the screen
```

This comment is redundant and adds nothing to the understanding of the line of code. It would be much better in this case to leave the comment out completely. If you find yourself almost repeating the C++ code, leave out that particular comment. Not every line of a C++ program should be commented. Comment only when a line or group of lines needs explaining, in English terms, to the people looking at the program.

If a comment does not span more than one line in your program file, you can start the comment with //. The comment is read from the // to the end of the line. If the comment does span more than one line, you can either start each subsequent line with a //, or you can wrap the comment by starting it with /* and ending it with *.

The following example shows the use of /* and */ as comments:

```
/* Print Visual C++ By Example
   on the screen */
cout << "Visual C++ By Example";
```

> **Note:** C++ comments usually begin with the // symbol.

Of course, it does not matter if you use uppercase letters, lowercase letters, or a mix of both in comments because C++ ignores comments. Most C++ programmers capitalize the first letter of sentences in comments, just as they would in everyday writing. Since people, not computers, read comments, use whatever case seems most appropriate to the message in the comment.

> **Caution:** C++ /* ... */ style comments cannot be nested. That is, you cannot put a comment within another comment. If you do, the C++ compiler will get confused when it sees the first comment end in the middle of the second one.

The following section of a C++ program is illegal because one comment resides within another:

```
sales = 3456.54 * bonus;
/* This is an example of a C++ program
   /* It does NOT
      comment correctly! */
   The first comment did not end before the second began. */
```

This sometimes confuses programmers who are just learning C++ but who know another programming language. In C++, you cannot comment out large sections of code just by inserting a /*...*/ pair at the beginning and end of the section if *any* lines within that section have comments on them. Sometimes programmers like to comment out several lines in a program so that the lines do not execute. This lets the programmer test the remaining lines independently of those commented out. If you were to try this, and nested comments resulted, the compiler would ignore the second begin comment marker (/*) and treat it as a comment. Then, when it encountered the first end comment marker (*/), it would end both comments and any code up to the final end comment marker would no longer be commented out. In the preceding example, the line The first comment did not end before the second began. */ would be compiled as if it were code, and would of course generate errors. A worse situation would be if there were legitimate code that you really didn't want to compile. It would compile anyway, but you wouldn't have any errors to warn you.

Comment As You Go

Put comments in your programs as you write them. You are most familiar with your program logic at the time you are typing the program in the editor. Some people put off including comments until after the program is written. More often than not, the comments never get put in, or only a half-hearted attempt is made.

If you comment as you write your code, you can glance up at the comments while working on later sections of the program, instead of having to decipher the previous code. This greatly helps when you want to look at something earlier in the program.

Examples

 1. Suppose that you want to write a C++ program to produce a fancy, boxed title with your name and flashing dots around it (like a marquee). The C++ code to do this may be difficult to understand and may not, by itself, be understandable to others who look at the program. Before such code, you might want to insert the following comment:

```
// The following few lines draw a fancy box around
// a name and then display flashing dots around the
// name to look like a Hollywood movie marquee.
```

This would not tell C++ to do anything, because a comment is not a C++ command. The comment would, however, make the next few lines of code more understandable to you and others. The comment explains in English, for the people reading the program, exactly what the program is getting ready to do.

 2. You should put the disk filename of the program in an early comment. In the C4FIRST.CPP program shown earlier, for example, the first line is the beginning of a comment:

```
// Filename: C4FIRST.CPP
```

The comment continues on the next two lines, but this part of it explains to anyone who might look at the program listing exactly which disk file it is in. Throughout this book, each program has a comment that includes a suggested filename under which the program can be stored. Each filename begins with Cx, where x is the chapter number in which the program appears—for example, C6VARPR.CPP and C10LNIN.CPP. This will help you find the programs in case another section of the book refers to them later.

> **Tip:** It also may be a good idea to put your name in a comment at the top of a program. If someone has to modify your program at a later date, that person may need to speak with you, the original programmer, before changing it.

The Sample Program Summarized

Now that you have an overview of a C++ program, its structure, and its comments, the rest of this chapter walks you through the entire sample program. Do not attempt to become a C++ expert after you complete this section—that is what the rest of the book is for! Just sit back and follow the discussion of the code.

As described earlier, the C4FIRST.CPP program contains several comments. The following are the first three lines of the program:

```
// Filename: C4FIRST.CPP
// Initial CPP program that demonstrates the C++ comments
// and shows a few variables and their declarations
```

This comment gives the filename and explains the purpose of the program. This is not the only comment in the program; others appear throughout the rest of the code. The next statement is as follows:

```
#include     <iostream.h>
```

An #include statement is an instruction to a part of the compiler called the preprocessor to include some additional information in your program. You will learn about the preprocessor in Chapter 7.

Following are the next two lines (following the blank separating line):

```
main()
{
```

This begins the main() function. Basically, the main() function's opening and closing braces enclose the body of this program and the instructions that actually execute. Many times, C++ programs contain more than one function, but they always contain one called main(). The main() function does not have to be the first one, but it usually is. The opening brace begins the first and only block of this program.

When this program is compiled and run, the computer looks for main() and starts executing whatever instruction follows main()'s opening brace. Here are the next four lines:

```
int      i;     // These 4 lines declare 4 variables
int      j;
char     c;
float    x;
```

These four lines declare variables. A *variable declaration* describes all variables used in that block of code. A C++ program takes data and processes it into meaningful results. All C++ programs include the following:

◆ Commands

◆ Data

The data is made up of *variables* and *constants*. As the name implies, a *variable* is data that can change (it is *variable*) as the program runs. A *constant* remains the same. In real life, a variable might be your age or salary. Both increase over time (if you are lucky!). Your first name and social security number are constants because they remain with you throughout your life and do not change.

Chapter 5, "Variables and Constants," fully explains these concepts. However, just for an overview of the sample program's elements, the following discussion explains variables and constants in this program.

C++ allows several kinds of constants. For now, you simply need to understand that a C++ constant is any number, character, word, or phrase. All the following are valid C++ constants:

```
5.6   -45   'Q'   "Mary"   18.67643   0.0
```

As you can see, some constants are numeric, and some are character-based. The single and double quotation marks around two of the constants are not part of the constants themselves. A single-character constant requires single quotes around it, whereas a string of characters, such as "Mary" requires double quotes.

If you look for the constants in the sample program, you will find the following:

```
4   7   'A'   9.087   4.5
```

A variable is like a box inside your computer that holds something. That something might be a number or character. You can have essentially as many variables as your program needs in order to hold data that changes in the program. However, be aware that there are some limitations on how much memory you can use imposed by the operating system and the amount of memory on your computer. Once you put a value into a variable, it stays in that variable until you change it or put something else in it.

Variables have names so that you can tell them apart. You use the *assignment operator*, the equal sign (=), to assign values to variables. The statement

```
sales = 25000;
```

puts the constant value 25000 into the variable named sales. In the sample program, you will find the following variables:

```
i   j   c   x
```

51

The four lines of code that follow the opening brace of the sample program declare these variables. This variable declaration lets the rest of the program know that two integer variables named i and j, as well as a character variable called c and a floating-point variable called x, will appear throughout the program. If the terms *integer* and *floating point* are new to you, they are basically two different types of numbers. Integers are whole numbers, and floating-point numbers contain decimal points.

You can see the variables being assigned values in the next few statements in the sample program:

```
i = 4;        // i and j are assigned integer constants

j = i + 7;

c = 'A';      // All character constants are enclosed in
              // single quotes

x = 9.087;    // x requires a floating-point value
              // since it was declared as a
              // floating-point variable

x = x * 4.5;  // Change what was in x with a formula
```

The first line puts a 4 in the integer variable i. The second line adds a 7 to the variable i's value to get an 11, which then gets assigned to (put into) the variable called j. The plus sign (+) in C++ works the same as on calculators. The other primary math operators are shown in Table 4.1.

Table 4.1. The primary math operators.

Operator	Meaning	Example
+	Addition	4 + 5
-	Subtraction	7 - 2
*	Multiplication	12 * 6
/	Division	48 / 12

The character constant A is assigned to the c variable. The number 9.087 is assigned to the variable called x, and then x is immediately overwritten with a new value: itself (9.087) times 4.5. This helps illustrate why computer designers use an asterisk (*) for multiplication and not a small x as people do when multiplying. The computer would confuse the variable x with the multiplication symbol x if both were allowed.

> **Tip:** If there are mathematical operators on the right side of the equal sign, the math is completely done before the assignment is performed.

The next line (after the comment) includes the following special, and at first confusing, statement:

```
cout << i << ' ' << j << ' '<< c << ' ' << x;
```

When the program runs and gets to this line, it prints the contents of the four variables to the screen.

The actual output from this line is as follows:

```
4 11 A 40.891499
```

Because the cout is the only one in the program, this is the only output the program produces. You might think that the program is rather long for such a small line of output. Once you learn more about C++, you will see much more useful programs.

The cout is not a C++ command but is actually the name of the *console output stream*; the <<s are overloaded operators defined by the stream classes. You'll learn about classes in Chapter 33; for now, cout is treated as if it were a function. The same applies to cin, which is the *console input stream*.

> **Note:** For the QuickWin programs in this book, the console input and output streams are assigned, respectively, to Stdin and Stdout. Refer to figure 3.4 in Chapter 3 for an example of cin and cout as they appear in the output window of a QuickWin program.

```
return 0;      // ALWAYS end programs and functions with
               // return

}
```

Put a *return* statement at the end of each function.

The return statement simply tells C++ that this function is finished and to return a value of zero to DOS.

The return statement is optional. C++ would know when it reached the end of the program without a return. It is a good programming practice, however, to put a return statement at the end of every function, including main(). Because some functions require a return statement (if you are returning values) but others do not, you will be better off learning the habit of using this statement instead of leaving one out when you really need it.

The closing brace after the return does three things in this program. It signals the end of a block (which was begun earlier with the opening brace), the end of the main() function, and the end of the program.

Summary

Now that you have a feel for what a C++ program looks like, it is time to begin considering the specifics of commands. This chapter focused on commenting your programs well. You also learned a little about variables and constants. The variables and constants hold the program's data; without them, the term *data processing* would no longer be meaningful.

Starting with the next chapter, you begin to write your own programs. Chapter 5 examines constants and variables, describes their uses, and explains how you choose names for them.

Review Questions

Answers to Review Questions are in Appendix B.

1. What must go before and after each multiline comment in a C++ program?

2. What is a variable?

3. What is a constant?

4. True or false: You can put a comment within another comment.

5. What are four C++ math operators?

6. What operator puts a value into a variable? (*Hint:* It is called the *assignment operator*.)

7. True or false: A variable can consist of only two types: integer and character.

8. What is the built-in function that writes output to the screen?

9. Is the following a variable name or a string constant?

   ```
   city
   ```

10. What, if anything, is wrong with the following C statement?

    ```
    RETURN;
    ```

Variables and Constants

To understand data processing with C++, you must understand how C++ creates, stores, and manipulates data. This chapter introduces the following topics:

- ♦ Variables and constants
- ♦ Naming and using C++ variables
- ♦ The types of C++ variables
- ♦ Declaring variables
- ♦ Assigning values to variables
- ♦ The types of C++ constants
- ♦ Special constants

Now that you have an overview of C++, you can begin to write your own programs. Before you are done with this chapter, you will be writing C++ programs from scratch.

Garbage in, garbage out!

You learned in the last chapter that C++ programs consist of commands and data. Data is the heart of all C++ programs; if you do not correctly declare or use variables and constants, your data will be inaccurate, and your results will be, too. An old computer adage says that if you have "Garbage in, you will get garbage out!" This is very true. Most of the time, people blame computers for mistakes that are made. The computers themselves are probably not to blame, but the data was most likely entered into the programs incorrectly.

This chapter focuses on numeric variables and numeric constants. If you are not a "numbers" person, don't fret. Working with numbers is the computer's job. You just have to understand how to let the computer know what you want it to do.

Variable Characteristics

Variables have characteristics. When you decide that your program needs another variable, you simply declare a new variable, and C++ makes sure that you get it. You can declare a C++ variable anywhere in a block of code, as long as you declare it before you use it. To declare a variable, you must understand its characteristics:

♦ Each variable has a name.

♦ Each variable has a type.

♦ A variable holds a value that you assign to it.

The following sections explain these characteristics.

Naming Variables

Because you can have many variables in a single program, you must assign names to them so that you can keep track of them. Variable names are unique, just as house addresses are unique. If two variables had the same name, C would not know which variable you wanted when you requested one of them.

Microsoft Visual C++ variable names can be as short as a single letter or as long as 247 characters. Their names must begin with a letter of the alphabet or an underscore (_). After the first letter or underscore, they can contain letters, numbers, and additional underscores.

> **Tip:** The underscore (_) helps separate parts of the variable name because spaces are not allowed in the name.

The following variable names are valid:

```
salary   aug91_sales  _i   index_age   amount

Salary   Aug91Sales   _i   IndexAge    Amount
```

Some C++ programmers prefer to use all lowercase letters for variable names, with underscores to separate the names into words, as shown on the first line above. A more recent trend uses mixed uppercase and lowercase, without the underscores, as shown on the second line. You do not have to follow either method, but you should know that, to the C++ compiler, uppercase letters in variable names are very different from lowercase letters. Therefore, each of the following four variables are completely different to your C++ compiler:

```
sales   Sales   SALES   sALES
```

Do not give a variable the name of a command or library function.

Be very careful with the Shift key when you type a variable name. Do not inadvertently change the case of a variable name throughout a program; if you do, C++ will think that they are distinct and separate variables and will not operate on them properly.

Variables cannot have the same name as a C++ command or library function. Watch out for these when naming variables. The following are examples of *invalid* variable names:

```
81 sales   Aug91+Sales   MY AGE   cout
```

Use Meaningful Variable Names

Although you can call a variable any name that fits the naming rules (as long as the name is not being used by another variable in the program), you should always use meaningful variable names. Use names that help describe the values held by the variables.

For example, keeping track of total payroll in a variable called `total_payroll` is more descriptive than using the variable name `XYZ34`. Even though both names are valid, `total_payroll` is easier to remember, and you have a good idea of what the variable holds by looking at its name.

Variable Types

Variables can hold different *types* of data. Table 5.1 lists the different types of C++ variables. If a variable holds an integer, for example, C++ assumes that no decimal point or fractional part (the part to the right of the decimal point) exists for the variable's value. Many types are possible in C++. For now, the most important types that you should concentrate on are `char`, `int`, and `float`. You can append the prefix `long` to make some variables hold larger values than they would otherwise hold. Using the `unsigned` prefix makes them hold positive numbers only.

Table 5.1. Possible C++ variable types.

Declaration Name	Type
char	Character
unsigned char	Unsigned character
signed char	Signed character (same as char)
int	Integer
unsigned int	Unsigned integer

continues

57

Table 5.1. Continued

Declaration Name	Type
signed int	Signed integer (same as int)
short int	Short integer
unsigned short int	Unsigned short integer
signed short int	Signed short integer (same as short int)
long	Long integer
long int	Long integer (same as long)
signed long int	Signed long integer (same as long int)
unsigned long int	Unsigned long integer
float	Floating-point
double	Double-precision floating-point
long double	Long-double precision floating-point

Declare all variables in a C++ program before you use them.

The next section describes each of these types in more detail. For now, you need to concentrate on the importance of declaring them before using them. You can declare a variable in two places:

◆ Anywhere within a block of code, as long as the variable is declared before it is referenced (used) in the block of code

◆ Before a function name, such as before main()

The first of these locations is the most common and is used throughout much this book. (If you declare a variable before a function name, the variable is called a *global* variable. Later chapters address the pros and cons of global variables.) To declare a variable, you must state its type followed by its name. In the last chapter, you saw a program that declared four variables in the following way.

Start of the main() *function.*
Declare the variables i *and* j *as integers.*
Declare the variable c *as a character.*
Declare the variable x *as a floating-point variable.*

```
main()
{
     int      i;    // These 4 lines declare 4 variables
     int      j;
     char     c;
     float    x;
     // Rest of program follows
```

This declares two integer variables named i and j. You have no idea what is inside those variables, however. You generally cannot assume that a variable holds zero or any other number until you assign a value to the variable. The first two lines basically tells C++ the following:

> "I am going to use two integer variables somewhere in this program. Be expecting them. I want them named i and j. When I put a value into i or j, I will ensure that the value is an integer and not a floating-point number or anything else."

The second line in this example declares a character variable called c. Only single characters should be placed there. A floating-point variable called x is declared next.

Examples

1. Suppose that you have to keep track of a person's first, middle, and last initials. Because an initial is obviously a character, it would be prudent to declare three character variables to hold the three initials. In C++, you can do that with the following statement:

```
main()
{
     char     first, middle, last;
     // Rest of program follows
```

This statement can go after the opening brace of main() and lets the rest of the program know that you will require these three character variables.

2. You also can declare these three variables on three separate lines, improving readability and maintainability:

```
main()
{
     char     first;
     char     middle;
     char     last;
     // Rest of program follows
```

3. Suppose that you want to keep track of a person's age and weight. If you want to store these values as whole numbers, they can probably go into integer variables. The following statement declares these variables:

```
main()
{
    int     age, weight;
    // Rest of program follows
```

4. The next section explores each of the variable types in detail. Despite the fact that there are so many types, you typically use character, integer, and floating-point variables more than any other. In short, character variables hold single characters, integer variables hold whole numbers, and floating-point variables hold numbers that contain decimal points.

Suppose that a teacher wants to keep track of a class average score, the average letter grade, and the number of students in the class. Note how all three common types of variables are used here:

```
main()
{
    char            letter_grade;
    float       class_avg;
    int             class_size;
    // Rest of program follows
```

Looking at Data Types

You may be wondering why it is important to have so many variable types. After all, a number is just a number. C++ has more data types than almost any other programming language. It turns out that the type of variable is critical, but knowing what type to use is not as difficult as it may first seem.

The character variable is easy to understand. This variable can hold only a single character. You cannot put more than a single character into a character variable.

> **Note:** C++ does not have a string variable, as do many other programming languages. You cannot hold more than a single character in a C++ character variable. To store a string of characters, you must use an *aggregate* variable type, which combines other fundamental types from table 5.1, to create an array. Chapter 6, "Character Strings and Character Arrays," explains this more fully.

Integer variables hold whole numbers. Although mathematicians may cringe at this definition, an *integer* is really just any number that does not contain a decimal point. All the following are integers:

```
45   -932   0   12   5421
```

Floating-point numbers contain decimal points. They are known as *real* numbers to mathematicians. Whenever you need to store a salary, a temperature, or any other number that may have a fractional part (a decimal portion), you must store the number in a floating-point variable. All the following are floating-point numbers, and any of the floating-point variables can hold them:

```
45.12   -2344.5432   0.00   .04594
```

Sometimes you have to keep track of very large numbers or very small numbers. Table 5.2 shows a list of ranges that each C++ variable type might hold. *Use this table only as a guide*; different compilers and different computers may allow for different ranges.

Table 5.2. Typical ranges that C++ variables hold.

Type	Range
char	−128 to 127
unsigned char	0 to 255
signed char	−128 to 127
int	−32768 to 32767
unsigned int	0 to 65535
signed int	−32768 to 32767
short int	−32768 to 32767
unsigned short int	0 to 65535
signed short int	−32768 to 32767
long int	−2147483648 to 2147483647
signed long int	−2147483648 to 2147483647
unsigned long int	0 to 4294967295
float	−3.4E+38 to 3.4E+38
double	−1.7E+308 to 1.7E+308
long double	−1.2E+4932 to 1.2E+4932

*Note: The floating-point ranges are shown in scientific notation To determine the actual range, take the number before the E (meaning exponent) and multiply it by 10 raised to the power after the plus sign. For example, a floating-point number (a type float) can contain a number as small as −3.4 * 10^{38}.*

Caution: Experienced C++ programmers know that they cannot count on using this exact table on every computer that uses C++. These ranges may be much different on another computer. Remember to use this table only as a guide.

Notice that long integers and long doubles tend to hold larger numbers (and therefore higher precision) than regular integers and regular double floating-point variables. This is true because of the larger number of memory locations used by many of the C++ compilers for these data types. Again, you cannot count on this always being the case, but it generally is.

Use Variables That Accommodate the Size of the Data

If the long variable types hold larger numbers than the regular ones, you might initially want to use long variables for all your data. This is not required in most cases and will slow down your program's execution.

As Appendix A explains, the more memory locations used by data, the larger that data can be. However, every time your computer has to access more storage for a single variable (which is usually the case for long variables), the CPU takes much longer to access it, calculate with it, and store it. As designed by Kernighan and Ritchie, the basic data types (`char`, `int`, and `float`) should be optimized for the computer, and in Visual C++, they are.

Use long variables only if you suspect your data will overflow the typical data-type ranges. Although the ranges will vary on other computers, you should have an idea of whether your numbers may exceed the computer's storage ranges. If you are working with extremely large numbers (or extremely small and fractional numbers), consider using long variables so that they hold the extra data width.

Generally, all numeric variables should be signed (the default) unless you know for certain that your data will contain only positive numbers. Some values, such as age and distance, are always positive. Other data can be negative. By making a variable an unsigned variable, you gain a little extra storage range, but that extra range of values must always be positive.

Obviously, you must be very aware of what kinds of data your variables will hold. You certainly do not always know exactly what all of them will hold, but you will have a general idea. If you want to store a person's age, for example, you know that a long integer variable would probably be a waste of space because nobody would live longer than a regular integer could hold.

At first, it may seem strange that table 5.2 states that character variables can hold numeric values. In C++, integers and character variables can be used interchangeably in many cases. As explained in Appendix A, each of the ASCII table characters has a unique number that corresponds to the character's location in the table. If you store a number in a character variable, C++ will actually treat the data as if it were the ASCII character which matched that number in the table. Conversely, you can store character data in an integer variable. C++ will find that character's ASCII number and store it instead of the character. Examples that help illustrate this appear a little later in this chapter.

Designating Long, Unsigned, and Floating-Point Constants

When you type a number, C++ interprets its type as the smallest type that can hold the number. For example, if you type **63**, C++ knows that this number will fit into a signed integer memory location. C++ will not treat the number as a long integer because 63 is not large enough to warrant a long integer constant size.

You can append a suffix character to numeric constants to override the default type, however. If you put an **L** at the end of an integer, C++ interprets that integer as a long integer. The number **63** is an integer constant, whereas the number **63L** is a long integer constant.

Assign the **U** suffix to designate an unsigned integer constant. The number **63** is, by default, a signed integer constant. If you type **63U**, however, C++ treats it as an unsigned integer. The suffix **UL** indicates an unsigned long constant.

C++ interprets all floating-point constants (numbers that contain decimal points) as double floating-point constants. This ensures the maximum accuracy in such numbers. If you used the constant **6.82**, C++ treats it as a double floating-point data type, even though it would fit in a regular float. You can append the floating-point suffix, **F**, or the long double floating-point suffix, **L**, to constants that contain decimal points in order to represent either a floating-point constant or a long double floating-point constant instead of the default double constant value.

You may rarely use these suffixes, but if you have to assign a constant value to an extended or unsigned variable, you may gain a little more accuracy if you append the **U**, **L**, **UL**, or **F** (their lowercase equivalents work, too) at the end of the constant.

Assigning Values to Variables

Now that you know about the C++ variable types, you are ready to learn how to put values into those variables. You do this with the *assignment* statement. The equal sign (=) is used for assigning values to variables. The format of the assignment statement is as follows:

```
variable = expression;
```

The *variable* is any variable you declared earlier. The *expression* is any variable, constant, expression, or combination that produces a resulting data type which is the same as the *variable*'s data type.

> **Tip:** Think of the equal sign (=) as a left-pointing arrow. Loosely, the equal sign means that you want to take whatever number, variable, or expression is on the right side of the equal sign and put it into the variable on the left side of the equal sign.

Examples

1. If you want to keep track of your current age, salary, and dependents, you can store these values in three C++ variables. You first declare the variables by deciding on correct types and good names for them. You then assign values to them. Later in the program, these values may change—for example, if the program calculates a new pay increase for you.

Good variable names are age, salary, and dependents. To declare these three variables, the first part of the main() function might look like this:

```
// Declare and store three values
main()
{
    int       age;
    float     salary;
    int       dependents;
```

Notice that you do not have to declare all integer variables together, but you can if you want. Once these variables are declared, the next three statements can assign them values, as in

```
age = 32;
salary = 25000.00;
dependents = 2;
```

Note that this program is not complete. After these assignment statements come other statements and then a closing brace.

2. The preceding example is not very long, and it does not do much. It does, however, illustrate using values and assigning them to variables. Do not put commas in values you assign to variables. Numeric constants should *never* contain commas. The following statement is invalid:

```
salary = 25,000.00;
```

3. You can assign variables to other variables, or mathematical expressions to other variables. Suppose that you stored your tax rate in a variable called tax_rate earlier in a program, and you decide to use your tax rate for your spouse's rate as well. At the proper point in the program, you can code the following:

```
spouse_tax_rate - tax_rate;
```

Putting the spaces around the equal sign is okay with the C++ compiler, but you do not have to include them. Use whatever you are most comfortable with.

The value in tax_rate will, at this line's point in the program, be copied to a new variable named spouse_tax_rate. The value in tax_rate will still be there after this line finishes. Of course, the assumption is that the variables were declared earlier in the program.

If your spouse's tax rate is going to be 40 percent of yours, you can assign an expression to the spouse's variables, as in

```
spouse_tax_rate = tax_rate * .40;
```

Any of the four mathematical symbols you learned in the last chapter, as well as all those you will learn later in this book, can be part of the expression you assign to a variable.

4. If you want to assign character data to a character variable, you must enclose the character in single quote marks. All C++ character constants must be enclosed in single quote marks.

The following section of a program declares three initial variables and then assigns three initials to them. The initials are character constants because they are enclosed within single quotes.

```
main()
{
    char     first, middle, last;
    first = 'G';
    middle = 'M';
    last = 'P';
    // Rest of program follows
```

Of course, you can later put other values into these variables if the program warrants it.

> **Caution:** Do not mix types. In most cases, C++ will let you, but the results are unpredictable. For example, you could have stored a floating-point constant in `middle`, as shown here:
>
> ```
> middle = 345.43244;    // Do not do this!
> ```
>
> If you did so, `middle` would hold a strange value that seems to be meaningless garbage. Make sure that values you assign to variables match the variable's type. The only major exception to this occurs when you assign an integer to a character variable, or a character to an integer variable, as you will see shortly.

5. C++ gives you the ability to declare *and* initialize variables with values at the same time. For example, the following section of code declares an integer `age`, a floating-point `salary`, and three character variables, and initializes them at the time of declaration:

```
main()
{
    int       age = 30;
    float     salary = 25000.00;
    char      first = 'G', middle = 'M', last = 'P';
    // Rest of program follows
```

This is a little easier than first declaring them and then initializing them with values. As the preceding chapter discussed, `cout` is used to print the values of variables and constants. Chapter 8, "Simple Input and Output," explains `cout` in more detail. Just as a preview, the following `cout` statements will print the variables declared in the preceding section of code:

```
cout << age << ' ' << salary << ' ';
cout << first << ' ' << middle << ' ' << last;
```

Putting all of these together into one commented program (albeit a short one), produces the following code:

```
// Filename: C5VAR.CPP
// Program that initializes and prints five variables

#include  <iostream.h>

main()
{
    int       age = 30;
    float     salary = 25000.00;
```

```
        char    first = 'G', middle = 'M', last = 'P';

        cout << age << ' ' << salary << ' ';
        cout << first << ' ' << middle << ' ' << last;
        return 0;
}
```

If you were to compile and run this program, you would see the following output:

```
30 25000 G M P
```

The numbers are not formatted very well (especially `salary`), but you will soon see how to produce output that looks the way you want it to look.

Special Constants

As with variables, C++ has several types of constants. Remember that a constant does not change. Integer constants are whole numbers that do not contain decimal points. Floating-point constants are numbers that contain a fractional portion (a decimal point with an optional value to the right of the decimal point).

Special Integer Constants

You already know that an integer is any whole number without a decimal point. C++ lets you assign integer constants to variables, use integer constants for calculations, and print integer constants with `cout`.

A regular integer constant cannot begin with a leading `0`. To C++, the number `012` is *not* the number twelve. If you precede an integer constant with a leading `0`, C++ interprets it as an *octal* constant. An octal constant is a base-8 number. The octal numbering system is not used much in today's computer systems. The newer versions of C++ retain octal capabilities for compatibility with previous versions when octal played a more important role in computers.

Another special integer that is possible in C++ *is* still greatly used today. It is a base-16 or *hexadecimal* constant. Appendix A describes the hexadecimal numbering system. If you want to represent a hexadecimal integer constant, append the `0x` prefix to it. In other words, all the following numbers are hexadecimal numbers:

```
0x10   0x2C4   0xFFFF   0X9
```

An octal integer constant contains a leading *0*, and a hexadecimal constant contains a leading *0x*.

Notice that it does not matter whether you use a lowercase `x` or an uppercase `X` after the leading zero, or a lowercase or an uppercase hexadecimal digit (for hexadecimal numbers A through F). If you write business application programs in C++, you might think that you'll never have the need for using hexadecimal, and you might be correct. However, for a complete understanding of C++, and your computer in general, you should be familiar with the fundamentals of hexadecimal numbers.

Table 5.3 shows a few integer constants represented in their regular decimal, hexadecimal, and octal notations. Each row contains the same number in all three bases.

Table 5.3. Integer constants represented in three bases.

Base-10 Decimal	Base-16 Hexadecimal	Base-8 Octal
8	0x08	010
10	0x0A	012
16	0x10	020
65536	0x10000	0200000
25	0x19	031

Note: Floating-point constants may begin with a leading zero. They will be properly interpreted by C++ because only integers are possible hexadecimal and octal constants.

Your Computer's Word Size Is Important

If you write many system programs that use hexadecimal numbers, you will probably want to store those numbers in unsigned variables. This keeps C++ from improperly interpreting positive numbers as negative ones.

For example, your computer stores integers in two-byte words. The hexadecimal constant 0xFFFF represents either –1 or 65535, depending on how the sign bit is interpreted. If you declare an unsigned integer, such as

```
unsigned int i_num = 0xFFFF;
```

C++ knows that you want it to use the sign bit as data and not as the sign. If, however, you declare the same value as a signed integer, as in

```
int i_num = 0xFFFF;    // The word "signed" is optional
```

C++ thinks that this is a negative number (–1) because the sign bit is turned on (if you were to convert 0xFFFF to binary, you would get 16 ones). Appendix A describes these concepts in more detail.

String Constants

A string constant is always enclosed in double quotes.

One type of C++ constant, called the *string constant*, does not have a matching variable. A string constant is *always* enclosed within double quote marks. Here are examples of string constants:

```
"C++ Programming"    "123"    " "    "4323 E. Oak Road"    "x"
```

Any string of characters between double quotes, as well as single characters between double quotes, is considered to be a string constant. A single space, word, or group of words between double quotes is a C++ string constant. If the string constant contains only numeric digits, it is *not* a number, but a string of numeric digits with which you cannot perform math. You can perform math with numbers only—not with string constants that contain numbers, or even a character constant that might contain a number (enclosed in a single quote).

> **Note:** A string constant is *any* character, digit, or group of characters enclosed in double quotes. A character constant is any character enclosed in single quotes.

The double quotes are never considered part of the string constant. The double quotes surround the string and simply inform your C++ compiler that the constant is a string constant, not some other type of constant.

You can print string constants easily. Simply put the string constants in a cout call, as in the following line.

Print Visual C++ By Example *to the screen.*

```
cout << "Visual C++ 1.5 By Example";
```

Examples

1. The following program displays a simple message to the screen. No variables are needed because no data is stored or calculated.

```cpp
// Filename: C5ST1.CPP
// Displays a string on the screen

#include  <iostream.h>

main()
{
    cout << "C++ programming is fun!";
    return 0;
}
```

Remember to make the last line in your C++ programs (before the closing brace) a `return` statement.

2. You will want to label the output from your programs. Do not print the value of a variable unless you also print a string constant that describes the variable. The following program computes sales tax for a sale and then prints the tax. Notice that a message is printed first, which tells the user of the program what the next number means.

```cpp
// Filename: C5ST2.CPP
// Computes sales tax and with an appropriate message

#include     <iostream.h>

main()
{
    float     sale, tax;
    float     tax_rate = .08;      // Sales tax percentage

    // Determine the amount of the sale
    sale = 22.54;

    // Compute the sales tax
    tax = sale * tax_rate;

    // Print the results
    cout << "The sales tax is: " << tax;

    return 0;
}
```

Here is the output of this program:

```
The sales tax is: 1.8032
```

The Tail of String Constants

An additional aspect of string constants sometimes confuses beginning C++ programmers. All string constants end with a zero. You do not see the zero, but C++ makes sure that the zero is stored at the end of the string in memory. Figure 5.1 shows what the string `"Visual C++ Program"` looks like in memory.

Figure 5.1

A string constant always ends with a zero in memory.

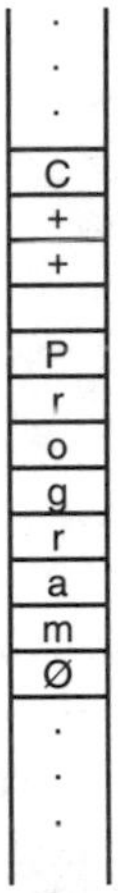

```
.
.
.
C
+
+

P
r
o
g
r
a
m
Ø
.
.
.
```

You do not have to worry about putting the zero at the end of a string constant; C++ does this for you whenever it stores a string. If your program were to contain the string `"Visual C++ Program"`, the compiler would recognize it as a string constant (from the double quotes) and store the zero at the end.

The zero, called the *string delimiter*, is important to C++. Without this delimiter, C++ would not know where the string constant ended in memory. (Remember that the double quotes are not stored as part of the string, so C++ cannot use them to determine where the string ends.)

The string-delimiting zero is *not* the same as a character zero. If you look at the ASCII table in Appendix C, you will see that the first entry, ASCII number 0, is the *null* character. This is actually what delimits strings in C++: the null, ASCII zero. (If you are unfamiliar with the ASCII table, read Appendix B for a review.) Sometimes you will hear that C++ string constants end in *ASCII 0*, or the *null zero*. This differentiates the string-delimiting zero from the character `'0'`, whose ASCII value is 48.

All string constants end in a null zero, sometimes called the binary zero or ASCII zero.

As explained in Appendix A, all memory locations in your computer hold bit patterns for characters. If the letter A is stored in memory, an A is not really there, but the binary bit pattern for the ASCII A (01000001) is stored there. Because the binary bit pattern for the null zero is 00000000, the string-delimiting zero is also called a *binary zero*.

To illustrate this concept further, figure 5.2 shows the bit patterns for the following string constant when stored in memory:

```
"I am 30."
```

Figure 5.2

The bit pattern showing the difference between the null zero and the character zero.

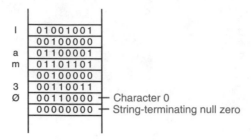

I	01001001
	00100000
a	01100001
m	01101101
	00100000
3	00110011
Ø	00110000 — Character 0
	00000000 — String-terminating null zero

This concept is fairly advanced, but you need to understand it before you continue. If you are new to computers, you should read Appendix A. Figure 5.2 shows how a string is stored in your computer's memory at the binary level. It is important for you to recognize that the character 0 inside the number 30 is not the same zero (at the bit level) as the string-terminating null zero. If it were, C++ would think that this string ended early (after the 3), which is incorrect.

The Length of Strings

Many times, your program needs to know the length of a string. This will become critical when you learn how to accept string input from the keyboard.

> **Note:** The length of a string is the number of characters up to, but not including, the delimiting null zero.

The length of a string constant does not include the null binary zero.

In other words, when you need to know how long a string constant is, or when you need to tell C++ how long it is (as you will see a little later), you need to count the number of characters in the string. Do not include the null character in that count, even though you know that C++ will add it to the end of the string.

Examples

1. The following are some string constants:

```
"0"      "C++"      "A much longer string constant"
```

2. Note these string constants and their corresponding string lengths:

String	Length
"C++"	3
"0"	1
"Hello"	5
""	0
"30 oranges"	10

Special Character Constants

All C++ character constants should be enclosed within single quotes. The single quotes are not part of the character, but they serve to delimit it. All the following are valid C++ character constants:

```
'w'   'W'   'C'   '7'   '*'   '='   '.'   'K'
```

C++ does not append a null zero to the end of character constants. Be aware that the following constants are very different to C++:

```
'R'   "R"
```

The first `'R'` is a single character constant. It is one character long, as *all* character constants (and variables) are one character long. The second `"R"` is a string constant because it is delimited by double quotes. Its length is also one, but it includes an extra null zero in memory so that C++ knows where the string ends. Because of this difference, you cannot mix character constants and character strings. Figure 5.3 shows how these two constants are stored in memory.

Figure 5.3

The character constant 'R' and the string constant "R" stored in memory.

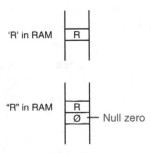

'R' in RAM | R

"R" in RAM | R / Ø — Null zero

All the alphabetic, numeric, and special characters on your keyboard can be character constants. There are some characters, however, that cannot be represented with your keyboard. These include some of the higher ASCII characters, such as the Spanish Ñ. Because you do not have keys for every character in the ASCII table, C++ provides a way for you to represent these characters by typing the character's ASCII hex number inside the single quotes.

For example, to store the Spanish Ñ in a variable, look up its hexadecimal ASCII number in Appendix C. You will find that it is A5. Prepend the prefix \x to it and enclose it in single quotes. Then C++ will know to use the special character. You can do this with the following code:

```
char sn='\xA5';     // Puts the Spanish N into the variable
                    // called sn
```

This is the way to store (or print) any character from the ASCII table, even if the character does not have a key on your keyboard.

The single quote marks still tell C++ that a *single* character is inside the quotes. Even though '\xA5' contains four characters inside the quotes, those four characters represent a single character, not a character string. If you were to include these four characters inside a string constant, C++ would treat them as a single character within the string. The string constant

```
"An accented a is \xA0"
```

is a C++ string that is 18 characters long. C++ will interpret the \xA0 character as the á, just as it should.

> **Caution:** If you are familiar with entering ASCII characters by typing their ASCII numbers with the Alt-*number* key (from the keypad), do not use this method in your C++ programs. Although the Visual C++ compiler supports the method, your program might not be portable to another C++ compiler.

Any character interpreted with a backslash (\), such as those in this discussion, are called *escape sequences* or *escape characters*. Table 5.4 shows some additional escape sequences that come in handy when you want to print special characters.

Table 5.4. Special C++ escape sequence characters.

Escape Sequence	Meaning
\a	Alarm (the terminal's bell)
\b	Backspace
\f	Formfeed (for the printer)
\n	Newline (carriage return and linefeed)
\r	Carriage return
\t	Tab
\v	Vertical tab
\\	Backslash (\)
\?	Question mark
\'	Single quote
\"	Double quote

Escape Sequence	Meaning
\ooo	Octal number
\xhh	Hexadecimal number
\0	The null zero (or binary zero)

> **Tip:** Include \n in a cout if you want it to skip to the next line.

Math with C++ Characters

Because C++ links characters so closely with their ASCII numbers, you can actually perform arithmetic on character data. Note the following section of code:

```
char  c;
c = 'T' + 5;      // Add 5 to the ASCII character
```

This actually stores a Y in c. The ASCII value of the letter T is 84. Adding 5 to 84 produces 89. Because the variable c is not an integer variable but is a character variable, C++ knows to put the ASCII character for 89 in c and not the number itself.

Conversely, you can store character constants in integer variables. If you do, C++ actually stores the matching ASCII number for that character. Note this section of code:

```
int i = 'P';
```

This does *not* put a letter P in i, because i is not a character variable. C++ assigns the number 80 to the variable, as 80 is the ASCII number for the letter P.

Examples

1. To print two names on two different lines, you include \n between them.

   Print Harry to the screen, drop cursor down to newline, and print Jerry.

   ```
   cout << "Harry" << '\n' << "Jerry";
   ```

   When the program gets to this line, it prints

   ```
   Harry
   Jerry
   ```

2. The following short program prints names to the screen in columns because the program assigns the \t (tab) escape sequence to a variable and then prints that variable between each pair of names:

```
// Filename: C5COLS.CPP
// Prints out names in columns to screen

#include  <iostream.h>

main()
{
    char    tab='\t';

    cout << "Harry" << tab << "Jerry" << "\n";
    cout << "Hal" << tab << "Joe" << "\n";
    cout << "Harriet" << tab << "Josephine";
    return 0;

}
```

The tab character causes the program to skip to the next tab stop before printing the second name on each line. When the program runs, it produces the following output:

```
Harry   Jerry
Hal     Joe
Harriet Josephine
```

3. Without these escape sequences, you would have no way to print double quote marks. Because double quote marks delimit strings, C++ would think that the string you were printing ended too early. The backslash and single quote cannot print regularly either; C++ interprets the backslash as an escape sequence prefix, and the single quote as a character constant delimiter. Therefore, the three escape sequences \", \\, and \' let you print these characters as the following program shows:

```
// Filename: C5SPEC2.CPP
// Prints quotes and a backslash

#include  <iostream.h>

main()
{
    cout << "Albert said, \"I will be going now.\" \n";
    cout << "The backslash character looks like this: \\
\n";
    cout << "I\'m learning C++ \n";
    return 0;
}
```

The \n is included to send the cursor to the next line after each cout. The output from this program is as follows:

```
Albert said, "I will be going now."
The backslash character looks like this: \
I'm learning C++
```

Summary

A firm grasp of C++'s foundation is critical to covering the material in more detail. This is one of the last general-topic chapters in this book. You learned about variable types and constant types, how to name variables, and how to assign values to them. These issues are important to your understanding of the rest of C++.

This chapter showed you how to store in variables almost every type of constant. There is no string variable, so you cannot store string constants in string variables, as you can in other programming languages. However, you can "fool" C++ into thinking that it has a string variable by using a character array to hold strings. The next chapter teaches this important concept.

Review Questions

Answers to Review Questions are in Appendix B.

1. Which of the following variable names are valid?

    my_name   89_sales   sales_89   a-salary

2. Which of the following constants are characters, strings, integers, and floating-point constants?

    0   -12.0   "2.0"   "X"   'X'   65.4   -708   '0'

3. How many variables do the following statements declare, and what are their types?

```
int     i, j, k;
char    c, d, e;
float   x = 65.43;
```

4. With what do all string constants end?

5. True or false: An unsigned variable can hold a larger value than a signed variable.

6. How many characters of storage does the following constant take?

    '\x41'

7. How is the following string stored at the bit level?

```
"Order 10 of them."
```

8. How is the following string (called a *null string*) stored at the bit level? (*Hint:* The length is zero, but there is still a terminating character.)

```
" "
```

Review Exercises

1. Write the C++ code to store in three variables: your weight (you can fib), height in feet, and shoe size. Declare the variables and assign them values in the body of the program.

2. Rewrite the program in the preceding exercise, adding proper cout statements to print the values to the screen. Use appropriate messages (by printing string constants) to describe the numbers that are printed.

3. Write a program that stores a value in every type of variable C++ allows. You must first declare each variable at the top of the program. Put numbers in the variables and print them out to see how C++ stores and prints them.

Character Strings and Character Arrays

Even though C++ has no string variables, you can emulate string variables by using character arrays. The concept of arrays may be new to you, but this chapter shows how easily you can declare and use them. Once you declare arrays, they can hold character strings, as if they were actual string variables.

This chapter introduces the following topics:

♦ Character arrays

♦ Assigning string values to character arrays

♦ Printing character arrays

♦ How character arrays differ from strings

After you finish this chapter, you'll be on your way to manipulating almost every type of variable C++ offers. Being able to manipulate characters and words is one thing that separates your computer from powerful calculators, giving the computer true data processing capabilities.

Character Arrays

A string constant can be stored in an array of characters.

There's a variable for almost every type of data in C++, but no variable exists that will hold character strings. The authors of the C++ language realized that users needed some way to store strings in variables. Instead of storing strings in string variables (some languages, such as BASIC and Pascal, have string variables), you must store them in an *array* of characters.

If you have never programmed before, an array will be new to you. Most programming languages allow the use of arrays. An *array* is a list (sometimes called a *table*) of variables. Suppose that you have to keep track of the sales of 100 salespersons. You could make up 100 variable names and assign each one a different salesperson's sales. You would have a difficult time keeping track of all those variable names, however. If you were to put them into an array of floating-point variables, you would have to keep track of only a single name (the array name) and then reference each of the 100 values with a numeric subscript.

Chapter 28, "Pointers and Arrays," covers processing arrays in more detail than this chapter. However, to work with character string data in your early programs, you need to become familiar with the concept of an array of characters, called a *character array*.

Because a string is simply a list of one or more characters, a character array is a perfect place to hold strings of information. Suppose that you want to keep track of a person's full name, age, and salary by placing them in variables. The age and salary are easy; there are variable types to hold those. You can code the following to declare those variables:

```
int      age;
float    salary;
```

There is no string variable that can hold the name, but you can create an array of characters (one or more character variables next to each other in memory) with the following declaration:

```
char name[ 15 ];
```

This reserves an array of characters. An array declaration always includes brackets ([ ]), which declare the storage that C++ needs to reserve for the array. This array will be 15 characters long, and the array name is name. You also can assign a value to the character array at the time you declare it. The following declaration statement not only declares the character array but also puts the name "Michael Jones" into it.

Declare the character array name as 15 characters long and assign Michael Jones *to that array.*

```
char name[ 15 ] = "Michael Jones";
```

Figure 6.1 shows what this array looks like in memory. Each of the 15 boxes of the array is called an *element*. Notice that there is a null zero (the string-terminating character) at the end of the string. Notice also that the last character of the array, the 15th element, has no data in it. There is a value there, even though the program didn't place any data there. It is not necessary to be concerned with what follows the string's null zero.

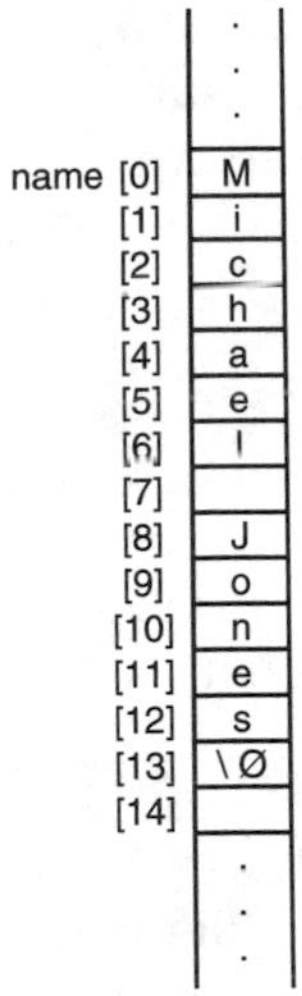

Figure 6.1

A character array
after being
declared and
assigned a string
value.

```
name [0]   M
     [1]   i
     [2]   c
     [3]   h
     [4]   a
     [5]   e
     [6]   l
     [7]
     [8]   J
     [9]   o
    [10]   n
    [11]   e
    [12]   s
    [13]   \Ø
    [14]
```

You can access individual elements in an array, or the array as a whole. This is the primary advantage of an array over a bunch of variables with different names. You can assign values to individual array elements by putting each element's location, called a *subscript*, in brackets. Note the following example:

```
name[ 3 ] = 'k';
```

This overwrites the h in the name with a k. The string now looks like the one in figure 6.2.

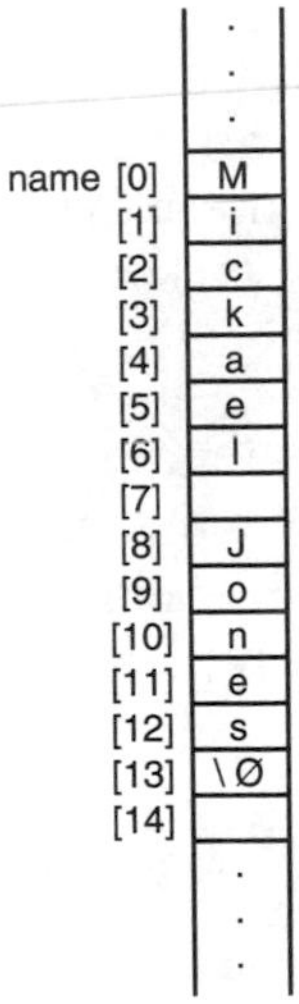

Figure 6.2

The array contents
after changing one
of the elements.

```
name [0]   M
     [1]   i
     [2]   c
     [3]   k
     [4]   a
     [5]   e
     [6]   l
     [7]
     [8]   J
     [9]   o
    [10]   n
    [11]   e
    [12]   s
    [13]   \Ø
    [14]
```

All array subscripts
start at 0.

All array subscripts start at zero. Therefore, to overwrite the first element, you have to use a 0 as the subscript. Assigning `name[ 3 ]`, as just shown, changes the fourth value in the array.

You can print the entire string, or more accurately, the entire array, with a single `cout`:

```
cout << name;
```

Notice that when you print an array, you don't put the brackets after the array name.

You must be sure that you reserve enough characters in the array to hold the entire string, including the terminating null zero. For example, the following will not work:

```
char name[ 5 ] = "Michael Jones";
```

This reserves only five characters for the array, but the name and its null zero take 14 characters. C++ will not give you an error if you try to do this; instead, C++ overwrites whatever follows the array `name` in memory. This will cause unpredictable results and is certainly not correct.

Always reserve enough array elements to hold the string, plus its terminating null character. It's easy to forget the null zero at the end, but don't. If your string contains 13 characters, it must have a 14th null zero, or the string will never be treated as a string. To help eliminate this error, C++ provides a shortcut. The following character array statements are exactly the same:

```
char horse[ 9 ] = "Stallion";
```

```
char horse[ ] = "Stallion";
```

If you assign a value to a character array at the same time you declare the character array, C++ counts the string's length, adds one for the null zero, and reserves that much array space for you.

Visual C++ will not allow you to declare a character array (or any other type of array) with empty brackets if you don't also assign values to the array at the same time. The statement

```
char people[ ];
```

does *not* reserve any space for the array called `people`. If you try to do this, Visual C++ will produce an error message when you compile the program because it does not know how much space to reserve for the array.

Character Arrays versus Strings

In the last section, you saw how to put a string in a character array. Strings can exist in C++ only as string constants or be stored in character arrays. As you read through this book, familiarizing yourself with the use of arrays and strings, you will become more comfortable with them. At this point, you should understand the following fundamental rule about C++ character arrays and character strings:

Strings must be stored in character arrays, but not all character arrays contain strings.

To understand this point, look at the two arrays illustrated in figure 6.3. The first one, called cara1, does *not* contain a string. It is, however, a character array, containing a list of several characters. The second array, called cara2, does contain a string because there is a null zero at the end.

Figure 6.3

Two character arrays, one containing characters and the other containing a character string.

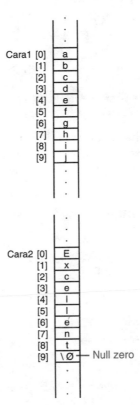

These arrays could be initialized with the following declaration statements:

Declare the array cara1 *with 10 individual characters.*
Declare the array cara2 *with the character string* Excellent.

```
char cara1[ 10 ] = { 'a', 'b', 'c', 'd', 'e', 'f', 'g',
                     'h', 'i', 'j' };
char cara2[ 10 ] = "Excellent";
```

If you want to put individual characters into an array, you must enclose the list of characters in braces, as shown in the preceding statements. You could also initialize cara1 later in the program, using assignment statements, as in the following example:

```
char cara1[ 10 ];
cara1[ 0 ] = 'a';
cara1[ 1 ] = 'b';
cara1[ 2 ] = 'c';
cara1[ 3 ] = 'd';
cara1[ 4 ] = 'e';
cara1[ 5 ] = 'f';
cara1[ 6 ] = 'g';
cara1[ 7 ] = 'h';
cara1[ 8 ] = 'i';
cara1[ 9 ] = 'j';     // Last element possible, since started
                      // with 0 subscript
```

This character array doesn't contain a null zero, so it does not contain a string of characters. It contains characters that can be stored there and used individually, but they cannot be treated as if they were a string in a program.

> **Caution:** You cannot assign string values to character arrays in a regular assignment statement, except when you declare them. A character array is not a string variable (the array is used only to hold a string), so the array cannot go on the left side of an equal sign.

The following program is *invalid*:

```
main()
{
    char     petname[ 20 ];      // Reserve space for
                                 // the pet's name
    petname = "Alfalfa";         // INVALID!
    cout << petname;
    return 0;
}
```

Because the pet's name was not assigned *at the time the character array was declared*, petname cannot be assigned a value later. The following program is allowed, however, because you can assign values individually to a character array:

```
main()
{
    char      petname[ 20 ];          // Reserve space for
                                      // the pet's name

    petname[ 0 ] = 'A';               // Assign values one
                                      // element at a time

    petname[ 1 ] = 'l';
    petname[ 2 ] = 'f';
    petname[ 3 ] = 'a';
    petname[ 4 ] = 'l';
    petname[ 5 ] = 'f';
    petname[ 6 ] = 'a';
    petname[ 7 ] = '\0';              // Needed to ensure that
                                      // this is a string!

    cout << petname;                  // Now the pet's name
                                      // prints properly

    return 0;

}
```

The petname character array now holds a string since the last character is a null zero. How long is the string in petname? It is seven characters long because the length of a string never includes the null zero.

You cannot assign more than 20 characters, which is this array's reserved space. However, you can store any string of 19 or fewer characters (leaving one for the null zero) in the array. If you put the "Alfalfa" string into the array and then assign a null zero to petname[3], as in

```
petname[ 3 ] = '\0';
```

the string in petname is now just three characters long. You have, in effect, shortened the string. There are still 20 characters reserved for petname, but the data inside it is the string "Alf", ending with a null zero.

There are many other ways to assign a string a value, such as using a strcpy() function. This is a library function that lets you copy a string constant into a string. To copy the "Alfalfa" pet name into the petname array, you could type the following:

```
strcpy(petname, "Alfalfa"); // Copy Alfalfa into the array
```

The *strcpy()* function puts string constants in string arrays.

The strcpy() function (for "string copy") assumes that the first value in its parentheses is a character array name and that the second value is a valid string constant, or another character array that holds a string. You must be sure that the first character array in the parentheses is long enough (has enough elements reserved) to hold whatever string you copy into it.

Other methods of initializing arrays are explored throughout this book.

Examples

1. Suppose that you want to keep track of your aunt's name in a program so that you can print the name. If your aunt's name is Ruth Ann Cooper, you have to reserve at least 16 elements—15 to hold the name and another element to hold the null character. The following statement properly reserves a character array to hold the name:

```
char aunt_name[ 16 ];
```

2. If you want to put your aunt's name in the array at the same time you reserve the array storage, you can do so with the following statement:

```
char aunt_name[ 16 ] = "Ruth Ann Cooper";
```

You could leave out the array size and let C++ count the number needed:

```
char aunt_name[ ] = "Ruth Ann Cooper";
```

3. Suppose that you want to keep track of three friends' names. The longest name is 20 characters (including the null zero). You just have to reserve enough character array space to hold each friend's name:

```
char friend1[ 20 ];
char friend2[ 20 ];
char friend3[ 20 ];
```

These declarations can go toward the top of the block, along with any integer, floating-point, or character variables you need to declare.

4. The following program asks the user for his or her first and last names. It then prints the user's initials to the screen by printing the first character in each name array. The program must print each array's 0 subscript because the first subscript of any array begins at 0, not 1.

```
// Filename: C6INIT.CPP
// Prints the user's initials

#include <iostream.h>

main()
{
    char    first[ 20 ];    // Holds the first name
    char    last[ 20 ];     // Holds the last name

    cout << "What is your first name? ";
    cin >> first;
    cout << "What is your last name? ";
    cin >> last;
```

```
     // Print the initials
     cout << "Your initials are " << first[0] << '.'
          << last[0] << '.';
     return 0;
}
```

5. The following program takes those three friend character arrays and
   assigns them string values in the three ways shown in this chapter:

```
// Filename: C6STR.CPP
// Stores and initializes 3 character arrays for 3 friends

#include     <iostream.h>
#include     <string.h>

main()
{
     // Declare all arrays and initialize the first one
     char     friend1[ 20 ] = "Johann Paul Johnson";
     char     friend2[ 20 ];
     char     friend3[ 20 ];

// Use a function to initialize the second array
     strcpy(friend2, "Julie L. Roberts");

     friend3[ 0 ] = 'A';        // Initialize the last string
                                // an element at a time
     friend3[ 1 ] = 'd';
     friend3[ 2 ] = 'a';
     friend3[ 3 ] = 'm';
     friend3[ 4 ] = ' ';
     friend3[ 5 ] = 'G';
     friend3[ 6 ] = '.';
     friend3[ 7 ] = ' ';
     friend3[ 8 ] = 'S';
     friend3[ 9 ] = 'm';
     friend3[ 10 ] = 'i';
     friend3[ 11 ] = 't';
     friend3[ 12 ] = 'h';
     friend3[ 13 ] = '\0';
```

```
    // Print all three names out
    cout << friend1 << '\n';
    cout << friend2 << '\n';
    cout << friend3 << '\n';
    return 0;
}
```

Obviously, the last method of initializing a character array with a string one element at a time is not used as often as the other ways.

Summary

This has been a short but powerful chapter. You learned about character arrays that hold strings. Even though C++ has no string variables, character arrays can hold string constants. After you put a string into a character array, you can print it or manipulate it as if it were a string.

Starting with the next chapter, you will begin to hone the C++ skills you are building. Chapter 7 introduces preprocessor directives. These directives are not really part of the C++ language, but they help you work with your source code as a whole before your program is compiled.

Review Questions

Answers to Review Questions are in Appendix B.

1. How would you declare a character array, called my_name, that will hold the following string constant?

   ```
   "This is C++"
   ```

2. How long is the preceding string?

3. How many bytes of storage does this string take?

4. What do all string constants end with?

5. How many variables do the following statements declare, and what are their types?

   ```
   char name[ 25 ];
   char address[ 25 ];
   ```

6. True or false: The following statement assigns a string constant to a character array.

```
myname[]="Kim Langston";
```

7. True or false: The following declaration puts a string into the character array called city.

```
char city[ ] = { 'M', 'i', 'a', 'm', 'i', '\0' };
```

8. True or false: The following declaration puts a string into the character array called city.

```
char city[ ] = { 'M', 'i', 'a', 'm', 'i' };
```

Review Exercises

1. Write the C++ code to store your weight (you can fib), height in feet, shoe size, and name in four variables. Declare the variables and then assign them values in the body of the program.

2. Rewrite the program in Exercise 1 by adding proper cout statements to print the values to the screen. Use appropriate messages (by printing string constants) to describe the values that are printed.

3. Write a program to store and print the names of your two favorite television programs. Store these programs in two character arrays. Initialize one of the strings (assign it the first program's name) at the time you declare the array. Initialize the second value in the body of the program with the strcpy() function. (*Hint:* Don't forget to use a #include for the strcpy() function. See Example 5.)

4. Write a program that puts 10 different initials into 10 elements of a single character array. Do not store a string-terminating null zero. Print the list backward, one initial on each line.

CHAPTER 7

Preprocessor Directives

As you might recall from Chapter 3, the C++ compiler routes your programs through a *preprocessor* before compiling your programs. The preprocessor could be called a "precompiler" because it changes your source code before the compiler sees it.

The preprocessor is so important to the C++ programming language that you should familiarize yourself with it before learning more commands within the language. Regular C++ commands do not affect the preprocessor. You must supply special non-C++ commands, called *preprocessor directives*, that the preprocessor looks at. These directives make changes to your source code before the C++ compiler looks at it.

This chapter introduces the following topics:

♦ Preprocessor directives

♦ The #include preprocessor directive

♦ The #define preprocessor directive

Almost every proper C++ program contains preprocessor directives. In this chapter, you learn about the two most common directives: #include and #define.

What Are Preprocessor Directives?

As indicated, preprocessor directives are commands you supply to the preprocessor. All preprocessor directives begin with a pound sign (#). Because they are not C++ commands but are C++ preprocessor commands, never put a semicolon at the end of a preprocessor directive. These directives typically begin in column 1 of your source program. They can begin in any column, but in the interest of code portability, stay with tradition and start each one in the first column on the line where the directive appears. Figure 7.1 shows a program that contains three preprocessor directives.

Figure 7.1

A program that contains three preprocessor directives.

```
// Filename: C7PRE.CPP
// C++ program that demonstrates preprocessor directives

#include <iostream.h>
#define AGE 28
#define MESSAGE "Hello, world."

main()
{
   int i = 10, age;  // i is assigned a value at declaration
                     // age is still UNDEFINED

   age = 5;          // Put 5 in the variable age

   i = i * AGE;   // AGE is not the same as the variable age

   cout << i << age << AGE;   // Print 280 5 28
   cout << MESSAGE;   // Hello, world gets printed on screen

   return;
}
```

Preprocessor directives temporarily change your source code.

Preprocessor directives are commands that you give to your C++ preprocessor to change your source code. These changes last only as long as the compile takes. Once you look at your source code again, the preprocessor will be through with your file, and its changes will no longer be in the file. Your preprocessor does not in any way compile your program or look at your actual C++ commands. Some beginning C++ students tend to get confused by this, but you will not be confused if you understand that your program has yet to be compiled when your preprocessor directives execute.

Similar to a word processor or an editor, a preprocessor does what these kinds of programs might do with your program. This analogy applies throughout this chapter.

The *#include* Preprocessor Directive

The #include preprocessor directive merges a disk file into your source program. Remember that a preprocessor directive is like a word processing command. Word processors are capable of file merging, just as the #include directive is. The #include preprocessor directive takes one of the following formats:

```
#include <filename>
```

```
#include "filename"
```

In the #include directive, the *filename* must be an ASCII text file (as your source file is) that resides on your disk. Examine Figure 7.2, which shows the contents of two files on disk. One file is called OUTSIDE, and the other file is called INSIDE. Notice that OUTSIDE includes the following preprocessor directive.

Include in your source file the file INSIDE.

```
#include <INSIDE>
```

Figure 7.2

Two files that illustrate the *#include* directive

The file called OUTSIDE contains the following text:

```
Now is the time for all good men

#include INSIDE

to come to the aid of their country.
```

The file called INSIDE contains the following text:

```
A quick brown fox jumped
over the lazy dog.
```

Assume that you are able to run the OUTSIDE file through the C++ preprocessor. The preprocessor finds the #include directive and replaces it with the entire file called INSIDE. In other words, the C++ preprocessor directive merges the INSIDE file into the OUTSIDE file, at the place of the #include. OUTSIDE is expanded to include its original text *plus* the merged text. Figure 7.3 shows what OUTSIDE looks like after the preprocessor finishes with the #include.

> OUTSIDE now includes the INSIDE file:
>
>
> Now is the time for all good men
>
> A quick brown fox jumped
> over the lazy dog.
>
> to come to the aid of their country.

The INSIDE file remains in its original form on the disk. Only the file that contains the #include directive is changed. Note that this change is *temporary*; that is, OUTSIDE is expanded by the included file only as long as it takes to compile the program.

Because the OUTSIDE and INSIDE files are not C++ programs, consider a few examples that are more usable to the C++ programming language. You might want to #include a file that contains common code you use often. Suppose that you print your name and address many times in your C++ programs. You *could* type the following few lines of code, which print your name and address, into each of your programs:

```
cout << "Kelly Jane Peterson\n";
cout << "Apartment #217\n";
cout << "4323 East Skelly Drive\n";
cout << "New York, New York\n";
cout << "            10012\n";
```

Instead of typing the same five lines everywhere you want your name and address printed, you can type them *once* and then save them in a file called MYADD.CPP. Afterward, you just type the following line when you want your name and address printed:

```
#include <myadd.cpp>
```

This method not only saves keystrokes but also maintains consistency and accuracy. (Sometimes this kind of repeated text is known as *boilerplate* text.)

You usually can use angle brackets (< >) or double quotes ("") around the included file name and get the same results. The angle brackets tell the preprocessor to look for the included file in a default include directory set up by your compiler. The double quotes inform the preprocessor to look for the included file first in the directory where the source code is stored, and if not found there, to look in the system include directory.

The *#include* directive is most often used for system header files.

Most of the time, you will see angle brackets around the included file name. If you want to include sections of code in other programs, be sure to store that code in the system include directory if you use angle brackets. Even though #include works well for inserted source code, there are more efficient ways to include common source code. You learn about these methods later in this book.

The preceding #include example for source code has served well in explaining what the #include preprocessor directive does. However, #include is not often used to include source code text, but to include special system files called *header* files. Header files inform C++ how it is to interpret the many library functions you use. Your C++ compiler comes with its own header files. When you installed your compiler, these header files were automatically stored on your disk in the system include directory. By convention, their file names always end in .h to distinguish them from regular C++ source code.

The most common header file for the examples in this book is named iostream.h. This gives your C++ compiler needed information about the library cout and cin functions, as well as other common library routines that perform input and output.

At this point, you do not have to understand fully the iostream.h file. You should, however, place this file before main() in every program you write. It is rare when a C++ program does *not* need iostream.h included, and it doesn't harm anything if you include iostream.h when it isn't needed.

Throughout this book, whenever a new library function is described, the matching header file for that function is also given. Because almost every C++ program that you write includes a cout to print to the screen, almost every program contains the following line:

```
#include <iostream.h>
```

In the last chapter, you saw the strcpy() function. Its header file is called string.h. Therefore, if you write a program that contains strcpy(), you should also include its matching header file at the time you include <iostream.h>. These items should go on separate lines:

```
#include <iostream.h>
#include <string.h>
```

The order of your include files does not matter as long as you include them before the functions that need them. Most C++ programmers include all their needed header files before the first function in the file.

These header files are nothing more than text files. You may want to search your disk with the editor and find one of them, such as iostream.h, so that you can look at it. It may seem very complex at this point, but there is nothing unusual about these files. If you do look at some of these files, do *not* change them in any way. If you make any changes, you may have to reload them from scratch to get them back.

Examples

1. The following program is very short. It includes the printing routine for name and address, which was just described. After printing the name and address, the program ends.

```
// Filename: C7INC1.CPP
// Illustrates the #include preprocessor directive

#include  <iostream.h>

main()
{
#include "myadd.cpp"
     return 0;
}
```

The double quotes are used because the file named MYADD.CPP is stored in the same directory as the source file. You should realize that if you type this program into your computer (after typing and saving the MYADD.CPP file) and then compile the program, the MYADD.CPP file is included only as long as it takes to compile the program. Your compiler will not see the file as shown here. The compiler will see (and think you typed) the following:

```
// Filename: C7INCL1.CPP
// Illustrates the #include preprocessor directive

#include  <iostream.h>

main()
{
     cout << "Kelly Jane Peterson\n";
     cout << "Apartment #217\n";
     cout << "4323 East Skelly Drive\n";
     cout << "New York, New York\n";
     cout << "             10012\n";
     return 0;
}
```

This explains what is meant by a preprocessor; the changes are made to your source code *before* it is compiled. Your original source code is restored as soon as the compile is finished. When you look at your program again, it is back in its original form, as originally typed, with the #include statement.

2. The following program copies a message into a character array and prints it to the screen. Because cout and strcpy() library functions are used, both of their header files should be included as well.

```
// Filename: C7INCL3.CPP
// Uses two header files

#include <iostream.h>
#include <string.h>

main()
{
    char message[ 20 ];

    strcpy(message, "This is fun!");
    cout << message;
    return 0;
}
```

The *#define* Preprocessor Directive

The #define preprocessor directive is also commonly used in many C++ programs. The #define directive may seem strange at first, but it really does nothing more than a word processor's find-and-replace command. The format of #define is as follows:

```
#define ARGUMENT1 argument2
```

#define replaces every occurrence of the first argument with the second argument.

ARGUMENT1 is a single word, containing no spaces. Use the same naming rules for the #define statement's first argument as for variables (refer to Chapter 5). It is traditional to use uppercase characters for *ARGUMENT1*; this is one of the few uses of uppercase in the C++ language. At least one space separates *ARGUMENT1* from *argument2*, which can be any character, word, or phrase. *argument2* can contain spaces or anything else you can type at the keyboard. Because #define is a preprocessor directive and not a C++ executable statement, do not put a semicolon at the end of it.

The #define preprocessor directive replaces the occurrence of *ARGUMENT1* everywhere in your program with the contents of *argument2*. In most cases, the #define directive should go before main(), along with the #include directive. Consider the following #define directive:

Define the constant AGELIMIT to 21.

```
#define AGELIMIT 21
```

If your program includes one or more occurrences of the word AGELIMIT, the preprocessor replaces every one of them with the number 21. Your compiler will interpret this as if you typed 21 instead of AGELIMIT, because the preprocessor finishes before your compiler sees the source code. Again, though, the change is temporary. After your program is compiled, you will see it as you originally typed it, with the #define and AGELIMITs still intact.

AGELIMIT is *not* a variable. Variables get declared and assigned values only when your program is compiled and run. The preprocessor changes your source file *before* it gets compiled.

#define creates defined constants.

You might wonder why you should go to this much trouble. If you wanted 21 everywhere AGELIMIT occurs, you could have typed 21 to begin with! The advantage to using #define instead of constants is that if the age limit ever changes (is reduced to 18, for example), you have to change only one line in the program; you do not have to look for every occurrence of 21 and change each one—and maybe miss one in the process.

Because the #define preprocessor directive lets you easily define and change constants, the replaced arguments of the #define are sometimes called *defined constants*. You can define any type of constant, including string constants. The following program contains a defined string constant that replaces a string in two places:

```
// Filename: C7DEF1.CPP
// Defines a string constant and uses it twice

#include <iostream.h>
#define MYNAME "Phil Ward"

main()
{
    char name[ ] = MYNAME;
    cout << "My name is " << name << '\n'; // Print the
                                           // array
    cout << "My name is " <<  MYNAME << '\n';  // Print the
                                               // defined constant
    return 0;
}
```

The reason that the first argument of the #define is in uppercase is to distinguish it from variable names in the program. Variables are usually entered in lowercase or MixedCase. Although your preprocessor and compiler would not get confused, people who look at your program can quickly scan it and tell which items are defined constants and which items are not. When they see an uppercase word (if you follow the recommended standard for the first #define argument), they will know to look at the top of the program for its actual defined value.

The fact that defined constants are not variables is made even clearer in the following program, which prints five values. Try to guess what those five values are before looking at the answer following the program.

```
// Filename: C7DEF2.CPP
// Illustrates that #define constants are not variables

#include <iostream.h>

#define X1 (b +c)
#define X2 (X1 + X1)
#define X3 (X2 * c + X1 - d)
#define X4 (2 * X1 + 3 * X2 + 4 * X3)

main()
{
    int  b = 2;     // Declare and initialize 4 variables
    int  c = 3;
    int  d = 4;
    int  e = X4;

    cout << e << "   " << X1 << "   " << X2 << "   " << X3
        << "   " << X4;
    return 0;
}
```

The following is the output from this program:

```
164   5   10   31   164
```

If you treated X1, X2, X3, and X4 as variables, you would not get the correct answers. X1 through X4 are not variables but defined constants. Before your program is compiled, the preprocessor looks at the first line and knows to change every occurrence of X1 to (b + c). This happens before the next #define is processed. Therefore, after the first #define, the source code looks like this:

```
// Filename: C7DEF2.CPP
// Illustrates that #define constants are not variables

#include <iostream.h>

#define X2 ((b + c) + (b + c))
#define X3 (X2 * c + (b + c) - d)
#define X4 (2 * (b + c) + 3 * X2 + 4 * X3)
```

```
main()
{
    int  b = 2;      // Declare and initialize 4 variables
    int  c = 3;
    int  d = 4;
    int  e = X4;

    cout << e << "   " << (b + c) << "   " << X2 << "   "
        << X3 << "   " << X4;
    return 0;
}
```

After the first `#define` finishes, the second one takes over and changes every occurrence of X2 to `((b + c) + (b + c))`. At that point, your source code looks like this:

```
// Filename: C7DEF2.CPP
// Illustrates that #define constants are not variables

include <iostream.h>

#define X3 (((b + c) + (b + c)) * c + (b + c) - d)
#define X4 (2 * (b + c) + 3 * ((b + c) + (b + c)) + 4 * X3)

main()
{
    int  b = 2;      // Declare and initialize 4 variables
    int  c = 3;
    int  d = 4;
    int  e = X4;

    cout << e << "   " << (b + c) << "   " << ((b + c) +
            (b + c)) << "   " << X3 << "   " << X4);
    return 0;
}
```

After the second `#define` finishes, the third one takes over and changes every occurrence of X3 to `(((b + c) + (b + c) * c + (b + c) - d)`. Your source code then looks like this:

```
// Filename: C7DEF2.CPP
// Illustrates that #define constants are not variables

#include <iostream.h>
```

```
#define X4 (2 * (b + c) + 3 * ((b + c) + (b + c)) + 4 *
       (((b +c) + (b + c)) * c + (b + c) - d))



main()
{
    int  b = 2;      // Declare and initialize 4 variables
    int  c = 3;
    int  d = 4;
    int  e = X4;

    cout << e << "  " << (b + c) << "  " << ((b + c) +
            (b + c) << "  " << (((b + c) + (b + c)) * c +
            (b + c) - d) << "  " << X4;
    return 0;

}
```

The source code is growing rapidly! After the third #define finishes, the fourth and last one takes over and changes every occurrence of X4 to (2 * (b + c) + 3 * ((b + c) + (b + c)) + 4 * (((b + c) + (b + c)) * c + (b + c) - d)). Your source code looks like this at this point:

```
// Filename: C7DEF2.CPP
// Illustrates that #define constants are not variables

#include <iostream.h>

main()
{
    int  b = 2; // Declare and initialize 4 variables
    int  c = 3;
    int  d = 4;
    int  e = (2 * (b + c) + 3 * ((b + c) + (b + c)) + 4 *
            (((b + c) + (b + c)) * c + (b + c) - d))

    cout << e << "  " << (b + c) << "  " << ((b + c) +
            (b + c) << "  " << (((b + c) + (b + c)) * c +
            (b + c) - d) << "  " << (2 * (b + c) + 3 *
            ((b + c) + (b + c)) + 4 * (((b + c) +
            (b + c)) * c + (b + c) - d));
    return 0;
}
```

This is what your compiler actually sees. You did not type this complete listing; you typed only the original listing that was first shown. The preprocessor expanded the source into this longer form, as though you *had* typed it this way.

C++ has an alternative to #define for defining constants. The keyword const placed before a variable accomplishes the same thing. Note the following lines:

```
const int     i = 12;
const char    c = 'A';
const float   f = 3.1415926;
```

i, c, and f are now constants and cannot be changed.

What are the advantages and disadvantages of using #define instead of const? They have to do with several points that haven't been made yet.

First, a #define allocates no storage, but a const variable does. This is important if you're trying to keep your executable program size to a minimum.

Second, a #define is visible from where it is in the source file all the way to the end of the file. That is, when the compiler does its search and replace, it will replace every instance from the point of definition on. A const variable has visibility only within the program block in which it is defined. In other words, if a const is defined inside a block bounded by braces ({ }), the const has no visibility outside its block. The search and replace is restricted.

The third point has to do with arrays. You can create an array, which is a list of values, by using a #define or a const variable. With arrays, the first point in favor of #define over const is reversed. Every time you use an array created by the #define, that array is duplicated. Every time you use an array created as a const variable, a reference to the variable is created; this takes less room in memory than making another copy of the array.

The following example may be extreme, but it illustrates how #define works on your source code and does not define any variables at all. The #define does nothing more than a word processor's find-and-replace command. Because of this, you can even rewrite the C++ language. If you are used to BASIC, you might be more comfortable by typing PRINT instead of C's cout when printing to the screen. The #define statement

```
#define PRINT cout
```

allows you to print in C++ with the following statements:

```
PRINT << "This is a new printing technique\n";
PRINT << "I could have used cout instead.\n";
```

This works because your compiler, by the time it sees the program, will see the following:

```
cout << "This is a new printing technique\n";
cout << "I could have used printf() instead.\n";
```

You cannot replace a defined constant if it resides in another string constant. For example, you cannot use the #define statement

```
#define AGE
```

to replace information in the following cout:

```
cout << "AGE";
```

AGE is a string constant and will print literally as it appears inside the double quotes. As long as the defined constant does not reside between double quotes, the processor will make the replacement.

Do Not Overuse #define

Many early C++ programmers enjoy redefining parts of the language to suit what they are used to in another language. The cout-to-PRINT example is just one illustration. You can virtually redefine any C++ statement or function so that it "looks" the way you like.

There is a danger here, and you should be wary of using #define for this purpose. Redefining the language becomes very confusing to others who may need to modify your programs later. In addition, as you become familiar with C++, you will start to use the true C++ language more and more. Any older programs that you redefined will be confusing to you.

If you are going to program in C++, use the language elements supplied by C++. Shy away from redefining commands in the language. The #define directive is a great way to define numeric and string constants. If those constants change, you have to change only one line in your program. Resist the temptation to define commands and built-in functions.

Examples

1. Suppose that you want to keep track of your company's target sales amount of $55,000.00. That target amount has not changed for the last two years. Because it probably will not change in the near future (sales are flat), you decide to start using a defined constant to represent the target sales amount. Then, if the target amount does change, you have to change it only on the #define line. The #define would look like this:

```
#define TARGETSALES 55000.00
```

This line defines a floating-point constant. You can then assign TARGETSALES to floating-point variables and print it, just as if you had typed 55000.00 throughout your program.

2. If you find yourself defining the same constants in many programs, you might consider putting them in their own file on disk and then include them. This saves typing the defined constants at the top of every program. If you stored that file in a file called MYDEFS.H in your program's directory, you could include it with the following #include statement:

```
#include "mydefs.h"
```

(To use angle brackets, you would have to store the file in your system's include directory.)

3. Defined constants are good for array sizes. Suppose that you declare an array for a customer's name. When you write the program, you know that you do not have any customer whose name is longer than 22 characters (including the null zero). Therefore, you can use the following:

```
#define CNMLENGTH 22
```

When you define the array, you could use this:

```
char cust_name[ CNMLENGTH ]
```

Other statements that need to know the array size also can use CNMLENGTH.

4. Many C++ programmers define a list of error messages. Once the messages are defined with easy-to-remember names, you can print those constants if an error occurs while maintaining consistency throughout your programs. You might see something like the following toward the top of C++ programs:

```
#define DISKERR "Your disk drive seems not to be working"
#define PRNTERR "Your printer is not responding"
#define AGEERR  "You cannot enter an age that small"
#define NAMEERR "You must enter a full name"
```

Summary

This chapter covered the #include and #define preprocessor directives. Although these are the only two preprocessor directives you know so far, they are the two used in most C++ programs. Although these directives are not executed, they change your source file by merging and defining constants in your programs.

The next chapter explains cout in more detail. There are many cout options that you will want to use as you write programs. You also will see a way to get keyboard input into your C++ programs.

Review Questions

Answers to Review Questions are in Appendix B.

1. True or false: You can define variables with the preprocessor directives.

2. Which preprocessor directive will merge another file into your program?

3. Which preprocessor directive will define constants throughout your program?

4. True or false: You can define character, string, integer, and floating-point constants with the #define directive.

5. Which happens first: your program is compiled or preprocessed?

6. When would you use the angle brackets in an #include statement, and when would you use double quotes?

7. Which are easier to change: defined constants or constants you type throughout a program? Why?

8. Which header file should be included in almost every C++ program you write?

9. True or false: The line

```
#define MESSAGE "Please press Enter to continue..."
```

would change the statement

```
cout << "MESSAGE";
```

10. What is the output from the following program?

```
// Filename: C7EXER.CPP

#include <iostream.h>
#define AMT1 a+a+a
#define AMT2 AMT1 - AMT1

main()
{
    int  a = 1;

    cout << "Amount is " << AMT2;
    return 0;
}
```

Review Exercises

1. Write a program that prints your name to the screen. Use a defined constant for the name. Do not use a character array and do not type your actual name inside the cout.

2. Suppose that your boss wants you to write a program that produces an exception report. If the company's sales are lower than $100,000.00 or more than $750,000.00, your boss wants the program to print a message accordingly. You will learn how to produce this type of report later in this book, but for now, write the #define statements that define these two floating-point constants.

3. Write the cout statements that print your name and birth date to the screen. Store these statements in a separate file. Write a second program that includes the first file to print your name and birth date. Be sure to include <iostream.h>, because the included file contains cout statements.

4. Write a nonsense program that defines 10 digits—0 through 9—as constants ZERO through NINE. Add these 10 defined digits together and print the results.

CHAPTER 8

Simple Input and Output

You have already seen the cout operator, which prints values to the screen. There is much more to cout than you have learned. Because the screen is such a common output device, you need to understand how to take advantage of cout to print data the way you want to see it. In addition, your programs will become more powerful if you learn to get input from the keyboard. cin is an operator that mirrors cout. Instead of sending output values to the screen, cin accepts values the user types at the keyboard.

The cout and cin operators offer the beginning C++ programmer easy-to-use input and output operators. The cout and cin operators are limited, but they enable you to easily send output from and receive input into your programs.

This chapter covers the following topics:

- Using the cout operator

- Using manipulators

- Using the cin operator

You will be surprised at how much more advanced your programs can be after you learn these input/output operators.

The *cout* Operator

cout sends output to the screen.

The cout operator sends data to the standard output device, which is the screen. The format of cout is a little different from that of regular C++ commands:

```
cout << data [ << data ];
```

The *data* can be variables, constants, expressions, or a combination of all three.

Note that in this book it is sometimes necessary to define C++ constructs that have an indefinite number of parameters or arguments, or that have optional parameters that may or may not be present. In such cases, the optional parameter appears in square brackets, [ ]. The text enclosed in square brackets may be present one or more times, or not at all.

Printing Strings

The easiest data to print with cout is a string. To print a string constant, you simply put the string constant after the cout operator. For example, to print the string "The rain in Spain", you type the following cout:

Print the phrase The rain in Spain to the screen.

```
cout << "The rain in Spain";
```

You must remember, however, that cout does *not* perform an automatic carriage return. This means that the screen's cursor will be left after the last character that is printed. Subsequent couts begin right next to the last character printed. To understand this better, try to predict the output from the following three cout operators:

```
cout << "Line 1";
cout << "Line 2";
cout << "Line 3";
```

These couts produce the output

```
Line 1Line 2Line 3
```

which is probably not what was intended. You must include the newline character, \n, whenever you want to move the cursor to the next line. The following three cout operators produce a three-line output:

```
cout << "Line 1\n";
cout << "Line 2\n";
cout << "Line 3\n";
```

Here is the output from these couts:

```
Line 1
Line 2
Line 3
```

The \n character sends the cursor to the next line no matter where you insert the character. The following three cout operators also produce the correct three-line output:

```
cout << "Line 1";
cout << "\nLine 2\n";
cout << "Line 3";
```

The second cout prints a new line before it prints anything else. It then prints its string followed by another new line. The third string prints on that new line.

You also can print strings stored in character arrays by putting the array name inside the cout. If you were to store your name in an array defined as

```
char my_name[ ] = "Lyndon Harris";
```

you could print the name with the following cout:

```
cout << my_name;
```

Examples

1. The following section of code prints three string constants on three different lines:

```
cout << "Nancy Carson\n";
cout << "1213 Oak Street\n";
cout << "Fairbanks, Alaska\n";
```

2. The following program stores a few values in three variables and prints the result:

```
// Filename: C8PRNT1.CPP
// Prints values in variables

#include <iostream.h>

main()
{
    char        first = 'E';      // Store some character,
    char        middle = 'W';     // integer, and
    char        last = 'C';       // floating-point
                                  // variables
```

```
int         age = 32;
int         dependents = 2;
float    salary = 25000.00;
float    bonus = 575.25;

// Print the results
cout << first << middle << last;
cout << age << dependents;
cout << salary << bonus;
return 0;
}
```

3. The preceding program does not help the user at all. The output is not labeled, and all of it prints on a single line. Here is the same program with a few messages printed before the numbers and some newline characters placed where they are needed.

```
// Filename: C8PRNT2.CPP
// Prints values in variables with appropriate labels

#include <iostream.h>

main()
{
    char        first = 'E';      // Store some character,
    char        middle = 'W';     // integer, and
    char        last = 'C';       // floating-point
                                  // variables
    int         age = 32;
    int         dependents = 2;
    float    salary = 25000.00;
    float    bonus = 575.25;

    // Print the results
    cout << "Here are the initials:\n";
    cout << first << middle << last << "\n\n";
    cout << "The age and number of dependents are:\n";
    cout << age << "    " << dependents << "\n\n";
    cout << "The salary and bonus are:\n";
    cout << salary << ' ' << bonus;
    return 0;
}
```

Note the output from this program:

```
Here are the initials:
EWC

The age and number of dependents are:
32    2

The salary and bonus are:
25000 575.25
```

The next section shows you how to limit the number of leading and trailing zeros that are printed.

4. The cout is often used to label output. Before printing an age, an amount, a salary, or any other numeric data, you should print a string constant that tells the user what the number means. The following cout lets the user know that the next number printed will be an age. Without this cout, the user may not know that the number is an age.

```
cout << "Here is the age that was found in our files:";
```

5. All four of the following couts produce different output because all four string constants are different:

```
cout << "Come back tomorrow\n";
cout << "Come  back  tomorrow\n";
cout << "cOME BACK TOMORROW\n";
cout << "C o m e   b a c k   t o   m o r r o w\n";
```

6. You can print a blank line by printing two newline characters next to each other (\n\n) after your string:

```
cout << "Prepare the invoices...\n\n";
```

7. If you need to print a table of numbers, you can use the \t tab character. Place the tab character between the numbers that print. The following program prints a list of team names and number of hits for the first three weeks of the season:

```
// Filename: C8TEAM.CPP
// Prints a table of team names and wins for three weeks

#include <iostream.h>

main()
{
    cout << "Parrots\tRams\tKings\tTitano\tChargers\n";
```

```
    cout << "3\t5\t3\t1\t0\n";
    cout << "2\t5\t1\t0\t1\n";
    cout << "2\t6\t4\t3\t0\n";
    return 0;
}
```

This program produces the following table. You can see that even though the names have different widths, the numbers print correctly beneath them. The \t character forces the next name or value into the next tab position (every eight characters).

```
Parrots Rams   Kings   Titans  Chargers
3       5       3       1       0
2       5       1       0       1
2       6       4       3       0
```

The *hex* and *oct* Manipulators

The hex and oct manipulators are used to print hexadecimal and octal numbers. Even if you store a hexadecimal number in an integer variable (with the leading 0x characters, such as 0x3C1), that variable will print as a decimal value. To print the value in hex, you must use the hex manipulator.

> **Tip:** You can print any integer value as a hexadecimal number if you use the hex conversion character. You do not have to store the integer as a hex number first.

Examples

1. Suppose that you are working on a systems program and need to add five hexadecimal values together to test the results. You can write a short C++ program that does just that. You then can print the answer as a hexadecimal number by using the hex manipulator. Note the following program:

```
// Filename: C8HEX.CPP
// Adds five hexadecimal numbers and prints the answer

#include <iostream.h>

main()
{
```

```
    // Store the five numbers to add together
    int     num1 = 0x4c, num2 = 0x52, num3 = 0xd1,
            num4 = 0xdc, num5 = 0x1f;
    int     hex_ans;        // This will hold the result

    hex_ans = num1 + num2 + num3 + num4 + num5;

    // Print the answer
    cout << "The hexadecimal numbers add up to:"
        << hex << hex_ans << " \n";
    return 0;
}
```

This program produces a single line of output:

```
The hexadecimal numbers add up to: 26a
```

2. If you use octal, you might need this type of routine to add octal (base-8) numbers. The preceding program can be rewritten with octal numbers and printed with the oct manipulator:

```
// Filename: C8OCT.CPP
// Adds five octal numbers and prints the answer

#include <iostream.h>

main()
{
    // Store the five numbers to add together
    int     num1 = 054, num2 = 067, num3 = 011, num4 = 031,
            num5 = 056;
    int     oct_ans;   // This will hold the result

    oct_ans = num1 + num2 + num3 + num4 + num5;

    // Print the answer
    cout << "The octal numbers add up to:"
        << oct << oct_ans << " \n";
    return 0;
}
```

This program produces the following output:

```
The octal numbers add up to: 203
```

The answer, 263, is an octal number (not a decimal) because you printed it with the oct manipulator.

3. Use of the hex or oct manipulator sets integer output to octal or hexa-decimal until another oct, hex, or dec manipulator is encountered. The dec manipulator returns output to decimal.

Other Manipulators

You can modify the way numbers print.

You have already seen the need for additional program output control. All floating-point numbers print with too many decimal places for most applications. What if you want to print only dollars and cents (two decimal places), or print an average with a single decimal place? If you want to control the way these conversion characters produce output, you need to use a parameterized manipulator.

You can specify how many print positions to use in printing a number by using the setw manipulator. For example, the following cout prints the number 456, using three positions (the length of the data):

```
cout << 456;
```

If 456 were stored in an integer variable, it would still use three positions to print, because the number of digits printed is 3. However, you can specify how many positions will print by using the setw manipulator, and you can specify what character will be used to fill extra spaces by using the setfill manipulator. The following cout prints the number 456 in five positions (with two leading spaces):

```
cout << setw(5) << setfill(' ') << 456;
```

You typically will use the setw manipulator when you want to print data in uniform columns. The following program shows you the importance of the width number. Each cout output is shown in the comment to its right.

```
// Filename: C8MOD1.CPP
// Illustrates various integer width cout modifiers

#include <iostream.h>
#include <iomanip.h>                 // note the header for
                                     // the manipulators


main()
{                                            // The output appears
below
    cout << 456 << 456 << 456         // 456456456
        << "\n";
    cout << setw(5) << 456 << setw(5)
        << 456 << setw(5) << 456      // 456  456  456
        << "\n";
    cout << setw(7) << 456 << setw(7)
          << 456 << setw(7) << 456;   // 456    456    456
return 0;
}
```

When you use a setw manipulator inside a conversion character, C++ right-justifies the number in the width you specify. When you specify an eight-digit width, C++ prints a value inside the eight digits, padding the number with leading blanks if it does not fill the whole width. Also, the setw manipulator affects only the next item sent to cout. That is why setw is used before each output item in the preceding example—to ensure that the width is properly set for each output item.

> **Note:** If you do not specify a width large enough to hold the number, C++ ignores your width request and prints the number in its entirety.

You can control the width of strings in the same manner, again with the setw manipulator. If you don't specify enough width to print the full string, C++ ignores the width. The mailing list application in the back of this book uses this technique to print names on mailing labels.

> **Note:** setw() becomes more important when you want to print floating-point numbers.

setprecision(2) tells C++ to print a floating-point number with two decimal places. C++ will round the fractional part, if necessary. The lines

```
cout << setiosflags(ios::fixed);
cout << setw(6) << setprecision(2) << 134.568767;
```

produce the following output:

```
134.57
```

Without the setw or setprecision manipulator, C++ would print the following:

```
134.568767
```

> **Tip:** When printing floating-point numbers, C++ always prints the entire portion to the left of the decimal (to maintain as much accuracy as possible), no matter how many positions wide you specify. Therefore, many C++ programmers ignore the setw manipulator for floating-point numbers and specify only the precision, as in setprecision(2).
>
> When you use setprecision, you usually will also want to use setiosflags(ios::) so that the output will be in decimal number format. Without the ios::fixed setting, the output may default to scientific notation, and the output from the preceding code sample would have been the first two significant digits of 134.568767, or 1.3e+002.

The `setiosflags` and `resetiosflags` manipulators are used to set certain global flags that the C++ iostream class uses in establishing the default behavior of its input and output. `setiosflags` sets the flags indicated; `resetiosflags` clears (or resets) them. These manipulators take as arguments any of the values shown in table 8.1. You may add these together.

Table 8.1. Arguments for *setiosflags* and *resetiosflags*.

Value	Meaning if Set
ios::skipws	Skip white space on input
ios::left	Left-adjust output
ios::right	Right-adjust output
ios::internal	Pad after the sign or base indicator
ios::dec	Decimal conversion
ios::oct	Octal conversion
ios::hex	Hexadecimal conversion
ios::showbase	Show base indicator on output
ios::showpoint	Show decimal point
ios::uppercase	Uppercase hexadecimal output
ios::showpos	Show '+' with positive integers
ios::scientific	Use scientific notation
ios::fixed	Use fixed notation
ios::unitbuf	Flush all streams after insertion
ios::stdio	Flush stdout, stderr after insertion

You will typically use the `setiosflags` and `resetiosflags` manipulators to change the justification or other appearance of your output. Unlike the manipulators you have used up to now, the effect of `setiosflags` and `resetiosflags` remains until another call to the manipulator changes the flag, or your program ends. The following program illustrates the use of `setiosflags` to switch between scientific and fixed notation when printing floating-point numbers.

```
// Filename: C8FLAG.CPP
// Illustrates the use of setiosflags

#include <iostream.h>
#include <iomanip.h>

main()
{
    float answer = 98.44;

    // first, print the answer with all default settings
    cout << "The answer is  ==> "
        << answer << "\n";

    // now, set output to scientific notation
    cout << "The scientific answer is  ==> "
        << setiosflags( ios::scientific )
        << answer << "\n";

    // now, switch back to fixed notation and print
    // twice to show that the flag stays in effect
    cout << "The fixed, wide answer is  ==> "
        << setiosflags( ios::fixed )
        << setw( 12 )
        << answer << "\n";
    cout << "The still fixed, but no longer wide, answer ==> "
        << answer;

    return 0;
}
```

When you run the program above, the output looks like the following:

```
The answer is  ==> 98.44
The scientific answer is  ==> 9.844000e+001
The fixed, wide answer is  ==>        98.44
The still fixed, but no longer wide, answer ==> 98.44
```

Examples

1. You saw earlier how the \t tab character can be used to print columns of data. The tab character is limited to eight columns. If you want more control of the width of your data, use a setw manipulator. The following program is a modified version of C8TEAM.CPP, xusing the width specifier instead of the tab character. This specifier ensures that each column is 10 characters wide.

```
// Filename: C8TEAMMD.CPP
// Prints a table of team names and wins for three weeks,
// using width-modifying conversion characters

#include <iostream.h>
#include <iomanip.h>

main()
{
    cout << setw(10) << "Parrots" << setw(10) << "Rams"
         << setw(10) << "Kings" << setw(10) << "Titans"
         << setw(10) << "Chargers" << "\n";
    cout << setw(10) << 3 << setw(10) << 5 << setw(10) << 2
         << setw(10) << 1 << setw(10) << 0 << "\n";
    cout << setw(10) << 2 << setw(10) << 5 << setw(10) << 1
         << setw(10) << 0 << setw(10) << 1 << "\n";
    cout << setw(10) << 2 << setw(10) << 6 << setw(10) << 4
         << setw(10) << 3 << setw(10) << 0 << "\n";
    return 0;
}
```

2. The following program is a payroll program. The output prints dollar amounts (to two decimal places).

```
// Filename: C8PAY1.CPP
// Computes and prints payroll data properly
// in dollars and cents

#include <iostream.h>
#include <iomanip.h>

main()
{
    char    emp_name[ ] = "Larry Payton";
    char    pay_date[ ] = "03/09/92";
    int     hours_worked = 40;
    float   rate = 7.50;          // Pay per hour
    float   tax_rate = .40;       // Tax percentage rate
    float   gross_pay, taxes, net_pay;

    // Compute the pay amount
    gross_pay = hours_worked * rate;
    taxes = tax_rate * gross_pay;
    net_pay = gross_pay - taxes;
```

```
    // Print the results
    cout << setiosflags( ios::fixed );
    cout << "As of: " << pay_date << "\n";
    cout << emp_name << " worked " <<hours_worked
        << " hours\n";
    cout << "and got paid " << setw(2)
        << gross_pay << "\n";
    cout << "After taxes of: " << setw(5)
        << taxes << "\n";
    cout << "his take-home pay was: " << setw(6)
        << net_pay << "\n";
    return 0;
}
```

The following is the output from this program. When you set the width to less than the contents of a variable, the setw modifiers have no effect and cout prints the entire contents of the number.

```
As of: 03/09/92
Larry Payton worked 40 hours
and got paid 300.000000
After taxes of: 120.000000
his take-home pay was: $180.000000
```

3. Most C++ programmers, and all users of a program like the preceding one, would agree that the six places after the decimal point make the output much more difficult to read. Here is the payroll program again, using the shortcut floating-point width method. Notice that the last three cout statements include no setw manipulator. C++ knows to print the full number to the left of the decimal, but only two places to the right.

```
// Filename: C8PAY2.CPP
// Computes and prints payroll data properly, using the
// shortcut modifier

#include <iostream.h>
#include <iomanip.h>

main()
{
    char    emp_name[ ] = "Larry Payton";
    char    pay_date[ ] = "03/09/92";
```

```
int        hours_worked = 40;
float      rate = 7.50;          // Pay per hour
float      tax_rate = .40;       // Tax percentage rate
float      gross_pay, taxes, net_pay;

// Compute the pay amount
gross_pay = hours_worked * rate;
taxes = tax_rate * gross_pay;
net_pay = gross_pay - taxes;

// Print the results
cout << setiosflags(ios::fixed);
cout << "As of: " << pay_date << "\n";
cout << emp_name << " worked " << hours_worked
     << " hours\n";
cout << "and got paid "
     << setprecision(2) << gross_pay
     << "\n";
cout << "After taxes of: "
     << setprecision(2) << taxes
     << "\n";
cout << "his take-home pay was: "
     << setprecision(2) << net_pay
     << "\n";
return 0;
}
```

The following program's output is much more readable:

```
As of: 03/09/92
Larry Payton worked 40 hours
and got paid 300.00
After taxes of: 120.00
his take-home pay was: 180.00
```

The *cin* Operator

You now understand how C++ represents data and variables, and you know how to print that data. There is one additional part of programming that you have not seen: inputting data into your programs.

In this book, until now, you have not written a program that allows external input of data. All data you worked with was assigned to variables within the program. However, this is not always the best way to get the data into your programs; you rarely know what your data is going to be when you write your programs. The data is known only when you run the programs (or another user runs them).

The *cin* operator stores keyboard input in variables.

You can use the `cin` operator to get input from the keyboard. When your programs reach the line with a `cin`, the user at the keyboard can enter values directly into variables. Your program can then process those variables and produce output. Figure 8.1 illustrates the difference between cout and cin.

Figure 8.1

The actions of
cout and *cin*.

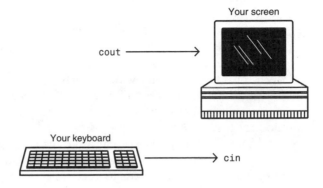

Your screen

cout ⟶

Your keyboard

⟶ cin

The *cin* Fills Variables with Values

There is a major difference between `cin` and the assignment statements (such as `i = 17;`) you have seen. Both fill variables with values. However, an assignment statement assigns specific values to variables *at programming time*. When you run a program with assignment statements, you know from the program's listing exactly what values will go into the variables, because you wrote the program to store those values there. Every time you run the program, the results are exactly the same since the same values go into (are *assigned* to) the same variables.

When you write programs that use `cin`, you have no idea what values will go into the `cin`'s variables because the values are not known *until the program is run and the user enters those values*. This means more flexible programs that can be used by a variety of people. Whenever the program is run, different results are printed, depending on what is typed at each `cin` in the program.

The `cin` has its drawbacks. If you understand the `cout` operator, however, `cin` should not pose much of a problem. Therefore, the next few chapters make use of `cin`, until you learn the more powerful (and flexible) input methods. The `cin` operator looks very much like `cout`, containing one or more variables to the right of the operator name. The format of `cin` is as follows:

```
cin [>> values];
```

> **Tip:** An easy way to remember which operator to use with `cin` and `cout` is to think of the arrows (>> and <<) as pointing in the direction the data flows. For `cin`, the data flows from the input >> to the program, and for `cout`, the data flows to the output << from the program.

The iostream.h header file contains the information C++ needs for `cin`, so include that file when using `cin`. The `cin` operator uses the same manipulators as the `cout` operator. The *values* are the variables into which the data will be placed.

The `cin` operator requires that the user type correct input. This is not always possible to guarantee!

As mentioned, `cin` poses a few problems. The `cin` operator requires that the user type the input *exactly* as `cin` expects it. Because you cannot control the user's typing, its accuracy cannot be ensured. You might want the user to enter an integer value followed by a floating-point value, which your `cin` operator call might expect, yet your user decides to enter something else! If that happens, there is not much you can do; the resulting input will be incorrect, and your C++ program has no reliable method for testing user accuracy.

For the next few chapters, you can assume that the user knows to enter the proper values. But for your own programs used by others, you will want to be on the lookout for additional methods to get better input, starting in Part V of this book.

Examples

1. If you want a program that computes a seven percent sales tax, you can use the `cin` statement to get the sales, compute the tax, and print the results, as shown in the following program:

```cpp
// Filename: C8SLTX1.CPP
// Gets a sales amount and prints the sales tax

#include <iostream.h>
#include <iomanip.h>

main()
{
    float     total_sale;   // User's sales amount
                            // will go here
    float     stax;

    // Get the sales amount from user
    cin >> total_sale;

    // Calculate sales tax
    stax = total_sale * .07;
```

```
        cout << setiosflags( ios::fixed);
        cout << "The sales tax for " << setprecision(2)
             << total_sale << " is " << setprecision (2)
             << stax;
        return 0;
}
```

If you run this program, it will wait for you to enter a value for the total
sale. After you press the Enter key, the program calculates the sales tax
and prints the results.

If you entered `10.00` as the sales amount, you would see the following
output:

```
The sales tax for 10.00 is 0.70
```

2. The preceding program is fine for introducing `cin` but contains a serious
problem. The problem is not in the code itself but in the assumption made
about the user. The program does not indicate what it expects the user to
enter. The `cin` assumes too much already, so your programs that use `cin`
should inform the user exactly what should be typed. The following
revision of this program prompts the user with an appropriate message
before getting the sales amount:

```cpp
// Filename: C8SLTX2.CPP
// Prompts for a sales amount and prints the sales tax

#include <iostream.h>
#include <iomanip.h>

main()
{
    float    total_sale;      // User's sales amount
                              // will go here
    float    stax;

    // Display a message for the user
    cout << "What is the total amount of the sale? ";

    // Get the sales amount from user
    cin >> total_sale;

    // Calculate sales tax
    stax = total_sale * .07;
```

```
cout << setiosflags( ios::fixed );
    cout << "The sales tax for " << setprecision(2)
            << total_sale << " is " << setprecision (2)
            << stax;
return 0;
}
```

Because the first `cout` does not contain a newline character, `\n`, the user's response to the prompt will appear directly to the right of the question mark.

3. When you use `cin` to input keyboard strings into character arrays, each new word causes `cin` to look for a new character array to store the input, and input ends for a given `cin` line when the user has entered as many separate words as `cin` is expecting and then presses the Enter key. Note that while this is convenient for a program like the one in this example, it also means that you must use a different input method if you want the user to be able to type in sentences. You will learn how to input sentences from the user in a later chapter. The following program asks the user to type their first and last names all at one time. `cin` will use the space between the names to store the first and last name in separate character arrays. The program then prints the names in reverse order.

```
// Filename: C8PHON1.CPP
// Program that gets the user's name and prints it
// to the screen as it would appear in a phone book

#include <iostream.h>
#include <iomanip.h>

main()
{
    char    first[ 20 ], last[ 20 ];

    cout << "Please type your first and last name==>";
    cin >> first >> last;
    cout << "\n\n";      //Print 2 blank lines
    cout << "In a phone book, your name would look
    ➡this:\n";
    cout << last << ", " << first;
    return 0;
}
```

A sample run from this program produced the following output:

```
What is your first name? Martha
What is your last name? Roberts


In a phone book, your name would look like this:
Roberts, Martha
```

4. Suppose that you want to write a program that does simple addition for your seven-year-old daughter. The following program prompts her for two numbers and then waits for her to type an answer. When she gives her answer, the program displays the correct result so that she can see how well she did. (Later you will learn how you can let her know immediately whether her answer is correct.)

```cpp
// Filename: C8MATH.CPP
// Program to help children with simple addition
// Prompts child for 2 values, after printing a title
message
#include <iostream.h>
#include <iomanip.h>

main()
{
    int     num1, num2, ans;
    int     her_ans;

    cout << "*** Math Practice ***\n\n\n";
    cout << " What is the first number? ";
    cin >> num1;
    cout << "What is the second number? ";
    cin >> num2;

    // Compute answer and give her a chance to wait for it
    ans = num1 + num2;

    cout << "\nWhat do you think is the answer? ";
    cin >> her_ans;      // Nothing is done with this

    // Print answer after a blank line
    cout << "\n" << num1 << " plus " << num2 << " is: "
         << ans << "\n\nHope you got it right!";
    return 0;
}
```

Summary

You now can print almost anything to the screen. By studying the manipulators and how they behave, you can control your output more thoroughly than ever before. Furthermore, because you can receive keyboard values, your programs are much more powerful. No longer do you have to know your data values when you write the program. You can ask the user to enter values into variables for you with `cin`.

You have the tools to begin writing programs that fit the data processing model of input -> process -> output. This chapter concludes the preliminary discussion of the C++ language. This part of the book provided an overview of the language and showed you enough of its elements so that you can begin writing useful programs as soon as possible.

The next chapter begins a new kind of discussion. You learn how C++'s math and relational operators work on data, and you learn the importance of the precedence table of operators.

Review Questions

Answers to Review Questions are in Appendix B.

1. What is the difference between `cout` and `cin`?

2. Why is displaying a prompt message important before using `cin` for input?

3. How many values are entered with the following `cin`?

```
cin >> i >> j >> k >> l;
```

4. Because both methods put values into variables, is there any difference between assigning values to variables and using `cin` to give them values?

5. What is the output produced by the following `cout`?

```
cout << "The backslash, \"\\\" character is special";
```

6. What is the result of the following `cout`?

```
cout << setw(8) << setprecision(3) << 123.456789;
```

Review Exercises

1. Write a program that prompts for the user's name and weight. Store these values in separate variables and print them to the screen.

2. Assume that you are a college professor who needs to average grades for 10 students. Write a program that prompts for 10 different grades and displays an average of them.

3. Modify the program in Exercise 2 to ask for each student's name as well as grade. Print the grade list to the screen, with each student's name and grade in two columns. Make sure that the columns align by using a setw manipulator on the grade. At the bottom, print the average of the grades. (*Hint:* Store the 10 names and 10 grades in different variables with different names.) This program is easy but takes about 30 lines, plus appropriate comments and prompts. Later you learn ways to streamline this program.

4. Write a program that prompts for the user's full name, hours worked, hourly rate, and tax rate, and then displays the taxes and net pay in the appropriate dollars and cents. (Store the first, middle, and last names in three separate character arrays.)

5. Modify the child's math program (C8MATH.CPP), shown earlier in this chapter, so that it practices subtraction, multiplication, and division after it finishes the addition.

6. This exercise tests your understanding of the backslash conversion character. Write a program that uses cout operators to produce the following illustration on the screen:

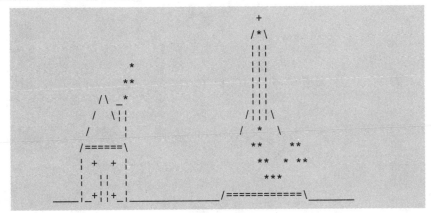

Part II

Using C++ Operators

CHAPTER 9

Using C++ Math Operators and Precedence

You may be dreading this chapter if you don't like math. Relax—C++ does all your math for you. You don't have to be good at math to understand how to program computers. The opposite is true. The computer is there to be your slave, follow your instructions, and do all the calculations.

This chapter shows how C++ computes by introducing these topics:

- C++'s primary math operators

- The operator precedence table

- Multiple assignments

- Compound operators

- Mixed data type conversions

- Type casting

Many people who dislike math actually enjoy learning how the computer does calculations. After seeing the operators and a few simple ways in which C++ uses them, you will feel comfortable putting calculations in your programs. Computers are very fast, and they can perform math operations many times faster than people.

The Primary Math Operators

C++ *math operators* are symbols used for addition, subtraction, multiplication, and division, as well as other similar operations. C++ operators are not always mathematical in nature, but many are. Table 9.1 lists the primary C++ operators and their meanings.

Table 9.1. The C++ primary operators and their meanings.

Symbol	Meaning
*	Multiplication
/	Division and integer division
%	Modulus or remainder
+	Addition
–	Subtraction

Most of these operators work in ways familiar to you. Multiplication, addition, and subtraction produce the same results (and the division operator usually does) that you get when you do these math functions with a calculator. Table 9.2 shows examples that illustrate four of these simple operators.

Table 9.2. Some typical results of using operators.

Formula	Result
4 * 2	8
64 / 4	16
80 – 15	65
12 + 9	21

Table 9.2 contains examples of *binary operations* performed with four operators. Do not confuse this term with binary numbers. When an operator is used between two constants or variables (or a combination of both), it is called a binary operator because it operates on two values. When you use these operators (as in assigning their results to variables), it does not matter whether you put spaces around the operators.

Note: Use the asterisk (*) for multiplication and not an *x*, which you normally use when you multiply by hand. An *x* cannot be used because C++ would confuse it with a variable called x. C++ would not know whether you wanted to multiply or use the value of that variable.

The Unary Operators

You can use the addition and subtraction operators by themselves. When you do, they are called *unary operators*. A unary operator operates on, or affects, a single value. For instance, you can assign a variable a positive or negative number by using a unary + or –. In addition, you can assign a variable another positive or negative variable by using a unary + or –.

Examples

1. The following section of code assigns four variables a positive or negative number. All the plus signs (+) and minus signs (–) are unary because they are not used between two values.

The variable a becomes equal to negative 25.
The variable b becomes equal to positive 25.
The variable c becomes equal to negative a.
The variable d becomes equal to positive b.

```
a = -25;   // Assign 'a' a negative 25
b = +25;   // Assign 'b' a positive 25 (The plus sign is
           // unneeded)
c = -a;    // Assign 'c' the negative of 'a' (25)
d = +b;    // Assign 'd' the positive of 'b' (The plus sign
           // is unneeded)
```

2. You generally don't have to use the unary plus sign. C++ assumes that a number or variable is positive even if you don't put a plus sign in front of it. The following four statements are equivalent to the last ones, except that these don't contain plus signs:

```
a = -25;   // Assign 'a' a negative 25
b =  25;   // Assign 'b' a positive 25
c = -a;    // Assign 'c' the negative of 'a' (-25)
d =  b;    // Assign 'd' the positive of 'b'
```

3. The unary negative comes in handy when you want to negate a single number or variable. The negative of a negative is positive. Therefore, the following short program assigns a negative number (using the unary -) to a variable and then prints the negative of that variable. Because it had a negative number to begin with, the cout produces a positive result.

```
// Filename: C9NEG.CPP
// The negative of a variable that contains a negative value

#include <iostream.h>

main()
{
    signed int     temp = -12;      // 'signed' is unneeded
                                    // since that is default

    cout << -temp;      // Produce a 12 on the screen
    return 0;
}
```

The variable declaration did not need the signed prefix because all integer variables are signed by default.

4. If you want to subtract the negative of a variable, make sure that you put a space before the unary minus sign. For example, the line

```
new_temp = old_temp - -inversion_factor;
```

temporarily negates the inversion_factor and then subtracts that negated value from new_temp.

Division and Modulus

The division operator (/) and the modulus operator (%) may operate in ways unfamiliar to you. They are usually as easy to use, though, as the other operators just discussed.

The modulus operator (%) computes the remainder of division.

The forward slash (/) always divides. However, it produces an integer division if integer values (constants, variables, or a combination of both) appear on both sides of the /. If there is a remainder, C++ discards it.

The percent sign (%) produces a modulus, or a remainder, of an integer division. This operator requires integers on both sides and will not work otherwise.

Examples

1. Suppose that you want to compute your weekly pay. The following program asks for your yearly pay, divides it by 52, and prints the results to two decimal places:

```
// Filename: C9DIV.CPP
// Displays user's weekly pay

#include <iostream.h>
#include <iomanip.h>

main()
{
    float     weekly, yearly;

    cout << "What is your annual pay? ";  // Prompt user
    cin >> yearly;

    weekly = yearly / 52;  // Compute the weekly
    cout << setiosflags( ios::fixed);
    cout << "\n\nYour weekly pay is "
        << setprecision(2) << weekly;
    return 0;
}
```

Because a floating-point number is used in the division, C++ produces a floating-point result. Here is a sample run from this program:

```
What is your annual pay? 38000.00
Your weekly pay is 730.77
```

2. Integer division does not round its results. If you divide two integers and the answer is not a whole number, C++ ignores the fractional part. The following couts help show this. The output that would result from each cout appears in the comment to the right of each line.

```
cout << 10 / 2 << " \n";      // 5  (no remainder)
cout << 300 / 100 << " \n";   // 3  (no remainder)
cout << 10 / 3 << " \n";      // 3  (discarded remainder)
cout << 300 / 165 << " \n";   // 1  (discarded remainder)
```

3. The modulus operator produces an integer remainder. If the preceding four couts used the modulus operator, the output would show only the remainder of each division, as in the following:

```
cout << 10 % 2 << " \n";      // 0  (no remainder)
cout << 300 % 100 << " \n";   // 0  (no remainder)
cout << 10 % 3 << " \n";      // 1  (Answer: 3 with '1'
                              // remaining)
cout << 300 % 165 << " \n";   // 135 (Answer: 1 with '135'
                              // remaining)
```

The modulus operator will come in handy for several types of applications once you learn a few more commands. You can use the modulus to make sure that the user entered an odd or even number and to check whether a year is a leap year, as well as test for several other helpful values.

The Order of Precedence

Knowing the meaning of the math operators is the first of two steps toward understanding C++ calculations. You also must understand the *order of precedence*. This order (sometimes called the *math hierarchy* or *order of operators*) determines exactly how C++ computes formulas. The precedence of operators is the same as that used in high school algebra courses. (Don't be frightened—this is the easy part of algebra!) To see how the order of precedence works, try to determine the result of the following simple calculation:

```
2 + 3 * 2
```

Perform multiplication, division, and modulus before addition and subtraction.

If you said 10, you would not be alone; many people would respond with 10. However, 10 is correct only if you interpret the formula from left to right. But what if you calculated the multiplication first? If you took the value of 3 * 2 and got an answer of 6, and then added 2 to it, you would end up with 8. This is exactly the answer—8—that C++ computes!

C++ always performs multiplication, division, and modulus first, and then performs addition and subtraction. Table 9.3 shows the order of the operators you have seen so far. There are many more levels to C++'s precedence table of operators than those shown in Table 9.3. Unlike most computer languages, C++ has 15 levels of precedence. Appendix D contains the complete table of precedence. In Appendix D, notice that in the precedence table multiplication, division, and modulus reside on level 3, one level higher than addition and subtraction, which are on level 4. In the next few chapters, you learn how to use the rest of the precedence table in your C++ programs.

Table 9.3. The order of precedence for the primary operators.

Order	Operators
First	Multiplication, division, modulus remainder (*, /, %)
Second	Addition, subtraction (+, –)

Examples

1. Following C++'s order of operators is easy if you look at the intermediate results one at a time. The three calculations in Figure 9.1 show you how to do this.

Figure 9.1

Sample calcualtions showing C++'s order of operators.

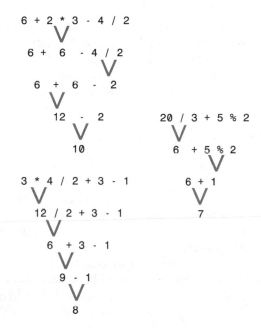

 2

2. Looking back at the order of precedence table again, you will notice that multiplication, division, and modulus are on the same level. This implies that there is no hierarchy on that level. If more than one of these operators appear in a calculation, C++ performs the math from left to right. The same is true of addition and subtraction; the leftmost calculation will be done first. Figure 9.2 shows an example.

Figure 9.2

Sample calculation
showing C++'s
order of operators
from left to right.

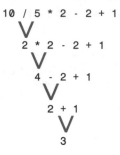

$$10 \ / \ 5 \ * \ 2 \ - \ 2 \ + \ 1$$
$$2 \ * \ 2 \ - \ 2 \ + \ 1$$
$$4 \ - \ 2 \ + \ 1$$
$$2 \ + \ 1$$
$$3$$

Because the division appears to the left of the multiplication, the division is computed first because both are on the same level in the precedence table (Appendix D).

You now should be able to follow the order of these C++ operators. You really do not need to worry about the math because C++ does all the work. However, you should understand the order of operators so that you will know how to structure your calculations. Now you are ready to see how you can override the order of precedence with parentheses.

Using Parentheses

If you want to override the order of precedence, put parentheses in your calculations. The parentheses actually reside on a level above the multiplication, division, and modulus in the precedence table. In other words, any calculation in parentheses—whether it is addition, subtraction, division, or something else—is always performed before the rest of the line. The other calculations are performed in their normal operator order.

Parentheses
override the
normal precedence
of math operators.

The first formula in this chapter, 2 + 3 * 2, produced an 8 because the multiplication was performed before addition. However, by adding parentheses around the addition, as in (2 + 3) * 2, the answer becomes 10.

In the precedence table shown in Appendix D, the parentheses reside on level 1, the highest level in the table. Being higher than the other levels means that the parentheses take precedence over multiplication, division, and all the other operators you have seen.

Examples

1. The calculations in Figure 9.3 illustrate how parentheses override the regular order of operators. These are the same three formulas shown in the last section, except that their results are calculated differently because of the use of parentheses.

Figure 9.3

The use of parentheses as the highest level of precedence.

```
                                              3 * 4 / 2 + (3 - 1)
                                                      V
                                              3 * 4 / 2 + 2
                                                    V
          6 + 2 * (3 - 4) / 2              12 / 2 + 2
                  V                              V
          6 + 2 * -1 / 2                    6 + 2
                V                              V
          6  + -2  / 2                         8
                  V
          6 +   - 1                       20 / (3 + 5) % 2
              V                                  V
              5                           20  / 8 % 2
                                                V
                                              2 % 2
                                                V
                                                0
```

2. If an expression contains parentheses within parentheses, C++ evaluates the contents of the innermost parentheses first. The expression in Figure 9.4 illustrates this.

Figure 9.4

The use of parentheses within parentheses.

```
          5 * (5 + (6 - 2) + 1)
                    V
          5 * (5 + 4 + 1)
                  V
            5 * (9 + 1)
                  V
            5 * 10
                V
              50
```

3. The following program produces an incorrect result, even though it looks as if it should work. See if you can spot the error.

Comments to identify your program.
Include the header file iostream.h.
Include the header file iomanip.h.
Start of the main() function.
  Declare the variables avg, grade1, grade2, and grade3
  as floating-point integers.
  Set the variable grade1 to 85.0.
  Set the variable grade2 to 80.0.
  Set the variable grade3 to 75.0.

The variable avg becomes equal to grade1 plus grade2 plus grade3 divided by 3.0.
Print to the screen The average is and the average of the 3 grade variables. Return from the main() function.

```
// Filename: C9AVG1.CPP
// Computes the average of three grades

#include <iostream.h>
#include <iomanip.h>

main()
{
    float      avg, grade1, grade2, grade3;

    grade1 = 85.0;
    grade2 = 80.0;
    grade3 = 75.0;
    avg = grade1 + grade2 + grade3 / 3.0;
    cout << setiosflags( ios::fixed );
    cout << "The average is " << setprecision(1) << avg;
    return 0;
}
```

The problem is that division is performed first. Therefore, the third grade is first divided by three, and then the other two grades are added to that result. To fix the problem, you just need to add one set of parentheses, as shown in the following:

```
// Filename: C9AVG2.CPP
// Computes the average of three grades

#include <iostream.h>
#include <iomanip.h>

main()
{
    float      avg, grade1, grade2, grade3;

    grade1 = 85.0;
    grade2 = 80.0;
    grade3 = 75.0;
    avg = (grade1 + grade2 + grade3) / 3.0;
    cout << setiosflags( ios::fixed );
    cout << "The average is " << setprecision(1) << avg;
    return 0;
}
```

Tip: Use plenty of parentheses in your C++ programs to make the order of operators clearer, even when you don't have to override their default order. It sometimes makes the calculations easier to understand when you later modify the program.

Shorter Is Not Always Better

When you program computers for a living, it is much more important to write programs that are easy to understand than to write programs that are short or include tricky calculations.

Maintainability is the computer industry's word for changing and updating programs originally written in a simple style. The business world is changing rapidly, and the programs that companies used for years must be updated to reflect the changing environment. Businesses do not always have the resources to write programs from scratch, so they have to make do with modifying the ones they have.

Years ago, when computer hardware was much more expensive, and when computer memories were much smaller, it was important that you write small programs, despite the problems they caused when they needed to be changed. This was aggravating when the original programmers left and someone else (you!) had to step in and modify another person's code.

Companies are realizing the importance of spending time to write programs that are easy to modify and that do not rely on tricks or "quick and dirty" routines that are hard to follow. You will be a more valuable programmer if you write clean programs, with lots of white space, many remarks, and straight-forward code. Put parentheses around formulas to make them clearer, and use variables for storing results in case you need the same answer later in the program. Break long calculations into several smaller ones.

Throughout this book, you will see tips on writing maintainable programs. You and your colleagues will appreciate these tips when you incorporate them into your own C++ programs.

The Assignment Statement

In C++, the assignment operator, =, is used more extensively than in other languages. So far, you have seen this operator used for the simple assignment of values to variables. This is consistent with its use in most programming languages. In C++, the assignment operator also can be used in other ways, such as for multiple assignment and compound assignment. This discussion illustrates these additional uses.

Multiple Assignment

If more than one equal sign appears in an expression, each = performs an assignment. This multiple use introduces a new aspect of the precedence order. Consider the following expression:

```
a = b = c = d = e = 100;
```

This may seem confusing at first, especially if you know other computer languages. To C++, the equal sign always means to "assign the value on the right to the variable on the left." This right-to-left order is described in Appendix D's precedence table. The third column in the table is labeled *Associativity*. The Associativity column describes the direction of the operation. The assignment operator associates from right to left, whereas some of the other operators associate from left to right.

Because the assignment associates from right to left, the preceding expression first assigns the 100 to the variable named e. This produces a value, 100, of the expression. In C++, all expressions produce values, typically the result of assignments. Therefore, this value (100) is then assigned to the variable d. The value of 100 is assigned to c, and then to b, and finally to a. Whatever values were in the five variables previous to this statement are replaced by 100 after the statement finishes.

C++ does not automatically set variables to zero before you use them, so you might want to zero them out before you use them with a single assignment statement. The following section of variable declarations and initialization is performed with multiple assignment statements:

```
#include <iostream.h>
main()
{
    int         ctr, num_emp, num_dep;
    float     sales, salary, amount;

    ctr = num_emp = num_dep = 0;
    sales = salary = amount = 0;
    // Rest of program follows
```

In C++, you can include the assignment statement almost anywhere in a program, even within another calculation. Consider the following statement:

```
value = 5 + (r = 9 - c);
```

This is a perfectly legal C++ statement. The assignment operator resides on the first level of the precedence table and always produces a value. Because its associativity is from right to left, the r is first assigned 9 - c, because the equal sign on the right is evaluated first. The subexpression (r = 9 - c) produces a value— whatever is placed into r—which is added to 5 before that result is stored in value.

Examples

1. Because C++ does not initialize variables to zero before you use them, you may want to include a multiple assignment operator to zero them out before using them. The following section of code ensures that all variables are initialized before the rest of the program uses them:

```
#include <iostream.h>
main()
(
        int        num_emp, dependents, age;
        float      salary, hr_rate, taxrate;

        // Initialize all variables to zero
        num_emp = dependents = age = hours = 0;
        salary = hr_rate = taxrate = 0.0;

        // Rest of program follows
```

2. The two statements

```
gross = hr_rate * hours;
salary = taxrate * gross;
```

can be combined into one with the multiple assignment operator, as in

```
salary = taxrate * (gross = hr_rate * hours);
```

Use these types of statements judiciously. Even though combining statements may be more efficient than using two statements, combined statements are not necessarily clearer to use.

Compound Assignment

Many times in programming, you will want to update the value of a variable. That is, you will need to take a variable's current value, add or multiply that value by an expression, and then assign it back to the original variable. The following assignment statement demonstrates this:

```
salary = salary * 1.2;
```

This expression multiplies the old value of salary by 1.2 (in effect, raising the value in salary by 20 percent) and then assigns it back to salary. C++ provides several operators, called *compound operators*, that you can use whenever the same variable appears on both sides of the equal sign. The compound operators are shown in Table 9.4.

Table 9.4. The compound operators.

Operator	Example	Equivalent
+=	bonus += 500;	bonus = bonus + 500;
-=	budget -= 50;	budget = budget - 50;
*=	salary *= 1.2;	salary = salary * 1.2;
/=	factor /= .50;	factor = factor / .50;
%=	daynum %= 7;	daynum = daynum % 7;

The compound operators are low in the precedence table. They are typically evaluated very late in equations that use them.

Examples

1. Suppose that you have been storing your factory's production amount in a variable called prod_amt, and your supervisor has just informed you of a new addition that needs to be applied to that production value. You could code this update in a statement that looks like the following:

```
prod_amt = prod_amt + 2.6;  // Add 2.6 to current production
```

Instead of this formula, you should use C++'s compound addition operator by coding the update in this way:

```
prod_amt += 2.6;  // Add 2.6 to current production
```

2. Suppose that you are a high school teacher who wants to adjust your students' grades upward. You gave a test that seemed too difficult, and the grades were not up to your expectations. If you had stored each student's grade in variables named grade1, grade2, grade3, and so on, you could update the grades from within a program with the following section of compound assignments:

```
grade1 *= 1.1;      // Increase each student's grade by 10%
grade2 *= 1.1;
grade3 *= 1.1;
// Rest of grade changes follow
```

3. The precedence of the compound operators requires important consideration when you decide how to code compound assignments. Notice in Appendix D that the compound operators are on level 14, much lower than the regular math operators. This means that you must be careful how you interpret them.

Suppose that you want to update the value of a sales variable with the following formula:

```
4 - factor + bonus
```

You could update the sales variable with the statement

```
sales += 4 - factor + bonus;
```

This applies the new formula, 4 - factor + bonus, to sales. This is *not* the same as the following:

```
sales = sales + 4 - factor + bonus;
```

Because the += operator is much lower in the precedence table than + or -, += is performed last and with right-to-left associativity. Therefore, the following two statements *are* equivalent:

```
sales += 4 - factor + bonus;

sales = sales + (4 - factor + bonus);
```

4. To give you a better idea of the compound operators and their precedence level, the following program uses each compound operator and prints a result based on the operators. The program and its output will help you understand how to use the compound operators and their levels in the precedence table.

```cpp
// Filename: C9CMP.CPP
// Illustrates each compound operator

#include <iostream.h>

main()
{
    int     i = 4;
    int     j = 8;
    int     k = 12;
    int     ans;            // Will hold various results

    ans = i + j;
    cout << ans << " \n";       // Print a 12
    ans += k;
    cout << ans << " \n";       // Print a 24
    ans /= 3;
    cout << ans << " \n";       // Print an 8
    ans -= 5;
    cout << ans << " \n";       // Print a 3
    ans *= 2;
```

```
    cout << ans << " \n";      // Print a 6
    ans %= 4;
    cout << ans << " \n";      // Print a 2

// Order of precedence affects the following
    ans *= 5 + 3;
    cout << ans << " \n";      // Print a 16
    ans += 4 - 2;
    cout << ans << " \n";      // Print an 18

    return 0;
}
```

Mixing Data Types in Calculations

C++ attempts to convert the smaller data type to the larger one in a mixed data type expression.

You can mix data types in C++, such as adding together an integer and a floating-point value. C++ will generally convert the smaller type to the larger type. If you add a double to an integer, for example, C++ first converts the integer to a double value and then performs the calculation. This produces the most accurate result possible. The automatic conversion of data types is only temporary; the converted value is back in its original data type as soon as the expression is finished.

If C++ converted two different data types to the smaller value's type, the higher-precision value would be *truncated* (shortened) too much, and accuracy would be lost. For example, in the following short program, the floating-point value of sales is added to an integer called bonus. Before computing the answer, C++ converts bonus to a floating-point value, which results in a floating-point answer.

```
// Filename: C9DATA.CPP
// Demonstrates mixed data type in an expression

#include <iostream.h>
#include <iomanip.h>

main()
{
    int        bonus = 50;
    float      salary = 1400.50;
    float      total;

    total = salary + bonus;   // bonus becomes
                              // floating-point temporarily
```

```
    cout << setiosflags( ios::fixed );
        cout << "The total is " << setprecision(2) << total;
        return 0;
}
```

Type Casting

Most of the time, you will not have to worry about C++'s automatic conversion of data types. However, problems can occur if you mix unsigned variables with variables of other data types. Because of differences between computer architecture, unsigned variables do not always convert to the larger data type. Therefore, loss of accuracy may result, and even incorrect results are possible.

You can override C++'s default conversions by specifying your own temporary type change, called *type casting*. When you type cast, you temporarily change a variable's data type from its declared data type to a new one. The format of a type cast is

```
(data type) expression
```

where data type can be any valid C++ data type, and the `expression` can be a variable, a constant, or an expression that combines both. The following line of code type casts the integer variable age into a double floating-point variable temporarily, so that it can be multiplied by the double floating-point factor.

Assign the variable `age_factor` the value of the variable age (now a double floating-point variable) and multiply by the variable `factor`.

```
    age_factor = (double)age * factor;   // Temporarily change
                                          // age to double
```

Examples

1. Suppose that you want to verify the interest calculation used by your bank on a loan. The interest rate is 15.5 percent, stored as 0.155 in a floating-point variable. The amount of interest you owe is computed by multiplying the interest rate by the amount of the loan balance, and then multiplying that by the number of days in the year since the loan was originated. The following program finds the daily interest rate by dividing the annual interest rate by 365, the number of days in a year. C++ must convert the integer 365 to a floating-point constant automatically because it is used in combination with a floating-point variable.

```
// C9INT1.CPP
// Calculates interest on a loan

#include <iostream.h>
#include <iomanip.h>

main()
{
    int         days = 45;  // Days since loan origination
    float       principal = 3500.00;    // Original loan amount
    float       interest_rate = 0.155; // Annual interest rate
    float       daily_interest;         // Daily interest rate

    daily_interest = interest_rate / 365;    // Compute
                                             // floating-point value

    // Since days is an integer, it too will be converted
    // to float next
    daily_interest = principal * daily_interest * days;
    principal += daily_interest;     // Update the principal
                                     // with interest
    cout << setiosflags( ios::fixed );
    cout << "The balance you owe is "
         << setprecision(2)
         << principal;
    return 0;
}
```

Here is the output of this program:

```
The balance you owe is 3566.88
```

2. Instead of letting C++ perform the conversion, you may want to type cast all mixed expressions to ensure that they convert to your liking. Here is the same program that appears in example 1, except that type casts are used to convert the integer constants to floating-point values before they are used.

```
// C9INT2.CPP
// Calculates interest on a loan using type casting

#include <iostream.h>
#include <iomanip.h>
```

```
main()
{
    int         days = 45;   // Days since loan origination
    float       principal = 3500.00;   // Original loan amount
    float       interest_rate = 0.155; // Annual interest rate
    float       daily_interest;        // Daily interest rate

    // Type cast days to float
    daily_interest = interest_rate / (float)365;

    // Since days is an integer, convert it to float too
    daily_interest = principal * daily_interest * (float)days;
    principal += daily_interest;       // Update the principal
                                       // with interest
    cout << setiosflags(ios::fixed);
    cout << "The balance you owe is "
        << setprecision(2)
        << principal;
    return 0;
}
```

The output from this program will be exactly the same as the output from
the first program.

Summary

You now understand C++'s primary math operators and the important precedence
table. You can group operations together with parentheses to override the default
precedence levels. Unlike some operators in other programming languages, every
operator in C++ has a meaning, no matter where the operator appears in an expression.
You can therefore use the assignment operator (=) in the middle of other expressions.

When performing math with C++, you must be aware of how C++ interprets data
types, especially when you mix them within the same expression. You can temporarily type cast a variable or constant in order to override its default data type.

This chapter introduced you to C++ operators. The next two chapters extend this
discussion to include relational and logical operators, which enable you to compare
data and compute accordingly.

Review Questions

Answers to Review Questions are in Appendix B.

1. What is the result of each of the following expressions?

   a. `1 + 2 * 4 / 2`

   b. `(1 + 2) * 4 / 2`

   c. `1 + 2 * (4 / 2)`

2. What is the result of each of these expressions?

   a. $9 \% 2 + 1$

   b. $(1 + (10 - (2 + 2)))$

3. Convert each of the following formulas into its C++ assignment equivalents:

   a. $a = \dfrac{3+3}{4+4}$

   b. $x = (a - b) * (a - c)2$

   c. $f = \dfrac{a1/2}{b1/3}$

   d. $d = \dfrac{(8 - x2)}{(x - 9)} - \dfrac{(4 * 2 - 1)}{x3}$

4. Write a short program that prints the area of a circle with a radius of 4 and pi = 3.14159. (The area of a circle is computed by `pi * radius2`.)

5. Write the assignment and `cout` statement that prints the remainder of 100 / 4.

Review Exercises

1. Write a program that prints each of the first 8 powers of 2—that is, 2^1, 2^2, 2^3, . . ., 2^8. Please include a comment to indicate your name at the top of the program. Print string constants that describe each answer printed. The first two lines of your output should look like this:

```
2 raised to the first power is: 2
2 raised to the second power is: 4
```

2. Change C9PAY.CPP, shown earlier in the chapter, so that it computes and prints a bonus of 15 percent of the gross pay. Taxes are not to be taken out of the bonus. After printing the four variables gross_pay, tax_rate, bonus, and gross_pay, print a check on the screen that looks like a printed check. Add string constants so that the program prints the name of the payee, and put your name as the payor at the bottom of the check.

3. Store in variables the weights and ages of three people. Print a table, with titles, of the weights and ages. At the bottom of the table, print the average of the weights and heights as well as their totals.

4. Assume that a video store employee worked 50 hours. She gets paid $4.50 for the first 40 hours, gets time and a half (1.5 times the regular pay rate) for the first 5 hours over 40, and gets double time for all hours over 45. Assuming a 28% tax rate, write a program that prints her gross pay, taxes, and net pay to the screen. Label each amount with appropriate titles (using string constants) and add appropriate comments in the program.

CHAPTER 10

Relational Operators

At times, you don't want every statement in your C++ program to execute whenever the program runs. So far, each program you have seen began executing at the top of the program and continued, line by line, until the last statement executed. Depending on your application, you may not always want this to happen.

In *data-driven* programs, the data dictates what the program does. For example, you would not want the computer to print paychecks for all of a company's employees every pay period; some employees may have taken a leave of absence, or they may be on a sales commission and didn't make a sale during a particular pay period. Printing paychecks with zero dollars would be ridiculous. You want the computer to print checks to employees who have pay coming to them, but not to others.

In this chapter, you learn how to create data-driven programs. Such programs do not execute the same way every time they are run. The use of *relational operators* makes this possible. These operators conditionally control other statements. The relational operators look at the constants and variables in the program and operate based on what they find. This may sound difficult, but it is very straightforward and intuitive.

This chapter introduces the following topics:

♦ Relational operators

♦ The `if` statement

♦ The `else` statement

Besides introducing these comparison commands, the chapter prepares you for much more powerful programs that are possible once you learn them.

Looking At Relational Operators

Relational operators compare data.

In addition to using the math operators discussed in the last chapter, you can use other operators to make data comparisons. These operators are called *relational operators*. They compare data, letting you know whether two variables are equal or not equal, or which one is less or more than the other. Table 10.1 lists the relational operators and their meanings.

Table 10.1. The relational operators.

Operator	Description
==	Equal to
>	Greater than
<	Less than
>=	Greater than or equal to
<=	Less than or equal to
!=	Not equal to

The six operators in Table 10.1 provide the foundation for comparing data in C++. Each operator always appears with two constants, variables, expressions, or a mix of these—one on each side of the operator. Many of the relational operators are probably familiar to you. You should learn them as well as you know the +, -, *, /, and % mathematical operators.

> **Note:** Unlike many programming languages, C++ tests for equality with a double equal sign (==). The single equal sign (=) is reserved for assignment of values only.

Examples

1. Assume that a program initializes four variables in this way:

```
int   a = 5;
int   b = 10;
int   c = 15;
int   d = 5;
```

The following statements are then true:

a is equal to d so a == d.

b is less than c so b < c.

c is greater than a so c > a.

h is greater than or equal to a so b >= a.

d is less than or equal to b so d <= b.

b is not equal to c so b != c.

These are not C++ statements but are statements of relational fact about the values in the variables. Relational logic is easy.

Relational logic always produces a *True* or *False* result. In some programming languages, you cannot directly use the True or False result of relational operators inside other expressions, but in C++ you can. You will soon see how to do this, but for now, the following True and False evaluations are correct:

A *True* relational result evaluates to 1.

A *False* relational result evaluates to 0.

Each of the examples presented previously in this section evaluates to a 1, or True, result.

2. Assuming the values in the last example's four variables, each of the following statements about those values is False (0):

a == b

b > c

d < a

d > a

a != d

b >= c

c <= b

You should study these statements to see why each one is False and evaluates to 0. The variables a and d are exactly equal to the same value (5), so neither is greater, nor less than the other.

You deal with relational logic in everyday life. Think of the following statements you might make:

"The generic butter costs less than the name brand."

"My child is younger than Johnny."

"Our salaries are equal."

"The dogs are not the same age."

Each of these statements is either True or False. There is no other possible outcome.

Watch the Signs!

Many people say that they are "not math-inclined" or "not very logical," and you may be one of them. As mentioned earlier, you do not have to be good in math to be a good computer programmer. And you should not be frightened by the term "relational logic"; you just saw that you use it all the time. Nevertheless, some people get confused about its meaning.

The two primary relational operators, less than (<) and greater than (>), are easy to remember. You may have been taught which is which in school, but you may have forgotten them. Actually, their symbols tell you what they mean.

The "arrow points" of the < and > indicate the smaller of the two values. Notice in the True statements in example 1 that the point of each < and > always goes toward the smaller number. The large, open part of the operators points to the larger values.

The relation is False if the point goes in the wrong direction. In other words, 4 > 9 is False because the point of the operator is pointing to the 9. Or, in English, "4 is greater than 9 is a False statement because 4 is really less than 9."

The *if* Statement

You incorporate relational operators in C++ programs with the `if` statement. This statement is called a *decision statement* because it tests a relationship, using the relational operators, and makes a decision about which statement to execute next, based on the result of that decision. The `if` statement has the following format:

```
if (condition)
    { A block of 1 or more C++ statements }
```

The `condition` includes any relational comparison and must be enclosed within parentheses. You saw several relational comparisons earlier, such as a == d and c < d. The `block of one or more C++ statements` is any possible C++ statement, such as an assignment or the `cout` operator, enclosed within braces. The block of the `if`, sometimes called the body of the `if` statement, is usually indented a few spaces for readability. This allows you to see at a glance exactly what executes if the *condition* is True.

If only one statement follows the `if`, the braces are not required, but they are helpful to include. The block will execute *only if the condition is True.* If the condition is False, C++ ignores the block and simply executes the next statement in the program following the `if` statement.

Basically, you can read an `if` statement in the following way: "If the condition is True, perform the block of statements inside the braces. Otherwise, the condition must be False, so do *not* execute the block but continue execution as though the `if` did not exist."

The `if` statement is used to make a decision. The block of statements following the `if` executes if the decision (the result of the relation) is True, and, if not, the block does not execute. As with relational logic, you use "if" logic every day. Consider the following:

> "If the day is warm, I will go swimming."

> "If I make enough money, I will build a new house."

> "If the light is green, go."

> "If the light is red, stop."

Each of these statements is *conditional*. That is, if and only *if* the condition is True will you complete the statement.

> **Caution:** Do not put a semicolon after the parentheses of the relational test. Semicolons go after each statement inside the block.

Expressions as Conditions

C++ always interprets any nonzero value as True and interprets zero as False. This allows you to insert regular nonconditional expressions within the `if` logic. To see this, consider the following section of code:

```
main()
{
    int     age = 21;      // Declare and assign age a
                           // value of 21

    if (age = 85)
    {
        cout << "You have lived through a lot!";
        // Rest of program goes here
```

The if statement makes a decision.

At first, it may seem as though the cout does not execute, *but it does*. Because a regular assignment operator, =, is used and not a relational operator, ==, C++ performs the assignment of 85 to age. As in all the assignments you saw in the last chapter, this produces a value for the expression of 85. Since 85 is nonzero, C++ interprets the if condition as True and performs the body of the if statement.

> **Note:** Mixing the relational equality test (==) and the regular assignment operator (=) is a common error made in C++ programs. The nonzero True test makes this bug even more difficult to find.
>
> The designers of C++ did not intend for this to confuse you. They wanted you to take advantage of this feature when you could. Instead of putting an assignment before an if and then testing the result of that assignment, you can combine the assignment and the if into a single statement.
>
> To test your understanding, would C++ interpret the following condition as True or False?
>
> ```
> if (10 == 10 == 10) ...
> ```
>
> Be careful. At first glance, it seems True, but C++ interprets the expression as False. The == operator associates from left to right, so the first 10 is compared to the second 10. Because they are equal, the result is 1 (for True) and the 1 is then compared to the third 10, which results in a 0 (False) result.

Examples

1. All the statements in this example are valid C++ if statements.

*If (the variable sales is greater than 5000),
    the variable bonus becomes equal to 500.*

```
if (sales > 5000)
{
    bonus = 500;
}
```

If this were part of a C++ program, the value inside the variable sales determines what happens next. If sales contains more than 5000, the next statement that executes is the one inside the block that initializes bonus. If sales contains 5000 or less, however, the block will not execute, and the line following the if's block will execute.

If (the variable age *is less than or equal to 21), print* You are a minor. *to the screen and go to a newline, print* What is your grade? *to the screen, and accept an integer from the keyboard.*

```
if (age <= 21)
{
    cout << "You are a minor.\n";
    cout << "What is your grade?";
    cin >> grade;
}
```

If the value in age is less than or equal to 21, the lines of code in the block will execute next. Otherwise, C++ skips the entire block and continues with the program.

If (the variable balance *is greater than the variable* low_balance*), print* Past due! *to the screen and move the cursor to a newline.*

```
if (balance > low_balance)
{
    cout << "Past due!\n";
}
```

If the balance is more than low_balance, execution of the program continues at the block, and the message Past due! prints to the screen. You can compare two variables as in this example, a variable to a constant as in previous examples, a constant to a constant (although that is rarely done), or an expression in place of any variable or constant. The following if statement shows an expression included in the if.

If (the variable pay *multiplied by the variable* tax_rate
equals the variable minimum*),*
   the variable low_salary *becomes equal to 1400.60.*

```
if (pay * tax_rate == minimum)
{
    low_salary = 1400.60;
}
```

The precedence table of operators in Appendix D includes the relational operators. They are on levels 6 and 7, lower than the other primary math operators. When using expressions such as this one, you can make them much more readable if you use parentheses, even though they are not required, around the expressions. Here is a rewrite of this if statement with ample parentheses.

If ((the variable pay multiplied by the variable `tax_rate`*)*
   equals the variable `minimum`*),*
   the variable `low_salary` *becomes equal to 1400.60.*

```
if ((pay * tax_rate) == minimum)
{
    low_salary = 1400.60;
}
```

2. Here is a simple program that computes the pay of a salesperson. The salesperson gets a flat pay of $4.10 per hour. If the sales are more than $8,500, the salesperson gets an additional $500. This is a good introductory example of conditional logic that depends on a relation of two values: sales and $8,500.

```cpp
// Filename: C10PAY1.CPP
// Calculates a salesperson's pay based on that person's
// sales

#include <iostream.h>
#include <iomanip.h>

main()
{
    char        sal_name[ 20 ];
    int         hours;
    float     total_sales, bonus, pay;

    cout << "\n\n";      // Print 2 blank lines
    cout << "Payroll Calculation\n";
    cout << "-----------------\n";

    // Ask the user for needed values
    cout << "What is salesperson's last name? ";
    cin >> sal_name;
    cout << "How many hours did the salesperson work? ";
    cin >> hours;
    cout << "What were the total sales? ";
    cin >> total_sales;

    bonus = 0;     // Initially, there is no bonus

    // Compute the base pay
    pay = 4.10 * (float)hours;      // Type cast the hours
```

```
    // Add bonus only if sales were high
    if (total_sales > 8500.00)
    {
        bonus = 500.00;
    }


    cout << setiosflags(ios::fixed);
    cout << sal_name << " made "
         << setprecision(2) << pay << " \n";
    cout << "and got a bonus of "
         << setprecision(2) << bonus << "\n";


    return 0;
}
```

Now take a look at the results of running this program twice, each time with different input values. Notice what the program does: It computes a bonus for one employee, but does not for the other. The $500 bonus is a direct result of the if statement. The assignment of $500 to bonus is executed only if the total_sales is more then $8,500.

```
Payroll Calculation
- - - - - - - - - - - - - - - - -
What is salesperson's last name? Harrison
How many hours did the salesperson work? 40
What were the total sales? 6050.64
Harrison made 164.00
and got a bonus of 0.00

Payroll Calculation
- - - - - - - - - - - - - - - - -
What is salesperson's last name? Robertson
How many hours did the salesperson work? 40
What were the total sales? 9800
Robertson made 164.00
and got a bonus of 500.00
```

3. When getting input from users, it is often wise to perform *data validation* on the values they type. If a user enters a bad value—for example, a negative number when you know the input cannot be negative—you can inform the user of the problem and ask that the input be reentered.

Not all data can be validated, but most of it can be checked to be certain that it's reasonable. For example, if you were writing a student record-keeping program to track each student's name, address, age, and other pertinent data, you could check to see whether the age falls within a reasonable range. If the user enters 213 for the age, you know that the value is incorrect. If the user enters -4 for the age, you know that the input value is also incorrect. Not all incorrect input can be checked. If the student is 21 and the user types 22, your program would have no way of knowing whether the age is correct, because 22 falls within a reasonable range.

The following program is a routine that requests an age and checks to make sure that it is more than 10. This test is certainly not foolproof—the user can still enter incorrect ages—but it does take care of extremely low values. If the user enters a bad age, the user is requested for it again, inside the if statement.

```cpp
// Filename: C10AGE.CPP
// Program to help ensure that age values are reasonable

#include <iostream.h>

main()
{
    int     age;

    cout << "\nWhat is the student's age? ";
    cin >> age;

    if (age < 10)
    {
        cout << "*** The age cannot be less than 10***\n";
        cout << "Try again...\n\n";
        cout << "What is the student's age? ";
        cin >> age;
        if (age < 10)
        {
            cout << "*** Sorry, you still haven't entered a
            ➥valid age.\n";
            return 0;
        }
    }

    cout << "Thank you.  You entered a valid age.\n";
    return 0;
}
```

This routine could be a section of a longer program. Later you learn how to prompt repeatedly for a value until a valid input is given.

If the entered age is less than 10, the user gets an error message. The program warns the user about the bad age before asking for it again.

Look at the result of running this program. Notice that the program knows, because of the if statement, whether age is more than 10.

```
What is the student's age? 3
*** The age cannot be less than 10 ***
Try again...


What is the student's age? 21
Thank you.  You entered a valid age.
```

4. Unlike many languages, C++ does not include a square operator. You can take the square of a number by multiplying it by itself. Because many computers don't allow integers to hold more than the square of 180, this program uses if statements to make sure that the number fits in an integer answer when it is computed.

The following program takes a value from the user and prints the square of it, unless it is more than 180. The message I cannot square numbers that large appears if the user types too large a number.

```cpp
// Filename: C10SQRT1.CPP
// Prints the square of the input value
// if the input value is less than 180

#include <iostream.h>

main()
{
    int     num, square;

    cout << "\n\n";     // Print 2 blank lines
    cout << "What number do you want to see the square of?";
    cin >> num;

    if (num < 180)
    {
        square = num * num;
        cout << "The square of " << num << " is " <<
square;
    }
```

```
if (num >= 180)
    {
        cout << "\n*** Square is not allowed for ";
        cout << "numbers over 180 ***";
        cout << "\nRun this program again and try ";
        cout << "a smaller value.";
    }

    cout << "\nThank you for requesting squares.";
    return 0;
}
```

Following are the results of a couple of sample runs from this program. Notice that both conditions work: If the user enters a number below 180, the user sees the square. If the user enters a larger number, an error message appears.

```
What number do you want to see the square of? 45
The square of 45 is 2025
Thank you for requesting squares.

What number do you want to see the square of? 212

*** Square is not allowed for numbers over 180 ***
Run this program again and try a smaller value.
Thank you for requesting squares.
```

This program will be improved when you learn to use else later in this chapter. The program's problem is its redundant check of the user's input. The variable num has to be checked once to print the square if it is below 180, and checked again for the error message if it is above 180.

5. The value of 1 for True or 0 for False can help save you an extra programming step that other languages do not necessarily allow you. To see how, examine the following section of code:

```
commission = 0;                     // Initialize commission

  if (sales > 10000)
  {
      commission = 500.00;
  }

  pay = net_pay + commission;    // commission is 0
                                 // unless high sales
```

This program can be streamlined and made more efficient by combining the if's relational test with the assignments to commission and pay, knowing that it will return 1 or 0:

```
pay = net_pay + (commission = (sales > 10000) * 500.00);
```

This single line does what the previous four lines did. Because the rightmost assignment has precedence, it gets computed first. The variable sales is compared to 10000. If it is more than 10000, a True result of 1 is returned. That 1 is multiplied by 500.00 and stored in commission. If sales is not more than 10000, however, 0 is the result, an 0 multiplied by 500.00 still leaves 0.

The value (500.00 or 0) that is assigned to commission becomes the value of that expression. That value is then added to net_pay and stored in pay.

The *else* Statement

The else statement never appears in a program without an if statement. This section introduces the else statement by showing you the popular if-else combination statement. Its format is as follows:

```
if (condition)
{
      A block of 1 or more C++ statements
}
else
{
      A block of 1 or more C++ statements
}
```

The first part of the if-else is identical to the if statement. If the *condition* is True, the block of C++ statements following the if executes. However, if the *condition* is False, the block of C++ statements following the else executes. Although the simple if statement determines only what happens when the *condition* is True, the if-else determines what happens if the *condition* is False. No matter what the outcome, the statement following the if-else executes next.

> **Note:** The following text describes the nature of if-else:
>
> If the condition is True, the entire block of statements following the if is performed.
>
> If the condition is False, the entire block of statements following the else is performed.

> **Tip:** You can compare characters, not just numbers. When you compare characters, C++ uses the ASCII table to determine which character is "less than" (lower in the ASCII table) the other. You cannot compare character strings or arrays of character strings directly with the relational operators.

Examples

1. The following program asks the user for a number. The program then prints a line indicating that the number is greater than zero or that it is not, using the if-else statement.

```cpp
// Filename: C10IFEL1.CPP
// Demonstrates if-else by printing whether an input value
// is greater than zero or not

#include <iostream.h>

main()
{
    int     num;

    cout << "What is your number? ";
    cin >> num;      // Get the user's number

    if (num > 0)
    {
        cout << "More than 0\n";
    }
    else
    {
        cout << "Less or equal to 0\n";
    }

    // No matter what the number was, the following executes
    cout << "\n\nThanks for your time!\n";
    return 0;
}
```

There is no need to test for *both* possibilities when you use an else. The if tests to see whether the number is greater than zero, and the else takes care of all other possibilities automatically.

2. The following program asks for the user's first name and stores it in a character array. The first character of the array is then checked to see whether it falls in the upper half of the alphabet. If it does, an appropriate message is displayed.

```cpp
// Filename: C10IFEL2.CPP
// Tests the user's first initial and prints a message

#include <iostream.h>

main()
{
    char     last[ 20 ];      // Holds the last name

    cout << "What is your last name? ";
    cin >> last;

    // Test the initial - must be uppercase
    if (last[ 0 ] <= 'P')
    {
        cout << "Your name is early in the alphabet.\n";
    }
    else
    {
        cout << "You have to wait a while ";
        cout << "for YOUR name to be called!";
    }
    return 0;
}
```

Notice that because a character array element is being compared to a character constant, you must enclose the character constant in single quotes. The data types on both sides of each relational operator must match.

3. The following program is a more complete payroll routine than you have seen. It uses the `if` statement to illustrate how to compute overtime pay. The logic goes something like this:

If an employee works 40 hours or fewer, the employee gets paid regular pay (the hourly pay times the number of hours worked). If the employee works over 40 hours, the employee gets one and a half times the hourly rate for the hours over 40. The employee still gets regular pay for the first 40 hours.

```cpp
// Filename: C10PAY2.CPP
// Computes the full overtime pay possibilities

#include <iostream.h>
#include <iomanip.h>

main()
{
    int         hours;
    float       ot, rp, rate, pay;

    cout << "\n\nHow many hours were worked? ";
    cin >> hours;
    cout << "\nWhat is the regular hourly pay? ";
    cin >> rate;

    ot = 0.0;       // set overtime to zero

    // Compute pay here
    // check for overtime
    if (hours > 40)
    {
        ot = 1.5 * rate * (float)(hours - 40);
    }

    // Regular pay
    if (hours >= 40)
    {
        rp = 40 * rate;
    }
    else
    {
        rp = (float)hours * rate;
    }

    pay = ot + rp;    // Add up regular plus overtime

    cout << setiosflags( ios::fixed );
    cout << "\nThe pay is " << setprecision(2) << pay
        << '\n';
    return 0;
}
```

4. The block of statements following the if can contain any valid C++ statement, even another if statement. This sometimes comes in handy.

The following program could be run to give an award to employees based on their years of service to your company. You are giving a gold watch to those with more than 20 years, a paperweight to those with more than 10 years, and a pat on the back to everyone else.

```cpp
// Filename: C10SERV.CPP
// Prints a message depending on years of service

#include <iostream.h>

main()
{
    int     yrs;

    cout << "How many years of service? ";
    cin >> yrs;      // Get the years employee has worked

    if (yrs > 20)
    {
        cout << "Give a gold watch\n";
    }
    else
    {
        if (yrs > 10)
        {
            cout << "Give a paper weight\n";
        }
        else
        {
            cout << "Give a pat on the back\n";
        }
    }
    return 0;
}
```

You should probably not rely on if-else-if to take care of too many conditions, because more than three or four conditions add confusion. You get into messy logic like this: "If this is True, then if this is True, then do something else if this is True, and so on...." The switch statement in a later chapter handles these types of multiple if selections better than a long if-else.

Summary

You now have the tools to write powerful data-driven programs. This chapter showed you how to compare constants, variables, and combinations of both by using the relational operators. The `if` and `if-else` statements rely on these comparisons of data to determine which code to execute next. You now can *conditionally execute* statements within your programs.

The next chapter goes one step further by combining relational operators to create logical operators (sometimes called compound conditions). These logical operators improve your program's ability to make selections based on data comparisons.

Review Questions

Answers to Review Questions are in Appendix B.

1. What operator tests for equality?

2. State whether the following relational tests are True or False:

    a. 4 >= 5

    b. 4 == 4

    c. 165 >= 165

    d. 0 != 25

3. True or false: `C++ is fun` will print on the screen when the following statement is executed.

```
if (54 <= 54)
{

    cout << "C++ is fun";

}
```

4. What is the difference between an `if` statement and an `if-else` statement?

5. Will the following `cout` execute?

```
if (3 != 4 != 1)
{

    cout << "This will print";

}
```

6. Using the ASCII table in Appendix C, state whether these character relational tests are True or False:

   a. 'C' < 'c'

   b. '0' > '0'

   c. '?' > ')'

Review Exercises

1. Write a weather-calculator program that asks for a list of the last five days' temperatures and prints Brrrr! whenever a temperature falls below freezing.

2. Write a program that asks for a number and prints the square and cube (the number multiplied by itself three times) of the input number if that number is more than 1. Otherwise, print nothing.

3. Ask the user for two numbers. Print a message telling how the first one relates to the second. In other words, if the user entered 5 and 7, you would print 5 is less than 7.

4. Prompt the user for an employee's pretax salary. Print the employee's salary taxes. The taxes are 10 percent if the employee made less than $10,000, 15 percent if the employee earned between $10,000 and $20,000, and 20 percent if the employee earned more than 20 percent.

CHAPTER 11

Logical Operators

By combining *logical operators* with relational operators, you can create more powerful data-testing statements. The logical operators are sometimes called *compound relational operators*. As C++'s precedence table shows, the relational operators take precedence over the logical operators when you combine them. The precedence table plays an important role in these types of operators.

In this chapter, you learn about the following topics:

♦ The && AND operator

♦ The ¦¦ OR operator

♦ The ! NOT operator

This chapter concludes your learning of the conditional testing that C++ allows. Presented here are many examples of if statements in programs that work on compound conditional tests.

Logical Operators

There may be times when you need to test more than one set of variables. You can combine more than one relational test into a *compound relational test* by using C++'s logical operators, shown in table 11.1.

Table 11.1. The logical operators.

Operator	Meaning
&&	AND
¦¦	OR
!	NOT

Logical operators are used for compound relational tests.

The first two logical operators, && and ¦¦, never appear by themselves. They typically go between two or more relational tests.

Tables 11.2, 11.3, and 11.4 illustrate how each of the logical operators work. These tables are called *truth tables*; they show how to achieve True results from an if statement that uses them. Take a minute to study the tables.

Table 11.2. The *&& AND* truth table.

Both sides of the operator must be True.

True AND True = True

True AND False = False

False AND True = False

False AND False = False

Table 11.3. The ¦¦ *OR* truth table.

One or the other side of the operator must be True.

True OR True = True

True OR False = True

False OR True = True

False OR False = False

Table 11.4. The *! NOT* truth table.

An opposite relation is produced.

NOT True = False

NOT False = True

The Use of Logical Operators

The True and False on each side of the operators represent a relational if test. For example, the following tests are valid if tests that use logical operators (sometimes called *compound relational operators*):

If ((the variable a is less than the variable b) AND (the variable c is greater than the variable d)), print Results are invalid. *to the screen.*

```
if ((a < b) && (c > d))
{

        cout << "Results are invalid.";

}
```

The variable a must be less than b and, at the same time, c must be greater than d, for the cout to execute. The if statement still requires parentheses around its complete conditional test.

```
if ((sales > 5000) || (hrs_worked > 81))
{

        bonus = 500;

}
```

The || is sometimes called the "inclusive or."

Here the sales must be more than 5000 or the hrs_worked must be more than 81 before the assignment executes.

```
if (!(sales < 2500))
{

        bonus = 500;

}
```

In this example, if sales is greater than or equal to 2500, bonus will be initialized. This illustrates an important programming tip: "Use ! sparingly." (Or, as some so wisely state, "Do not use ! or your programs will not be ! (unclear).") It would be much clearer to rewrite the preceding example by turning it into a positive relational test:

```
if (sales >= 2500)
{

        bonus = 500;

}
```

The ! operator is sometimes helpful, especially when testing for end-of-file conditions later. Most of the time, you can avoid ! by using reverse logic:

!(var1 == var2) is exactly the same as (var1 != var2)

!(var1 <= var2) is exactly the same as (var1 > var2)

!(var1 >= var2) is exactly the same as (var1 < var2)

!(var1 != var2) is exactly the same as (var1 == var2)

!(var1 > var2) is exactly the same as (var1 <= var2)

!(var1 < var2) is exactly the same as (var1 >= var2)

Notice that the overall format of the if statement is retained when you use logical operators, but the relational test has been expanded to include more than one relation. You can even have three or more tests:

```
if ((a == B) && (d == f) || (1 = m) || !(k != 2)) ...
```

This is a little too much, however, and good programming practice dictates using, at most, two relational tests inside a single if statement. If you need to combine more than two tests, use more than one if statement.

As with other relational operators, you use these logical operators in everyday conversation. Note some examples:

"If my pay is high *and* my vacation time is long, we can go to Italy this summer."

"If you take the trash out *or* clean your room, you can watch TV tonight."

"If you are *not* good, you will be punished."

Internal Truths

The True or False results of relational tests occur internally at the bit level. For example, consider the following if test:

```
if (a == 6) ...
```

To determine the truth of the relation, (a == 6), the computer takes a binary 6, or 00000110, and compares it, bit by bit, to the variable a. If a contains 7, a binary 00000111, the result of the equal test is False because the right bit (called the least significant bit) is different.

C++'s Logical Efficiency

C++ attempts to be more efficient than other languages. If you combine multiple relational tests with one of the logical operators, C++ will not always interpret the full expression. This ultimately makes your programs run faster, but you should be aware of some dangers. Given the conditional test

```
if ((5 > 4) || (sales < 15) && (16 != 15)) ...
```

C++ "looks at" only the first condition, (5 > 4), and realizes that it doesn't have to look further. Because (5 > 4) is True, and because True || (or) anything that follows is still True, C++ will not bother with the rest of the expression. The same holds for the following:

```
if ((7 < 3) && (age > 15) && (initial == 'D')) ...
```

C++ looks only at the first condition, which is False. Because False && (and) anything else that follows will also be False, C++ does not interpret the expression to the right of (7 < 3). Most of the time, this will not pose a problem, but you should be aware that the following expression may not fulfill your expectations:

```
if ((5 > 4) || (num = 0)) ...
```

The (num = 0) assignment will never execute because C++ has to interpret only the (5 > 4) to see whether the entire expression is True or False. Because of this danger, do not include assignment expressions in the same condition as a logical test. The single if condition

```
if ((sales > old_sales) || (inventory_flag = 'Y')) ...
```

should be broken into two statements, such as

```
inventory_flag) = 'Y';
if ((sales > old_sales) || (inventory_flag)) ...
```

so that inventory_flag will always be assigned the 'Y' value, no matter how (sales > old_sales) tests.

Examples

1. The Summer Olympics are held every four years, each year that is divisible evenly by 4. The U.S. Census is taken every 10 years, at the start of each decade, in each year that is evenly divisible by 10. The following short program asks for a year and then tells the user whether it is a year of the Summer Olympics or the year of the census, or both. The program uses relational operators, logical operators, and the modulus operator to determine the output.

```
// Filename: C11YEAR.CPP
// Determines if it is Summer Olympics year, U.S. Census
year,
// or both

#include <iostream.h>

main()
{
    int     year;

    // Ask for a year
    cout << "What is a year for the test? ";
    cin >> year;

    // Test the year
    if ((year % 4) == 0 && (year % 10) == 0)
    {
        cout << "\nBoth Olympics and U.S. Census!\n";
    }
    else
    {
        if ((year % 4) == 0)
        {
            cout << "\nSummer Olympics only\n";
        }
        else
        {
            if ((year % 10) == 0)
            {
                cout << "\nUS Census only\n";
            }
            else
            {
                cout << "\nNeither\n";
            }
        }
    }
    return 0;
}
```

2. Now that you know about compound relations, you can write an age-checking program like C9AGE.CPP, presented in the preceding chapter. C9AGE.CPP ensured that the age was above 10. There is another way that you can validate input to be sure that it's reasonable. The following program includes a logical operator in its `if` statement to see whether the age is greater than 10 and below 100. If both are True, the program knows that the user entered a valid age.

```cpp
// Filename: C11AGE.CPP
// Program to help ensure that age values are reasonable

#include <iostream.h>

main()
{
    int     age;

    cout << "What is your age? ";
    cin >> age;
    if ((age > 10) && (age < 100))
    {
        cout << "\nYou entered a valid age.\n";
    }
    else
    {
        cout << "\n*** The age must be ";
        cout << "between 10 and 100 ***\n";
    }
    return 0;
}
```

Compare this program to C9AGE.CPP in Chapter 9. This one is clean and easy to follow.

3. The following program might be used by a video store to calculate a discount based on the number of rentals a customer makes and the customer's status. Customers are classified as R for Regular or as S for Special Status. Special Status customers have been members of the rental club for more than one year. They automatically get a 50-cent discount on all rentals. The store also holds value days several times a year. On value days, all customers get the 50-cent discount. Special Status customers do not get an additional 50 cents off during value days because every day is a discount for them.

The program asks for the customer status and whether it is a value day. The program then uses the ¦¦ operator to test for the discount. Even before you started learning C++, you might look at this problem with the following idea:

> If a customer has Special Status or if it is a value day, deduct 50 cents from the rental.

This is basically the idea of the if decision in the program. Even though Special Status customers do not get an additional discount on value days, there is one final if test for them that prints an extra message at the bottom of the screen's bill.

```cpp
// Filename: C11VIDEO.CPP
// Program to compute video rental amounts and give
// appropriate discounts based on the day or customer status

#include <iostream.h>
#include <iomanip.h>

main()
{
    float         tape_charge, discount, rental_amt;
    char          first_name[ 15 ];
    char          last_name[ 15 ];
    int           num_tapes;
    char          val_day, sp_stat;

    cout << "\n\n *** Video Rental Computation ***\n";
    cout << "        ------------------------\n";
    // Underline title

    tape_charge = 2.00;        // The before-discount tape
                               // fee per tape

    // Get input data
    cout << "\nWhat is customer's first name? ";
    cin >> first_name;
    cout << "What is customer's last name? ";
    cin >> last_name;

    cout << "\nHow many tapes are being rented? ";
    cin >> num_tapes;

    cout << "Is this a Value day (Y/N)? ";
    cin >> val_day;
```

```
cout << "Is this a Special Status customer (Y/N)? ";
cin >> sp_stat;

// Calculate rental amount
discount = 0.0;        // Increase the discount IF they
                       // are eligible
if ((val_day == 'Y') || (val_day == 'y')
    || (sp_stat == 'Y') || (sp_stat == 'y'))
{
    discount = 0.5;
}
else
{
    discount = 0;
}
rental_amt = (num_tapes * tape_charge) - (discount
* num_tapes);
}

// Print the bill
cout << setiosflags(ios::fixed);
cout << "\n\n** Rental Club **\n\n";
cout << first_name << ' ' << last_name
     << " rented " << num_tapes << " tapes\n";
cout << "The total was "
     << setprecision(2) << rental_amt << "\n";
cout << "The discount was "
     << setprecision(2) << discount << " per tape\n";

// Print extra message for Special Status customers
if ((sp_stat == 'Y') || (sp_stat == 'y'))
{
    cout << "\nThank them for being ";
    cout << "a Special Status customer";
}
return 0;
}
```

Figure 11.1 shows the output from a sample run of this program. Notice that Special Status customers get the extra message at the bottom of the screen. This program, because of its if statements, will perform differently depending on the data entered. No discount is applied for Regular customers on nonvalue days.

Figure 11.1

The logical *if* helps give special discounts to certain customers.

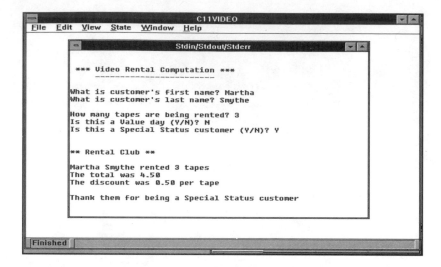

```
┌──────────────────────────────────────────────────────────────┐
│ ─                        C11VIDEO                       ▼ ▲ │
│ File  Edit  View  State  Window  Help                        │
│  ┌────────────────────────────────────────────────────┐      │
│  │ ─              Stdin/Stdout/Stderr            ▼ ▲ │      │
│  │                                                    │      │
│  │   *** Video Rental Computation ***                 │      │
│  │   --------------------------                       │      │
│  │                                                    │      │
│  │  What is customer's first name? Martha             │      │
│  │  What is customer's last name? Smythe              │      │
│  │                                                    │      │
│  │  How many tapes are being rented? 3                │      │
│  │  Is this a Value day (Y/N)? N                      │      │
│  │  Is this a Special Status customer (Y/N)? Y        │      │
│  │                                                    │      │
│  │                                                    │      │
│  │  ** Rental Club **                                 │      │
│  │                                                    │      │
│  │  Martha Smythe rented 3 tapes                      │      │
│  │  The total was 4.50                                │      │
│  │  The discount was 0.50 per tape                    │      │
│  │                                                    │      │
│  │  Thank them for being a Special Status customer    │      │
│  │                                                    │      │
│  └────────────────────────────────────────────────────┘      │
│ ┌──────────┐                                                 │
│ │ Finished │                                                 │
│ └──────────┘                                                 │
└──────────────────────────────────────────────────────────────┘
```

The Precedence of Logical Operators

The math precedence order you read about in Chapter 9 did not include the logical operators. To be thorough, you should be familiar with the entire order, presented in Appendix D. As you can see, the math operators take precedence over the relational operators, and the relational operators take precedence over the logical operators.

You might wonder why the relational and logical operators are included in a precedence table. The following statement helps show why:

```
if ((sales < min_sal * 2 && yrs_emp > 10 * sub) ...
```

Without the complete order of operators, it would be impossible to determine how such a statement would execute. According to the precedence order, the `if` statement executes like this:

```
if ((sales < (min_sal * 2)) && (yrs_emp > (10 * sub))) ...
```

This still may be confusing, but it is less so. The two multiplications are performed first, followed by the operators < and >. The && is performed last because it is lowest in the order of operators.

To avoid such ambiguity problems, use plenty of parentheses, even if the default precedence order is intended. It is also wise to resist combining too many expressions inside a single `if` relational test.

Notice that `||` (OR) has lower precedence than `&&` (AND). Therefore, the following `if` tests are equivalent:

```
if ((first_initial == 'A') && (last_initial == 'G')
    || (id == 321)) ...
if (((first_initial == 'A') && (last_initial == 'G'))
    || (id == 321)) ...
```

The second test is clearer because of the parentheses, but the precedence table makes the tests identical.

Summary

This chapter extended the if statement to include the &&, ||, and ! logical operators. These operators allow you to combine more than one relational test into a single test. C++ does not always have to look at every relational operator when you combine several in an expression. This chapter concludes the explanation of the if statement.

The next chapter explains the rest of the regular C++ operators. As you saw in this chapter, the precedence table is very important to the C++ language. When evaluating expressions, keep the precedence table in mind (or at your fingertips) at all times.

Review Questions

Answers to Review Questions are in Appendix B.

1. What are the three logical operators?

2. The following compound relational tests produce True or False comparisons. Determine which are True and which are False.

    a. ! (true || false)

    b. (true && false) && (false || true)

    c. ! (true && false)

    d. true || (false && false) || false

3. Consider the following statement:

```
int i = 12, j = 10, k = 5;
```

What are the results (True or False) of the following statements? (*Hint:* Remember that C++ interprets *any* nonzero statement as True.)

    a. i && j

    b. 12 - i || k

    c. j != k && i != k

4. What is the value printed in the following program? (*Hint:* Do not be confused by the assignment operators on each side of the ||.)

```
// Filename: C11LOGO.CPP
// Logical operator test

#include <iostream.h>

main()
{
    int     f, g;

    g = 5;
    f = 8;
    if ((g = 25) ¦¦ (f = 35))
    {
        cout << "g is " << g << " and f got changed to: "
             << f << '\n';
    }
    return 0;
}
```

Review Exercises

1. Write a program to determine whether the user entered an odd, positive number. Use a single compound `if` statement.

2. Write a program that asks the user for two initials. Print a message informing the user whether the first initial falls alphabetically before the second.

3. Write a number-guessing game. Assign a variable called `number` a value at the top of the program. Give a prompt that asks for five guesses. Get the user's five guesses with a single `cin`. See whether any guess matches the `number` and print an appropriate message if one does.

4. Write a tax-calculation routine. A family pays no tax if its members' combined salaries are less than $5,000. The family pays a 10 percent tax if the combined salaries are between $5,000 and $9,999, and a 20 percent tax if the combined salaries are between $10,000 and $19,999. Otherwise, the family pays a 30 percent tax.

CHAPTER 12

Additional C++ Operators

There are several other C++ operators that you should learn. C++ has more operators than most programming languages. If you are not familiar with all the operators, you might think that C++ programs are cryptic and difficult to follow. C++'s heavy reliance on its operators and operator precedence makes it efficient, which means that your programs run smoother and faster.

This chapter introduces the following topics:

♦ The ?: conditional operator

♦ The ++ increment operator

♦ The -- decrement operator

♦ Postfix and prefix operation

♦ The sizeof operator

♦ The , sequence point operator

Most of the operators described in this chapter are unlike those found in any other programming language. Even if you have programmed in other languages for many years, you may be surprised at the power of some of these operators.

The *?:* Conditional Operator

The *conditional operator* is a ternary operator.

The conditional operator, ?:, is C++'s only ternary operator. A *ternary* operator requires three operands (instead of the single and double operands of unary and binary operators). The conditional operator is used to replace if-else logic in some situations. The format of the conditional operator is

```
conditional_expression ? expression1 : expression2;
```

where `conditional_expression` is any expression in C++ that results in a True (nonzero) or False (zero) answer. If the result of the `conditional_expression` is True, `expression1` executes. If the result of the `conditional_expression` is False, `expression2` executes. Only one of the expressions following the question mark ever executes. Put a single semicolon at the end of `expression2`. The internal expressions, such as `expression1`, should not have a semicolon.

Figure 12.1 shows the conditional operator a little more clearly.

Figure 12.1

The format of the conditional operator.

```
                              If conditional        If conditional
                              expression is         expression is
                                  True                  False
                                execute               execute
                                  this                  this
                                   ↓                     ↓
conditional_expression ? expression1 : expression2 ;
```

```
                          If sales > 8000      If sales is not
           Example:         execute             > 8000 only
                              only                execute
                              this                  this
                               ↓                     ↓
           (sales > 8000) ?  bonus = 500  :  bonus = 0 ;
```

If you require simple if-else logic, the conditional operator usually provides a more direct and succinct method, although you should always prefer readability over compact code.

To get a glimpse of how useful the conditional operator is, consider the following section of code:

If (the variable a is greater than the variable b), the variable ans becomes equal to 10. Otherwise, the variable ans becomes equal to 25.

```
if (a > b)
{
    ans = 10;
}
else
{
```

```
        ans = 25;


}
```

You can easily rewrite this kind of if-else code with a single conditional operator, as in the following example.

If the variable a is greater than the variable b, the variable ans becomes equal to 10; otherwise, ans becomes equal to 25.

```
a > b ? (ans = 10) : (ans = 25);
```

Because the conditional operator has very low precedence, parentheses are not required around the *conditional_expression* to make this work. However, they usually improve readability. This statement could be rewritten, using parentheses, as shown in the following:

```
(a > b) ? (ans = 10) : (ans = 25);
```

Because each C++ expression has a value—in this case, the value being assigned—this statement can be made even more succinct, without loss of readability, by assigning ans the answer to the left of the conditional:

```
ans = (a > b) ? (10) : (25);
```

This expression now says the following: if a is more than b, assign ans a 10; otherwise, assign ans a 25. Almost any if-else statement can be rewritten as a conditional, and a conditional can be rewritten as an if-else. You should practice converting one to the other to acquaint yourself with the conditional operator's purpose.

Tip: Any valid C++ statement can be the *conditional_expression*, including all relational and logical operators, as well as any combination of them.

Examples

1. Suppose that you are looking over your early C++ programs and you notice the following section of code:

```
if (production > target)
{
    target *= 1.10;
}
else
```

```
{
     target *= .90;
}
```

You realize that such a simple if-else statement can be rewritten with a conditional operator and that more efficient code will result. You can change the code to this single statement:

```
(production > target) ? (target *= 1.10) : (target *= .90);
```

2. Using a conditional operator, you can write a routine to find the lowest value between two variables. This is sometimes called a *minimum routine*. The statement to do this is as follows:

```
minimum = (var1 < var2) ? var1 : var2;
```

If var1 is less than var2, the value of var1 is assigned to minimum. If var2 is less, it is assigned to minimum. If the variables are equal, var2 is assigned to minimum (because it doesn't matter which one is assigned).

3. A maximum routine can be written just as easily:

```
maximum = (var1 > var2) ? var1 : var2;
```

4. Taking the preceding examples a step further, you can test for the sign of a variable. The following conditional expression assigns -1 to the variable called sign if testvar is less than 0, 0 to sign if testvar is 0, and +1 to sign if testvar is more than 1:

```
sign = (testvar < 0) ? -1 : (testvar > 0);
```

It might be easy to spot why the less-than test results in -1, but the sec ond part may be confusing. This technique works well because of C++'s 1 (True) and 0 (False) return values from a relational test. If testvar is 0 or greater, sign is assigned the answer to (testvar > 0). The value of (testvar > 0) will be 1 if True (therefore, testvar is more than 0) or 0 if testvar is equal to 0.

This technique takes advantage of C++'s efficiency and conditional operator very well. It may be helpful to rewrite this statement with a typical if-else. Here is the same problem written with a typical if-else statement:

```
if (testvar < 0)
{
     sign = -1;
}
else
```

```
{

    sign = (testvar > 0);

}      // testvar can be only 0 or more here
```

The ++ and -- Increment and Decrement Operators

C++ offers two unique operators that add 1 to variables or subtract 1 from variables. These are the increment (++) and decrement (--) operators. Table 12.1 shows how these operators relate to other types of expressions you have seen. Notice that the ++ or -- can go on either side of the variable it modifies. If the ++ or -- appears on the left, it is known as a *prefix* operator. If the operator appears on the right, it is a *postfix* operator.

Table 12.1. The ++ and -- operators.

Operator	Example	Description	Equivalent	Statements
++	i++;	Postfix	i = i + 1;	i += 1;
++	++i;	Prefix	i = i + 1;	i += 1;
--	i--;	Postfix	i = i - 1;	i -= 1;
--	--i;	Prefix	i = i - 1;	i -= 1;

Whenever you need to add 1 to a variable or subtract 1 from a variable, use one of these operators. As table 12.1 shows, if you need to increment or decrement just a single variable, these operators provide the means to do so.

The choice you use, prefix or postfix, does not matter if you are incrementing or decrementing single variables on lines by themselves. However, when you combine these two operators with other operators in a single expression, you must be aware of their differences. Consider the following section of a program. (All variables in the next few examples are integers because the increment and decrement work only on integer variables.)

Increment and Decrement Efficiencies

The increment (++) and decrement (--) operators are straightforward, efficient methods to add 1 to a variable or subtract 1 from a variable. Often you need to do this when counting or processing loops, which are covered in Part III of this book.

These two operators compile directly into their assembly language equivalents. Almost all computers include, at their lowest binary machine-language commands, increment and decrement instructions. If you use C++'s increment and decrement operators, you ensure that they will compile into these low-level equivalents.

If, however, you code expressions to add or subtract 1, such as i = i - 1, as you would in other programming languages, you do not ensure that the C++ compiler will compile this instruction into its machine-language efficient equivalent.

The variable a becomes equal to 6.
The variable b becomes equal to the variable a incremented once - 1.

```
a = 6;
b = ++a - 1;
```

++ adds 1 to a variable, and -- subtracts 1 from a variable.

What are the values of a and b after these two statements finish? The value of a is easy to determine; it gets incremented in the second statement, so the value is 7. However, b is either 5 or 6, depending on *when* the variable a increments. To determine when a increments, consider the following rules:

- ◆ If a variable is incremented or decremented with a prefix operator, the increment and decrement occur *before* the variable's value is used in the rest of the expression.

- ◆ If a variable is incremented or decremented with a postfix operator, the increment and decrement occur *after* the variable's value is used in the rest of the expression.

In the preceding code, a contains a prefix increment. Therefore, its value is first incremented to 7, and then the 1 gets subtracted from the 7. The result, 6, is assigned to b. If a postfix increment had occurred, as in the following:

```
a = 6;
b = a++ - 1;
```

the a would still be 7, but a 5 would be assigned to b because a did not increment until after its value was used in the expression. The precedence table in Appen dix C shows that prefix operators contain higher precedence than almost every other operator, especially postfix increments and decrements that occur last.

Tip: If the order of prefix and postfix confuses you, break your expressions into two lines of code, putting the increment or decrement before or after the expression that uses it. The preceding example could be rewritten as

```
a = 6;
b = a - 1;
a++;
```

There is now no doubt as to when a gets incremented. Despite this tip, you should learn how these operators work because they are efficient and easy to use.

Even parentheses cannot override the postfix rule. Consider the following statement:

```
x = p + (((amt++)));
```

There are too many unneeded parentheses here, but even the redundant paren theses are not enough to increment amt before adding its value to p. Postfix increment and decrement *always* occur after their variables are used in the sur rounding expression.

Caution: Do not attempt to increment or decrement an expression. You can apply these operators only to variables. The following expression is *invalid*:

```
sales = ++(rate * hours);   // NOT ALLOWED!
```

Examples

1. As with all other C++ operators, keep the precedence table in mind when evaluating expressions that use increment and decrement. Figure 12.2 shows some examples that illustrate these operators.

2. The precedence table takes on even more meaning when you see a section of code like that shown in figure 12.3.

Figure 12.2

Examples of C
operators and the
precedence table.

```
          int i = 1;
          int j = 2;
          int k = 3;
          ans = i++ + j - --k;


              i++ + j - 2


                 2  - 2


                   0
```

Then i increments by 1 to its final value of 2.

```
          int i = 1;
          int j = 2;
          int k = 3;
          ans = ++i * j - k--;


              2 * j - k--


                 4  - k--


                   1
```

Then k decrements by 1 to its final value of 2.

3. Considering the precedence table, and more importantly, what you know about C++'s relational efficiencies, what is the value of ans in the following section of code?

```
int     i=1, j=20, k=-1, l=0, m=1, n=0, o=2, p=1;
ans = i ¦¦ j-- && k++ ¦¦ ++l && ++m ¦¦ n-- & !o ¦¦ p--;
```

At first, this seems to be extremely complicated. Nevertheless, you can simply glance at it and determine the value of ans, as well as the ending value of the rest of the variables.

Recall that when C++ performs a relation ¦¦ (OR), it ignores the right side of the ¦¦ if the value on the left is True (any nonzero value is True). Because True or any other value is still True, C++ does not think that it has to look at the values on the right. Therefore, C++ performed this expression in the following way:

Figure 12.3

Another example
of C++ operators
and the
precedence table.

```
                    int i = 0;
                    int j = -1;
                    int k = 0;
                    int l = 1;

                    ans = i++ && ++j || k || l++

                        i++ && 0 || k || l++

                           0  || k || l++

                           0    || l++

                                 1
```

Then i and l increment by 1 to their final values of 1 and 2.

```
ans = i || j-- && k++ || ++l && ++m || n-- & !o || p--;
      |
      1 (true)
```

Because i is true, C++ knows that the entire expression is True and ignores the rest of it after the first ||. Therefore, *every other increment and decrement expression is ignored.* The result is that only ans is changed by this expression, and the rest of the variables, j through p, are never incremented or decremented, even though several of them contain increment and decrement operators. If you use relational operators, be aware of this problem and break out all increment and decrement operators into statements by themselves before relational statements.

The *sizeof* Operator

Another operator in C++ does not look like an operator at all but looks like a library function. It is the sizeof operator. If you think of sizeof as a function call, you will not get too confused, because sizeof works in a similar way. The sizeof operator has one of the following formats:

```
sizeof data

sizeof(data type)
```

The sizeof operator is a unary operator because it operates on a single value. This operator produces a result that is the size, in bytes, of the *data* or *data type* specified. Because most data types and variables require different amounts of internal storage on different computers, the `sizeof` operator was provided to allow for consistent programs across different kinds of computers.

> **Tip:** Most C++ programmers use parentheses around the `sizeof` argument, whether that argument is *data* or *data type*. Because parentheses are required around *data type* arguments and are optional around *data*, you may want to get in the habit of using them all the time.

The *sizeof* operator returns the size, in bytes, of its argument.

The `sizeof` operator is sometimes called a *compile-time operator*. At compile time, not runtime, the compiler replaces each occurrence of `sizeof` in your program with an `unsigned` integer value. The `sizeof` is used in advanced C++ programming.

If you use an array as the `sizeof` argument, C++ returns the size, in bytes, of the number of bytes you originally reserved for the array. The data in the array, even if it is a short string inside a character array, has nothing to do with the array's size.

Example

Suppose that you want to know the size, in bytes, of floating-point variables for your computer. You can determine this by putting the word `float` in parentheses, as shown in the following program:

```
// Filename: C12SIZE1.CPP
// Prints the size of floating-point values

#include <iostream.h>

main()
{
    cout << "The size of floating-point variables ";
    cout << "on this computer is: " << sizeof(float) << '\n';
    return 0;
}
```

This program will produce different results on different kinds of computers. You can use any valid data type as the `sizeof` argument. When you directly print `sizeof` results, as shown here, type cast the `sizeof` to an integer in order to print it properly with `%d`. Compiled under Visual C++, this program produces the following output:

```
The size of floating-point variables on this computer is: 4
```

The Comma Operator

An additional operator (,), sometimes called a *sequence point*, is used a little differently from most C++ operators. The comma operator does not directly operate on data but produces a left-to-right evaluation of expressions. The comma allows you to put more than one expression, separated by commas, on a single line.

You have already seen one use of the sequence point comma when you learned how to declare and initialize variables. In the following section of code, the comma separates statements. Because the comma associates from left to right, the first variable, i, is declared and initialized before the second variable, j.

```
main()
{
    int     i = 10, j = 25;



    // Rest of program follows
```

The comma is *not* a sequence point when used inside function parentheses but is said to *separate arguments*.

Examples

1. You can put more than one expression on a line by using the comma as a sequence point. Note the following program:

```
// Filename: C12COM1.CPP
// Illustrates the sequence point

#include <iostream.h>

main()
{
    int     num, sq, cube;

    num = 5;

    // Calculate the square and cube of the number
    sq = (num * num), cube = (num * num * num);

    cout << "The square of " << num << " is " << sq
         << " and the cube is " << cube << "\n";
    return 0;
}
```

This technique is not necessarily recommended because it does not add anything to the program and even decreases readability. The square and cube are probably better computed on two separate lines.

2. The comma allows for some interesting statements. Consider the following section of code:

```
i = 10;
j = (i = 12, i + 8);
```

When this section of code finishes, j has the value of 20, even though this is not necessarily clear. In the first statement, i is assigned 10. In the second statement, the comma causes the i to be assigned a value of 12, and then i + 8, or 20, is assigned to j.

3. In the following section of code, ans is assigned the value of 12, because the assignment before the comma is performed first. Despite the right-to-left associativity of the assignment operator, the comma's sequence point lastly forces the assignment of 12 into x before x is assigned to ans.

```
ans = (y = 8, x = 12);
```

When this completes, y contains an 8, x contains a 12, and ans contains a 12 also.

Summary

You now have learned almost every operator in the C++ language. The conditional, increment, and decrement operators make C++ stand apart from many other programming languages. As with all operators, you must be aware of the precedence table at all times when using these operators.

The sizeof and sequence point operators are unlike most other operators. The sizeof is a compile-time operator that works in a manner similar to the #define preprocessor directive; sizeof is replaced by its value at compile time. The sequence point operator (,) lets you put multiple statements on a line or within a single expression. However, you should reserve this operator for initializing variables because it may be unclear if combined with other expressions.

The next chapter discusses the *bitwise* operators. They operate on a very low binary level on your computer's variables. There are programmers who have programmed in C++ for years but have yet to learn the bitwise operators. If you are just learning C++ and are not interested in doing bit-level operations, you may want to skim the next chapter and come back to it later when you need those operators.

Review Questions

Answers to Review Questions are in Appendix B.

1. Which set of statements does the conditional operator replace?

2. Why is the conditional operator called a ternary operator?

3. Rewrite the following conditional operator as an `if-else`:

```
ans = (a == b) ? c + 2 : c + 3;
```

4. True or false: The following statements produce the same result.

```
var++;

var = var + 1;
```

5. Why is using the increment and decrement operators more efficient than using the addition and subtraction operators?

6. What is a sequence point?

7. Can the output of the following section of code be determined?

```
age = 20;
cout << "You are now " << age << ", and will be "
<< age++ << " in one year";
```

8. What is the output of the following section of a program?

```
char    name[ 20 ] = "Mike";
cout << "The size of name is: " << sizeof(name);
```

Review Exercises

1. Write a program that prints the numbers 1 to 10. Use 10 different couts and only one variable called `result` to hold the value before each cout. Use the increment operator to add 1 to `result` before each cout.

2. Write a program that asks for the user's age. Using a single cout that includes a conditional operator, print the following if the age is over 21:

```
You are not a minor.
```

Otherwise, print the following:

```
You are still a minor.
```

This cout may be long, but it helps illustrate how the conditional operator can be used within other statements when the `if-else` cannot.

3. Use the conditional operator, not `if-else` statements, to write a tax-calculation routine. A family pays no tax if the members' combined salaries are less than $5,000. The family pays a 10 percent tax if the combined salaries are between $5,000 and $9,999, and 20 percent tax if the combined salaries are between $10,000 and $19,999. Otherwise, the family pays a 30 percent tax. This is similar to an exercise in the preceding chapter, except for the conditional operator.

CHAPTER 13

Bitwise Operators

This chapter introduces the *bitwise operators*. They operate on internal representations of data, not just "values in variables," as the other operators do. Bitwise operators require an understanding of Appendix A's binary numbering system and of your PC's memory. If you don't think you are ready to tackle the bitwise operators, you can skim this chapter and come back to it later.

Some people program in C++ for years and don't know the bitwise operators. Nevertheless, understanding them can help improve the efficiency of your programs and enable you to operate at a level deeper than many programming languages allow.

In this chapter, you learn about the following topics:

♦ The bitwise logical operators

♦ Performing bitwise operations internally

♦ The bitwise shift operators

This chapter concludes the discussion of C++ operators for a while. After you master this chapter, you will be able to perform almost any operation on your C++ variables and constants.

Bitwise Logical Operators

There are four bitwise logical operators, shown in table 13.1. Because these operators work on the binary representation of integer data, systems programmers can manipulate internal bits in memory and variables. The bitwise logical operators are not just for systems programmers, however. Application programmers can also improve portions of their programs by learning how to use these operators.

Table 13.1. The bitwise logical operators.

Operator	Meaning
&	Bitwise AND
¦	Bitwise inclusive OR
^	Bitwise exclusive OR
~	Bitwise 1's complement or bitwise NOT

Bitwise logical
operators perform
bit-by-bit
operations on
internal data.

Each bitwise logical operator performs a bit-by-bit operation on internal data. Bitwise operators apply only to char, int, and long variables and constants, not to floating-point data. Because binary numbers consist of 1s and 0s, these 1s and 0s (called *bits*) are manipulated to produce the desired result of each bitwise operator.

Before looking at examples, you should understand tables 13.2 through 13.5. They contain truth tables that describe the actions of the bitwise operators on the internal bit patterns of an int (or char or long).

Table 13.2. The bitwise & (AND) truth table.

First Bit	AND	Second Bit	Result
1	&	1	1
1	&	0	0
0	&	1	0
0	&	0	0

In bitwise truth tables, you can replace the 1 and 0 with True and False, respectively, to better understand the result. For the & (AND) bitwise truth table, both bits being operated on with & must be True for the result to be True. In other words, "True AND True is equal to True."

Tip: By replacing the 1s and 0s with True and False, you might be able to relate the bitwise operators to the regular logical operators && and ¦¦, which you used with if comparisons.

Table 13.3. The bitwise ¦ (*OR*) truth table.

First Bit	OR	Second Bit	Result
1	¦	1	1
1	¦	0	1
0	¦	1	1
0	¦	0	0

The | bitwise operator is sometimes called the inclusive bitwise OR operator. Either side of the | operator, or both sides, must be 1 (True) for the result to be 1 (True).

Table 13.4. The bitwise ^ (exclusive *OR*) operator.

First Bit	XOR	Second Bit	Result
1	^	1	0
1	^	0	1
0	^	1	1
0	^	0	0

For bitwise ^, one side or the other must be 1, but not both sides.

The ^ bitwise operator is called the *exclusive bitwise* OR operator. Either side of the ^ operator must be 1 (True) for the result to be 1 (True), but both sides cannot be 1 (True) at the same time.

Table 13.5. The bitwise ~ (1's complement) operator.

1's Complement	Bit	Result
~	1	0
~	0	1

The ~ bitwise operator, called the bitwise 1's complement operator, reverses each bit to its opposite value.

> **Note:** The bitwise 1's complement does *not* negate a number. As Appendix A shows, the PC uses a 2's complement to negate numbers. The bitwise 1's complement reverses the bit pattern of numbers but does not add the additional 1, as the 2's complement requires.

You can test and change individual bits inside variables to check for patterns of data. The examples in the next section help illustrate the bitwise logical operators.

Examples

1. If you apply the bitwise & operator to the numbers 9 and 14, you get a result of 8. Figure 13.1 shows why this is so. When the binary values of 9 (1001) and 14 (1110) are operated on with a bitwise &, the resulting bit pattern is 8 (1000).

Figure 13.1

Performing the bitwise & on two numbers.

```
  1   0   0   1   (9)
  ↓   ↓   ↓   ↓
  &   &   &   &
  1   1   1   0   (14)
= 1   0   0   0   (8)
```

In a C++ program, you could code this bitwise operation in the following way.

result becomes equal to the binary value of 9, which is 1001, AND the binary value of 14, which is 1110.

```
result = 9 & 14;
```

The result variable will hold 8, which is the result of the bitwise &. The 9 or 14 (or both) also could be stored in variables, with the same result.

2. When applying the bitwise ¦ operator to the numbers 9 and 14, you get 15. When the binary values of 9 (1001) and 14 (1110) are operated on with a bitwise ¦, the resulting bit pattern is 15 (1111). The reason is that the result's bits are 1 (True) in every position in which a bit is 1 in either of the two numbers.

In a C++ program, you could code this bitwise operation as follows:

```
result = 9 ¦ 14;
```

The `result` variable will hold 15, which is the result of the bitwise ¦. The 9 or 14, or both, could also be stored in variables, with the same result.

3. The bitwise ^, when applied to 9 and 14, produces a 7. The bitwise ^ will set the resulting bit to 1 if one number's bit or the other number's bit is on, but not both.

In a C++ program, you could code this bitwise operation as follows:

```
result = 9 ^ 14;
```

The result variable holds 7, which is the result of the bitwise ^. The 9, the 14, or both the 9 and 14, could also be stored in variables, with the same result.

4. The bitwise ~ simply negates each bit. The bitwise ~ is a unary bitwise operator because you can apply it to only a single value at one time. The bitwise ~ applied to 9 will result in several values, depending on the size of the 9 and whether the 9 is a `signed` value or not, as shown in figure 13.2.

Figure 13.2

Performing the bitwise ~ on the number 9.

```
~  1  0  0  1  (9)
=  0  1  1  0  (6)
```

In a C++ program, you could code this bitwise operation as follows:

```
unsigned char  uc_result = ~9;

signed char    sc_result = ~9;

unsigned int   ui_result = ~9;

signed int     si_result = ~9;

unsigned long  ul_result = ~9;

signed long    sl_result = ~9;
```

The `uc_result` variable will hold 246, the result of the bitwise ~ on the `unsigned char` 9. The `sc_result` variable will hold –10, the result of the bitwise ~ on the `signed char` 9. The `ui_result` variable will hold 65526, the result of the bitwise ~ on the `unsigned int` 9. The `si_result` variable will hold –10, the result of the bitwise ~ on the `signed int` 9. The `ul_result` variable will hold 4294967286, the result of the bitwise ~ on the `unsigned` long 9. The s1_result variable will hold –10, the result of the bitwise ~ on the signed long 9. In any case, the 9 could have been stored in a variable, with the same result.

5. You can take advantage of the bitwise operators to perform tests on data that you couldn't perform as efficiently in other ways.

Suppose that you want to know whether the user typed an odd or even number (assuming that the input is integers). You could use the modulus operator (%) to see whether the remainder, after dividing the input value by 2, is 0 or 1. If the remainder is 0, the number is even. If the remainder is 1, the number is odd.

The bitwise operators are more efficient than other operators because bitwise operators directly compare bit patterns without using any mathematical operations. Because a number is even if its bit pattern ends in 0, and odd if its bit pattern ends in 1, you also can test for odd or even numbers by applying the bitwise & to the data and to a binary 1. This technique is more efficient than using the modulus operator. The following program tells the user whether the input value is odd or even.

Comments to identify the file.
Include the header file iostream.h.
Start of the main() loop.
Declare the variable input as an integer.
Print the statement What number do you want me to test? *on-screen.*
Obtain a value for input from the user.
If the least-significant bit of input is 1, print the statement The number <the actual number that the user entered> *is odd.*
If the least significant bit of input is 0, print the statement The number <the actual number that the user entered> *is even.*

```cpp
// Filename: C13ODEV.CPP
// Uses a bitwise & to see if a number is odd or even

#include <iostream.h>

main()
{
    int  input;    // Will hold user's number

    cout << "What number do you want me to test? ";
```

```
    cin >> input;

    if (input & 1) // True if result is 1; otherwise, it is
                    // False (0)
    {
        cout << "The number " << input << " is odd\n";
    }
    else
    {
        cout << "The number " << input << " is even\n";
    }
return 0;
}
```

6. The only difference between the bit patterns for uppercase and lowercase characters is bit number 5 (the third bit from the left, as shown in Appendix A). For lowercase letters, bit 5 is a 1. For uppercase letters, bit 5 is a 0. Figure 13.3 shows how A and B differ from a and b by a single bit.

Figure 13.3

The difference between uppercase and lowercase ASCII letters.

```
ASCII  A  is  01000001    (hex 41, decimal 65)
ASCII  a  is  01100001    (hex 61, decimal 97)
              |_____ Only bit 5 is different

ASCII  B  is  01000010    (hex 42, decimal 66)
ASCII  b  is  01100010    (hex 62, decimal 98)
              |_____ Only bit 5 is different
```

To convert a character to uppercase, you have to turn off (change to a 0) bit number 6. You can apply a bitwise & to the input character and 223 (which is 11011111 in binary) to turn off bit 6 and convert any input character to its uppercase equivalent. If the number is already in uppercase, this bitwise & will not change it.

The 223 (binary 11011111) is called a *bit mask* because it masks off (just as masking tape masks off areas to be painted) bit 6 so that it becomes 0, if it isn't already a 0. The following program does this to ensure that the user typed uppercase characters when asked for initials:

```
// Filename: C13UPCS1.CPP
// Converts the input characters to uppercase if they aren't
// already

#include <iostream.h>
```

```
#define   BITMASK   (0xDF)        // 11011111 in binary

main()
{
    char   first, middle, last;  // Will hold user's
initials

    cout << "What is your first initial? ";
    cin >> first;
    cout << "What is your middle initial? ";
    cin >> middle;
    cout << "What is your last initial? ";
    cin >> last;

    // Ensure that initials are in uppercase
    first = first & BITMASK;      // Turn off bit 6 if
    middle = middle & BITMASK;    // it isn't already
    last = last & BITMASK;        // turned off

    cout << "Your initials are: " << first << ' '
        << middle << ' ' << last << '\n';
    return 0;
}
```

The following output shows what happens when two of the initials are typed with lowercase letters. The program converts them to uppercase before printing them again. Although there are other ways to convert letters to lowercase, none are as efficient as using the & bitwise operator.

```
What is your first initial? g
What is your middle initial? M
What is your last initial? p
Your initials are: G M P
```

Compound Bitwise Operators

As with most of the mathematical operators, you can combine the bitwise operators with the equal sign (=) to form *compound bitwise operators*. When you want to update the value of a variable, using a bitwise operator, you can shorten the expression by using the compound bitwise operators. Table 13.6 describes the compound bitwise operators.

Table 13.6. The compound bitwise operators.

Operator	Description
&=	Compound bitwise AND assignment
¦=	Compound bitwise inclusive OR assignment
^=	Compound bitwise exclusive OR assignment

The preceding example for converting lowercase initials to their uppercase equivalents can be rewritten with compound bitwise & operations:

```cpp
// Filename: C13UPCS2.CPP
// Converts the input characters to uppercase if they aren't
// already

#include <iostream.h>

#define   BITMASK   (0xDF)       // 11011111 in binary

main()
{
    char first, middle, last;  // Will hold user's initials

    cout << "What is your first initial? ";
    cin >> first;
    cout << "What is your middle initial? ";
    cin >> middle;
    cout << "What is your last initial? ";
    cin >> last;

    // Ensure that initials are in uppercase
    first &= BITMASK;        // Turn off bit 6 if it isn't
    middle &= BITMASK;       // already turned off
    last &= BITMASK;

    cout << "Your initials are: " << first << ' '
         << middle << ' ' << last << '\n';
    return 0;
}
```

Mathematics of the Binary Bitwise Operators

There are three important mathematical properties of the binary bitwise operators. The first property is *associativity*: the action of any of the binary bitwise operators on any three objects does not depend on how the three objects are grouped. Note the following examples:

```
(A | B) | C = A | (B | C)

(A & B) & C = A & (B & C)

(A ^ B) ^ C = A ^ (B ^ C)
```

The second property is *commutativity*: the action of any of the binary bitwise operators on any two objects does not depend on the order in which the objects are given. Note these examples:

```
A | B = B | A

A & B = B & A

A ^ B = B ^ A
```

The third property is that of having an *identity value*: each of the binary bitwise operators has an identity, which is a value e for which A ° e = e ° A = A, where ° represents the operator. Note some examples:

```
A | 0 = 0 | A = A

A & 1 = 1 & A = A

A ^ 0 = 0 ^ A = A
```

The important thing to remember about this last property is that it applies, as the binary bitwise operators do, bit by bit. Although this isn't a problem for the inclusive and exclusive OR operators, it can be a problem for the AND operator. When applying the AND operator, don't forget to include enough 1 bits for the bits you don't want to touch.

Bitwise Shift Operators

Table 13.7 shows the bitwise shift operators. The bitwise shift operators shift bits inside a number to the left or right. The number of bits shifted depends on the value to the right of the bitwise shift operator. The formats of the bitwise shift operators are as follows:

```
value << number_of_bits

value >> number_of_bits
```

The value can be an integer or character variable, or a constant. The `number_of_bits` determines how many bits will be shifted. Figure 13.4 shows what happens when the number 29 (binary 00011101) is left-shifted three bits with a bitwise left shift (<<). Notice that each bit "shifts over" to the left three times, and 0s fill in from the right. If this were a bitwise right shift (>>), the 0s would fill in from the left as the rest of the bits are shifted to the right three times.

Figure 13.4
Shifting the bits in binary 29 to the left.

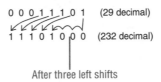

Table 13.7. The bitwise shift operators.

Operator	Description
<<	Bitwise left shift
>>	Bitwise right shift

Caution: The results of bitwise shift operators are not consistent when applied to `signed` values. On the PC, the sign bit *propagates* with each shift. That is, for every shift position, the sign bit shifts, but the original sign is retained as well. The end result is that negative numbers fill in from the left with 1s and not with 0s, when a bitwise right shift is applied to them.

You have probably noticed that the bitwise shift operators are the same operators used in `cout` and `cin`. This advanced feature of C++ is called *operator overloading*. Although a detailed treatment of operator overloading is beyond the scope of this book, rest assured that the Visual C++ compiler can understand from context which meaning you intend. You have already been using an overloaded operator with `cin >>` and `cout <<`.

Examples

1. The following program takes two values and shifts them three bits to the left and then to the right. This program illustrates how to code the bitwise left- and right-shift operators.

```
// Filename: C13SHFT1.CPP
// Demonstrates bitwise left- and right-shift operators

#include <iostream.h>

main()
{
    int     num1 = 25;          // 00011001 binary
    int     num2 = 102;         // 01100110 binary
    int     shift1, shift2;     // Will hold shifted numbers

    shift1 = num1 << 3;     // Bitwise left shift
    cout << "25 shifted left 3 times is " << shift1
        << " \n";
    shift2 = num2 << 3;     // Bitwise left shift
    cout << "102 shifted left 3 times is " << shift2
        << " \n";

    shift1 = num1 >> 3;     // Bitwise right shift
    cout << "25 shifted right 3 times is " << shift1
        << " \n";
    shift2 = num2 >> 3;     // Bitwise right shift
    cout << "102 shifted right 3 times is " << shift2
        << " \n";

    return 0;
}
```

Following is the output for this program:

```
25 shifted left 3 times is 200
102 shifted left 3 times is 816
25 shifted right 3 times is 3
102 shifted right 3 times is 12
```

2. You should know another useful feature of bitwise shifting. If you bitwise left-shift a variable by a certain number of bit positions, the result will be the same as multiplying that same number by a power of 2. In other words, 15 left-shifted 4 times results in the same value as 15 times 2^4, or 15 times 16, which equals 240.

If you bitwise right-shift a number by a certain number of bit positions, the result will be the same as dividing that same number by a power of 2. In other words, 64 right-shifted by 2 results in the same value as 64 divided by 2^2, or 64 divided by 4, which equals 16. This property is retained in signed arithmetic by the sign propagation feature mentioned earlier. For this reason, a shift right on an unsigned value is often referred to as a logical shift right, and a shift right on a signed value is often referred to as an arithmetic shift right.

If you have to multiply or divide a variable by a power of 2, you can do it much faster by simply shifting the number. In fact, this is an optimization frequently used internally by the Visual C++ compiler. Consider the following program:

```
// Filename: C13SHFT2.CPP
// Demonstrates multiplication and division by
// bitwise shifting

#include <iostream.h>

main()
{
    signed int    num1 = 15;        // Numbers to be shifted
    signed int    num2 = -15;
    unsigned int  num3 = 15;
    unsigned int  num4 = 0x8000;

    num1 = num1 << 4;      // Multiply num1 by 16
    num2 = num2 >> 3;      // Divide num2 by 8
    num3 = num3 << 2;      // Multiple num3 by 4
    num4 = num4 >> 1;      // divide num4 by 2

    cout << "15 multiplied by 16 is " << num1 << " \n";
    cout << "-15 divided by 8 is " << num2 << " \n";
    cout << "15 multiplied by 4 is " << num3 << " \n";
    cout << "0x8000 divided by 2 is 0x" << hex << num4
         << " \n";

    return 0;
}
```

Compound Bitwise Shift Operators

As with most of the mathematical operators, you can combine the bitwise operators with the equal sign (=) to form *compound bitwise shift operators*. When you want to update the value of a variable, using a bitwise shift operator, you can shorten the expression by using the compound bitwise operators, shown in table 13.8.

Table 13.8. The compound bitwise shift operators.

Operator	Description
<<=	Compound bitwise left shift
>>=	Compound bitwise right shift

The preceding example that demonstrates math by use of shift operators can be rewritten with compound bitwise & operations:

```
// Filename: C13SHFT3.CPP
// Demonstrates multiplication and division by
// bitwise shifting

#include <iostream.h>

main()
{
    signed int     num1 = 15;        // Numbers to be shifted
    signed int     num2 = -15;
    unsigned int   num3 = 15;
    unsigned int   num4 = 0x8000;

    num1 <<= 4;        // Multiply num1 by 16
    num2 >>= 3;        // Divide num2 by 8
    num3 <<= 2;        // Multiple num3 by 4
    num4 >>= 1;        // divide num4 by 2

    cout << "15 multiplied by 16 is " << num1 << " \n";
    cout << "-15 divided by 8 is " << num2 << " \n";
    cout << "15 multiplied by 4 is " << num3 << " \n";
    cout << "0x8000 divided by 2 is 0x" << hex << num4
         << " \n";

    return 0;
}
```

Summary

Because the bitwise operators work at the bit level, they often are not used in application programs. You must be comfortable with the binary numbering system before you can fully understand their operations. However, the bitwise operators offer a very efficient method of changing individual bits or groups of bits in variables. With these operators, you can test for odd and even numbers, multiply and divide by powers of two, and perform other tasks for which you would normally use less efficient operators and commands.

The bitwise operators, despite their efficiency, do not always lend themselves to readable code. Generally, most people reserve them for systems-level programming and use the easier-to-read, higher-level operators for most data processing.

Review Questions

Answers to Review Questions are in Appendix B.

1. What are the four bitwise logical operators, the three compound bitwise logical operators, and the two bitwise shift operators?

2. What is the result of each of the following bitwise True-False expressions?

   a. `1 ^ 0 & 1 & 1 | 0`

   b. `1 & 1 & 1 & 1`

   c. `1 ^ 1 ^ 1 ^ 1`

   d. `~(1 ^ 0)`

3. True or false: 7 (binary 111) can be used as a bit mask to test whether the rightmost three bits in a variable are 1s.

4. What is the difference between the bitwise ~ (1's complement) and 2's complement?

Review Exercises

1. Write a program that converts an entered uppercase letter to a lowercase letter by applying a bit mask and one of the bitwise logical operators. If the character is already in lowercase, do not change it.

2. Write a program that asks the user for a number. Multiply that number by each power of 2, from 2^1 to 2^7, and then divide that number by each power of 2, from 2^1 to 2^7. Use shift operators, not math operators.

3. Write a program that swaps the contents of two variables without using any other variable. Use one of the bitwise variables.

Part III

C++ Constructs

while Loops

The capabilities to repeat tasks make computers good tools for processing large amounts of information. This chapter and the next few chapters present C++ constructs. *Constructs* are the control and looping commands in programming languages. C++ constructs include powerful but succinct and efficient looping commands similar to those of other programming languages you may already know.

The while loops let your programs repeat a series of statements, over and over, as long as a certain condition is met. Computers don't get bored when performing the same tasks repeatedly. That's one reason why they are so important in business data processing.

This chapter introduces the following topics:

♦ The while loop

♦ The do-while loop

♦ The exit() function

♦ The break statement

♦ Counters and totals

After completing this chapter, you will know the first of several methods available in C++ for repeating sections of a program. This chapter's discussion of loops includes one of the most important uses for looping: creating counter and total variables.

The *while* Statement

The while statement is one of several C++ construct statements. A construct (from *construc*tion) is a programming language statement or a series of statements that controls looping. The while is a looping statement. Looping statements control execution of a series of other statements, causing parts of a program to execute repeatedly as long as a certain condition is met.

The format of the while statement is

```
while (test expression)
    {
        block of one or more C++ statements;
    }
```

The parentheses around the test expression are required. As long as the test expression is True (nonzero), the block of one or more C++ statements will execute repeatedly until the test expression becomes False (evaluates to zero). If you want to execute just one statement in the body of the while loop, you do not have to enclose the statement in braces. Each statement within the body of the while loop requires semicolons at the end.

The body of the *while* loop executes repeatedly as long as the *test expression* is True.

The test expression usually contains relational and possibly logical operators. These operators provide the True-False condition checked for in the test expression. If the test expression is False when the program reaches the while loop for the first time, the entire body of the while loop will not execute at all. Whether the body of the while loop executes zero times, one time, or many times, the statements following the while loop's closing brace execute when the test expression becomes False.

Because the test expression determines when the loop finishes, the body of the while loop *should* change variables used in the test expression. Otherwise, the test expression will never change, and the while loop will repeat forever. This is known as an *infinite loop* and should be avoided.

> **Tip:** If the body of the while loop contains only one statement, the braces surrounding it are not required. It is a good habit, however, to enclose all while loop statements with braces. If you later have to add more statements to the body of the while loop, the braces will already be there.

The Concept of Loops

You use the loop concept throughout your day-to-day life. Whenever you have to repeat a certain procedure several times, you are performing a loop, just as your computer does with the while construct. Suppose that you are wrapping holiday gifts. Here are the looping steps, in a while-like format, that you go through to wrap them:

```
while (There are still unwrapped gifts)
{

    Get the next gift;
    Cut the wrapping paper;
    Wrap the gift;
    Put a bow on the gift;
    Fill out a name card for the gift;
    Put the wrapped gift with the others;

}
```

If you had 3, 15, or 100 gifts to wrap, you would go through this procedure (loop) repeatedly until every gift was wrapped. For a less physical example that might be more easily computerized, suppose that you want to add up all the checks you wrote last month. You perform the following step:

While there are still checks from last month, add the amount of the next check to the total.

The body of the pseudocode `while` loop has only one statement, but that statement must be performed until you have added up all the checks from last month. When this loop ends (when there are no more checks from last month), you will have the total.

The body of the `while` loop can contain one or more C++ statements, even additional `while` loops. Your program will be more readable if you indent the body of a while loop a few spaces to the right. The following examples illustrate this.

Examples

1. Some of the programs you saw in earlier chapters required user input with `cin`. If the user did not enter the appropriate values, the programs displayed an error message and asked the user once more. This was fine, but now that you understand the `while` loop construct, you should put the error message inside a loop, so that the user sees it not once but continually, until the user types the proper input values.

   The following program is short, but it demonstrates a `while` loop used to ensure valid user input. The program asks the user whether to continue with the program. You might want to incorporate this program into a larger one that needs the user's permission to continue. Place a prompt, such as the one shown here, at the bottom of a screenful of text. The text will remain on-screen until the user tells the program to continue with the rest of the execution.

Comments to identify the program.
Include the header file iostream.h.
Start of the main() *function.*
Declare the variable ans as a character.
Print to the screen Do you want to continue (Y/N)?
Obtain a character from the keyboard.
While the character typed is not a Y *or an* N *(or a y or*
an n), go through the loop.
Print to the screen You must type a Y or an N.
Print to the screen Do you want to continue (Y/N)?
Obtain another character from the keyboard.
Return.

```
// Filename: C14WHIL1.CPP
// Input routine to ensure that user types a correct response
// This routine might be part of a larger program.

#include <iostream.h>

main()
{
    char    ans;

    cout << "Do you want to continue (Y/N)? ";
    cin >> ans;      // Get user's answer

    while ( (ans != 'Y') && (ans != 'y') && (ans != 'N')
          && (ans != 'n') )
    {
        cout << "\nYou must type a Y or an N\n";
            // Warn and ask again
        cout << "Do you want to continue (Y/N) ?";
        cin >> ans;
    }    // Body of while loop ends here

    return 0;
}
```

Notice that there are two cin functions that do the very same thing. An
initial cin, outside the while loop, must be used to get an answer for which
the while loop can check. If the user types something other than Y or N (or
y or n), the program prints an error message, asks for another answer, and

loops back to check the answer again. This method of data-entry validation is preferred to giving the user only one additional chance to get it right.

The while loop tests the expression at the top of the loop. This is why the loop may never execute; if the test is initially False, the loop will not execute even once. Notice the following output from this program. The program will repeat indefinitely, until the relational test is True (until the user types Y, y, N, or n).

```
Do you want to continue (Y/N)? k

You must type a Y or an N
Do you want to continue (Y/N)? c

You must type a Y or an N
Do you want to continue (Y/N)? s

You must type a Y or an N
Do you want to continue (Y/N)? 5

You must type a Y or an N
Do you want to continue (Y/N)? Y
```

2. The following program is an example of an *invalid* while loop. See if you can find the problem.

```cpp
// Filename: C14WHBAD.CPP
// Bad use of a while loop

#include <iostream.h>

main()
{
    int     a = 10, b = 20;

    while (a > 5)
    {
        cout << "a is " << a << ", and b is " << b

            << " \n";
        b = 20 + a;
    }
    return 0;
}
```

This `while` loop is an example of an infinite loop. It is vital that at least one of the statements inside the `while` changes a variable in the `test expression` (in this example, the variable a); otherwise, the condition will always be True. Because a does not change inside the `while` loop, the program will never end without the user's intervention.

> **Tip:** If you inadvertently write an infinite loop, you will have to stop the program yourself. This typically means pressing Ctrl-Break, if not Ctrl-Alt-Del.

3. The following program asks for the user's first name and then uses a `while` loop to count the characters in the name. This is a string-length program. That is, it counts the number of characters in the name until it reaches the null zero. The length of a string is the number of characters in a string up to, but not including, the null zero.

```cpp
// Filename: C14WHIL2.CPP
// Counts the number of letters in the user's first name

#include <iostream.h>

main()
{
    char    name[ 15 ];    // Will hold user's first name
    int     count = 0;     // Will hold total characters in
                           // name

    // Get the user's first name
    cout << "What is your first name? ";
    cin >> name;

    while (name[ count ] != 0)      // Loop until the null
                                    // zero is reached
    {
        count++;                    // Add 1 to the count
    }

    cout << "Your name has " << count << " characters\n";
    return 0;
}
```

The loop continues as long as the value of the next character in the name array is more than zero. Because the last character in the array will be a null zero, the test will fail on the name's last character, and the statement following the body of the loop will continue.

> **Note:** A library function called strlen() determines the length of strings. You learn about this function in Chapter 23, "Character, String, and Numeric Functions."

4. The string-length program's while loop is not as efficient as it should be. A while loop fails when its test expression is zero, so there is no need for the inequality-to-zero test. By changing the test expression, as the following program shows, you can improve the efficiency of the string-length count.

```cpp
// Filename: C14WHIL3.CPP
// Counts the number of letters in the user's first name

#include <iostream.h>

main()
{
    char    name[ 15 ];    // Will hold user's first name
    int     count = 0;     // Will hold total characters in
                           // name

    // Get the user's first name
    cout << "What is your first name? ";
    cin >> name;

    while (name[ count ])  // Loop until the null zero
                           // is reached
    {
        count++;           // Add 1 to the count
    }

    cout << "Your name has " << count << " characters\n";
    return 0;
}
```

The *do-while* Loop

The do-while statement controls the do-while loop. This loop is similar to the while loop, except that with do-while the relational test occurs at the *bottom* of the loop. This ensures that the body of the loop executes at least once. The do-while loop tests for a positive relational test; as long as the test is True, the body of the loop continues to execute.

The format of the do-while loop is as follows:

```
do
{
    block of one or more C++ statements;
}
while (test expression)
```

The body of the *do-while* loop executes at least once.

As with the while statement, the test expression must have parentheses around it.

Examples

1

1. The following program is just like the earlier program with the while loop (C14WHIL1.CPP) except that a do-while loop is used instead. Notice the placement of the test expression. Because it is at the end of the loop, the user input does not have to appear before the loop and then again in the body of the loop.

```
// Filename: C14WHIL4.CPP
// Input routine to ensure that user types a correct response
// This routine might be part of a larger program.

#include <iostream.h>

main()
{
    char     ans;

    do
    {
        cout << "\nYou must type a Y or an N\n";
                // Warn and ask again
        cout << "Do you want to continue (Y/N) ?";
        cin >> ans;
    }      // Body of while loop ends here
    while ((ans != 'Y') && (ans != 'N'));
    return 0;
}
```

2. Suppose that you are entering sales amounts into the computer to calculate extended totals. You need the computer to print the quantity sold, part number, and extended total (quantity times the price per unit). You could use the following program:

```cpp
// Filename: C14INV1.CPP
// Gets inventory information from user and prints
// an inventory detail listing with extended totals

#include <iostream.h>
#include <iomanip.h>

main()
{
    int         part_no, quantity;
    float       cost, ext_cost;

    cout << "*** Inventory Computation ***\n\n";    // Title
    // Get inventory information
    do
    {
        cout << "What is the next part number ";
        cout << "(-999 to end)? ";
        cin >> part_no;
        if (part_no != -999)
        {
            cout << "How many were bought? ";
            cin >> quantity;
            cout << "What is the unit price ";
            cout << "of this item? ";
            cin >> cost;
            ext_cost = cost * quantity;
            cout << setiosflags( ios::fixed );
            cout << "\n" << quantity << " of # "
                << part_no << " will cost "
                << setprecision(2) << ext_cost;
            cout << "\n\n\n";    // Print two blank lines
        }
    }
    while (part_no != -999);        // Loop only if part
                                    // number is not -999

    cout << "End of inventory computation\n";
    return 0;
}
```

Figure 14.1 shows the output from this program.

Figure 14.1

Displaying
extended
inventory totals
on-screen.

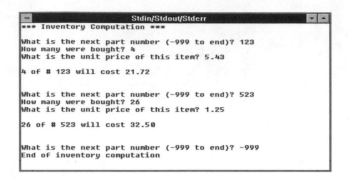

```
┌─┬──────────────────────Stdin/Stdout/Stderr──────────────────┬─┬─┐
│*** Inventory Computation ***                                       │
│What is the next part number (-999 to end)? 123                     │
│How many were bought? 4                                             │
│What is the unit price of this item? 5.43                           │
│                                                                    │
│4 of # 123 will cost 21.72                                          │
│                                                                    │
│                                                                    │
│What is the next part number (-999 to end)? 523                     │
│How many were bought? 26                                            │
│What is the unit price of this item? 1.25                           │
│                                                                    │
│26 of # 523 will cost 32.50                                         │
│                                                                    │
│                                                                    │
│What is the next part number (-999 to end)? -999                    │
│End of inventory computation                                        │
└────────────────────────────────────────────────────────────────────┘
```

The do-while loop controls the entering of the customer sales information. Notice the trigger that ends the loop. If the user enters -999 for the part number, the do-while loop quits because no part number –999 exists in the inventory.

This program can be improved in several ways. The invoice should be printed to the printer, not to the screen. You learn how to direct your output to a printer in Part V, "Character, Input, Output, and String Functions." The inventory total (the total amount of the entire order) should also be computed. You learn how to total such data in the section "Counters and Totals" later in this chapter.

The *if* Loop versus the *while* Loop

Some beginning programmers confuse the if statement with the loop constructs. The while and do-while loops repeat a section of code a number of times, depending on the condition being tested. The if statement may or may not execute a section of code, but if the section does execute, it executes only once.

Use an if statement when you want to conditionally execute a section of code once, and use a while or do-while loop if you want to execute the section of code more than once. The following example shows the differences between the if statement and the two while loops.

```
if (conditional test)

{

                    // Body of if statements

}

while (conditional test)

{

                    // Body of while statements

}

do

{

                    // Body of do statements

while (conditional test)
```

Body executes only once if test is True

Test at top of loop

Body loops continuously as long as test is true

Test at top of loop

exit() and break

C++ provides a way to leave a program early (before its natural finish) with the exit() function. The format of exit() is as follows:

```
exit(status);
```

status is an int variable or constant. In DOS, the status is sent to the operating system's *error-level* environment variable where the status can be tested by batch files.

The *exit()* function provides an early exit from your programs.

Often something happens in a program that requires the program's termination. What occurs may be a major problem such as a disk drive error, or the user may simply indicate a desire to to quit the program. (You can tell this by giving the user a special value to type in cin functions that triggers the user's intent.) You can put the exit() function on a line by itself or anywhere a C++ statement or function can appear. Typically, exit() is placed in the body of an if statement to end the program early, depending on the result of a relational test.

You should include the stdlib.h header file when using `exit()`. This file defines the operation of `exit()` to your program. Whenever you use a function in a program, you should know its corresponding #include header file, which is listed in the library reference manual.

Instead of exiting an entire program, you can use the break statement to exit the current loop. The format of break is

```
break;
```

The *break* statement ends the current loop.

The break statement goes anywhere in a C++ program that another statement can go, but break typically appears in the body of a `while` or `do-while` loop so that you can leave the loop early. The following examples illustrate the `exit()` function and the `break` statement. The `break` statement is covered more extensively in Chapter 16.

> **Note:** The `break` statement exits only the most current loop. If you have a program with a `while` loop within another `while` loop, `break` exits only the loop in which the break statement exists.

Examples

1. Following is a simple program that shows how the `exit()` function works. This program looks as if it prints several messages on-screen. Because of the `exit()` early in the program, however, the program quits immediately after `main()`'s opening brace.

```cpp
// C14EXIT1.CPP
// Quits very early because of exit() function

#include <iostream.h>
#include <stdlib.h>    // Required for exit()

main()
{
    exit(0);           // Force program to end here

    cout << "C++ programming is fun.\n";
    cout << "I like learning Visual C++ by example!\n";
    cout << "C++ is a powerful language ";

    cout << "that is not difficult to learn.";

    return 0;
}
```

2. The break statement is not intended to be as strong a program exit as the exit() function. Whereas exit() ends the entire program, break quits only the loop that is active at the time. In other words, break is usually placed inside a while or do-while loop to make the program think that the loop is finished. The statement following the loop executes after a break occurs, but the program does not quit, as it does with exit().

The following program appears to print C++ is fun! until the user types N or n to stop it. The program prints the message only once, however, because the break statement forces an early exit from the loop.

```
// Filename: C14BRK.CPP
// Demonstrates the break statement

#include <iostream.h>

main()
{
    char    user_ans;

    do
    {
        cout << "C++ is fun! \n";
        break;      // Cause early exit
        cout << "Do you want to see ";
        cout << "the message again (N/Y)? ";
        cin >> user_ans;
    }
    while (user_ans == 'N' && user_ans == 'n');

    cout << "That's all for now\n";
    return 0;
}
```

This program always produces the following output:

```
C++ is fun!
That's all for now
```

You can tell from this program's output that the break statement does not allow the do-while loop to reach its natural conclusion but causes the loop to finish early. The final cout prints because the entire program does not exit with the break statement; only the current loop exits.

3. Unlike the break in the last program, break is usually placed after an if statement. This makes it a *conditional break*. The break occurs only if the relational test of the if statement is True.

A good illustration of this is the inventory program you saw earlier (C14INV1.CPP). Even though the user enters -999 to quit the program, an additional if test is needed inside the do-while. The -999 ends the do-while loop, but the body of the do-while still needs an if test so that the remaining quantity and cost prompts are not given.

If you insert a break after the test for the end of the user's input, as shown in the next program, the do-while does not need the if test. The break quits the do-while as soon as the user signals the end of the inventory by entering -999 as the part number.

```
// Filename: C14INV2.CPP
// Gets inventory information from user and prints
// an inventory detail listing with extended totals

#include <iostream.h>
#include <iomanip.h>

main()

{
    int         part_no, quantity;
    float       cost, ext_cost;

    cout << "*** Inventory Computation ***\n\n";    // Title

    // Get inventory information
    do
    {
        cout << "What is the next part number ";
        cout << "(-999 to end)? ";
        cin >> part_no;
        if (part_no == -999)
        {
```

```
                  break;
            }     // Exit the loop if no more part numbers
        cout << "How many were bought? ";
        cin >> quantity;
        cout << "What is the unit price of this item? ";
        cin >> cost;
        ext_cost = cost * (float)quantity;
        setiosflags( ios::fixed );
        cout << "\n" << quantity << " of # "
              << part_no << " will cost "
              << ext_cost;
        cout << "\n\n\n";          // Print two blank lines
    }
    while (part_no != -999);    // Loop only if part number
                                // is not -999

    cout << "End of inventory computation\n";
    return 0;
}
```

4. The following program might be used to control two other programs. It illustrates how C++ can pass information to DOS with exit(). This is your first example of a *menu* program. Like a menu in a restaurant, a menu program lists possible choices. The user decides which choice from the menu's options the computer is to perform.

This program returns a 1 or 2 to its operating system, depending on the user's selection. The operating system then tests the exit value and handles the running of the appropriate program.

```
// Filename: C14EXIT2.CPP
// Asks user for selection and returns that selection
// to the operating system with exit()

#include <iostream.h>
#include <stdlib.h>

main()
{
```

```
int     ans;

do
{
    cout << "Do you want to:\n\n";
    cout << "\t1.  Run the word processor \n\n";
    cout << "\t2.  Run the database program \n\n";
    cout << "What is your selection? ";
    cin >> ans;
}
while ((ans != 1) && (ans != 2));          // Ensure that
                                           // user enters 1 or 2

exit(ans);      // Return value to operating system
return 0;
}
```

Counters and Totals

Counting is important for many applications. For example, you might need to know how many customers you have or how many people in a class scored above an average. Or you might want to count how many checks you wrote last month with your computerized checkbook system.

Before developing C++ routines to count occurrences, think of how you count in your mind. If you were adding up a total number of items, such as the stamps in your stamp collection or the number of wedding invitations you sent out, you would do the following:

Start at 0 and add 1 to it for each item you are counting. When you finish, you have the total number (the total count) of items.

This is all you do when counting with C++. Assign 0 to a variable and add 1 to it every time you process another data value. The increment operator (++) is especially useful when counting.

Examples

1. To illustrate the use of a counter, the following program prints Computers are fun! exactly 10 times on-screen. You could write a program that actually had 10 cout operators, but that would not be very elegant. It would also be too cumbersome to have 5,000 cout operators if you wanted to print that same message 5,000 times.

By adding a while loop and a counter that stops after a certain total is reached, you can control the printing, as the following program shows:

```cpp
// Filename: C14CNT1.CPP
// Program to print a message 10 times

#include <iostream.h>

main()
{
    int     ctr = 0;    // Holds the number of times printed

    do
    {
        cout << "Computers are fun!\n";
        ctr++;      // Add one to the count, after each cout
    }
    while (ctr < 10); // Print again if fewer than 10 times
    return 0;

}
```

The following is the output from this program. Notice that the message prints exactly 10 times.

```
Computers are fun!
Computers are fun!
Computers are fun!
Computers are fun!
Computers are fun!
Computers are fun!
Computers are fun!
Computers are fun!
Computers are fun!
Computers are fun!
```

The heart of the counting process in this program is the following statement.

Increment the variable ctr by 1.

```cpp
ctr++;
```

You learned earlier that the increment operator adds 1 to a variable. In this program, the counter variable is incremented each time the do-while loops. Because the only operation performed on this line is the increment of ctr, the prefix increment (++ctr) would produce the same result.

2. Notice that the last program not only added to the counter variable but also performed a loop a specific number of times. This is a common method of conditionally executing parts of a program a fixed number of times.

The following program is a password program. A password is stored in an integer variable. The user must correctly enter the matching password in three attempts. If the user does not type the correct password in three tries, the program ends. This is a common method that dial-up computers use; they let the caller try the password a fixed number of times, and then hang up the phone if that limit is exceeded. This helps deter people from trying hundreds of different passwords at one sitting.

If the user guesses the correct password within three tries, a secret message is displayed.

```cpp
// Filename: C14PASS1.CPP
// Program to prompt for a password and check it against an
// internal one

#include <iostream.h>
#include <stdlib.h>

main()
{
    int     stored_pass = 11862;
    int     num_tries = 0;          // The counter for
                                    // password attempts

    int     user_pass;

    while (num_tries < 3)           // Loop only 3 times
    {
        cout << "\nWhat is the password ";
        cout << "(You get 3 tries...)? ";
        cin >> user_pass;
        num_tries++;                // Add 1 to counter
        if (user_pass == stored_pass)
        {
            cout << "You entered the correct password.\n";
            cout << "The cash safe is behind ";
            cout << "the picture of the ship.\n";
            exit(0);
        }
```

```
        else
        {
            cout << "You entered the wrong password.\n";
            if (num_tries == 3)
            {
                cout << "Sorry, you get no more chances";
            }
            else
            {
                cout << "You get " << 3 - num_tries
                    << " more tries...\n";
            }
        }
    }     // End of while loop
    exit(1);
}
```

This program gives the user three chances just in case one or two typing errors occur. Following three attempts, however, the program quits after refusing to let the user see the secret message.

3. The following program is a letter-guessing game. It includes a message that tells the user how many tries were made before guessing the letter. A counter counts the number of tries. Figure 14.2 shows the program's output.

```
// Filename: C14GUES.CPP
// Letter-guessing game

#include <iostream.h>

main()
{
    int     tries = 0;
    char    comp_ans, user_guess;

    // Save the computer's letter
    comp_ans = 'T';      // Change to a different letter
                         // if desired

    cout << "I am thinking of a letter...";
    do
    {
```

```
            cout << "What is your guess? ";
            cin >> user_guess;
            tries++;              // Add 1 to the guess-counting
                                  // variable
            if (user_guess > comp_ans)
            {
                cout << "Your guess was too high\n";
                cout << "\nTry again...\n";
            }
            if (user_guess < comp_ans)
            {
                cout << "Your guess was too low\n";
                cout << "\nTry again...\n";
            }
        }
        while (user_guess != comp_ans);      // Quit when match
                                             // found

        // User got it right, let the user know
        cout << "*** Congratulations!  You got it right! \n";
        cout << "It took you only " << tries
             << " tries to guess.";
        return 0;
}
```

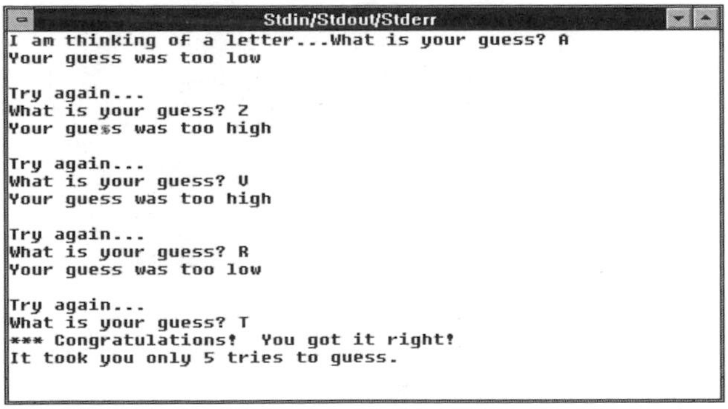

Figure 14.2

Counting the number of guesses.

```
 _                    Stdin/Stdout/Stderr              ▼ ▲
I am thinking of a letter...What is your guess? A
Your guess was too low

Try again...
What is your guess? Z
Your guess was too high

Try again...
What is your guess? U
Your guess was too high

Try again...
What is your guess? R
Your guess was too low

Try again...
What is your guess? T
*** Congratulations!  You got it right!
It took you only 5 tries to guess.
```

Producing Totals

Writing a routine that adds up values is as easy as counting. Instead of adding 1 to the counter variable, you add a value to the total variable. If you want to find the total dollar amount of checks you wrote in December, for example, you would do the following: start at 0 (nothing) and add to that each check written in December. Instead of building a count, you are building a total.

When you want C++ to add up values, initialize a total variable to zero and add each value to the total until you have gone through all the values. The following examples show you how to produce totals.

Examples

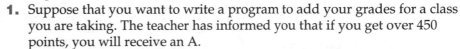

1. Suppose that you want to write a program to add your grades for a class you are taking. The teacher has informed you that if you get over 450 points, you will receive an A.

The following program keeps asking you for values until you type -1. The -1 is a signal that you are finished entering grades and you want to see the total. The program also prints a congratulatory message if you earn an A.

```cpp
// Filename: C14GRAD1.CPP
// Adds up grades and determines if an A was made

#include <iostream.h>
#include <iomanip.h>

main()
{
    float    total_grade=0.0;
    float    grade;   // Holds individual grades

    do
    {
        cout << "What is your grade? (-1 to end) ";
        cin >> grade;
        if (grade >= 0.0)
        {
            total_grade += grade;
        }    // Add to total
    }
    while (grade >= 0.0);    // Quit when -1 entered
```

```
        // Control begins here if no more grades
        cout << setiosflags(ios::fixed);
        cout << "\n\nYou made a total of "
            << setprecision(1)
            << total_grade << " points\n";
        if (total_grade >= 450.00)
        {
            cout << "** You made an A!!";
        }

        return 0;
    }
```

Notice that the -1 response does *not* get added into the total grade. The program checks for -1 before adding to total_grade. Figure 14.3 shows the output from this program.

Figure 14.3

Computing the total grade.

```
                    Stdin/Stdout/Stderr
What is your grade? (-1 to end) 87
What is your grade? (-1 to end) 89
What is your grade? (-1 to end) 96
What is your grade? (-1 to end) 78
What is your grade? (-1 to end) 99
What is your grade? (-1 to end) 87
What is your grade? (-1 to end) 89
What is your grade? (-1 to end) -1


You made a total of 625.0 points
** You made an A!!
```

2. The following program is an extension of the grade-calcuation program. The program here not only totals the grades but also computes an average.

The program must know how many grades were entered before the average calculation can work. This is a subtle problem; the number of grades entered is unknown in advance. Therefore, every time the user enters a valid grade (not -1), the program must add 1 to a counter as well as add that grade to the total variable. This kind of routine, which combines a counter with totaling, is common in many programs. Figure 14.4 shows the result of running this program.

```
// Filename: C14GRAD2.CPP
// Adds up grades, computes average, and determines if an
// A was made

#include <iostream.h>
#include <iomanip.h>
```

```
main()
{
    float        total_grade = 0.0;
    float        grade_avg = 0.0;
    float        grade;
    int          grade_ctr = 0;

    do
    {
        cout << "What is your grade? (-1 to end) ";
        cin >> grade;
        if (grade >= 0.0)
        {
            total_grade += grade;      // Add to total
            grade_ctr ++;              // Add to count
        }
    }
    while (grade >= 0.0);      // Quit when -1 entered

    // Control begins here if no more grades
    if (grade_ctr != 0)
    {
        grade_avg = (total_grade / grade_ctr);   // Compute
                                                  // average
        cout << setiosflags(ios::fixed);
        cout << "\nYou made a total of "
             << setprecision(1)
             << total_grade << " points.\n";
        cout << "Your average was " << setprecision(1)
             << grade_avg << " \n";
        if (total_grade >= 450.0)
        {
            cout << "** You made an A!!";
        }
    }
    return 0;
}
```

Figure 14.4

Computing the total grade and the average.

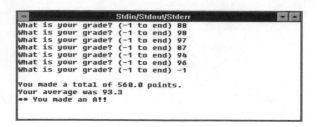

```
                    Stdin/Stdout/Stderr
What is your grade? (-1 to end) 88
What is your grade? (-1 to end) 98
What is your grade? (-1 to end) 97
What is your grade? (-1 to end) 87
What is your grade? (-1 to end) 94
What is your grade? (-1 to end) 96
What is your grade? (-1 to end) -1

You made a total of 560.0 points.
Your average was 93.3
** You made an A!!
```

Summary

This chapter shows you two ways to produce a C++ loop: the `while` loop and the `do-while` loop. The two variations of the `while` loop differ in how they test the end of the loop. The `while` loop tests at the top, and the `do-while` loop tests at the bottom. The end result is that the body of the `do-while` always executes at least once. To add to the `while` loop's flexibility, you learned the `exit()` function, which terminates a program, and the `break` statement, which terminates the current loop.

You also learned about counters and totals, which are two of the most important applications of loops. Your computer is a wonderful tool for adding and counting because of the repetitive capability of the `while` loop.

The next chapter extends your knowledge of loops by showing you how to create a *determinate* loop called the `for` loop. The `for` loop is useful when you want a section of code to loop for a specific number of times.

Review Questions

Answers to Review Questions are in Appendix B.

1. What is the difference between the `while` loop and the `do-while` loop?

2. What is the difference between a counter variable and a total variable?

3. Which C++ operator is most useful for counting?

4. True or false: The braces are not required around the body of `while` and `do-while` loops.

5. What is wrong with the following code?

```
while (sales > 50)
      cout << "Your sales are very good this month.\n";
      cout << "You will get a bonus for your high sales\n";
```

6. What file must you include as a header file if you use `exit()`?

7. How many times will this `cout` print?

```
int     a = 0;
do
    {
    cout << "Caroful \n";
    a++;
    }
while (a > 5);
```

8. How can you inform DOS of the program exit status?

9. What is printed in the following section of code?

```
a = 1;
while (a < 4)
{
    cout << "This is the outer loop\n";
    a++;
    while (a <= 25)
    {
        break;
        cout << "This prints 25 times\n";
    }
}
```

10. In program C14GRAD2.CPP, what could have happened if you hadn't checked for a grade counter of zero?

Review Exercises

1. Write a program with a `while` loop that prints the numbers from 10 to 20, adding a blank line between the numbers.

2. Write a weather-calculator program that asks for a list of the last 10 day's temperatures, computes the average, and prints the results. You will have to compute the total as the input occurs, and then divide that total by 10 to find the average. Use a `while` loop for the 10 repetitions.

3. Rewrite the program in Exercise 1, using a `do-while` loop.

4. Write a program similar to the weather-calculator program in Exercise 2 but make it a general-purpose program that computes the average of any number of days. You will have to count the number of temperatures entered so that you'll have that count when you compute the final average.

5. Write a program to produce your own ASCII table on-screen. Do not print the first 31 characters, because they are nonprintable.

for Loops

The for loop offers a way to repeat sections of your program a specific number of times. Unlike the while and do-while loops, the for loop is called a *determinate loop*. This means that at programming time you can usually determine exactly how many times the loop will take place. You saw that the while and do-while loops loop until a certain condition is met. The for loop does that and more; it continues looping until a specific count (up or down) is reached. Once the final for loop count is reached, execution continues at the next statement in the sequence.

This chapter introduces the following topics:

♦ The for loop

♦ Nested for loops

The for loop is a helpful way of looping through a section of code when you want to count or total amounts. Although the for loop does not replace the while and do-while loops, there are instances in which the for loop is more readable than a corresponding while loop.

The *for* Statement

The for statement encloses one or more C++ statements that form the body of the loop; the statements in the loop repeat continuously a certain number of times. As the programmer, you control the number of times the loop repeats.

The format of the for loop is as follows:

```
for (start expression; test expression; count expression)
    {
        Block of one or more C++ statements;
    }
```

The *for* loop loops for a specific number of times.

The *start expression* is an expression that C++ evaluates before the loop begins. This expression is typically an assignment statement (such as `ctr = 1;`) but can be any legal expression you specify. C++ looks at and evaluates the *start expression* only once, at the top of the loop, and never evaluates the *start expression* again.

> **Caution:** Do not put a semicolon after the right parenthesis. If you do, the `for` loop will think that the body of the loop is zero statements long! It will continue looping, doing nothing each time, until the *test expression* becomes False.

Every time the body of the loop repeats, the *count expression* executes, typically incrementing or decrementing a variable. The *test expression* evaluates to True (nonzero) or False (zero) and determines whether the body of the loop will repeat again.

> **Tip:** If only one C++ statement resides in the for loop's body, the braces are not required but are recommended. If you add more statements later, the braces will be there already, and you will not inadvertently leave them out.

The Concept of *for* Loops

You use the concept of `for` loops in day-to-day life. Whenever you have to repeat a certain procedure a specified number of times, that procedure is a good candidate for a computerized `for` loop.

To illustrate further the concept of a `for` loop, suppose that you need to put up 10 new shutters on your house. You must do the following steps for each shutter:

Move the ladder to the location of the next shutter.

Take a shutter, hammer, and nails up the ladder.

Hammer the shutter to the side of the house.

Climb down the ladder.

Because you have 10 shutters, you must perform each of these steps exactly 10 times. After 10 times, the job is finished. You loop through a procedure that has several steps. These steps are the body of the loop. It is certainly not an endless loop because there is a fixed number of shutters; you run out of shutters after 10 of them.

For a less physical example that might be more easily computerized, suppose that you have to fill out three tax returns for each of your teenage children. For each child, you must perform the following steps:

Add up the total income.

Add up the total deductions.

Fill out a tax return.

Put it in an envelope.

Mail it.

You then must repeat this procedure two more times.

Notice how the sentence before these five steps begins: "For each child...." This signals a construct similar to the for loop.

> **Note:** The for loop tests at the top of the loop. If the *test expression* is False when the for loop begins, the body of the loop will never execute.

The Choice of Loops

You can write any loop construct with a for loop, while loop, or do-while loop. All these loop constructs are candidates for virtually any loop you need C++ to perform. The for loop is a good choice when you want to count or loop a specific number of times.

Although the while and do-while loops continue looping until a certain condition is met, the for loop continues until a certain value is reached. Because of the close connection of C++'s True-False test to an expression's result (an expression is True if it is nonzero), any loop construct can be used for any loop your programs require.

Generally, you will use for loops when you want a determinate loop that iterates until a specific incremented (or decremented) value is reached. You will reserve while loops for looping until a False condition is met.

Examples

1. To give you a glimpse of the for loop's capabilities, the first program in this example contains a for loop, and the second program does not. The first program is a counting program. Look at the program and its output. The results basically speak for themselves and illustrate the for loop very well.

The following is a program with a for loop.

Comments to identify the program.
Include the header file iostream.h.
Start of the main() function.
Declare the variable ctr as an integer.
Start at the variable ctr equal to 1 and go through
the loop, incrementing ctr by 1, while the variable
ctr is less than or equal to 10.
Print to the screen the value of ctr.
Return from the main() function.

```
// Filename: C15FOR1.CPP
// Introduces the for loop

#include <iostream.h>

main()
{
    int     ctr;

    for (ctr = 1; ctr <= 10; ctr++)        // Start ctr at 1,
                                  // increment through loop
    {
        cout << ctr << "\n";      // Body of for loop
    }
    return 0;
}
```

The program's output is as follows:

```
1
2
3
4
5
6
7
8
9
10
```

Now look at the same program with a while loop.

Comments to identify the program.
Include the header file iostream.h.
Begin the program by calling the main() *function.*
Initialize ctr *to 1.*
If ctr <= 10 *is True, perform body of loop (do the* cout
operator and increment ctr *by 1).*
If it is False (evaluates to 0), skip the loop and
continue with the rest of the program.
Return from the main() *function.*

```
// Filename: C15WHI1.CPP
// Simulating a for loop with a while loop

#include <iostream.h>

main()
{
    int     ctr = 1;

    while (ctr <= 10)
    {
        cout << ctr << "\n";     // Body of while loop
        ctr++;
    }

    return 0;
}
```

Notice that the for loop is a cleaner way of controlling the looping process. The for loop does several things that a while loop will not do unless you write extra statements.

With for loops, you do not have to write extra code to initialize variables and increment or decrement them. You can see at a glance (in the expressions within the for statement) exactly how the loop will execute. This is not the case with the while loop, which forces you to look inside the loop to see how it is controlled.

2. Both of the following programs add the numbers from 100 to 200. The first program uses a for loop, and the second program does not. The first example shows how using a *start expression* other than 1 starts the loop with a bigger *count expression*.

Here is a program with a for loop:

```cpp
// Filename: C15FOR2.CPP
// Demonstrates totaling by using a for loop

#include <iostream.h>

main()
{
    int     total, ctr;

    total = 0;      // Will hold total of 100 to 200

    for (ctr = 100; ctr <= 200; ctr++)  // ctr is 100, 101,
                                         // 102, ..., 200
    {
        total += ctr;
    }               // Add value of ctr each iteration

    cout << "The total is " << total << "\n";
    return 0;
}
```

Here is the same program without a for loop:

```cpp
// Filename: C15WHI2.CPP
// A totaling program that uses a do while loop
#include <iostream.h>

main()
{
    int     total = 0;      // Initialize total
    int     num = 100;      // Starting value

    do
    {
        total += num;       // Add to total
        num++;              // Increment counter
    }
    while (num <= 200);
    cout << "The total is " << total << "\n";
    return 0;
}
```

Both programs produce the following output:

```
The total is 15150
```

The body of the loop in both programs executes only 100 times. The starting value is 100, not 1 (as in the last example). Note that the for loop is less complex than the do-while loop because the initialization, testing, and incrementing are performed in the single for statement.

> **Tip:** Notice how the body of the for loop is indented. This is a good habit to develop; it makes the beginning and end of the loop's body easier to follow.

3. The body of the for loop can have more than one statement. The following program requests five pairs of data values: children's first names and their ages. It then prints the name of the child's teacher, based on the child's age. This program illustrates a for loop with couts, a cin, and an if statement in its body. Because there are exactly five children to check, the for loop ensures that the program ends after the fifth child is checked.

```cpp
// Filename: C15FOR3.CPP
// Program that receives input on five children and prints
// the names of their teachers inside a loop

#include <iostream.h>

main()
{
    char    child[ 25 ];  // Holds child's first name
    int     age;          // Holds child's age
    int     ctr;          // The for loop counter variable

    for (ctr = 1; ctr <= 5; ctr++)
    {
        cout << "What is the next child's name? ";
        cin >> child;
        cout << "What is the child's age? ";
        cin >> age;
        if (age <= 5)
        {
            cout << "\n" << child
                 << " has Mrs. Jones for a teacher\n";
        }
        if (age == 6)
```

```
        {
                cout << "\n" << child
                        << " has Miss Smith for a teacher\n";
        }
        if (age >= 7)
        {
                cout << "\n" << child
                        << " has Mrs. Anderson for a teacher\n";
        }
    }              // Quits after 5 times

    return 0;
}
```

Figure 15.1 shows the output from this program. You will be able to improve the program after you learn to use the switch statement in Chapter 17, "The switch and goto Statements."

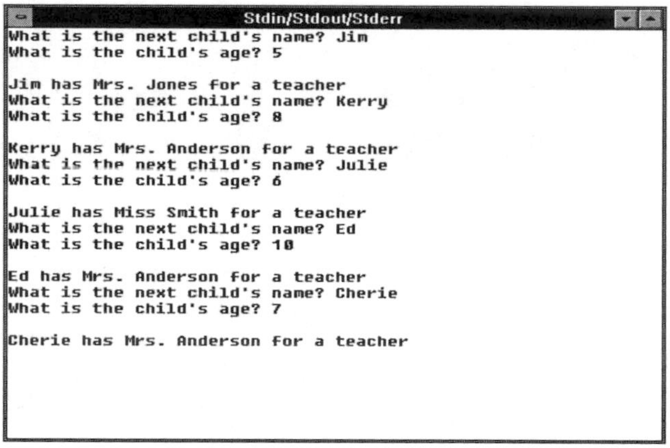

Figure 15.1

Input values inside a *for* loop.

```
                    Stdin/Stdout/Stderr
What is the next child's name? Jim
What is the child's age? 5

Jim has Mrs. Jones for a teacher
What is the next child's name? Kerry
What is the child's age? 8

Kerry has Mrs. Anderson for a teacher
What is the next child's name? Julie
What is the child's age? 6

Julie has Miss Smith for a teacher
What is the next child's name? Ed
What is the child's age? 10

Ed has Mrs. Anderson for a teacher
What is the next child's name? Cherie
What is the child's age? 7

Cherie has Mrs. Anderson for a teacher
```

4. The preceding examples use an increment as the count expression. You can make the for loop increment the loop variable by any value. It does not have to be a 1.

The following program prints the even numbers from 1 to 20, followed by the odd numbers from 1 to 20. To do this, 2 (instead of 1) is added to the counter variable each time the loop executes.

```
// Filename: C15EVOD.CPP
// Prints the first few odd and even numbers

#include <iostream.h>

main()
{
    int    num;     // The for loop variable

    cout << "Even numbers below 21\n";    // Title
    for (num = 2; num <= 20; num += 2)
    {
        cout << num << " ";
    }                  // Print every other number

    cout << "\nOdd numbers below 20\n";    // A second title
    for (num = 1; num <= 20; num += 2)
    {
        cout << num << " ";
    }            // Print every other number
    cout << "\n";
    return 0;
}
```

The first `for` loop variable, `num`, is 2 and not 1. If it were 1, the number 1 would print first, as it does in the odd-number section. This program contains two loops. The body of each loop consists of the single `cout` function.

Two of the `cout`s, the titles, are not part of either loop. If they were, the titles would print before each number prints. The result of running this program is as follows:

```
Even numbers below 21
2 4 6 8 10 12 14 16 18 20
Odd numbers below 20
1 3 5 7 9 11 13 15 17 19
```

5. You can decrement the loop variable as well. If you do, the value is subtracted from the loop variable each time through the loop. The following example is a rewrite of the counting program, producing the reverse effect by showing a countdown:

```
// Filename: C15CNTD1.CPP
// Countdown to the lift-off

#include <iostream.h>

main()
{
    int     ctr;

    for (ctr = 10; ctr != 0; ctr—)
    {
        cout << ctr << "\n";
    }            // Print ctr as it counts down
    cout << "*** Blast off! ***";
    return 0;
}
```

When decrementing a loop variable, the initial value should be larger than the end value being tested for. In this case, 10 is counted down to 1. The loop variable, ctr, decrements each time. You can see how easy it is to control a loop by looking at this program's output:

```
10
 9
 8
 7
 6
 5
 4
 3
 2
 1
*** Blast off! ***
```

6. You can make a for loop test for something other than a constant value. The following program combines much of what you have learned so far. It asks for student grades and computes an average. Because there may be a different number of students each semester, the program first asks the user for the number of students whose grades are about to be entered. The program then loops until the user enters that many scores, and computes the average based on the total and the number of grades entered.

Tip: This countdown program's for loop illustrates a redundancy you can eliminate in code, thanks to C++. The *test expression*, ctr != 0;, tells the for loop to continue looping until ctr equals zero. If ctr becomes zero, however, that is a False value in itself; there is no reason to add the additional != 0, except for clarity. The for loop can be rewritten as

```
for (ctr = 10; ctr; ctr—)
```

without loss of meaning and with more efficiency. This technique is such an integral part of C++ that you should become comfortable with it. You have very little loss of clarity once you get used to writing your code this way.

```cpp
// Filename: C15FOR4.CPP
// Computes a grade average with a for loop

#include <iostream.h>
#include <iomanip.h>
#include <stdlib.h>            // Why?...

main()
{
    float        grade, avg;
    float        total = 0.0;
    int          num;          // Total number of grades
    int          loopvar;      // Used to control for loop

    cout << "\n*** Grade Calculation ***\n\n";     // Title
    cout << "How many students are there? ";
    cin >> num;     // Get total number to enter
    if (num < 1)
    {
        exit(0);
    }

    for (loopvar = 1; loopvar <= num; loopvar++)
    {
        cout << "\nWhat is the next student's grade? ";
        cin >> grade;
        total += grade;
    }    // Keep a running total
```

```
    avg = total / num;
    cout << setiosflags( ios::fixed );
    cout << "\n\nThe average of this class is: "
         << setprecision(1) << avg << "\n";
    return 0;
}
```

Neither the total nor the average calculations have to be changed if the number of students changes, because of the way the for loop is set up.

7. Characters and integers are so closely associated in C++ that you can actually increment character variables in a for loop. The following program prints the letters A through Z with a simple for loop:

```
// Filename: C15FOR5.CPP
// Prints the alphabet with a simple for loop

#include <iostream.h>

main()
{
    char    letter;

    cout << "Here is the alphabet\n";
    for (letter = 'A'; letter <= 'Z'; letter++)  // Loops
                                     // 'A' through 'Z'
    {
        cout << letter << " ";
    }
    cout << "\n";
    return 0;
}
```

The program produces the following output:

```
Here is the alphabet
A B C D E F G H I J K L M N O P Q R S T U V W X Y Z
```

8. You can leave any of the for loop's expressions blank. The following for loop leaves all the expressions blank (they are called *null expressions*):

```
for ( ; ; )
{

    cout << "Over and over...";

}
```

This executes forever in an infinite loop. Although you should avoid infinite loops, your program might dictate that you leave one expression or another in a for loop blank. If you already initialized the *start expression* earlier in the program, you would be wasting computer time to repeat that expression in the for loop, and C++ does not require it. The following program leaves the *start expression* and the *count expression* blank, leaving only the for loop's *test expression*.

```
// Filename: C15FOR6.CPP
// Uses only the test expression in the for loop to count
// by 5s

#include <iostream.h>

main()
{
    int     num = 5;                        // Starting value

    cout << "\nCounting by 5s: \n";       // Title
    for ( ; num <= 100; )  // Only contains test expression
    {
        cout << num << "\n";
        num += 5;  // Increment expression outside of loop
    }              // End of the loop's body
    return 0;
}
```

Note the following output from this program, which illustrates the optional for loop expressions. Most of the time, you will need to leave out just one of them. If you find yourself using a for loop without two of its expressions, you might want to consider replacing it with a while or do-while loop.

```
Counting by 5s:
5
10
15
20
25
30
35
40
45
50
```

```
55
60
65
70
75
80
85
90
95
100
```

Nested *for* Loops

Use nested loops when you want to repeat a loop more than once.

Any C++ statement can go inside the body of a `for` loop—even another `for` loop! When you put a loop within a loop, you are creating *nested loops*. The clock in a sporting event works like a nested loop. You might think that this is stretching an analogy a little far, but it truly works. A football game counts down from 15 minutes to 0. It does this four times. The first countdown is a loop going from 15 to 0 (for each minute), and that loop is nested within another loop counting from 1 to 4 (for each of the four quarters).

Whenever your program needs to repeat a loop more than once, it is a good candidate for a nested loop. The following example shows two outlines of nested loops. You can think of the inside loop as looping "faster" than the outside loop. In the first outline, the `for` loop, counting from 1 to 10, is the inside loop. It loops faster because the variable `in` goes from 1 to 10 before the outside loop, the variable `out`, finishes its first iteration. Because the outside loop does not repeat until the body of the loop ends, the inside `for` loop has a chance to finish in its entirety. When the outside loop finally does iterate a second time, the inside loop starts all over again.

```
for (out = 1; out <= 100; out++)

    {

        for (in =1; in <= 10; in++)

        {

            // Body of inside loop                          Inside loop

        }

    }
```

Outside loop

```
for (out = 1; out <= 100; out++)

{

    for (in1 = 1; in1 <= 5; in1++)

    {

            // Body of 1st inside loop

    }

    for (in2=1;in2<=5;in2++)

    {

            // Body of 2nd inside loop

    }

}
```

1st inside loop

2nd inside loop

Outside
loop

The second outline shows two loops within an outside loop. Both of the inside loops execute in their entirety before the outside loop finishes its first iteration. When the outside loop starts its second iteration, the two inside loops repeat all over again.

Notice the order of the braces in each of the outlines. The inside loop *always* finishes, and therefore its ending brace must come before the outside loop's ending brace. Indentation makes this much clearer because you can "line up" the braces of each loop.

To sum up nested loops, follow this rule of thumb:

In nested loops, the inside loop or loops execute completely before the outside loop's next iteration.

Nested loops become important later when you use them for array and table processing.

Examples

1. The following program contains a nested loop (a loop within a loop). The inside loop counts and prints from 1 to 5. The outside loop counts from 1 to 3. Therefore, the inside loop repeats, in its entirety, three times. In other words, this program prints the values 1 to 5 and prints them three times.

```
// Filename: C15NEST1.CPP
// Prints the numbers from 1 to 5 three times, using a
// nested loop

#include <iostream.h>

main()
{
    int     times, num;     // Outer and inner for
                            // loop variables

    for (times = 1; times <= 3; times++)
    {
        for (num = 1; num <= 5; num++)
        {
            cout << num << "\n";
        }   // Inner loop body
    }       // End of outer loop

    return 0;
}
```

Notice that the inside loop, which prints from 1 to 5, repeats three times.

The indentation maintains the standard of `for` loops; every statement in each loop is indented a few spaces. Because the inside loop is already indented, its body is indented another few spaces.

Here is the result of running this program:

```
1
2
3
4
5
1
2
3
```

```
4
5
1
2
3
4
5
```

2. The outside loop's counter variable changes each time through the loop. If one of the inside loop's control variables is the outside loop's counter variable, you see effects like those shown in the following program:

```cpp
// Filename: C15NEST2.CPP
// An inside loop controlled by the outer loop's counter
// variable

#include <iostream.h>

main()
{
    int     outer, inner;

    for (outer = 5; outer >= 1; outer—)
    {
        for (inner = 1; inner != outer; inner++)
        {
            cout << inner << "\n";
        }   // End of inner loop
    }
    return 0;
}
```

Note the following output from this program. The inside loop repeats five times (as outer counts down from 5 to 1) and prints from 4 to 1 numbers.

```
1
2
3
4
1
2
3
1
2
1
```

Table 15.1 shows the two variables being traced through this program. Sometimes you have to "play computer" when learning a new concept such as nested loops. By executing a line at a time and writing down each variable's contents, you can produce this table.

Tip (for Mathematicians): The for statement is identical to the mathematical summation symbol. When you write programs to simulate the summation symbol, the for statement is an excellent candidate. A nested for statement is good for double summations.

For example, the summation

```
i = 30
Σ   (i / 3 * 2)

i = 1
```

can be rewritten as

```
total = 0;
for (i = 1; i <= 30; i++)
{

    total += (i / 3 * 2);

}
```

Table 15.1. Tracing the output of C15NEST2.CPP.

Variable Outer	Value Inner
5	1
5	2
5	3
5	4
4	1
4	2
4	3
3	1

Variable	Value
Outer	Inner
3	2
2	1

3. A factorial is a mathematical number used in probability theory and statistics. A *factorial* of any number is the multiplied product of every number from 1 to that number. For instance, the factorial of 4 is 24 because

$$4 * 3 * 2 * 1 = 24$$

The factorial of 6 is 720 because

$$6 * 5 * 4 * 3 * 2 * 1 = 720$$

The factorial of 1 is 1 by definition.

Nested loops are good candidates for writing a factorial number-generating program. The following program asks the user for a number and then prints the factorial of that number:

```
// Filename: C15FACT.CPP
// Computes the factorial of numbers through the
// user's number

#include <iostream.h>

main()
{
    int     outer, num, fact, total;

    cout << "What factorial do you want to see? ";
    cin >> num;

    for (outer = 1; outer <= num; outer++)
    {
        total = 1;  // Initialize total for each factorial
        for (fact = 1; fact <= outer; fact++)
        {
            total *= fact;

        }    // Compute each factorial
    }
```

```
        cout << "The factorial for " << num << " is " << total
            << "\n";
        return 0;
}
```

The program's output is as follows:

```
What factorial do you want to see? 7
The factorial for 7 is 5040
```

You can run this program, entering different values when asked, and see various factorials. Be careful, however, because factorials multiply quickly, and a factorial of 11 or so will no longer fit in an int variable.

Summary

This chapter showed you how to control loops. Instead of writing extra code around a while loop, you can use the for loop to control the number of iterations at the time you define the loop. All for loops contain three parts: a *start expression*, a *test expression*, and a *count expression*.

You have now seen C++'s three loop constructs: the while loop, the do-while loop, and the for loop. These are similar but behave differently in the testing or initialization of loops. None of the three loops is better to use than another. Your programming problem should dictate which loop is appropriate.

The next chapter shows you additional ways to control the loops you write.

Review Questions

Answers to Review Questions are in Appendix B.

1. What is a loop?

2. True or false: The body of a for loop contains, at most, one statement.

3. What is a nested loop?

4. Why would you want to leave one or more expressions out of the for statement's parentheses?

5. Which loop "moves faster"—the inside loop or the outside loop?

6. What is the output from the following program?

```
for (ctr = 10; ctr >= 1; ctr -= 3)
{

    cout << "ctr \n";

}
```

7. True or false: A `for` loop is better to use than a `while` loop when you know in advance exactly how many iterations a loop requires.

8. What happens when the *test expression* becomes False in a `for` statement?

9. True or false: The following program contains a valid nested loop.

```
for (i = 1; i <= 10; i++);
{
    for (j = 1; j <= 5; j++)
    {
        cout << i << " " << j << "\n";
    }
}
```

10. What is the output of the following section of code?

```
start = 1;
end = 5;
step = 1;

for ( ; start >= end; )
{
    cout << i << "\n";
    start += step;
    end—;
}
```

Review Exercises

1. Write a program that prints the numbers from 1 to 15 on-screen. Use a `for` loop to control the printing.

2. Write a program that prints the values from 15 to 1 on-screen. Use a `for` loop to control the printing.

3. Write a program that uses a `for` loop to print every odd number from 1 to 100.

4. Write a program that asks for the user's age. Use a `for` loop to print `Happy Birthday!` for every year of the age.

5. Write a program that uses a `for` loop to print the ASCII characters from 32 to 255 on-screen.

6. Using the ASCII table numbers, write a program that prints the following output, using a nested `for` loop:

```
A
AB
ABC
ABCD
ABCDE
```

Hint: The outside loop should loop from 1 to 5, and the inside loop's start variable should be 65 (the value of ASCII "A").

CHAPTER 16

Advanced Control of *for* Loops: *break* and *continue*

This chapter focuses on two techniques for refining control of a for loop: the break statement and the continue statement. These statements allow you the power (depending on the data being processed) to break out of a for loop early or to skip processing the rest of the loop body.

This chapter covers the following topics:

♦ Using break inside a for loop

♦ Using the continue statement

The *break* and *for* Statements

The for loop was designed to execute a loop a specified number of times. There may be rare instances when the for loop should quit before the for's counting variable has reached its final value, however. As with while loops, you can use the break statement to quit a for loop early.

The break statement goes in the body of the for loop. Programmers rarely put break on a line by itself; it almost always appears after an if test. If the break were on a line by itself, the loop would always quit early, defeating the purpose of the body of the for loop.

Examples

1. The following program shows what can happen when C++ encounters an unconditional `break` statement—that is, one *not* proceeded by an `if` statement.

Comments to identify the program
Include the header file iostream.h.
Start of the main() function.
Declare the variable num as an integer.
Print `Here are the numbers from 1 to 20` *on-screen*
and return to the next line.
The variable num starts at 1 and is incremented by 1
while num is less than or equal to 20.
Print the value of num and return to the next
line.
Break immediately out of the for loop.
Print `That's all, folks!` *on-screen.*
Return out of the main() function.

```cpp
// Filename: C16BRAK1.CPP
// A for loop defeated by the break statement

#include <iostream.h>

main()
{
    int     num;


    cout << "Here are the numbers from 1 to 20\n";
    for (num = 1; num <= 20; num++)
    {
        cout << num << "\n";
        break;      // This exits the for loop immediately
    }

    cout << "That's all, folks!";
    return 0;
}
```

This program's output is as follows:

```
Here are the numbers from 1 to 20
1
That's all, folks!
```

Notice that the break immediately terminates the for loop before it has completed one cycle. The for loop might as well not be in this program.

2. The following program is an improved version of the program in Example 1. This program asks whether the user wants to see another number. If the user does, the for loop continues its next iteration. If the user does not, the break statement terminates the for loop.

```cpp
// Filename: C16BRAK2.CPP
// A for loop running at the user's request

#include <iostream.h>

main()
{
    int     num;           // Loop counter variable
    char    ans;

    cout << "Here are the numbers from 1 to 20\n";

    for (num = 1; num <= 20; num++)
    {
        cout << num << "\n";
        cout << "Do you want to see another (Y/N)? ";
        cin >> ans;
        if ((ans == 'N') || (ans == 'n'))
        {
            break;      // Will exit the for loop if
                        // user wants
        }
    }

    cout << "\nThat's all, folks!";
    return 0;
}
```

Note the following sample run of this program. The for loop prints 20 numbers, as long as the user does not answer N or n to the prompt. Otherwise, the break takes over and terminates the for loop early. The statement after the body of the loop always executes next if the break occurs.

```
Here are the numbers from 1 to 20
1
Do you want to see another (Y/N)? Y
2
Do you want to see another (Y/N)? Y
3
Do you want to see another (Y/N)? Y
4
Do you want to see another (Y/N)? Y
5
Do you want to see another (Y/N)? Y
6
Do you want to see another (Y/N)? Y
7
Do you want to see another (Y/N)? Y
8
Do you want to see another (Y/N)? Y
9
Do you want to see another (Y/N)? Y
10
Do you want to see another (Y/N)? N
That's all, folks!
```

If you nest one loop inside another, the break terminates the "most active" loop—that is, the innermost loop in which the break statement resides.

3. Use the *conditional* break (an if statement followed by a break) when you are missing data. When you process data files or large amounts of user data entry, you might expect 100 input numbers and get only 95; you could use a break to terminate the for loop before it cycles through its 96th iteration.

Suppose that the teacher using C15FOR4.CPP, the grade-averaging program presented in the last chapter, entered an incorrect number of total students. Maybe she typed 16 when there were only 14 students. The preceding for loop would loop 16 times, no matter how many students there really were, because that loop relies on the teacher's count.

The following grade-averaging program is more sophisticated. It asks the teacher for the total number of students, but if the teacher wants to, she can enter -99 as a student's score. The –99 does not actually get averaged in but is used as a trigger value to break out of the for loop before its normal conclusion. A counter has to be placed in the loop as well, because the total number of grades entered may not match the number the teacher originally entered.

```
// Filename: C16BRAK3.CPP
// Computes a grade average with a for loop,
// allowing for an early exit with a break statement

#include <iostream.h>
#includo <iomanip.h>

main()
{
    float       grade, avg;
    float       total = 0.0;
    int         num, count = 0;  // Total number of grades
                                 // and counter
    int         loopvar;         // Used to control for
loop

    cout << "\n*** Grade Calculation ***\n\n";     // Title
    cout << "How many students are there? ";
    cin >> num;     // Get total number to enter

    for (loopvar = 1; loopvar <= num; loopvar++)
    {
        cout << "\nWhat is the next student's grade? ";
        cout << "(-99 to quit) ";
        cin >> grade;
        if (grade < 0.0)   // A negative number triggers
                           // break
        {
            break;         // Leave the loop early
        }
        count++;
        total += grade;    // Keep a running total
    }

    if (count != 0)
    {
        avg = total / count;
        cout << setiosflags( ios::fixed );
        cout << "\n\nThe average of this class is: "
             << setprecision(1) << avg << "\n";
    }
    return 0;
}
```

Notice that the grade is tested for less than zero, not −99.0. Floating-point values do not compare well for equality (because of their bit-level representations). No grade will be negative, so any negative number will trigger the break statement. Here is how this program works:

```
*** Grade Calculation ***

How many students are there? 10

What is the next student's grade? (-99 to quit) 87

What is the next student's grade? (-99 to quit) 97

What is the next student's grade? (-99 to quit) 67

What is the next student's grade? (-99 to quit) 89

What is the next student's grade? (-99 to quit) 94

What is the next student's grade? (-99 to quit) -99

The average of this class is: 86.8
```

The *continue* Statement

The *continue* statement causes C++ to skip the remaining statements in a loop.

The continue statement does the opposite of the break; instead of exiting a loop early, continue forces the computer to perform *another* iteration of the loop. If you put a continue statement in the body of a for or while loop, the computer ignores any statement in the loop that follows continue.

The format of continue is

```
continue;
```

You will use the continue statement when data in the body of the loop is bad, out of bounds, or unexpected. Instead of acting on the bad data, you might want to loop back to the top of the loop and get another data value. The following examples help illustrate the use of continue.

Tip: The continue statement forces a new iteration of any of the three loop constructs: the for loop, the while loop, and the do while loop.

The following example shows the difference between the break and continue statements.

```
for (i = 0; i <= 10; i++)

{

        break;

        cout << "loop it\n";    // Never prints

}

// Rest of program
```

break terminates loop immediately

```
for (i = 0; i <= 10; i++)

{

        continue;

        cout << "loop it\n";    // Never prints

{

// Rest of program
```

continue causes loop to perform another iteration

Examples

1

1. The following program appears to print the numbers 1 through 10, each followed by C++ Programming. It doesn't. The continue in the body of the for loop causes an early finish to the loop. The first cout in the for loop executes, but the second cout does not execute because of the continue.

```
// Filename: C16CON1.CPP
// Demonstrates use of continue statement

#include <iostream.h>

main()
{
    int     ctr;

    for (ctr = 1; ctr <= 10; ctr++)      // Loop 10 times
    {
```

```
            cout << ctr << " ";
            continue;               // Cause body to end early
            cout << "C++ Programming\n";
      }
      cout << "\n";
      return 0;
}
```

Note this program's output:

```
1 2 3 4 5 6 7 8 9 10
```

If you have such warnings enabled, Visual C++ gives you a warning message when you compile this type of program. The compiler recognizes that the second cout is unreachable code since it will never execute because of the continue. Therefore, most programs do not use a continue, except after an if statement. This makes it a conditional continue statement, which is much more useful. The next two examples demonstrate the conditional use of continue.

2. The following program asks the user for five lowercase letters, one at a time, and prints their uppercase equivalents. The program uses the ASCII table to ensure that the user entered lowercase letters. (These are the letters whose ASCII numbers range from 97 to 122.) If the user does not type a lowercase letter, the program ignores it with the continue statement.

```
// Filename: C16CON2.CPP
// Prints uppercase equivalents of 5 lowercase letters

#include <iostream.h>

main()
{
      char    letter;
      int     ctr;

      for (ctr = 1; ctr <= 5; ctr++)
      {
            cout << "Please enter a lowercase letter ";
            cin >> letter;
            if ((letter < 'a') || (letter > 'z')) // See if
                                                   // out of range
            {
                  continue;    // Go get another
            }
```

```
            letter -= 32;      // Subtract 32 from ASCII value
                               // to get uppercase
            cout << "The uppercase equivalent is: "
                 << letter << "\n";
    }
    return 0;
}
```

Because of the `continue` statement, only lowercase letters get converted to uppercase.

3. Suppose that you want to average the salaries of employees who made over $10,000 a year in your company, but you have only their monthly gross pay figures. The following program prompts for each employee's monthly salary, annualizes it (by multiplying it by 12), and computes an average. It does not average in any salary that is less than $10,000 a year. The `continue` ensures that those salaries are ignored in the average calculation, letting the other salaries fall through.

If you enter -1 as the monthly salary, the program quits and prints the result of the average.

```
// Filename: C16CON3.CPP
// Average salaries over $10,000 annually

#include <iostream.h>
#include <iomanip.h>

main()
{
    float    month, year;   // Monthly and yearly salaries
    float    avg = 0.0, total = 0.0;
    int      count = 0;

    do
    {
        cout << "What is the next monthly salary ";
        cout << "(-1 to quit)? ";
        cin >> month;
        if (month < 0.0)
        {
            break;      // Quit if user entered -1
        {
```

```
    if ((year = month * 12.00) < 10000.00)   // Do not
                                              // add low salaries
        {
            continue;
        }

        count++;              // Add 1 to valid counter
        total += year;        // Add yearly salary to total
    }
    while (month > 0.0);

    if (count)
    {
        avg = total / (float)count;       // Compute average
        cout << setiosflags(ios::fixed);
        cout << "\n\nThe average of high salaries is $"
             << setprecision(2)
             << avg << "\n";
    }
    return 0;
}
```

Notice that this program uses both a `continue` statement and a `break` statement. The program does one of three things, depending on the user's input: adds to the total, continues another iteration if the salary is too low, or completely exits the `while` loop (and average calculation) if the user types a -1.

Following is the output from a sample run of this program:

```
What is the next monthly salary (-1 to quit)? 500.00
What is the next monthly salary (-1 to quit)? 2000.00
What is the next monthly salary (-1 to quit)? 750.00
What is the next monthly salary (-1 to quit)? 4000.00
What is the next monthly salary (-1 to quit)? 5000.00
What is the next monthly salary (-1 to quit)? 1200.00
What is the next monthly salary (-1 to quit)? -1



The average of high salaries is $36600.00
```

Summary

In this chapter, you learned several more ways to use and modify your program's loops. By adding timing loops, continue statements, and break statements, you can better control how the loop behaves. Being able to exit early (with the break statement) or continue the next loop iteration early (with the continue statement) allows more freedom in processing different types of data.

The next chapter shows you a construct of C++ that does not loop but relies on the break statement to work properly. This construct is the switch statement, which makes your program's choices much easier to program.

Review Questions

Answers to Review Questions are in Appendix B.

1. What are timing loops for?

2. Why would timing loop ranges have to be adjusted for different types of computers?

3. Why do continue and break statements rarely appear without an if statement controlling them?

4. What is the output from this section of code?

```
for (i = 1; i <= 10; i++)
{
    continue;
    cout << "***** \n";
}
```

5. What is the output from this section of code?

```
for (i = 1; i <= 10; i++)
{
    cout << "***** \n";
    break;
}
```

6. To perform a long timing loop, you generally have to use a nested loop. Why?

Review Exercises

1. Write a program that prints C++ is fun on-screen for 10 seconds. You may have to adjust the timing loop a while to make it work on your computer.

2. Make the program in Exercise 1 flash the message C++ is fun on and off for 10 seconds. (*Hint:* You may have to use several timing loops.)

3. Write a grade-averaging program for a class of 20 students. Ignore any grade less than 0 and continue until all 20 student grades are entered, or until the user types -99 to end early.

4. Write a program that prints the numbers from 1 to 15 in one column. To the right of each even number, print the square of that number. To the right of each odd number, print the cube (the number raised to the 3rd power) of that number.

CHAPTER 17

The *switch* and *goto* Statements

The switch statement improves on the if and else-if constructs by streamlining the multiple-choice decisions your programs make. The switch statement does not replace the if statement but is better to use when your programs have to perform one of many different actions.

The switch and break statements work together. Almost every switch statement you use will include at least one break statement in its body. As a conclusion to Part III on C++ constructs, this chapter presents the goto statement for completeness, although you will use it rarely.

The following topics are introduced in this chapter:

- ♦ The switch statement
- ♦ The goto statement

If you have mastered the if statement, you should have little trouble with the concepts presented here. By learning the switch statement, you will be able to write menus and multiple-choice data-entry programs with ease.

The *switch* Statement

The switch statement, sometimes called the *multiple-choice statement*, lets your program choose from several alternatives. The format of the switch statement is a little longer than that of other statements you have seen. Its format is as follows:

```
switch (expression)
{
case (expression1):
    one or more C++ statements;
case (expression2):
    one or more C++ statements;
case (expression3):
    one or more C++ statements;
  :
  :
default:
    one or more C++ statements;
}
```

The *expression* can be any int or char expression, constant, or variable. The subexpressions—*expression1*, *expression2*, and so on—can be any other int or char constant. The number of case expressions following the switch line is determined by your application. The *one or more C++ statements* can be any block of C++ code.

The default line is optional; not all switch statements include a default line, although most do. It does not have to be the last line of the switch body.

If the *expression* matches the first case *expression1*, the statements to the right of *expression1* execute. If the *expression* matches the second case *expression2*, the statements to the right of *expression2* execute. If none of the case expressions match that of the switch *expression*, the default case block executes.

The case expression does not have to have parentheses around it, but their use sometimes helps differentiate the value to make it easier to find.

Use the *switch* statement when your program makes a multiple-choice selection.

> **Tip:** Use a break statement after each case block to keep execution from "falling through" to the rest of the case statements.

The use of the switch statement is easier than its format might lead you to believe. Anywhere an if-else-if combination of statements can go, you can usually use a clearer switch statement instead. The switch statement is much easier to follow than an if within an if within an if, as you had to write until now.

The if and else-if combinations of statements are not hard to use or that difficult to follow. When the relational test that determines the choice is complex and contains many && and || operators, the if may be a better candidate. The switch statement is preferable when multiple-choice possibilities are based on a single constant, a variable, or an expression.

The following examples clarify the switch statement. They compare switch and if statements to help you see the difference.

Examples

1. Suppose that you want to write a program to teach your child how to spell numbers. The program should ask the child for a number, type out a message repeating the number as a numeral, and then give the spelling.

   The program assumes that the child enters a number from 1 to 5. The following program uses the if-else-if combination to accomplish the beeping-counting program.

Comments to identify the program.
Include the header file iostream.h.
Comment to identify what is about to happen in the program.
Globally define the typed output messages.
Start of the main() function.
   Declare the variable num as an integer.
   Comment to identify what is about to happen in the program.
   Print to the screen Please enter a number.
   Obtain an integer from the keyboard.
   Comment to identify what is about to happen in the program.
   If the variable obtained is equal to a 1, cause the computer to print out the spelling of 1, followed by a newline.
      Otherwise, if the variable obtained is equal to a 2, cause the computer to print out the spelling of 2, followed by a newline.
         Otherwise, if the variable obtained is equal to a 3, cause the computer to print out the spelling of 3, followed by a newline.

Otherwise, if the variable obtained is equal to a 4, cause the computer to print out the spelling of 4, followed by a newline.

 Otherwise, if the variable obtained is equal to a 5, cause the computer to print out the spelling of 5, followed by a newline.

Return from the `main()` *function.*

```
// Filename: C17SPEL1.CPP
// Spells out numbers, using if/else statements

#include <iostream.h>

// define the messages, to avoid retyping
#define THE_NUMB "The number "
#define IS_SPELL " is spelled "

main()
{
    int     num;

    // Get a number from the child (you may have to help
    // the child)
    cout << "Please enter a number ";
    cin >> num;

    // Use multiple if statements to beep
    if (num == 1)
    {
        cout << THE_NUMB << num
            << IS_SPELL << "\"one\"\n";
    }
    else
    {
        if (num == 2)
        {
            cout << THE_NUMB << num
                << IS_SPELL << "\"two\"\n";
        }
        else
```

```
        {
            if (num == 3)
            {
                cout << THE_NUMB << num
                    << IS_SPELL << "\"three\"\n";
            }
            else
            {
                if (num == 4)
                {
                    cout << THE_NUMB << num
                        << IS_SPELL << "\"four\"\n";
                }
                else
                {
                    if (num == 5)
                    {
                        cout << THE_NUMB << num
                            << IS_SPELL
                            << "\"five\"\n";
                    }
                }
            }
        }
    }
    return 0;
}
```

This program assumes that if the child enters something other than 1 through 5, no output is produced. The program takes advantage of the #define preprocessor directive to define the standard parts of the output messages.

One drawback to this type of "if within an if" program is reduced readability. By the time you indent the body of each if and else, the program is shoved too far to the right. There is room for no more than five or six possibilities. More important, this type of logic is difficult to follow. Because it involves a multiple-choice selection, a switch statement is much better to use, as the following, improved version shows:

```cpp
// Filename: C17SPEL2.CPP
// Spells out numbers, using a switch

#include <iostream.h>

// define the messages, to avoid retyping
#define THE_NUMB "The number "
#define IS_SPELL " is spelled "

main()
{
    int     num;

    // Get a number from the child (you may have to help
    // the child)
    cout << "Please enter a number ";
    cin >> num;

    switch (num)
    {
        case 1:
            cout << THE_NUMB << num << IS_SPELL <<
"\"one\"\n";
            break;
        case 2:
            cout << THE_NUMB << num << IS_SPELL <<
"\"two\"\n";
            break;
        case 3:
            cout << THE_NUMB << num << IS_SPELL <<
"\"three\"\n";
            break;
        case 4:
            cout << THE_NUMB << num << IS_SPELL <<
"\"four\"\n";
            break;
        case 5:
            cout << THE_NUMB << num << IS_SPELL <<
"\"five\"\n";

            break;
    }
    return 0;
}
```

This version is much clearer than the previous one. It is obvious that the value of num controls the execution. Only the case that matches num will execute. The indentation helps separate the cases from each other.

Should the child type a number other than 1 through 5, no output is produced because there is not a case expression to match any other value, nor is there a default case.

If two or more of the case expressions are the same, this is an error; the program will not compile.

2. If the child did not type a 1, 2, 3, 4, or 5, nothing happened in the preceding program. Here is the same program modified to take advantage of the default option. The default block of statements executes if none of the previous cases matched.

```cpp
// Filename: C17SPEL3.CPP
// Spells out numbers, using a switch

#include <iostream.h>

// define the messages, to avoid retyping
#define THE_NUMB "The number "
#define IS_SPELL " is spelled "

main()
{
    int     num;

    // Get a number from the child (you may have to help
    // the child)
    cout << "Please enter a number ";
    cin >> num;

    switch (num)
    {
        case 1:
            cout << THE_NUMB << num << IS_SPELL <<
"\"one\"\n";
            break;
        case 2:
            cout << THE_NUMB << num << IS_SPELL <<
"\"two\"\n";
```

```
            break;
        case 3:
            cout << THE_NUMB << num << IS_SPELL <<
"\"three\"\n";
            break;
        case 4:
            cout << THE_NUMB << num << IS_SPELL <<
"\"four\"\n";
            break;
        case 5:
            cout << THE_NUMB << num << IS_SPELL <<
"\"five\"\n";
            break;
        default:
            cout << "You must enter a number ";
            cout << "from 1 to 5\n";
            cout << "Please run this program again\n";
            break;
    }
    return 0;
}
```

The break at the end of the default case might seem redundant. After all, there are no other case statements that will execute by "falling through" from the default case. It is a good habit to put a break after the default case anyway. If you move the default higher in the switch (it does not have to be the last switch option), you are more inclined to move the break with it (where it is then needed).

3. To show the importance of using break statements in each case expression, here is the same spelling program without any break statements:

```
// Filename: C17SPEL4.CPP
// A program that incorrectly spells, using a switch

#include <iostream.h>

// define the messages, to avoid retyping
#define THE_NUMB "The number "
#define IS_SPELL " is spelled "
```

```
main()
{
    int     num;

    // Get a number from the child (you may have to help
    // the child)
    cout << "Please enter a number ";
    cin >> num;

    switch (num)
    {
        case 1:
            cout << THE_NUMB << num << IS_SPELL <<
            ➥"\"one\"\n";
        case 2:
            cout << THE_NUMB << num << IS_SPELL <<
            ➥"\"two\"\n";
        case 3:
            cout << THE_NUMB << num << IS_SPELL <<
            ➥"\"three\"\n";
        case 4:
            cout << THE_NUMB << num << IS_SPELL <<
            ➥"\"four\"\n";
        case 5:
            cout << THE_NUMB << num << IS_SPELL <<
            ➥"\"five\"\n";
        default:
            cout << "You must enter a number ";
            cout << "from 1 to 5\n";
            cout << "Please run this program again\n";
            break;
    }
    return 0;
}
```

If the child types a 1, the program prints five different spellings, and then adds insult to injury by telling them they didn't enter a proper number! The break is not there to stop the execution from falling through to the other cases. Unlike other programming languages, such as Pascal, C++'s switch statement requires that you handle the case code in this way.

This is not necessarily a drawback. The trade-off of having to specify breaks gives more control in how you handle the specific cases, as shown in the next example.

4. The following program controls the printing of end-of-day sales totals. The program first asks for the day of the week. If the day is Monday through Thursday, a daily total prints. If the day is a Friday, a weekly total, as well as a daily total, prints. If the day happens to be the end of the month, a monthly sales total prints.

In reality, these totals would come from the disk drive instead of being assigned at the top of the program. Furthermore, instead of individual sales figures being printed, a full daily, weekly, and monthly report of many sales totals would probably be printed. You are on your way to learning more about expanding the power of your C++ programs in the upcoming chapters. For now, concentrate on the switch statement and its possibilities.

The daily sales figures, the daily and weekly sales figures, and the daily, weekly, and monthly sales figures are handled through a hierarchy of cases. Because the daily amount is the last case, it is the only report printed if the day of the week is Monday through Thursday. If the day of the week is Friday, the second case executes, printing the weekly sales total and then falling through to the daily total (since Friday's total has to be printed as well). If it is the end of the month, the first case executes, falling through to the weekly total and then to the daily sales total. In this example, the use of a break statement would be harmful. Other languages that do not offer this "fall through" flexibility are more limiting.

```cpp
// Filename: C17SALE.CPP
// Prints daily, weekly, and monthly sales totals

#include <iostream.h>
#include <iomanip.h>

main()
{
    // Later these figures will come from a disk file
    // instead of being so obviously assigned as they
    // are here
    float     daily = 2343.34;
    float     weekly = 13432.65;
    float     monthly = 43468.97;
    char      ans;
    int       day;                 // Day value to trigger
                                   // correct case
```

```
// Month will be assigned 1 through 5 (for Mon - Fri)
// or 6 if it is the end of the month. Assume weekly
// AND daily prints if it is the end of month no matter
// what the day is.
cout << "Is this the end of the month? (Y/N) ";
cin >> ans;
if ((ans=='Y') || (ans=='y'))
{
    day = 6;        // Month value
}
else
{
    cout << "What day number, 1 through 5 ";
    cout << "(for Mon-Fri) is it? ";
    cin >> day;
}

cout << setiosflags( ios::fixed );
switch (day)
{
    case 6:
        cout << "The monthly total is: $"
            << setprecision(2)
            << monthly << "\n";
    case 5:
        cout << "The weekly total is: $"
            << setprecision(2) << weekly << "\n";
    default:
        cout << "The daily total is: $"
            << setprecision(2) << daily << "\n";
}
return 0;
}
```

5. The order of the case statements is not fixed. You can rearrange them to make them more efficient. If you know that most of the time only one or two cases will be selected, put those cases toward the top of the switch statement.

For example, most of the company's employees in the preceding program are engineers, yet their option is third in the case statements. By rearranging the case statements so that Engineering is at the top, you will speed up this program. C++ will not have to scan two case expressions that it rarely executes.

```cpp
// Filename: C17DEPT2.CPP
// Prints message, depending on the department entered

#include <iostream.h>

main()
{
    char    choice;

    do      // Display menu and ensure that the user enters
            // a correct option
    {
        cout << "\nChoose your department:\n";
        cout << "S - Sales\n";
        cout << "A - Accounting\n";
        cout << "E - Engineering\n";
        cout << "P - Payroll\n";
        cout << "What is your choice? ";
        cin >> choice;
        // Convert choice to uppercase (if the user
        // entered lowercase) with the ASCII table
        if ((choice >= 'a') && (choice <= 'z'))
        {
            choice -= 32;       // Subtract enough to make
                                // uppercase
        }
    }
    while ((choice != 'S') && (choice != 'A')
          && (choice != 'E') && (choice != 'P'));

        // Put the Engineering first since it occurs most
        // often

    switch (choice)
    {
        case 'E':
            cout << "\n Your meeting is at 2:30\n";
            break;
```

```
            case 'S':
                    cout << "\n Your meeting is at 8:30\n";
                    break;
            case 'A':
                    cout << "\n Your meeting is at 10:00\n";
                    break;
            case 'P':
                    cout << "\n Your meeting has been
                    ➡canceled\n";
                    break;
        }
        return 0;
}
```

6. When you use menus, it is best to give the user a chance to do nothing. Perhaps the user started the program and then decided against continuing. If so, the user may not want to do *any* option on the menu. Most programmers give the user a chance to exit earlier than the normal conclusion of the program, as the following example shows. The menu now has a fifth option. If the user types Q, the program exits to the operating system early.

```
// Filename: C17DEPT3.CPP
// Prints message, depending on the department entered,
// giving the user a chance to stop the program early

#include <iostream.h>
#include <stdlib.h>


main()
{
    char      choice;

    do      // Display menu and ensure that the user enters
            // a correct option
        {
        cout << "\nChoose your department:\n";
        cout << "S - Sales\n";
        cout << "A - Accounting\n";
        cout << "E - Engineering\n";
        cout << "P - Payroll\n";
        cout << "Q - Quit the program\n";
        oout << "What is your choice? ";
```

```
            cin >> choice;
            // Convert choice to uppercase (if the user
            // entered lowercase) with the ASCII table
            if ((choice >= 'a') && (choice <= 'z'))
            {
                choice -= 32;      // Subtract enough
                                   // to make uppercase
            }
    }
    while ((choice != 'S') && (choice != 'A')
           && (choice != 'E') && (choice != 'P')
           && (choice != 'Q'));

    // Put the Engineering first since it occurs most
    // often

    switch (choice)
    {
        case 'E':
            cout << "\n Your meeting is at 2:30\n";
            break;
        case 'S':
            cout << "\n Your meeting is at 8:30\n";
            break;
        case 'A':
            cout << "\n Your meeting is at 10:00\n";
            break;
        case 'P':
            cout << "\n Your meeting has been
canceled\n";
            break;
        case 'Q':
            exit(0);       // Give the user a chance
                           // to change mind
            break;
    }
    return 0;
}
```

The *goto* Statement

Early programming languages did not offer the flexible constructs that C++ gives you, such as `for` loops, `while` loops, and `switch` statements. The only means of looping and comparing was with the `goto` statement. C++ still includes a `goto`, but the other constructs are more powerful, more flexible, and easier to follow in a program.

The `goto` statement causes your program to jump to a different location, instead of executing the next statement in the sequence. The format of the `goto` statement is as follows

```
goto statement label
```

The *goto statement* causes execution to jump to a statement other than the next one in order.

A `statement label` is named just as variables are (refer to Chapter 5, "Variables and Constants"). A `statement label` cannot have the same name as another variable being used in the program, or as a C++ command or function. If you use a `goto` statement, there must be a `statement label` somewhere else in the program to which the `goto` can branch. Execution then continues at the statement with the `statement label`.

The `statement label` precedes a line of code. Follow all such labels with a colon (:). C++ then knows that they are labels and will not get them confused with variables. You haven't seen such labels in the C++ programs so far in this book because none of the programs needed them. These labels are optional, unless you have a `goto` that branches to one.

Each of the following four lines of code has a different `statement label`. These lines are not a program, but individual lines that might be included in a program. Notice that each `statement label` goes to the left of its line:

```
pay:        cout << "Place checks in the printer \n;

Again:      cin >> name;

EndIt:      cout << "That is all the processing.\n";

CALC:       amount = (total / .5) * 1.15;
```

These labels are not intended to replace comments, although their label names should reflect something of the code that follows. Such labels give `goto` statements a tag to go to. When your program gets to the `goto`, it branches to the statement labeled by the `statement label`. The program then continues to execute sequentially until the next `goto` changes the order again (or until the program ends).

> **Tip:** Use identifying line labels. A repetitive calculation deserves a label such as `CalcIt` and not `x15z`. Even though both are allowed, the first one is a better indication of the code's purpose.

Use *goto* Judiciously

The goto statement is not considered a good programming statement when overused. There is a tendency to include too many gotos in a program, especially for beginning programmers. When a program branches all over the place, following its execution becomes as difficult as trying to trace a single strand of spaghetti through a plate of noodles. This is called *spaghetti code*—really!

Using a few gotos, here and there, is not necessarily a bad practice. Usually, however, you can substitute better code. To eliminate gotos and write more structured programs, you should use the other looping and **switch** constructs shown in the last few chapters. They are better alternatives to the goto statement.

The goto statement should be used judiciously. Starting with the next chapter, you will begin to break your programs into smaller modules called *functions*. As you write more and more functions, the goto statement becomes less important.

For now, become familiar with the goto statement so that you can under-stand programs that use it. Some day, you might be called on to fix someone's code that contains the goto statement. The first thing you will probably do is substitute something else for the goto statement!

Examples

1. The following program has a problem, directly the result of the goto, but is one of the best illustrations of the goto statement. The program consists of an *endless loop* (sometimes called an *infinite loop*). The first three lines (after the opening brace) execute, and then the fourth line, the goto, causes execution to loop back to the beginning and repeat the first three lines. The goto continues to do this forever until you press the Ctrl-Break key combination. Figure 17.1 shows the result of running this program.

Comments to identify the program.
Include the header file iostream.h.
Start of the main() function.
Label the line as Again:
    and print This message *to the screen and return to*
    the next line.
    Tab over and print keeps repeating *and return*
    to the next line.

*Tab over twice and print over and over and
return to the next line.
Go to the line labeled as* Again:.
Return out of the main() *function.*

```cpp
// Filename: C17GOTO1.CPP
// Program to show use of goto
// (This program ends only when user presses Ctrl-Break.)

#include <iostream.h>

main()
{
Again:
    cout << "This message\n";
    cout << "\t keeps repeating\n";
    cout << "\t\t over and over\n";

    goto Again;       // Repeat continuously

    return 0;
}
```

Figure 17.1

A "repeat printing"
program.

Of course, this is a silly example. You do not want to write programs with
infinite loops. Because the goto is a statement best preceded with an if,
eventually the goto will stop branching without intervention needed on the
user's part.

2. The following program is one of the worst-written programs ever! It is the epitome of spaghetti code! However, do your best to follow it and understand its output. By understanding its flow, you will increase your understanding of the goto. You also will appreciate the fact that the rest of this book uses the goto only when needed to make the program clearer.

```cpp
// Filename: C17GOTO2.CPP
// Program that demonstrates overuse of goto

#include <iostream.h>

main()
{
    goto Here;
First:    cout << "A\n"; goto Final;
There:    cout << "B\n"; goto First;
Here:     cout << "C\n"; goto There;
Final:    return 0;
}
```

At first glance, this program appears to print the first three letters of the alphabet, but the gotos make them print in reverse order: C, B, A. Although the program is not well designed, some indentation of the lines without *statement labels* will make the program a little more readable. Indenting allows you to quickly separate the *statement labels* from the rest of the code, as you can see in the following program:

```cpp
// Filename: C17GOTO3.CPP
// Program that demonstrates overuse of goto

#include <iostream.h>
main()
{
    goto Here;

First:
    cout << "A\n";
    goto Final;

There:
```

```
        cout << "B\n";
        goto First;

Here:
        cout << "C\n";
        goto There;

Final:
        return 0;
}
```

This program's listing is slightly easier to follow than the last one, even though they do the very same thing. In this book, the rest of the programs that use *statement labels* use indentation also.

You certainly realize that this output would be better produced by the following three lines:

```
cout << "C\n";
cout << "B\n";
cout << "A\n";
```

The goto warning is worth repeating: use goto sparingly and only when its use makes the program more readable and maintainable. Usually, there are better commands to use.

Summary

You have now seen the switch statement and its related options. It can help improve the readability of a complicated if-else-if selection. The switch is especially good when several outcomes are possible based on a certain choice. You can also use the exit() function to end a program earlier than its normal conclusion if the user prefers.

The goto statement causes an unconditional branch and can be difficult to follow at times. However, you should be acquainted with as much C++ as possible to prepare yourself to work on programs that others have written. The goto is not used much these days, and you almost always can find a better construct to use.

This ends the control section of the book. The next section introduces user-written functions. You have been using some of the library functions (such as cout and cin), and now you are ready to write your own.

Review Questions

Answers to Review Questions are in Appendix B.

1. How does goto change the order in which parts of a program would normally execute?

2. What statement can substitute for an if-else-if construct?

3. What statement usually ends each case statement in a switch?

4. True or false: The order of your case statements has no bearing on the efficiency of your program.

5. Rewrite the following section of code, using a switch statement:

```
if (num == 1)
{
     cout << "Alpha";
}
else if (num == 2)
{
     cout << "Beta";
}
else if (num == 3)
{
     cout << "Gamma";
}
else
{

     cout << "Other";

}
```

6. Rewrite the following program, using a do-while loop:

```
Ask:
     cout << "What is your first name? ";
     cin >> name);
     if ((name[0] < 'A') || (name[0] > 'Z'))
     {
         goto Ask;       // Keep asking until the user
                         // types a valid letter
     }
```

Review Exercises

1. Write a program, using the `switch` statement, that asks for the user's age and prints the following messages: You can vote! if the user is 18 or older, You can adopt! if the user is 21 or older, and Are you REALLY that young? for any other age.

2. Write a program, driven by a menu, for your local TV cable company. Here is how it charges:

If you live within 20 miles outside the city limits, you pay $12.00 a month. If you live within 20 to 30 miles outside the city limits, you pay $23.00 a month. If you live within 30 to 50 miles outside the city limits, you pay $34.00 a month. No one living outside 50 miles gets the service. Use a menu to prompt for the user's living range from the city.

3. Write a program that calculates parking fees for a multilevel parking garage. Ask whether the driver is in a car or truck. Charge the driver $2.00 for parking the first hour, $3.00 for the second hour, and $5.00 for more than 2 hours. For a truck, add an extra $1.00 to the total fee. (*Hint:* Use one `switch` statement and one `if` statement.)

4. Modify the preceding program to charge varying fees depending on the time of day the car or truck is parked. If the car or truck is parked before 8 a.m., charge the fees given in Exercise 3. If the car or truck is parked after 8 a.m. and before 5 p.m., charge an extra usage fee of 50 cents. If the car or truck is parked after 5 p.m., deduct 50 cents from the computed price. You will have to prompt the user for the starting time in a menu that includes the following:

a. Before 8 a.m.

b. Before 5 p.m.

c. After 5 p.m.

Part IV

*Variable Scope and
Modular Programming*

CHAPTER 18

Writing C++ Functions

A computer doesn't get bored. It performs the same input, output, and computations your programs require, as long as you want it to. You can take advantage of the computer's repetitive nature by looking at your programs in a new way: as a series of small routines that execute whenever you need them, as many times as necessary.

This chapter approaches its subject a little differently from the preceding chapters. It concentrates on teaching the need for writing your own *functions*, which are modules or sections of code that you execute and control from the `main()` function. So far, all programs in this book have consisted of one single, long function called `main()`. As you learn here, `main()`'s primary purpose is to control the execution of other functions that follow it.

This chapter covers the following topics:

♦ The need for functions

♦ Tracing functions

♦ Writing functions

♦ Calling functions

The chapter stresses the use of *structured programming*, sometimes called *modular programming*. C++ was designed to make it easy for you to write a program in several modules instead of as one long program. By breaking programs into several smaller routines (functions), you can better isolate problems, write correct programs faster, and produce programs that are much easier to maintain.

An Overview of Functions

When you approach an application problem that needs to be programmed, it's best not to sit down at the keyboard and start typing. Instead, think about the program and what you need it to do. One of the best ways to attack a program is to start with the overall program's goal and then break it into several smaller tasks. You should never lose sight of the overall goal of the program, but you should try to think of how the individual pieces fit together to accomplish this goal.

When you finally do sit down to start coding the program, continue to think in terms of the pieces that fit together. Do not approach a program as if it were one giant program, but continue to write the small pieces individually.

This approach does not mean that you should write separate programs to do everything. You can keep individual pieces of the overall program together if you write functions.

C++ programs should consist of many small functions.

C++ programs are not like BASIC or FORTRAN programs. C++ was designed to force you to think in a modular, subroutine-like, functional style. Good C++ programmers write programs that consist of many small functions, even if their programs execute one or more of the functions only once. The functions work together to produce a program that solves an application problem.

> **Tip:** You should not code one very long program. Instead, write several smaller routines, called functions. One of them must be called `main()`, which is always the first function that executes.

All programs must have a main() function.

The location of `main()` does not have to be the first function in a program, but usually `main()` is. Even when `main()` is not the first function in the code, it will be the first one to execute.

Breaking a Program into Functions

If your program does very much, break it up into several functions. Each function should do one primary task. For example, if you were writing a C++ program to get a list of characters from the keyboard, alphabetize them, and print them to the screen, you *could* write all of this in one big function—all in `main()`, as the C++ skeleton (program outline) in listing 18.1 shows.

Listing 18.1. A nonstructured *main()* function skeleton.

```
main()
{
    // :
    // C++ code to get a list of characters
    // :
```

```
        // C++ code to alphabetize the characters
        // :
        // C++ code to print the alphabetized list on screen
        // :

        return 0;
}
```

The skeleton in Listing 18.1 is *not* a good way to write the program. Even though you could type this program in just a few lines of code, it would be much better to get in the habit of breaking up every program into distinct tasks. You should not use main() to do everything—in fact, you should use main() to do very little except call each of the other functions that actually do the work.

A better way to organize this program is to write separate functions for each task the program is to do. This does not mean that each function should be only one line long, but make sure that each function acts as a building block and performs only one distinct task in the program.

The skeleton in listing 18.2 shows a much better way to write the program just described.

Listing 18.2. A modular skeleton of the same program, using separate functions for each task.

```
main()
{
    getletters();      // Call a function that gets the
                       // numbers
    alphabetize();     // Call a function that alphabetizes
                       // the letters
    printletters();    // Call a function that prints
                       // letters on the screen
    return 0;          // Return to DOS
}

getletters()
{
    // :
    // C++ code to get a list of characters
    // :

    return;     // Return to main()
}
```

```
alphabetize()
{
    // :
    // C++ code to alphabetize the characters
    // :
    //
    return;      // Return to main()
}


printletters()
{
    // :
    // C++ code to print the alphabetized list on screen
    // :

    return;      // Return to main()
}
```

Although the program outlined in Listing 18.2 takes longer to type, the program is much better organized. The only thing that main() does is to control the other functions by showing, in one place, the order in which they are called. Each separate function completes its task and then returns to main(), which calls the next function until there are no more functions. The main() function then returns control to DOS.

> **Tip:** A good rule of thumb is that a function should not occupy more than one screen length. If it does, you are probably doing too much in the function and should break it into two or more functions.

The *main()* function is usually a calling function that controls the rest of the program.

Until now, you have typed the full program in the first function, main(). From this point on, in all but the smallest of programs, main() will simply be a control of other functions that do the work.

These listings are not intended to be examples of real C++ programs but are skeletons, or outlines, of programs. From these types of outlines, it is easier to write the actual full program. Before going to the keyboard to write such a program, you know that the program will have four distinct sections: a primary function-calling main() function, a keyboard data-entry function, an alphabetizing function, and a printing function.

You should never lose sight of your original programming problem. With the approach just described, you never do! Look again at the main() calling routine in listing 18.2. Notice that you can glance at main() and get a feel for the overall program, without the rest of the program's statements getting in the way. This is a good example of structured, modular programming. A large programming problem has been broken into distinct, separate modules called functions, and each function performs one primary job in a few C++ statements.

More on Function Mechanics

Until this point, very little has been said about naming and writing functions, but you probably understand many of the goals of listing 18.2. A C++ function generally has the following properties:

1. Each function must have a name.

2. A function name is made up and assigned by you, the programmer, and follows the naming rules for variables. A function name can have up to 247 characters, must begin with a letter or underscore (_), and can contain letters, numbers, and the underscore.

3. Each function name has one set of parentheses immediately following it. This helps you (and C++) distinguish functions from variables. The parentheses may or may not have something inside them. So far, all such parentheses in this book have been empty.

4. The body of each function, starting immediately after the closing parenthesis of the function name, must be enclosed by braces. This means that a block of one or more statements makes up the body of each function.

Although the outline shown in listing 18.2 is a good example of structured code, it can be improved (besides putting the actual C++ statements inside it to make it work). It may be better to use the underscore character (_) or MixedCase in the function names. Do you see how `get_letters()` and `print_letters()` or `GetLetters()` and `PrintLetters()` are much easier to read than `getletters()` and `printletters()`?

> **Caution:** Be sure to use the underscore character (_) and not a hyphen (-) when naming functions and variables. If you use a hyphen, C++ will produce misleading error messages because a hyphen is not a legal character in a function name, but it is valid as an arithmetic operator, which is how C++ would treat it.

Use meaningful function names. *CalcBalance()* is more descriptive than *xy3()*.

Listing 18.3 shows an example of a C++ function. You already can tell a lot about this function. You know that it isn't a complete program because it does not contain a `main()` function. All programs must have a `main()` function. The function name is `CalcIt`. You know this because parentheses follow the name. These parentheses happen to have something in them. The body of the function is enclosed within a block of braces. Inside that block is a smaller block, the body of the `while` loop. A return statement is the last line of the function.

> **Tip:** Not every function requires a `return` statement as its last line, but including a `return` is recommended. It helps show your intent to return to the calling function at that point. Later you will see when the `return` is required, but for now, getting in the habit of including it will pay off.

Listing 18.3. A function called *calc_it()*.

```
CalcIt(int     n)
{
    // Function to print the square of a number
    int     square = 0;

    while (square <= 250)
    {
        square = n * n;
        cout << "The square of " << n << " is "
            << square << "\n";
        n++;
    }    // A block within the function
    return;

}
```

Calling and Returning Functions

You have been reading a lot about *function calling* and *returning control*. Although you may already understand these phrases from the description of functions so far, an illustration of a function call may be helpful.

A function call is like a temporary program detour.

A function call in C++ is like a detour on a highway. You are traveling along in the primary function called `main()` and then run into a function-calling statement. You must temporarily leave the `main()` function and go execute the function's code. Once that function finishes (its `return` statement is reached), program control reverts back to `main()`. When you finish the detour, you end up back in your main routine to continue the trip (hopefully!). Control continues as `main()` continues to call other functions.

> **Note:** Generally, the primary function that controls function calls and their order is called a *calling function*. The functions controlled by the calling function are called the *called functions*.

A complete C++ program, with functions, will make all of this very clear. The following program, named C18FUN1.CPP, prints several messages to the screen. Each message printed is determined by the order of the functions.

Before worrying too much about what this program does, take a little time to study its structure. You ought to be able to see that three functions are defined in the program: main(), next_fun(), and third_fun(). The three functions appear sequentially, one after the other. The body of each is enclosed within braces, and each function has a return statement at the end of it.

```cpp
// C18FUN1.CPP
// This program illustrates function calls

#include <iostream.h>

void     next_fun(void)    // Second function - parentheses
                           // always required
{
    cout << "Inside next_fun()\n";  // No variables defined
                                    // in function
    return;                 // Control is now returned
                            // to main()
}

void     third_fun(void)  // Last function called in program
{
    cout << "Inside third_fun()\n";
    return;                 // Always return from
                            // all functions
}

main()      // main() is ALWAYS the first C function executed
{
    cout << "First function called is always main()\n";
    next_fun();     // Second function is called here
    third_fun();    // This function is called here
    cout << "main() is completed\n";  // All control
                                      // returns here
    return 0;               // Control is returned to DOS
}                           // This brace concludes main()
```

Following is the output of this program:

```
First function called is always main()
Inside next_fun()
Inside third_fun()
main() is completed
```

Figure 18.1 shows a trace of this program's execution. Notice that main() controls which of the other functions are called, as well as their order. Control *always* returns to the calling function once the called function finishes.

Figure 18.1

Tracing the
function calls.

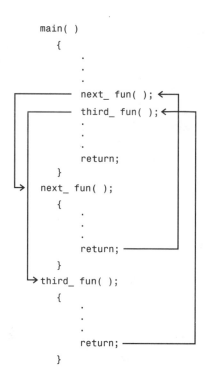

Notice that the user functions are preceded by void and include void inside the parentheses. C++, being a strongly typed language, requires this. Its meaning will be discussed in Chapter 21, "Function Return Values and Prototypes."

To call a function, you just type its name, including the parentheses, and then a semicolon. Remember that semicolons follow all executable statements in C++, and a function call (sometimes called a *function invocation*) is an executable statement.

The execution is the function's code being called. Any function can call any other function. It just happens that main() is the only function that calls other user-written functions in this program.

You can tell that the following statement is a function call:

```
print_total();
```

Because print_total is not a C++ command or library function name, it must be the name of a variable or user-written function. Only function names end with the parentheses, so print_total(); must be a function call or the start of a function's code. Of these two possibilities, it must be a call to a function because it ends with a semicolon. Without the semicolon, it would have to be the start of a function definition.

When you define a function—that is, when you type the function name and its subsequent code inside braces—you *never* follow the name with a semicolon. Notice in the previous program that main(), next_fun(), and third_fun() have no semicolons where these functions appear in the body of the program. Only in main(), where these two functions are called, does a semicolon follow the function names.

> **Caution:** You cannot define one function within another. All function code must be listed sequentially, one after the other, throughout the program. A function's closing brace must appear before another function's code can be listed.

Examples

1. Suppose that you are writing a program to do the following:

Ask for the user's department. If the user is in accounting, the user should receive the accounting department's report; if in engineering, the engineering department's report; and if in marketing, the marketing department's report.

Following is a skeleton of such a program. The code for main() is shown in its entirety. The switch statement is a perfect function-calling statement for such a multiple-choice selection. Only a skeleton of the other functions is shown.

```
// Skeleton of a departmental report program

#include <iostream.h>

void     acct_report(void)
{
    // :
    // Accounting report code goes here
    // :

    return;
}

void     eng_report(void)
{
    // :
    // Engineering report code goes here
    // :

    return;
}

void    mtg_report()
{
    // :
    // Marketing report code goes here
    // :

    return;
}

main()
{
    int     choice;

    do
    {
        cout << "Choose your department from ";
        cout << "the following list\n";
        cout << "\t1.  Accounting\n";
        cout << "\t2.  Engineering\n";
        cout << "\t3.  Marketing\n";
```

```
            cout << "What is your choice? ";
            cin >> choice;
    }
    while ((choice < 1) || (choice > 3)); // Ensure 1, 2,
                                          // or 3


    switch (choice)
    {
        case    1:
            acct_report();   // Call accounting function
            break;           // Don't fall through
        case    2:
            eng_report();    // Call engineering function
            break;
        case    3:
            mtg_report();    // Call marketing function
            break;
    }
    return 0;       // Program returns to DOS when done
}
```

The body of switch statements usually contains function calls. You can tell that these case statements execute functions. For example, acct_report();, which is the first line of the first case, is not a variable name or C++ command, but is the name of a function defined in the program. If the user enters a 1 at the menu, the function called acct_report() executes. When acct_report() finishes, control returns to the first case body, whose break; statement causes the switch to end. The main() function returns to DOS (or to your integrated C++ environment if you are using it) when its return statement executes.

2. In the preceding example, the main() routine is not very modular. The displaying of the menu should be done in a separate function. Remember that main() should do very little except control other functions that do all the work.

Here is a rewrite of this sample program, with a fourth function added that prints the menu to the screen. This is truly a modular example in which each function performs a single task. Again, the first three functions show only skeleton code because the goal of these examples is to illustrate function calling and returning.

```
// 2nd skeleton of a departmental report program

#include <iostream.h>

void     menu_print(void)
{
    cout << "Choose your department from ";
    cout << "the following list\n";
    cout << "\t1.  Accounting\n";
    cout << "\t2.  Engineering\n";
    cout << "\t3.  Marketing\n";
    cout << "What is your choice? ";
    return;      // Return to main()
}

void     acct_report(void)
{
    // :
    // Accounting report code goes here
    // :

    return;
}

void     eng_report(void)
{
    // :
    // Engineering report code goes here
    // :

    return;
}

void     mtg_report(void)
{
    // :
    // Marketing report code goes here
    // :

    return;
}
```

```
main()
{
    int      choice;

    do
    {
        menu_print();    // Call a function to do printing
                         // of menu
        cin >> choice;
    }
    while ((choice < 1) || (choice > 3)); // Ensure 1, 2,
                                          // or 3

    switch (choice)
    {
        case    1:
                acct_report();  // Call accounting function
                break;          // Don't fall through
        case    2:
                eng_report();   // Call engineering function
                break;
        case    3:
                mtg_report();   // Call marketing function
                break;
    }
    return 0;      // Program returns to DOS when done
}
```

3. Because readability is the key, programs broken into separate functions result in better code that is easier to read. You can write and test each function, one at a time. Once you write a general outline of the program, you can list a bunch of function calls in `main()` and define their skeletons after `main()`.

The body of each function will initially consist of `return` statements, so the program compiles in its skeleton format. As you complete each function, you can compile and test the program *as you write it*. This approach results in more accurate programs sooner. The separate functions allow others who might later modify the program to "zero in" on the code they need to change, without affecting the rest of the program.

Another useful habit, popular with many C++ programmers, is to separate functions from each other with a comment consisting of a line of asterisks (*) or hyphens (-). This makes it easy, especially in longer programs, to see where a function begins and ends. Following is another listing of the preceding program but with separating comments that help break up the program listing, making it even easier to see the four separate functions:

```cpp
// 3nd skeleton of a departmental report program

#include <iostream.h>

void     menu_print(void)
{
    cout << "Choose your department from ";
    cout << "the following list\n";
    cout << "\t1.  Accounting\n";
    cout << "\t2.  Engineering\n";
    cout << "\t3.  Marketing\n";
    cout << "What is your choice? ";
    return;    // Return to main()
}

//***********************************************************

void     acct_report(void)
{
    // :
    // Accounting report code goes here
    // :

    return;
}

//***********************************************************

void     eng_report(void)
{
    // :
    // Engineering report code goes here
    // :

    return;
}

//***********************************************************
```

```
void     mtg_report(void)
{
    // :
    // Marketing report code goes here
    // :

    return;
}


//**********************************************************

main()
{
    int     choice;

    do
    {
        menu_print();     // Call a function to do printing
                          // of menu
        cin >> choice;
    }
    while ((choice < 1) ¦¦ (choice > 3)); // Ensure 1, 2,
                                          // or 3

    switch (choice)
    {
        case     1:
            acct_report(); // Call accounting function
            break;         // Don't fall through
        case     2:
            eng_report();  // Call engineering function
            break;
        case     3:
            mtg_report();  // Call marketing function
            break;
    }
    return 0;      // Program returns to DOS when done
}
```

Because of space limitations, not all program listings in this book show functions separated in this manner. You might find, however, that your listings are easier to follow if you put the separating comments between your functions.

4. You can execute a function more than once simply by calling it from more than one place in a program. If you put a function call in the body of a loop, the function will execute repeatedly until the loop finishes.

The following program uses functions to print the message C++ is Fun! both forward and backward several times on-screen. Notice that main() does not make every function call. The second function, name_print(), calls the function named reverse_print(). Trace the execution of the program's couts. Figure 18.2 shows the output from the program to help you trace its execution.

```cpp
// Filename: C18FUN2.CPP
// Prints C++ is Fun! several times on the screen

#include <iostream.h>

//************************************************************

void     ReversePrint(void)
{
    // Print several C++ is Fun! messages, in reverse,
    // separated by tabs
    cout << "!nuF si ++C\t!nuF si ++C\t!nuF si ++C\t\n";
    return;       // Return to name_print()
}

//************************************************************

void     NamePrint(void)
{
    // Print C++ is Fun! across a line, separated by tabs
    cout << "C++ is Fun!\tC++ is Fun!\t";
    cout << "C++ is Fun!\tC++ is Fun!\n";
    cout << "C + +  i s  F u n !\tC + +  i s  F u n !\t";
    cout << "C + +  i s  F u n !\n";

    ReversePrint();      // Call next function from here
    return;                  // Return to main()
}

//************************************************************

void     OnePerLine(void)
{
```

```
        // Print C++ is Fun! down the screen
        cout << "C\n+\n+\n \ni\ns\n \nF\nu\nn\n!\n";
        return;              // Return to main()
}


main()
{
    int     ctr;         // To control loops

    for (ctr = 1; ctr <= 5; ctr++)
    {
        NamePrint();  // Call function 5 times
    }

    OnePerLine();      // Call last function once
    return 0;
}
```

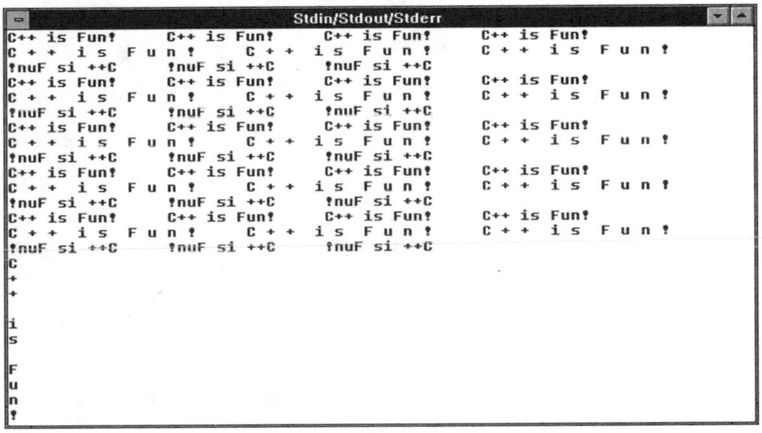

Figure 18.2

A message printed
several times
on-screen.

Summary

You now have been exposed to truly structured programs. Instead of typing long programs, you can break them up into separate functions. That way, you can isolate your routines so that surrounding code doesn't get in the way when you are concentrating on a section of your program.

There is a little more complexity to functions that you should know, involving the way variable values are recognized by all the program's functions. The next chapter shows you how variables are handled between functions and helps strengthen your structured programming skills.

Review Questions

Answers to Review Questions are in Appendix B.

1. True or false: A function must always include a `return` statement as its last command.

2. What is the name of the first function executed in a C++ program?

3. Which is better—one long function, or several smaller functions? Why?

4. How do function names differ from variable names?

5. How can you use comments to help visually separate functions from each other?

6. What is wrong with the following section of a program?

```cpp
void    CalcIt(void)
{
    cout << "Getting ready to calculate the square of 25\n";

    sq_25()
    {
        cout << "The square of 25 is: "
            << (25 * 25) << "\n";
        return;
    }

    cout << "That is a big number!\n";
    return;
}
```

7. Is the following a variable name, a function call, a function definition, or an expression?

```cpp
scan_names();
```

CHAPTER 19

Variable Scope

The concept of *variable scope* is most important when you write functions. Variable scope determines which functions recognize certain variables. If a function recognizes a variable, the variable is visible to that function. Variable scope protects variables in one function from other functions. If a function does not need access to a variable, that function should not be able to see or change the variable.

This chapter introduces the following topics:

♦ Local variables

♦ Global variables

♦ Passing arguments

♦ Receiving parameters

♦ Automatic and static variables

The concept introduced in the last chapter, multiple functions, is much more useful when you learn about local and global variable scope.

Global versus Local Variables

If you have programmed in BASIC only, the concept of local and global variables may be new to you. In many interpreted versions of BASIC, all variables are global. That is, the entire program knows what every variable is and has the capability to change any variable. If you use a variable called SALES at the top of the program, even the last line in the program can use SALES. (If you don't know BASIC, don't despair—this is one habit you won't have to break!)

Global variables can be dangerous. Parts of a program can inadvertently change a variable that shouldn't be changed. Suppose that you need to write a program to keep track of grocery store inventory. You might keep track of sale percentages, discounts, retail prices, wholesale prices, produce prices, dairy prices, delivered prices, price changes, sales tax percentages, holiday markups, post-holiday markdowns, and so on.

The huge number of prices in such a system would be confusing. You would have to write a program to keep track of each kind of prices, and it would be easy to call the dairy prices `d_prices` but also call the delivered prices `d_prices`. Either C++ will disallow it (it will not let you define the same variable twice), or you will overwrite a value used for something else. Whatever happens, keeping track of all the different, but similarly named, prices will make the program confusing to write.

Global variables are visible across many program functions. Such variables can be dangerous because code can inadvertently overwrite a variable that has been initialized elsewhere in the program. It is better to have every variable local in your program; that way, only the functions that should be able to change the variables can do so.

A local variable can be seen (and changed) only from within the function in which the variable is defined. Therefore, if a function defines a variable as local, that variable's scope is protected. The variable cannot be used, changed, or erased from any other function without special programming that you learn about in Chapter 20, "Passing Values."

If you use only one function, `main()`, the question of global versus local variables is moot. You know, after reading the last chapter, that single-function programs are not recommended, however. It's best to write modular, structured programs made up of many smaller functions. When you type functions into your program, you must understand how to define variables to be local to the functions that need them.

Defining Variable Scope

When you first read about variables in Chapter 5, "Variables and Constants," you learned about two methods of defining variables:

♦ You can define a variable after the opening brace of a block of code (usually at the top of a function).

♦ You can define a variable before a function name, such as `main()`.

Until now, all the program examples in this book have contained variables defined with the first method. You have yet to see the second way used.

Because most of these programs consisted entirely of a single function called `main()`, there was no reason to distinguish the two methods. It is only when you use multiple functions in programs that these two variable definitions become critical.

Local variables are visible only in the block in which they are defined. These two methods of variable definitions describe the way local and global variables are defined. The following rules, specific to local and global variables, are very important:

♦ A variable is local if, and only if, you define it after an opening brace of a block, typically at the top of a function.

♦ A variable is global if, and only if, you define it outside a function.

All variables you have seen so far have been local. They were all defined after the opening braces of `main()`; therefore, they were local to `main()`, and only `main()` could use them. Other functions would have no idea that these variables existed, as they belonged to `main()` only. Once the function (or block) ends, all its local variables are destroyed.

> **Tip:** All local variables go away when their block ends. A global variable is visible from its point of definition down into the source file.

A global variable is visible ("known") from its point of definition down into the source file. That is, if you define a global variable, any line in the rest of the program, no matter how many functions and lines of code follow, will be able to use that variable.

Examples

1. The following section of code defines two local variables, `i` and `j`:

```
main()
 {
     int  i, j;      // Local since defined after brace

     // Rest of main() goes here
 }
```

These variables are visible to `main()` and not to any other function that might follow or be called by `main()`.

2. The following section of code defines two global variables, g and h:

```
int   g, h;           // Global since defined before a function

  main()
  {
     // main()'s code goes here
  }
```

It really doesn't matter if your #include lines go before or after global variable declarations.

3. Global variables can appear before any function. In the following program, main() uses no variables at all. However, both functions before main() can use sales and profit because these variables are global.

```
// Filename: C19GLO.CPP
// Program that contains 2 global variables

#include <iostream.h>
#include <iomanip.h>

float     sales, profit; // 2 global variables

void third_fun(void)
{
     cout << "In the third function: \n";
     cout << "The sales in 3rd function is: "
          << setprecision(2) << sales << "\n";
     cout << "The profit in 3rd function is: "
        << setprecision(2) << profit << "\n";
    // If sales and profit were local, they would not be
    // visible by more than one function
     return;
}

void do_fun(void)
{
     sales = 20000.00;   // This variable is visible from
                         // this point down.
     profit = 5000.00;   // So is this one. They are both
                         // global.
     cout << "The sales in the 2nd function is: "
```

```
              << setiosflags(ios::fixed) << setprecision(2)
              << sales << "\n";
     cout << "The profit in the 2nd function is: "
              << setprecision(2) << profit << "\n\n";
     third_fun();          // Call 3rd function to show that
                           // globals are visible
     return;
   }


   main()
   {
     cout << "No variables defined in main()\n\n";
     do_fun();            // Call the first function
     return 0;
   }
```

A global variable is visible from its point of definition down into the program. Statements appearing before global variable definitions cannot use those variables. Figure 19.1 shows the result of running the preceding program.

Figure 19.1

A demonstration
of global variables.

```
                         Stdin/Stdout/Stderr
No variables defined in main()

The sales in the 2nd function is: 20000.00
The profit in the 2nd function is: 5000.00

In the third function:
The sales in 3rd function is: 20000.00
The profit in 3rd function is: 5000.00
```

Tip: Declare all global variables at the top of your programs. Even though you can define such variables later, between any two functions, you will be able to spot the variables faster when making changes to your programs.

4. The following program uses both local and global variables. It should now be obvious to you that j and p are local and that i and z are global.

```
// Filename: C19GLLO.CPP
// Program with both local and global variables
// Global Variables        Local Variables
```

```
//      i, z                        j, p

#include <iostream.h>
#include <iomanip.h>

float     z = 9.0;  // Global variable since defined before
                    // a function

void pr_again(void)
{
    int  j = 5;     // Local to pr_again() only

    cout << j << " " << z << "\n";
          // This couldn't print p or i!
    return;   // Return to main()
}

int  i = 0;            // Global variable since defined outside
                       // main()

main()
{
    float     p;   // Local to main() only

    p = 9.0;           // Put value in global variable
    cout << i << "  " << p << " " << z << "\n";
    // Print global i and local p
    pr_again();    // Call next function
    return 0;      // Return to DOS
}
```

Even though j is defined in a function that main() calls, main() cannot use j because j is local to pr_again(). When pr_again() finishes, j completely goes away. The variable z is global from its point of definition on. That is why pr_again() could not print i. The function pr_again() cannot print p because p is a local variable to main() only.

Make sure that you can recognize local and global variables before continuing. A little study here makes the rest of the chapter very easy.

5. Two variables, local to two different functions, can have the same name. They are distinct variables, even though their names are identical.

The following short program uses two variables, both named age. They have two different values, and they are considered two very different variables. The first age is local to main(), and the second age is local to get_age().

```cpp
// Filename: C19LOC2.CPP
// Two different local variables with the same name

#include <iostream.h>

void get_age(void)
{
    int  age;       // A different age - this one is local
                    // to get+age()

    cout << "What is your age again? ";
    cin >> age;
    return;
}

main()
{
    int  age;

    cout << "What is your age? ";
    cin >> age;

    get_age();      // Call the second function
    cout << "main()'s age is still: " << age << "\n";
    return 0;
}
```

The output of this program is shown next. Study it carefully. Notice that main()'s last cout << does not print the newly changed age. Instead, cout << prints the only age known to main()— the age that is local to main(). Even though these variables have the same name, main()'s age has nothing to do with get_age()'s age. They might as well have different variable names.

```
What is your age? 28
What is your age again? 56
main()'s age is still 28
```

You should be careful when naming variables. Having two variables with the same name is misleading. It would be easy to get confused when changing this program later. If these variables truly need to be separate, name them differently, such as old_age and new_age, or ag1 and ag2. That convention helps you see immediately that they are quite different.

6. There are a few times when overlapping the names of local variables does not add to confusion, but you should be careful about overdoing it. Sometimes programmers use the same variable name as the name of the counter variable in a for loop. The following program illustrates an acceptable use of two local variables with the same name:

```cpp
// Filename: C19LOC3.CPP
// Using two local variables with the same name as counting
// variables

#include <iostream.h>

void do_fun(void)
{
    int   ctr;

    for (ctr = 10; ctr >= 0; ctr—)
    {
        cout << "do_fun()'s ctr is: " << ctr << "\n";
    }
    return;         // Return to main()
}

main()
{
    int   ctr;      // Loop counter

    for (ctr = 0; ctr <= 10; ctr++)
    {
        cout << "main()'s ctr is: " << ctr << "\n";
    }
    do_fun();       // Call second function
    return 0;
}
```

Although this is a nonsense program that simply prints 0 through 10 and then prints 10 through 0, the use of ctr in both functions is not a problem. These variables do not hold important data that will be processed; instead, they serve as for loop counting variables. Calling them both ctr will cause little confusion as their use is limited to control for loops only. Because a for loop initializes and increments variables, neither function relies on the other's ctr to do anything.

7. Be very careful about creating local variables with the same names in the same function. If a local variable is defined early in a function and another local variable with the same name is defined again inside a new block, C++ uses only the innermost variable, until its block ends.

The following example helps clarify this confusing problem. The program contains one function with three local variables. See if you can find the three variables.

```cpp
// Filename: C19MULI.CPP
// Program with multiple local variables called i

#include <iostream.h>

main()
{
    int   i;          // Outer i

    i = 10;
    {
        int   i;    // New block's i

        i = 20;    // Outer i STILL holds a 10
        cout << i << " " << i << "\n";      // Print 20 20
        {
            int   i;    // Another new block and local
                        // variable

            i = 30;    // Innermost i only
            cout << i << " " << i << " " << i << "\n";
                // Print 30 30 30
        }              // Innermost i is now gone forever
    }          // Second i is gone forever (its block ended)
    cout << i << " " << i << " " << i << "\n";
        // Print 10 10 10
    return 0;
}          // main() ends and so does its variables
```

All local variables are local to the block in which they are defined. This program has three blocks, each one nested within another. Because you can define local variables immediately after an opening brace of a block, there are three distinct i variables in this program.

The local i disappears completely when its block ends (that is, when the closing brace is reached). C++ always prints the variable it sees as the "most local."

Use Global Variables Rarely

You may be asking yourself, "So why do I need to know about global and local variables?" At this point, that's an understandable question, especially if you've programmed only in BASIC until now. Here is the bottom line: global variables can be dangerous. Code can inadvertently overwrite a variable that was initialized in another place in the program. It is better to have every variable in your program be local to the function that needs to access it.

Please read that last sentence once more. Even though you now know how to make variables global, you should not do so! Try to stay away from ever using another global variable. It may seem easier to use global variables when writing programs with more than one function; if you make every variable that is used by every function global, you never have to worry whether or not one is visible to a certain function. However, a function can accidentally change a global variable when the function has no right to do so. If you keep variables local to functions that need them, you protect their values and keep your programs, both the code and the data, fully modular.

The Need for Passing Variables

You just learned the difference between local and global variables. You saw that by making your variables local, you protect their values because the function that sees a variable is the only one that can modify the variable.

What do you do, though, if you have a local variable that you want to use in two or more functions? In other words, you may need a variable to be typed from the keyboard in one function, yet that same variable needs to be printed in another function. If the variable is local to the first function, how can the second function access it?

If two functions need to share a variable, you have two alternatives. One way is to declare the variable globally. This alternative is bad because you want only those two functions to "see" the variable, yet all functions could "see" it if it were global. The better way is to pass the local variable from one function to another. This alternative has a big advantage— the variable is known only to the two functions, and the rest of the program will not be able to access the variable.

> **Caution:** Never pass a global variable. This method is a bit confusing to those who have to read the code in the future. Besides, the global variable is already visible to all functions following its definition.

You pass an argument when you pass one local variable to another function.

When you pass a local variable from one function to another, you are passing an argument from the first function to the next. You can pass more than one argument (variable) at a time if you want several local variables sent from one function to another. The receiving function receives parameters (variables) from the function that sent them. You should not worry too much about what you call these variables—either arguments or parameters. The important thing is that you are simply sending local variables from one function to another.

> **Note:** You already passed arguments to parameters when you passed data to the `cout` statement. The constants, variables, and expressions in the `cout` statement were arguments. The library `cout` function received those values (called parameters on its receiving end) and displayed them.

You need to know some additional terminology before you look at examples. When a function passes parameters, it is called the *calling function*. The function that receives those arguments (called parameters when they are received) is called the *receiving function*. Figure 19.2 shows a diagram that explains these new terms.

Figure 19.2

The calling and receiving functions.

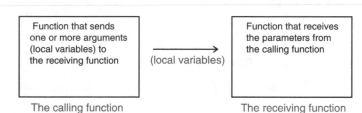

To pass a local variable from one function to another, you must place the local variable in parentheses in both the calling and receiving functions. For example, the local and global examples presented earlier did not pass local variables from `main()` to `do_fun()`. If a function name has empty parentheses, nothing is being passed to it. Given this, the following line passes two variables, `total` and `discount`, to a function called `do_fun()`:

```
do_fun(total, discount);
```

It is sometimes said that a variable or function is defined. This has absolutely nothing to do with the #define preprocessor directive that defines constants. You define variables with such statements as these:

```
int       i, j;
int       m = 9;
float     x;
char      ara[ ] = "Tulsa";
```

These statements tell the program that these variables are needed and you want them reserved. A function is defined when the C++ compiler reads the function's first statement that describes the name and any variables that may have been passed to it. Never follow a function definition with a semicolon, but always follow the statement that calls a function with a semicolon.

Note: To some C++ purists, a variable is declared only when you write int i;, and it is truly defined only when you assign it a value such as i = 7;. They say that the variable is both declared and defined when you declare it and assign it a value at the same time, such as int i = 7;.

The following program contains two function definitions, main() and pr_it().

The start of the main() function.
   Initialize the integer variable i to 5.
   Call the pr_it function, passing the i variable with the value of 5.
   Jump down to the function pr_it.
      Print the value of i to the screen and return to the next line.
      Return to the main() function.
      Return to DOS.

```
main()                   // The main() function definition
{
     int  i = 5;         // Define an integer variable

     pr_it(i);           // Call the pr_it() function and
                         // pass it i
     return 0;           // Return to DOS
}

void pr_it(int i)        // The pr_it() function definition
{
     cout << i << "\n";  // Call the cout function
     return;             // Return to main()
}
```

Because a passed parameter is treated like a local variable in the receiving function, the cout in pr_it() prints a 5, even though main() was the function that initialized this variable.

When you pass arguments to a function, the receiving function has no idea of the data types of the incoming variables. Therefore, you must include each parameter's data type in front of the parameter's name. In the preceding example, the definition of pr_it() (the first line of the function) contains the type, int, of the incoming variable i. Notice that the main() calling function does not need to indicate the variable type. In this example, main() already knows what type of variable i is (an integer); only pr_it() needs to know that i is an integer.

> **Tip:** C++ requires you to declare the type of the parameters in the receiving function. Precede each parameter in the function's parentheses with int, float, or whatever each passed variable's data type is.

Examples

1. Following is a main() function that contains three local variables. main() passes one of the variables to the first function, and two of the variables to the second function.

```cpp
// Filename: C19LOC1.CPP
// Passes 3 local variables to functions

#include <iostream.h>
#include <iomanip.h>


void pr_init(char initial)      // NEVER put a semicolon after
                                // a function definition
{
    cout << "Your initial is really " << initial << "? \n";
    return;                     // Return to main()
}

void pr_other(int age, float salary)    // MUST type BOTH
                                        // parameters
{
    setiosflags( ios::fixed );
    cout << "You look young for " << age << "\n";
    cout << "And $" << salary
```

```
            << " is a LOT of money!";
      return;                    // Return to main()
}

main()
{
      char      initial;        // 3 variables local to main()
      int       age;
      float     salary;

      // Fill these variables in main()
      cout << "What is your initial? ";
      cin >> initial;
      cout << "What is your age? ";
      cin >> age;
      cout << "What is your salary? ";
      cin >> salary;
      pr_init(initial);          // Call pr_init() and pass it
                                 // initial

      pr_other(age, salary);     // Call pr_other() and pass
                                 // it other 2

      return 0;
}
```

2. A receiving function can contain its own local variables. As long as the names are not the same, these local variables will not conflict with the passed ones. In the following program, the second function receives a passed variable from main() and also defines its own local variable called price_per.

```
// Filename: C19LOC4.CPP
// Second function has its own local variable

#include <iostream.h>
#include <iomanip.h>

void compute_sale(int gallons)
{
      float     price_per = 12.45;  // Local to
                                    // compute_sale()

      cout << "The total is: $" << setprecision(2)
            << (price_per * (float)gallons) << "\n";
```

```
        // Had to type cast gallons since it was integer
        return;                        // Return to main()
}


main()
{
    int  gallons;

    cout << "Richard's Paint Service\n";
    cout << "How many gallons of paint did you buy?";
    cin >> gallons;            // Get gallons in main()
    compute_sale(gallons);     // Compute total in function
    return 0;
}
```

3. The following sample lines test your skill at recognizing calling and receiving functions. Being able to recognize the difference is half the battle of understanding them.

```
do_it()
```

The preceding code must be the first line of a new function because no semicolon appears at the end of the line.

```
do_it2(sales);
```

This calls a function called do_it2(). The calling function passes the variable called sales to do_it2().

```
pr_it(float total)
```

This is the first line of a function that receives a floating-point variable from the calling function. All receiving functions must specify the type of each variable being passed.

```
pr_them(float total, int number)
```

This is the first line of a function that receives two variables; one is a floating-point variable, and the other is an integer. This line cannot be calling the function pr_them because no semicolon appears at the end of the line.

Automatic and Static Variables

The terms *automatic* and *static* describe what happens to local variables when a function returns to the calling procedure. By default, all local variables are automatic. This means that local variables are erased completely when their function ends. To declare a variable as an automatic variable, prefix its definition with the word `auto`. Because all local variables are automatic by default, the `auto` is optional. Look at the two statements after `main()`'s opening brace:

```
main()
{
    int          i;
    auto float   x;
    // Rest of main() goes here
```

Both of these statements declare automatic local variables. Because `auto` is the default, x does not really need it. C++ programmers rarely use the `auto` keyword, as all local variables are automatic by default.

Automatic variables are local and disappear when their function ends. The opposite of an automatic variable is a static variable. All global variables are static. Local static variables are not erased when their functions end. If local, a static variable retains its value when its function ends, in case the function is ever called a second time. To declare a variable as static, place the keyword `static` in front of the variable when you define it. The following section of code defines three variables: i, j, and k. The variable i is automatic, but j and k are static.

```
my_fun()                    // Start of new function definition
{
    int          i;
    static int   j = 25;    // Both j and k are static
                            // variables
    static int   k = 30;
```

If local variables are static, their values remain in case the function is called again. Always assign an initial value to a static variable when you declare it, as in the last two lines of the preceding code. That initial value will be placed there only the first time `my_fun()` executes. If you do not assign a static variable an initial value, C++ will initialize the static variable to zero.

> **Tip:** Static variables are good to use when you write functions that keep track of a count or that add to a total when called. If the counting or total variables were local and automatic, their values would disappear when the function ended, destroying the totals.

Rules for Automatic and Static Variables

A local automatic variable disappears when its block ends. All local variables are automatic by default. You can either prefix a variable (at its definition time) with the auto keyword or leave it off; the variable will still be automatic, and its value will be destroyed when the block in which the variable is local ends.

A local static variable does not lose its value when its function ends. The static variable remains local to that function. When the function is called after the first time, the static variable's value is still in place. As noted, you declare a static variable by placing the static keyword before a variable's definition.

Examples

1. Consider the following program:

```
// Filename: C19STA1.CPP
// Attempts to use a static variable without a static
// declaration
#include <iostream.h>

void triple_it(int ctr)
{
    int  total, ans;   // Local automatic variables

    // Triple whatever value is passed to it and add up
    // the total

    total = 0;      // Will hold total of all numbers
                    // tripled

    ans = ctr * 3; // Triple number passed
    total += ans;  // Add up triple numbers as this is
                   // called

    cout << "The number " << ctr
         << ", multiplied by 3 is: " << ans << "\n";

    if (total > 100)
    {
        cout << "The total of the triple numbers ";
        cout << "is over 100\n";
    }
```

```
        return;
    }

main()
{
    int  ctr;        // Used for the for loop to call
                     // a function 10 times

    for (ctr = 1; ctr <= 10; ctr++)
    {
        triple_it(ctr);      // Pass function called
                             // triple_it() the ctr

    }
    return 0;
}
```

This is a nonsense program that does not do much, yet if you look at it, you may sense that something is wrong. The program passes numbers from 1 to 10 to the function called `triple_it`. The function triples the number and prints it.

The variable called `total` is initially set to 0. The idea is to add up the triple numbers and print a message when the total of the triples goes over 100. However, that `cout` will never execute. Each of the 10 times this subroutine is called, `total` gets set back to 0 again. `total` is an automatic variable whose value is erased and initialized each time its procedure is called. The next example fixes this problem.

2. If you want `total` to retain its value, even after the procedure ends, you have to make it static. A local variable is automatic by default, so the `static` keyword overrides the default and makes the variable static. The variable's value is then retained each time the subroutine is called.

The following program corrects the intent of the preceding program:

```
// Filename: C19STA2.CPP
// Uses a static variable with the static declaration

#include <iostream.h>

void triple_it(int ctr)
{
    static int    total = 0;     // Local and static
    int           ans;           // Local and automatic
```

```
        // Triple whatever value is passed to it and add up
        // the total

        // total will be set to 0 only the FIRST time this
        // function is called

        ans = ctr * 3; // Triple number passed
        total += ans;  // Add up triple numbers as this is
                       // called

        cout << "The number " << ctr
             << ", multiplied by 3 is: " << ans << "\n";

        if (total > 100)
        {
            cout << "The total of the triple numbers ";
            cout << "is over 100\n";
        }
        return;
    }

main()
{
    int  ctr;      // Used for the for loop to call
                   // a function 10 times

    for (ctr = 1; ctr <= 10; ctr++)
    {
        triple_it(ctr);      // Pass function called
                             // triple_it() the ctr
    }
    return 0;
}
```

Figure 19.3 shows this program's output. Notice that the function's cout is triggered, even though total is a local variable. Because total is static, its value is not erased when the function finishes. When the function is called a second time by main(), total's previous value (when you left the routine) is still there.

Figure 19.3
Using a static
variable.

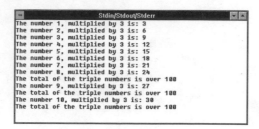

This does not mean that local static variables become global. The main program cannot refer to, use, print, or change total because it is local to the second function. *Static* simply means that the local variable's value will still be there if the program calls that function again.

Three Issues of Parameter Passing

To have a complete understanding of multiple functions, you need to learn three additional concepts:

1. Passing arguments (variables) by value (or "by copy")

2. Passing arguments (variables) by address (or "by reference")

3. Returning values from functions

The first two items deal with the way local variables are passed and received. The third item describes the way that receiving functions send values back to the calling functions. The next chapter focuses on these methods of passing parameters and returning values.

Summary

The concept of parameter passing is important to know because local variables are better than global ones; local variables are protected in their own functions but are shared among other functions. If the local data is to remain in those variables, in case the function is called again in the same program, the variables should be made static; if they are automatic, their values would disappear.

Most of the information in this chapter will become clearer as you use functions in your own programs. The next chapter provides more detail about the passing of parameters and shows two different ways to pass them.

Review Questions

Answers to Review Questions are in Appendix B.

1. True or false: Even though it is not required, a function should always include a `return` statement as its last command.

2. What is a local variable called when it is passed an argument or a parameter?

3. True or false: A function that is passed variables from another function cannot have its own local variables as well.

4. What must appear inside the receiving function's parentheses, besides the variables passed to it?

5. If a function keeps track of a total or count every time it is called, should the counting or total variable be automatic or static?

6. When would you pass a global variable to a function?

7. How many arguments are there in the following statement?

```
cout << "The rain has fallen " << rainf << " inches.\n";
```

Review Exercises

1. Write a program to ask for the following in `main()`:

    The age of the user's dog

   Write a second function, called `people()`, that computes the dog's age in "people" years (multiplying the dog's age by 7 to get the equivalent people years).

2. Write a function that counts the number of times the function is called. Name the function `count_it()`. Do not pass it anything. Print the following message in the body of `count_it()`:

    ```
    The number of times this function has been called is: ##
    ```

   ## is the actual number.

   (*Hint:* Because the variable must be local, make it static and initialize it to zero when you first define it.)

3. The following program contains several problems, some of which produce errors. One problem (for a hint, find all global variables) is not an error but is a bad location of a variable declaration. See if you can spot some of the problems in the program and rewrite it so that it works better.

```cpp
// Filename: C19BAD.CPP
// Program with bad uses of variable declarations

#include <iostream.h>

#define NUM 10

char city[ ] = "Miami";
int  count;

main()
{
    int  abc;

    count = NUM;
    abc = 5;
    do_var_fun();

    cout << abc << " " << count << " " << pgm_var << " "
        << xyz;
    return 0;
}

int  pgm_var = 7;

void do_var_fun(void)
{
    char xyz = 'A';

    xyz = 'b';
    cout << xyz << " " << pgm_var << " " << abc << " "
        << city;
    return;
}
```

CHAPTER 20

Passing Values

C++ provides two methods for passing variables between functions. This chapter explores both methods. The one you use depends on how you want to use the passed variables—whether or not you want to change the passed variables in the called function.

The concepts discussed here are not new to the C++ language. Other programming languages—such as Pascal, FORTRAN, and QBasic—pass parameters with similar techniques. A computer language must have the capability to pass information between functions in order to be truly structured.

This chapter introduces the following topics:

♦ Passing variables by value

♦ Passing arrays by address

♦ Passing nonarrays by address

Pay close attention to this chapter; it explains these special passing issues. Most of the programs in the rest of the book rely on the methods described in this chapter.

Passing by Value (or by Copy)

The phrases *passing by value* and *passing by copy* mean the same thing in computer terms. Some textbooks and C++ programmers say that arguments are passed by value, and some say that they are passed by copy. Both describe one of the two methods by which arguments are passed to receiving functions. (The other method, covered later in this chapter, is called *passing by address* or *passing by reference*.)

> **Note:** When an argument (local variable) is passed *by value*, a copy of the variable's value is assigned to the receiving function's parameter. If more than one variable is passed by value, a copy of each variable's value is assigned to the receiving function's parameters.

When passing by value, a copy of the variable's value is passed to the receiving function.

Figure 20.1 shows the action of passing an argument by value. The actual variable i is not passed, but the *value* of i, 5, is passed to the receiving function. There is not just one variable called i; there are actually two variables. The first variable is local to main(), and the second variable is local to pr_it(). Both variables have the same name, but because they are local to their respective functions, no conflict exists. The variable does not have to be called i in both functions; the value of i is sent to the receiving function, so it does not matter what the receiving function called the variable that receives the value.

Figure 20.1

Passing the variable *i* by value.

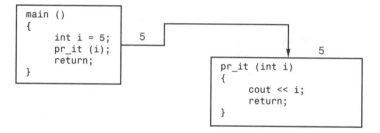

In this case, when passing and receiving variables among functions, the variables have retained the *same* names. Even though they are not the same variables, they hold the same value. In this example, the value of 5 is passed from main()'s i to pr_it()'s i.

Because a copy of i's value is passed to the receiving function (and *not* the actual variable), if pr_it() changed i, that function would be changing only its copy of i, not main()'s i. You have a technique to pass a copy of a variable to a receiving function, but the receiving function cannot modify the calling function's variable. You therefore have true separation of functions and variables.

All C++'s nonarray variables that you have seen so far are passed by value. You do not have to do anything special to pass variables by value except to pass them in the calling function's argument list, and receive them in the receiving function's parameter list.

> **Note:** The default method for passing parameters is by value, as just described, unless you pass arrays. Arrays are always passed by address, the other method described later in this chapter.

Examples

1. The following program asks for the user's weight. The program then passes the weight to a function that calculates the equivalent weight on the moon. Notice that the second function uses the passed value and calculates with it. After the weight is passed to the second function, that function can treat it as though it were a local variable.

Comments to identify the program.
Include the header file iostream.h.
Start of the moon() *function.*
   Take the value of weight *and divide it by 6.*
   Print You weigh only X pounds on the moon! *to the screen.*
   Return out of the moon() *function.*
Start of the main() *function.*
   Declare the variable weight *as an integer.*
   Print How many pounds do you weigh? *to the screen.*
   Obtain an integer from the keyboard.
   Call the moon() *function and pass it the variable* weight.
   Return out of the main() *function.*

```cpp
// Filename: C20PASS1.CPP
// Calculates the user's weight in a second function

#include <iostream.h>

void    moon(int weight)    // Declare the passed parameter
{
    // Moon weights are 1/6th that of Earth weights
    weight /= 6;                // Divide the weight by 6

    cout << "You weigh only " << weight
        << " pounds on the moon!\n";
    return;                    // Return to main()
}

main()
{
    int    weight;    // main()'s local weight

    cout << "How many pounds do you weigh? ";
    cin >> weight;
```

```
    moon(weight);       // Call the moon() function and pass
                        // it the weight
    return 0;           // Return to DOS
}
```

The output of this program is as follows:

```
How many pounds do you weigh? 120
You weigh only 20 pounds on the moon!
```

2. You can rename a passed variable in the receiving function. That variable is distinct from the calling function's variable. Following is the same program that is in example 1, except that the receiving function calls the passed variable earth_weight. A new variable, moon_weight, which is local to the receiving function, is used for the moon's equivalent weight.

```cpp
// Filename: C20PASS2.CPP
// Calculates the user's weight in a second function

#include <iostream.h>

void    moon(int earth_weight)          // Declare the passed
                                        // parameter
{
    int     moon_weight;

    // Moon weights are 1/6th that of Earth weights
    moon_weight = earth_weight / 6;  // Divide the weight
                                     // by 6

    cout << "You weigh only " << moon_weight
         << " pounds on the moon!\n";
    return;                             // Return to main()
}

main()
{
    int     weight;     // main()'s local weight

    cout << "How many pounds do you weigh? ";
    cin >> weight;
    moon(weight);       // Call the moon() function and
                        // pass it the weight
    return 0;           // Return to DOS
}
```

The resulting output is identical to that of the first program. Renaming the passed variable changes nothing.

3. You can pass the same variable to more than one receiving function. Here is the same program from Example 2, but now there are two different receiving functions. The additional function computes and prints the equivalent weight on Jupiter.

```cpp
// Filename: C20PASS3.CPP
// Calculates the user's weight in multiple functions

#include <iostream.h>

void    moon(int earth_weight)          // Declare the passed
                                        // parameter
{
    int    moon_weight;

    // Moon weights are 1/6th that of Earth weights
    moon_weight = earth_weight / 6;   // Divide the weight
                                      // by 6

    cout << "You weigh only " << moon_weight
         << " pounds on the moon!\n";
    return;                             // Return to main()
}
void    jupiter(int earth_weight)       // Declare the passed
                                        // parameter
{
    float    jupiter_weight;

    // Jupiter weights are 2.64 times that of Earth weights
    jupiter_weight = earth_weight * 2.64;

    cout << "You weigh " << jupiter_weight
         << " pounds on Jupiter!\n";
    return;                             // Return to main()
}

main()
{
    int    weight;   // main()'s local weight
```

```
cout << "How many pounds do you weigh? ";
cin >> weight;

moon(weight);      // Call the moon() function and
                   // pass it the weight
jupiter(weight);   // Do the same with jupiter()

return 0;          // Return to DOS
}
```

Here is the output from this program:

```
How many pounds do you weigh? 120
You weigh only 20 pounds on the moon!
You weigh 316.8 pounds on Jupiter!
```

4. The following program passes three variables, of three different types, to the receiving function. In the receiving function's parameter list, each of these variable types must be declared.

This program prompts the user for three values in the `main()` function. `main()` then passes those variables to the receiving function, which calculates and prints values related to those passed variables. Notice again that when the receiving function modifies a variable passed to it, it does *not* affect the calling function's variable. When variables are passed by value, the value—not the variable—is passed.

```
// Filename: C20PASS4.CPP
// Gets grade information for a student

#include <iostream.h>

void     check_grade(char lgrade, float average, int tests)
{
    switch (tests)
    {
        case    0:
            cout << "You will get your current grade of "
                << lgrade << "\n";
            break;
        case 1:
            cout << "You still have time to ";
            cout << "bring your average ";
            cout << "of " << average <<
                " up.   Study hard!\n";
```

```
                    break;
            default:
                    cout << "Relax — You still have ";
                    cout << "plenty of time.\n";
                    break;
        }
    return;
}


main()
{
    char        lgrade;    // Letter grade
    int         tests;     // Number of tests yet taken
    float       average;   // Student's average based on
                           // 4.0 scale

    cout << "What letter grade do you want? ";
    cin >> lgrade;
    cout << "What is your current test average? ";
    cin >> average;
    cout << "How many tests do you have left? ";
    cin >> tests;

    check_grade(lgrade, average, tests);  // Call function
                        // and pass 3 variables by value
    return 0;
}
```

Passing by Address

The phrases "passing by address" and "passing by reference" mean the *very same thing*. Some textbooks and C++ programmers say that arguments are passed by address, and some say that they are passed by reference. This interchangeable usage was fine for C programmers, but C++ has added another method of passing variables known as *reference variables*, which are not quite the same thing as "passing by reference."

To avoid confusion, this book uses "passing by address" to mean the technique discussed in the following part of this chapter, and "reference passing" to refer to the C++ style reference variable. The first part of this chapter described the passing of arguments by value (or by copy). This section describes the passing of arguments by address. The final section of this chapter describes reference passing.

When a variable is passed by address, the address of the variable is passed to the receiving function.

When you pass an argument (local variable) by address, the variable's address is assigned to the receiving function's parameter. (If you pass more than one variable by address, each of their addresses is assigned to the receiving function's parameters.)

All variables in memory (RAM) are stored at memory addresses. Figure 20.2 illustrates addresses of memory. If you want more detail on your memory's internal representation, refer to Appendix A.

Figure 20.2

Memory addresses.

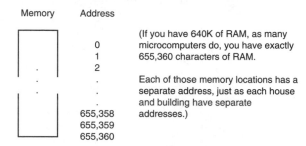

When you tell C++ to define a variable (such as int i;), you are requesting that C++ find a blank place in memory and assign that memory's address to i. When your program prints or uses the variable called i, C++ knows to go to i's address and print what is there.

Note how five variables are defined:

```
int        i;
float      x = 9.8;
char       ara[ 2 ] = {'A', 'B'};
int        j = 8, k = 3;
```

C++ might arbitrarily place these variables in memory at the addresses shown in figure 20.3.

Figure 20.3

After variables are defined and placed in memory.

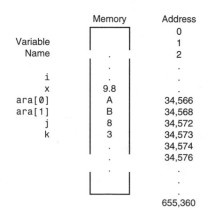

You don't know what is in the variable called i because you have not yet put anything in it. Before you use i, you should initialize it with a value. (All variables except character variables usually take more than one byte of memory.)

As noted, the address of the variable—not its value—is copied to the receiving function when you pass a variable by address. In C++, *all arrays are passed by address*. (Actually, a copy of the array's address is passed, but you will understand this better when you learn more about arrays and pointers in Part VI of this book.) The following important rule holds true for programs that pass by address:

> Every time you pass a variable by address, if the receiving function changes the variable, it is also changed in the calling function.

Therefore, if you pass an array to a function and that function changes the array, the change will still be with the array when the function returns to the calling function. Unlike passing by value, passing by address enables you to change a variable in the receiving function and keep the change in effect in the calling function. The following sample program helps illustrate this concept.

All C++ arrays are passed by address.

```
// Filename: C20ADD1.CPP
// Program that passes by address

#include <iostream.h>
#include <string.h>

void     change_it(char c[ 4 ]) // You MUST tell the
                                // function that c is an array
{
    cout << c << "\n";      // Print as it is passed
    strcpy(c, "USA");       // Change the array, both here
                            // AND in main()

    return;
}

main()
{
    char     name[ 4 ] = "ABC";

    change_it(name);        // Pass by address since it is
                            // an array
    cout << name << "\n";   // Called function can change
                            // array

    return 0;
}
```

Following is the output of this program:

```
ABC
USA
```

At this point, you should have no trouble understanding that the array is passed from main() to the function called change_it(). Even though change_it() calls the array c, that function refers to the same array passed to it, which was called name in the main() function.

Figure 20.4 shows how the array is passed. The value of the array is not passed from name to c, but both arrays are the same thing.

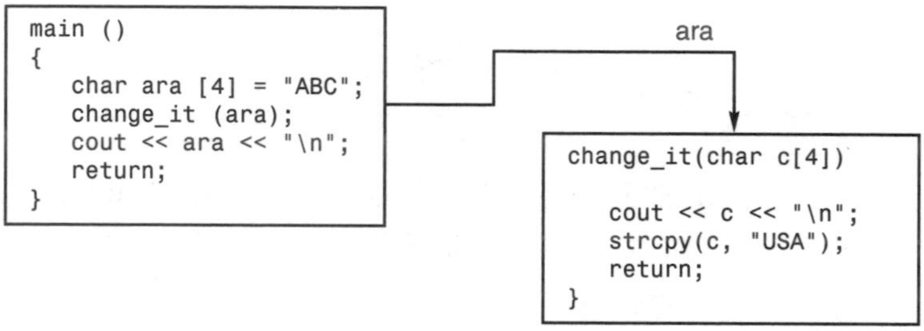

Figure 20.4

Passing an array by address.

```
main ()
{
    char ara [4] = "ABC";
    change_it (ara);
    cout << ara << "\n";
    return;
}
```

ara

```
change_it(char c[4])

    cout << c << "\n";
    strcpy(c, "USA");
    return;
}
```

Before going any further, a few additional comments are needed. Because the actual address of name is passed to the function, even though the array is called c in the receiving function, c is still the same array as name. Figure 20.5 shows how C++ accomplishes this at the memory address level.

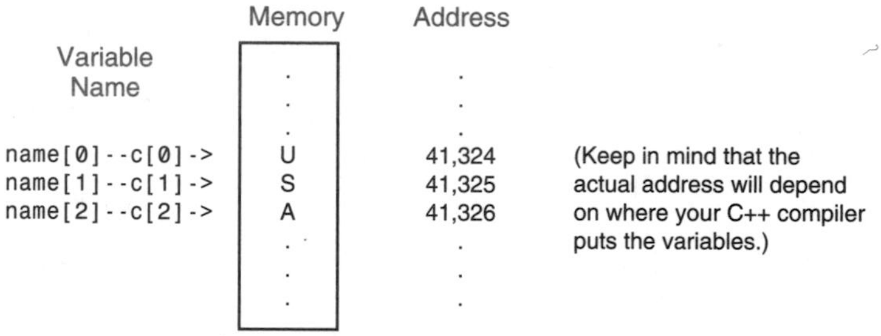

Figure 20.5

The array being passed is the same as that of the receiving function, despite the different names.

Variable Name	Memory	Address	
name[0]--c[0]->	U	41,324	(Keep in mind that the
name[1]--c[1]->	S	41,325	actual address will depend
name[2]--c[2]->	A	41,326	on where your C++ compiler puts the variables.)

The variable array is referred to as name in main(), but as c in change_it(). The address of name is copied to the receiving function, so the variable gets changed no matter what it is called in either function. Because change_it() changes the array, it is also changed in main().

Examples

1. You can now use a function to fill an array with user input. The following program asks for the user's first name in the function called get_name(). As the user types the name in the array, the name is also being typed into main()'s array. main() then passes the array to pr_name(), where it is printed.

You should realize that if arrays were passed by value, this program would not work. Only the array value would be passed to the receiving functions.

```
// Filename: C20ADD2.CPP
// Gets a name in an array and then prints it,
// using separate functions

#include <iostream.h>

void    get_name(char name[ 25 ])     // Pass the array
                                      // by address
{
    cout << "What is your first name? ";
    cin >> name;
    return;
}

void    print_name(char name[ 25 ])
{
    cout << "\n\n Here it is: " << name << "\n";
    return;
}

main()
{
    char    name[ 25 ];

    get_name(name);        // Get the user's name
    print_name(name);      // Print the user's name
    return 0;
}
```

When you pass an array, be sure to specify the array's type in the receiving function's parameter list. If the preceding program declared the passed array with

```
get_name(char name)
```

the function get_name() would think that it were being passed a single character variable, *not* a character array. You don't have to put the array size in the brackets. The following statement would work as the first line of get_name():

```
get_name(char name[ ])
```

Most C++ programmers put the array size in the brackets to help future readers of the code remember the size of the array, even though it isn't necessary.

2. Many programmers pass character arrays to functions in order to erase the arrays. Here is a function called clear_it(). It expects two parameters: a character array and the total number of elements declared for that array. The array is passed by address (as all arrays are), and the number of elements, num_els, is passed by value (as all nonarrays are). When the function finishes, the array will be cleared (all its elements will be set to null zero). Subsequent functions that use the array will then have a fresh array.

```
clear_it(char ara[ 10 ], int num_els)
{
    int      ctr;

    for (ctr = 0; ctr <= num_els; ctr++)
        {
        ara[ ctr ] = '\0';
        }
    return;
}
```

The ara brackets do not need to have a number, as indicated in the last example. The 10 in this example simply serves as a placeholder for the brackets. Any value (or no value) that you want to substitute will work too.

Passing Nonarrays by Address

You can pass nonarrays by address as well.

You should now understand the difference between passing variables by value and by address. You can pass arrays by address and pass nonarrays by value. You can override the default passing by value for nonarrays if you want. This is not always recommended because the called function can damage values in the calling function, but it is sometimes helpful.

If you want a nonarray variable changed in a receiving function, and you want the change also kept in the calling function, you must override C++'s default (passing by value) and pass the variable by address. (You will better understand this section once you learn how arrays and pointers relate.) To pass a nonarray by address, you must do the following:

1. Precede the variable in the calling function with an ampersand (&) symbol.

2. Precede the variable in the receiving function with an asterisk (*) everywhere the variable appears.

This technique might sound strange, and it is at this point. Not many C++ programmers override the default passing by value. When you learn about pointers, you will have little need for this technique. Most C++ programmers do not like to clutter their code with those extra ampersands and asterisks, but they know they can use them if necessary.

The next section demonstrates how to pass nonarray variables by address.

Examples

1. The following program passes a nonarray variable by address from `main()` to a function. The function changes the variable and returns to `main()`. Because the variable is passed by address, `main()` recognizes the new value.

```cpp
// Filename: C20ADD3.CPP
// Demonstrates passing nonarrays by address

#include <iostream.h>

void    do_fun(int *amt)      // Inform function of passing
                              // by address
{
    *amt = 85;                // Assign new value to amt
    cout << "In do_fun(), amt is " << *amt << "\n";
    return;
}
```

```
main()
{
    int     amt;

amt = 100;           // Assign a value in main()
    cout << "In main(), amt is " << amt << "\n";
    do_fun(&amt);        // The & means to pass it by address
    cout << "After return, amt is " << amt
            << " in main()\n";
    return 0;
}
```

The output of this program is as follows:

```
In main(), amt is 100
In do_fun(), amt is 85
After return, amt is 85 in main()
```

Notice that amt changed in the receiving function. Because amt was passed by address, it gets changed also in the calling function.

2. You can use a function to get the user's keyboard values, and main() will recognize those values as long as you pass them by address. The following program calculates the cubic feet in a swimming pool by requesting the length, width, and depth in one function; calculates the cubic feet of water in another function; and then prints the answer in a third function. The purpose of main() is clearly to be a controlling function, passing variables between the functions by address.

```
// Filename: C20POOL.CPP
// Calculates cubic feet in a swimming pool

#include <iostream.h>

void    get_values(int *length, int *width, int *depth)
{
    cout << "What is the pool's length? ";
    cin >> *length;
    cout << "What is the pool's width? ";
    cin >> *width;
    cout << "What is the pool's average depth? ";
    cin >> *depth;
    return;
```

```
}

void    calc_cubic(int *length, int *width,
                   int *depth, int *cubic)
{
    // This may look confusing, but you MUST precede each
    // variable with an asterisk.
    *cubic = (*length) * (*width) * (*depth);
    return;
}

void    print_cubic(int *cubic)
{
    cout << "\nThe pool has " << *cubic << " cubic feet\n";
    return;
}


main()
{
    int     length, width, depth, cubic;

    get_values(&length, &width, &depth);
    calc_cubic(&length, &width, &depth, &cubic);
    print_cubic(&cubic);
    return 0;
}
```

The output of the program is as follows:

```
What is the pool's length? 16
What is the pool's width? 32
What is the pool's average depth? 6

The pool has 3072 cubic feet
```

C++ References

Visual C++ has another, much easier way to pass variables to a receiving function when you need to modify the original variable in the receiving function. It is known as *reference passing*, or a *reference variable*, or more simply, a *reference*. A *reference*, in this context, is not the same as the phrase *pass by reference*, which you have already learned refers to passing an address. A C++ *reference* is a new variable type that contains the address of another variable. At first, that may sound confusing, and you might (justifiably) wonder why bother with something that uses the same term, but in a different way, to mean almost the same thing.

There is one advantage to using *references* that shows up immediately—programs that pass *references* instead of addresses (or *pass by reference*) are easier to read, but you can still modify their values, just like a variable that has been passed by address. There are other benefits to *references* when you start working with classes and overloaded operators, but for now just concentrate on learning how to use a reference to pass a variable to a receiving function.

The syntax of passing a *reference* is quite simple.

1. In the calling function, just use the variable name, without any special symbols.

2. In the receiving function's parameter list, put an ampersand (&) immediately before each variable that is to receive a reference. The parameter list is the only place you need to use the ampersand in the receiving function. In the main body of the function, you again just use the variable name.

The following examples show how to use C++ *references*.

Examples

1. In this example, you write a function that will receive a *reference* by preceeding the receiving parameter names with an ampersand (&) in the function declaration. You do not need to use any special symbols in the function body when you use the variable.

```
// Filename: C20REF1
// Gets user's weight into a passed reference variable

#include <iostream.h>

void    get_weight( int& weight)  // & signals a reference
{
    cout << "How much do you weigh? ";
    cin >> weight;          // no special symbol,
                            // just use it.

    return;
}

main()
{
```

```
        int user_weight;

        get_weight( user_weight );      // looks just like
                                        // pass by value
        cout << "\nYou said that you weigh "
             << user_weight << " pounds.\n";
        return 0;
    }
```

Notice that in the get_weight() function, the ampersand is present only in the parameter list and is not used in the function body. In main(), the user_weight variable also is passed without any special symbol. As the output below shows, however, user_weight was modified by the get_weight() function.

Following is the output of the preceding example:

```
How much do you weigh? 145

You said that you weigh 145 pounds.
```

2. Here is the pool volume program you wrote earlier in which variables were passed by address. This version uses *references* instead. Compare the two program listings. Which one is easier to read and understand?

```
// Filename: C20POOL2.CPP
// Calculates cubic feet in a swimming pool

#include <iostream.h>

void    get_values(int& length, int& width, int& depth)
{
    cout << "What is the pool's length? ";
    cin >> length;
    cout << "What is the pool's width? ";
    cin >> width;
    cout << "What is the pool's average depth? ";
    cin >> depth;
    return;
}

void    calc_cubic(int &length, int &width,
                   int &depth, int &cubic)
```

```
{
     // This is much easier to read
     // (and to type)
     cubic = length * width * depth;
     return;
}

void     print_cubic(int& cubic)
{
     cout << "\nThe pool has " << cubic << " cubic feet\n";
     return;
}

main()
{
     int     length, width, depth, cubic;

     get_values(length, width, depth);
     calc_cubic(length, width, depth, cubic);
     print_cubic(cubic);
     return 0;
}
```

The output of the above program is the same as the original pool volume program.

You now know three ways to pass values to a function: pass by value, pass by address, and reference passing. The following example shows how these three methods look, all in the same program. Notice that you can use all three in one function call! (Not very many C++ programmers would choose to do so, however.)

```
void     called_func( int amt,

                      int *ans,

                      int &diff)
{

     *ans = amt * 5;

     diff = *ans - amt;
```

```
}

void    main()
{

    int amt = 5;
    int ans = 0;
    int diff = 0;


    called_func( amt,



            &ans,



            diff);


}
```

Summary

You now have a complete understanding of the various ways to pass data to functions. Because you will be using local variables as much as possible, you need to know how to pass them between functions so that they can share data, yet keep the data away from functions that don't need it.

There are three ways to pass data: by value, by address, and as a reference. When you pass data by value, which is the default method for nonarrays, only a copy of the variable's contents is passed. If the receiving function modifies its parameters, those variables are not modified in the calling function. When you pass data by address, as is done with arrays and nonarray variables preceded by an ampersand (&) in the calling function, the receiving function can change the data in both functions.

You can also pass a variable by reference by preceeding it with an ampersand (&) in the receiving function's parameter list, instead of in the calling function. When you use this method, you do not need to use extra symbols in the calling function or the body of the receiving function.

When passing values, you must ensure that they match in number and type. If you do not match them, the Visual C++ compiler will display error messages and not compile your program. This checking by C++ will prevent many potential problems. Suppose that you pass an array and a floating-point variable, but in the receiving function, you receive a floating-point variable followed by an array. The data would not get to the receiving function properly because the parameter data types do not match the variables being passed. The next chapter shows you how Visual C++ protects against such a disaster by using prototypes with all functions.

Review Questions

Answers to Review Questions are in Appendix B.

1. What kind of variable is always passed by address?

2. What kind of variable is always passed by value?

3. True or false: If a variable is passed by value, it is also passed by copy.

4. If a variable is passed to a function by value and the function changes that variable, will it be changed in the receiving function?

5. If a variable is passed to a function by address and the function changes that variable, will it be changed in the receiving function?

6. What is wrong with the following function?

```
do_fun(x, y, z)
{
    cout << "The variables are: " << x << ", " << y
        << ", and " << z;
    return;
}
```

7. If you pass an array *and* a nonarray variable to a function at the same time, which of the following is correct?

   a. Both variables are passed by address.

   b. Both variables are passed by value.

   c. One variable is passed by address, and the other variable is passed by value.

Review Exercises

1. Write a `main()` function and a second function that `main()` calls. Ask for the user's income in `main()`. Pass the income to the second function and print a congratulatory message if the user makes more than $50,000 or an encouragement message if the user makes less.

2. Write a three-function program, consisting of the following functions:

```
main()
fun1()
fun2()
```

Declare a 10-element character array in `main()`, fill it with the letters A through J in `fun1()`, and print that array backward in `fun2()`.

3. Write a program whose `main()` function passes a number to a function called `print_aster()`. The `print_aster()` function prints that many asterisks on a line, across the screen. If `print_aster()` is passed a number greater than 80, display an error, because most screens will not be able to print more than that. When finished, return control to `main()` and then return to the operating system.

4. Write a function that is passed two integer values by address. The function should declare a third local variable. Use the third variable as an intermediate variable and swap the values of both integers passed. In other words, if the calling function passes it `old_pay` and `new_pay`, as in

```
swap_it(old_pay, new_pay);
```

the function `swap_it()` should reverse the two values so that the `old_pay` and `new_pay` values are swapped when control is returned to the calling function.

5. Rewrite the program from Exercise 4 to use passed references instead of pass by address.

CHAPTER 21

Function Return Values and Prototypes

So far, you have passed all variables to functions in one direction: a calling function passes data to a receiving function. You have yet to see how data is passed back *from* the receiving function to the calling function. When you pass variables by address, or pass a reference, the data gets changed in both functions, but this is different from actually passing data back. This chapter shows you how to write functions that return values, which will greatly increase your programming power.

Once you begin to pass and return values, you also need to prototype every function you write. Visual C++ requires that all functions be prototyped. This is one way in which Visual C++ helps you ensure the accuracy of passed and return values.

This chapter, introduces the following topics:

♦ Returning values from functions

♦ Prototyping functions

♦ Understanding header files

This chapter concludes this book's coverage of functions. After you read the chapter, your programs will be truly modular. You will have the tools to write better, more powerful, and more accurate programs once you complete your understanding of functions and how to use them.

Function Return Values

Put the return value at the end of the *return* statement.

Until now, all functions in this book have been subroutines. A *subroutine* is a function that is called from another function but does not return any values. The difference between subroutines and functions that return values in C++ is not as critical as in other languages. All functions, whether they are subroutines or functions that return values, are defined in the same way. You can pass variables to each of them, as you have seen in this part of the book.

Functions that return values offer a new approach to using functions. Instead of data being passed in one direction, from calling function to receiving function, you can pass data back from a function to its calling function. When you want to return a value from a function to its calling function, put the return value after the return statement. To make the return value clearer, many programmers put parentheses around the return value, as in the following:

```
return (return value);
```

> **Caution:** Do not return global variables. This action is redundant because their values are already known throughout the code.

The calling function must have a use for the return value. Suppose that you write a function to calculate the average of three integer variables passed to it. If you return the average, the calling function will have to receive that return value. The following example helps illustrate this principle:

```cpp
// Filename: C21AVG.CPP
// Calculates the average of three input values

#include <iostream.h>

int     calc_av(int num1, int num2, int num3)
{
    int     local_avg;   // Holds average for these numbers

    local_avg = (num1 + num2 + num3) / 3;
    return (local_avg);
}


main()
{
    int     num1, num2, num3;
    int     avg;     // Will hold the return value
```

```
      cout << "Please type three numbers ";
      cout << "(such as 23, 54, 85)\n";
      cout << "Hit enter after each number.\n";
      cout << "  First number  ==> ";
      cin >> num1;
      cout << "  Second number ==> ";
      cin >> num2;
      cout << "  Third number  ==> ";
      cin >> num3;

      // Call the function, passing the numbers, and accept
      // return value
      avg = calc_av(num1, num2, num3);
      cout << "\n\n  The average is ==> " << avg << "\n";
      return 0;
   }
```

Note this sample output from the program:

```
Please type three numbers (such as 23, 54, 85)
Hit enter after each number.
  First number  ==> 121
  Second number ==> 19
  Third number  ==> 406


  The average is ==> 182
```

Study this program carefully. It is like many programs you have seen, but a few additional points should be considered now that the function returns a value. It may help to walk through this program a few lines at a time.

Put the function's return type before its name.

The early part of main() is similar to that of many programs in previous chapters. It declares its local variables—three for the user input, and one for the calculated average. The cout and cin are familiar to you. The function call to calc_av() is familiar too; it passes three variables—num1, num2, and num3—to the calc_av() by value. (If the function passed them by address, an ampersand (&) would have to precede each argument, as discussed in Chapter 20.)

The receiving function, calc_av(), looks like others you have seen except that the first line, the function's definition line, has one addition: the int before its name. This is the type of the return value. You must always precede a function name with its return data type. If you don't specify a type, C++ assumes that the return type is int. Without the return type indicated, this program would work just as well because an int return type would be assumed.

> **Note:** Although C++ assumes an int return type if no return type is specified, most experienced C++ programmers prefer to always specify the return type, even if the return type is *void*. This helps protect against errors in the same way as function prototypes, which are covered later in this chapter.

Since the variable local_avg, which is being returned from calc_av(), is an integer, the integer return type is placed before calc_av()'s name.

You can also see that the return statement of calc_av() includes the return value, local_avg. This is the variable being sent back to the calling function, main(). You can return only a single variable to a calling function. Note this rule for returning variables:

> Even though a function can receive more than one parameter, it can return only a single value to the calling function. If a receiving function is to modify more than one value from the calling function, you must pass the parameters by address; you cannot return multiple values by using a return statement.

Once the receiving function, calc_av(), returns the value, main() must do something with that returned value. So far, you have seen function calls on lines by themselves. Notice in main() that the function call appears on the right side of the following assignment statement:

```
avg = calc_av(num1, num2, num3);
```

When the calc_av() function returns its value (the average of the three numbers), that value *replaces* the function call. If the average computed in calc_av() is 40, the C++ compiler "sees" the following statement in place of the function call:

```
avg = 40;
```

You typed a function call to the right of the equal sign, but the program replaces the function call with its return value when the return takes place. In other words, a function that returns a value becomes that value. You *must* put such a function where you would put any variable or constant, usually to the right of an equal sign, or in an expression or cout. The following line is an incorrect way to call calc_av():

```
calc_av(num1, num2, num3);
```

If you used this line, C++ would have nothing to do with the return value of 40 (or whatever it happens to be).

Note: Function calls that return values usually never appear on lines by themselves. Because the function call is replaced by the return value, you should do something with that return value—for example, assign it to a variable or use it in an expression. Return values can be ignored, but doing so usually defeats the purpose of using them.

Examples

1. The following program passes a number to a function called `doub()`. The function doubles the number and returns the result.

```cpp
// Filename: C21DOUB.CPP
// Doubles the user's number

#include <iostream.h>

int     doub(int num)
{
    int     d_num;

    d_num = num * 2;     // Double the number
    return (d_num);      // Return the result
}


main()
{
    int     number;   // Holds user's input
    int     d_number; // Will hold double the user's input

    cout << "What number do you want doubled? ";
    cin >> number;
    d_number = doub(number);     // Assign return value
    cout << number << " doubled is " << d_number << "\n";
    return 0;
}
```

The program produces output like the following:

```
What number do you want doubled? 5
5 doubled is 10
```

2. Function return values can be used anywhere that constants, variables, and expressions are used. Notice that the following program is quite similar to the preceding one. The difference is found in main(). The function call is performed, not on a line by itself, but from within a cout.

This call is a nested function call. You call the cout, using the return value from one of the program's functions, named doub(). Because the call to doub() is replaced by its return value, the cout has enough information to proceed as soon as doub() returns. This keeps main() a little cleaner from the extra variable called d_number, although you must use your own judgment as to whether the program is easier to maintain. Sometimes it is wise to include function calls within other expressions. At other times, it may be clearer to call the function and assign its return value to a variable before using it.

```cpp
// Filename: C21DOUB2.CPP
// Doubles the user's number

#include <iostream.h>

int     doub(int num)
{
    int     d_num;

    d_num = num * 2;    // Double the number
    return (d_num);     // Return the result
}


main()
{
    int     number;     // Holds user's input

    cout << "What number do you want doubled? ";
    cin >> number;
    // The 3rd cout parameter is replaced with
    // a return value
    cout << number << " doubled is " << doub(number)
        << "\n";

    return 0;
}
```

3. The following program asks the user for a number. The number is then passed to a function called sum(), which adds together the numbers from 1 to that number. In other words, if the user types 6, the function returns the result of the following calculation:

$$1 + 2 + 3 + 4 + 5 + 6$$

This is known as the *sum-of-the-digits calculation*, and it is sometimes used for depreciation in accounting.

```cpp
// Filename: C21SUMD.CPP
// Computes the sum of the digits

#include <iostream.h>

int     sum(int num)
{
    int     ctr;            // Local loop counter
    int     sumd = 0;       // Local to this function

    if (num <= 0) // Check to see if parameter is too small
    {
        sumd = num;         // Return parameter if too small
    }
    else
    {
        for (ctr = 1; ctr <= num; ctr++)
        {
            sumd += ctr;
        }
    }
    return (sumd);
}


main()
{
    int     num, sumd;

    cout << "Please type a number ";
    cin >> num;
    sumd = sum(num);
    cout << "The sum of the digits is " << sumd << "\n";
    return 0;
}
```

The output of this program is as follows:

```
Please type a number 6
The sum of the digits is 21
```

4. The following program contains two functions that return values. The first function, maximum(), returns the higher of two numbers entered by the user. The second function, minimum(), returns the lower number.

```cpp
// Filename: C21MINMX.CPP
// Finds minimum and maximum values in functions

#include <iostream.h>

int     maximum(int num1, int num2)
{
    int     max;      // Local to this function only

    max = (num1 > num2) ? (num1) : (num2);
    return (max);
}

int     minimum(int num1, int num2)
{
    int     min;      // Local to this function only

    min = (num1 < num2) ? (num1) : (num2);
    return (min);
}


main()
{
    int     num1, num2;      // User's 2 numbers
    int     min, max;

    cout << "Please type two numbers (such as 46, 75)\n";
    cout << "Press Enter after each number.\n";
    cout << "  First Number  ==> ";
    cin >> num1;
    cout << "  Second Number ==> ";
    cin >> num2;
    max = maximum(num1, num2);  // Assign return value of
                                // each function to variables
```

```
        min = minimum(num1, num2);
        cout << "\n  The minimum number is " << min << "\n";
        cout << "   The maximum number is " << max << "\n";
        return 0;
}
```

Note the following output:

```
Please type two numbers (such as 46, 75)
Press Enter after each number.
   First Number  ==> 99
   Second Number ==> 13


   The minimum number is 13
   The maximum number is 99
```

If the user types the same number twice, the minimum and maximum numbers will be the same.

These two functions can be passed any two integer values. In a simple example like this one, the user already knows which number is higher or lower. The purpose is to show how to code return values. You might want to use similar functions in a more useful application, such as finding the highest-paid employee from a payroll disk file.

Function Prototypes

The word *prototype* is sometimes defined as a model. In C++, a function prototype models the actual function. Before completing your study of functions, parameters, and return values, you must understand how to prototype each function in a program.

You should prototype all functions in your programs. By prototyping them, you inform C++ of the function's parameter types and its return value, if any. You do not always need to prototype functions, but it is always recommended. Sometimes a prototype is mandatory before your functions will work properly.

A simple example will help clarify the need for prototyping. Listing 21.1 contains a program that asks the user for a temperature in Celsius and then converts that temperature to Fahrenheit. The parameter and the return type are both floating-point values. You know the return type is a floating-point value because of the word *float* before the function convert()'s definition. See whether you can follow this program. Except for the Celsius calculation, the program is similar to other programs you have seen in this book.

Listing 21.1. A program that converts Celsius to Fahrenheit.

```
// Filename: C21TEMP.CPP
// Converts the user's Celsius to Fahrenheit

#include <iostream.h>
#include <iomanip.h>

main()
{
    float       c_temp;     // Holds user's Celsius temperature
    float       f_temp;     // Holds converted temperature

    cout << "What is the Celsius temperature to convert? ";
    cin >> c_temp;

    f_temp = convert(c_temp);    // Convert the temperature

    cout << "The Fahrenheit equivalent is "
         << setprecision(1) << f_temp << "\n";
    return 0;
}

float       convert(float c_temp)  // Return var and parameter
                                   // are both float
{
    float       f_temp;            // Local variable

    f_temp = c_temp * (9.0 / 5.0) + 32.0;
    return (f_temp);
}
```

You must prototype all functions.

If you run the preceding program, the Visual C++ compiler refuses to compile it. Yet this program seems like many others you have seen. The primary difference is that you referred to the function before it occurred in your code. In other words, the function had not yet been prototyped. C++ requires that each function be prototyped before you can refer to it.

All the programs you have written so far defined their functions before those functions were used. These definitions served the double purpose of furnishing both a prototype and the definition of the function. However, it is often desirable to defer definition of a function until later in the program. This is especially true in large programs. The way out of this dilemma is to create a *prototype* for the function.

To prototype a function, copy the function's definition line to the top of your program (immediately before or after the `#include <stdio.h>` line is fine). Place a semicolon at the end of the copied line, and you have the prototype. Because the definition line (the function's first line) contains the return type, the function name, and the type of each argument, the function prototype serves (to the program) as a model of the function that is to follow.

If a function does not return a value, or if that function has no arguments passed to it, Visual C++ still requires you to prototype it. Use the keyword void in place of a return type. If there are no parameters, you can either use void or just leave the parameter area empty. (You still need the parentheses, though.) Even main() can be prototyped. Listing 21.2 shows the preceding program corrected with the proto- type lines. Because there are two functions, main() and convert(), there are two prototypes.

Listing 21.2. Temperature-conversion program corrected with prototypes.

```
// Filename: C21TEMP.CPP
// Converts the user's Celsius to Fahrenheit

#include <iostream.h>
#include <iomanip.h>

float    convert(float c_type);    // convert()'s prototype

int    main(void)
{
    float    c_temp;   // Holds user's Celsius temperature
    float    f_temp;   // Holds converted temperature

    cout << "What is the Celsius temperature to convert? ";
    cin >> c_temp;

    f_temp = convert(c_temp);    // Convert the temperature

    cout << setiosflags( ios::fixed );
    cout << "The Fahrenheit equivalent is "
         << setprecision(1) << f_temp << "\n";
    return 0;
}

float    convert(float c_temp)  // Return var and parameter
                                // are both float
{
```

```
    float      f_temp;              // Local variable

    f_temp = c_temp * (9.0 / 5.0) + 32.0;
    return (f_temp);
}
```

All functions must match their prototypes. You don't have to list individual parameter names in the function's prototype parentheses, only the data types of each parameter.

You can look at a prototype and determine whether it is a prototype or function definition (the function's first line) by whether it has a semicolon at the end.

Prototyping Is Safe

Prototyping protects you from the possibility of your own programming mistakes. Suppose that you wrote a function which expected two arguments: an integer followed by a floating-point value. Here is the definition line of such a function:

```
my_fun(int num, float amount)
```

What if you were to try to pass my_fun() incorrect data types? (If you called this function by passing it two constants, a floating-point value followed by an integer would result.) Consider the following example:

```
my_fun(23.43, 5);   // Call the my_fun() function
```

The function would *not* receive correct parameters. The function is expecting an integer followed by a floating-point value, but you did the opposite and sent it a floating-point value followed by an integer. But because Visual C++ required you to prototype your function, when you try to compile the above mistake, the compiler displays an error message and does not produce a compiled program.

If you fail to follow the usage defined by the prototype, your compiler informs you of the problem, and you can correct it. Without prototypes, the compiler would not be able to detect this kind of error. The program would compile, but the results would be wrong. The program would be difficult to debug, at best. This was a common problem with C that was corrected in C++.

Prototyping helps C++ protect your programs from function programming errors.

Prototype All Functions

You must prototype every function in your program, as the earlier example showed. The prototype defines for the program which functions follow, their return types, and their parameter types.

Think about how you would prototype cout. You don't always pass it the same types of parameters because you print different data with each cout. Prototyping functions that you write is easy; the prototype is basically the first line in the function. Prototyping functions that you don't write may seem difficult. It isn't—in fact, you have already done it in each program in this book!

When the designers of C++ required that all functions should be prototyped, they realized also that you cannot prototype library functions, so they did that for you by placing their prototypes in special files called header files on your disk. You have been including the cout and cin prototype in each program with the following statement:

```
#include <iostream.h>
```

Header files contain library function prototypes.

Inside the file iostream.h is a prototype of many of C++'s input and output functions. By prototyping these functions, you ensure that you cannot pass bad values to such functions. If you do, C++ will catch the problem.

Prototyping is the primary reason why you always need to include the matching header file when using one of C++'s library functions. The strcpy() function you saw in earlier chapters requires the following line:

```
#include <string.h>
```

This is the header file for the strcpy() function. Without this file, the program will not compile.

> **Tip:** If you are working in the Visual C++ editor and need to know the name of the header file for a function or need to see its prototype so that you can code the right parameters, type the name of the function, put the cursor somewhere in the name, and press F1. Visual C++ will bring up a Help screen that shows you the function's prototype, and the name of the header file to include.

Examples

1. The following program asks the user for a number in main() and passes that number to ascii(). The ascii() function then returns the ASCII character of the user's number. This program illustrates a character return type. Functions can return any data type.

```
// Filename: C21ASC.CPP
// Prints the ASCII character of the user's number
// Prototypes follow

#include <iostream.h>

char    ascii(int num);
```

```
int     main(void)
{
    int     num;
    char    asc_char;

    cout << "What is an ASCII number? ";
    cin >> num;

    asc_char = ascii(num);
    cout << "The ASCII character for " << num
        << " is " << asc_char << "\n";
    return 0;
}

char    ascii(int num)
{
    char    asc_char;

    asc_char = (char)num;
    return (asc_char);
}
```

The output of this program is as follows:

```
What is an ASCII number? 67
The ASCII character for 67 is C
```

2. Suppose that you need to calculate net pay for a company. You will find yourself multiplying the hours worked by the hourly pay and then deducting taxes to compute the net pay. The following program includes a function that does these tasks. It requires three arguments: the hours worked, the hourly pay, and the tax rate (as a floating-point decimal, such as .30 for 30%). The function returns the net pay. The main() calling program tests this by sending three different payroll values to the function and then prints the three return values.

```
// Filename: C21NPAY.CPP
// Defines a function that computes net pay

#include <iostream.h>
#include <iomanip.h>

float     netpayfun(float hours, float rate, float taxrate);
```

```
int     main(void)
{
    float     net_pay;

    net_pay = netpayfun(40.0, 3.50, .20);

    oout << setiosflags( ios::fixed );
    cout << "The pay for 40 hours at $3.50/hr., ";
    cout << "and a 20% tax rate is: ";
    cout << setprecision(2) << net_pay << "\n";
    net_pay = netpayfun(50.0, 10.00, .30);
    cout << "The pay for 50 hours at $10.00/hr., ";
    cout << "and a 30% tax rate is: ";
    cout << setprecision(2) << net_pay << "\n";
    net_pay = netpayfun(10.0, 5.00, .10);
    cout << "The pay for 10 hours at $5.00/hr., ";
    cout << "and a 10% tax rate is: ";
    cout << setprecision(2) << net_pay << "\n";

    return 0;
}

float     netpayfun(float hours, float rate, float taxrate)
{
    float     gross_pay, taxes, net_pay;

    gross_pay = (hours * rate);
    taxes = (taxrate * gross_pay);
    net_pay = (gross_pay - taxes);
    return (net_pay);
}
```

Summary

You now have seen how to build your own collection of functions. When you write a function, you might want to use it in several programs; there is no need to reinvent the wheel. Many programmers write useful functions and use them in more than one program.

You now understand the importance of prototyping functions. You know how to prototype all your own functions and how to include the appropriate header file when using one of the library functions.

The rest of this book uses the concepts presented in Parts I through IV so that you can take advantage of separate, modular functions and local data. You are now ready to learn more about how C++ performs input and output. The next chapter shows you the theory behind C++'s I/O and introduces more library functions.

Review Questions

Answers to Review Questions are in Appendix B.

1. How do you declare a function return type?

2. What is the maximum number of return values a function can return?

3. What are header files for?

4. What is the default function return type?

5. True or false: A function that returns a value can be passed only a single parameter.

6. How do prototypes protect the programmer from bugs?

7. Why do you not need to return global variables?

8. Consider the following function prototype:

```
float my_fun(char a, int b, float c);
```

What is the return type? How many parameters are being passed to my_fun()? What are their types?

Review Exercises

1. Write a program that contains two functions. The first function returns the square of the integer passed to it, and the second function returns the cube. As with all programs from this point on, prototype all functions, including main().

2. Write a function that returns the double-precision area of a circle, given the double-precision radius passed to it. The formula to calculate the radius of a circle is

area = 3.14159 * radius * radius

3. Write a function that returns the value of a polynomial (the return value), given this formula:

$$9x^4 + 15x^2 + x^1$$

Assume that x is passed from main() and was supplied by the user.

Part V

*Character, Input, Output,
and String Functions*

CHAPTER 22

Device and Character I/O

Unlike many programming languages, C++ contains no input or output commands. C++ is an extremely *portable* language; this means that a C++ program which compiles and runs on one computer will be able to compile and run on another type of computer. Most incompatibilities between computers reside in their input/output devices. Each device requires a different method of performing I/O (input/output).

By putting all I/O capabilities in common functions supplied with each computer's compiler instead of in C++ statements, the designers of C++ ensured that programs were not tied to specific hardware for input and output. A compiler has to be modified for every computer for which it is written. This ensures that the compiler works with the computer and all its devices. The compiler writers write I/O functions for each machine; when your C++ program writes a character to the screen, the program works whether you have a color PC screen or a UNIX X/ Windows terminal.

This chapter shows you additional ways to perform input and output of data other than with the cin and cout operators you have seen so far. With its character-based I/O functions, C++ gives you the basic I/O functions needed for writing powerful data entry and printing routines.

This chapter introduces the following topics:

♦ Stream input and output

♦ Redirecting I/O

♦ Printing to the printer

♦ Character I/O functions

♦ Buffered and nonbuffered I/O

By the time you finish this chapter, you will understand the fundamental, built-in I/O functions available in C++. Performing character input and output, one character at a time, may sound like a slow method of I/O. You will soon see that character I/O actually gives you the ability to create more powerful I/O functions than are possible with the `cin` and `cout` operators.

Stream and Character I/O

C++ views input and output from all devices as a stream of characters.

C++ views all input and output as streams of characters. Whether your program gets input from the keyboard, a disk file, a modem, or a mouse, C++ sees only a stream of characters. C++ does not know (or care) what type of device is supplying the input. C++ lets the operating system take care of the device specifics. The designers of C++ want your programs to operate on characters of data without regard to the physical method that is taking place.

This stream I/O means that you can use the same functions to get input from the keyboard as from the modem. You can use the same functions to write to a disk file, printer, or screen. Of course, you need some way of routing that stream input or output to the proper device, but each program's I/O functions work similarly. Figure 22.1 illustrates this concept.

Figure 22.1

All I/O is viewed as a character stream to C++.

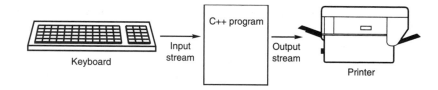

The Newline Special Character: \n

Portability is the key to C++'s success. Few companies have the resources to rewrite every program they use when changing computer equipment. They need a programming language that works on many platforms (hardware combinations). C++ achieves true portability better than almost any other programming language.

It is because of portability that C++ uses the generic newline character, \n, instead of the specific carriage return and linefeed sequences other languages use. This is why C++ uses \t for tab, as well as all the other control characters used in I/O functions.

If C++ relied on specific ASCII code to represent these special characters, your programs would not be portable. You would be writing a C++ program on one computer, using a carriage return value such as 12, but 12 may not be the carriage return value on another type of computer.

By using the newline character and the rest of the control characters available in C++, you ensure that your programs will work on any computer on which they are compiled. A specific compiler will substitute its computer's actual codes for the control codes in your programs.

Standard Devices

Table 22.1 shows a listing of standard I/O devices. C++ always assumes that input will come from stdin, meaning the *standard input device*. It is usually the keyboard, although you can reroute this default. C++ assumes that all output will go to stdout, or the *standard output device*. There is nothing magical in the words stdin and stdout, although if you have never heard of them, that is fine because many people see them for the first time in C++.

Table 22.1. Standard devices in C++.

Description	C++ Name	MS-DOS Name
Screen	stdout	CON:
Keyboard	stdin	CON:
Printer	stdprn	PRN: or LPT1:

continues

Table 22.1. Continued

Description	C++ Name	MS-DOS Name
Serial port	stdaux	AUX: or COM1:
Error messages	stderr	CON:
Disk files	None	Filename

Take a moment to study Table 22.1. It may seem confusing that three devices are named CON:. MS-DOS knows the difference between the screen device called CON: (which stands for console) and the keyboard device called CON: from the context of the data stream. If you send an output stream (a stream of characters) to CON:, MS-DOS knows to route it to the screen. If you request input from CON:, MS-DOS knows to get it from the keyboard. (These defaults hold true as long as you have not redirected these devices, as explained later in this chapter.) MS-DOS sends all error messages to the screen (CON:) as well.

> **Note:** Chapter 21, "Sequential Files," teaches you how to route I/O to a second printer or serial port.

Printing Formatted Output to the Printer

ofstream lets your program write to the printer.

Sending program output to the printer is easy with the ofstream function. The format of ofstream is as follows:

```
ofstream device(device_name);
```

> **Note:** ofstream uses the fstream.h header file.

The next example shows how you can combine cout and ofstream to write to both the screen and the printer.

Example

The following program asks for the user's first and last names. It then prints the full name, last name first, on the printer.

```
// Filename: C22FPR1.CPP
// Prints a name on the printer

#include <fstream.h>

main()
{
    char     first[ 20 ];
    char     last[ 20 ];

    cout << "What is your first name? ";
    cin >> first;
    cout << "What is your last name? ";
    cin >> last;

    // Send names to the printer
    ofstream prn("PRN");
    prn << "In a phone book, your name looks like this: \n";
    prn << last << ", " << first << "\n";
    return 0;
}
```

Character I/O Functions

Because all I/O is actually character I/O, C++ provides many functions for performing character input and output. The cout and cin functions are called *formatted I/O operators*, which give you formatting control over your input and output. The cout and cin functions are not character I/O functions.

There's nothing wrong with using cout for formatted output, but cin has many problems, as you have seen. In this discussion, you learn how to write character input routines that replace cin, as well as how to use character output functions to prepare you for Chapters 32 and 33 on disk files.

The *get()* and *put()* Functions

get() inputs characters from any standard devices; *put()* outputs characters to any standard devices.

The most fundamental character I/O functions are get() and put(). The get() function inputs a single character from the standard input device (the keyboard if you don't redirect it). The put() function outputs a single character to the standard output device (the screen if you don't redirect it from the operating system).

The format of get() is as follows:

```
device.get(char_var);
```

The *device* can be any standard input device. If you were getting character input from the keyboard, you would use cin as the device. If you had initialized your modem and wanted to receive characters from it, you would use ifstream to open the modem device and read from it.

The format of put() is as follows:

```
device.put(char_val);
```

You output character data with put(). The *char_val* can be a character variable, expression, or constant. The *device* can be any standard output device. To write a character to your printer, you would open PRN with ofstream.

Examples

1. The following program asks for the user's initials, one character at a time. Notice that the program uses both cout and put(). The cout is still very useful for formatted output, such as messages to the user. Writing individual characters is best achieved with put().

   The program has to call two get() functions for each character typed. When you answer a get() prompt, by typing a character and then pressing Enter, C++ sees that input as a stream of two characters. The get() first gets the letter you typed and then gets the \n (the newline character, supplied to C++ when you press Enter). Examples that follow fix this double get() problem.

```
// Filename: C22CH1.CPP
// Introduces get() and put()

#include <fstream.h>

main()
{
    char    in_char;      // Holds incoming initial
    char    first, last;  // Holds converted first and
                          // last initials

    cout << "What is your first name initial? ";
    cin.get(in_char);     // Wait for first initial
    first = in_char;
    cin.get(in_char);     // Ignore newline
    cout << "What is your last name initial? ";
```

```
cin.get(in_char);      // Wait for last initial
    last = in_char;
    cin.get(in_char);      // Ignore newline
    cout << "\nHere they are: \n";
    cout.put(first);
    cout.put(last);
    return 0;
}
```

The output of this program is as follows:

```
What is your first name initial? G
What is your last name initial? P

Here they are:
GP
```

2. You can add carriage returns for better spacing of the output. To print the two initials on two separate lines, use put() to write a newline character to cout, as shown in the following program:

```
// Filename: C22CH2.CPP
// Introduces get() and put() and uses put() to output
// newline

#include <fstream.h>

main()
{
    char      in_char;    // Holds incoming initial
    char      first, last; // Holds converted first and
                           // last initials

    cout << "What is your first name initial? ";
    cin.get(in_char);      // Wait for first initial
    first = in_char;
    cin.get(in_char);      // Ignore newline
    cout << "What is your last name initial? ";
    cin.get(in_char);      // Wait for last initial
    last = in_char;
    cin.get(in_char);      // Ignore newline
    cout << "\nHere they are: \n";
    cout.put(first);
    cout.put('\n');
```

```
cout.put(last);
    return 0;
}
```

3. It may be clearer to define the newline character as a constant. At the top of the preceding program, you could use the following:

```
#define NEWLINE '\n'
```

The put() could then read as follows:

```
cout.put(NEWLINE);
```

Some programmers prefer to define their character formatting constants and refer to them by name. It's up to you if you think that this is clearer, or if you want to continue using the '\n' character constant in put().

Buffered and Unbuffered Character I/O

The get() function is a *buffered* input function. That is, as you type characters, the data does not immediately go into your program but instead goes into a buffer. The buffer is a section of memory managed by C++ (and has nothing to do with your PC's type-ahead buffers).

Figure 22.2 shows how a buffered input function works. When your program gets to a get(), the program temporarily waits as you type the input. The program doesn't see the characters at all, because they are going to the buffer of memory. There is practically no limit to the size of the buffer; it will keep filling up with input until you press Enter. When you press Enter, the computer releases the buffer to your program.

Figure 22.2

get( ) input goes to a buffer, which is released when you press Enter.

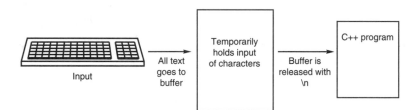

Most PCs allow either buffered or nonbuffered input. The getch() function, discussed later in this chapter, is nonbuffered. With get(), all input is buffered, which affects the timing of your program's input. The program receives no characters from get() until Enter is pressed. Therefore, if you ask a question, such as

```
Do you want to see the report again (Y/N)?
```

and use get() for input, the user can answer Y, but the program does not know it until the user presses Enter. The Y and the Enter keystrokes are then sent, one character at a time, to the program where the input is processed. If you want immediate response to a user's typing (as with INKEY$, if you are familiar with BASIC), you will have to use getch().

> **Tip:** If you use buffered input, the user can type a string of characters, in response to a loop with get(), getting characters and correcting the input with a Backspace keystroke, if desired, before pressing Enter. If the input is nonbuffered, the Backspace keystroke is treated as just another character of data.

Examples

When getting characters, you may have to discard the newline keystroke.

1. C22CH2.CPP must discard the newline character. It did so by assigning the input character, from get(), to an extra variable. Obviously, the get() returns a value (the character typed). In this case, it's okay to ignore that return value by not using the character returned by get(). You know that the user will have to press Enter (to end the input), so discarding the character with an unused get() function call is acceptable.

2. cin is very limited when used for inputting strings, such as names and sentences. The cin operator allows only one word to be entered at a time. If you asked for a user's full name with the lines

```
cout << "What are your first and last names? ";
cin >> names;      // Get name into character array names
```

the array names would receive only the first name; cin ignores all data to the right of the first space.

However, there is a better way. get() has an alternate format. The alternate format has 3 parameters, not just one. get() with three parameters is used like this:

```
char in_string[25];
int num_char = 25;
char delim = '\n';
cin.get( in_string, num_char, delim );
```

The code above will get characters into the buffer until there have been 24 characters entered (Why 24 characters, and not 25? See the following *Tip*.), or the user presses the Enter key. Actually, you can make the input stop on any character—that is the purpose of delim. It is the *delimiting* character. When the user types the delimiting character, input to the buffer is ended, and the resulting buffer is copied into in_string.

> **Tip:** get(), as used in the preceding example, will read in one character less than num_char. It then uses the remaining character to add the terminating null (\0) to the end of the input_string.

Following is an example of using this form of cin. The program is not very "user-friendly."

```
// Filename: C22GET1.CPP
// Introduces get() and put() and uses put() to output
// newline

#include <iostream.h>

main()
{
    char in_string[50];    // input area
    int num_char = 20;     // number of characters to get
    char delim = 'd';

    cout << "Please type the alphabet, in order.\n";
    cout << "It is important that you use lower case.\n";
    cout << "Start NOW! ==> ";

    cin.get( in_string, num_char, delim );

    cout << "I didn't really want the whole alphabet.\n";
    cout << in_string << " was enough.";

    return 0;
}
```

Run this program several times. Experiment with different sequences of input characters. Notice that no matter what you type, after you press the Enter key the program only outputs back the characters up to the lower-case *d*, or the first 19 characters if no lowercase *d* was typed before that point.

Note, too, that you still have to press the Enter key to signal that you are finished typing, the delimiter character only stops input to the buffer. You can prove that by typing more than 19 characters without typing a lowercase *d*. (input_string was deliberately defined to be larger than num_char to illustrate this point.) Figure 22.3 shows the output from this program when more than 19 characters are entered without typing a *d* before pressing Enter.

Figure 22.3

get( ) with a defined buffer size and delimiter.

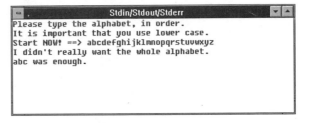

```
Stdin/Stdout/Stderr
Please type the alphabet, in order.
It is important that you use lower case.
Start NOW! ==> abcdefghijklmnopqrstuvwxyz
I didn't really want the whole alphabet.
abc was enough.
```

3. This example shows more about the nature of the input buffer. Even though characters returned to the cin.get() statement end at the lowercase *k*, the other typed input is still in the buffer and is retrieved with the following call to cin << more_str.

```cpp
// Filename: C22GET2.CPP
// Introduces get() and put() and uses put() to output
// newline

#include <iostream.h>

main()
{
    char in_string[50];    // input area
    char more_str[50];     // input area
    int num_char = 27;     // number of characters to
    ➥get
    char delim = 'k';

    cout << "Please type the alphabet, in order.\n";
    cout << "It is important that you use lower case.
    ➥\n";
    cout << "Start NOW! ==> ";

    cin.get( in_string, num_char, delim );

    cout << "\nI didn't really want the whole
    ➥alphabet.\n";
```

```
    cout << in_string << " was enough.\n";

    cin >> more_str;
    cout << "I threw away the " << more_str << "\n";

    return 0;
}
```

Figure 22.4 shows the output from this program when the entire alphabet is entered. The first letters, up to but not including the delimiter, are output first. The remainder of the input is then retrieved into more_str and printed with another cout.

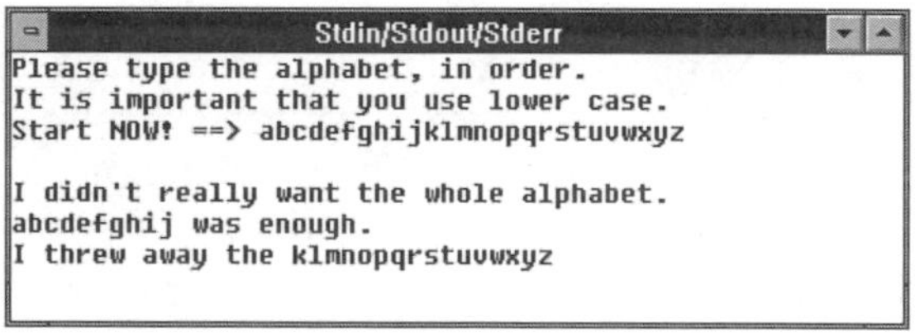

Figure 22.4

Reading the unused characters in the buffer.

```
Stdin/Stdout/Stderr
Please type the alphabet, in order.
It is important that you use lower case.
Start NOW! ==> abcdefghijklmnopqrstuvwxyz

I didn't really want the whole alphabet.
abcdefghij was enough.
I threw away the klmnopqrstuvwxyz
```

4. You can build your own input function, using get(), which doesn't have a single-word limitation. When you want to get a string of characters from the user, such as first and last names, you can call the get_in_str() function, shown in the following program.

The main() function defines an array and prompts the user for a name. After the prompt, the program calls the get_in_str() function and builds the input array, one character at a time, using get(). The function keeps looping, using the while loop, until the user presses Enter (signaled by the newline character, \n) *or* until the maximum number of characters are typed.

You might want to use this function in your own programs. Be sure to pass it a character array and an integer that holds the maximum array size. (You don't want the input string to be longer than the character array that will hold it.) When control returns to main(), or to whatever function called get_in_str(), the array will have the user's full input, spaces and all.

```
// Filename: C22IN.CPP
// Program that builds an input string array, using get()

#include <fstream.h>
```

```
#define MAX 25      // Size of character array to be typed in

//**********************************************************
// The following function requires that a string and the
// maximum length of the string be passed to it. It accepts
// input from the keyboard and will send keyboard input into
// the string. On return, the calling routine has access to
// the string.
//**********************************************************

void    get_in_str(char str[ ], int len)
{
    int     i = 0;          // Index
    char    input_char;     // Character typed

    cin.get(input_char);    // Get next character in string
    while (i < (len - 1) && (input_char != '\n'))
    {
        str[ i ] = input_char; // Build string a character
                               // at a time
        i++;
        cin.get(input_char);   // Get next character in
                               // string
    }
    str[ i ] = '\0';   // Make the char array into a string
    return;
}
int     main(void)
{
    char    input_str[ MAX ]; // Keyboard input will fill
                              // this
    cout << "What is your full name? ";
    get_in_str(input_str, MAX);     // String from keyboard
    cout << "After return, your name is " << input_str
        << "\n";
    return 0;
}
```

> **Note:** The loop checks for **len** - **1** to save room for the null terminating zero at the end of the input string.

Summary

You should now understand the generic method that C++ programs use for input and output. By writing to standard I/O devices, you have portability with C++. If you write a program for one computer, it will work on another. If C++ were to write directly to specific hardware, programs would not work on every computer.

If you still want to use the formatted I/O functions, such as cout, you can do so. The ofstream() function lets you write formatted output to any device, including the printer.

Although the methods of character I/O may seem primitive (and they are), they provide flexibility because you can build on them to create your own input functions. One of the C++ functions used most often, a string-building character I/O function, was demonstrated in the C22IN.CPP program in this chapter.

The next two chapters introduce many character and string functions, including string I/O functions. The string I/O functions build on the principles presented here. You will be surprised at the extensive character- and string-manipulation functions available in the language as well.

Review Questions

Answers to Review Questions are in Appendix B.

1. Why are there no input or output commands in C++?

2. True or false: If you use the character I/O functions to send output to stdout, the output always goes to the screen.

3. What is the difference between getch() and get()?

4. What function sends formatted output to devices other than the screen?

5. What are the MS-DOS redirection symbols?

6. What nonstandard function, which is most similar to getch(), echoes the input character to the screen as the user types it?

7. True or false: When using get(), the program receives your input as you type it.

8. Which keystroke releases the buffered input to the program?

9. True or false: Using devices and functions described in this chapter, you can write one program that sends some output to the screen, some to the printer, and some to the modem.

Review Exercises

1. Write a program that asks the user for five letters and prints them backward, first to the screen and then to the printer.

2. Write a miniature typewriter program, using `get()` and `put()`. Loop while getting a line of input (until the user presses Enter without typing any text) and then write that line to the printer. Because `get()` is buffered, nothing goes to the printer until the user presses Enter at the end of each line of text. (Use the string-building input function shown in C22IN.CPP.)

3. Add a `putch()` inside the first loop of C22GCH1.CPP (this chapter's first `get()` program) so that the characters are echoed to the screen as the user types them.

4. A *palindrome* is a word or phrase spelled the same forward and backward. Two sample palindromes are

```
Madam, I'm Adam
Golf? No sir, prefer prison flog!
```

Write a C++ program that asks the user for a phrase. Build the input, one character at a time, using a character input function such as `get()`. Once you have the full string (store it in a character array), test the phrase to see whether it is a palindrome. You will have to filter out special characters (nonalphabetic), storing only alphabetic characters to a second character array. You must also convert the characters, as you store them, to uppercase. The first palindrome becomes

```
MADAMIMADAM
```

Using one or more `for` or `while` loops, you can now test the phrase to see whether it is a palindrome. Print the result of the test on the printer. Sample output should look like this:

```
"Madam, I'm Adam" is a palindrome.
```

CHAPTER 23

Character, String, and Numeric Functions

C++ provides many built-in functions in addition to the strcpy() function and the cout and cin operators presented in this book. These library functions increase your productivity and save you programming time. You do not have to write as much code because they perform many useful tasks for you.

This chapter introduces the following topics:

- ◆ Character-testing functions
- ◆ Character-conversion functions
- ◆ String-testing functions
- ◆ String-manipulation functions
- ◆ String I/O functions
- ◆ Mathematical functions
- ◆ Trigonometric functions
- ◆ Logarithmic and exponential functions
- ◆ Random-number processing

Character Functions

This section explores many of the character functions available in the C++ language. Generally, you pass character arguments to the functions, and they return values you can store or print. By using these functions, you off-load a lot of work to C++, letting it do some of the tedious manipulation of your character and string data.

The character functions return True (nonzero) or False (0) results, based on characters you pass to them.

Several functions test for certain characteristics of your character data. With these functions, you can test whether your character data is alphabetic (uppercase or lowercase) or numeric, and much more. You must pass a character variable or constant argument to these functions (by placing the argument in the function parentheses) when calling them. All the functions return a True (nonzero) or False (0) result, so you can test their return values inside an `if` statement or a `while` loop.

> **Note:** All character functions discussed in this chapter are prototyped in the ctype.h header file. Be sure to include ctype.h at the top of any program that uses these functions.

Alphabetic and Digit Testing

The following functions test for alphabetic conditions:

◆ `isalpha(c)`. Returns True (nonzero) if *c* is an uppercase or a lowercase letter. A False (0) value is returned if anything other than a letter is passed to this function.

◆ `islower(c)`. Returns True (nonzero) if *c* is a lowercase letter. A False (0) value is returned if anything other than a lowercase letter is passed to this function.

◆ `isupper(c)`. Returns True (nonzero) if *c* is an uppercase letter. A False (0) value is returned if anything other than an uppercase letter is passed to this function.

Remember that any nonzero value is considered to be True in C++, and 0 is always False. If you use these functions' return values in a relational test, the True return value is not always 1 (it might be any nonzero value), but it will always be considered True for the test.

The following functions test for numeric characters:

◆ `isdigit(c)`. Returns True (nonzero) if *c* is a digit from 0 through 9. A False (0) value is returned if anything other than a digit is passed to this function.

Note: Even though some of the character functions test for digits, the arguments are still considered to be character data and cannot be used in mathematical calculations, unless you want to calculate using ASCII values of characters.

♦ `isxdigit(c)`. Returns True (nonzero) if *c* is any of the hexadecimal digits 0 through 9, A through F, or *a* through *f*. A False (0) value is returned if anything other than a hexadecimal digit is passed to this function. (See Appendix A for more information on the hexadecimal numbering system.)

The following function tests for numeric or alphabetic arguments:

♦ `isalnum(c)`. Returns True (nonzero) if *c* is a digit from 0 through 9 or an alphabetic character (either uppercase or lowercase). A False (0) value is returned if anything other than a digit or letter is passed to this function.

Caution: You can pass only character values and integer values (holding ASCII values of characters) to these functions. You cannot pass an entire character array to character functions. If you want to test the elements of a character array, you must pass the array one element at a time.

Example

The following program asks for the user's initials. If the user types anything other than alphabetic characters, the program displays an error and asks again.

Comments to identify the program.
Include the header file iostream.h.
Include the header file ctype.h.
Start of the main() *function.*
> *Declare the variable* initial *to a character.*
> *Print* What is your first initial? *to the screen.*
> *Obtain a character from the keyboard.*
> *While the character was not an alphabetic character, go through the loop.*
>> *Print* That was not a valid initial! *to the screen.*
>> *Print* What is your first initial? *to the screen.*
>> *Obtain another character from the keyboard.*
> *Print* Thanks! *to the screen.*
> *Return from the* main() *function.*

```
// Filename: C23INI.CPP
// Asks for initials and tests to ensure that they are
// correct

#include <iostream.h>
#include <ctype.h>

main()
{
    char    initial;

    cout << "What is your first initial? ";
    cin >> initial;
    while (!isalpha(initial))
    {
        cout << "\nThat was not a valid initial!\n";
        cout << "\nWhat is your first initial? ";
        cin >> initial;
    }

    cout << "\nThanks!\n";
    return 0;
}
```

This program shows one use of the ! (NOT) operator that is clear. The program continues to loop while the entered character is not alphabetic.

Special Character-Testing Functions

Some character functions are useful if you need to read from a disk file, a modem, or another operating system device from which you route input. These functions are not used as much as the character functions you saw in the last section, but these functions may be useful for testing specific characters for readability.

The following list describes the rest of the character-testing functions:

◆ iscntrl(c). Returns True (nonzero) if c is a *control character* (any character numbered 0 through 31 from the ASCII table). A False (0) value is returned if anything other than a control character is passed to this function.

◆ isgraph(c). Returns True (nonzero) if c is a printable character (a noncontrol character), except for a space. A False (0) value is returned if a space or anything other than a printable character is passed to this function.

♦ `isprint(c)`. Returns True (nonzero) if c is a printable character (a noncontrol character) from ASCII 32 to ASCII 127, including a space. A False (0) value is returned if anything other than a printable character is passed to this function.

♦ `ispunct(c)`. Returns True (nonzero) if c is any *punctuation character* (any printable character other than a space, letter, or digit). A False (0) value is returned if anything other than a punctuation character is passed to this function.

♦ `isspace(c)`. Returns True (nonzero) if c is a space, newline (\n), carriage return (\r), tab (\t), or vertical tab (\v) character. A False (0) value is returned if anything other than a space character is passed to this function.

Character-Conversion Functions

tolower() and *toupper()* return lowercase arguments and uppercase arguments, respectively.

Instead of testing characters, the two remaining functions can actually change characters to their lowercase or uppercase equivalents. The following list describes these functions:

♦ `tolower(c)`. Converts c to lowercase. Nothing is changed if you pass `tolower()` a lowercase letter or a nonalphabetic character.

♦ `toupper(c)`. Converts c to uppercase. Nothing is changed if you pass `toupper()` an uppercase letter or a nonalphabetic character.

These two functions return their changed character values. Typically, programmers change a character in the following ways:

```
c = tolower(c);
```

```
c = toupper(c);
```

In these two statements, the character variable named c gets changed to its lowercase and uppercase equivalents.

These functions are quite useful for user input. Suppose that you ask the user a yes or no question, such as

```
Do you want to print the checks (Y/N)?
```

Without knowing `toupper()` and `tolower()`, you would have to check for both Y and y before printing the checks. (The user may or may not type an uppercase letter for the answer.) Instead of testing for both conditions, you can convert the character to uppercase and then test for Y.

Example

Following is a program that prints an appropriate message for a user who is a girl or a user who is a boy. The program tests for G or B after converting the user's input to uppercase. No check for lowercase has to be done.

Comments to identify the program.
Include the header file iostream.h.
Include the header file ctype.h.
Start of the main() *function.*
  Declare the variable ans *as a character.*
  Print Are you a Girl or a Boy (G/B)? *to the screen.*
  Assign the variable ans *to the value entered from the keyboard.*
  Accept the Enter from the keyboard.
  Change the value of ans *to uppercase.*
  If ans *is a G, print* You look like a princess today! *to the screen and skip to the next line. Then break out of the switch.*
  If ans *is a B, print* You look handsome today! *to the screen and skip to the next line. Then break out of the switch.*
  If a G or B is not entered, print Your answer doesn't make sense! *to the screen and skip to the next line. Then break out of the switch.*
  Return from the main loop.

```cpp
// Filename: C23GB.CPP
// Tests if a G or a B is entered by user

#include <iostream.h>
#include <ctype.h>

main()
{
    char    ans;       // Holds user's response
    char    c;         // To catch newline

    cout << "Are you a Girl or a Boy (G/B)? ";
    cin.get(ans);      // Get answer
    cin.get(c);        // Discard newline
    ans = toupper(ans);     // Convert answer to uppercase
    switch (ans)
    {
```

```
        case       'G':
               cout << "You look like a princess today!\n";
               break;
        case       'B':
               cout << "You look handsome today!\n";
               break;
        default:
               cout << "Your answer doesn't make sense!\n";
               break;
     }
     return 0;
}
```

The output from this program is as follows:

```
Are you a Girl or a Boy (G/B)? B
You look handsome today!
```

String Functions

Some of the most powerful built-in C++ functions are the string functions. They perform much of the tedious work you have been writing code for so far, such as inputting strings from the keyboard and comparing strings.

As with the character functions, there is no need to reinvent the wheel by writing code for tasks when built-in functions will do them for you. Use these functions as much as possible. Now that you have a good grasp of the basics of C++, you can master the string functions. They let you concentrate on your program's primary purpose instead of spending time coding your own string functions.

String-Manipulation Functions

A handful of string functions can be used for string testing and conversion. You have already seen one of the string functions, strcpy(), which copies a string of characters into a character array.

> **Note:** All string functions presented in this section are prototyped in the string.h header file. Be sure to include string.h at the top of any program that uses the string functions.

The string-manipulation functions work on character arrays that contain strings or on string constants.

The following list describes some string functions that test or manipulate strings:

◆ strcat(*s1*, *s2*). Concatenates (merges) the string *s2* onto the end of the character array *s1*. The array *s1* must have enough reserved elements to hold both strings.

◆ strcmp(*s1*, *s2*). Compares the string *s1* with *s2* on an alphabetic, element-by-element basis. If *s1* alphabetizes before *s2*, strcmp() returns a negative value. If *s1* and *s2* are exactly the same, strcmp() returns a 0. If *s1* alphabetizes after *s2*, strcmp() returns a positive value.

◆ strlen(*s1*). Returns the length of *s1*. Remember that the length of a string is the number of characters up to but not including the null zero. The number of characters actually defined for the character array has nothing to do with the length of the string.

> **Tip:** Before using strcat() to concatenate (merge) strings, use sizeof() to ensure that the target string (the string being contatenated to) is large enough to hold both strings. (strlen() only tells you how many characters are stored in a character array, not how many characters are allocated in the array. sizeof() will tell you how many characters are allocated in an array.)

String Input/Output Functions

In the last chapter, you used a character input function, get(), to build input strings. Now that you have seen a few string functions, you can begin to use the string input and output functions. Although the string-building functions show you the specifics of the language, these string I/O functions are much easier to use than writing character input functions.

The following list describes the string input and output functions:

◆ gets(*s*). Stores input from stdin (usually directed to the keyboard) in a string named *s*.

◆ puts(*s*). Outputs string *s* to stdout (usually directed to the screen by the operating system).

◆ fgets(*s*, *len*, *dev*). Stores input from the standard device specified by *dev* (such as stdin or stdaux) in the string *s*. If more than *len* characters are input, fgets() discards the excess characters.

◆ fputs(*s*, *dev*). Outputs string *s* to the standard device specified by *dev*.

These four functions make the input and output of strings easy. The functions work in pairs. That is, strings input with gets() are usually output with puts(). Strings input with fgets() are usually output with fputs().

gets() inputs strings, and *puts()* outputs strings.

When getting strings with `gets()` or `fgets()`, an Enter keystroke terminates the input. Each of these functions handles string-terminating characters in a slightly different manner. Table 23.1 shows the differences.

Table 23.1. String I/O functions handle newlines and nulls differently.

Function	Newlines and Nulls
`gets()`	A newline input becomes a null zero (\0).
`puts()`	A null at the end of a string becomes a newline character (\n).
`fgets()`	A newline input stays, and a null zero is added after it.
`fputs()`	The null zero is dropped, and no newline character is added.

Therefore, when entering strings with `gets()`, C++ places a string-terminating character in the string at the point where Enter is pressed. This creates the input string. (Without the null zero, the input would not be a string.) When you output a string, the null zero at the end of the string becomes a newline character. This is good because you typically prefer a newline at the end of a line of output (to put the cursor on the next line).

Because `fgets()` and `fputs()` can input and output strings from devices such as disk files and telephone modems, it may be critical that the incoming newline characters are retained for the data's integrity. When outputting strings to these devices, you do not want C++ to insert extra newline characters.

One final function, `fflush()`, is worth noting although it is not a string function. `fflush()` flushes (empties) whatever standard device is listed in its parentheses. To flush the keyboard of all its input, you code the following:

```
fflush(stdin);
```

When you are doing string input and output, sometimes an extra newline character gets into the keyboard buffer. A previous answer to `gets()` or `getc()` might have an extra newline that you forgot to discard. When a program seems to ignore a `gets()`, you might have to insert `fflush(stdin)` before the `gets()`.

Flushing the standard input device causes no harm, and using `fflush()` can clear the input stream so that your next `gets()` works properly. You can also flush standard output devices with `fflush()` to clear the output stream of any characters you may have sent to it.

> **Note:** The header file for `fflush()` is stdio.h.

Example

To show you how easy it is to use `gets()` and `puts()`, the following program requests the name of a book from the user with a single `gets()` function call. The program then prints the book title with `puts()`.

Identify the program with comments.
Include the header file iostream.h.
Include the header file stdio.h.
Include the header file string.h.
Start of the main() function.
    Declare the character array book with 30 elements.
    Print What is a book title? to the screen.
    Assign the array book the string that is entered from the keyboard.
    Display the string that is stored in the array book to an output device, probably your screen.
    Print Thanks for the book! to the screen and move to the next line.
    Return from the main() function.

```
// C23GPS1.CPP
// Gets and puts strings

#include <iostream.h>
#include <stdio.h>
#include <string.h>
```

```
main()
{
    char     book[ 30 ];

    puts("What is a book title? ");
    fflush(stdout);
    gets(book);      // Get an input string
    puts(book);      // Display the string
    puts("Thanks for the book!\n");
    return 0;
}
```

The output of this program is as follows:

```
What is a book title?
Mary and Her Lambs
Mary and Her Lambs
Thanks for the book!
```

Converting Strings to Numbers

At times, you will need to convert numbers stored in character strings to a numeric data type. C++ provides the following functions:

♦ atoi(s). Converts s to an integer. The name stands for *a*lphabetic *to integer*.

♦ atol(s). Converts s to a long integer. The name stands for *a*lphabetic *to long* integer.

♦ atof(s). Converts s to a floating-point number. The name stands for *a*lphabetic *to* floating-point.

Note: These three ato() functions are prototyped in the stdlib.h header file. Be sure to include stdlib.h at the top of any program that uses the ato() functions.

The string must contain a valid number. The following string can be converted to an integer:

```
"1232"
```

The string must hold a string of digits short enough to fit in the target numeric data type. The following string cannot be converted to an integer with the atoi() function:

```
"-1232495.654"
```

This string can be converted to a floating-point number with the atof() function.

C++ cannot perform any mathematical calculations with such strings, even if they contain digits that represent numbers. Therefore, you must convert a string into its numeric equivalent before performing arithmetic with it.

> **Note:** If you pass a string to an ato() function and that string does not contain a valid representation of a number, the ato() function returns 0.

These functions will become more useful later, after you learn about disk files, pointers, and command-line arguments.

Numeric Functions

In this section, you are introduced to some of the C++ numeric functions. As with string functions, these library functions save you time by converting and calculating numbers so that you don't have to write functions to do such tasks. Many of these functions are trigonometric and advanced math functions. You may use some of them rarely, but they are available in case you need them.

Mathematical Functions

These numeric functions return double-precision values.

There are several built-in numeric functions that return results based on numeric variables and constants passed to them. Even if you write very few science and engineering programs, some of these functions will be useful to you.

> **Note:** All mathematical and trigonometric functions are prototyped in the math.h header file. Be sure to include math.h at the top of any program that uses these functions.

The following list describes the numeric functions:

◆ ceil(x). Rounds up to the nearest integer. This function is sometimes called the *ceiling function*.

◆ fabs(x). Returns the absolute value of x. The absolute value of a number is its positive equivalent. Absolute value is used for distances (which are always positive), accuracy measurements, age differences, and other calculations that require a positive result.

♦ `floor(x)`. Rounds down to the nearest integer.

♦ `fmod(x, y)`. Returns the floating-point remainder of (x divided by y), with the same sign as x. y cannot be zero. Because the modulus operator (%) works with integers only, this function was supplied to find the remainder of floating-point number divisions.

♦ `pow(x, y)`. Returns x raised to the y power, or x^y. If x is less than or equal to zero, y must be an integer. If x equals zero, y cannot be negative.

♦ `sqrt(x)`. Returns the square root of x. x must be greater than or equal to zero.

The *n*th Root

There are no functions that return the *n*th root of a number, only the square root. In other words, you cannot call a function that gives you the fourth root of 65,536. By the way, 16 is the fourth root of 65,536 because 16 times 16 times 16 times 16 equals 65,536.

You can use a mathematical trick to simulate the *n*th root, however. C++ lets you raise a number to a fractional power, so with the `pow()` function, you can raise a number to the *n*th root by raising it to the (1/*n*) power. For example, to find the fourth root of 65,536, you type something like the following:

```
root = pow(65536.0, (1.0/4.0));
```

Caution: The decimal points keep the numbers in floating-point format. If you left them as integers, as in

```
root = pow(65536, (1/4));
```

C++ would produce incorrect results. The `pow()` and most of the other mathematical functions require floating-point values as arguments.

To store the 7th root of 78,125 in a variable called **root**, you type

```
root = pow(78125.0, (1.0/7.0));
```

This stores 5.0 in **root** since 5^7 equals 78,125.

Knowing how to compute the *n*th root comes in handy in scientific programs and financial applications, such as time value of money problems.

Example

The following program uses the fabs() function to compute the difference between two ages.

```
// Filename: C23ABS.CPP
// Prints the difference between two ages

#include <iostream.h>
#include <math.h>

main()
{
    float    age1, age2, diff;

    cout << "\nWhat is the first child's age? ";
    cin >> age1;
    cout << "What is the second child's age? ";
    cin >> age2;
    // Calculate the positive difference
    diff = fabs(age1 - age2);    // Determine the absolute
                                 // value
    cout << "\nThey are " << diff << " years apart.\n";
    return 0;
}
```

This program's output is as follows:

```
What is the first child's age? 10
What is the second child's age? 12

They are 2 years apart.
```

Because of `fabs()`, the order of the ages does not matter. Without absolute value, this program would produce a negative age difference if the first age were less than the second age. Because the ages are relatively small, floating-point variables are used in this example. C++ automatically converts floating-point arguments to double when passing them to `fabs()`.

Trigonometric Functions

The following functions are available for trigonometric applications:

◆ `cos(x)`. Returns the cosine of the angle x. x is expressed in radians.

◆ `sin(x)`. Returns the sine of the angle x. x is expressed in radians.

◆ `tan(x)`. Returns the tangent of the angle x. x is expressed in radians.

These functions are probably the least-used functions in most programs. This is not meant to belittle the work of scientific and mathematical programmers who need them; thank goodness that C++ supplies these functions! Otherwise, programmers would have to write their own functions to perform these three basic trigonometric calculations.

> **Tip:** If you need to pass an angle, expressed in *degrees*, to these functions, convert the angle in degrees to radians by multiplying the degrees by (pi / 180.0). Pi is approximately 3.14159.

Logarithmic and Exponential Functions

The following three highly mathematical functions are sometimes used in business and mathematics:

♦ exp(x). Returns the base of the natural logarithm (e) raised to a power specified by x (e^x). e is approximately 2.718282.

♦ log(x). Returns the natural logarithm of the argument x, mathematically written as $\ln(x)$. x must be positive.

♦ log10(x). Returns the base-10 logarithm of the argument x, mathematically written as $\log 10(x)$. x must be positive.

Random-Number Processing

Random events happen every day of your life. You wake up, and it might be raining or sunny. You may have a good day or a bad day. You may get a phone call, or you may not. Your stock portfolio may go up or down in value. Random events are especially important in games; part of the fun of games is the luck involved with the roll of the dice or the draw of a card, when combined with your playing skills.

Simulating random events is important for a computer also. Computers, however, are finite machines. That is, given the same input, they always produce the same output. This can result in very boring game programs.

The *rand()* function produces random integer numbers.

The designers of C++ knew this and found a way to overcome it. They wrote a function, rand(), for generating random numbers. With it, you can get a random number to compute a dice roll or to draw a card randomly.

To call the rand() function and assign the returned random number to test, you use the following line.

Assign the variable test a random number returned from the rand() function.

```
test = rand();
```

The `rand()` function returns an integer from 0 to 32767. Never use an argument in the `rand()` parentheses. Each time you call `rand()` in the same program, you will get a different number.

If you run the *same* program that uses `rand()` over and over, `rand()` returns the same set of random numbers. One way to get a different set of random numbers is to call the `srand()` function. Its format is as follows:

```
srand(seed);
```

seed is an integer variable or constant. If you don't call `srand()`, C++ assumes a *seed* value of 1. The *seed* value reseeds (resets) the random number generator, so the *next* random number is based on the new *seed* value. If you were to run a program that uses `rand()`, and you called `srand()` with a different *seed* value at the beginning of the program, `rand()` would return a different random number.

> **Note:** The `rand()` and `srand()` functions are prototyped in the stdlib.h header file. Be sure to include stdlib.h at the top of any program that uses `rand()` or `srand()`.

Why Do They Make Us Do This?

There is much debate among C++ programmers concerning the random number generator. Many of them think that random numbers should be *truly* random and that programmers should not have to seed the generator themselves. These programmers believe that C++ should do its own internal seeding when you ask for a random number, thereby taking the burden of *randomness* off the programmers' backs.

However, many applications would no longer work if the random number generator were seeded for you. Computer simulations are used all the time in business, engineering, and research to approximate the pattern of real-world events. Researchers need to be able to duplicate these simulations, over and over. Even though the events inside the simulations may be random to each other, the running of the simulations cannot be random if researchers are to study several different effects.

Mathematicians and statisticians also need to repeat random number patterns for their analyses, especially when working with risk, probability, and gaming theory.

Because so many computer users need to repeat their random number patterns, the designers of C++ have wisely chosen to give you, the programmer, the option of keeping the same random patterns or changing them. The advantages outweigh by far the burden of including an extra `srand()` function call!

If you do want to produce a different set of random numbers every time your program runs, you can use `randomize()` to initialize the random number generator randomly. It is implemented as a macro that calls the `time()` function, so you should include time.h.

Summary

By including the ctype.h header file, you can test and convert characters the user types. There are many useful purposes for these character functions, such as converting a user's responses to questions to uppercase letters. That way, you can easily test the user's answers.

The string I/O functions give you more ease and control over both string and numeric input. You can get a string of digits from the keyboard and convert the digits to a number with the `ato()` functions. The string-comparison and concatenation functions let you test and change the contents of more than one string.

Functions save you programming time because they do some of the computing tasks for you, leaving you time to concentrate on your programs. There are numeric functions that round numbers, manipulate numbers, produce trigonometric and logarithmic results, and produce random numbers.

This chapter concludes the discussion of C++'s standard library functions. After mastering the concepts in this chapter, you will be ready to learn more about arrays and pointers, discussed in Part VI.

Review Questions

Answers to Review Questions are in Appendix B.

1. How do the character-testing functions differ from the character-conversion functions?

2. What are the two string input functions?

3. What is the difference between `floor()` and `ceil()`?

4. What will the following nested function return?

```
isalpha(islower('s'));
```

5. If the character array `str1` contains the string `Peter`, and the character array `str2` contains `Parker`, what does `str2` contain after the following line of code?

```
strcat(s2, s1);
```

6. What is the output of the following cout?

```
cout << floor(8.5) << " " << ceil(8.5);
```

7. True or false: The isxdigit() and isgraph() functions could return the same value, depending on the character passed to them.

8. Assume that you declare a character array with the following statement:

```
char ara[5];
```

Now suppose that the user types Programming in response to the following statement:

```
fgets(ara, 5, stdin);
```

Would ara contain Prog, Progr, or Programming?

9. True or false: The following statements print the same results.

```
cout << pow(64.0, (1.0/2.0));
```

```
cout << sqrt(64.0);
```

Review Exercises

1. Write a program that asks for the user's age. If the user types anything other than two digits, display an error message.

2. Write a program that stores a password in a character array called pass. Ask the user for the password. Use strcmp() to let the user know whether the proper password was typed. Use the string I/O functions for all the program's input and output.

3. Write a program that rounds the numbers –10.5, –5.75, and 2.75 in two different ways (up and down).

4. Write a program that asks for the user's name. Print the name in reverse case; in other words, print the first letter of each name in lowercase and print the rest of the name in uppercase.

5. Write a program that asks the user for five movie titles. Print the longest title. Use only the string I/O functions and the string-manipulation functions shown in this chapter.

6. Write a program that computes the square root, cube root, and fourth root of the numbers from 10 to 25.

7. Ask for the user's favorite song title. Discard all the special characters in the title. Print the words in the title, one word per line. If the title is *My True Love Is Mine, Oh, Mine!*, the output should look like this:

```
My
True
Love
Is
Mine
Oh
Mine
```

8. Ask the user for 10 first names of children. Using `strcmp()` on each pair of names, write a program to print the name (in each pair) that comes first in the alphabet.

Part VI

Arrays and Pointers

CHAPTER 24

Introducing Arrays

This chapter discusses different types of arrays. You are already familiar with the character array, which is the only way to store a string of characters in C++. Character arrays are not the only kind of arrays you can use, however. There is an array for every data type in C++. Learning how to process these arrays will improve the efficiency and power of your programs.

This chapter introduces the following topics:

♦ Array basics: names, data types, and subscripts

♦ Initializing an array at declaration time

♦ Initializing an array during program execution

♦ Selecting elements from arrays

The sample programs in this chapter and the next few chapters are some of the most advanced you will see in this book. Arrays are not difficult, but their power lends them to advanced programs.

Array Basics

An array is a list of two or more variables with the same name.

Although you have seen a special use of arrays as character strings, a little review of arrays is needed. An array is a list of two or more variables with the same name. Not every list of variables is an array. The following four variables do not count as an array:

```
sales
bonus_92
first_initial
ctr
```

This is a list of four variables, but they do not make up an array because each variable has a different name. You might wonder how more than one variable can have the same name; that seems to violate the rules of variables. If two variables have the same name, how will C++ know which one you want when you use the name of one of them?

Array variables are distinguished from each other by a *subscript*. A subscript is a number, inside brackets, that differentiates one *element* of an array from another. Elements are the individual variables in an array.

Suppose that you want to store a person's name in a character array called name. You can use either of the following definitions:

```
char name[ ] = "Ray Krebbs";

char name[ 11 ] = "Ray Krebbs";
```

Because C++ knows to reserve an extra element for the null zero at the end of every string, you don't have to specify the 11 as long as you initialize the array with a value. You know that the variable name is an array because brackets follow its name. The array has a single name called name, which contains 11 elements. The array is stored in memory (see Figure 24.1). Each element is a character. You can manipulate individual elements in the array by their subscripts.

Figure 24.1

Storing a character array in memory.

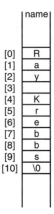

Note: All array subscripts begin with 0.

For instance, the following cout function prints Ray's initials.

Print the first and fifth elements of the array name.

```
cout << name[ 0 ] << ". " << name[ 4 ];
```

You can define an array as any data type in C++. You can have integer arrays, long integer arrays, double floating-point arrays, short integer arrays, and so on. C++ knows that you are defining an array instead of a single nonarray variable when you put brackets after the array name. For example, the following line defines an array, called ages, of five integers:

```
int  ages[ 5 ];
```

The first element in the ages array is ages[0]. The second element is ages[1], and the last element is ages[4]. This declaration of ages does not assign values to the elements, so you do not know what is in ages, and your program cannot assume that it contains zeros or anything else.

Following are some more array definitions:

```
int  weights[ 25 ], sizes[ 100 ]; // Declare 2 integer arrays

float    salaries[ 8 ];            // Declare 1 floating-point
                                   // array

double   temps[ 50 ];             // Declare 1 double floating-
                                  point
                                  // array

char letters[ 15 ];               // Declare a character array
```

When you declare an array, you instruct C++ to reserve a specific number of memory locations for that array. C++ will protect those elements. In the preceding four lines of code, if you assign a value to letters[2], you will not overwrite any data in weights, sizes, salaries, or temps. If you assign a value to sizes[94], you will not overwrite data stored in weights, salaries, temps, or letters.

Each element in an array occupies the same amount of storage as a nonarray variable of the same data type. In other words, each element in a character array occupies one byte of memory. Each element in an integer array occupies two bytes of memory. The same is true for every other data type.

In your programs, you can reference elements by using formulas for subscripts. As long as the subscript can evaluate to an integer, you can use a constant, a variable, or an expression for the subscript. All the following reference individual elements of arrays:

```
ara[ 4 ]

sales[ ctr + 1 ]

bonus[ month ]

salary[ month[ i ] * 2 ]
```

Array elements
follow each other
in memory, with
nothing between
them.

All array elements are stored in a contiguous, back-to-back fashion. This is important to remember, especially when you write more advanced programs. You can *always* count on an array's first element preceeding the second, the second element placed immediately before the third, and so on. There is no "padding" of memory; that is, C++ ensures (and guarantees) that there is no extra space between array elements. This holds true for character arrays, integer arrays, floating-point arrays, and every other array data type. If a floating-point value on your computer occupies four bytes of memory, the *next* element in a floating-point array *always* begins four bytes after the preceding element.

The Size of Arrays

The `sizeof()` function returns the number of bytes needed to hold its argument. If you use `sizeof()` to request the size of an array name, `sizeof()` returns the number of bytes *reserved* for the entire array.

Suppose that you declared an integer array of 100 elements called `scores`. If you were to produce the size of the array, as in

```
n = sizeof(scores);
```

n would hold 200. `sizeof()` always returns the reserved amount of storage, no matter what data is in the array. Therefore, a character array's contents, even if the array holds a very short string, do not affect the size of the array that was originally reserved in memory.

If you request the size of an individual array element, however, such as

```
n = sizeof(scores[ 6 ]);
```

n would hold 2.

You must never go out of bounds of an array. Suppose that you want to keep track of five employees' exemptions and their five salary codes. You can reserve two arrays to hold this data:

```
int  exemptions[ 5 ];   // Holds up to 5 employee exemptions

char sal_codes[ 5 ];    // Holds up to 5 employee codes
```

Figure 24.2 shows how C++ reserves memory for these arrays. Notice that C++ knows to reserve five elements for `exemptions` from the array declaration. C++ starts reserving memory for `sal_codes` after it reserves all five elements for the `exemptions`. If you were to declare several more variables, either locally or globally, after these two lines, C++ would always protect the five elements for `exemptions` and `sal_codes`.

C++ protects only
as many array
elements as you
specify.

Figure 24.2

Memory locations
of two arrays.

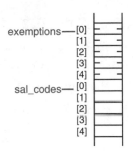

C++ does its part to protect your array data, so you must too. If you reserve five elements for `exemptions`, you have five integer array elements referred to as `exemptions[ 0 ]`, `exemptions[ 1 ]`, `exemptions[ 2 ]`, `exemptions[ 3 ]`, and `exemptions [ 4 ]`. C++ *will not protect more than five elements for* `exemptions`! If you were to put a value into an `exemptions` element that you did not reserve, such as

```
exemptions[ 6 ] = 4;      // Assign a value to an out-of-range
                          // element
```

C++ lets you do so, but the results are damaging! C++ overwrites other data—in this case, `sal_codes[ 2 ]` and `sal_codes[ 3 ]`, because they were reserved where the sixth element of the integer array `exemptions` would be placed. Figure 24.3 shows the damaging results of assigning a value to an out-of-range element.

Figure 24.3

Memory storage
after overwriting
part of *sal_codes*.

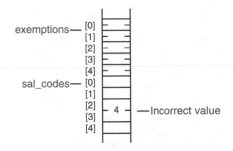

> **Caution:** Unlike most programming languages, C++ allows you to assign values to out-of-range (nonreserved) subscripts. You must be careful not to do this; if you do, you will overwrite other data or code.

Although you can define an array of any data type, you cannot declare an array of strings. A string is not a C++ variable data type. You learn how to hold multiple strings in an arraylike structure in Chapter 28, "Pointers and Arrays."

Initializing Arrays

You must assign values to array elements before using them. Here are the two ways to initialize elements in an array:

♦ Initialize the elements at declaration time

♦ Initialize the elements in the program

> **Note:** C++ automatically initializes global arrays to null zeros. All global character array elements are therefore null, and all numeric array elements contain zero. You should limit your use of global arrays. If you do use them, explicitly initialize them to zero, even though C++ does this for you, to clarify your intentions.

Initializing Elements at Declaration Time

You already know how to initialize character arrays that hold strings when you define the arrays. You simply assign the array a string. For example, the following declaration reserves six elements in a character array called city:

```
char city[ 6 ];      // Reserve space for city
```

If you also want to initialize city with a value, you can use the following code:

```
char city[ 6 ] = "Tulsa"; // Reserve space and initialize city
```

The 6 is optional because C++ counts the elements needed to hold Tulsa, plus an extra element for the null zero at the end of the quoted string.

You can reserve a character array and initialize it, a single character at a time, by using braces around the character data. The following line of code declares an array called initials and initializes it with eight characters:

```
char initials[ 8 ] =
    { 'Q', 'K', 'P', 'G', 'V', 'M', 'U', 'S' };
```

The array initials is *not a string!* Its data does not end in a null zero. There is nothing wrong with defining an array of characters like this one, but you must remember that you cannot treat the array as if it were a string. Do not use string functions with it, or attempt to print the array as a string.

Using the braces, you can initialize any type of array. For example, if you want to initialize an integer array that holds five children's ages, you can use the following declaration:

```
int  child_ages[ 5 ] =
    { 2, 5, 6, 8, 12 }; // Declare and initialize array
```

If you want to keep track of the last three years' total sales, you can declare an array and initialize it at the same time with this declaration:

```
double    sales[ ] =
     { 454323.43, 122355.32, 343324.96 };
```

As with character arrays, you do not have to state explicitly the array size when declaring and initializing an array of any type. C++ knows, in this case, to reserve three double floating-point array elements for sales. Figure 24.4 shows the memory representation of child_ages and sales.

Figure 24.4

Memory representation of two arrays.

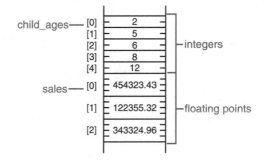

Note: You cannot initialize an array, using the assignment and braces, *after* you declare it. You can initialize arrays in this manner only when you declare them. If you want to fill an array with data after you declare the array, you must do so element by element, or by using functions as described later in this chapter.

C++ zeros all array values that you do not explicitly define at declaration time.

Although C++ does not automatically zero-out (or initialize to *any* value) array elements, if you initialize some but not all the elements when you declare the array, C++ will finish the job for you by assigning the rest of the elements to zero.

Suppose that you need to reserve array storage for three preceding months of profit figures as well as the next three months of profit figures. You need to reserve six elements of storage, but you know values for only the first three elements. You can initialize the array in this way:

```
double    profit[ 6 ] =
     { 67654.43, 46472.34, 63451.93 };
```

Because you explicitly initialized the three elements, C++ initializes the rest of them to zero. If you were to print the entire array, one element per line, with an appropriate cout, you would get the following results:

```
67654.43
46472.34
63451.93
00000.00
00000.00
00000.00
```

Tip: To initialize all elements of a large array to zero at the same time, declare the entire array and initialize its first value to zero. C++ finishes assigning the rest of the array to zero.

Caution: Always declare an array with the maximum number of subscripts, unless you initialize the array at the same time. The following array declaration is illegal:

```
int  count[ ];   // BAD array declaration!
```

C++ will not know how many elements to reserve for count, so it reserves *none*. The Visual C++ compiler will print out an error and refuse to compile the program. This protects you from an error; if you were to assign values to count's nonreserved elements, you probably would overwrite other data.

You can leave the brackets empty only when you assign values to the array, such as in the following:

```
int  count[ ] =

    { 15, 9, 22, -8, 12 };   // Good definition
```

C++ can tell, from the list of values, how many elements to reserve. In this case, C++ reserves five elements for count.

Examples

1. Suppose that you want to keep track of the stock market averages for the preceding 90 days. Instead of storing the averages in 90 different variables, you can easily store them in an array:

```
float    stock[ 90 ];
```

The rest of the program can assign values to the averages.

2. You just finished taking classes at a local university and want to average your six class scores. The following program initializes an array for the school name and for the six classes. The body of the program averages each of the six scores.

```cpp
// Filename: C24ARA1.CPP
// Averages six test scores

#include <iostream.h>

main()
{
    char        s_name[ ] = "Tri Star University";
    float    scores[ 6 ] =
           { 88.7, 90.4, 76.0, 97.0, 100.0, 86.7 };
    float     average = 0.0;
    int          ctr;

    // Compute total of scores
    for (ctr = 0; ctr < 6; ctr++)
    {
         average += scores[ ctr ];
    }
    // Compute the average
    average /= (float)6;
    cout << "At " << s_name << ", your class average is "
         << average << ".\n";
    return 0;
}
```

This program's output is as follows:

```
At Tri Star University, your class average is 89.8.
```

Notice that the use of arrays makes processing lists of information much easier. Instead of averaging six differently named variables, you can use a for loop to step through the array elements. The advantage to arrays is that you can average even 1,000 numbers with a simple for loop. If the 1,000 variables were not arrays but were individually named, you would have to write a lot of code just to add them together.

3. The following program is an expanded version of the preceding one. This program prints the six scores before computing the average. Notice that you have to print array elements individually; there is no way to print an entire array in a single cout. (Of course, you can print an entire character array, but only if it holds a null-terminated string of characters.)

```cpp
// Filename: C24ARA2.CPP
// Prints and averages six test scores

#include <iostream.h>

void    pr_scores(float scores[ 6 ])
{
    // Print the six scores
    int     ctr;

    cout << "Here are your scores:\n";      // Title
    for (ctr = 0; ctr < 6; ctr++)
        cout << scores[ ctr ] << "\n";
    return;
}


int     main(void)
{
    char            s_name[ ] = "Tri Star University";
    float       scores[ 6 ] =
        { 88.7, 90.4, 76.0, 97.0, 100.0, 86.7 };
    float       average = 0.0;
    int             ctr;

    // Call function to print scores
    pr_scores(scores);
    // Compute total of scores
    for (ctr = 0; ctr < 6; ctr++)
    {
        average += scores[ ctr ];
    }
    // Compute the average
    average /= (float)6;
    cout << "At " << s_name << ", your class average is "
        << average << ".\n";
    return 0;
}
```

To pass any array to a function, you just specify the array's name. In the receiving function's parameter list, you must state the array type and provide brackets that tell the function that it is an array.

4. To improve the maintainability of your programs, define all array sizes with the #define preprocessor directive. What if you plan to take only four classes next semester but you want to use this same program? You can modify it by changing all the 6s to 4s, but if you have defined the array size with a defined constant, you will need to alter only one line to change the program's subscript limits. Notice how the following program uses a defined constant for the number of classes throughout the program:

```cpp
// Filename: C24ARA3.CPP
// Prints and averages six test scores

#include <iostream.h>

#define     CLASS_NUM      (6)

void     pr_scores(float scores[ CLASS_NUM ])
{
    int     ctr;

    cout << "Here are your scores:\n";     // Title
    for (ctr = 0; ctr < CLASS_NUM; ctr++)
        cout << scores[ ctr ] << "\n";
    return;
}


int     main(void)
{
    char          s_name[ ] = "Tri Star University";
    float     scores[ CLASS_NUM ] =
        { 88.7, 90.4, 76.0, 97.0, 100.0, 86.7 };
    float     average = 0.0;
    int          ctr;

    // Call function to print scores
    pr_scores(scores);
```

```
    // Compute total of scores
    for (ctr = 0; ctr < CLASS_NUM; ctr++)
    {
        average += scores[ ctr ];
    }
    // Compute the average
    average /= (float)CLASS_NUM;
    cout << "At " << s_name << ", your class average is "
        << average << ".\n";
    return 0;
}
```

For a simple example like this, using a defined constant for the maximum subscript may not seem like a big advantage. If you were writing a larger program that processed several arrays, however, changing the defined constant at the top of the program is much easier than searching the program for each occurrence of that array reference.

Using defined constants for array sizes has the added advantage of protecting you from going out of the subscript bounds. You don't have to remember the subscript when looping through arrays; you can use the defined constant instead.

Initializing an Array in the Program

Rarely will you know the contents of arrays when you declare them. Usually, you fill an array with user input or from a disk file's data. The for loop is a perfect tool for looping through arrays when you fill them with values.

> **Caution:** An array name cannot appear on the left side of an assignment statement.

You cannot assign one array to another. Suppose that you want to copy an array called total_sales to a second array called saved_sales. You *cannot* do this with the following assignment statement:

```
saved_sales = total_sales;      // INVALID!
```

Instead, you have to copy the arrays one element at a time, using a loop, as in the following section of code.

Initialize the variable ctr to 0 and increment it by 1 while the variable ctr is less than ARRAY_SIZE.
    Write the ctr'th element of the total_sales array to the ctr'th element of the saved_sales array.

```
for (ctr = 0; ctr < ARRAY_SIZE; ctr++)
{

    saved_sales[ ctr ] = total_sales[ ctr ];

}
```

The following examples illustrate methods for initializing arrays within the program. After learning about disk processing later in the book, you will learn to read array values from a disk file.

Examples

1. The following program uses the assignment operator to assign 10 temperatures to an array:

```
// Filename: C24ARA4.CPP
// Fills an array with 10 temperature values

#include <iostream.h>

#define NUM_TEMPS 10

main()
{
    float       temps[ NUM_TEMPS ];
    int         ctr;

    temps[ 0 ] = 78.6;      // Subscripts ALWAYS begin at 0
    temps[ 1 ] = 82.1;
    temps[ 2 ] = 79.5;
    temps[ 3 ] = 75.0;
    temps[ 4 ] = 75.4;
    temps[ 5 ] = 71.8;
    temps[ 6 ] = 73.3;
    temps[ 7 ] = 69.5;
    temps[ 8 ] = 74.1;
    temps[ 9 ] = 75.7;
    // Print the temps
    cout << "Daily temperatures for the last "
         << NUM_TEMPS << " days:\n";
    for (ctr = 0; ctr < NUM_TEMPS; ctr++)
    {
        cout << temps[ ctr ] << "\n";
    }
    return 0;
}
```

2. The following program uses a `for` loop to assign eight integers from the user's input, using `cin`. The program then prints the total of the numbers.

```
// Filename: C24TOT.CPP
// Totals 8 input values from the user

#include <iostream.h>

#define NUM 8

main()
{
    int    nums[ NUM ];
    int    ctr;
    int    total = 0;   // Holds total of user's 8 numbers

    for (ctr = 0; ctr < NUM; ctr++)
    {
        cout << "Please enter the next number...";
        cin >> nums[ ctr ];
        total += nums[ ctr ];
    }
    cout << "The total of the numbers is " << total <<
    ➡"\n";
    return 0;
}
```

3. You don't have to access the elements of an array in the same order in which you initialized the array. Chapter 25, "Array Processing," shows you how to change the order of an array. You can use the subscript to "pick out" items from a list (array) of values.

The following program requests sales data for the last 12 months. The program then waits until another user types a month number. That month's sales are then printed, without the values for the surrounding months getting in the way. This is how you would begin to build a search program to find requested data: store the data in an array (or in a disk file that can be read into an array, as you see in Chapters 32 and 33) and then wait for a request from the user to see only specific pieces of that data.

```
// Filename: C24SAL.CPP
// Stores 12 months of sales and prints selected ones

#include <iostream.h>
#include <ctype.h>
```

```
#include <conio.h>
#include <iomanip.h>

#define NUM 12

main()
{
    float    sales[ NUM ];
    int      ctr;
    int      req_month;      // Holds user's request
    char     ans;

    cout.setf(ios::fixed);
    cout.setf(ios::showpoint);

    // Fill the array
    cout << "Please enter the twelve monthly "
        << "sales values\n";
    for (ctr = 0; ctr < NUM; ctr++)
    {
        cout << "What are sales for month number "
            << (ctr + 1) << "\n";
        cin >> sales[ ctr ];
    }

    // Wait for a requested month
    for (ctr = 0; ctr < 25; ctr++)
        cout << "\n";   // Clear the screen
    cout << "*** Sales Printing Program ***\n";
    cout << "Prints any sales from the last " << NUM
        << " months\n\n";
    do
    {
        cout << "\nWhat month (1-" << NUM
            << ") do you want to see a sales value for?";
        cin >> req_month;

        // Adjust for zero-based subscript
        cout << "Month " << req_month << "'s sales are "
            << setprecision(2) << sales[ req_month - 1 ]
            << "\n";
        cout << "\nDo you want to see another (Y/N)? ";
        cin >> ans;
        ans = toupper(ans);
    }
    while (ans == 'Y');
    return 0;
}
```

Figure 24.5 shows the second screen from this program. After the 12 sales values are entered into the array, any or all of them can be requested, one at a time, simply by supplying the month number (the number of the subscript).

Figure 24.5

Printing sales values entered into the array.

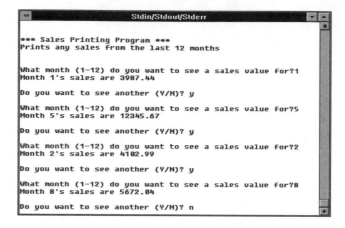

```
                        Stdin/Stdout/Stderr
*** Sales Printing Program ***
Prints any sales from the last 12 months


What month (1-12) do you want to see a sales value for?1
Month 1's sales are 3987.44

Do you want to see another (Y/N)? y

What month (1-12) do you want to see a sales value for?5
Month 5's sales are 12345.67

Do you want to see another (Y/N)? y

What month (1-12) do you want to see a sales value for?2
Month 2's sales are 4102.99

Do you want to see another (Y/N)? y

What month (1-12) do you want to see a sales value for?8
Month 8's sales are 5672.04

Do you want to see another (Y/N)? n
```

Notice the helpful screen-clearing routine that prints 25 newline characters. This routine scrolls the screen until it is blank.

Summary

You now know how to declare and initialize arrays of various data types. You can initialize an array when you declare it or in the body of your program. Array elements are much easier to process than many variables with different names.

Useful sorting and searching techniques are available to make your programs extremely powerful. The next chapter describes these techniques and shows you other ways to access array elements.

Review Questions

Answers to Review Questions are in Appendix B.

1. True or false: A single array can hold several values of different data types.

2. How do C++ programs tell one array element from another if the elements have identical names?

3. Why must you initialize an array before using it?

4. Look at the following definition of an array called `weights`:

```
int  weights[ 10 ] = { 5, 2, 4 };
```

What is the value of `weights[ 5 ]`?

5. Recall how character arrays are passed to functions. If you change a passed integer array in a function, does the array change also in the calling function?

6. How does C++ initialize global array elements?

Review Exercises

1. Write a program to store six of your friends' ages in a single array. Store each of the six ages by using the assignment operator. Print the ages on-screen.

2. Modify the preceding program to print the ages backward.

3. Write a simple data program to track a radio station's ratings (1, 2, 3, 4, or 5) for the last 18 months. Use `cin` to initialize the array with the ratings. Print the ratings on the screen with an appropriate title.

4. Write a program to store the numbers from 1 to 100 in an array of 100 integer elements. Remember that the subscripts begin at 0 and end at 99.

5. Write a program that a small business owner can use to track customers. Assign each customer a number (starting at 0). When a customer comes into the store, store that customer's sales in an element that matches a number for that customer (the next, unused array element). When the store owner signals the end of the day, print a report of each customer number and matching sales, with a total sales at the bottom, along with the average sales per customer.

CHAPTER 25

Array Processing

C++ provides many ways to access arrays. If you have programmed with other computer languages, some of C++'s array-indexing techniques will be unfamiliar to you. Arrays in the C++ language are closely linked with pointers. Chapter 27, "Pointers," describes the many ways that pointers and arrays interact.

Because pointers are so powerful, and because understanding arrays provides a good foundation for learning about pointers, this chapter describes in detail how to reference arrays and discusses the different types of array processing. You learn how to search an array for one or more values, find the highest and lowest values in an array, and sort an array into numeric or alphabetic order.

This chapter introduces the following topics:

♦ Searching arrays

♦ Finding the highest and lowest values in arrays

♦ Sorting arrays

♦ Advanced subscripting with arrays

Many programmers see the use of arrays as a turning point. Understanding array processing will make your programs not only more accurate but also more powerful.

Searching Arrays

Array elements do not always appear in the most appropriate order.

Arrays are one of the primary means by which data is stored in C++ programs. Many types of programs lend themselves to processing lists (arrays) of data, such as an employee payroll program, scientific research of several chemicals, or customer account processing. As mentioned in Chapter 24, array data is usually read from a disk file. Upcoming chapters describe disk file processing. For now, you should know how to manipulate arrays so that you see the data exactly the way you want to see it.

In the preceding chapter, you learned how to print the elements of arrays in the same order in which you entered the data. This is sometimes done, but it is not always the best method for looking at data.

Suppose that a high school uses C++ programs for its grade reports, and the principal wants to see the top 10 grade-point averages. You cannot print the first 10 grade-point averages in the list of student averages because the top 10 grade points may not (and probably do not) appear as the first 10 array elements. Because the grade points are not in any sequence, the program would have to sort the array elements into numeric order (from high to low grade points), or search the array for the 10 highest grade points.

You need a method for putting arrays in a specific order. This is called *sorting* an array. When you sort an array, you put that array's elements in a specific order, such as alphabetic order or numeric order. A dictionary is in alphabetic order, and so is a phone book.

You also can reverse the order of a sort, called a *descending sort*. If you wanted to look at a list of all employees in descending salary order, for example, the names of the highest-paid employees would be printed first.

Figure 25.1 shows a list of eight numbers in an array called unsorted. The middle list of numbers is an ascending sorted version of unsorted. The third list of numbers is a descending sorted version of unsorted.

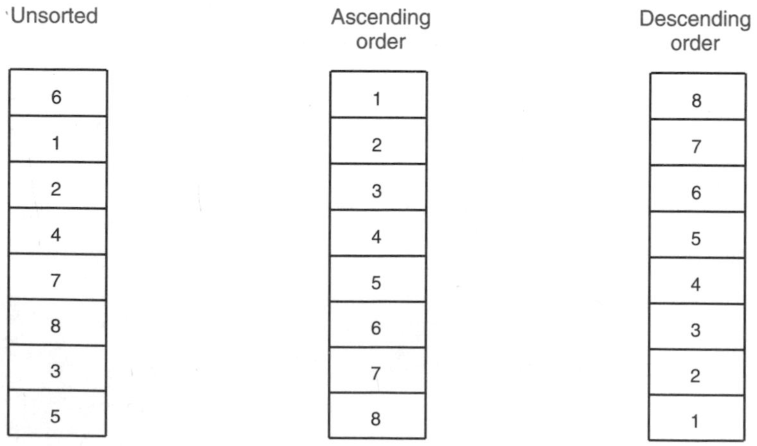

Figure 25.1

A list of unsorted numbers sorted in both ascending and descending order.

Before learning to sort, you need to know a preliminary step—how to search an array for a value. What if one of those students receives a grade change? The computer has to be able to access that student's grade in order to change it (without affecting the others). As the next section shows, programs can search for specific array elements.

> **Note:** C++ provides a method for sorting and searching lists of strings, although you cannot fully understand how to do this until you learn about pointers, beginning in Chapter 27, "Pointers." The sorting and searching examples and algorithms in this chapter on array processing demonstrate sorting and searching arrays of numbers. The same concepts will apply (and will actually be much more usable for real-world applications) when you learn how to store lists of names in C++.

Searching for Values

You do not have to sort an array to find its extreme values.

You do not need to know any new commands to search an array for a value. Basically, the `if` and `for` loop statements are all you need. To search an array for a specific value, look at each element in the array, using the `if` statement to compare the elements to see whether they match. If they do not, keep searching down the array. If you run out of array elements before finding the value, the value is not in the array.

You can perform several different kinds of searches. For example, you might need to find the highest or lowest value in a list of numbers. This is helpful when you have lots of data and you want to know the extremes of the data (such as the highest and lowest sales region in your division). In addition, you can search an array to see whether it contains a matching value. For example, you can determine whether an item is already in an inventory by searching a part number array for a match.

The following programs illustrate some of these array-searching techniques.

Examples

1. To find the highest number in an array, compare each element with the first one. If you find a higher value, it becomes the basis for the rest of the array. If you continue until you reach the end of the array, you will have the highest value, as the following program shows:

```
// Filename: C25HIGH.CPP
// Finds the highest value in the array
```

```
#include <iostream.h>

#define SIZE 15

main()
{
    // Put a bunch of numbers in the array
    int     ara[ SIZE ] =
        { 5, 2, 7, 8, 36,
          4, 2, 86, 11, 43,
          22, 12, 45, 6, 85 };
    int     high_val, ctr;

    high_val = ara[ 0 ];        // Initialize with first array
                                // element
    for (ctr = 1; ctr < SIZE; ctr++)
    {     // Store current value if it is higher than
          // highest so far
        if (ara[ ctr ] > high_val)
        {
            high_val = ara[ ctr ];
        }
    }
    cout << "The highest number in the list is "
        << high_val << ".\n";
    return 0;
}
```

This program's output is as follows:

```
The highest number in the list is 86.
```

You save the element only if its value is higher than the value of the one to which you are comparing it. Finding the smallest number in an array is just as easy except that you compare the elements to see whether each succeeding array value is less than the lowest value found so far.

2. The following program finds the highest and lowest values. It stores the first array element in *both* the highest and lowest variables to begin the search. This ensures that each element after the first one is tested to see whether it is higher or lower than the first element.

This example also uses the rand() function, discussed in Chapter 23, to fill the array with random values from 0 to 99. The modulus operator (%) and 100 are applied to whatever value rand() produces. The program prints the entire array before starting the search for the highest and lowest values. Figure 25.2 shows the output of this program.

```
// Filename: C25HILO.CPP
// Finds the highest and lowest values in the array

#include <time.h>
#include <iostream.h>
#include <stdlib.h>

#define SIZE 15

main()
{
    time_t  timeval;             // used to seed random function
    int     ara[ SIZE ];
    int     high_val, low_val, ctr;

    // Fill array with random numbers from 0 to 99
    srand( (unsigned)time(&timeval) );
    for (ctr = 0; ctr < SIZE; ctr++)
    {
        ara[ ctr ] = rand() % 100;
    }

    // Print the array to the screen
    cout << "Here are the " << SIZE
        << " random numbers:\n";      // Title
    for (ctr = 0; ctr < SIZE; ctr++)
    {
        cout << ara[ ctr ] << "\n";
    }
    cout << "\n\n";                 // Print a blank line

    high_val = ara[ 0 ];      // Initialize both high_val
    low_val  = ara[ 0 ];      // and low_val to 1st element

    // go through array
    // Store current value in high or low if it is
    // higher or lower than highest or lowest so far
    for (ctr = 1; ctr < SIZE; ctr++)
    {
        if (ara[ ctr ] > high_val)
            high_val = ara[ ctr ];
        if (ara[ ctr ] < low_val)
            low_val = ara[ ctr ];
    }

    cout << "The highest number in the list is "
        << high_val << ".\n";
    cout << "The lowest number in the list is "
        << low_val << ".\n";
    return 0;
}
```

Figure 25.2

Printing the
highest and lowest
values in a list of
random numbers.

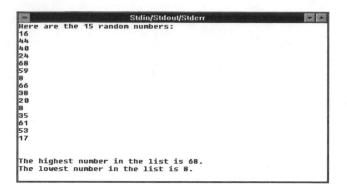

```
Stdin/Stdout/Stderr
Here are the 15 random numbers:
16
44
40
24
68
59
8
66
38
20
8
35
61
53
17

The highest number in the list is 68.
The lowest number in the list is 8.
```

3. The following program fills an array with part numbers from an inventory.
Use your imagination; the inventory array would normally fill more of the
array, be initialized from a disk file, and be part of a larger set of arrays
holding descriptions, quantities, costs, selling prices, and so on. For this
example, assignment statements initialize the array. The important idea to
learn from this program is not the array initialization but the method for
searching the array. Figure 25.3 shows the program's output.

Note: If the newly entered part number is already on file, the program
tells the user. Otherwise, the part number is added to the end of the
array.

```cpp
// Filename: C25SERCH.CPP
// Searches a part number array for the input value. If
// the entered part number is not in the array, it is added.
// If the part number is in the array, a message is printed.

#include <iostream.h>

#define MAX 100


void    fill_parts(long int parts[ MAX ])
{
    // Assign 5 part numbers to array for testing
    parts[ 0 ] = 12345;
    parts[ 1 ] = 24724;
    parts[ 2 ] = 54154;
    parts[ 3 ] = 73496;
```

```
    parts[ 4 ] = 83925;
    return;
}


int     main(void)
{
    long int     search_part;   // Holds user request
    long int     parts[ MAX ];
    int          ctr;
    int          num_parts = 5; // Beginning inventory count

    fill_parts(parts);       // Fill the first 5 elements
    do
    {
        cout << "\n\nPlease type a part number ";
        cout << "...(-9999 ends program) ";
        cin >> search_part;
        if (search_part == -9999)
            break;      // Exit loop if user wants
        // Scan array to see if part is in inventory
        for (ctr = 0; ctr < num_parts; ctr++)
            // Check each item
        {
            if (search_part == parts[ctr])
                // If in inventory...
            {
                cout << "\nPart " << search_part
                    << " is already in inventory";
                break;
            }
            else
            {
                if (ctr == (num_parts - 1))
                    // If not there, add it
                {
                    parts[ num_parts ] = search_part;
                    // Add to end of array
                    num_parts++;
                    cout << "\n" << search_part
                        << " was added to inventory\n";
                    break;
                }
            }
        }
    }
    while (search_part != -9999); // Loop until user
                                  // signals end
    return 0;
}
```

443

Figure 25.3

Searching a table of part numbers.

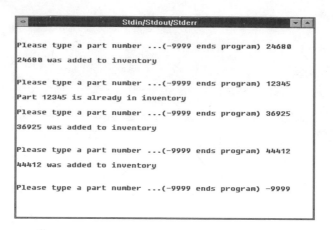

```
                        Stdin/Stdout/Stderr
Please type a part number ...(-9999 ends program) 24680

24680 was added to inventory

Please type a part number ...(-9999 ends program) 12345

Part 12345 is already in inventory

Please type a part number ...(-9999 ends program) 36925

36925 was added to inventory

Please type a part number ...(-9999 ends program) 44412

44412 was added to inventory

Please type a part number ...(-9999 ends program) -9999
```

Sorting Arrays

At times, you may need to sort one or more arrays. Suppose that you took a list of numbers, wrote each number on a separate piece of paper, and threw all the pieces into the air. The steps you would follow in trying to put the numbers in order, shuffling and changing the order of the pieces, are similar to what your computer goes through to sort numbers or character data.

Because sorting arrays requires exchanging values of elements, you should first learn the technique for swapping variables. Suppose that you have two variables named score1 and score2. What if you wanted to reverse their values (putting score2 into the score1 variable, and score1 into the score2 variable)? You could *not* use the following method:

```
score1 = score2;      // Does NOT swap the two values
score2 = score1;
```

Why doesn't this work? In the first line, the value of score1 gets replaced with score2's value; when the first line finishes, both score1 and score2 contain the same value. Therefore, the second line cannot work.

To swap two variables, you need to use a third variable to hold the intermediate result. (That's the only purpose of the third variable.) For instance, to swap score1 and score2, use a third variable, called hold_score, as in the following code:

```
hold_score = score1;      // These 3 lines properly swap
score1 = score2;          // score1 and score2
score2 = hold_score;
```

This code exchanges the two values in the two variables.

There are several different ways to sort arrays. Some of the methods are the *bubble sort*, the *quick sort*, and the *shell sort*. The basic goal of each method is to compare each array element to another array element and then swap them if the higher one is less than the other one.

The theory behind these sorts is beyond the scope of this book; however, the bubble sort is one of the easiest methods to follow. Values in the array are compared to each other, a pair at a time, and swapped if they are not in back-to-back order. The lowest value eventually "floats" to the top of the array, like a bubble in a glass of soda.

> The lowest value in a list "floats" to the top with the bubble sort algorithm.

Figure 25.4 shows a list of numbers before, during, and after a bubble sort. The bubble sort steps through the array, comparing pairs of numbers, to see whether they need to be swapped. Several passes may have to be made through the array before it is finally sorted (that is, no more passes are needed). Other types of sorts improve on the bubble sort; its procedure is easy to program but slower than many of the other methods.

The sample programs that follow show the bubble sort in action.

Figure 25.4

Sorting a list of numbers with the bubble sort.

First Pass

3	2	2	2
2	3	3	3
5	5	1	1
1	1	5	4
4	4	4	5

Second Pass

2	2
3	1
1	3
4	4
5	5

Third Pass

2	1
1	2
3	3
4	4
5	5

Fourth Pass

1
2
3
4
5

Examples

1. This program assigns 10 random numbers, between 0 and 99, to an array and then sorts it.

A nested for loop, as shown in the sort_array() function, is perfect for sorting numbers in the array. Nested for loops provide a nice mechanism for working on pairs of values, swapping them if needed. As the outside loop counts down the list, referencing each element, the inside loop compares each of the remaining values with those array elements.

```cpp
// Filename: C25SORT1.CPP
// Sorts and prints a list of numbers

#define MAX 10

#include <time.h>
#include <iostream.h>
#include <stdlib.h>


void    fill_array(int ara[ MAX ])
{
    // Put random numbers in the array
    time_t  timeval;   // used to seed the rand function
    int     ctr;

    srand( (unsigned)time(&timeval) );
    for (ctr = 0; ctr < MAX; ctr++)
        ara[ ctr ] = (rand() % 100);   // Force # to
                                       // 0-99 range
    return;
}

void    print_array(int ara[ MAX ])
{
    // Print the array
    int     ctr;
    for (ctr = 0; ctr < MAX; ctr++)
        cout << ara[ ctr ] << "\n";
    return;
}
```

```cpp
void     sort_array(int ara[ MAX ])
{
    // Sort the array
    int     temp;          // Temporary variable to swap with
    int     ctr1, ctr2;    // Need 2 loop counters to swap
                           // pairs of numbers

    for (ctr1 = 0; ctr1 < (MAX - 1); ctr1++)
    {
        for (ctr2 = (ctr1 + 1); ctr2 < MAX; ctr2++)
            // Test pairs
        {
            if (ara[ ctr1 ] > ara[ ctr2 ])
                // Swap if this pair
            {
                temp = ara[ ctr1 ]; // is not in order
                ara[ ctr1 ] = ara[ ctr2 ];
                ara[ ctr2 ] = temp; // "float" the
                                          // lowest to highest
            }
        }
    }
    return;
}


int     main(void)
{
    int     ara[ MAX ];

    fill_array(ara);       // Put random numbers in the array
    cout << "Here are the unsorted numbers:\n";
    print_array(ara);      // Print the unsorted array
    sort_array(ara);       // Sort the array
    cout << "\nHere are the sorted numbers:\n";
    print_array(ara);      // Print the newly sorted array
    return 0;
}
```

Figure 25.5 shows the output of this program. If any two randomly generated numbers are the same, the bubble sort will work properly, placing them next to each other in the list.

Figure 25.5

Printing a sorted list of numbers.

```
                  Stdin/Stdout/Stderr
Here are the unsorted numbers:
58
14
78
10
49
1
40
69
87
66

Here are the sorted numbers:
1
10
14
40
49
58
66
69
78
87
```

2. The following program is just like the preceding one, except that this program prints the list of numbers in descending order.

A descending sort is as easy to write as an ascending sort. With the ascending sort (from low to high values), you compare pairs of values, testing to see whether the first value is greater than the second one. With a descending sort, you test to see whether the first value is less than the second one.

To produce a descending sort, use the < (less than) logical operator when swapping array elements.

```
// Filename: C25SORT2.CPP
// Sorts and prints a list of numbers in descending order

#define MAX 10

#include <time.h>
#include <iostream.h>
#include <stdlib.h>


void    fill_array(int ara[ MAX ])
{
    // Put random numbers in the array
    time_t  timeval;   // use to seed rand function
    int     ctr;

    srand( (unsigned)time(&timeval) );
    for (ctr = 0; ctr < MAX; ctr++)
        ara[ ctr ] = (rand() % 100);       // Force # to
                                           // 0-99 range

    return;
}
```

```
void     print_array(int ara[ MAX ])
{
    // Print the array
    int     ctr;
    for (ctr = 0; ctr < MAX; ctr++)
        cout << ara[ ctr ] << "\n";
    return;
}

void     sort_array(int ara[ MAX ])
{
    // Sort the array
    int     temp;         // Temporary variable to swap with
    int     ctr1, ctr2;   // Need 2 loop counters to swap
                          // pairs of numbers

    for (ctr1 = 0; ctr1 < (MAX - 1); ctr1++)
    {
        for (ctr2 = (ctr1 + 1); ctr2 < MAX; ctr2++)
            // Test pairs
            // Notice the difference in descending (here)
            // and ascending
        {
            if (ara[ ctr1 ] < ara[ ctr2 ])
                // Swap if this pair
            {
                temp = ara[ ctr1 ]; // is not in order
                ara[ ctr1 ] = ara[ ctr2 ];
                ara[ ctr2 ] = temp; // "float" the
                                    // highest to lowest
            }
        }
    }
    return;
}

int     main(void)
{
    int     ara[ MAX ];

    fill_array(ara);       // Put random numbers in the array
    cout << "Here are the unsorted numbers:\n";
    print_array(ara);      // Print the unsorted array
    sort_array(ara);       // Sort the array
    cout << "\n\nHere are the sorted numbers:\n";
    print_array(ara);      // Print the newly sorted array
    return 0;
}
```

> **Tip:** You can save the preceding programs' sort functions in two files named `sort_ascend` and `sort_descend`. When you need to sort two different arrays, `#include` these files inside your own programs. Even better, compile each of these routines separately and link the one you need to your program.

You can sort character arrays as easily as you sort numeric arrays. C++ uses the ASCII table for its sorting comparisons. Notice that in the ASCII table in Appendix C, numbers sort before letters and uppercase letters sort before lowercase letters.

Advanced Referencing of Arrays

The array notation you have seen so far is common in computer programming languages. Most languages use subscripts inside brackets (or parentheses) to refer to individual array elements. For example, you know the following array references describe the first and fifth elements of the array called `sales` (remember that the starting subscript is always 0):

```
sales[ 0 ]
sales[ 4 ]
```

C++ provides another approach to referencing arrays. Even though the title of this section includes the word *Advanced*, this array-referencing method is not difficult. It is very different, though, especially if you are familiar with another programming language's approach.

An array name is the address of the starting element of the array.

There is nothing wrong with referring to array elements in the manner you have seen. However, the approach described here, unique to C++, will be helpful when you learn about pointers in upcoming chapters. Actually, C++ programmers who have programmed for several years rarely use the subscript notation you have seen.

In C++, an array's name is not just a label for you to use in programs. To C++, the array name is the actual address where the first element begins in memory. Suppose that you define an array called `amounts` with the following statement:

```
int     amounts[ 6 ] =
    { 4, 1, 3, 7, 9, 2 };
```

Figure 25.6 shows how this array is stored in memory. The figure shows the array beginning at address 405,332. (The actual addresses of variables are determined by the computer when you load and run your compiled program.) Notice that the name of the array, `amounts`, is located somewhere in memory and contains the address of `amounts[ 0 ]`, or 405,332.

Figure 25.6

The array name
amounts holds
the address of
amounts[0].

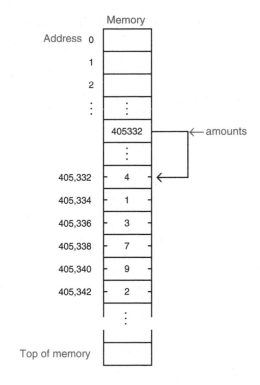

You can refer to an array by using its regular subscript notation or modifying the address of the array. Both of the following items refer to the third element of amounts:

```
amounts[ 3 ]
```

```
(amounts + 3)[ 0 ]
```

Because C++ considers the array name to be an address in memory that contains the location of the first array element, nothing keeps you from using a different address as the starting address and referencing from there. Taking this one step farther, each of the following items *also* refers to the third element of amounts:

```
(amounts + 0)[ 3 ]

(amounts + 2)[ 1 ]

(amounts - 2)[ 5 ]

(1 + amounts)[ 2 ]

(3 + amounts)[ 0 ]

(amounts + 1)[ 2 ]
```

You can print any of these array elements with a cout function.

> **Caution:** The hierarchy table in Appendix D shows that array subscripts have precedence over addition and subtraction. Therefore, you must enclose an array name in parentheses if you want to modify the name. The following examples are not equivalent:
>
> ```
> (2 + amounts)[ 1 ]
>
>  + amounts[ 1 ]
> ```
>
> The second example takes the value of `amounts[ 1 ]` (which is 1 in this sample array) and adds 2 to it (resulting in a value of 3).

This second method of array referencing might seem like more trouble than it is worth, but learning to reference arrays in this way will make your transition to pointers much easier. An array name is actually a pointer because the array contains the address of the first array element (it "points" to the start of the array).

When printing strings inside character arrays, referencing the arrays by their modified addresses is more useful than referencing the arrays with integers. Suppose that you stored three strings in a single character array. You could initialize the array with the following statement:

```
char names[ ] =
    { 'T', 'e', 'd', '\0',
      'E', 'v', 'a', '\0',
      'S', 'a', 'm', '\0' };
```

Figure 25.7 shows how this array might look in memory. The array name, names, contains the address of the first element, names[0] (the letter T).

You have yet to see a character array that holds more than one string, but C++ allows such an array. The problem is how you reference (especially how you print) the second and third strings. If you were to print this array (as you have been doing) with

```
cout << names;
```

C++ would print

```
Ted
```

cout prints characters starting at the array's address until the null zero is reached.

As mentioned in Chapter 8, "Simple Input and Output," cout prints the string starting at the address of the specified array. Without a different way to reference the array, you would have no method of printing the three strings inside the single array (without resorting to printing them one element at a time).

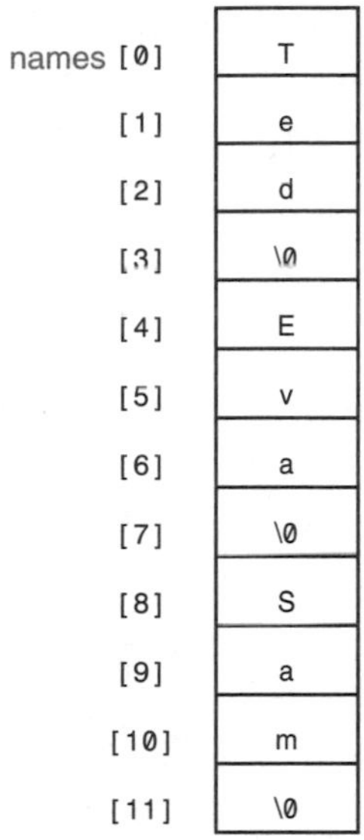

Figure 25.7

Storing more than
one string in a
single character
array.

names [0]	T
[1]	e
[2]	d
[3]	\0
[4]	E
[5]	v
[6]	a
[7]	\0
[8]	S
[9]	a
[10]	m
[11]	\0

Because cout requires a starting address, you can print the three strings with the following cout function calls:

```
cout << names;        // Print Ted
cout << names + 4;    // Print Eva
cout << names + 8;    // Print Sam
```

To test your understanding, what will the following cout function calls print?

```
cout << names + 1;
cout << names + 6;
```

The first cout prints ed, the string starting at the address specified (names + 1), and stops printing when it gets to the null zero. The second cout prints a. Adding 6 to the address at names produces the address where the a is located. The "string" is only one character long because the null zero appears in the array immediately after the a.

In summary of character arrays, the following refer to individual array elements (single characters):

```
names[ 2 ]
(names + 1)[ 1 ]
```

You can print both of these elements as characters but *not* as strings.
The following refer to addresses only:

```
names
(names + 4)
```

You can print both of these elements as strings but *not* as characters.

The next sample program is a little different from most of those you have seen. This example does not perform real-world work but helps you become familiar with this new method of array referencing. The next few chapters expand on this method.

Example

The following program stores the numbers from 100 to 600 in an array and then prints elements with the new method of array subscripting:

```cpp
// Filename: C25REF1.CPP
// Prints elements of an integer array in different ways

#include <iostream.h>

main()
{
    int    num[ 6 ] =
         { 100, 200, 300, 400, 500, 600 };

    cout << "num[0] is \t" << num[ 0 ] << "\n";
    cout << "(num + 0)[ 0 ] is \t" << (num + 0)[ 0 ]
         << "\n";
    cout << "(num - 2)[ 2 ] is \t" << (num - 2)[ 2 ]
         << "\n\n";
    cout << "num[ 1 ] is \t" << num[ 1 ] << "\n";
    cout << "(num + 1)[ 0 ] is \t" << (num + 1)[ 0 ]
         << "\n";
    cout << "(num - 5)[ 4 ] is \t" << (num - 5)[ 4 ]
         << "\n\n";
    cout << "num[ 5 ] is \t" << num[ 5 ] << "\n";
    cout << "(num + 5)[ 0 ] is \t" << (num + 5)[ 0 ]
         << "\n";
    cout << "(num + 2)[ 3 ] is \t" << (num + 2)[ 3 ]
         << "\n\n";
    cout << "(3 + num)[ 1 ] is \t" << (3 + num)[ 1 ]
         << "\n";
    cout << "3 + num[ 1 ] is \t" << 3 + num[ 1 ] << "\n";
    return 0;
}
```

Figure 25.8 shows this program's output. The output for (num-5)[4] may be different on your computer because the computed offset into the array is actually one position before the first element of the array. This is a common error that you need to be careful to avoid in your own programs.

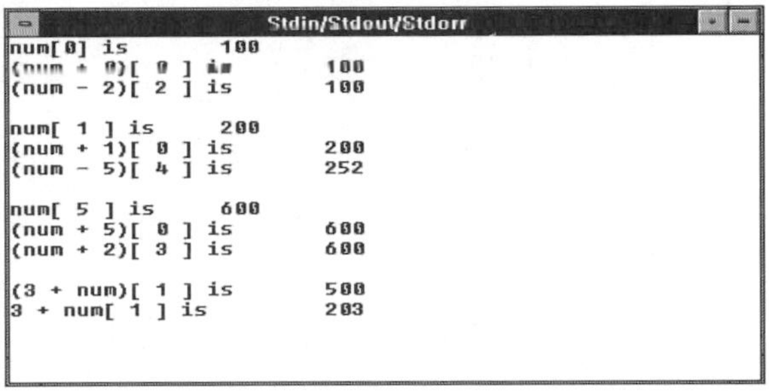

Figure 25.8

The output of various array references.

```
                    Stdin/Stdout/Stderr
num[0] is          100
(num + 0)[ 0 ] is          100
(num - 2)[ 2 ] is          100

num[ 1 ] is        200
(num + 1)[ 0 ] is          200
(num - 5)[ 4 ] is          252

num[ 5 ] is        600
(num + 5)[ 0 ] is          600
(num + 2)[ 3 ] is          600

(3 + num)[ 1 ] is          500
3 + num[ 1 ] is          203
```

Summary

You are beginning to see the true power of programming languages. Arrays enable you to search and sort lists of values. Sorting and searching are what computers do best; they can quickly scan hundreds and even thousands of values, looking for a match. Scanning files of paper by hand to look for just the right number takes much more time. By stepping through arrays, your programs can quickly scan, sort, calculate, or print a list of values. You now have the tools to sort lists of numbers as well as to search for values in a list.

You will use the concepts presented in this chapter to search and sort lists of string data as well, once you learn a little more about the way C++ manipulates strings and pointers. In building a solid foundation for this and other more advanced material, you now know how to reference array elements without using conventional subscripts.

Chapter 26, "Multidimensional Arrays," shows you how to keep track of arrays in a different format, called a *matrix*. Not all lists of data lend themselves to matrices, but you should be prepared when you need them.

Review Questions

Answers to Review Questions are in Appendix B.

1. True or false: You must access an array in the same order in which you initialized it.

2. Where did the bubble sort get its name?

3. Are the following values sorted in ascending or descending order?

| 33 | 55 | 78 | 78 | 90 | 102 | 435 | 859 | 976 | 4092 |

4. How does C++ use the name of an array?

5. Look at this array definition:

```
char teams[ ] =
        { 'E', 'a', 'g', 'l', 'e', 's', '\0',
          'R', 'a', 'm', 's', '\0' };
```

What is printed with each of the following statements?

   a. `cout << teams;`

   b. `cout << teams + 7;`

   c. `cout << (teams + 3);`

   d. `cout << teams[ 0 ];`

   e. `cout << (teams + 0)[ 0 ];`

   f. `cout << (teams + 5);`

   g. `cout << (teams - 200)[ 202 ]);`

Review Exercises

1. Write a program to store six of your friends' ages in a single array. Assign the ages in random order. Print the ages, from lowest to highest, on-screen.

2. Modify the preceding program to print the ages in descending order.

3. Using the new approach of subscripting arrays, rewrite the programs in Exercises 1 and 2. Always put a 0 in the subscript brackets, modifying the address instead. Use `(ages + 3)[ 0 ]` instead of `ages[ 3 ]`.

4. Sometimes *parallel arrays* are used in programs that must track more than one list of values that are related. Suppose that you have to maintain an inventory, tracking the integer part numbers, prices, and quantities of each item. This task requires three arrays: an integer part-number array, a floating-point price array, and an integer quantity array. Each array has the same number of elements (the total number of parts in the inventory).

Write a program to maintain such an inventory. Reserve enough elements for 100 parts in the inventory. Present the user with an input screen. When the user enters a part number, search the part number array. Once you locate the position of the part, print the corresponding price and quantity. If the part does not exist, allow the user to add it to the inventory, along with the matching price and quantity.

Multidimensional Arrays

Some data fits into lists, as shown in the preceding chapters; other data is better suited for tables of information. The preceding chapters focused on single-dimensional arrays—that is, an array that represents a list of values but has only one subscript. This chapter takes arrays one step further by covering *multidimensional arrays*. These arrays, sometimes called *tables* or *matrices*, have at least two dimensions: rows and columns. Sometimes they have even more dimensions.

This chapter covers the following topics:

♦ Multidimensional arrays

♦ Reserving storage for multidimensional arrays

♦ Putting data into multidimensional arrays

♦ Using nested `for` loops to process multidimensional arrays

If you understood single-dimensional arrays, you should have no trouble understanding arrays with more than one dimension.

Understanding Multidimensional Arrays

A multidimen-
sional array has
more than one
subscript.

A *multidimensional array* is an array with more than one subscript. A single-dimensional array is a list of values, but a multidimensional array simulates a table of values, or even multiple tables of values. The most commonly used table is a two-dimensional table (an array with two subscripts).

Suppose that a softball team wants to keep track of its players' hits. The team played 10 games, and there are 15 players on the team. Table 26.1 shows the team's record of hits.

Table 26.1. A softball team's record of hits.

Player Name	1	2	3	4	5	6	7	8	9	10
Adams	2	1	0	0	2	3	3	1	1	2
Berryhill	1	0	3	2	5	1	2	2	1	0
Downing	1	0	2	1	0	0	0	0	2	0
Edwards	0	3	6	4	6	4	5	3	6	3
Franks	2	2	3	2	1	0	2	3	1	0
Grady	1	3	2	0	1	5	2	1	2	1
Howard	3	1	1	1	2	0	1	0	4	3
Jones	2	2	1	2	4	1	0	7	1	0
Martin	5	4	5	1	1	0	2	4	1	5
Powers	2	2	3	1	0	2	1	3	1	2
Smith	1	1	2	1	3	4	1	0	3	2
Smithtown	1	0	1	2	1	0	3	4	1	2
Townsend	0	0	0	0	0	0	1	0	0	0
Ulmer	2	2	2	2	2	1	1	3	1	3
Williams	2	3	1	0	1	2	1	2	0	3

The softball table is a two-dimensional table. It has rows (the first dimension) and columns (the second dimension). You would call this a two-dimensional table with 15 rows and 10 columns. (Generally, the number of rows is specified first.)

A three-dimensional table has three dimensions: depth, rows, and columns.

Each row has a player's name, and each column has a game number associated with it; but these are not part of the actual data. The data consists only of 150 values (15 rows times 10 columns equals 150 data values). The data in a two-dimensional table, just as with arrays, is always the same type of data; in this case, every value is an integer. If it were a table of salaries, every element would be a floating-point value.

The number of dimensions—in this case, two of them—corresponds to the dimensions in the physical world. The single-dimensional array is a line or list of values. Two dimensions represent length and width. You write on a piece of paper in two dimensions; two dimensions represent a flat surface. Three dimensions represent length, width, and depth. You have seen 3-D movies. Not only do the images have length (height) and width, but they also (appear to) have depth. Figure 26.1 shows what a three-dimensional array looks like if it has a depth of four, six rows, and three columns. Notice that a three-dimensional table resembles a cube of blocks.

Figure 26.1

A representation of a three-dimensional table (a cube).

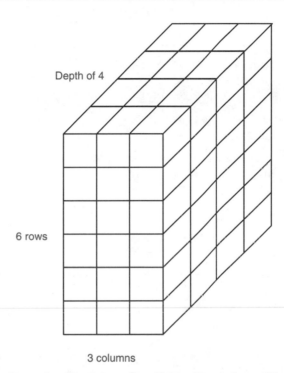

Depth of 4

6 rows

3 columns

It is difficult to visualize more than three dimensions. However, you can think of each dimension after three as another occurrence. In other words, a list of one player's season hit record could be stored in an array. The team's hit record (as shown earlier) is two-dimensional. The league, made up of several teams' hit records would represent a three-dimensional table. Each team (the depth of the table) would have rows and columns of hit data. If there are two leagues, the second league could be considered another dimension (another set of data).

C++ gives you the capability to store several dimensions, although real-world data rarely requires more than two or three dimensions.

Reserving Multidimensional Arrays

When you reserve a multidimensional array, you must let C++ know that the array has more than one dimension. Put more than one subscript in brackets after the array name. You must put a different number, in brackets, for each dimension in the table. For example, to reserve the team data from Table 26.1, you use the following multidimensional array declaration.

Declare the integer array `teams` *with 15 rows and 10 columns.*

```
int  teams[ 15 ][ 10 ];// Reserve a two-dimensional table
```

Caution: Unlike other programming languages, C++ requires that you enclose *each* dimension in brackets. Do not reserve multidimensional array storage like this:

```
int  teams[ 15, 10 ];    // INVALID table declaration
```

Properly reserving the `teams` table produces a table with 150 elements. The elements' subscripts look like those in figure 26.2.

Columns

Figure 26.2

Subscripts for the softball team table.

Rows

[0] [0]	[0] [1]	[0] [2]	[0] [3]	[0] [4]	[0] [5]	[0] [6]	[0] [7]	[0] [8]	[0] [9]
[1] [0]	[1] [1]	[1] [2]	[1] [3]	[1] [4]	[1] [5]	[1] [6]	[1] [7]	[1] [8]	[1] [9]
[2] [0]	[2] [1]	[2] [2]	[2] [3]	[2] [4]	[2] [5]	[2] [6]	[2] [7]	[2] [8]	[2] [9]
[3] [0]	[3] [1]	[3] [2]	[3] [3]	[3] [4]	[3] [5]	[3] [6]	[3] [7]	[3] [8]	[3] [9]
[4] [0]	[4] [1]	[4] [2]	[4] [3]	[4] [4]	[4] [5]	[4] [6]	[4] [7]	[4] [8]	[4] [9]
[5] [0]	[5] [1]	[5] [2]	[5] [3]	[5] [4]	[5] [5]	[5] [6]	[5] [7]	[5] [8]	[5] [9]
[6] [0]	[6] [1]	[6] [2]	[6] [3]	[6] [4]	[6] [5]	[6] [6]	[6] [7]	[6] [8]	[6] [9]
[7] [0]	[7] [1]	[7] [2]	[7] [3]	[7] [4]	[7] [5]	[7] [6]	[7] [7]	[7] [8]	[7] [9]
[8] [0]	[8] [1]	[8] [2]	[8] [3]	[8] [4]	[8] [5]	[8] [6]	[8] [7]	[8] [8]	[8] [9]
[9] [0]	[9] [1]	[9] [2]	[9] [3]	[9] [4]	[9] [5]	[9] [6]	[9] [7]	[9] [8]	[9] [9]
[10] [0]	[10] [1]	[10] [2]	[10] [3]	[10] [4]	[10] [5]	[10] [6]	[10] [7]	[10] [8]	[10] [9]
[11] [0]	[11] [1]	[11] [2]	[11] [3]	[11] [4]	[11] [5]	[11] [6]	[11] [7]	[11] [8]	[11] [9]
[12] [0]	[12] [1]	[12] [2]	[12] [3]	[12] [4]	[12] [5]	[12] [6]	[12] [7]	[12] [8]	[12] [9]
[13] [0]	[13] [1]	[13] [2]	[13] [3]	[13] [4]	[13] [5]	[13] [6]	[13] [7]	[13] [8]	[13] [9]
[14] [0]	[14] [1]	[14] [2]	[14] [3]	[14] [4]	[14] [5]	[14] [6]	[14] [7]	[14] [8]	[14] [9]

The far-right dimension always represents columns; the next dimension represents rows, and so on.

If you needed to keep track of three teams, and each team has 15 players and played 10 games, you could dimension an array as follows:

```
int  teams[ 3 ][ 15 ][ 10 ];  // Reserve a 3-dimensional
                              // table
```

This dimensions three occurrences of the team table shown in figure 26.2.

When dimensioning a two-dimensional table, always put the maximum number of rows first, and the maximum number of columns second. C++ always uses 0 as the starting subscript of each dimension. The last element, the lower right element of the teams table, would be teams[2][14][9].

Examples

1. Suppose that you want to keep track of utility bills for the year. You can store 12 months of 4 utilities in a two-dimensional table of floating-point amounts, as shown in the following array declaration:

```
float    utilities[ 12 ][ 4 ];    // Reserve 48 elements
```

You can compute the total number of elements in a multidimensional array by multiplying the subscripts. Because 12 times 4 is 48, there are 48 elements in this array (12 rows, 4 columns). Each of these elements is a floating-point data type.

2. If you were keeping track of five years' worth of utilities, you would have to add an extra dimension. The first dimension is the years, the second dimension is the months, and the last dimension is the individual utilities. You would reserve storage as follows:

```
float    utilities[ 5 ][ 12 ][ 4 ]; // Reserve 240 elements
```

Mapping Arrays to Memory

C++ approaches multidimensional arrays a little differently from most programming languages. By using subscripts, you really do not have to understand the internal representation of multidimensional arrays. Most C++ programmers believe, however, that a deeper understanding of these arrays is important, especially when programming advanced applications.

A two-dimensional array is actually an *array of arrays*. You program multidimensional arrays as though they were tables with rows and columns. A two-dimensional array is really a single-dimensional array, and *each* of its elements is not an integer, floating-point, or character value; but each element is another array.

Knowing that a multidimensional array is an array of other arrays is critical when passing and receiving such arrays. C++ passes all arrays, including multi-dimensional arrays, by address. Suppose that you are using an integer array called scores, reserved as a five by six table. You can pass scores to a function called print_it():

```
print_it(scores);    // Pass table to a function
```

The function print_it() has to know the type of parameter being passed to it. print_it() must know also that the parameter is an array. If the table is one-dimensional, you can receive it as

```
print_it(int scores[ ])          // Works only if scores
                                 // is 1-dimensional
```

or

```
print_it(int scores[ 10 ])       // Assuming scores have 10
                                 // elements
```

If scores is a multidimensional table, you *must* designate each pair of brackets and put the maximum number of subscripts in the brackets, as in

```
print_it(int scores[ 5 ][ 6 ])   // Let print_it() know
                                 // about dimensions
```

or

```
print_it(int scores[ ][ 6 ])     // Let print_it() know
                                 // about dimensions
```

Notice that you do *not* have to explicitly state the number of elements in the first dimension when passing multidimensional arrays, but you must explicitly state the number of elements in the other dimensions. If scores were a three-dimensional table, dimensioned as 10 by 5 by 6, you would pass it to print_it() as

```
print_it(int scores[ 10 ][ 5 ][ 6 ])  // Let print_it() know
                                      // about dimensions
```

or

```
print_it(int scores[ ][ 5 ][ 6 ])   // Only first dimension
                                    // is optional
```

C++ stores multi-dimensional arrays in row order.

Generally, you do not need to worry much about the way tables are physically stored. Even though a two-dimensional table is actually an array of arrays (and each of *those* arrays would contain another array if the table were three-dimensional), you can program multidimensional arrays as if they were stored in row-and-column order by using subscripts.

Multidimensional arrays are stored in *row order*. Suppose that you want to keep track of a three by four table. Figure 26.3 shows how that table (and its subscripts) can be visualized. Despite the table-like feel of such a two-dimensional table, your memory is still sequential storage. C++ has to map multidimensional arrays to single-dimensional memory, and it does so in row order.

Figure 26.3

Mapping a two-dimensional table to memory.

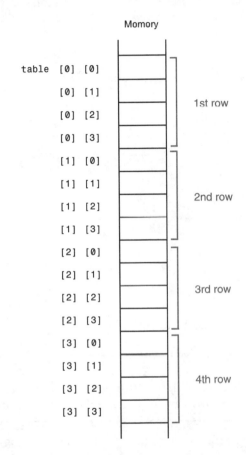

Each row fills memory before the next row is stored. The bottom of figure 26.3 shows how a three by four table is mapped to memory. The entire first row, `table[ 0 ][ 0 ]` through `table[ 0 ][ 3 ]`, is stored first in memory before any of the second row. Because a table is really an array of arrays, and because you learned earlier that array elements are always stored sequentially in memory, the first row (array) completely fills memory before the second row. Study figure 26.3 to learn how two-dimensional arrays map to memory.

Defining Multidimensional Arrays

C++ is not picky about the way you define a multidimensional array when you initialize it at declaration time. As with single-dimensional arrays, you initialize multidimensional arrays with braces that designate dimensions. Because a multidimensional array is an array of arrays, you can nest braces together when initializing them.

The following three array definitions fill the arrays ara1, ara2, and ara3, as shown in figure 26.4.

```
int   ara1[ 5 ] =
      { 8, 5, 3, 25, 41 };      // 1-dimensional array

int     ara2[ 2 ][ 4 ] =
{
      { 4, 3, 2, 1 },
      { 1, 2, 3, 4 }
};

int   ara3[ 3 ][ 4 ] =

{

      { 1, 2, 3, 4 },

      { 5, 6, 7, 8 },

      {9, 10, 11, 12 }

};
```

Notice that the multidimensional arrays are stored in row order. In ara3, the first row gets the first four elements of the definition (1, 2, 3, and 4).

Tip: To make a multidimensional array initialization match the array's subscripts, some programmers like to visualize how arrays are filled. Because C programs are free-form, you can initialize **ara2** and **ara3** as follows:

```
int ara2[2][4]={{4, 3, 2, 1},      // Does exactly the
                {1, 2, 3, 4}};     // same thing as
                                   // before
int ara3[3][4]={{1, 2, 3, 4},
                {5, 6, 7, 8},
                {9, 10, 11, 12}};  // Visually more
                                   // obvious
```

Figure 26.4

Table contents after initialization.

ara1

	[0]	[1]	[2]	[3]	[4]
	8	5	3	25	41

Columns

ara2

Rows		0	1	2	3
	0	4	3	2	1
	1	1	2	3	4

Columns

ara3

Rows		0	1	2	3
	0	1	2	3	4
	1	5	6	7	8
	2	9	10	11	12

C++ does not mind if you initialize a multidimensional array as if it were a single-dimensional array. You have to make sure that you keep track of the row order if you do this. For example, the following two definitions reserve storage and initialize ara2 and ara3:

```
int     ara2[ 2 ][ 4 ] =
        { 4, 3, 2, 1, 1, 2, 3, 4 };
int     ara3[ 3 ][ 4 ] =
        { 1, 2, 3, 4, 5, 6, 7, 8, 9, 10, 11, 12};
```

There is no difference in initializing ara2 and ara3 with and without the nested braces. The nested braces seem to show the dimensions and how C++ fills them a little better, but the choice of using nested braces is yours.

> **Tip:** Multidimensional arrays (unless they are global) are *not* initialized to specific values unless you assign them values at declaration time or in the program. As with single-dimensional arrays, if you initialize one or more of the elements, but not all of them, C fills the rest with zeros. If you want to zero-out an entire multidimensional array, you can use the following:
>
> ```
> float     sales[ 3 ][ 4 ][ 7 ][ 2 ] =
>       { 0.0 };      // Fill all of sales with zeros
> ```

One last point to consider is how multidimensional arrays are viewed by your compiler. Many people program in C++ for years but never understand how tables are stored internally. As long as you use subscripts, a table's internal representation should not matter. Once you learn about pointer variables, however, you might need to know how C++ stores your tables in case you want to reference them with pointers (as shown in the next few chapters).

Figure 26.5 shows the way C++ stores a three by four table in memory. Unlike the elements of a single-dimensional array, each element is stored contiguously, but look at how C++ views the data. Because a table is an array of arrays, the array name contains the address of the start of the primary array. Each of those elements points to the array it contains (the data in each row). This coverage of table storage is for your information only. As you become more proficient in C++ and write more powerful programs that manipulate internal memory, you may want to review this method, used by C++ for table storage.

Figure 26.5

Internal represen-
tation of a two-
dimensional table.

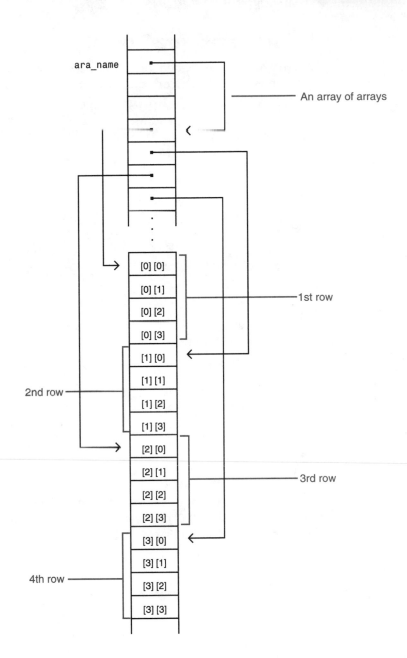

ara_name

An array of arrays

[0] [0]
[0] [1]
[0] [2]
[0] [3]

1st row

[1] [0]
[1] [1]
[1] [2]
[1] [3]

2nd row

[2] [0]
[2] [1]
[2] [2]
[2] [3]

3rd row

[3] [0]
[3] [1]
[3] [2]
[3] [3]

4th row

Tables and *for* Loops

Nested `for` loops are good candidates for looping through every element of a multidimensional table. For example, the code

```
for (row = 0; row < 2; row++)
{
    for (col = 0; col < 3; col++)
        cout << row << "  " << col << "\n";
}
```

produces the following output:

```
0    0
0    1
0    2
1    0
1    1
1    2
```

These are exactly the subscripts, in row order, for a two-row by three-column table that is dimensioned with

```
int     table[ 2 ][ 3 ];
```

Notice that there are as many `for` loops as there are subscripts in the array (two). The outside loop represents the first subscript (the rows), and the inside loop represents the second subscript (the columns). The nested `for` loop steps through each element of the table.

You can use `cin()`, `get()`, and other input functions to fill a table, and you can assign values to the elements when declaring the table. Usually the data comes from data files on disk. Regardless of what method actually stores values in multidimensional arrays, nested `for` loops are excellent control statements for stepping through the subscripts. The next examples illustrate how nested `for` loops work with multidimensional arrays.

Nested loops work well with multidimensional arrays.

Examples

1. The following statement reserves enough memory elements for a television station's ratings (A through D) for one week:

```
char     ratings[ 7 ][ 48 ];
```

This statement reserves enough elements to hold seven days (the rows) of ratings for each 30-minute time slot (48 of them in a day).

Every element in a table is always the same type. In this case, each element is a character variable. Some of them can be initialized with the following assignment statements:

```
shows[ 3 ][ 12 ] = 'B';    // Store B in 4th row, 13th column
shows[ 1 ][ 5 ] = 'A';     // Store C in 2nd row, 6th column
cin.get(shows[ 6 ][ 20 ]);
```

2. A computer company sells two sizes of diskettes: 3 1/2 inch and 5 1/4 inch. Each diskette comes in one of four capacities: single-sided, double-density; double-sided, double-density; single-sided, high-density; and double-sided, high-density.

The diskette inventory is well suited for a two-dimensional table. The company determined that the diskettes have the following retail prices:

	Single-Sided, Double-Density	Double-Sided, Double-Density	Single-Sided, High-Density	Double-Sided, High-Density
3 ½"	2.30	2.75	3.20	3.50
5 ¼"	1.75	2.10	2.60	2.95

The company wants to store the price of each diskette in a table for easy access. The following program does that with assignment statements:

```
// Filename: C26DISK1.CPP
// Assigns diskette prices to a table

#include <iostream.h>
#include <iomanip.h>

main()
{
    float       disks[ 2 ][ 4 ];  // Table of disk prices
    int         row, col;

    disks[ 0 ][ 0 ] = 2.30;    // Row 1, Column 1
    disks[ 0 ][ 1 ] = 2.75;    // Row 1, Column 2
    disks[ 0 ][ 2 ] = 3.20;    // Row 1, Column 3
    disks[ 0 ][ 3 ] = 3.50;    // Row 1, Column 4
    disks[ 1 ][ 0 ] = 1.75;    // Row 2, Column 1
    disks[ 1 ][ 1 ] = 2.10;    // Row 2, Column 2
    disks[ 1 ][ 2 ] = 2.60;    // Row 2, Column 3
    disks[ 1 ][ 3 ] = 2.95;    // Row 2, Column 4
```

```
        // Print the prices
        cout.setf(ios::fixed);
        cout.setf(ios::showpoint);
        for (row = 0; row < 2; row++)
        {
            for (col = 0; col < 4; col++)
                cout << "$" << setprecision(2)
                        << disks[ row ][ col ] << "\n";
        }
        return 0;
}
```

This program displays the following prices:

```
$2.30
$2.75
$3.20
$3.50
$1.75
$2.10
$2.60
$2.95
```

The program prints the prices one line at a time and without any descriptive titles. Although this output is not labeled, the program illustrates how you can use assignment statements to initialize a table and how nested for loops can print the elements.

3. The preceding diskette inventory would be displayed better if the output had descriptive titles. Before you add titles, you should know how to print a table in its native row-and-column format.

Typically, you use a nested for loop, like the one in the preceding example, to print rows and columns. You should not output a newline character with every cout, however. If you do, you will see one value per line, as in the preceding output, which is not the row-and-column format of the table.

You do not want to see every diskette price on one line, but you want each row of the table printed on a separate line. You must insert a cout << "\n"; to send the cursor to the next line each time the row number changes. Printing newlines after each row prints the table in its row-and-column format, as the following program shows:

```
// Filename: C26DISK2.CPP
// Assigns diskette prices to a table and prints them in a
// table format
```

```
#include <iostream.h>
#include <iomanip.h>

main()
{
    float       disks[ 2 ][ 4 ];  // Table of disk prices
    int         row, col;

    disks[ 0 ][ 0 ] = 2.30;       // Row 1, Column 1
    disks[ 0 ][ 1 ] = 2.75;       // Row 1, Column 2
    disks[ 0 ][ 2 ] = 3.20;       // Row 1, Column 3
    disks[ 0 ][ 3 ] = 3.50;       // Row 1, Column 4
    disks[ 1 ][ 0 ] = 1.75;       // Row 2, Column 1
    disks[ 1 ][ 1 ] = 2.10;       // Row 2, Column 2
    disks[ 1 ][ 2 ] = 2.60;       // Row 2, Column 3
    disks[ 1 ][ 3 ] = 2.95;       // Row 2, Column 4
    // Print the prices
    cout.setf(ios::fixed);
    cout.setf(ios::showpoint);
    for (row = 0; row < 2; row++)
    {
        for (col = 0; col < 4; col++)
            cout << "$" << setprecision(2)
                 << disks[row][col] << "\t";
        cout << "\n";      // Print a new line each row
    }
    return 0;
}
```

The output of the disk prices in their native table order is as follows:

$2.30	$2.75	$3.20	$3.50
$1.75	$2.10	$2.60	$2.95

4. To add descriptive titles, simply print a row of titles before the first row of values and then print a new column title before each column, as shown in the following program. Figure 26.6 shows the program's output.

```
// Filename: C26DISK3.CPP
// Assigns diskette prices to a table
// and prints them in a table format with titles

#include <iostream.h>
#include <iomanip.h>
```

```
main()
{
    float       disks[ 2 ][ 4 ];     // Table of disk prices
    int         row, col;

    disks[ 0 ][ 0 ] = 2.30;   // Row 1, Column 1
    disks[ 0 ][ 1 ] = 2.75;   // Row 1, Column 2
    disks[ 0 ][ 2 ] = 3.20;   // Row 1, Column 3
    disks[ 0 ][ 3 ] = 3.50;   // Row 1, Column 4
    disks[ 1 ][ 0 ] = 1.75;   // Row 2, Column 1
    disks[ 1 ][ 1 ] = 2.10;   // Row 2, Column 2
    disks[ 1 ][ 2 ] = 2.60;   // Row 2, Column 3
    disks[ 1 ][ 3 ] = 2.95;   // Row 2, Column 4
    cout.setf(ios::fixed);
    cout.setf(ios::showpoint);
    // Print the top titles
    cout << "\tSingle-sided,\tDouble-sided,"
        << "\tSingle-sided,\tDouble-sided,\n";
    cout << "\tDouble-density\tDouble-density"
        << "\tHigh-density\tHigh-density\n";
    // Print the prices
    for (row = 0; row < 2; row++)
    {
        if (row == 0)
            cout << "3 1/2\"\t";
        else
            cout << "5 1/4\"\t";
        for (col = 0; col < 4; col++)
            cout << "$" << setprecision(2)
                << disks[row][col] << "\t\t";
        cout << "\n"; // Print a new line each row
    }
    return 0;
}
```

Figure 26.6

The table of disk prices with titles.

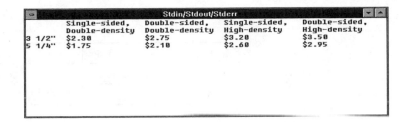

	Single-sided, Double-density	Double-sided, Double-density	Single-sided, High-density	Double-sided, High-density
3 1/2"	$2.30	$2.75	$3.20	$3.50
5 1/4"	$1.75	$2.10	$2.60	$2.95

Summary

You now know how to create, initialize, and process multidimensional arrays. Although not all data fits into the compact format of tables, some data does. Using nested `for` loops makes stepping through a multidimensional array straightforward.

One of the limitations of a multidimensional array is that each element must be the same data type. This keeps you from being able to store several kinds of data in tables. Upcoming chapters show you how to store data in different ways to overcome this limitation of tables.

Review Questions

Answers to Review Questions are in Appendix B.

1. What statement reserves a two-dimensional table of integers, called `scores`, with five rows and six columns?

2. What statement reserves a three-dimensional array of four tables of character variables, called `initials`, with 10 rows and 20 columns?

3. Consider the following statement:

```
int    weights[ 5 ][ 10 ];
```

Which subscript (first or second) represents rows, and which represents columns?

4. How many elements are reserved with the following statement?

```
int    ara[ 5 ][ 6 ];
```

5. Examine the following table of integers in a table called ara:

4	1	3	5	9
10	2	12	1	6
25	42	2	91	8

What values do the following elements contain?

a. ara[2][2]

b. ara[0][1]

c. ara[2][3]

d. ara[2][4]

6. What control statement is best used for stepping through multidimensional arrays?

7. Consider this section of a program:

```
int     grades[ 3 ][ 5 ] = {80, 90, 96, 73, 65,
                            67, 90, 68, 92, 84,
                            70, 55, 95, 78, 100 };
```

What are the values of the following?

a. grades[2][3]

b. grades[2][4]

c. grades[0][1]

Review Exercises

1. Write a program that stores and prints the numbers from 1 to 21 in a three by seven table. (*Hint:* Remember that C++ begins subscripts at 0.)

2. Write a program that reserves storage for three years' worth of sales data for five salespeople. Use assignment statements to fill the table with data and print it out, one value per line.

3. Instead of using assignment statements, use the cin function to fill the salespeople's data in the preceding exercise.

4. Write a program that tracks the grades for five classes, each having 10 students. Input the data, using the cin function. Print the table in its native row-and-column format.

CHAPTER 27

Pointers

C++ reveals its true power through pointer variables. *Pointer variables* (or *pointers*, as they are generally called) are variables that contain addresses of other variables. All variables that you have seen so far have held data values. You understand that variables hold various data types: character, integer, floating-point, and so on. Pointer variables contain the location of regular data variables. In effect, a pointer variable *points* to the data because the variable holds the address of the data.

When first learning C++, students of the language tend to shy away from pointers, thinking that they will be difficult. But pointers don't have to be difficult. In fact, after you work with them for a while, you will think that pointers are easier to use than arrays (and much more flexible).

This chapter introduces the following topics:

- What pointers are
- Pointers of different data types
- The address of (&) operator
- The dereferencing (*) operator
- Arrays of pointers

Pointers offer a highly efficient means of accessing and changing data. Because a pointer contains the actual address of data, your compiler has less work to do when finding that data in memory. Pointers do not have to link data to specific variable names. A pointer can point to an unnamed data value. With pointers, you gain a "different view" of your data.

Pointer Variables

Pointers contain addresses of other variables.

Pointers are variables. They follow all the usual naming rules of regular, nonpointer variables. As with regular variables, you must declare pointer variables before you use them. There is a type of pointer for every data type in C++; there are integer pointers, character pointers, floating-point pointers, and so on. You can declare global pointers (although global pointers, as with regular variables, are not usually recommended) or local pointers, depending on where you declare them.

About the only difference between pointer variables and regular variables is what they hold. Pointers do not contain data, but *addresses* of data. If you need a quick review of addresses and memory, see Appendix A.

C++ has two pointer operators:

& The "address of" operator

* The dereferencing operator

Don't let these operators throw you. You have seen them before! The & is the bitwise AND operator (see Chapter 13, "Bitwise Operators"), and the * means, of course, multiplication. These are called *overloaded* operators. They perform more than one function, depending on how you use them in your programs. C++ does not confuse * with multiplication when you use this symbol as a dereferencing operator with pointers.

Whenever you see & used with pointers, think of the phrase "address of." The & operator always produces the memory address of whatever it precedes. The * operator, when used with pointers, either declares a pointer or dereferences the pointer's value. The next sections explain these operators.

Declaring Pointers

Because you must declare all pointers before using them, the best way to begin learning about pointers is to see how to declare and define them. Actually, declaring pointers is almost as easy as declaring regular variables. After all, pointers are variables.

If you need to declare a variable that is to hold your age, you might use the following variable declaration:

```
int     age = 30;     // Declare a variable to hold my age
```

Declaring age like this does several things. Because C++ knows that you will need a variable called age, C++ reserves storage for that variable. C++ knows also that you will store only integers in age, not floating-point or double floating-point data. You also have requested that C++ store the value of 30 in age after it reserves storage for it.

Where did C++ store age in memory? You, as programmer, do not really care where C++ decided to store age. You do not need to know the variable's address because you will never refer to age by its address. If you want to calculate or print with age, you will call it by its name, age.

Suppose that you want to declare a pointer variable. This pointer variable will not hold your age but will *point* to age, the variable that holds your age. (Why you would want to do this will be made clear in this chapter and the next few chapters.) p_age or pAge might be a good name for this pointer variable. It is assumed that C++ stored age at address 350,606, although your C++ compiler arbitrarily determines the address of age, and it could be anything.

Tip: Make your pointer variable names meaningful.

The name pAge by itself has nothing to do with pointers except that it is the name selected for the pointer to age. pAge could just as easily be named house, x43344, space_trek, or whatever else you wanted to call it. You can name variables anything, as long as you follow the naming rules for variables. This reinforces the idea that a pointer is just a variable that you must reserve in your program. Make up meaningful variable names, even for pointer variables. pAge is a good name for a variable that points to age. The names ptr_age and ptr_to_age are appropriate too.

What's in a Name?

When you begin looking at C++ code written by other programmers, you will notice that there are many different ways of forming meaningful names. Some programmers prefer to use all lowercase and separate the parts of the name with underscore characters. These programmers would use **p_age** to name a pointer to age. Other programmers like to use MixedCase, without the underscores; they would use **pAge** for this variable name.

So far, in this book, most of the examples have used the underscore naming style. To help you become accustomed to the other style, the rest of this book will use the MixedCase style. This style also frequently prepends a letter to the name which helps identify what kind of variable is being named. An **int** or **float** variable for age would then be named **nAge**.

To declare the pAge pointer variable, you must do the following:

```
int*    pAge;    // Declare an integer pointer
```

As with the declaration for age, this line reserves a variable called pAge. It is not a normal integer variable, however. Because of the dereferencing operator, *, C++ knows that this is to be a pointer variable.

Remember that the * is *not* part of the variable name. When you later use pAge, you will not always prefix the name with the *, unless you are dereferencing it at the time (as later examples will show).

> **Tip:** Whenever an * appears in a variable definition, the variable being declared is *always* a pointer variable.

Consider the declaration for pAge if the asterisk were not there; C++ would think that you were declaring a regular integer variable. The * is important because it tells C++ to interpret p_age as a pointer variable instead of as a normal, data variable.

Where to Put the *

C++ can be very fussy about what it will accept or not accept. By now you have probably seen how loudly the compiler complains if you forget an opening or closing parenthesis or the semicolon on the end of a statement.

But surprisingly, C++ is much less fussy about where you put the * when you declare a pointer. The only rule is that only the * and whitespace may be between the variable type declaration and the variable name. All four declarations below are valid:

```
int*pAge;
int * pAge;
int *pAge;
int* pAge;
```

Few C++ programmers would use the first two styles above. But the camp is approximately equally divided between the last two. The Microsoft Foundation Classes use the last style in the list, the one with the asterisk adjacent to the variable type. This book will use that style so that you will be accustomed to seeing it.

Assigning Values to Pointers

Pointers point to data of their own type.

pAge is an integer pointer. This is very important. pAge can point only to integer values, never to floating-point values, double values, or even characters. If you needed to point to a floating-point variable, you might declare the pointer as

```
float*   pPrice;      // Declare a floating-point pointer
```

As with any automatic variables, C++ does not initialize pointers when you declare them. If you declare pAge as previously described, and you want pAge to point to age, you have to explicitly assign pAge to the address of age:

```
pAge = &age;          // Assign the address of age to p_age
```

What value is now in pAge? You do not know exactly, but you do know that it is the address of age, wherever that is.

Instead of assigning the address of age to pAge with an assignment operator, you can declare and initialize pointers at the same time. The next two lines declare and initialize both age and pAge:

```
int     age = 30;           // Declare a regular integer
                            // variable, putting 30 in it
int*    pAge = &age;        // Declare an integer pointer,
                            // initializing it with the
                            // address of age
```

These two lines produce the variables described previously.
If you want to print the value of age, you can use the following cout:

```
cout << age;                // Print the value of age
```

Or you can print the value of age with this cout:

```
cout << *pAge;              // Dereference p_age
```

The dereferencing operator produces the value *where the pointer points to*. Without the *, the second cout would print an address (the address of age). The * means to print the value at that address.

You can assign age a different value with the following statement:

```
age = 41;              // Assign age a new value
```

Or you can assign age a value in this way:

```
*pAge = 41;
```

This line says, "Take the value being pointed to by pAge and assign it 41."

> **Tip:** The * appears before a pointer variable in only two places: when you declare a pointer variable and when you dereference a pointer variable (to find the data it points to).

Pointers and Parameters

You may recall from Chapter 20, "Passing Values," that you can override C++'s normal default of passing by copy (also known as passing by value) by passing a variable preceded by an &, and putting an asterisk before the parameter everywhere it appears in the receiving function. The following function call passes tries by address to the receiving function called pr_it():

```
pr_it(&tries);   // Pass integer tries to pr_it() by address
                 // (tries would normally pass by copy)
```

The function `pr_it()` receives the address of `tries`, in effect, receiving `tries` by address:

```
void     pr_it(int* tries)   // Receive tries by address
                             // (dereference its value)
{
    *tries++;      // This changes tries in calling AND
                   // receiving functions.
    return;
}
```

Now that you understand the `&` and `*` operators, you can understand the passing of nonarray parameters to functions by address. (Arrays default to passing by address without requiring that you use `&` and `*`.)

Examples

1. The following section of a program declares three regular variables of three different data types, as well as pointers that point to those variables:

```
char      Initial= 'Q';        // Declare three regular
int       Num = 40;            // variables of three
                               // different types
float     Sales = 2321.59;

char*     pInitial = &Initial;   // Declare three
int*      pNum     = &Num;       // pointers
float*    pSales   = &Sales;
```

2. As with regular variables, you can initialize pointers with assignment statements. You do not have to initialize pointers when you declare them. The next few lines of code are equivalent to the code in the preceding example:

```
char      Initial;          // Declare three regular variables
int       Num;              // of three different types
float     Sales;

char*     pInitial;         // Declare three pointers but
int*      pNum;             // do not initialize them yet
float*    pSales;

Initial = 'Q';              // Initialize the regular
Num     = 40;               // variables with values
Sales   = 2321.59;

pInitial = &Initial;        // Initialize the pointers with
pNum     = &Num;            // the addresses of their
pSales   = &Sales;          // corresponding variables
```

Notice that you do not put the * operator before the pointer variable names when assigning them values. You prefix a pointer variable with * only if you are dereferencing it.

> **Note:** In this example, the pointer variables could have been assigned the addresses of the regular variables before they were assigned values. There would be no difference in the operation. The pointers are assigned the addresses of the regular variables no matter what data is in the regular variables.

Keep the data type of each pointer consistent. Do *not* assign a floating-point variable to an integer's address. For example, you cannot make the assignment statement

```
pInitial = &Sales;     // INVALID pointer assignment
```

because `pInitial` can point only to character data, not to floating-point data.

3. Examine the following program closely. It shows more about pointers and the pointer operators, & and *, than several pages of text could explain:

```cpp
// Filename: C27POINT.CPP
// Demonstrates the use of pointer declarations and
// operators

#include <iostream.h>

main()
{
    int     Num = 123;          // A regular integer variable
    int*    pNum;               // Declare an integer pointer

    cout << "Num is " << Num << "\n";  // Print value of
Num
    cout << "The address of Num is "
         << (unsigned long)&Num << "\n";

    pNum = &Num;        // Put address of Num in pNum,
                        // in effect, making pNum point
                        // to Num (no * in front of pNum)
    cout << "*pNum is " << *pNum << "\n"; // Print value
                                          // of num
    cout << "pNum is " << (unsigned long)pNum << "\n";
                        // Print location of num
    return 0;
}
```

Following the output of this program:

```
Num is 123
The address of Num is 848246030
*pNum is 123
pNum is 848246030
```

If you run this program, you will probably get different results for the value of pNum, because your compiler will place num at a different location, depending on your memory setup. The actual address is moot, though. Because the pointer pNum will always contain the address of num, and because you can dereference pNum to get num's value, the actual address is not critical.

4. The following program includes a function that swaps the values of any two integers passed to it. You may recall that a function can return only a single value. Therefore, you could not write, before now, a function that changed two different values and returned both values to the calling function.

To swap two variables (reversing their values for sorting as you saw in Chapter 25, "Array Processing"), you need the ability to pass both variables by address. Then, when the function reverses the variables, the calling function's variables will also be swapped.

Notice the function's use of dereferencing operators before each occurrence of num1 and num2. You don't care which addresses num1 and num2 are stored at, but you have to make sure that you dereference whatever addresses were passed to the function.

Be sure to pass arguments with the prefix & to functions that receive by address, as shown here in main().

```cpp
// Filename: C27SWAP.CPP
// Program that includes a function which swaps any two
// integers passed to it

#include <iostream.h>

void    swap_them(int* num1, int* num2)
{
    int     temp;       // Variable that holds in-between
                        // swapped value

    temp = *num1;       // The asterisks ensure that the
                        // calling function's variables are
                        // ones worked on in this function
```

```
                            // and not copies of them.
    *num1 = *num2;
    *num2 = temp;
    return;
}



main()
{
    int i = 10, j = 20;

    cout << "\n\nBefore swap, i is " << i
        << " and j is " << j << "\n\n";
    swap_them(&i, &j);
    cout << "\n\nAfter swap, i is " << i
        << " and j is " << j << "\n\n";
    return 0;
}
```

Arrays of Pointers

If you need to reserve many pointers for many different values, you might want to declare an *array of pointers*. You know that you can reserve an array of characters, integers, long integers, and floating-point values, as well as an array of every other data type available. You can also reserve an array of pointers, with each pointer being a pointer to a specific data type.

The following line reserves an array of 10 integer pointer variables:

```
int*      pIarray[ 10 ];    // Reserve an array of 10 integer
                            // pointers
```

Figure 27.1 shows how C++ views this array. Each element holds an address (after being assigned values) that *points* to other values in memory. Each value pointed to must be an integer. You can assign an element from pIarray an address, just as you would for nonarray pointer variables. You can make pIarray[4] point to the address of an integer variable named age by assigning it, as shown here:

```
pIarray[ 4 ] = &age;   // Make pIarray[ 4 ] point to
                       // address of age
```

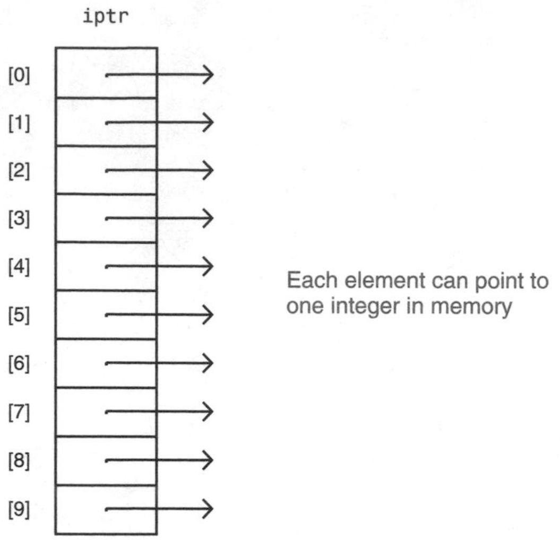

Figure 27.1

An array of 10
integer pointers.

The following line reserves an array of 20 character pointer variables:

```
char*    pCharArr[ 20 ];   // Array of 20 character pointers
```

Some beginning C++ students start getting confused when they see such a declaration. Pointers are one thing, but reserving storage for arrays of pointers tends to bog down students. Reserving storage for arrays of pointers is easy to understand. Take away the asterisk from the last declaration, as in the following:

```
char     pCharArr[ 20 ];
```

You have just reserved a simple array of 20 characters. Adding the asterisk informs C++ to go one step further: instead of wanting an array of character variables, you want an array of character-pointing variables. Instead of each element being a character variable, each element holds an address that points to characters.

Reserving arrays of pointers will be much more meaningful when you learn about structures in the next few chapters. As with regular, nonpointer variables, an array makes processing several variables much easier. You can use a subscript to reference each variable (element) without having to use a different variable name for each value.

Summary

Declaring and using pointers may seem like a lot of trouble at this point. Why assign *pNum a value when it is easier (and clearer) to assign a value directly to num? If you are asking yourself (and this book!) that question, you probably understand everything you should from this chapter, and you are ready to begin seeing the true power of pointers: combining array processing and pointers.

Review Questions

Answers to Review Questions are in Appendix B.

1. What kind of variable is reserved in each of the following?

    a. `int*     a;`

    b. `char*    cp;`

    c. `float*   dp;`

2. What words should spring to mind when you see the & operator?

3. What is the dereferencing operator?

4. How would you assign the address of the floating-point variable `salary` to a pointer called `pSal`?

5. True or false: You must define a pointer with an initial value when declaring it.

6. Examine the following two sections of code:

```
int    i;
int*   pti;
i = 56;
pti = &i;


int    i;
int    *pti;
pti = &i;      // These two lines are reversed from the
i = 56;        // preceding example.
```

Is the value of `pti` the same after the fourth line of each section?

7. Now look at the this section of code:

```
float    pay;
float*   pPay;
pay  = 2313.54;
pPay = &pay;
```

What is the value of each of the following (answer "Invalid" if it cannot be determined)?

    a. `pay`

    b. `*pPay`

    c. `*pay`

    d. `&pay`

8. What does the following declare?

```
double*    ara[ 4 ][ 6 ];
```

a. An array of double floating-point values

b. An array of double floating-point pointer variables

c. An invalid declaration statement

> **Note:** Because this is a theory-oriented chapter, exercises are saved until you master the next chapter, "Pointers and Arrays."

CHAPTER 28

Pointers and Arrays

Arrays and pointers are closely related in the C++ programming language. You can address arrays as if they were pointers, and pointers as if they were arrays. Being able to store and access pointers and arrays means that you can store strings of data in array elements. Without pointers, you could not do this because there is no fundamental string data type in C++; there are no string variables, only string constants.

This chapter introduces the following topics:

♦ Array names and pointers

♦ Character pointers

♦ Pointer arithmetic

♦ Ragged-edge arrays of string data

You will use the concepts presented here for much of your future programming in C++. Pointer manipulation is very important to the C++ programming language.

Array Names as Pointers

An array name is just a pointer, nothing more. Suppose that you have the following array declaration:

```
int    ara[ 5 ] =
    { 10, 20, 30, 40, 50 };
```

If you printed ara[0], you would see 10. By now, you fully understand and expect this value to appear.

An array name
is a pointer.

But what if you were to print *ara? Would that print anything? If so, what? If you thought that an error would print because ara is not a pointer but an array, you would be wrong. An array name is a pointer. If you print *ara, you would also see 10.

Recall how arrays are stored in memory. figure 28.1 reviews how ara is mapped in memory. The array name, ara, is nothing more than a pointer that points to the first element of the array. If you dereference that pointer, you dereference the value stored at the first element of the array, which is 10. Dereferencing ara is exactly the same thing as referring to ara[0] because both produce the same value.

Figure 28.1

Storing the array
ara in memory.

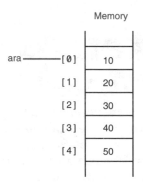

You now see that you can reference an array with subscripts or with pointer dereferencing. Can you use pointer notation to print the third element of ara? Yes, and you already have the tools to do so. The following cout prints ara[2] (the third element of ara) without using a subscript:

```
cout << *(ara + 2);     // Print ara[ 2 ]
```

The expression *(ara + 2) is not vague at all, as long as you remember that an array name is just a pointer that always points to the array's first element. *(ara + 2) takes the address stored in ara, adds 2 to the address, and dereferences *that* location. All the following hold true:

ara + 0 points to ara[0]

ara + 1 points to ara[1]

ara + 2 points to ara[2]

ara + 3 points to ara[3]

ara + 4 points to ara[4]

Therefore, to print, store, or calculate with an array element, you can use either subscript notation or pointer notation. Because an array name contains the address of the array's first element, you must dereference the pointer to get the element's value.

Internal Locations

C++ knows the internal data-size requirements of characters, integers, floating-points, and the other data types on your computer. Therefore, because `ara` is an integer array and each element in an integer array consumes two bytes of storage, C++ adds 2 or 4 to the address if you reference arrays as just shown.

Even though you may write `*(ara + 3)` to refer to `ara[ 3 ]`, C++ really adds 6 to the address of `ara` to get the third element. C++ does not add an actual 3. You don't have to worry about this because C++ handles these internals. When you write `*(ara + 3)`, you are actually requesting that C++ add three integer addresses to the address of `ara`. If `ara` were a floating-point array, C++ would add three floating-point addresses to `ara`.

Pointer Advantages

An array name is a pointer constant.

An array name is actually a unique type of pointer. When an array is initialized, the array identifier (array name) is given a value which points to the block of memory that will be used by the array. An array name is a *pointer constant*, not a pointer variable. You cannot change the pointer value represented by an array name because you cannot change constants. This explains why you cannot assign an array new values during a program's execution. For example, even if cname is a character array, the following is not valid in C++:

```
cname = "Christine Chambers";    // INVALID array assignment
```

The value of the array name, cname, cannot be changed because it is a constant that points to the array's preallocated block of memory. You would not attempt the following because you cannot change the constant 5 to any other value:

```
5 = 4 + 8 * 2;                   // INVALID assignment
```

C++ knows that you cannot assign anything to 5, and will give you an error if you attempt to change 5. C++ knows also that the pointer value represented by an array name is a constant and that you cannot change an array to another value. You can assign values to an array at declaration time. During execution, after the array has been declared, you must either assign values to one element at a time, or by using functions such as `strcpy()`.

The most important reason to learn pointers is this: pointers (except arrays referenced as pointers) are variables. You *can* change a pointer variable, which makes processing virtually any data, including arrays, much more powerful and flexible.

Examples

1. By changing pointers, you make them point to different values in memory. The following program shows how to change pointers. The program first defines two floating-point values. A floating-point pointer points to the first variable, v1, and is used in the cout. The pointer is then changed so that it points to the second floating-point variable, v2.

```
// C28PTRCH.CPP
// Changes the value of a pointer variable

#include <iostream.h>

main()
{
    float     v1 = 676.54;      // Define 2 floating-point
                                // variables
    float     v2 = 900.18;
    float     *p_v;        // Define a floating-point pointer

    p_v = &v1;                   // Make pointer point to v1
    cout << "The first value is " << *p_v << "\n";
        // Print 676.54
    p_v = &v2;      // Change the pointer so it points to v2
    cout << "The second value is " << *p_v << "\n";
        // Print 900.18
    return 0;
}
```

Because they are able to change pointers, most C++ programmers use pointers instead of arrays. Sometimes, because arrays are easy to declare, programmers declare arrays and then use pointers to reference those arrays. If the array data changes, the pointer helps to change it.

2. You can reference arrays with pointer notation, and you can reference pointers with array notation. The following program declares an integer array and an integer pointer that points to the start of the array. The array and pointer values are printed with subscript notation. Afterward, the program uses array notation to print the array and pointer values.

Study the following program carefully. You will see the inner workings of arrays and pointer notation.

```cpp
// Filename: C28ARPTR.CPP
// References arrays like pointers and references pointers
// like arrays

#include <iostream.h>

main()
{
    int     ctr;
    int     iara[ 5 ] =
        { 10, 20, 30, 40, 50 };
    int     *iptr;

    iptr = iara; // Make iptr point to array's first
    ➥element
    // This would also work: iptr = &iara[ 0 ];
    cout << "Using array subscripts:\n";
    cout << "iara" << "\t" << "iptr\n";
    for (ctr = 0; ctr < 5; ctr++)
        cout << iara[ ctr ] << "\t" << iptr[ ctr ] << "\n";
    cout << "\nUsing pointer notation:\n";
    cout << "iara" << "\t" << "iptr\n";
    for (ctr = 0; ctr < 5; ctr++)
        cout << *(iara + ctr) << "\t"
            << *(iptr + ctr) << "\n";
    return 0;
}
```

This program's output is as follows:

```
Using array subscripts:
iara    iptr
10      10
20      20
30      30
40      40
50      50
```

```
Using pointer notation:
iara     iptr
10       10
20       20
30       30
40       40
50       50
```

Using Character Pointers

A character pointer can point to the first character of a string.

The ability to change pointers is useful when you are working with character strings in memory. You have the ability to store strings in character arrays or to point to strings with character pointers. Consider the following two string definitions:

```
char      cara[ ] = "C++ is fun";    // An array holding
                                     // a string
char*     cptr = "Visual C++ By Example"; // A pointer to
                                          // the string
```

Figure 28.2 shows how C++ stores these two strings in memory. C++ stores them basically the same way. You are familiar with the array definition. When assigning a string to a character pointer, C++ finds enough free memory to hold the string, and assigns the address of the first character to the pointer. Apart from the changeability of the two pointers (the array name and the character pointers), the preceding two string definition statements do exactly the same thing.

Because cout prints strings, starting at the array or pointer name until the null zero is reached, you can print each of these strings with the following cout statements:

```
cout << "String 1: " << cara << "\n";
cout << "String 2: " << cptr << "\n";
```

Notice that you print strings in arrays and strings pointed to in the same way. Up to this point, you may have wondered what advantage one method of storing strings has over the other. The seemingly minor difference between these stored strings makes a big difference when you change them.

Suppose that you want to store the string Hello in the two strings. You *cannot* assign the string to the array in this way:

```
cara = "Hello";      // INVALID
```

Figure 28.2

Storing two
strings as arrays.

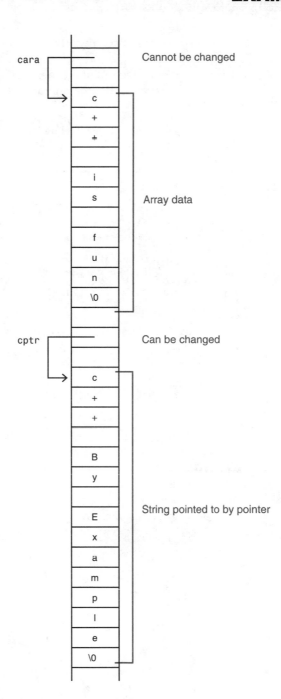

Because you cannot change the array name, you cannot assign it a new value. The only way to change the contents of the array is to assign characters from the string to the array, one element at a time, or to use a built-in function such as strcpy(). You can, however, make the character pointer point to the new string, as in the following:

```
cptr = "Hello";      // Change the pointer so that it points
                     // to the new string
```

Tip: If you want to store user input in a string, pointed to by a pointer, you first must reserve enough storage for that input string. The easiest way to do this is to reserve a character array and then assign a character pointer to the beginning element of that array, like this:

```
char  input[ 81 ];      // Holds a string as long as
                        // 80 characters
char* iptr = input;     // Could also have done this:
                        // char *iptr = &input[ 0 ];
```

Now you can input a string by using the pointer, as in

```
cin >> iptr;            // Make sure that iptr points
                        // to the string typed by user
```

You can use pointer manipulation, arithmetic, and modification on the input string.

Examples

1. Suppose that you want to store your sister's full name and then print it. Instead of using arrays, you can use a character pointer. The following program does just that:

```
// Filename: C28CP1.CPP
// Stores a name in a character pointer

#include <iostream.h>

main()
{
    char*    c = "Bettye Lou Horn";

    cout << "My sister's name is " << c << "\n";
    return 0;
}
```

This program prints the following:

```
My sister's name is Bettye Lou Horn
```

2. Now suppose that you need to change a string pointed to by a character pointer. If your sister married, changing her last name to Henderson, your program can show both strings:

```cpp
// Filename: C28CP2.CPP
// Illustrates changing a character string

#include <iostream.h>

main()
{
    char*    c = "Bettye Lou Horn";

    cout << "My sister's maiden name was " << c << "\n";
    c = "Bettye Lou Henderson";   // Assign new string to c
    cout << "My sister's married name is " << c << "\n";
    return 0;
}
```

The output is as follows:

```
My sister's maiden name was Bettye Lou Horn
My sister's married name is Bettye Lou Henderson
```

3. Do not use character pointers to change string constants. This can confuse the compiler, and you will probably not get the results you expect. The following program is similar to those you just saw. Instead of making the character pointer point to a new string, this example attempts to change the contents of the original string.

```cpp
// Filename: C28CP3.CPP
// Illustrates changing a character string improperly

#include <iostream.h>

main()
{
    char*    c = "Bettye Lou Horn";

    cout << "My sister's maiden name was " << c << "\n";

    c += 11;     // Make c point to the last name
                 // (the 12th character)
```

```
    c = "Henderson";      // Assign new string to c
    cout << "My sister's married name is " << c << "\n";
    return 0;
}
```

The program seems to change the last name from Horn to Henderson, but it does not. The output of this program is as follows:

```
My sister's maiden name was Bettye Lou Horn
My sister's married name is Henderson
```

Why didn't the full string print? Because the address pointed to by c was incremented by 11, c still points to Henderson, so that was all that printed.

4. You might guess at a way to fix the preceding program. Instead of printing the string stored at c after assigning it to Henderson, you might want to decrement it by 11 so that it points to its original location, the start of the name. The code to do this is show here, but it does not work as expected. Study the program before reading the explanation.

```
// Filename: C28CP4.CPP
// Illustrates changing a character string improperly

#include <iostream.h>

main()
{
    char*    c = "Bettye Lou Horn";

    cout << "My sister's maiden name was " << c << "\n";
    c += 11;      // Make c point to the last name
                  // (the 12th character)
    c = "Henderson";      // Assign new string to c
    c -= 11;      // Make c point to its
                  // original location (???)
    cout << "My sister's married name is " << c << "\n";
    return 0;
}
```

This program will produce garbage at the second cout. There are actually two string constants in this program. When you first assign c to Bettye Lou Horn, C++ reserves space in memory for the constant string and puts the starting address of the string in c.

When the program then assigns c to Henderson, C++ finds room for *another* character constant, as shown in figure 28.3. If you subtract 11 from the location of c, after it points to the new string Henderson, c points to an area of memory that is not used by your program. There is no guarantee that printable data appears before the string constant Henderson. If you want to manipulate parts of the string, you will have to do so an element at a time, just as you would with arrays.

Figure 28.3

Two string constants appear in memory because two string constants are used in the program.

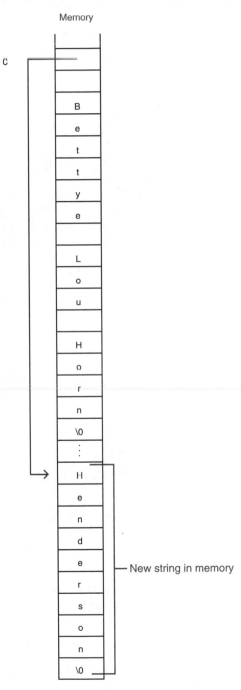

Memory

New string in memory

Pointer Arithmetic

You saw an example of pointer arithmetic when you accessed array elements with pointer notation. By now, you should be comfortable with the fact that both of these array/pointer references are identical:

```
ara[ sub ]
*(ara + sub)
```

You can increment or decrement a pointer. If you increment a pointer, the address inside the pointer variable increments. The pointer does not always increment by 1, however.

Suppose that `f_ptr` is a floating-point pointer that points to the first element of an array of floating-point numbers. `f_ptr` might be initialized as follows:

```
float     fara[ ] =
      { 100.5, 201.45, 321.54, 389.76, 691.34 };
float* f_ptr = fara;
```

Figure 28.4 shows what these variables look like in memory. Each floating-point value in this example takes four bytes of memory.

Figure 28.4

A floating-point array and a pointer.

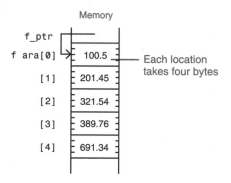

If you print the value of `*f_ptr`, you will see `100.5`. Suppose that you incremented `f_ptr` by one with the following statement:

Incrementing a pointer may add more than one byte to the pointer.

```
f_ptr++;
```

C++ does *not* add 1 to the address in `f_ptr` even though it seems as though 1 should be added. In this case, because floating-point values take four bytes each on this machine, C++ adds 4 to `f_ptr`. How does C++ know how many bytes to add to `f_ptr`? C++ knows from the pointer's declaration how many bytes of memory pointers take. This is why the data type of pointers is so important.

After incrementing f_ptr, if you were to print *f_ptr, you would see 201.45, the second element in the array. If C++ added only 1 to the address in f_ptr, f_ptr would point only to the second byte of 100.5. This would print garbage to the screen.

> **Note:** When you increment a pointer, C++ adds one data type size (in bytes) to the pointer, not 1. When you decrement a pointer, C++ subtracts one data type size (in bytes) from the pointer.

Examples

1. The following program defines an array with five values. An integer pointer is then initialized to point to the first element in the array. The rest of the program prints the dereferenced value of the pointer and then increments the pointer so that it points to the next integer in the array.

   So that you can see what is going on, the size of integer values is printed at the bottom of the program. Because integers take two bytes, C++ increments the pointer by 2 in order to point to the next integer. (The integers are two bytes apart from each other.)

```cpp
// Filename: C28PTI.CPP
// Increments a pointer through an integer array

#include <iostream.h>

main()
{
    int     iara[ ] =
        { 10, 20, 30, 40, 50 };
    int*    ip = iara;      // The pointer points to
                            // the start of the array

    cout << *ip << "\n";
    ip++;      // 2 is actually added
    cout << *ip << "\n";
    ip++;      // 2 is actually added
    cout << *ip << "\n";
    ip++;      // 2 is actually added
    oout << *ip << "\n";
    ip++;      // 2 is actually added
    cout << *ip << "\n\n";
```

```
      cout << "The integer size is " << sizeof(int)
          << " bytes on this machine";
      return 0;
}
```

The output of this program is as follows:

```
10
20
30
40
50

The integer size is 2 bytes on this machine
```

2. Here is the same program, but using a character array and a character
pointer. Because a character takes only one byte of storage, incrementing a
character pointer actually adds just 1 to the pointer; only 1 is needed since
the characters are just one byte apart from each other.

```
// Filename: C28PTC.CPP
// Increments a pointer through a character array

#include <iostream.h>

main()
{
    char    cara[ ] =
        { 'a', 'b', 'c', 'd', 'e' };
    char*   cp = cara;    // The pointer points to
                          // the start of the array

    cout << *cp << "\n";
    cp++;       // 1 is actually added
    cout << *cp << "\n";
    cp++;       // 1 is actually added
    cout << *cp << "\n";
    cp++;       // 1 is actually added
    cout << *cp << "\n";
    cp++;       // 1 is actually added
    cout << *cp << "\n\n";
    cout << "The character size is " << sizeof(char)
        << " byte on this machine";
    return 0;
}
```

3. The following program shows the many ways you can add to, subtract from, and reference arrays and pointers. The program defines a floating-point array and a floating-point pointer. The body of the program prints the values from the array, using array and pointer notation.

```
// Filename: C28ARPT2.CPP
// Comprehensive reference of arrays and pointers

#include <iostream.h>

main()
{
    float     ara[ ] =
        { 100.0, 200.0, 300.0, 400.0, 500.0 };
    float*    fptr;      // Floating-point pointer

    // Make pointer point to array's first value
    fptr = &ara[ 0 ];      // Could also have been this:
                           // fptr = ara;

    cout << *fptr << "\n";     // Print 100.0
    fptr++;     // Point to NEXT floating-point value
    cout << *fptr << "\n";     // Print 200.0
    fptr++;     // Point to NEXT floating-point value
    cout << *fptr << "\n";     // Print 300.0
    fptr++;     // Point to NEXT floating-point value
    cout << *fptr << "\n";     // Print 400.0
    fptr++;     // Point to NEXT floating-point value
    cout << *fptr << "\n";     // Print 500.0
    fptr = ara;     // Point back to first element again
    cout << *(fptr + 2) << "\n";  // Print 300.00 but do
                                  // NOT change fptr
    // Reference both array and pointer using subscripts
    cout << (fptr + 0)[ 0 ] << "  " << (ara + 0)[ 0 ]
        << "\n"; // 100.0   100.0
    cout << (fptr + 1)[ 0 ] << "  " << (ara + 1)[ 0 ]
        << "\n"; // 200.0   200.0
    cout << (fptr + 4)[ 0 ] << "  " << (ara + 4)[ 0 ]
        << "\n"; // 500.0   500.0
    // Reference both array and pointer, using subscripts
    // Notice that subscripts are based from addresses that
    // begin before the data in the array and pointer.
```

```
        cout << (fptr - 1)[ 2 ] << "   " << (ara - 1)[ 2 ]
              << "\n"; // 200.0  200.0
        cout << (fptr - 20)[ 23 ] << "  " << (ara - 20)[ 23 ]
              << "\n"; // 400.0  400.0
        return 0;
    }
```

This program's output is as follows:

```
100.0
200.0
300.0
400.0
500.0
300.0
100.0   100.0
200.0   200.0
500.0   500.0
200.0   200.0
400.0   400.0
```

Arrays of Strings

An array of character pointers defines a ragged-edge array.

You are now ready for one of the most useful applications of character pointers: storing arrays of strings. Actually, you cannot store an array of strings, but you can store an array of character pointers, and each character pointer can point to a string in memory.

By defining an array of character pointers, you define a *ragged-edge array*. This array is similar to a two-dimensional table, with one exception: instead of each row being the same length (the same number of elements), each row contains a different number of characters.

The words *ragged-edge* derive from word processing. A word processor can typically print text fully justified or with a ragged-right margin. The columns in a newspaper are fully justified because both the left and the right columns align evenly. Letters you write by hand or type on typewriters generally have ragged-right margins. It is very difficult to type so that each line ends in exactly the same column on the right.

All two-dimensional tables you have seen so far have been the fully justified kind. If you declare a character table with 5 rows and 20 columns, for example, each row contains the same number of characters. You could define the table with the following statement:

```
char     names[ 5 ][ 20 ] =
{
      { "George" },
      { "Michelle" },
      { "Joe" },
      { "Marcus" },
      { "Stephanie" }
};
```

This table is shown in figure 28.5. Notice that much of the table is wasted space. Each row takes 20 characters, even though the data in each row has far fewer characters. The unfilled elements contain null zeros because C++ zeros-out all elements you do not initialize in arrays. This type of table uses too much memory.

Figure 28.5

A fully justified table.

Columns

names

Rows

	0	1	2	3	4	5	6	7	8	9	10	11	12	13	14	15	16	17	18	19
0	G	e	o	r	g	e	\0													
1	M	i	c	h	e	l	l	e	\0											
2	J	o	e	\0																
3	M	a	r	c	u	s	\0													
4	S	t	e	p	h	a	n	i	e	\0										

Most of table is wasted

To fix the memory-wasting problem of fully justified tables, you should declare a single-dimensional array of character pointers. Each pointer points to a string in memory, and the strings do *not* have to be the same length.

The definition for such an array is as follows:

```
char*  names[ 5 ] =
{
      { "George" },
      { "Michelle" },
      { "Joe" },
      { "Marcus" },
      { "Stephanie" }
};
```

This array is single-dimensional. The definition should not confuse you, although it is something you have not seen. The asterisk before names makes this an array of pointers. The type of pointers is character. The strings are *not* being assigned to the array elements, but they are being *pointed to* by the array elements. Figure 28.6 shows this array of pointers. The strings are stored elsewhere in memory. Their actual locations are not critical because each pointer points to the starting character. The strings waste no data; each string takes only as much memory as needed by the string and its terminating zero. This gives the data its ragged-right appearance.

Figure 28.6

The array that points to each of the five strings.

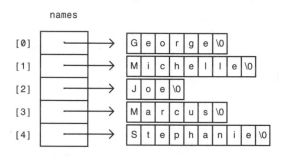

To print the first string, you use the following cout:

```
cout << *names;          // Print George
```

To print the second string, you use this cout:

```
cout *(names + 1);       // Print Michelle
```

Whenever you dereference any pointer element, using the * dereferencing operator, you access one of the strings in the array. You can use a dereferenced element anywhere you use a string constant or character array (with strcpy(), strcmp(), and so on).

Tip: Working with pointers to strings is *much* more efficient than working with the strings. For instance, it takes a lot of time to sort a list of strings if they are stored as a fully justified table. It is much faster to sort strings pointed to by a pointer array. You just swap pointers during the sort, not entire strings.

Examples

1. Here is a full program that uses the pointer array with five names. The for loop controls the cout function, printing each name in the string data. You now can see why learning about pointer notation for arrays pays off!

```
// Filename: C28PTST1.CPP
// Prints strings pointed to by an array

#include <iostream.h>

main()
{
    char*    name[ 5 ] =
    {
        { "George" },    // Define a ragged-edge array
        { "Michelle" }, // of pointers to strings
        { "Joe" },
        { "Marcus" },
        { "Stephanie" }
    };
    int    ctr;

    for (ctr = 0; ctr < 5; ctr++)
        cout << "String #" << ctr + 1 << " is "
        << *(name + ctr) << "\n";
    return 0;
}
```

The output of this program is as follows:

```
String #1 is George
String #2 is Michelle
String #3 is Joe
String #4 is Marcus
String #5 is Stephanie
```

2. The following program stores the days of the week in an array. When the user types a number from 1 to 7, the day of the week that matches that number (with Sunday being 1) is displayed. The program dereferences the pointer that points to that string.

```
// Filename: C28PTST2.CPP
// Prints the day of the week based on an input value

#include <iostream.h>

main()
{
    char*    days[ ] =
    {
```

```
            "Sunday",      // The seven separate sets
            "Monday",      // of braces are optional.
            "Tuesday",
            "Wednesday",
            "Thursday",
            "Friday",
            "Saturday"
    };
    int     day_num;

    do
    {
        cout << "What is a day number (from 1 to 7)? ";
        cin >> day_num;
    }
    while ((day_num < 1) || (day_num > 7));
        // Ensure accurate number
    day_num--;      // Adjust for subscript
    cout << "The day is " << *(days + day_num) << "\n";
    return 0;
}
```

Summary

You now understand the foundation of C++'s pointers and array notation. Once you master this material, you are on your way to thinking in C++ as you design your programs. C++ programmers know that C++'s arrays are pointers in disguise, and program them accordingly.

Using ragged-edge arrays offers two advantages. You can hold arrays of string data without wasting extra space, and you can quickly change the pointers without having to move the string data around in memory.

As you progress into advanced C++ concepts, you will appreciate the time you spend on pointer notation. The next chapter introduces a new topic, *structures*. Structures let you store data in a more unified way than simple variables allow.

Review Questions

Answers to Review Questions are in Appendix B.

1. What is the difference between an array name and a pointer?

2. Assume that `ipointer` points to integers that take two bytes of memory. If you performed the statement

```
ipointer += 2;
```

how many bytes are added to `ipointer`?

3. Which of the following items are equivalent, assuming that `iary` is an integer array and that `iptr` is an integer pointer that points to the start of the array?

a. `iary` and `iptr`

b. `iary[ 1 ]` and `iptr + 1`

c. `iary[ 3 ]` and `*(iptr + 3)`

d. `(iary - 4)[ 9 ]` and `iary[ 5 ]`

e. `*iary` and `iary[ 0 ]`

f. `iary[ 4 ]` and `*iptr + 4`

4. Why is it more efficient to sort a ragged-edge character array than a fully justified string array?

5. Look at the following array and pointer definition:

```
int     ara[ ] =
    { 1, 2, 3, 4, 5, 6, 7, 8, 9, 10 };
int*    ip1;
int*    ip2;
```

Which of the following are allowed?

a. `ip1 = ara;`

b. `ip2 = ip1 = &ara[ 3 ];`

c. `ara = 15;`

d. `*(ip2 + 2) = 15; // Assuming ip2 and ara are equal`

Review Exercises

1. Write a program to store the names of your family members in a character array of pointers. Print the names.

2. Write a program that asks the user for 15 daily stock market averages and stores those averages in a floating-point array. Using only pointer notation, print the array forward and backward. Using only pointer notation, print the highest and lowest stock market quotes in the list.

3. Modify the bubble sort shown in Chapter 25, "Array Processing," so that it sorts with pointer notation. Add this bubble sort to the program in Exercise 2, printing the stock market averages in ascending order.

4. Write a program that requests 10 song titles from the user. Store the titles in an array of character pointers (a ragged-edge array). Print the original titles, print the alphabetized titles, and print the titles in reverse alphabetic order (from Z to A).

Part VII

Data Structures

CHAPTER 29

Structures

Structures enable you to group data together and to work with that data as a whole. Business data processing uses the concepts of structures in almost every program. Being able to manipulate several variables as a single group makes programs easier to manage.

This chapter introduces the following topics:

♦ Structure definitions

♦ Initializing structures

♦ The dot (.) operator

♦ Structure assignment

♦ Nested structures

Structure Variables

Structures can have members of different data types.

A *structure* is a collection of one or more variable types. As you know, the elements in an array must be the same data type, and you must refer to the entire array by its name. Each element (called a *member*) in a structure can be a different data type.

Suppose that you want to use a structure to keep track of your CD music collection. You might want to track the following pieces of information about each CD:

Title

Artist

Number of songs

Cost

Date bought

This CD structure would have five members.

> **Tip:** If you have programmed in other computer languages or used a database program, C++ structures are analogous to file records, and members are analogous to fields in those records.

After deciding on the members, you must decide what data types to use for the members. Both the title and the artist can be character arrays, the number of songs can be an integer, the cost can be a floating-point value, and the date can be another character array. This information is represented in the following table.

Member Name	Data Type
Title	Character array of 25 characters
Artist	Character array of 19 characters
Number of songs	Integer
Cost	Floating-point
Date bought	Character array of 8 characters

A structure tag is a label for the structure's format.

Each structure you define can have an associated structure name, called a *structure tag*. Structure tags are not required in most cases, but generally it is best to define one for each structure in your program. The structure tag is *not* a variable name. Unlike array names that reference arrays as variables, a structure tag is just a label for the structure's format.

You name structure tags yourself, using the naming rules of variables. If you give the CD structure a structure tag named cd_collection, you are telling C++ that the tag called cd_collection looks like two character arrays, followed by an integer, a floating-point value, and a final character array.

A structure tag is a newly defined data type.

A structure tag is actually a newly defined data type that you, the programmer, define. When you want to store an integer, you do not have to define what an integer is. C++ already knows. However, when you want to store a CD collection's data, C++ does not know what format your CD collection will take. You have to tell C++ (using the example described in this section) that you need a new data type. That data type will be your structure tag called cd_collection, and it will look like the structure just described (two character arrays, an integer, a floating-point value, and another character array).

Note: No memory is reserved for structure tags. A structure tag is your own data type. C++ does not reserve memory for the integer data type until you declare an integer variable. C++ does not reserve memory for a structure until you declare a structure variable.

Figure 29.1 contains the CD structure, graphically showing the data types within the structure. Notice that there are five members, and each member is a different data type. The entire structure is called `cd_collection`, which is the structure tag.

Figure 29.1

The *cd_collection* structure.

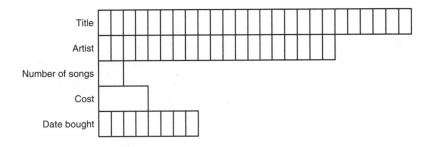

Examples

1. Suppose that you are asked to write a program for a company's inventory system. The company had been using a card-file inventory system that tracks the following items:

> Item name
>
> Quantity in stock
>
> Quantity on order
>
> Retail price
>
> Wholesale price

This is a perfect use for a structure containing five members. Before defining the structure, you need to determine the data type of each member by asking questions about the range of data. For example, you must know the largest item name and the most quantity that will ever be on order to ensure that your data types will hold the data. You then decide to use the following structure tag and data types:

Structure tag: *inventory*

Member	Data Type
Item name	Character array of 20 characters
Quantity in stock	`long int`
Quantity on order	`long int`
Retail price	`double`
Wholesale price	`double`

2. Suppose that the same company wants you to write a program to keep track of its monthly and annual salaries, printing a report at the end of the year that shows each month's individual salaries and the annual salaries at the end of the year.

What would the structure look like? Be careful! This type of data probably does not need a structure. Because all the monthly salaries will be the same data type, a floating-point or double floating-point array will hold the monthly salaries nicely without the complexity of a structure.

Structures are useful for keeping track of data that must be grouped together, such as inventory data, a customer's name and address data, or an employee data file.

Defining Structures

To define a structure, you must use the `struct` statement. `struct` defines for your program a new data type with more than one member. The format of the `struct` statement is as folows:

```
struct [structure tag]
{
    member definition;
    member definition;
        :
    member definition;
} [one or more structure variables];
```

As mentioned earlier, the `structure tag` is optional (hence, the brackets in the format). Each `member definition` is a normal variable definition, such as `int i;` or `float sales[ 20 ];` or any other valid variable definition, including variable pointers if the structure requires a pointer as a member. At the end of the structure's definition and before the final semicolon, you can specify one or more structure variables.

If you specify a structure variable, you request C++ to reserve space for that variable. C++ knows that the variable is not an integer, character, or any other internal data type; C++ knows that the variable will be a type that looks like the structure. It may seem strange that the members themselves do not reserve storage, but they don't. Storage is reserved when you declare a structure variable. This will be made clear in the examples that follow.

Following is how you declare the CD structure:

```
struct cd_collection
{
    char        title[ 25 ];
    char        artist[ 20 ];
    int         num_songs;
    float       price;
    char        date_bought[ 8 ];
} cd1, cd2, cd3;
```

Before going any further, you should be able to answer the following questions about this structure:

1. What is the structure tag?

2. How many members are there?

3. What are the member data types?

4. What are the member names?

5. How many structure variables are there?

6. What are their names?

The structure tag is called `cd_collection`. There are five members: two character arrays, an integer, a floating-point value, and a character array. The member names are `title`, `artist`, `num_songs`, `price`, and `date_bought`. The three structure variables are `cd1`, `cd2`, and `cd3`.

Often you can visualize structure variables as looking like a card-file inventory system. Figure 29.2 shows how you might keep your CD collection in a 3-by-5 card file, each CD taking one card (representing each structure variable). The information about the CD (the structure members) is on each card.

If you had 1,000 CDs, you would have to declare 1,000 structure variables. Obviously, you would not want to list that many structure variables at the end of a structure definition. To help define structures for a large number of occurrences, you must define an *array of structures*. Chapter 30, "Arrays of Structures," shows you how to do that. For now, just familiarize yourself with structure definitions.

Figure 29.2

Using a card-file
CD inventory
system.

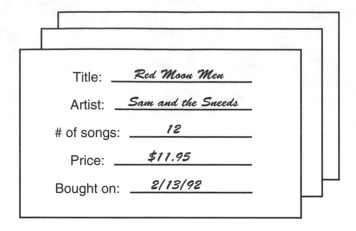

Examples

1. Following is a structure definition of the inventory application described
earlier in this chapter:

```
struct inventory
{
    char        item_name[ 20 ];
    long int    in_stock;
    long int    order_qty;
    float       retail;
    float       wholesale;
} item1, item2, item3, item4;
```

Four inventory structure variables are defined. Each structure variable—
item1, item2, item3, and item4—looks like the structure.

2. Suppose that a company wants to track its customers and personnel. The
following two structure definitions create five structure variables for each
structure. This example (with five employees and five customers) is very
limited, but serves to show how structures can be defined.

```
struct employees
{
    char        emp_name[ 25 ];     // Employee full name
    char        address[ 30 ];      // Employee address
    char        city[ 10 ];
    char        state[ 2 ];
    long int    zip;
    double      salary;             // Annual salary
} emp1, emp2, emp3, emp4. emp5;
```

```
struct customers
{
    char         cust_name[ 25 ];      // Customer full name
    char         address[ 30 ];        // Customer address
    char         city[ 10 ];
    char         state[ 2 ];
    long int     zip;
    double       balance;              // Balance owed to company
} cust1, cust2, cust3, cust4, cust5;
```

Similar data is in each structure. A little later in this chapter, you learn how to consolidate similar member definitions by creating nested structures.

Tip: Put comments to the right of members to document the purpose of the members.

Initializing Structure Data

You can define a structure's data when you declare the structure.

Members of a structure are initialized in two ways. You can initialize members when you declare a structure, or you can initialize a structure within the body of the program. Most programs lend themselves to the second method because you do not always know structure data when you write your program.

Following is an example of a structure declared and initialized at the same time:

```
struct cd_collection
{
    char         title[ 25 ];
    char         artist[ 20 ];

    int          num_songs;
    float        price;
    char         date_bought[ 8 ];
} cd1 =
    {
        "Red Moon Men",
        "Sam and the Sneeds",
        12,

        11.95,

        "02/13/92"

    };
```

When you first learn about structures, you may be tempted to initialize members individually inside the structure, as in the following:

```
char     artist[ 20 ] = "Sam and the Sneeds";     // INVALID
```

You cannot initialize individual members because they are *not* variables. You can only assign values to variables. The only structure variable in the preceding structure is cd1. The braces must enclose the data when you initialize the structure variables, just as the braces enclose data when you initialize arrays.

This method of initializing structure variables gets tedious when there are several structure variables (as there usually are). Putting the data into several variables, with each set of data enclosed in braces, gets messy and takes too much space in your code.

More important, you will usually not know the contents of the structure variables. Generally, the user enters the data to be stored in structures, or you read the data from a disk file.

Use the dot (.) operator to initialize members of structures.

A better approach to initializing structures is to use the *dot (.) operator*. With it, you can initialize individual members of a structure variable within the body of your program. You can treat each structure member almost as if it were a regular, nonstructure variable.

The format of the dot operator is as follows:

```
structure_variable_name.member_name
```

A structure variable name must always precede the dot operator, and a member name must always appear after the dot operator. Using the dot operator is quite easy, as the following examples illustrate.

Examples

1. Following is a simple program that uses the CD collection structure and the dot operator to initialize the structure. Notice that the program treats members as if they were regular variables when combined with the dot operator.

```
// Filename: C29ST1.CPP
// Structure initialization with the CD collection

#include <iostream.h>
#include <string.h>

main()
{
    struct     cd_collection
    {
        char          title[ 25 ];
```

```
            char        artist[ 20 ];
            int         num_songs;
            float       price;
            char        date_bought[ 8 ];
        } cd1;

        // Initialize members here
        strcpy(cd1.title, "Red Moon Men");
        strcpy(cd1.artist, "Sam and the Sneeds");
        cd1.num_songs = 12;
        cd1.price = 11.95;
        strcpy(cd1.date_bought, "02/13/92");
        // Print the data to the screen
        cout << "Here is the CD information:\n\n";
        cout << "Title: " << cd1.title << "\n";
        cout << "Artist: " << cd1.artist << "\n";
        cout << "Songs: " << cd1.num_songs << "\n";
        cout << "Price: " << cd1.price << "\n";
        cout << "Date bought: " << cd1.date_bought << "\n";
        return 0;
}
```

Note the output of the program:

```
Here is the CD information:

Title: Red Moon Men
Artist: Sam and the Sneeds
Songs: 12
Price: 11.95
Date bought: 02/13/92
```

2. By using the dot operator, you can get structure data from the keyboard with any of the data input functions you know, such as cin and get().

The following program asks the user for student information. To keep the example reasonably short, only two students are defined in the program. Figure 29.3 shows the program's output.

```
// Filename: C29ST2.CPP
// Structure input with student data

#include <iostream.h>
#include <stdio.h>
#include <string.h>
```

```
main()
{
    struct      students
    {
        char          name[ 25 ];
        int           age;
        float         average;
    } student1, student2;

    // Get two students' data
    cout << "What is first student's name? ";
    cout.flush();
    gets(student1.name);
    cout << "What is the first student's age? ";
    cin >> student1.age;
    cout << "What is the first student's average? ";
    cin >> student1.average;
    fflush(stdin);      // Clear input buffer for next input
    cout << "What is second student's name? ";
    cout.flush();
    gets(student2.name);

    fflush( stdout );
    cout << "What is the second student's age? ";
    fflush( stdout );
    cin >> student2.age;
    cout << "What is the second student's average? ";
    fflush( stdout );
    cin >> student2.average;
    fflush( stdin );
    // Print the data
    cout << "\n\nHere is the student ";
    cout << "information you entered:\n\n";
    cout << "Student #1:\n";
    cout << "Name:    " << student1.name << "\n";
    cout << "Age:     " << student1.age << "\n";
    cout << "Average: " << student1.average << "\n\n";
    cout << "Student #2:\n";
    cout << "Name:    " << student2.name << "\n";
    cout << "Age:     " << student2.age << "\n";
    cout << "Average: " << student2.average << "\n";
    return 0;
}
```

Figure 29.3

For this program, the user has filled structure variables with values.

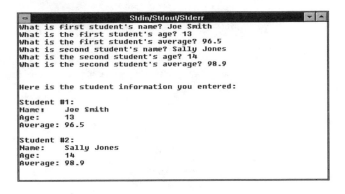

```
                    Stdin/Stdout/Stderr
What is first student's name? Joe Smith
What is the first student's age? 13
What is the first student's average? 96.5
What is second student's name? Sally Jones
What is the second student's age? 14
What is the second student's average? 98.9


Here is the student information you entered:

Student #1:
Name:    Joe Smith
Age:     13
Average: 96.5

Student #2:
Name:    Sally Jones
Age:     14
Average: 98.9
```

Define structures globally; define structure variables locally.

3. Structure variables are passed by copy, not by address as with arrays. There-fore, if you fill a structure in a function, you must return the structure to the calling function in order for that function to recognize the structure. Or you must use global structure variables, which are generally not recommended.

There is a good solution to the local/global structure problem. Define your structures globally without *any* structure variables; define all your struc-ture variables locally to the functions that need them. As long as your structure definition is global, you can declare local structure variables from that structure. All upcoming examples in this book use this method.

This is where the structure tag plays an important role. Use the structure tag to define local structure variables. The following program is similar to the preceding one. Notice that the student structure is defined globally with *no structure variables*. In each function, local structure variables are declared through references to the structure tag. The structure tag keeps you from having to redefine the structure members every time you define a new structure variable.

```cpp
// Filename: C29ST3.CPP
// Structure input with student data passed to functions

#include <iostream.h>
#include <stdio.h>
#include <string.h>

struct      students     // A global structure
{
    char          name[ 25 ];
    int           age;
    float         average;
};                       // No memory reserved yet
```

```
students     fill_structs(students student_var)
{
    // Get students' data
    fflush(stdin);     // Clear input buffer for next input
    cout << "What is student's name? ";
    cout.flush();
    gets(student_var.name);
    cout << "What is the student's age? ";
    cin >> student_var.age;
    cout << "What is the student's average? ";
    cin >> student_var.average;
    return (student_var);
}

void    pr_students(students student_var)
{
    cout << "\nName:    " << student_var.name << "\n";
    cout << "Age:     " << student_var.age << "\n";
    cout << "Average: " << student_var.average << "\n";
    return;
}

int    main(void)
{
    students     student1, student2;    // Define 2
                                        // local variables

    // Call function to fill structure variables
    student1 = fill_structs(student1);  // student1 is
                                        // passed by copy, so it
                                        // must be returned for
                                        // main() to recognize it.
    student2 = fill_structs(student2);

    // Print the data
    cout << "\n\nHere is the student ";
    cout << "information you entered:\n";
    pr_students(student1);   // Print first student's data
    pr_students(student2);   // Print second student's data
    return 0;
}
```

The prototype and definition of the `fill_structs()` function may seem complicated, but they follow the same pattern you have seen throughout this book. Before a function name, you must declare `void` or put the return data type if the function returns a value. `fill_structs()` does return a value, and the type of value it returns is `students`. This shows that to C++ a `students struct` is really a new data type.

4. Because structure data is nothing more than regular variables grouped together, feel free to calculate with structure members. As long as you use the dot operator, you can treat structure members like other variables.

The following example asks for a customer's balance and uses a discount rate (included in the customer's structure) to calculate a new balance. To keep the example short, the structure's data is initialized at variable declaration time.

This program does not actually require structures because only one customer is used. Individual variables could be used, but they would not illustrate calculating with structures.

```
// Filename: C29CUST.CPP
// Updates a customer balance in a structure

#include <iostream.h>

struct     customer_rec
{
    char         cust_name[ 25 ];
    double       balance;
    float        dis_rate;
};

main()
{
    customer_rec     customer =
        { "Steve Thompson", 2431.23, .25 };

    cout << "Before the update, " << customer.cust_name;
    cout << " has a balance of " << customer.balance
        << "\n";
    // Update the balance
    customer.balance *= (1.0 - customer.dis_rate);
    cout << "After the update, " << customer.cust_name;
    cout << " has a balance of " << customer.balance
        << "\n";
    return 0;
}
```

5. You can copy one structure variable to another structure variable as long as both structures have the same format. The member variables of the structures will be copied, variable by variable.

Being able to copy one structure variable to another will be more meaningful in Chapter 30, "Arrays of Structures," but the concept is very easy to apply.

The following program declares three structure variables but initializes only the first one with data. The other two structure variables are then initialized when the first structure variable is assigned to them.

```cpp
// Filename: C29STCPY.CPP
// Demonstrates assigning one structure to another

#include <iostream.h>

struct      student
{
    char        st_name[ 25 ];
    char        grade;
    int         age;
    float       average;
};

main()
{
    student     std1 =
        { "Joe Brown", 'A', 13, 91.4 };
    student     std2, std3;     // Not initialized

    std2 = std1;    // Copy each member of std1 to std2
    std3 = std1;    // and std3
    cout << "The contents of std2:\n";
    cout << std2.st_name << ", " << std2.grade << ", ";
    cout << std2.age << ", " << std2.average << "\n\n";
    cout << "The contents of std3:\n";
    cout << std3.st_name << ", " << std3.grade << ", ";
    cout << std3.age << ", " << std3.average << "\n\n";
    return 0;
}
```

The program's output is as follows:

```
The contents of std2
Joe Brown, A, 13, 91.4

The contents of std3
Joe Brown, A, 13, 91.4
```

Notice that each member of std1 is assigned to std2 and std3 with two single assignments.

Nested Structures

C++ enables you to nest one structure definition within another. This saves time when you are writing programs that use similar structures. You have to define the common members only once in their own structure and then use that structure as a member in another structure.

Consider the following two structure definitions:

```
struct      employees
{
    char        emp_name[ 25 ];      // Employee full name
    char        address[ 30 ];       // Employee address
    char        city[ 10 ];
    char        state[ 2 ];
    long int    zip;
    double      salary;              // Annual salary
};

struct      customers
{
    char        cust_name[ 25 ];     // Customer full name
    char        address[ 30 ];       // Customer address
    char        city[ 10 ];
    char        state[ 2 ];
    long int    zip;
    double      balance;      // Balance owed to company
};
```

These structures hold very different data. One structure is for employee data, and the other structure is for customer data. Even though the data should be kept separate (you don't want to send a customer a paycheck!), the structure definitions have a lot of overlap and can be consolidated if you create a third structure:

```
struct     address_info
{
    char          address[ 30 ];   // Common address
                                    // information
    char          city[ 10 ];
    char          state[ 2 ];
    long int      zip;
};
```

This structure can then be used *as a member* in the other structures in this way:

```
struct     employees
{
    char                    emp_name[ 25 ];   // Employee
                                              // full name
    address_info e_address;     // Employee address
    double              salary;        // Annual salary
};

struct     customers
{
    char                    cust_name[ 25 ];  // Customer
                                              // full name
    address_info c_address;     // Customer address
    double              balance;        // Balance owed
                                        // to company
};
```

You must realize that there is a total of three structures, with the tags address_info, employees, and customers. How many members does the employees structure have? If you answered three, you are correct. There are three members in both employees and customers. employees has the structure of a character array, followed first by the address_info structure and then by the double floating-point member salary. Figure 29.4 shows how these structures look graphically.

Once you define a structure, it is then a new data type in the program and can be used anywhere that a data type (such as int, float, and so on) can appear.

You can assign values to members by using the dot operator. To assign the customer balance a number, you can type something like the following:

```
customer.balance = 5643.24;
```

The nested structure might appear to pose a problem. How can you assign a value to one of the nested members? When you use the dot operator, you must nest it just as you nest the structure definitions. To assign a value to the customer's ZIP code, you use the following:

```
customer.c_address.zip = 34312;
```

To assign a value to the employee's ZIP code, you use this:

```
employee.e_address.zip = 59823;
```

Figure 29.4

Defining a nested structure.

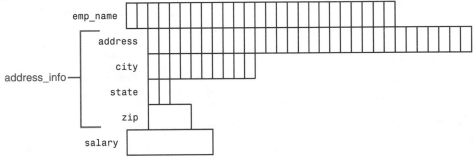

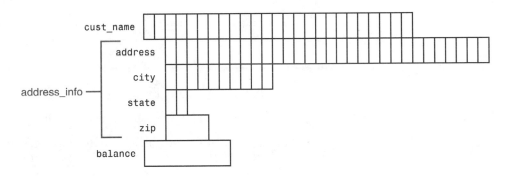

Summary

Structures enable you to group data together in more flexible ways than arrays allow. The structures can contain members of different data types. You can initialize the structures either at declaration time or during program execution with the dot (.) operator.

Structures become even more powerful when you declare arrays of structure variables. The next chapter shows you how to declare several structure variables without giving each one a different name. This enables you to step through structures more quickly with loop constructs.

Review Questions

Answers to Review Questions are in Appendix B.

1. What is the difference between structures and arrays?

2. What are the individual elements of a structure called?

3. What are the two ways to initialize members of a structure?

4. Do you pass structures by copy or by address?

5. True or false: The following structure definition reserves storage in memory.

```
struct      crec
{
    char      name[ 25 ];
    int       age;
    float     sales[ 5 ];
    long      int num;
};
```

6. Should you declare a structure globally or locally?

7. Should you declare a structure variable globally or locally?

8. How many members does the following structure declaration contain?

```
struct      item
{
    int               quantity;
    part_rec          item_desc;
    float             price;
    char              date_bought[8];
};
```

Review Exercises

1. Write a structure that a video store can use in a program to track the video tape inventory. Make sure that the structure includes the tape's title, length of the tape (in minutes), cost of the tape, rental price of the tape, and date of the movie's release.

2. Write a program that uses the structure declared in the preceding exercise. Define three structure variables and initialize them *when you declare the variables* with data. Print the data to the screen.

3. Write a teacher's program that keeps track of 10 student names, ages, letter grades, and IQs. Use 10 different structure variable names and get the data for the students in a for loop from the keyboard. Print the data on the printer when the teacher finishes entering the information for all the students.

CHAPTER 30

Arrays of Structures

This chapter builds on the preceding chapter by showing you how you can create many structures for your data. After creating an array of structures, you can store multiple occurrences of your data values.

Arrays of structures are good for storing a complete employee file, an inventory file, or any other set of data that fits within the structure format. Whereas arrays provide a handy way to store several values of the same type, arrays of structures let you store together several values of different types, grouped as structures.

This chapter introduces the following topics:

- Creating arrays of structures

- Initializing arrays of structures

- Referencing elements from a structure array

- Arrays as members

Many C++ programmers use arrays of structures as a prelude to storing data in a disk file. You can input and calculate your disk data in arrays of structures and then store those structures in memory. Arrays of structures also provide a means of holding data you read from the disk.

Declaring Arrays of Structures

Declaring an array of structures is easy. You specify the number of reserved structures inside array brackets when you declare the structure variable. Consider the following structure definition:

```
struct      stores
{
    int          employees;
    int          registers;
    double       sales;
} store1, store2, store3, store4, store5;
```

This structure is easy to understand because no new commands are used in the structure declaration, which creates five structure variables. Figure 30.1 shows how C++ stores these five structures in memory. Each of the structure variables has three members—two integers followed by a double floating-point value.

Figure 30.1

The structure of *store1, store2, store3, store4,* and *store5.*

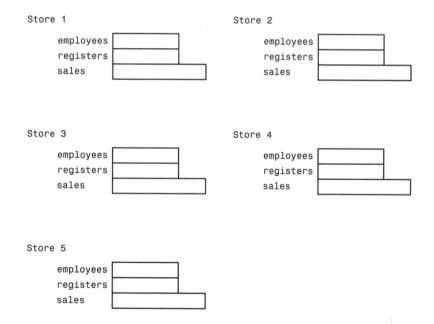

If the fourth store increases its employees by three, you can update the store's employee count with the following assignment statement:

```
store4.employees += 3;    // Add 3 to this store's
                          // employee count
```

Suppose that the fifth store just opened and you want to initialize its members with data. If the stores are a chain and the new store is similar to one of the others, you might begin initializing the store's data by assigning each of its members the same data as that of another store:

```
store5 = store2;          // Define initial values for the
                          // store5 members
```

Such structure declarations are fine for a small number of structures, but if the stores are a national chain, five structure variables will not be enough. What if there are 1,000 stores? You would not want to create 1,000 different store variables and work with each one individually. It would be much easier to create an array of store structures.

Consider the following structure declaration:

```
struct      stores
{
    int         employees;
    int         registers;
    double      sales;
} store[ 1000 ];
```

In one quick declaration, this code creates 1,000 store structures, each containing three members. Figure 30.2 shows how these structure variables appear in memory. Notice the name of each individual structure variable: store[0], store[1], store[2], and so on.

> **Caution:** Be careful that you do not run out of memory when creating a large number of structures. Arrays of structures quickly consume valuable memory. You may have to create fewer structures, storing more data in disk files and less data in memory.

The element store[2] is an array element. This element, unlike the others you have seen, is a structure variable. Therefore, it contains three members, each of which you can reference with the dot operator (.).

The dot operator works the same way for structure array elements as for regular structure variables. If the number of employees for the fifth store (store[4]) increases by three, you can update the structure variable as follows:

```
store[ 4 ].employees += 3;    // Add 3 to this store's
                              // employee count
```

Figure 30.2

An array of the
store structures.

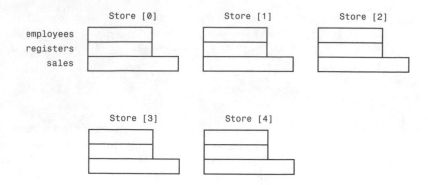

You can assign complete structures to one another by using array notation also. To assign all the members of the 20th store to the 45th store, you can do the following:

```
store[ 44 ] = store[ 19 ];      // Copy all members from the
                                // 20th store to the 45th
```

The rules of arrays are still in force here. The elements of the array called store are the *very same data type*. The data type of store is struct stores. As with any array, the elements have to be the same data type; you cannot mix data types within the same array. This array's data type happens to be a structure you created, containing three members. The data type for store[316] is exactly the same for store[981] and store[74].

The name of the array, store, is a pointer constant to the starting element of the array, store[0]. Therefore, you can use pointer notation to reference the stores. To assign store[60] the same value as store[23], you can reference the two elements as follows:

```
*(store + 60) = *(store + 23);
```

You can also mix array and pointer notation, and get the same results, as in the following:

```
store[ 60 ] = *(store + 23);
```

You also can increase the sales of store[8] by 40 percent with pointer or subscript notation:

```
store[ 8 ].sales = (*(store + 8)).sales * 1.40;
```

The extra pair of parentheses is required because the dot operator has precedence over the dereferencing symbol in C++'s hierarchy of operators (see Appendix D). Of course, in this case, the code is not helped by the pointer notation, and the following is a much clearer way to increase the sales by 40 percent:

```
store[ 8 ].sales *= 1.40;
```

Keep Your Array Notation Straight

You would never access the member `sales` like this:

```
store.sales[ 8 ] = 3234.54;      // INVALID
```

Array subscripts follow array elements only. `sales` is not an array; it was declared as being a double floating-point number. `store` can never be used *without* a subscript (unless you are using pointer notation).

Here is a corrected version of the preceding assignment statement:

```
store[ 8 ].sales = 3234.54;      // Correctly assigns
                                 // the value
```

The following examples build an inventory data-entry system for a mail order firm, using an array of structures. There is very little new that you have to know when working with arrays of structures. Concentrate on the notation for accessing arrays of structures and their members so that you can get comfortable with this notation.

Examples

1. Suppose that you work for a mail order company that sells disk drives. You are given the task of writing a tracking program for the 125 different drives you sell. You must keep track of the following information:

> Storage capacity in megabytes
>
> Access time in milliseconds
>
> Vendor code (A, B, C, or D)
>
> Cost
>
> Price

Because there are 125 different disk drives in the inventory, the data will fit nicely into an array of structures. Each array element is a structure containing the five members described in this list.

The following structure definition defines the inventory:

```
struct      inventory
{
    long int    storage;
    int         access_time;
    char         vendor_code;
```

```
        double    cost;
        double    price;
    } drive[ 125 ];      // Define 125 occurrences
                         // of the structure
```

2. When working with a large array of structures, your first concern should be how the data will be input into the array elements. The application will determine the best method of data entry.

If you are converting from an older computerized inventory system, for example, you will have to write a conversion program that reads the inventory file in its native format and saves it to a new file in the format needed by your C++ programs. This is no easy task, requiring that you have extensive knowledge of the system you are converting from.

If you are writing a computerized inventory system for the first time, your job is a little easier because you do not need to worry about converting the old files. You must still realize that someone has to type the data into the computer. You will have to write a data entry program that receives each inventory item from the keyboard and saves the item to a disk file. You should give the user a chance to edit inventory data to correct any data that may have been typed incorrectly.

One of the reasons that this book does not introduce disk files until the last chapters is that disk file formats and structures share a common bond. Once you store data in a structure, or more often in an array of structures, you can easily write that data to a disk file with straightforward disk I/O commands.

The following program takes the array of disk drive structures shown in the preceding example and adds a data entry function so that the user can enter data into the array of structures. The program is menu-driven. The user has a choice, when starting the program, to add data, print data to the screen, or exit the program. Because you have yet to see disk I/O commands, the data in the array of structures goes away when the program ends. As noted, saving those structures to disk will be an easy task after you learn C++'s disk I/O commands. For now, concentrate on the manipulation of the structures.

This program is longer than many you have seen in this book, but if you have followed the discussion of structures and the dot operator, you should have little trouble following the code.

```
// Filename: C30DSINV.CPP
// Data entry program for a disk drive company

#include <iostream.h>
#include <stdio.h>
#include <stdlib.h>

struct     inventory      // Global structure definition
{
    long int  storage;
    int       access_time;
    char      vendor_code;
    float     cost;
    float     price;
};    // No structure variables defined globally

void    disp_menu(void)
{
    cout << "\n\n*** Disk Drive Inventory System ***\n\n";
    cout << "Do you want to:\n\n";
    cout << "\t1. Enter new item in inventory\n\n";
    cout << "\t2. See inventory data\n\n";
    cout << "\t3. Exit the program\n\n";
    cout << "What is your choice? ";
    return;
}

inventory    enter_data(void)
{
    inventory     disk_item; // Local variable to
                             // fill with input

    cout << "\n\nWhat is the next drive's ";
    cout << "storage in bytes? ";
    cin >> disk_item.storage;
    cout << "What is the drive's access time in ms? ";
    cin >> disk_item.access_time;
    cout << "What is the drive's vendor code ";
    cout << "(A, B, C, or D)? ";
    cin >> disk_item.vendor_code;
    fflush(stdin);      // Discard carriage return
    cout << "What is the drive's cost? ";
```

```
     cin >> disk_item.cost;
     cout << "What is the drive's price? ";
     cin >> disk_item.price;
     return (disk_item);
}

void    see_data( inventory disk[ 125 ], int num_items)
{
     int    ctr;

     cout << "\n\nHere is the inventory listing:\n\n";
     for (ctr = 0; ctr < num_items; ctr++)
     {
          cout << "Storage: " << disk[ ctr ].storage
               << "\t";
          cout << "Access time: " << disk[ ctr ].access_time
               << "\n";
          cout << "Vendor code: " << disk[ ctr ].vendor_code
               << "\t";
          cout << "Cost: $" << disk[ ctr ].cost << "\t";
          cout << "Price: $" << disk[ ctr ].price << "\n";
     }
     return;
}

int    main(void)
{
     inventory    disk[ 125 ];   // Local array
                                 // of structures
     int          ans;
     int          num_items = 0;    // Number of
                                    // total items in the
inventory

     do
     {
          do
          {
               disp_menu();  // Display menu of user choices
               cin >> ans;   // Get user's request
          }
          while ((ans < 1) || (ans > 3));
```

```
        switch (ans)
        {
            case 1:
                // Enter disk data
                disk[ num_items ] = enter_data();
                num_items++; // Increment number of items
                break;
            case 2:
                // Display disk data
                see_data(disk, num_items);
                break;
            default:
                break;
        }
    }
    while (ans != 3);  // Quit program when user is through
    return 0;
}
```

Figure 30.3 shows an item being entered into the inventory file. Figure 30.4 shows the inventory listing being displayed on-screen. There are many features and error-checking functions you can add, but this program is the building block to a more comprehensive inventory system. You can easily adapt the program to a different type of inventory—such as a video tape collection, a coin collection, or any other tracking system—just by changing the structure definition and the member names throughout the program.

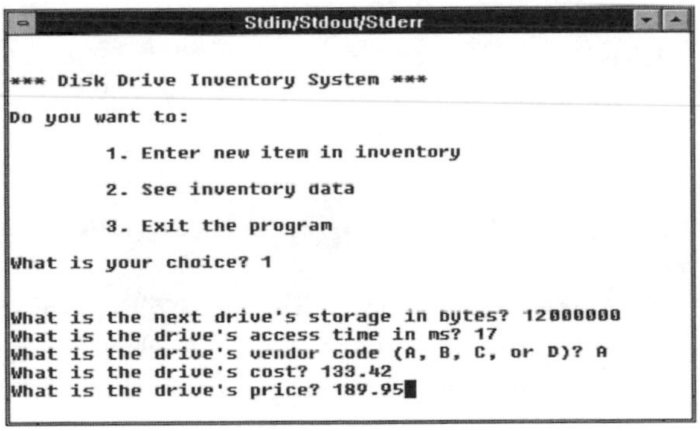

Figure 30.3

Entering inventory information.

```
*** Disk Drive Inventory System ***

Do you want to:
            1. Enter new item in inventory
            2. See inventory data
            3. Exit the program
What is your choice? 1

What is the next drive's storage in bytes? 12000000
What is the drive's access time in ms? 17
What is the drive's vendor code (A, B, C, or D)? A
What is the drive's cost? 133.42
What is the drive's price? 189.95
```

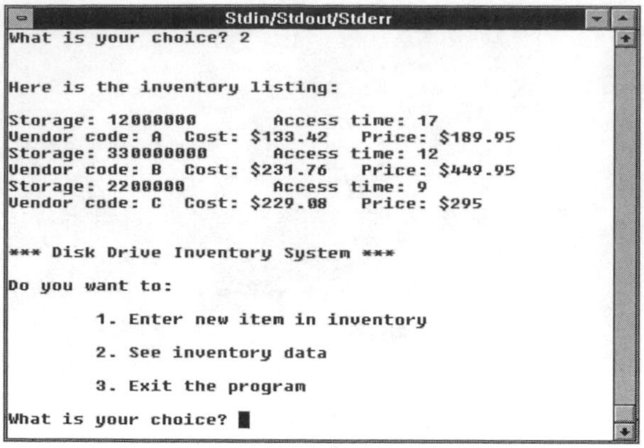

Figure 30.4

Displaying
inventory data.

```
┌─────────────── Stdin/Stdout/Stderr ───────────────┐
│What is your choice? 2                              │
│                                                    │
│Here is the inventory listing:                      │
│                                                    │
│Storage: 12000000      Access time: 17             │
│Vendor code: A  Cost: $133.42   Price: $189.95     │
│Storage: 330000000     Access time: 12             │
│Vendor code: B  Cost: $231.76   Price: $449.95     │
│Storage: 2200000       Access time: 9              │
│Vendor code: C  Cost: $229.08   Price: $295        │
│                                                    │
│                                                    │
│*** Disk Drive Inventory System ***                │
│                                                    │
│Do you want to:                                     │
│                                                    │
│        1. Enter new item in inventory             │
│                                                    │
│        2. See inventory data                      │
│                                                    │
│        3. Exit the program                        │
│What is your choice? █                              │
└────────────────────────────────────────────────────┘
```

Arrays as Members

Members of structures can themselves be arrays. Array members pose no new problem, but you have to be careful when you access individual array elements. Keeping track of arrays of structures that contain array members might seem like a lot of work on your part, but there is really nothing to it.

Consider the following structure definition. This statement declares an array of 100 structures, each structure holding payroll information for a company. Two of the members, name and department, are arrays.

```
struct       payroll
{
    char        name[ 25 ];          // Employee name array
    int         dependents;
    char        department[ 10 ]; // Department name array
    float       salary;
} employee[ 100 ];      // An array of 100 employees
```

Figure 30.5 shows what these structures look like. The first and third members are arrays. name is an array of 25 characters, and department is an array of 10 characters.

Suppose that you need to save the 25th employee's initial in a character variable. Assuming that initial is already declared as a character variable, the following statement assigns the employee's initial to initial:

```
initial = employee[ 24 ].name[ 0 ];
```

The double subscripts may look confusing, but the dot operator requires a structure variable on its left (employee[24]) and a member on its right (name's first array element). Being able to refer to member arrays makes the processing of character data in structures simple.

Figure 30.5

The payroll data.

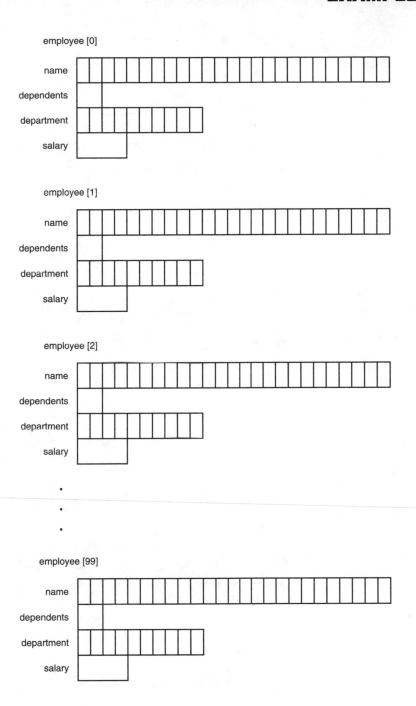

Examples

1. Suppose that an employee gets married and wants her name changed in the payroll file. (She happens to be the 45th employee in the array of structures.) Given the payroll structure just described, the following assigns a new name to her structure:

```
// Assign a new name
strcpy(employee[ 44 ].name, "Mary Larson");
```

When you refer to a structure variable with the dot operator, you can use regular commands and functions to process the data in the structures.

2. A bookstore wants to catalog its inventory of books. The following program creates an array of 10 structures. Each structure contains several types of variables, including arrays. This program is the data entry portion of a larger inventory system. Study the references to the members to see how member arrays are used.

```cpp
// Filename: C30BOOK.CPP
// Bookstore data entry program

#include <iostream.h>
#include <stdio.h>
#include <ctype.h>

struct      inventory
{
    char        title[ 25 ];            // Book's title
    char        pub_date[ 19 ];         // Publication date
    char        author[ 20 ];           // Author's name
    int         num;                    // Number in stock
    int         on_order;               // Number on order
    float       retail;                 // Retail price
};

main()
{
    inventory     book[ 10 ];
    int           total = 0;  // Total books
                              // in inventory
    char          ans;

    do      // Program enters data into the structures
    {
        cout << "Book #" << (total + 1) << ":\n";
```

```
            cout << "What is the title? ";
            cout.flush();
            gets( book[ total ].title );
            cout << "What is the publication date? ";
            cout.flush();
            gets( book[ total ].pub_date );
            cout << "Who is the author? ";
            cout.flush();
            gets( book[ total ].author );
            cout << "How many books of this title are there? ";
            cin >> book[ total ].num;
            cout << "How many are on order? ";
            cin >> book[ total ].on_order;
            cout << "What is the retail price? ";
            cin >> book[ total ].retail;

            fflush(stdin);
            cout << "\nAre there more books? (Y/N) ";
            cin >> ans ;
            fflush( stdin );
            ans = toupper(ans);      // Convert to uppercase
            if (ans == 'Y')
            {
                total++;
                continue;
            }
        }
    while (ans == 'Y');
    return 0;
}
```

There is a lot more needed to make this a usable inventory program. An exercise at the end of this chapter recommends ways you can improve this program (adding a printing routine and an author and title search). One of the first things you should do is put the data entry routine in a separate function to make the code more modular. Because this example is so short and the program performs only one task (data entry), there is no advantage to putting the data entry task in a separate function.

> **Caution:** There is only a limited amount of memory available for allocating arrays of structures. If your structure is starting to become large, as in the preceding example, you should not count on being able to allocate a large array. This limit is imposed by the way memory is addressed on most DOS computers, not by the amount of memory installed on your computer.
>
> There are two solutions to this dilemma. One is to find a way to use more of the memory which is installed on your computer. This is an advanced topic which is beyond the scope of this book.
>
> The other solution to limitations used by memory is to use a disk file to store your data and only keep the current "record" in memory. That is the reason for the existence of database management systems. You will learn some of the fundamentals of using disk storage in your programs in the next two chapters.

3. Here is a comprehensive example of the steps you might go through to write a C++ program. You are getting to the point where you understand enough of the C++ language to start writing some advanced programs.

Assume that you are hired to write a magazine inventory system by a local bookstore. You need to track the following:

> Magazine title (maximum of 25 characters)
>
> Publisher (maximum of 20 characters)
>
> Month (1, 2, 3, ..., 12)
>
> Publication year
>
> Number of copies in stock
>
> Number of copies on order
>
> Price of magazine (dollars and cents)

Suppose that there is a projected maximum of 1,000 magazine titles that the store will ever carry. This means that you need 1,000 occurrences of the structure, not a total of 1,000 magazines. Here is a good structure definition for such an inventory:

```
struct      mag_info
{
    char            title[ 25 ];
    char            pub[ 25 ];
    int             month;
    int             year;
    int             stock_copies;
    int             order_copies;
    float           price;
} mags[ 1000 ];      // Define 1,000 occurrences
```

Because this program will consist of more than one function, it is best to declare the structure globally and the structure variables locally within the functions that need them.

This program needs three basic functions: a `main()` controlling function, a data entry function, and a data printing function. There is a lot more you can add, but this is a good start for an inventory system. To keep the length of this example reasonable, assume that the user wants to enter several magazines and then print them out. (To make the program more usable, you would want to add a menu so that the user can control when to add and print the information, as well as add more error-checking and editing capabilities.)

Here is an example of the complete data entry and printing program with prototypes. The arrays of structures are passed between the functions from `main()`.

```
// C30MAG.CPP
// Magazine inventory program for adding and displaying
// a bookstore's magazines

#include <iostream.h>
#include <stdio.h>
#include <ctype.h>

struct      mag_info
{
    char            title[ 25 ];
    char            pub[ 25 ];
    int             month;
    int             year;
    int             stock_copies;
    int             order_copies;
    float           price;
```

```
};

mag_info    fill_mags( mag_info mag)
{
    cout << "\n\nWhat is the title? ";
    cout.flush();
    gets(mag.title);
    cout << "Who is the publisher? ";
    cout.flush();
    gets(mag.pub);
    cout << "What is the month (1, 2, ..., 12)? ";
    cin >> mag.month;
    cout << "What is the year? ";
    cin >> mag.year;
    cout << "How many copies in stock? ";
    cin >> mag.stock_copies;
    cout << "How many copies on order? ";
    cin >> mag.order_copies;
    cout << "How much is the magazine? ";
    cin >> mag.price;
    return (mag);
}

void    print_mags( mag_info mags[], int mag_ctr)
{
    int     i;

    for (i = 0; i <= mag_ctr; i++)
    {
        cout << "\n\nMagazine " << (i + 1) << "\n";
        cout << "\nTitle: " << mags[ i ].title << "\n";
        cout << "\tPublisher: " << mags[ i ].pub << "\n";
        cout << "\tPub. Month: "
            << mags[ i ].month << "\n";
        cout << "\tPub. Year: "
            << mags[ i ].year << "\n";
        cout << "\tIn-stock: "
            << mags[ i ].stock_copies << "\n";
        cout << "\tOn order: "
            << mags[ i ].order_copies << "\n";
        cout << "\tPrice: " << mags[ i ].price << "\n";
    }
```

```
        return;
}

int     main(void)
{
    mag_info        mags[ 10 ];
    int             mag_ctr = 0; // Number of
                                 // magazine titles
    char            ans;

    do
    {    // Assume that there will be at least
         // one magazine filled
        mags[ mag_ctr ] = fill_mags(mags[ mag_ctr ]);
        cout << "Do you want to enter another magazine? ";
        cout.flush();
        fflush(stdin);
        cin.get(ans);
        fflush(stdin);      // Discard carriage return
        if (toupper(ans) == 'Y')
            mag_ctr++;
    }
    while (toupper(ans) == 'Y');

    print_mags(mags, mag_ctr);

    return 0;       // Return to operating system
}
```

Summary

You have now mastered structures and arrays of structures. There are many useful inventory and tracking programs ready to be written by you, using structures. By being able to create arrays of structures, you can now create multiple occurrences of data.

Earlier in this chapter you read a caution that arrays of structures can rapidly become too large to store in memory, and you also read that one solution to this problem is to store your data in a disk file. The next chapter will introduce you to sequential disk files.

Review Questions

Answers to Review Questions are in Appendix B.

1. True or false: All elements in an array of structures must be the same type.

2. What is the advantage of creating an array of structures instead of using individual variable names for each structure variable?

3. Consider the following structure declaration:

```
struct     item
{
    char        part_no[ 8 ];
    char        descr[ 20 ];
    float       price;
    int         in_stock;
} inventory[ 100 ];
```

a. How would you assign a price of 12.33 to the 33rd item's in stock quantity?

b. How would you assign the first character of the 12th item's part number the value of 'x'?

c. How would you assign the 97th inventory item the same value as the 63rd?

4. Now look at this structure declaration:

```
struct     item
{
    char        desc[ 20 ];
    int         num;
    float       cost;
} inventory[ 25 ];
```

What is wrong with each of the following statements?

a. item[1].cost = 92.32;

b. strcpy(inventory.desc, "Widgets");

c. inventory.cost[10] = 32.12;

Review Exercises

1. Write a program that stores an array of friends' names, phone numbers, and addresses and then prints them two ways: the full name and address, and just the name and phone number for a phone listing.

2. Add a sort function to the preceding program so that you can print your friends' names in alphabetic order. (*Hint:* You will have to make the member holding the names a character pointer.)

3. Expand on the data entry program (C30BOOK.CPP) by adding features to make it more usable, such as searching books by author and title, and printing an inventory of books on order.

CHAPTER 31

Sequential Files

So far, every example in this book has processed data that resided inside the program listing or came from the keyboard. You assigned constants and variables to other variables and created new data values from expressions. The programs also received input with cin, gets(), and the character input functions.

The data that is created by the user and assigned to variables with assignment statements is sufficient for some applications. With the large volumes of data that most real-world applications need to process, however, you need a better way of storing that data. For all but the smallest computer programs, disk files offer the solution.

After storing data on disk, the computer helps you enter, find, change, and delete the data. The computer and C++ are simply tools to help you manage and process data. This chapter focuses on disk file processing concepts and shows you the first of two methods of disk access: *sequential file access*.

This chapter introduces the following topics:

♦ An overview of disk files

♦ The types of files

♦ Processing data on the disk

♦ Sequential file access

♦ File I/O functions

After reading this chapter, you will be ready to tackle the more advanced methods of accessing random files, covered in the next chapter. If you have programmed computerized data files with another programming language, you might be surprised at how C++ borrows from other programming languages, especially BASIC, when working with disk files. If you are new to disk file processing, you will find tht disk files are simple to create and read.

Why Use a Disk?

Disks hold more data than can fit in computer memory.

The typical computer system has much less memory storage than hard disk storage. Your disk drive holds more data than can fit in your computer's RAM. This is the primary reason for using the disk for your data. The disk memory, because it is nonvolatile, also lasts longer; when you power-off your computer, the disk memory is not erased, whereas RAM is erased. Furthermore, when your data changes, you (or more important, your users) do not have to edit the program and look for a set of assignment statements. Instead, the users run previously written programs that make changes to the disk data.

All of this makes programming more difficult at first because programs have to be written to change the data on the disk. However, nonprogrammers can then use the programs and modify the data without knowing how to program.

The capacity of your disk makes it a perfect place to store your data as well as your programs. Think about what would happen if all data had to be stored with a program's assignment statements. What if the Social Security office in Washington, D.C., asked you to write a C++ program to compute, average, filter, sort, and print each person's name and address in its files? Would you want your program to include millions of assignment statements? Not only would you not want the program to hold that much data, but the program could not do so because only relatively small amounts of data fit in a program before you run out of RAM.

By storing data on your disk, you are much less limited because you have more storage. Your disk can hold as much data as you have disk capacity. If your disk requirements grow, you can usually increase your disk space, whereas you cannot always add more RAM to your computer.

When working with disk files, C++ does not have to access much RAM because C++ reads data from your disk drive and processes it only parts at a time. Not all your disk data has to reside in RAM for C++ to process it. C++ reads some data, processes it, and then reads some more. If C++ requires disk data a second time, it rereads that place on the disk.

Types of Disk File Access

Your programs can access files in two ways: through sequential access and random access. Your application determines the method you should choose. The access mode of a file determines how you read, write, change, and delete data from the file. Some of your files can be accessed in both ways, sequentially and randomly, as long as your programs are written properly and the data lends itself to both types of file access.

A sequential file has to be accessed in the same order in which the file was written. This is analogous to cassette tapes: you play music in the same order it was recorded. (You can quickly fast-forward or rewind songs that you do not want to listen to, but the order of the songs dictates what you do to play the song you want.)

It is difficult, and sometimes impossible, to insert data in the middle of a sequential file. How easy is it to insert a new song in the middle of two other songs on a tape? The only way to add or delete records from the middle of a sequential file is to create a completely new file that combines both old and new songs. It may seem that sequential files are limiting, but it turns out that many applications lend themselves to sequential file processing.

Unlike sequential files, random access files can be accessed in any order you want. Think of data in a random access file as you would songs on a compact disc or record; you can go directly to any song you want without having to play or fast-forward the other songs. If you want to play the first song, the sixth song, and then the fourth song, you can do so. The order of play has nothing to do with the order in which the songs were originally recorded. Random file access sometimes takes more programming but rewards that effort with a more flexible file access method. Chapter 32, "Random Access Files," discusses how to program for random access files.

Sequential File Concepts

You can perform the following operations on sequential disk files:

♦ Create disk files

♦ Add to disk files

♦ Read from disk files

Again, your application determines what you need to do. If you are creating a disk file for the first time, you must create the file and write the initial data to it. Suppose that you want to create a customer data file. You need to create a new file and write your current customers to that file. The customer data might originally be in arrays, arrays of structures, pointed to with pointers, or typed into regular variables by the user.

As your customer base grows, you can add new customers to the file. When you add to the end of a file, you *append* to that file. As customers enter the store, you read their information from the customer data file.

Customer disk processing brings up one disadvantage of sequential files. Suppose that a customer moves and wants you to change his or her address in your files. Sequential access files do not lend themselves well to changing data stored in them. It is also difficult to remove information from sequential files. Random files, described in the next chapter, provide a much easier approach to changing and removing data. The primary approach to changing or removing data from a sequential access file is to create a new one from the old one, using the updated data. Because of the ease of updating provided with random access files, this chapter concentrates on creating, reading, and adding to sequential files.

Opening and Closing Files

Before you can create, write to, or read from a disk file, you must open the file. This is analogous to opening a file cabinet before working with a file stored in the cabinet. Once you are done with a cabinet's file, you close the file door. You also must close a disk file when you finish with it.

When you open a disk file, you just have to inform C++ of the file name and what you want to do (write to, add to, or read from). C++ and MS-DOS work together to make sure that the disk is ready and to create an entry in your file directory (if you are creating a file) for the file name. When you close a file, C++ writes any remaining data to the file, releases the file from the program, and updates the file directory to reflect the file's new size.

> **Caution:** You must ensure that the FILES= statement in your CONFIG.SYS file is large enough to hold the maximum number of disk files you will have open, with one file left over for your C++ program itself. If you are unsure about how to do this, check your DOS reference manual or a beginner's book on DOS.

Before you can open a file, you need to tell C++ that you are going to be working with a file. You do this by declaring a *file stream* variable. You then use the *file stream* variable to read and write your file. A *file stream* is similar to the cin and cout objects you are already familiar with, but it is designed for disk operations.

To open a file, you call the open() function. To close a file, you call the close() function. Following is how you declare a *file stream*, and the formats of the open() and close() function calls:

```
offstream fstr                  // declare a file stream
fstr.open(file_name, access);   // open the stream
fstr.close();                   // close the stream
```

Your operating system handles the exact location of your data in the disk file. You don't want to worry about the exact track and sector number of your data on the disk. Therefore, you will let the *file stream* point to the data you are reading and writing. Your program has only to manage the *file stream* while C++ and MS-DOS take care of locating the actual physical data.

The *file_name* is a string (or a character pointer that points to a string) containing a valid file name for your computer. The *file_name* can contain a complete disk and directory path name. You can specify the file name in uppercase or lowercase letters. The *access* can be one of the values from table 31.1.

Table 31.1. Possible access modes.

Mode	Description
app	Open the file for appending (adding to it).
ate	Seek to end of file on opening it.
in	Open file for reading.
out	Open file for writing.
binary	Open file in binary mode.
trunc	Discard contents if file exists.
nocreate	If file doesn't exist, open fails.
noreplace	If file exists, open fails unless appending or seeking to end of file on opening.

The default mode for file access is text. A text file is an ASCII file, compatible with most other programming languages and applications. Text files do not always contain text in the word processing sense of the word. Any data you need to store can go in a text file. Programs that read ASCII files can read data you create as C++ text files.

Binary Modes

If you specify binary access, C++ creates or reads the file in a binary format. Binary data files are "squeezed." That is, they take less space than text files. The disadvantage of using binary files is that other programs cannot always read the data files. Only C++ programs that are written to access binary files can read and write to them. The advantage of binary files is that you save disk space because your data files are more compact. Other than including the access mode in the open() function, you use no additional commands to access binary files with your C++ programs.

The binary format is a system-specific file format. In other words, not all computers will be able to read a binary file created on another computer.

If you open a file for writing, C++ creates the file. If a file by that name *already* exists, C++ overwrites the old file with no warning. You must be careful when opening files so that you do not overwrite existing data you want to save.

If an error occurs during the opening of a file, C++ will not open the file. Instead, C++ sets a status switch inside the *file stream* to show that an error has occurred. You then can check the status switch to see if it is safe to continue using the file. For example, if you open a file for output but use a disk name that is invalid, C++ will not be able to open the file and will set the status switch. Always check the status switch when writing disk file programs in order to ensure that the file opened properly.

Following is a sample of testing the status switch:

```
fstr.open( "testfile.dat", ios::out );
if ( !fstr.good() )  // check the status switch
{
      error processing here...
```

Table 31.2 shows the functions that check the status switch. The two you will use most often are good() and eof().

Table 31.2. Status–checking functions.

Mode	Description
good()	Returns non-zero value if operation was successful.
bad()	Returns non-zero value if a serious I/O error occurred.
eof()	Returns non-zero value if end of file was reached.
fail()	Returns non-zero value if a serious I/O error or a possibly recoverable I/O formatting error occurred.
rdstate()	Returns the stream's status flag.
clear()	Clears the stream's status flag.

Tip: Beginning programmers like to open all files at the beginning of their programs and close them at the end. This is not always best. Open files immediately before you access them and close them when you are done with them. This protects the files, keeping them open only as long as needed. A closed file is more likely to be protected in the unlikely (but possible) event of a power failure or computer breakdown.

This part of the chapter has included a lot of file access theory. The following examples help illustrate these concepts.

Examples

1. Suppose that you want to create a file for storing your house payment records for the last year. Following are the first few lines in the program, which would create a file called HOUSE.DAT on your disk:

```
#include <fstream.h>

main()
{
    ofstream      fstr;      // Declare a file stream
                             // for writing
    fstr.open("house.dat", ios::out); // Create the file
```

The rest of the program writes data to the file. The program never has to refer to the filename again but will use the *file stream* variable to refer to the file. Examples in the next few sections illustrate how this is done. There is nothing special about *file stream*, other than its name (although the name is meaningful in this case). You can name file pointer variables XYZ or a908973 if you like, but these names would not be meaningful.

You must include the fstream.h header file because it contains the definition for the ofstream and ifstream declarations. You don't have to worry about the physical specifics. The *file stream* will "point" to data in the file, as you write it. Put the declarations in your programs where you declare other variables and arrays.

> **Tip:** Because files are not part of your program, you might find it useful to declare file pointers globally. Unlike data in variables, file pointers usually don't need to be kept local.

Before ending the program, you should close the file. The following close() function closes the house file:

```
    fstr.close();      // Close the house payment file
```

2. If you like, you can put the complete path name in the file name parameter. The following line opens the household payment file in a subdirectory on the d: disk drive:

```
    fstr.open("d:\mydata\house.dat", ios::out);
```

3. You can store a file name in a character array or point to it with a character pointer. Each of the following sections of code are equivalent:

```
char     fn[ ] = "house.dat"; // Filename in character array
fstr.open(fn, ios::out);      // Create the file

char*     myfile = "house.dat";  // Filename pointed to
fstr.open(myfile, ios::out);     // Create the file

// Let the user enter the filename
cout << "What is the name of the household file? ";
gets(filename);        // Filename must be an array
                       // or character pointer
fstr.open(filename, ios::out);  // Create the file
```

No matter how you specify the file name when opening the file, close the file with the file pointer. The following `close()` function closes the open file, no matter which method you used to open the file:

```
fstr.close();       // Close the house payment file
```

4. You should check the status switch after `open()` to ensure that the file opened properly. Here is code after `open()` that checks for an error:

```
#include <fstream.h>

main()
{
    ofstream      fstr;        // Declare a file pointer

    fstr.open("house.dat", ios::out); // Create the file
    if (!fstr.good())      // check status flag
        cout << "Error opening file.\n";
    else
    {

        // Rest of output commands go here

    }
}
```

5. You can open and write to several files in the same program. Suppose that you want to read data from a payroll file and create a backup payroll data file. You would have to open the current payroll file using the `in` reading mode, and the backup file in the `out` output mode.

For each open file in your program, you must declare a different file stream. The file streams that your input and output statements use determine which file they operate on. If you have to open many files, you can declare an array of file streams.

Following is a way you can open the two payroll files:

```
#include <fstream.h>

ifstream      file_in;       // Input file
ofstream      file_out;      // Output file

main()
{
     file_in.open("payroll.dat", ios::in);   // Existing file
     file_out.open("payroll.BAK", ios::out);   // New file
```

When you finish with these files, be sure to close them with the following two `close()` function calls:

```
file_in.close();
file_out.close();
```

Writing to a File

Any input or output function that requires a device will perform input and output with files. You have seen most of these functions already. The following are the most common file I/O functions:

```
get()
put()

gets()
puts()
```

You can also use the *file stream* as you use `cout` or `cin`. The following function call reads three integers from a file declared by `fstr`:

```
fstr >> num1 >> num2 >> num3;    // Read three variables
```

There is always more than one way to write data to a disk file. Most of the time, more than one function will work. If you write a bunch of names to a file, for example, both `puts()` and `fstr <<` will work. You can also write the names by using `put()`. You should use whichever function you are most comfortable with for the data being written. You can use `fstr <<`, `puts()`, or `put()` to place a newline character (`\n`) at the end of each line in your file. `fstr <<` and `puts()` are probably easier to use than `put()`, but any of these three will do the job.

> **Tip:** Each line in a file is called a *record*. By putting a newline character at the end of file records, you make the input of those records easier.

Examples

1. The following program creates a file called NAMES.DAT. The program writes five names to a disk file, using `fp <<`.

```cpp
// Filename: C31WR1.CPP
// Writes 5 names to a disk file

#include <fstream.h>

ofstream    fp;

main()
{
    fp.open("NAMES.DAT", ios::out);   // Create a new file

    fp << "Michael Langston\n";
    fp << "Sally Redding\n";
    fp << "Jane Kirk\n";
    fp << "Stacy Grady\n";
    fp << "Paula Hiquet\n";
    fp.close();                        // Release the file
    return 0;
}
```

For simplicity, no error checking was done on the `open()`. The next few examples check for the error.

NAMES.DAT is a text data file. If you like, you can read this file into Visual C++'s text editor, or you can use the MS-DOS TYPE command to display this file on-screen. If you display NAMES.DAT, you see the following:

```
Michael Langston
Sally Redding
Jane Kirk
Stacy Grady
Paula Hiquet
```

2. The following file writes the numbers from 1 to 100 to a file called NUMS.1:

```
// Filename: C31WR2.CPP
// Writes 1 to 100 to a disk file

#include <fstream.h>

ofstream    fstr;

main()
{
    int     ctr;

    fstr.open("NUMS.1", ios::out);      // Create a new file
    if (!fstr.good())
        cout << "Error opening file.\n";
    else
    {
        for (ctr = 1; ctr < 101; ctr++)
            fstr << ctr << " ";
    }
    fstr.close();
    return 0;
}
```

The numbers are not written one per line, but with a space between them. The format of the `fstr` << determines the format of the output data. When writing data to disk files, keep in mind that you will have to read the data later. You will have to use "mirror image" input functions to read the data you output to files.

Writing to a Printer

The `open()` function and other output functions were not designed just to write to files. They were designed to write to any device, including files, the screen, and the printer. If you need to write data to a printer, you can treat it as if it were a file. The following program opens a file pointer, using the MS-DOS name for a printer located at LPT1 (the first parallel printer port):

```
// Filename: C31PRNT.CPP
// Prints to the printer device
```

```
#include <fstream.h>

ofstream      prnt;      // Will point to the printer

main()
{
    prnt.open("LPT1", ios::out);
    prnt << "Printer line 1\n";      // 1st line printed
    prnt << "Printer line 2\n";      // 2nd line printed
    prnt << "Printer line 3\n";      // 3rd line printed
    prnt << "\f";                    // formfeed
    prnt.close();
    return 0;
}
```

Make sure that your printer is turned on and has paper before you run this program. When you run it, the following lines are printed:

```
Printer line 1
Printer line 2
Printer line 3
```

Adding to a File

You can easily add data to an existing file or create new files by opening the file in append access mode. Data files on the disk are rarely static; they grow almost daily as business increases. Being able to add to data already on the disk is very useful indeed.

A file you open for append access (using ios::app) does not have to exist. If the file exists, C++ appends data to the end of the file when you write the data. If the file does not exist, C++ creates the file (just as when you open a file for write access).

Example

The following program adds three more names to the NAMES.DAT file created earlier:

```
// Filename: C31AP1.CPP
// Adds 3 names to a disk file

#include <fstream.h>

ofstream      fstr;
```

```
main()
{
    fstr.open("NAMES.DAT", ios::app);     // Add to file
    fstr << "Johnny Smith\n";
    fstr << "Laura Hull\n";
    fstr << "Mark Brown\n";
    fstr.close();     // Release the file
    return 0;
}
```

Following is the contents of the file with the three names added:

```
Michael Langston
Sally Redding
Jane Kirk
Stacy Grady
Paula Hiquet
Johnny Smith
Laura Hull
Mark Brown
```

> **Note:** If the file did not exist, C++ would create it and store the three names in the file.

Basically, you have to change only the open() function's access mode to turn a file-creation program into a file-appending program.

Reading from a File

Once the data is in a file, you need to be able to read that data. You must open the file in a read access mode. There are several ways to read data. You can read character data a character at a time or a string at a time. The choice depends on the format of the data.

Files must exist if you open them for read access.

Files you open for read access (using ios::in) must exist already; otherwise, C++ sets an error condition in the status switch. You cannot read a file that does not exist.

Another event happens when reading files. Eventually, you read *all* the data. Subsequent reading produces errors because there is no more data to read. C++ provides a solution to the end-of-file occurrence. If you attempt to read from a file that you have read all the data from, C++ sets the end-of-file condition in the status switch. Some read functions also return a zero to indicate that nothing was read. To find the end-of-file condition, be sure to check the status switch for eof(), or the read function for a zero return value when reading input from files.

Examples

1. The following program asks the user for a file name and prints the contents of the file to the screen. If the file does not exist, the program displays an error message. When the read operation reaches end-of-file, `fin.get(in_char)` returns a zero. (The `while` interprets the zero as "false" and terminates the while-loop.)

```
// Filename: C31RE1.CPP
// Reads and displays a file

#include <fstream.h>
#include <stdlib.h>

ifstream      fin;

main()
{
    char      filename[ 12 ];   // Will hold user's filename
    char      in_char;          // Input character

    cout << "What is the name of the file ";
    cout << "you want to see? ";
    cin >> filename;
    fin.open(filename, ios::in);
    if (!fin.good())
    {
        cout << "\n\n*** That file does not exist ***\n";
        exit(0);      // Exit program
    }
    while (fin.get(in_char))
        cout << in_char;
    fin.close();
    return 0;
}
```

Figure 31.1 shows what happens when the NAMES.DAT file is requested. Because newline characters are in the file at the end of each name, the names appear on-screen, one name per line. If you attempt to read a file that does not exist, the program displays the following message:

```
*** That file does not exist ***
```

Figure 31.1

Reading and
displaying a
disk file.

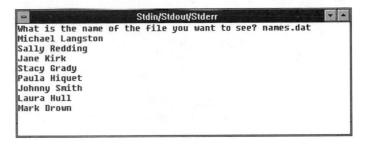

```
 ═                  Stdin/Stdout/Stderr              ▼ ▲
What is the name of the file you want to see? names.dat
Michael Langston
Sally Redding
Jane Kirk
Stacy Grady
Paula Hiquet
Johnny Smith
Laura Hull
Mark Drown
```

2. The following program reads one file and copies it to another file. You
might want to use such a program to back up important data in case the
original file gets damaged.

This program must open two files, the first for reading and the second
for writing. The file pointer determines which of the two files is being
accessed.

```cpp
// Filename: C31RE2.CPP
// Makes a copy of a file

#include <fstream.h>
#include <stdlib.h>

ifstream    infl;
ofstream    outfl;

main()
{
    char    in_filename[ 12 ];  // Will hold original
                                // filename
    char    out_filename[ 12 ]; // Will hold backup
                                // filename
    char    in_char;            // Input character

    cout << "What is the name of the file ";
    cout << "you want to back up? ";
    cin >> in_filename;
    cout << "What is the name of the file ";
    cout << "you want to copy " << in_filename
         << " to? ";
    cin >> out_filename;
    infl.open(in_filename, ios::in);
```

```
if (!infl.good())
   {
        cout << "\n\n*** %s does not exist ***\n";
        exit(0);      // Exit program
   }
outfl.open(out_filename, ios::out);
if (!outfl.good())
   {
        cout << "\n\n*** Error opening %s ***\n";
        exit(0);      // Exit program
   }
cout << "\nCopying...\n";      // Waiting message
while (infl.get(in_char))
        outfl.put(in_char);
cout << "\nThe file is copied.\n";
infl.close();
outfl.close();
return 0;
}
```

Summary

This chapter showed you how to perform two of the most important requirements of data processing: writing and reading to and from disk files. Before now, you could only store data in variables. The short life of variables (they last only as long as your program is running) made long-term storage of data impossible. Now you can save large amounts of data in disk files for processing later.

Reading and writing sequential files involves learning more concepts than actual commands or functions. The open() and close() functions are the most important ones discussed in this chapter. You are already familiar with most of the I/O functions needed to get data to and from disk files.

The next chapter, which concludes this book's discussion of disk files, shows you how to create and use random access files. By programming with such files, you will be able to read selected data from a file, as well as change data without having to rewrite the entire file.

Review Questions

Answers to Review Questions are in Appendix B.

1. What are the three ways to access sequential files?

2. What advantages do disk files have over holding data in memory?

3. How do sequential files differ from random access files?

4. What happens if you open a file for read access and the file does not exist?

5. What happens if you open a file for write access and the file already exists?

6. What happens if you open a file for append access and the file does not exist?

7. How does C++ inform you that you have reached the end-of-file condition?

Review Exercises

1. Write a program that creates a file containing the following data:

   Your name

   Your address

   Your phone number

   Your age

2. Write a second program that reads and prints the data file created in the preceding exercise.

3. Write a program that takes that same data and writes it to the screen, one word per line.

4. Write a program for PCs that backs up two important files: AUTOEXEC.BAT and CONFIG.SYS. Call the backup files AUTOEXEC.SAV and CONFIG.SAV.

5. Write a program that reads a file and creates a new file with the same data, with one exception: reverse the case on the second file. Everywhere uppercase letters appear in the first file, write lowercase letters to the new file. Everywhere lowercase letters appear in the first file, write uppercase letters to the new file.

CHAPTER 32

Random Access Files

Random file access enables you to read or write any data in a disk file without having to read or write every piece of data before it. You can quickly search for, add, retrieve, change, and delete information in a random access file. Although you need a few new functions to access files randomly, you will find that the extra effort pays off in flexibility, power, and speed of disk access.

In this chapter, you learn about the following topics:

♦ Random access files

♦ File records

♦ The seekg() function

♦ Special-purpose file I/O functions

This chapter concludes *Visual C++ 1.5 By Example*. With C++'s sequential and random access files, you can do everything you would ever want to do with disk data.

Random File Records

Random files exemplify the power of data processing with C++. Sequential file processing is slow unless you read the entire file into arrays and process them in memory. As explained in the preceding chapter, however, you have much more disk space than RAM, and most disk files do not even fit in your RAM at one time. Therefore, you need a way to quickly read individual pieces of data from a file in any order needed and to process them one at a time.

A record to a file is like a structure to variables.

Generally, you read and write file records. A record to a file is analogous to a C++ structure. A *record* is a collection of one or more data values (called *fields*) that you read and write to disk. Generally, you store data in structures and write the structures to disk, where they are called records. When you read a record from disk, you generally read that record into a structure variable and process it with your program.

Unlike most programming languages, C++ does not require that all disk data be stored in record format. Typically, you write a stream of characters to a disk file and access that data either sequentially or randomly by reading it into variables and structures.

The process of randomly accessing data in a file is simple. Think about the data files of a large credit card organization. When you make a purchase, the store calls the credit card company to get an authorization. There are millions of people in the credit card company's files. There is no way that the credit card company could read every record from the disk (sequentially) that comes before yours in a timely manner. Sequential files do not lend themselves to quick access. It is not feasible in many instances to look up individual records in a data file with sequential access.

The credit card company must use a random file access so that its computers can go directly to your record, just as you go directly to a song on a compact disk or record album. The functions you use are different from the sequential functions, but the power that results from learning the added functions is worth the effort.

You do not have to rewrite the entire file to change random access file data.

Reading and writing files randomly is similar to thinking of the file as a big array. With arrays, you know that you can add, print, or remove values in any order. You do not have to start at the first array element, sequentially looking at the next one, until you get the element you need. You can view your random access file in the same way, accessing the data in any order.

Most random file records are fixed-length records. That is, each record (usually a row in the file) takes the same amount of disk space. Most of the sequential files you read and wrote in the preceding chapter were variable-length records (except for the examples that wrote structures to the disks). When you are reading or writing sequentially, there is no need for fixed-length records because you input each value one character, word, string, or number at a time, looking for the data you want. With fixed-length records, your computer can better calculate exactly where the search record is located on the disk.

Although you waste some disk space with fixed-length records (because of the spaces that pad some of the fields), the advantages of random file access make up for the "wasted" disk space.

> **Tip:** With random access files, you can read or write records in any order. Therefore, even if you want to perform sequential reading or writing of the file, you can use random access processing and "randomly" read or write the file in sequential record number order.

Opening Random Access Files

Just as with sequential files, you must open random access files before reading or writing to them. You can use any of the read access modes mentioned in the preceding chapter (such as ios::in) if you will *only* read a file randomly. However, to modify data in a file, you must open the file in one of the update modes listed in the last chapter and repeated in table 32.1.

Table 32.1. Random access update modes.

Mode	Description
app	Opens the file for appending (adding to it).
ate	Seeks to end of file on opening it.
in	Opens file for reading.
out	Opens file for writing.
binary	Opens file in binary mode.
trunc	Discards contents if file exists.
nocreate	If file doesn't exist, open fails.
noreplace	If file exists, open fails unless appending or seeking to end of file on opening.

There is really no difference between sequential files and random files in C++. The difference between the files is not physical but lies in the method you use to access and update them.

Examples

1. Suppose that you want to write a program to create a file of friends' names. The following `open()` function call does the job, assuming that `fstr` is declared as a file stream:

```
fstr.open("NAMES.DAT", ios::out);
if (!fstr.good())
    cout << "\n*** Cannot open file ***\n");
```

No update `open()` access mode is needed if you are only creating the file. However, what if you wanted to create the file, write names to it, and give the user a chance to change any of the names before closing the file? You would then have to open the file as follows:

```
fstr.open("NAMES.DAT", ios::in | ios::out);
if (!fstr.good())
    cout << "\n*** Cannot open file ***\n");
```

This lets you create the file and then change the data you wrote to the file.

2. With random files, just as with sequential files, the only difference in using a binary `open()` access mode is that the file you create will be more compact and will save disk space. You will not, however, be able to read that file from other programs as an ASCII text file. The preceding `open()` function can be rewritten to create and allow updating of a binary file. All other file-related commands and functions work for binary files just as they do for text files. Here is the modified code:

```
fstr.open("NAMES.DAT", ios::in | ios::out | ios::binary);
if (fstr.good())
    cout << "\n*** Cannot open file ***\n");
```

The *seekg()* Function

You can use *seekg()* to read forward or backward from any point in a file.

C++ provides a function that allows you to read to a specific point in a random access data file. This is the `seekg()` function. The format of `seekg()` is

```
file_stream.seekg(long_num, origin);
```

The file_stream is the file stream for the file you want to access, initialized with an open() statement. *long_num* is the number of bytes in the file you want to skip. C++ will not read this many bytes but will literally skip the data by the number of bytes specified in *long_num*. Skipping the bytes on the disk is much faster than reading them. If *long_num* is negative, C++ skips backward in the file (allowing for rereading of data several times). Because data files can be large, you must declare *long_num* as a long integer to hold a large amount of bytes.

The *origin* is a value that tells C++ where to begin the skipping of bytes specified by *long_num*. The *origin* can be any of the three values shown in table 32.2.

Table 32.2. Possible *origin* values.

Description	Value
Beginning of file	ios::beg
Current file position	ios::cur
End of file	ios::end

The words ios::beg, ios::cur, and ios::end are defined in fstream.h.

> **Note:** Actually, the file stream plays a much more important role than just "pointing to the file" on the disk. The file stream continually knows the exact location of the *next byte to read or write*. In other words, as you read data, from either a sequential file or a random access file, the file stream increments (internally) with each byte read. By using seekg(), you can move the file stream forward or backward in the file.

Examples

1. No matter how far into a file you have read, the following seekg() function positions the file stream back to the beginning of a file:

```
fstr.seekg(0L, ios::beg);  // Position the file pointer
                           // at the beginning
```

The constant 0L passes a long integer 0 to the seekg() function. Without the L, C++ would think you were trying to pass a regular integer, and this would not match the prototype for seek() that is located in fstream.h. Chapter 5, "Variables and Constants," explained the use of data type suffixes on numeric constants, but the suffixes have not been used again until now.

This seekg() function literally reads "move the file pointer 0 bytes from the beginning of the file."

2. The following example reads a file named MYFILE.TXT twice, once to send the file to the screen and once to send the file to the printer. Three file streams are used, one for each device—the file, the screen (cout), and the printer.

```cpp
// Filename: C32TWIC.CPP
// Writes a file to the printer, rereads it, and sends it
// to the screen

#include <fstream.h>
#include <stdlib.h>

ifstream    in_file;  // Input file stream
ofstream    prnt;     // Printer stream

main()
{
    char    in_char;

    in_file.open("MYFILE.TXT", ios::in);
    if (!in_file.good())
    {
        cout << "\n*** Error opening MYFILE.TXT ***\n";
        exit(0);
    }
    while (in_file.get(in_char))
        cout << in_char;            // Output characters
    in_file.seekg(0L, ios::beg);    // Reposition file pointer
    prnt.open("LPT2", ios::out);    // Open printer device
    while (in_file.get(in_char))
        prnt << in_char;            // Output characters
                                    // to the printer
    prnt.close();                   // Always close all
                                    // open files

    in_file.close();
    return 0;
}
```

You can also close and then reopen a file to position the file stream back at the beginning, but using seekg() is a more efficient method.

Of course, regular I/O functions could be used to write to the screen, instead of opening the screen as a separate device.

3. The following `seekg()` function positions the file pointer at the 30th byte in the file. (The next byte read will be the 31st byte.)

```
file_ptr.seekg(30L, ios::beg);      // Position file pointer
                                    // at the 30th byte
```

This `seekg()` function literally reads "move the file pointer 30 bytes from the beginning of the file."

If you write structures to a file, you can quickly seek any structure in the file by using the `sizeof()` function. Suppose that you want the 123rd occurrence of the structure tagged with `inventory`. You would search with this `seekg()` function:

```
file_ptr.seekg((123L * sizeof(struct inventory)), ios::beg);
```

4. The following program writes the letters of the alphabet to a file called ALPH.TXT. The `seekg()` function is then used to read and display the ninth and eighteenth letters (I and R).

```
// Filename: C32ALPH.CPP
// Stores the alphabet in a file and then reads 2 letters
// from it

#include <fstream.h>
#include <stdlib.h>

fstream     fstr;

main()
{
    char    ch;      // Will hold A through Z

    // Open in update mode so that you can read
    // file after writing to it
    fstr.open("alph.txt", ios::in | ios::out);
    if (!fstr.good())
    {
        cout << "\n*** Error opening file ***\n";
        exit(0);
    }
    for (ch = 'A'; ch <= 'Z'; ch++)
        fstr << ch;      // Write letters
```

```
        cout << "Seeking to letter 8.\n";
        fstr.seekg(8L, ios::beg);    // Skip 8 letters, point to H
        fstr >> ch;   // read next character, which is I
        cout << "The ninth character is " << ch << "\n";
        cout << "Moving 8 more letters. \n";
        fstr.seekg(8L, ios::cur);  // Skip 8 letters, point to Q
        fstr >> ch;  // Read next character, which is R
        cout << "The 9th character past I is " << ch << "\n";
        fstr.close();
        return 0;
    }
```

In the preceding program, the first seekg moves eight characters into the alphabet, then the fstr >> reads the next character in the file. The stream is then moved eight more characters past the I. Finally, the next character, R, is read.

5. To point to the end of a data file, you can use the seekg() function to position the file pointer at the last byte. Subsequent seekg()s should then use a negative *long_num* value to skip backward in the file. The following seekg() function makes the file stream point to the end of the file:

```
    fstr.seekg(0L, ios::end);      // Position file pointer
                                   // at the end
```

This seekg() function literally reads "move the file stream 0 bytes from the end of the file." The file stream now points to the end-of-file marker, but you can then seekg() backward to get to other data in the file.

6. The following program reads the ALPH.TXT file (created in Example 4) backward, printing each character as it skips back in the file:

```
// Filename: C32BACK.CPP
// Reads and prints a file backward

#include <fstream.h>
#include <stdlib.h>

ifstream       fstr;

main()
{
    int        ctr;     // Step through the 26 letters
                        // in the file
    char       in_char;
```

```
        fstr.open("ALPH.TXT", ios::in);
        if (!fstr.good())
        {
            cout << "\n*** Error opening file ***\n";
            exit(0);
        }
        fstr.seekg(-1L, ios::end);       // Point to last byte
                                         // in the file
        for (ctr = 0; ctr < 26; ctr++)
        {
            fstr >> in_char;
            cout << in_char;
            fstr.seekg(-2L, ios::cur);
        }
        fstr.close();
        return 0;
    }
```

This program also uses `ios::beg` for *origin*. The last `seekg()` in the program seeks two bytes backward from the *current* position—not the beginning or end, as in the previous examples. The `for` loop toward the end of the program performs a "skip two bytes back, read one byte forward" method to skip backward through the file.

7. The following program performs the same actions as Example 4 (C32ALPH.CPP), but with one addition. When the letters I and R are found, the letter *x* is written over the I and R. The `seekg()` must be used to back up one byte in the file to overwrite the letter just read.

```
// Filename: C32CHANG.CPP
// Stores the alphabet in a file, reads 2 letters from it,
// and changes each of them to x

#include <fstream.h>
#include <stdlib.h>


fstream     fstr;


main()
{
    char     ch;       // Will hold A through Z
```

```
// Open in update mode so that you can read file
// after writing to it
fstr.open("alph.txt", ios::in | ios::out);
if (!fstr.good())
{
    cout << "\n*** Error opening file ***\n";
    exit(0);
}
for (ch = 'A'; ch <= 'Z'; ch++)
    fstr << ch;      // Write letters
fstr.seekg(8L, ios::beg);   // Skip 8 letters, point to I
fstr >> ch;
// Change the I to an x
fstr.seekg(-1L, ios::cur);
fstr << 'x';
cout << "The ninth character is " << ch << "\n";
fstr.seekg(8L, ios::cur);  // Skip next 8 from current
fstr >> ch;
cout << "The 9th next character is " << ch << "\n";
// back up & change that one
fstr.seekg(-1L, ios::cur);
fstr << 'x';
fstr.close();
return 0;
}
```

The file named ALPH.TXT now looks like this:

```
ABCDEFGHxJKLMNOPQxSTUVWXYZ
```

This program forms the basis of a more complete data file management program. After you master the seekg() function and become more familiar with disk data files, you can begin to write programs that store more advanced data structures and access them.

Other Helpful I/O Functions

Several more disk I/O functions are available that you might find useful. They are mentioned here for completeness. When you write more powerful programs in

C++, you will find a use for many of these functions when performing disk I/O. Each of the following functions is prototyped in the fstream.h header file:

♦ read(*array*, *count*). Reads the amount of data specified by the integer *count* into the array or pointer specified by *array*. read() is called a *buffered I/O* function. read() lets you read a lot of data with a single function call.

♦ write(*array*, *count*). Writes *count array* bytes to the file specified. write() is a buffered I/O function. write() lets you write a lot of data in a single function call.

♦ remove(*filename*). Erases the file named by *filename*. remove() returns a 0 if the file was successfully erased or −1 if an error occurred.

Many of these functions, as well as other built-in I/O functions you will learn in your C++ programming career, are helpful functions that you can duplicate by using what you already know.

The buffered I/O file functions let you read and write entire arrays (including arrays of structures) to the disk in a single function call.

Examples

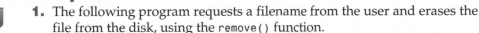

1. The following program requests a filename from the user and erases the file from the disk, using the remove() function.

```
// Filename: C32ERAS.CPP
// Erases the file specified by the user

#include <stdio.h>
#include <iostream.h>

main()
{
    char    filename[ 12 ];

    cout << "What is the filename you want me to erase? ";
    cin >> filename;
    if (remove(filename) == -1)
        cout << "\n*** I could not remove the file ***\n";
    else
        cout << "\nThe file " << filename <<
                " is now removed\n";
    return 0;
}
```

2. The following function could be part of a larger program that gets inventory data, in an array of structures, from the user. This function is passed the array name and the number of elements (structure variables) in the array. The write() function then writes the complete array of structures to the disk file pointed to by fstr.

```
void write_str(struct inventory items[ ], int inv_cnt)
{
      fstr.write(items, inv_cnt * sizeof(struct inventory));
      return;
}
```

If the inventory array had 1,000 elements, this one-line function would still write the entire array to the disk file. The read() function can be used to read the entire array of structures from the disk in a single function call.

Summary

C++ supports random access files with several functions. These include error checking, file pointer positioning, opening of files, and closing of files. You now have the tools you need to save your C++ program data to the disk for storage and retrieval.

Review Questions

Answers to Review Questions are in Appendix B.

1. What is the difference between records and structures?

2. True or false: You have to create a random access file before reading from it randomly.

3. What happens to the file stream as you read from a file?

4. What are the two buffered file I/O functions?

5. What are two methods for positioning the file stream at the beginning of a file?

6. What are the three starting positions (the *origins*) in the seekg() function?

7. What is wrong with the following program?

```
#include <fstream.h>

ifstream     fstr;

main()
{
    char     in_char;

    fstr.open(ios::in | ios::binary);
    if (fstr.get(in_char))
        cout << in_char;      // Write to the screen
    fp.close();
    return 0;
}
```

Review Exercises

1. Write a program that asks the user for a list of five names and writes the names to a file. Rewind the file and display its contents on-screen, using the seekg() and get() functions.

2. Rewrite the preceding program so that it displays every other character in the file of names.

3. Write a program that reads characters from a file. If the input character is a lowercase letter, change it to uppercase. If the input character is uppercase, change it to lowercase. Do not change other characters in the file.

4. Write a program that displays the number of nonalphabetic characters in a file.

5. Write a grade-keeping program for a teacher. Let the teacher enter up to 10 students' grades. Each student has three grades for the semester. Store the student names and their three grades in an array of structures and store the data on the disk. Make the program menu-driven. Let the teacher have the options of adding more students, looking at the file's data, or printing the grades to the printer with a calculated class average.

Part VIII

Object-Oriented Programming

CHAPTER 33

Classes

Classes are a powerful part of Visual C++. They distinguish C++ from C. In fact, before the name C++ was coined, the language was called "C with classes." Classes are often called the most important feature of C++, and they are the main focus of object-oriented programming.

This chapter covers the following topics:

♦ What a class is

♦ Member variables and member functions

♦ Using Classes

♦ Class member visibility

You will be working with classes for the next several chapters of this book. This chapter introduces the basics of designing and using a class.

Defining a Class

A class is a user defined data type.

A class is a user-defined data type that can have both *member variables* and *member functions*. Class member variables can be of any type, including user-defined data types. The member functions can manipulate the member variables, create and destroy class variables, and even redefine C++'s operators to act on the class objects. A class only defines a new data type, it does not declare any variables of that data type.

Methods or Members?

Some books on C++ use another term for member functions—*methods*. Still others use the term *operation*. All three terms refer to the same thing. The different usage came about because the developers of other object-oriented languages used other terms for these concepts that seemed better suited to the syntax of their languages. For example, books that teach the Smalltalk language will use *method* to refer to what we call *member functions.*

To define a class, you use the `class` statement. The format of the `class` statement is as follows:

```
class [class name]
{
[access specifier:]
    member definition;
    member definition;
    member definition;
    .
    .
    .
} [one or more class variables];
```

If this looks familiar, it should. This is almost identical to the format of the structure statement you learned earlier in this book. In many ways, a class is the same as a structure. But there are some important differences, too. The rest of this chapter will teach you some of those differences.

There are two kinds of class members: *member variables*, and *member functions*. Class members also have a new attribute that hasn't been seen before: *access specifiers* or *visibility*. Visibility is controlled through *access specifiers*, which will be covered at the end of this chapter. For now, just remember that you can control the visibility, or access, of class members. The rest of this book will use the term visibility to refer to this concept.

Member Variables

A class may have one or more *member variables*. Member variables can be any defined data type, including user defined data types. Because a class is a user defined data type, one class may have member variables that are actually instances of other classes.

The *member variables* of a class are exactly like the variables in a structure. Suppose that you want to define a class to represent a circle. What member variables would you want to have in such a class? You would probably want to know things like the radius of the circle, and where the circle was to be located (x-y coordinates). To define a Circle class which contains a circle's radius and its location, you use the following format:

```
// A circle class
class Circle
{
public:
    float     rad;            // Radius of circle
    float     x, y;           // Coordinates of circle
};
```

The `Circle` class has three member variables: `rad`, `x`, and `y`. So far, there isn't much to distinguish the circle class from a `struct` except for the label `public:`. `public:` is an *access specifier*. *Access specifiers* will be discussed at the end of this chapter. For now, you can ignore it.

Example

The following sample program uses this circle class:

```
// Filename: C33CLAS1.CPP
// Simple Circle Class demo

#include <iostream.h>

// A circle class
class Circle
{
public:
    float     rad;         // Radius of circle
    float     x, y;      // Coordinates of circle
};

main()
{
    Circle  cir;
    float    crad = 3.5;
    cir.rad = crad;
    cout << "The radius is ==>" << cir.rad;

    return 0;
}
```

In this program, `cir` is a variable of type `Circle`. It is allocated with a syntax that is exactly like the `float` declared on the next line. You can declare a variable whose type is a class exactly the same way you would use a built in variable type. You learned how to declare and use structure variables in Chapter 29, and this is the same technique.

The next two lines of the program access the member variables of the class using the dot(.) operator, the same as for members of a struct.

Member Functions

So far, the circle class doesn't do anything different than a structure. You will change that now by adding some *member functions*. *Member functions* are functions defined within a class that act on the member variables in the class. The use of member functions is one of the features that distinguishes a class from a struct.

> **Note:** Technically, C++ allows you to define and use member functions within a `struct` just as you are doing here for a `class`. However, generally accepted C++ practice uses member functions only in classes, not in structures.

Figure 33.1 shows the Circle class with some member functions added, and now the class begins to take on some useful additional characteristics.

Figure 33.1

A Circle Class.

- Values used in class
- comment
- begin class
- access specifier
- member variables
- constructor
- destructor
- member functions
- end class

```
#define PI 3.414

// A circle class

class Circle
{
public:
    float       m_rad;        // Radius of circle
    float       m_x, m_y;     // Coordinates of circle

    Circle(float xcoord, float ycoord, float radius)
    {
        m_x = xcoord; m_y = ycoord; m_rad = radius;
    }

    ~Circle() { }

    float       radius()
    {
        return m_rad;
    }

    float       circumference()
    {
        return m_rad * 2 * PI;
    }
};
```

The member functions added to the `Circle` class are `Circle(float xcoord, float ycoord, float radius)`, `~Circle()`, `circumference()`, and `radius()`. Circle is definitely not a `struct` anymore.

Naming Member Variables

You may have wondered why all the member variable names in the circle class have a prefix of `m_`. This is what is called a *naming convention*. Its purpose is to help identify these variables in other program code as member variables of a class. In most large programs, the class definition will be in a separate file from the main program code. By using this convention, it is easy for the programmer to tell which variables are class members and which ones are not. This convention is used extensively in the Microsoft Foundation Classes that you will study in the last part of this book.

Note that the `m_` has no special meaning to C++, it is merely a convenient way to help you tell when you are working with a class member variable.

Constructors and Destructors

A constructor function always has the same name as its class.

Two of the member functions in figure 33.1 have special purposes. The first function, `Circle(float xcoord, float ycoord, float radius)`, is a *constructor* function. A constructor function always has the same name as its class.

Note: The act of declaring a new variable whose type is a class (or struct) is called "declaring an *instance*" of the class.

The constructor function is called automatically by C++ whenever a variable of that class type is created. Constructor functions are used to initialize the member variables of a class variable. A *constructor function* is one that allows you to create a class variable and initialize it all at once. Class variables can be relatively complex to create and initialize; class constructors automate the procedure of creating and initializing the class variable, and eliminate the likelihood of missing a step or performing a step incorrectly.

A destructor function has the same name as its class, but with a tilde (~) prefix.

The other special function is `~Circle`. This is the destructor function. Note that it also has the same name as the class, but with a *tilde* (~) as a prefix.

Whereas the constructor function allocates memory to create a class variable, the *destructor function* gives back the memory, effectively destroying the class variable. The destructor may perform other activities, such as print out the final values of the class member variables (useful for debugging).

The destructor function is called automatically whenever a variable of that class type goes out of scope or is deliberately destroyed. The destructor function takes no arguments and returns no value. You'll notice also that this destructor doesn't do anything, which is true of most destructors. If your destructor function does nothing, you don't have to create one; as soon as the class variable is no longer in existence, the memory allocated for it is returned to the system. Similarly, if you don't need to do anything specific for a constructor, you don't need one; Visual C++ will allocate memory for a class variable when you create it.

Other Member Functions

Figure 33.1 shows two other functions added to the circle class. These functions are named radius() and circumference(). The radius() function merely returns the current value stored in the rad member variable. You will learn more about why you would use a function to get the value of a member variable in the last part of this chapter.

The circumference() function calculates the value of the circumference of the circle and returns that value to the calling function.

You access these member functions exactly the same way you access a member variable. The following code declares a variable named cir of type Circle, and then gets the circumference of cir by calling the circumference() member function.

```
Circle     cir;
cout << cir.circumference();
```

The circumference() member function is accessed using the dot (.) operator, exactly the same as a member variable.

Member Functions and Memory

You may be wondering how much memory is taken by the member functions of your class when you declare a variable from the class. Does each variable declared from a class cause memory to be allocated for both the member variables and the member functions? The answer is, of course, no. The internal code used by C++ to manipulate the built in data types is not duplicated every time you declare an int or a char, and neither is the code in your class member functions. No matter how many variables of a given class you declare in your program, there will only be one copy of the code for that class. Only the class data causes memory to be allocated, not the member functions.

Here is the complete circle class. The destructor will print out a message when a variable of this class is destroyed to help you see when the destructor is called. Notice the filename on the first line. The .H extension means that this file will be used as an include file in other programs. Take a moment now to enter this program into Visual C++, then save it with the name C33CIR1.H. You will use this same class definition in the next several examples by adding an #include statement to the beginning of each program.

```
// Filename: C33CIR1.H
// A circle class definition

#include <iostream.h>
#include <string.h>

#define PI 3.414

// A cirolo class
class Circle
{
public:

    // member variables
    float     m_rad;        // Radius of circle
    float     m_x, m_y;     // Coordinates of circle
    char      m_name[20];   // let us identify the circle

    // constructor
    Circle(float xcoord, float ycoord, float radius,
           char* name)
    {
        m_x = xcoord; m_y = ycoord; m_rad = radius;
        strcpy( m_name, name);
        cout << "Circle " << m_name << " constructed.\n";
    }

    // destructor
    ~Circle()
    {
        cout << "Destroying Circle " << m_name << "\n";
    }

    // member functions
    float circumference()
    {
        return (m_rad * 2 * PI);
    }

    float radius()
    {
        return m_rad;
    }
};
```

> **Caution:** Be sure to include a carriage return on the end of the last line in any file you plan to use for an include file. The preprocessor expects a carriage return at the end of an included file and will generate lots of strange errors that are very difficult to relate to the real source of the problem.

Using a Class

Now that you have defined a circle class it is time to see how it is used. The following examples illustrate how to use a class to declare variables and how to manipulate those variables in your program.

Examples

1. The following example shows the constructor and destructor functions in operation.

```
// Filename: C33CIR1.CPP
// Demonstrates constructor, member variables, and destructor

#include "c33cir1.h"   // include the class definition
#include <iostream.h>

main()
{
    // declare a Circle variable
    Circle cir( 2,4,1.5,"Test one");

    // print out the Circle's member variables
    cout << "Circle name is " << cir.m_name << "\n";
    cout << "Radius is " << cir.m_rad << "\n";
    cout << "x-y coordinates are: x=" << cir.m_x
         << " y=" << cir.m_y << "\n\n";

    // about to destroy the circle
    cout << "End program\n"
         << "Circle will self-destruct!\n\n";
    return 0;
}
```

When the variable cir is declared, the constructor is called. After cir is constructed, the program prints out the content of its member variables by directly accessing each one through the dot (.) operator. Finally, when the program ends, cir goes out of scope and the Circle destructor is called. The output from this program is as follows:

```
Circle Test one constructed.
Circle name is Test one
Radius is 1.5
x-y coordinates are: x=2 y=4

End program
Circle will self-destruct!

Destroying Circle Test one
```

2. The circle class also has two member functions defined. radius() returns the value stored in the m_rad member variable. circumference() calculates the circumference of the circle using the stored radius and returns the answer.

```cpp
// Filename: C33CIR2.CPP
// Demonstrates using member functions

#include "c33cir1.h"    // include the class definition
#include <iostream.h>

main()
{
    // declare a Circle variable
    Circle cir( 2,4,1.5,"Test two");

    // print out some information about it.
    cout << "Circle name is " << cir.m_name << "\n";

    // use the radius() function instead of the member
    // variable
    cout << "\tIt's Radius is " << cir.radius() << "\n";

    // have the circle tell you its circumference
    cout << "\tand it's circumference is: "
        << cir.circumference() << "\n\n";

    return 0;
}
```

The output from this program is as follows:

```
Circle Test two constructed.
Circle name is Test two
        It's Radius is 1.5
        and it's circumference is: 10.242

Destroying Circle Test two
```

3. A circle variable's values can be changed after it is created, and a circle variable can be passed to other functions. This example shows a circle variable being passed to print_cir(), a function which retrieves information from the circle and prints it.

```cpp
// Filename: C33CIR3.CPP
// Demonstrates using member functions

#include "c33cir1.h"    // include the class definition
#include <iostream.h>

void print_cir( Circle c )
{
    // print out some information about the passed circle
    cout << "Circle name is " << c.m_name << "\n";
    cout << "\tIt's Radius is " << c.radius() << "\n";
    cout << "\tand it's circumference is: "
        << c.circumference() << "\n";
    cout << "Leaving print_cir function.\n\n";
}

main()
{
    float x = 2;
    float y = 4;
    float radi = 2.5;
    char name[20] = "Test Circle";

    // declare a circle and print its values
    Circle cir( x, y, radi, name);
    print_cir( cir );
    cout << "Returned from print_cir.\n\n";

    // now, get some new values for the circle
    cout << "Enter a new radius for the circle ==>";
```

```
    cin >> radi;
    cir.m_rad = radi;
    strcpy( cir.m_name, "Changed Circle" );

    // print out the circle's new information
    print_cir( cir );
    cout << "Returned from print_cir.\n\n";

    return 0;
}
```

Figure 33.2 shows the output from this program. Notice the extra `Destroying circle` messages. In Chapter 20, you learned about parameters that were passed by value, which really meant "pass by copy." That is what happened here. C++ created a copy of the Circle parameter for the `print_cir()` function. When the function returned, C++ destroyed the copy, which in turn caused a call to the Circle class destructor, `~Circle()`.

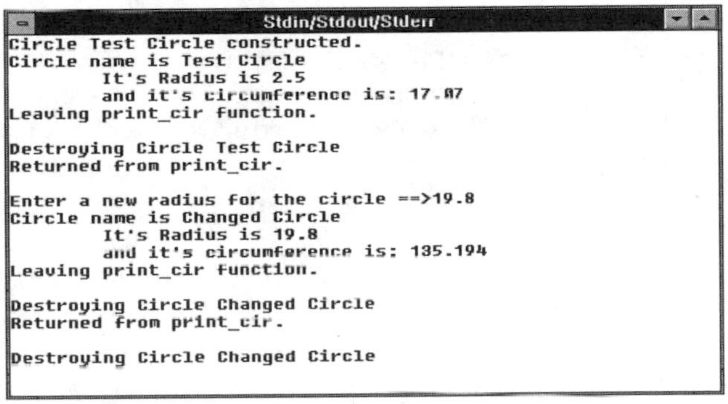

Figure 33.2

Passing a class variable to a function.

```
                      Stdin/Stdout/Stderr
Circle Test Circle constructed.
Circle name is Test Circle
        It's Radius is 2.5
        and it's circumference is: 17.07
Leaving print_cir function.

Destroying Circle Test Circle
Returned from print_cir.

Enter a new radius for the circle ==>19.8
Circle name is Changed Circle
        It's Radius is 19.8
        and it's circumference is: 135.194
Leaving print_cir function.

Destroying Circle Changed Circle
Returned from print_cir.

Destroying Circle Changed Circle
```

Passing a Class Variable by Address

In the last example in the previous section, you learned that C++ makes a copy of a class variable when it is passed to a function, just the same as for the built-in types such as `int` and `float`. You also saw that the copy was destroyed, and the class destructor function was called when the function returned to the calling program. This copying can be very "expensive" when a class has a lot of member variables, and the "expense" can show up in reduced speed of your program. If your class contained a very large array of character strings, for example, the entire array would have to be copied.

You also know that when a variable is passed by copy, any changes made to the variable in the called function are lost when the called function returns to the calling function. Now you should better understand why the changes are lost—because the copy of the variable is destroyed when the called function returns.

Just as there are times you want to change the value of an int or float in a called function, there are times you want to change the value of a class member variable in a called function.

There is also the problem of "expensive" copies which must be resolved when efficiency is an important requirement in your program.

Both requirements can be satisfied by one of two techniques. Take a moment and think about what you learned in Chapter 20 about passing by address and passing by reference. Because a class variable can be treated just like a built in type, it is also possible to pass a class variable to a calling function by address, or by reference, and the technique is exactly the same for a class as it was for an int or a float.

Here is a short review of the methods discussed in Chapter 20. To pass a variable by address, put an ampersand (&) in front of the variable name in the calling function, and put an asterisk (*) in front of the variable name in the prototype of the called function. To pass a variable by reference, put an ampersand (&) in front of the variable name in the prototype of the called function.

When a class variable is passed to a called function by address, you must use a slightly different syntax to reference the members of the variable in the body of the called function. Instead of referring to members using the dot (.) notation of the preceding examples, you use "arrow" notation. The "arrow" is formed from a dash (-), immediately followed by a right arrow (>). The arrow looks like this: ->. Another name for this notation is *pointer* notation. The arrow "points" to the member.

In the short function below, a Circle class variable named theCir is being passed to the function by address. The function assigns a value of 4.5 to a member of theCir, and then calls theCir's Circumference() function in a cout statement.

```
void ChangeCir( Circle* theCir )
{
    theCir->m_rad = 4.5;
    cout << theCir->Circumference();
    .
    .
    .
```

When you pass a class variable to a called function by reference, you use ordinary dot notation in the function body. Following is the same function, but now theCir is passed by reference.

```
void ChangeCir( Circle& theCir )
{
    theCir.m_rad = 4.5;
```

```
          cout << theCir.Circumference();
      .
      .
      .
```

The following example illustrates both techniques; passing a class variable by address, and passing a class variable by reference.

Examples

1. The following example shows a variable of class Circle being passed to functions using all three of the techniques you have studied. The printCir function uses pass by copy. The other two functions use pass by address and pass by reference. Figure 33.3 shows the output from this program.

```cpp
// Filename: C33CIR4.CPP
// Demonstrates using member functions

#include "c33cir1.h"   // include the class definition
#include <iostream.h>

// A Circle variable is passed by address and the radius
// member variable is changed.
void passCirByAddress( Circle* c )
{
    // print out some information about the passed circle
    cout << "Circle passed by address.\n";
    c->m_rad = c->m_rad * 1.5;   // use "arrow" notation
}

// A Circle variable is passed by reference and the radius
// member variable is changed.
void passCirByReference( Circle& c )
{
    // print out some information about the passed circle
    cout << "Circle passed by reference.\n";
    c.m_rad = c.m_rad * 6.5;
}

void printCir( Circle c )
{
    // print out some information about the passed circle
    cout << "Circle name is " << c.m_name;
```

```
        cout << "\tand it's Radius is " << c.radius() << "\n";
        cout << "Leaving printCir function.\n";

        c.m_rad = c.m_rad * 1.5; // won't have any effect
}

main()
{
    float x = 2;
    float y = 4;
    float radi = 2.5;
    char name[20] = "Test Circle";

    // declare a circle and print its values
    Circle cir( x, y, radi, name);
    cout << "\n***********Original Circle\n";
    printCir( cir );

    // now, use pass by address to change the radius
    // and print out the circle's new information
        cout << "\n\n***********Change Circle in pass by
    ➥address\n";
    passCirByAddress( &cir );
    printCir( cir );

    // now, use pass by reference to change the radius
    // and print out the circle's new information
        cout << "\n\n***********Change Circle in pass by
    ➥reference\n";
    passCirByReference( cir );
    printCir( cir );

    return 0;
}
```

Figure 33.3

Passing a class variable to a function by address and by reference.

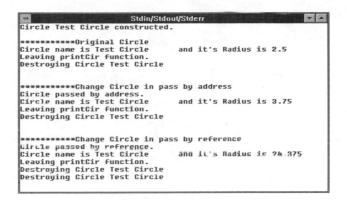

```
                        Stdin/Stdout/Stderr
Circle Test Circle constructed.

***********Original Circle
Circle name is Test Circle        and it's Radius is 2.5
Leaving printCir function.
Destroying Circle Test Circle


***********Change Circle in pass by address
Circle passed by address.
Circle name is Test Circle        and it's Radius is 3.75
Leaving printCir function.
Destroying Circle Test Circle


***********Change Circle in pass by reference
Circle passed by reference.
Circle name is Test Circle        and it's Radius is 24.375
Leaving printCir function.
Destroying Circle Test Circle
Destroying Circle Test Circle
```

Function Overloading

A class can have more than one version of a member function. This is called *function overloading*. You can have more than one version of any member function except the destructor. Overloading is the technique of defining more than one version of the same function name. How do you (and the C++ compiler) know what the overloaded function is doing or which version to use at what time? You create a different *prototype* for each of the different purposes.

With more than one prototype, each of which has the same function name, you have to give the functions different parameter lists so that the compiler can figure out which version of the function you intend to use. This supplies the context to the compiler and informs the compiler which overloaded function you intend to use.

You may be asking yourself what advantages there are to this technique. At first thought it would appear to be very confusing, and like many other useful techniques it can be misused. One area where function overloading is not confusing is in the matter of class constructors. You will often want to be able to construct an instance of a class before you know what values will be assigned to the class member variables. There are other times when you might want to initialize an instance of a class with the values from another instance of the same class. Overloaded constructor functions are an ideal method to provide for a variety of ways to construct an instance of a class.

It is also possible to overload operators—+, -, =, ==, >, and so on. You have already been working with one such set of overloaded operators—the << and >> operators you have used with cout and cin. Chapter 35, "Introduction to Class Libraries," contains another example. When used properly, overloaded operators can greatly simplify and clarify what your classes are doing.

Here is how overloaded constructors look in a class definition:

```
class Circle
{
public:

    Circle()     // default constructor
    {
        m_x = m_y = 0;
        m_rad = 1;
    }

    Circle(float xcoord, float ycoord, float radius)
    {
        m_x = xcoord; m_y = ycoord; m_rad = radius;
    }

    Circle( Circle& cir )
    {
        m_x   = cir.x;
        m_y   = cir.y;
        m_rad = cir.rad;
    }

    ~Circle() { }

    float     m_rad;        // Radius of circle
    float     m_x, m_y;     // Coordinates of circle
};
```

The preceding class contains three constructors. The first one does not take any parameters. A constructor that does not take any parameters is called the *default constructor*. The default constructor is called when you declare a variable of a class type without specifying any arguments. The following two lines both cause a call to the default constructor:

```
Circle cir1;
Circle cir2();
```

The second constructor is the kind you have been using in this chapter. The third constructor has one parameter—a reference to a variable of the same class. A constructor of this format is also called a *copy constructor*. If you define a copy constructor for a class, C++ will call your copy constructor whenever a copy of a variable of that class type is needed, such as when the variable is passed to a function by copy.

Class Member Visibility

In Chapter 19 you learned that global variables are accessible, or visible, to all functions in a program, but that variables declared inside a function are not. Likewise, individual members of a class can be made accessible to all users of the class—or not.

Accessibility of class members is controlled by *access specifiers*. The following are the three possible *access specifiers*: public, private, and protected. The third one, protected, will be covered in the following chapter when you learn about inheritance. The rest of this chapter discusses public and private.

Access specifiers have the format of the specifier name followed by a colon (:). By convention, most C++ programmers align the access specifiers with the left margin, but C++ does not require them to be there.

Whenever C++ encounters an access specifier in a class definition, all class members from that point forward in the definition have the designated accessibility. The specifier remains in effect until another access specifier is encountered or the end of the class definition is reached. See whether you can tell what accessibility each member of the following class will have.

```
class Person
{
    char* underwear;
    int GetDressed( );
public:
    char* shirt;
private:
    char* thoughts;
    char* dreams;
};
```

It should be obvious in the preceding definition that shirt is public and that thoughts and dreams are private. But what about underwear and the GetDressed() function? They are private because the default access for members of a class is private. All members of a class are assumed to be private unless otherwise specified. (A structure can have access specifiers, but its default access is public.)

Public Access

Public access means that all users of the class have access to the public member of the class. If the member is a variable, users of the class can access and change the variable freely. If the member is a function, all users of the class can call the function. Public access is what determines how a user of the class interacts with the class.

Private Access

Private access means that only other members of the class can access a member. If a class member, either a variable or a function, is specified to be private, no user of the class can access it. Based on the Person class above, the following would cause C++ to generate an error:

```
Person candidate;
cout << candidate.underwear;    // ERROR!
```

There are many reasons why you might want to make a class member private. Suppose that you wanted to make sure that nobody could change a member variable unless their change was verified. You would make the variable private and provide a public member function that would verify the new value of the variable. You would update the variable if the new value was valid. By the same token, you might have some member functions that do internal manipulation within the class that no user would ever need to call. The proper way to define these functions is private.

Examples

1. The following example shows the private and public access specifiers in use. Figure 33.4 shows the program's output.

```
// Filename: C33ACCT.CPP
// Demonstrates using member functions

#include <iostream.h>
#include <string.h>

class Account
{
public:
    char      m_Name[20];
    char      m_AcctNo[9];
private:
    float     m_Balance;

public:
    Account(char* name, char* acct)
    {
        strcpy(m_Name, name);
        strcpy(m_AcctNo, acct);
        m_Balance = 0;
    }
    ~Account() { };
```

```
    float balance() {return m_Balance;}

    float deposit(float amt)
    {
        m_Balance += amt;
        return m_Balance;
    }

    float withdraw(float amt)
    {
        if (amt > m_Balance)
        {
            cout << "Attempt to overdraw account "
                << m_Name << " rejected.\n";
            return m_Balance;
        }
        else
        {
            m_Balance -= amt;
            return m_Balance;
        }
    }
};

main()
{
    Account acct( "Josephine Smythe", "0097428" );
    float tranAmt;
    float bal;
    char trnType;

    do
    {
        cout << "\nEnter Transaction for account "
            << acct.m_AcctNo << "-"
            << acct.m_Name << "\n";
        cout << "Or 0 if you are finished.\n";

        cout << "Transaction Amount ==> ";
        cin >> tranAmt;
```

```
        if (tranAmt == 0 )
                break;
        cout << "Transaction Type (D or W) ==> ";
        cin >> trnType;
        if (trnType == 'D')
        {
                bal = acct.deposit( tranAmt );
                cout << "\tDeposit  \t"
                        << tranAmt << "\t"
                        << "Balance\t" << bal << "\n";
        }
        else
        {
                bal = acct.withdraw( tranAmt );
                cout << "\tWithdraw\t"
                        << tranAmt << "\t"
                        << "Balance\t" << bal << "\n";
        }
    } while ( 1 );  // always true, exit at break

    cout << acct.m_Name
        << "\n\t\tEnding Balance = " << acct.balance();

    return 0;
}
```

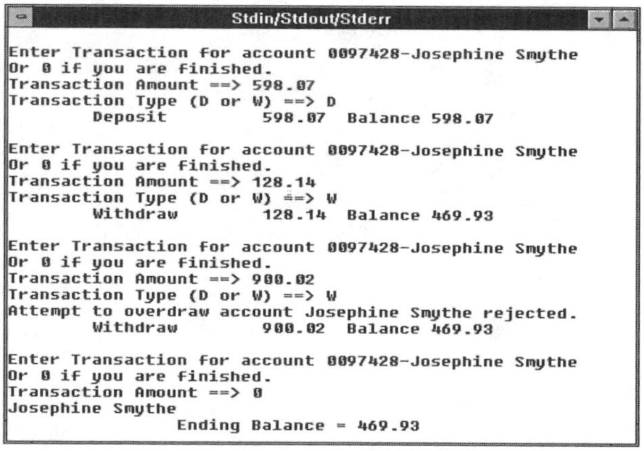

Figure 33.4

Using a class which has a private data member.

```
Stdin/Stdout/Stderr

Enter Transaction for account 0097428-Josephine Smythe
Or 0 if you are finished.
Transaction Amount ==> 598.07
Transaction Type (D or W) ==> D
        Deposit          598.07  Balance 598.07

Enter Transaction for account 0097428-Josephine Smythe
Or 0 if you are finished.
Transaction Amount ==> 128.14
Transaction Type (D or W) ==> W
        Withdraw         128.14  Balance 469.93

Enter Transaction for account 0097428-Josephine Smythe
Or 0 if you are finished.
Transaction Amount ==> 900.02
Transaction Type (D or W) ==> W
Attempt to overdraw account Josephine Smythe rejected.
        Withdraw         900.02  Balance 469.93

Enter Transaction for account 0097428-Josephine Smythe
Or 0 if you are finished.
Transaction Amount ==> 0
Josephine Smythe
              Ending Balance = 469.93
```

Summary

This chapter introduced you to classes, class members, member functions, and access specifiers. You have learned how classes can be used to build powerful new data types for your programs.

The next two chapters cover more information about classes and class libraries. You are now getting into the heart of object-oriented programming.

Review Questions

Answers to Review Questions are in Appendix B.

1. What are the two types of class members?

2. Is a constructor always necessary?

3. Is a destructor always necessary?

4. What is the default visibility of a class member?

5. How do you make a class member visible outside its class?

Review Exercises

1. Modify the Circle class to include a copy constructor and write a program that passes a Circle variable to a function by copy to show the copy constructor in use. You might want to add a cout to the copy constructor so that you can see it being called.

2. Construct a class for handling personnel records. Use the following member variables and keep them private:

```
char      name[ 25 ];
float     salary;
char      date_of_birth[ 9 ];
```

Create a constructor to initialize the record with its necessary values, and a constructor that simply creates an uninitialized record. Create member functions to alter the individual's name, salary, and date of birth.

CHAPTER 34

Inheritance and Polymorphism

Classes like the ones you learned about in the previous chapter are very powerful constructs in their own right. With classes you can create new data types that can be manipulated like the built-in data types. C++ has additional features that make classes even more powerful and useful. You will learn about these features in this chapter.

This chapter covers the following topics:

♦ Multiple-file programs

♦ Inheritance

♦ Parent and child classes

♦ Overriding functions

♦ Virtual functions

Multiple-File Programs

Before going farther with C++ and classes, you should learn about a way of organizing your programs that is used on virtually every C++ program except the very smallest and most limited programs. Most C++ programs are actually made up of many smaller programs. This organization makes it easier to maintain the program and also allows more than one programmer to work on the same program. In this section, you will learn the techniques for organizing and managing this type of program.

You are already applying one technique of multiple program management when you use *include* files. Those files contain the function prototypes for all of the library functions that come with C++. No matter how many times a function or class is used in a program, it only needs to be defined in one include file.

In the last chapter, you created your own include file for the circle class to save having to type in the whole class each time. That file, the C33CIR.H file, includes both the class prototype and the class function code in the same file. Normal practice with classes is to separate the class prototype into a header file (.H extension, or sometimes .HPP), and the actual class code into a program file (.CPP). The header file is sometimes called the *class interface*, and the program code is referred to as the *class implementation*. The Microsoft Foundation Classes library is organized this way, and so is all of the code generated by Application Wizard that you will study in the last part of this book.

Use Projects to manage multiple-file programs.

The other technique used to manage a program that has more than one source file is to create a list of the program's source files in a special type of file called the *project*. A project contains a list of all the files needed to compile a complete program, and instructions that tell Visual C++ how to "make" the files into the final program. The utility that reads a project file and manages the process of creating a program is called a *make program*. Another name for the project file is the *make* file and when you create a Visual C++ project file it is named with a .MAK extension.

To create a project file in Visual C++, pull down the **P**roject menu in Application Workbench and click on **N**ew. You then will see the New Project dialog. Figure 34.1 shows the New Project dialog. Fill in the name you want to give the project in the Project **N**ame field. Use the name you want Visual C++ to give to your completed program. Figure 34.1 shows the name filled in with C34CIR1, so the resulting program from this project will be named C34CIR1.EXE. Next, click on the arrow on the right end of the field marked Project **T**ype and then choose Quickwin application [.EXE]. Finally, if the Use Microsoft Foundation Classes box is checked, remove the checkmark by clicking on the box. Now click the OK button and Visual C++ will create your project file.

Figure 34.1

The New Project dialog.

The project file you just created does not have any programs assigned to the project yet, so Visual C++ will give you a chance to assign them now by bringing up the Project Edit dialog. The Project Edit dialog is shown in figure 34.2 with C34CIR.CPP assigned to the project. The box in the upper left area of the dialog labeled File **N**ame contains a list of all program files in the current directory. To assign one of them to the project, click on the name of the file you want to assign so that it is highlighted, and then click on the **A**dd button. The name of the file that was selected in the File **N**ame box will appear in the box labeled **F**iles in Project on the bottom of the dialog. This box lists all of the files currently contained in the project. Notice that there are not any .H files listed. These files will be automatically included when one of the program files refers to them.

Figure 34.2

The Edit Project dialog.

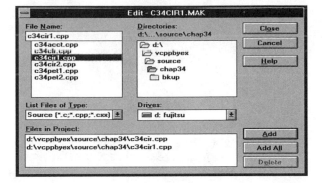

In the following example, you create a small project from the Circle class. The example is long, but when you finish it you will be well equipped to work with multiple-file programs.

Example

1. This example walks you through the process of creating a multiple-file program and then "making" an executable program from the multiple files.

First create a header file for the Circle class. Type it in as shown below, and save it with the file name in the comment at the top of the file. This file will contain only the prototype of the Circle class. None of the functions will have any code.

```
// Filename: C34CIR.H
// Circle Class header

class Circle
{
public:

    // member variables
    float    m_rad;        // Radius of circle
    float    m_x, m_y;     // Coordinates of circle
    char     m_name[20];   // let us identify the circle
```

```
        // constructor
        Circle(float xcoord, float ycoord, float radius,
              char* name);

        // destructor
        ~Circle() {  };

        // member functions
        float circumference();

        float radius();
};
```

Notice how the class definition contains the class member variables and function prototypes for the member functions. Each prototype ends with a semicolon (;), the same as a function prototype for a function that is not part of a class.

Type in the implementation file for the Circle class as shown in the following file. There are two things to study in this file. First, all #include statements are in this file, not the header, and there is an #include for the class header file, too.

```
// Filename: C34CIR.CPP
// Implementation file for the circle class

#include <iostream.h>
#include <string.h>

#include "C34CIR.H"

#define PI 3.414

// constructor
Circle::Circle(float xcoord, float ycoord, float radius,
              char* name)
{
    m_x = xcoord; m_y = ycoord; m_rad = radius;
    strcpy( m_name, name);
}

// member functions
float Circle::circumference()
{
```

```
        return (m_rad * 2 * PI);
}
float Circle::radius()
{
        return m_rad;
}
```

The second and most important thing you should study is the strange appearance of the class member functions. Each function name has the class name added to the front, with a double colon (::) separating the class name from the function name. The double colon is called the *scope resolution operator*. This operator tells C++ that the function name to the right of the operator is a member of the class name to the left of the operator. The line Circle::radius() means "The radius function of the Circle class." You did not need to use this operator when your functions were defined within the class prototype.

As with the header file, save this file with the file name at the top of the listing. When you have finished typing the file, you can compile it to check for syntax errors, but you do not need to make an executable program because there is not a main() function. The best way to do this is to use the Compile option from the **Project** menu instead of the **Build** option you have been using.

> **Tip:** Use the Com**p**ile option to check for syntax errors in a single program file when you are working with multiple file programs. It is often easier to correct your syntax errors this way.

Now that you have defined the circle class in separate files, it will only take a few lines of code to write a simple program that uses the Circle class. Type in the following program and save it with the file name at the top, but do not compile it yet.

```
// Filename: C34CIR1.CPP
// Program that uses externally defined circle class

#include <iostream.h>

#include "c34cir.h"

void main()
{
```

```
// define a circle variable
Circle cir( 4, 3, 3.5, "Test One");

// print out some information about cir
cout << cir.m_name << " circumference is "
    << cir.circumference();
}
```

You can do most of the rest of this example by just clicking with the mouse. You aren't quite finished with the Circle, though. You haven't inherited it yet.

The final step of this example is to create a project and then make the program. Follow the instructions above to open the New Project dialog box. Give the project a name of C34CIR1.CPP, make sure that you are building a QuickWin program without Microsoft Foundation Classes, and click OK. In the Edit dialog box, add the files C34CIR.CPP and C34CIR1.CPP to the project, and then click the Close button. There will be some brief activity while Visual C++ analyzes the project; then it will be ready for use. To create a finished program from this project, pull down the **P**roject menu and click **B**uild C34CIR1.CPP. Visual C++ will compile both of the .CPP files in the project and then link them together into a finished program. As a final check on your work, run the completed program. The output of this simple program might seem quite anti-climactic after all the work involved, but you have just mastered the basics of one of the most powerful and frequently used tools in Visual C++.

Inheriting the Wheel

C++ provides a way for you to create a class that has all the capabilities of another class and then adds additional capabilities of its own. This capability is called *inheritance.*

Suppose that another programmer gives you a copy of a class he developed. He tells you about some additions and improvements that were being made to the class and says that you can have the improved version when it is ready. Now suppose that you want to use this class, but you also need it to do something that it does not currently do, and the other programmer does not plan to add the feature to the original class. What will you do? If you change the code that was given to you, you will have to make the same changes to the new version when it is ready. You could wait for the new version before proceeding and then make your changes, but that only delays your project, and there is still the question of later updates being made to the original class. Neither option is very appealing, is it? What if you don't have the source code for the class, only a header file? This is where inheritance comes in.

Through inheritance, you can add new features to a class or change the way an existing feature works, without changing the original class. With inheritance you don't have to change anything in the original class—you don't even need the original class source code. Instead, you *derive* your own class from the original and then make the changes in your *derived* class. When one class inherits from another class, the original class is called the *base*, or *parent*, class and the new class is called the *derived*, or *child*, class. Figure 34.3 shows this relationship for a base class called `Employee` and a derived class called `HourlyEmployee`. The arrow points from the derived, or child class, to the base, or parent class.

Figure 34.3

Base and Derived Classes.

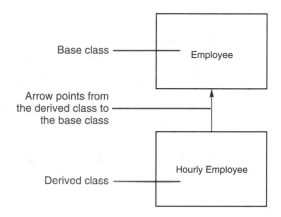

The C++ format for deriving a class from another class is as follows:

```
class HourlyEmployee : public Employee
```

Here a class named `HourlyEmployee` is derived from a class named `Employee`. The colon (:), followed by the words `public Employee` tell C++ that `HourlyEmployee` is being derived from another class named `Employee`. The `public` keyword is the `public` access specifier, but here it means that member variables and functions that are public in `Employee` will also be public to users of `HourlyEmployee`. When you use a variable of type `HourlyEmployee`, you can refer to member functions and variables of both class `HourlyEmployee` and of its base class, `Employee`.

Examples

1. In this example you use the `Circle` class from earlier in this chapter. If you did not type in that example, type in the first two files, C34CIR.H and C34CIR.CPP, and save them with those names.

This example shows you how to add a draw function to the `Circle` class by deriving a class named `myCircle` from `Circle`. Type the example the way it is shown. The format of the `myCircle` constructor will be explained shortly. For now, just notice that it looks similar to the class declaration that makes `Circle` the base class of `myClass`. The example uses some graphics functions to draw the circle, but that is not the point of the example, so there is only minimum explanation of how the drawing is done. Type in the code and save the file with the name at the top of the program.

```cpp
// Filename: C34CIR2.CPP
// Demonstrates adding a capability

#include <iostream.h>
#include <graph.h>  // needed for graphics
#include <io.h>      // needed for Quickwin menu control

#include "c34cir.h"   // include the class definition

class myCircle : public Circle
{
public:
    myCircle( float x, float y, float rad, char* name )
            : Circle( x, y, rad, name ) { }
    void Draw()
    {
        int    dia = m_rad * 2;  // diameter

        //  Draw the circle, using Quickwin graphics
        _setvideomode( _MAXRESMODE );
        _setcolor( 15 );     // white for background
        _floodfill( 0,0,7);  // fill background
        _setcolor( 4 );       // red for circle
        _ellipse( _GFILLINTERIOR,   // draw circle
                m_x, m_y, m_x + dia, m_y + dia );
        _wmenuclick( _WINTILE); // tile the 2 windows
    }
};

void main()
{
    // declare a Circle variable
    myCircle cir( 40,40,80,"Test two");

    // print out some information about it.
    cout << "Circle name is " << cir.m_name << "\n";
```

```
        cout << "\tIt's Radius is " << cir.radius() << "\n";

        // have the circle draw itself
        cir.Draw();
}
```

To compile this example, you first must create a project that includes the base class, Circle's program file. Name the project C34CIR2, and add the files C34CIR.CPP and C34CIR2.CPP to the project. Now you can build the program.

This program will produce different output than you have been seeing! Quickwin opened a second window and drew the circle in color. Figure 34.4 shows the output from this program. The color circle is attention getting, but also notice that the circle name and radius still printed out in the other window, even though the myCircle class did not have m_name or radius() members defined. It had *inherited* those members from its base class, and C++ used the base class members to satisfy the references to them in a myCircle variable.

Figure 34.4

Output from program to draw the circle.

More about Base and Derived Classes

You now know how to derive a child class from a base, or parent class, and add functionality to the child class that did not exist in its parent. Just as there often are rules that determine the relationship between a human parent and child, however, there are also rules that determine how a parent and child class interact. In this section we will look at the relationship from the derived, or child class's point of view.

Construction

Look back at the example you just completed in the previous section. In program C34CIR2.CPP you derived your own class named myCircle, from Circle. When you typed in the example, you used a different syntax for the constructor. Here is that constructor again:

```
myCircle( float x, float y, float rad, char* name )
        : Circle( x, y, rad, name ) { }
```

The difference in this constructor is the second line, the one with the colon and what looks like the base class's constructor. That line is just what it looks like—a call to `Circle`'s constructor with the parameters that were passed to `myCircle`'s constructor. The line ends with a set of braces, which simply indicates to C++ that `myCircle` will not have any constructor instructions of its own. The call to the parent class constructor occurs before control is passed to the child class constructor instructions.

Access Specifiers

In the last chapter you learned that there are three access specifiers: `public`, `private`, and `protected`. When a class member is declared to be `private`, it is private from even a child class, not just other users of the class. There often are times when you want a child class to be able to access certain members of its parent, but hide those members from external users of either class. That is where `protected` comes in. The `protected` access specifier makes class members act as if they were `private` to outside users of the class, but as if they were `public` to any child classes derived from the parent. The child can freely access the protected members of its parent, but outside users cannot. Listing 34.1 revisits the `Person` class of Chapter 33, but now there are some `protected` members as well.

Listing 34.1. Protected class members.

```
class Person
{
private:
    char* underwear;
    int GetDressed( );
public:
    char* shirt;
protected:
    char* thoughts;
    char* dreams;
};
```

A child class derived from the `Person` class can access the `thoughts` and `dreams` members of `Person`, but those members would still be inaccessible to users of either the Person class or any of its children. The private: specifier at the beginning of the class is redundant—class members are private by default—but is included for clarity.

Overriding Functions

Suppose that you have a class that has all of the data members and functions you want, but one of the member functions doesn't perform its job quite the way you want. You have already learned how to add functionality in a child class by adding new functions. You can also change how an existing function behaves by overriding it in a derived class.

To override a base class function in your derived class, declare an identical function prototype in the derived class, and then provide instructions for the function to perform the way you want. Listing 34.2 shows a fragment of a base class definition for a class named Account which has a member function named withdraw(), and a fragment of a derived class named lineOfCreditAccount() that overrides the withdraw() member by defining a member function with an identical prototype.

Listing 34.2. Overriding a base class member function.

```
class Account
{
     float withdraw( float amt );
. . . rest of class


class lineOfCreditAccount : public Account
{
     float withdraw( float amt );
. . . rest of class
```

When you declare an instance of the lineOfCreditAccount class shown in listing 34.2 and call the withdraw() member function for that variable, C++ does not invoke the base class member with that name, but instead uses the member function defined in lineOfCreditAccount.

You can also call the base class version of a member function from within the overridden function in a derived class. You do this by using the scope resolution operator. Listing 34.3 shows the implementation of a withdraw() member function for lineOfCreditAccount. This function tests a member variable that contains the credit limit amount. If the credit limit is 0, the base class withdraw() function is used, otherwise the child class function continues processing. The scope resolution operator is used to tell C++ to call the base class version of withdraw().

Listing 34.3. Calling an overridden base class function.

```
float lineOfCreditAccount::withdraw( float amt )
{
    if ( m_nCreditLimit == 0 )
        return Account::withdraw( amt );
. . . rest of function
```

Example

1. This example illustrates the protected access specifier in use, (and overriding a base class member function in a derived class.) The base class is named Account. It represents what might be a simple checking account at a bank. This is basically the same account class you worked with in the last chapter, which will not allow the account to be overdrawn. The derived class is named lineOfCreditAccount, and it will allow the account to be overdrawn, up to a predefined credit limit. The main program shows the derived class in use for some simple transactions.

First type in the header file and save it as C34ACCT.H.

```
// Filename: C34ACCT.H
// Header for the Account Class

#include <iostream.h>
#include <string.h>

class Account
{
public:
    char     m_Name[20];
    char     m_AcctNo[9];

protected:      // let derived classes use balance
    float    m_Balance;

public:
    Account(char* name, char* acct)
    {
        strcpy(m_Name, name);
        strcpy(m_AcctNo, acct);
        m_Balance = 0;
    }
    ~Account() { };
```

```
    float balance() {return m_Balance;}

    float deposit(float amt)
    {
        m_Balance += amt;
        return m_Balance;
    }

    float withdraw(float amt)
    {
        if (amt > m_Balance)
        {
            cout << "Attempt to overdraw account "
                << m_Name << " rejected.\n";
            return m_Balance;
        }
        else
        {
            m_Balance -= amt;
            return m_Balance;
        }
    }
};
```

Type in the main program file and save it as C34ACCT.CPP. You do not need to create a project for this program because there is only one program file. The header will be included by the preprocessor because of the #include directive. Figure 34.5 shows the program's output.

```
// Filename: C34ACCT.CPP
// Demonstrates adding member functions

#include <iostream.h>
#include <iomanip.h>
#include <string.h>
#include <math.h>        // for fabs() function

#include "C34ACCT.H"

class lineOfCredAccount : public Account
{
    float m_Rate;
    float m_Limit;
```

```
public:
    lineOfCredAccount(char* name, char* acct, float rate,
    ➥float limit)
        :Account( name, acct )
    {
        m_Rate = rate;
        m_Limit = limit;
    }
    float postInterest()
    {
        if ( m_Balance >= 0 ) // if not on credit
            return 0;         // don't charge interest

        float intAmt = m_Rate / 360  * m_Balance;
        m_Balance = m_Balance + intAmt;
        return fabs(intAmt);
    }

    float withdraw(float amt)
    {
        // if limit is zero
        //      use base class withdrawal method
        if (m_Limit == 0)
            return Account::withdraw( amt );

        // if withdrawal would put them over their
        // credit limit, reject the withdrawal, too.
        if ( abs(m_Balance - amt) > m_Limit )
        {
            cout << "Attempt to exceed Credit Limit "
                 << m_Name << " rejected.\n";
            return m_Balance;
        }

        // OK to withdraw, so do it
        if (amt > m_Balance)
            cout << "\n\tCredit Issued, ";
        m_Balance -= amt;
        cout << setiosflags( ios::fixed );
        if ( m_Balance < 0 )
        {
            cout << "\n\tOverdraft charge "
```

```
                                    << setprecision(2) << 10.00;
                        m_Balance -= 10.00;  // charge overdraft fee
                }
                return m_Balance;
        }
};

main()
{
        // create a line of credit account, rate 6.5%
        lineOfCredAccount acct( "Josephine Smythe",
                                "0097428", .065, 2000.00 );
        float tranAmt;
        float bal;
        char trnType;

        do
        {
                cout << "\nEnter Transaction for account "
                        << acct.m_AcctNo << "-"
                        << acct.m_Name << "\n";
                cout << "Or 0 if you are finished.\n";

                cout << "Transaction Amount ==> ";
                cin >> tranAmt;
                if (tranAmt == 0 )
                        break;
                cout << "Transaction Type (D or W) ==> ";
                cin >> trnType;
                cout << setiosflags( ios::fixed );
                if (trnType == 'D')
                {
                        bal = acct.deposit( tranAmt );
                        cout << "\tDeposit  \t";
                }
                else
                {
                        bal = acct.withdraw( tranAmt );
                        cout << "\tWithdraw\t";
                }
                cout << setprecision( 2 ) << tranAmt << "\t"
                        << "Balance\t"
```

```
                    << setprecision( 2 ) << bal << "\n";
        } while ( 1 );  // always true, exit at break

        tranAmt = acct.postInterest();
        if ( tranAmt != 0 )
            cout << "\t Interest Charge\t"
                    << setprecision( 2 ) << tranAmt;

        cout << "\n" << acct.m_Name
            << "\n\t\tEnding Balance = " << acct.balance();

        return 0;
}
```

Figure 34.5

Output from the
Line of Credit
Account program.

```
┌──────────────────────── Stdin/Stdout/Stderr ────────────────────────┐
│Enter Transaction for account 0097428-Josephine Smythe              │
│Or 0 if you are finished.                                           │
│Transaction Amount ==> 250.00                                       │
│Transaction Type (D or W) ==> W                                     │
│                                                                    │
│        Credit Issued,                                              │
│        Overdraft charge 10.00  Withdraw         250.00  Balance -260.00│
│Enter Transaction for account 0097428-Josephine Smythe              │
│Or 0 if you are finished.                                           │
│Transaction Amount ==> 1900.00                                      │
│Transaction Type (D or W) ==> W                                     │
│Attempt to exceed Credit Limit Josephine Smythe rejected.           │
│        Withdraw          1900.00 Balance -260.00                   │
│Enter Transaction for account 0097428-Josephine Smythe              │
│Or 0 if you are finished.                                           │
│Transaction Amount ==> 0                                            │
│         Interest Charge         0.05                               │
│Josephine Smythe                                                    │
│              Ending Balance = -260.05                              │
└────────────────────────────────────────────────────────────────────┘
```

Polymorphism

So far you have been learning about the relationship between base and derived classes from the viewpoint of the derived, or child class. You have learned how to add abilities to a class and how to override some existing behavior of a class. However, there are many times when it is necessary to be able to deal with the relationship in the other direction—from base class to derived class.

Real life is full of examples where a group of people, things, ideas, and so on all share a common feature or action, but each member of the group has a different version of the feature or performs the action in a different way. This type of relationship is called *polymorphism*.

For example, consider house pets that make a noise. This group might include dogs, cats, and birds. Each one makes sounds through their mouth, but each one's sound is different. Or consider a shape drawing program that needs to be able to draw many different shapes, but each shape is drawn a different way.

The "Is-A" Relationship

Figure 34.6 shows an example of such a relationship. The figure shows a base class named Shape, and several derived classes representing different types of shapes. Each derived class has its own draw() member function, which yields the results shown in the figure.

Figure 34.6

Several classes derived from Shape.

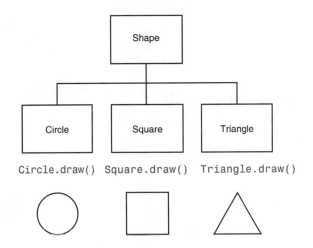

You already know how to use the derived classes to create and draw various shapes as needed. But suppose that you wanted to store shapes in an array without regard to what type of shape you were storing. C++ will not allow you to create an array of one type and then store variables of another type in that array. When one class is derived from another class, however, variables of the derived class type can also be treated as if they were variables of the base class type. For the example in figure 34.6, you could say that "A Square is a Shape." Note that this relationship does not go the other way—you cannot say that a Shape is a Square.

Now you can create an array to store shapes, regardless of what type of shape is being stored. The syntax is just like any other array:

```
Shape* shapeArr[3];
```

The preceding line will create an array to hold three pointers to variables of type Shape. Because a Square (or a Circle, or a Triangle) *is-a* Shape, you can store any of these in the array.

Example

1. This program defines a base class named housePet, and then derives three child classes from housePet named dog, cat, and bird. Each class, including the base class, has an identically prototyped speak() function, but each one "speaks" with a different sound. Because the base class doesn't represent any particular pet, it doesn't have anything intelligent to say.

The classes are tested in the main program. An array is allocated to hold three housePets, and then a dog, cat, and bird are allocated and pointers to them are stored in the array. Finally, a for loop goes through the array and invokes each housePet's speak() function.

```cpp
// Filename: C34PET1.CPP
// Demonstrates storing multiple types in an array

#include <iostream.h>

class housePet
{
public:
    void speak() { cout << "huh?\n"; }

};

class dog : public housePet
{
public:
    void speak() { cout << "woof\n"; }
};

class cat : public housePet
{
public:
    void speak() { cout << "meow\n"; }
};

class bird : public housePet
{
public:
    void speak() { cout << "chirp\n"; }
};

void main()
```

```
{
    housePet* myHouse[3];
    dog Fido;
    cat Puff;
    bird Tweety;
    Fido.speak();
    Puff.speak();
    Tweety.speak();
    myHouse[0] = &Fido;
    myHouse[1] = &Puff;
    myHouse[2] = &Tweety;
    for (int i = 0; i < 3; i++ )
        myHouse[i]->speak();
}
```

This program shows how you can store variables of derived classes in
an array that has been declared to hold variables of the base class type.
When each derived class variable is used to invoke the speak function, the
expected output is produced. When the final step loops through the array
and asks each "pet" to "speak," however, the result is not quite what we
had in mind. The output is as follows:

```
woof
meow
chirp
huh?
huh?
huh?
```

The output shows that C++ called the base class speak() function instead
of the various derived class functions when the pointers in the array were
used to invoke the speak function. This happened even though the pointers stored in the array pointed to derived class variables because C++ did
not have a way to know that the speak() function was overriden in the
derived classes. The next section shows you how to fix this.

Virtual Functions

You just learned that you can store variables of several types of derived class in an
array that was allocated to store the variables of the base class. When you access
member functions, however, the only ones that are accessible are those of the base
class. In the preceding example, you wanted the output to be the individual
"voices" of each pet.

The ability to perform this kind of operation is called *polymorphism*. Polymorphism is a big word for what amounts to a fairly simple idea. It is formed from two root words—*poly*, which simply means *many*, and *morph*, which means *shape*, or *form*. So *polymorphism* simply means many shapes or forms (or actions, or voices, or whatever.)

C++ implements polymorphism through something called a *virtual function*. When you define a function as a *virtual function* in a base class, and then override that same function in derived classes, C++ will call the appropriate derived class version of the function in situations like the last example. To declare a virtual function, you use the `virtual` keyword in the function prototype. The code below declares `speak()` to be a virtual function in class `housePet`.

```
class housePet
{
virtual  void  speak();
... rest of class
```

Example

1. This program uses the `virtual` keyword to make `speak()` a virtual function in the `housePet` base class.

```
// Filename: C34PET2.CPP
// Demonstrates virtual functions

#include <iostream.h>

class housePet
{
public:
    virtual void speak() { cout << "huh?\n"; }

};

class dog : public housePet
{
public:
    void speak() { cout << "woof\n"; }
};

class cat : public housePet
{
public:
    void speak() { cout << "meow\n"; }
```

```
};

class bird : public housePet
{
public:
     void speak() { cout << "chirp\n"; }
};

void main()
{
     housePet* myHouse[3];
     dog Fido;
     cat Puff;
     bird Tweety;
     Fido.speak();
     Puff.speak();
     Tweety.speak();
     myHouse[0] = &Fido;
     myHouse[1] = &Puff;
     myHouse[2] = &Tweety;
     for (int i = 0; i < 3; i++ )
          myHouse[i]->speak();
}
```

When you run this program, the results show that the same virtual speak() function is called both through the specific variable, and when called through an array of housePets. The output from this program is as follows:

```
woof
meow
chirp
woof
meow
chirp
```

Summary

In this chapter you learned how to use two extremely powerful capabilities of C++ classes: inheritance and polymorphism. These two capabilities form the basis for building extremely versatile and powerful libraries of classes such as the Microsoft Foundation Classes you will learn about in the last part of this book. The next chapter introduces you to the basics of class libraries.

Review Questions

Answers to Review Questions are in Appendix B.

1. What is a make file?

2. What is the purpose of the scope resolution operator?

3. Write the beginning of a class definition for a class named `myComputer` that will be derived from a base class named `Computer`?

4. What is `protected:`?

5. True or False: When you override a base class member function in a derived class, the base class function can no longer be used.

6. How do you make C++ call a function in a derived class when you only have a pointer to the base class?

Review Exercise

1. Create a base shape class with a virtual `draw()` member function, and then derive two new classes from shapes representing a Circle and Square and implement `draw()` functions for each derived class. Finally, write a program that will store at least one of each derived shape in an array of Shapes; go through the array and have each stored shape draw itself on-screen.

CHAPTER 35

Introduction to Class Libraries

In Chapter 7, you learned that C++ comes with several libraries of functions that you can use in your programs, and throughout this book you have been using those functions. Just as there are libraries of functions, there are also libraries of classes that you can use just as easily as the function libraries you have already been using.

This chapter covers the following topics:

♦ What are Class Libraries

♦ Advantages of Class Libraries

♦ The CString Class

♦ Collection Classes

In this chapter you will learn some of the basic methods of using class libraries, and then how to apply those methods to two of the general purpose classes that come with Visual C++.

What Are Class Libraries?

A library can contain both functions and classes.

Throughout the preceding chapters you have been using some of the functions from the large function libraries that come with C++. A *function library* is just a collection of useful functions, gathered in one place, with function prototypes provided in separate header files. The functions themselves are already compiled and kept in a file called, appropriately, a library. Library files have an extension of .LIB. By convention, the library files that come with Visual C++ are stored in a directory named LIB.

Classes can be collected into libraries, too. Class libraries are also kept in a library file with a .LIB extension, and in fact it is permissible to mix functions and classes in the same library.

Class libraries exist for many purposes. Usually a class library addresses one specific purpose or problem. You have been using one small class library for most of this book. It is called the iostream class library, and its purpose is to provide an object-oriented interface to input and output operations.

In this chapter, you learn about the Microsoft Foundation Class library's general purpose classes, a small subset of the larger Microsoft Foundation Class library. The General Purpose Classes provide some common utility objects that can be used with both MS-DOS and Microsoft Windows applications.

Advantages of Class Libraries

C++ is a powerful programming language by itself, but when it is used to create and use class libraries, its power is multiplied in several ways. Class libraries can be designed to provide capabilities that aren't available in C++ in a way that makes the new capabilities behave like an extension of the language. You will study one such class in this chapter, a class that gives C++ the string handling abilities that it doesn't have built in.

Another power of class libraries is their capability to simplify the process of learning a very complex skill, such as writing Microsoft Windows programs. Learning to write a Windows program in straight C++ using the Microsoft Windows Software Development Kit (SDK) is a long, difficult process. But one type of class library, known as an *application framework*, provides classes designed to encapsulate the ugly, difficult aspects of the Windows interface, so that you can concentrate on what you want the application to do.

One final advantage of class libraries comes from C++'s inheritance feature. You can extend or modify the capabilities of the library without changing or duplicating any of the library's code.

How to Use a Class Library

There are two aspects to using a class library. The first is the easy part—including the library in your program. To use a class library in your own program, you first need to find out what the names of the header (.H) files are, and ensure that Visual C++ can find them when it compiles your program. Second, you need to make sure that the compiler knows where the library files (.LIB) are located, and tell Visual C++ which library files to use. For the Microsoft Foundation Class library, the Setup program has already configured Visual C++ to know the locations of the header and library files and which libraries to use for various types of projects. As you work through the examples in this chapter, and the last part of the book, you will learn the names of the Microsoft Foundation Class library header files. There are only a few that you need to learn.

The other aspect of using a class library is learning your way around the library. A major class library, such as MFC (Microsoft Foundation Classes), is very complex and rich in features. As you start to learn how to use MFC, you will begin to appreciate how much it can do, and you may become a bit frustrated if you don't grasp it all immediately. Don't let that stop you from pushing ahead. As with anything else worthwhile, there are rich rewards ahead if you persist and master this powerful tool.

The best way to start learning how to use a class library is to actually use it. Set yourself some simple but nontrivial task, and set out to solve it. A personal calendar and to-do list, or a program to draw simple floor plans for a house would fall in this category. While you are working on the problem, study the documentation. Try to set in your mind some of the capabilities of the library. You may not need all the features right away, but as new problems arise for you to solve in your development, it is better to have a vague memory that a class or function that might solve that problem exists than to have to pore over the documentation wondering if anything in there can help you.

This book will help you get started on learning MFC, but it is only intended to be a brief introduction. For a more detailed look at the Microsoft Foundation Classes, see Que's *Using Visual C++*.

The *CString* Class

In Chapter 6, you learned that C++ does not have a true character string data type as a built-in type. Beginning programmers, or programmers who come to C++ after using a language that does have such a data type, often spend a long time learning to use C++ character arrays as strings because the syntax seems unnatural and the functions can be tricky to use. There are other limitations to character arrays as strings. For example, how do you increase the size of the array once it has been declared? It can be done, but it is tricky and awkward. Errors in resizing character arrays are a frequent source of bugs in conventional C++ programs. All of these factors—awkward syntax, difficult manipulation, error-prone operations—make character strings an excellent candidate for a class.

The CString class is a class for creating and manipulating character strings. It lets you create CString variables that can be manipulated like the built-in data types, and in a manner that is much more natural than C++ character arrays. CString variables also are variable in length, so you do not need to know how long a string will be when you create the variable; and if the size of the string changes, the variable changes its size to fit the string.

Using *CStrings*

You use a CString much the same as you would use any built-in variable, or any class variable such as the Circle class you used in the previous chapters. You can declare an empty CString as follows:

```
CString  myStr;
```

Or, you can declare a CString variable and assign a character constant to it in the same statement:

```
CString  myStr = "This is my string.";
```

An alternative form of the declaration uses a constructor, as shown here:

```
CString  myStr("This is my string.");
```

Once you declare a CString variable, you can manipulate it in the expected ways. You can assign a new value to it:

```
myStr = "This is still my string.";
```

Or you can assign another CString to it:

```
myStr = theirStr;
```

Finally, you can assign the contents of a character array to it:

```
char aName[20];
strcpy( aName, "Their string here");
myStr = aName;
```

A CString variable can be passed to a function just like any other variable. You can pass it by value, as a pointer, or as a reference. The syntax is the same for a CString variable as it is for an int, or any other built-in type. Listing 35.1 shows a function that accepts three CString variables:

Listing 35.1. Passing a *CString* variable to a function.

```
void  doSome(CString str1, CString* str2, CString& str3)
{
    cout << str1;
    cout << *str2; // dereference the pointer
    cout << str3;
}

main()
{
    CString s1, s2, s3;
    s1 = "one";
    s2 = "two";
    s3 = "three";
    doSome(s1, &s2, s3);
}
```

In Listing 35.1, s1 is passed to doSome by value, s2 is passed by address, or pointer, and s3 is passed by reference. The three CString variables are passed, and used, exactly the same as an int or a float.

Quickwin and the Microsoft Foundation Classes

Quickwin was intended to be an easy way to port existing DOS programs to the Windows environment. As such, it is a hybrid environment that doesn't always respond the way you would expect. This is especially true with a class library such as the Microsoft Foundation Class library, which is intended primarily for Windows application development under the full Windows interface.

It is possible to use the general purpose classes from Microsoft Foundation Classes in a Quickwin application, but you must take special steps to do so. The following paragraphs describe how to use the general purpose classes with Quickwin.

First, using the Visual Workbench or other program editor, type in the following lines of code and save them as C35MFCQW.H in the directory where you are doing the examples in this book. If you have the source code disk, this file is included in the directory for this chapter.

```
#ifdef _WINDOWS
    #undef _WINDOWS
    #define _DOS
    #include <afx.h>  // main MFC header file
    #undef _DOS
    #define _WINDOWS
#endif
```

Each example in this chapter refers to this file in an #include statement at the top of the file.

Before you compile an example, you need to change some of the compile and link options. To set up Application Workbench to properly compile a Quickwin application that uses the General Purpose classes, follow these steps:

1. Pull down the Application Workbench **O**ptions menu and choose Project to open the Project Options dialog.

2. Make sure that the Use Microsoft Foundation Classes box is not checked.

3. Click on the **L**inker button to open up the Linker Options dialog box.

continues

> **4.** In the Linker Options dialog box, make sure that the Prevent Use of Extended Dictionary box is checked.
>
> **5.** Finally, in the Libraries box, add the name of the medium-model foundation class DOS library to the beginning of the list. That name will be `mafxcrd` for the debug version, or `mafxcr` for the non-debug version. These libraries would have been installed in your MFC\LIB directory if you chose to install the DOS libraries. Users of Visual C++ 1.0 Standard Edition may not have these libraries.
>
> You will need to change the above options whenever you return to Visual Workbench, but the changes will stay in effect throughout each session.

Examples

> **Caution:** Before doing the examples in this chapter, be sure to read and follow the sidebar titled "Quickwin and the Microsoft Foundation Classes." These examples will not compile properly if you do not follow the instructions in the sidebar.

1. This example reads characters into a character array from the keyboard, then converts the characters into a `CString` and prints the `CString` on the console.

```
// Filename: C35CSTR1.CPP
// Demonstrates allocating a CString

#include <iostream.h>
#include "c35mfcqw.h"      // QuickWin works around file

#define MAXIN 80
void main()
{
    char inBuff [MAXIN +1];   // buffer for input
    CString promptMsg;  // CString for displaying messages
    CString inName;
```

```
        // Display input prompt
        promptMsg = "\nPlease enter a name ==>";
        cout << promptMsg;

        // Get input and store
        cin.get(inBuff, MAXIN);
        inName = inBuff;

        // if the CString is empty
        if( inName.IsEmpty() )
        {
            promptMsg = "\nYou didn't enter anything.";
            cout << promptMsg;
            return;
        }

        // Display back the name
        promptMsg = "\nThanks for the name. You Entered ==>";
        cout << promptMsg << inName;
    }
```

The first thing to notice in this example is how easily you can replace the contents of a CString after it is created. The CString variable promptMsg is allocated at the beginning of the program, and then new values are assigned to it every time the program needs to output a message. The syntax is exactly the same as you would use to assign a new value to an int or a float.

This example also shows that a CString is able to change its length depending on what you store in it. Both promptMsg and inName are initially empty, but later are filled with strings of varying lengths.

Notice that you can't use a CString in the cin.get(). That capability has not been defined for CString. So, you still have to use a character array to receive the input. Once the input has been read into the inBuff character array, however, it is very easy to assign it to a CString and then do any further manipulation on the CString. Later examples will show you some of the more advanced capabilities of CString that make the assignment very worthwhile.

 2. CString variables can be stored in an array, just like any other variable type. This program will accept up to five names from the console and store them as CString variables in an array. The program then prints the array, along with the sizes of the names. Figure 35.1 shows the output from a sample run of the program.

```cpp
// Filename: C35CSTR2.CPP
// Demonstrates CStrings stored in an array

#include <iostream.h>
#include "c35mfcqw.h"    // QuickWin works around file

#define MAXIN    80
#define MAXNAMES 5

void main()
{
    char inBuff[MAXIN + 1]; // input buffer
    CString aNames[5];      // array of 5 CStrings
    int numNames = 0;       // number entered so far

    cout << "Enter up to " << MAXNAMES << " names.\n";
    cout << "Quit before " << MAXNAMES
         << " by hitting Enter without typing a name.\n";

    // Accept names from input until 5 names have
    // been entered or user enters an empty name.
    do
    {
        cout << "Enter Name ==>";
        cin.getline(inBuff,MAXIN);
        if ( strlen(inBuff) == 0 ) // empty name
            break;                 // quit the loop
        aNames[ numNames ] = inBuff;
        numNames++;
    } while ( numNames < MAXNAMES );

    cout << "\nYou entered \n";
    cout << "No.\tLength\tName\n";
    for( int i = 0; i < numNames; i++ )
    {
        cout << i+1 << "\t"
             << aNames[i].GetLength() << "\t"
             << aNames[i] << "\n" ;
    }
}
```

Figure 35.1

Storing *CString* variables in an array.

```
┌──────────────────────── Stdin/Stdout/Stderr ──────────────────────┐
│ Enter up to 5 names.                                              │
│ Quit before 5 by hitting Enter without typing a name.            │
│ Enter Name ==>Tom Tomlinson                                      │
│ Enter Name ==>Dick Smith                                         │
│ Enter Name ==>Harry Jones                                        │
│ Enter Name ==>Joe Wikert                                         │
│ Enter Name ==>Janice J. Anderchild                               │
│                                                                  │
│ You entered                                                      │
│ No.     Length   Name                                            │
│ 1       13       Tom Tomlinson                                   │
│ 2       10       Dick Smith                                      │
│ 3       11       Harry Jones                                     │
│ 4       10       Joe Wikert                                      │
│ 5       20       Janice J. Anderchild                            │
│                                                                  │
└──────────────────────────────────────────────────────────────────┘
```

Overloaded Operators

In Chapter 33 you learned about overloaded functions and how you can define more than one version of a function. C++ also allows you to overload an operator.

You have already been using some overloaded operators. Every time you use cin and cout, you are using overloaded versions of the << and >> operators. Recall that in Chapter 13 these two operators were used as the bitwise shift operators. With the cin and cout objects, the same operators are called the *stream insertion operators*.

When an operator is overloaded, C++ uses the context where the operator is used to determine what action to associate with it. That is how C++ knows that when it sees a << with a cout, it should use the cout stream insertion function and not try to do a bitwise shift.

CString makes good use of overloaded operators to allow you to use a CString in much more natural-looking ways. You have even been using one of the CString overloaded operators in the previous examples, and it looked so natural you may not have even realized that you were using an overloaded operator. Look back at one of those examples for lines where a value is assigned to a CString. Following is one such line from the first example:

```
promptMsg = "\nPlease enter a name ==>";
```

This line of code looks perfectly normal. It assigns the character string inside the quotes on the right-hand side of the = sign to the CString variable, promptMsg, on the left-hand side. It looks normal, that is, until you remember the lessons of Chapter 6 where you learned that you cannot assign values to an already declared character array in a regular assignment statement. If promptMsg had been defined as a normal character array, you would have to use the strcpy function to assign it a new value.

CString has *overloaded* the assignment operator (the equal sign), so that a member function of CString is called whenever C++ encounters an equal sign with a CString on one side and a character expression (or another CString) on the other side. The member function of CString knows how to copy one character expression into another, so the statement works as you would expect. Now it makes perfect sense to write statements like the following:

```
CString strOne, strTwo;
strOne = "This is a string";
strTwo = strOne;
```

CString uses the + sign for concatenation.

CString has several other very useful overridden operators that allow you to perform comparisons on CString variables and to perform "arithmetic" on them. The overridden operators are normally used for arithmetic, but in CString they are used to *concatenate* CStrings. Concatenation is the process of attaching one string to the end of another or combining two or more strings into a longer string. So when you use the CString concatenation operators, the result is to join two character strings together. The following shows how to use the CString concatenation operators:

```
CString strOne, strTwo, strThree;
strOne = "Now is the time for all good";
strTwo = " people";
strThree = strOne + strTwo;
strThree += " to learn C++.";
```

After this sequence of instructions, strThree would contain the phrase:

```
Now is the time for all good people to learn C++.
```

The plus sign (+) causes strTwo to be joined to the end of strOne. The result of this is assigned to strThree. (strOne and strTwo are unaffected, as would be expected.) Finally, a character string constant is "added" to strThree. This looks far more natural, and is much easier to remember than the equivalent string functions. Table 35.1 shows the CString overloaded operators.

Table 35.1. *CString* overloaded operators.

Operator	Overloaded Meaning
=	Assigns a new value to a CString
+	Concatenates CStrings
+=	Adds one string to the end of another

Operator	Overloaded meaning
[ ]	Accesses a single character in a CString
==	Compares for equal
<=, =>, etc.	Other Boolean comparisons. All expected comparisons are supported.

If you have programmed in a language that supports string operations, you are already familiar with the use of these operators. In Chapter 6 you learned that C++ does not have string variables, which is true because a class such as CString can be made to act like a part of the language; however, now you can create and manipulate CStrings, and C++ has gained a way to use string variables.

Examples

1. This example demonstrates the CString concatenation operators. A name is read in as two variables, one for first name and another for last name, and stored in separate CString variables for first name and last name. The name is then formatted for printing in a third CString by concatenating the two parts of the name, along with a comma separator. The concatenated name is then printed.

```cpp
// Filename: C35CSTR3.CPP
// Demonstrates CString concatenation

#include <iostream.h>
#include "c35mfcqw.h"      // QuickWin work around file

void main()
{
    char inBuff[80];
    CString lastName, firstName, printName;

    cout << "Enter a person's first name ==>";
    cin.getline(inBuff,80);
    firstName = inBuff;
    cout << "Now, please enter their last name ==>";
    cin.getline(inBuff,80);
    lastName = inBuff;

    printName = lastName + ", " + firstName;
    cout << "\nThe name you entered is " << printName;
}
```

2. This example demonstrates the CString comparison operators. Two names are read and stored in CString variables. The CString comparison operators are used to determine which name comes first in the alphabet.

```
// Filename: C35CSTR4.CPP
// Demonstrates CString comparison operators

#include <iostream.h>
#include "c35mfcqw.h"      // QuickWin workaround file

void main()
{
    char inBuff[80];
    CString NameOne, NameTwo;

    cout << "Please enter two person's last names.\n\n";
    cout << "Enter the first one ==>";
    cin.getline(inBuff,80);
    NameOne = inBuff;
    cout << "Now, please enter the second one ==>";
    cin.getline(inBuff,80);
    NameTwo = inBuff;

    if ( NameOne == NameTwo )
        cout << "\nThe two names are the same.";
    else
    {
        if (NameOne < NameTwo)
            cout << "\n" << NameOne << " comes before "
                << NameTwo << " in the alphabet";
        else
            cout << "\n" << NameTwo << " comes before "
                << NameOne << " in the alphabet";
    }
}
```

Following is the output from a sample run of this program. This type of comparison could easily be used to sort a long list of names.

```
Please enter two person's last names.
Enter the first one ==>Joe Jones
Now, please enter the second one ==>Joan Jones

Joan Jones comes before Joe Jones in the alphabet
```

Collections

A collection is a group of related items.

One of the most important groups of classes in the general purpose classes is the collection classes. A *collection* is simply a convenient place in memory to hold a group of related variables. Collections play a vital role in many programs. Some places where a collection could be used include all the controls in a Windows dialog, or all the open windows in a program.

The general purpose classes include three types of collections: arrays, lists, and maps. For each type of collection, there are classes for most of the built-in types, plus a CString collection, and one that will hold variables of any class that has been derived from a common class named CObject. This chapter covers arrays and lists, which are the most frequently used classes by far. You will be working with collections of CString variables, but the same techniques can be used with collections of other variable types as well.

A Better Way Than C Arrays

You have already used the pure C++ implementation of one kind of collection—the array. C++ arrays are very useful, but they have some annoying limitations. The biggest limitation of C++ arrays is sizing. C++ does not provide a way for you to change the size of an array after it has been declared. This can be a serious limitation in any situation where you can't know in advance how many elements you will need to store. (Which is more often the case than not.) If you pick a size for the array that you hope will be big enough "most of the time," you can be sure of two things: First, most of the time it will be bigger than you need; second, occasionally it won't be big enough. There are ways to work around this limitation, but they are difficult to master and their implementation can clutter up your code.

This is where the general purpose collection classes come in. These collections are able to dynamically change their size when you store new elements, or remove elements. You don't have to know how large a collection will be when you declare it.

Building an Array of CStrings

The collection classes can dynamically change their size.

In C++, you declare arrays with statements similar to the following:

```
float   fNumb[10];
CString sArray[5];
```

The preceding lines declare arrays of 10 floating-point numbers and five CStrings. To declare an array of any other type, you change the data type on the left end of the line to the type you want.

The collection classes work a bit differently. To declare an array to hold CStrings, use the following syntax:

```
CStringArray   arrNames;
```

Here you have declared a variable called arrNames, which is a CStringArray. So far, that is all that is known about the array. It doesn't yet have any variables stored in it. It doesn't even have a size yet.

You can add members to a CStringArray in several ways. The simplest is to just start adding elements to the array with the Add member function. The following line adds a CString variable named strOne to a CStringArray named theArray.

```
theArray.Add( strOne );
```

The Add function adds the element to the end of a CStringArray. You also can add elements to the beginning or middle of a CStringArray. To add an element to the beginning or middle of an CStringArray, you use the InsertAt member function. InsertAt takes three parameters: the index to insert at, the CString variable to insert, and the number of times to repeat the insert. (You can insert multiple elements at one time.) If you leave off the number to insert, one element is inserted. If you pass a NULL as the CString to be inserted, you can insert an empty element. The following is an example of InsertAt:

```
theArray.InsertAt( 0, strOne );
```

The preceding line inserts the variable strOne at index 0 in the array and pushes all other elements down by one. It has the effect of adding an element to the beginning of the array instead of the end. You can insert an element anywhere in the array. You can even insert an element at a position past the current end of the array. When you insert an element past the current end of the array, CStringArray automatically adds empty elements between the end of the array and the index you specify.

> **Caution:** There is a limit to how large you can grow a CStringArray, or any of the other collection classes. The limit is determined by the size of an int variable for the machine you are programming. On an MS-DOS PC, the largest number you can represent with an int is 32767, so that is the most elements you can store in a collection.

Using the Array

After a CStringArray is declared and populated with elements, you can use several functions to learn things about the array and to manage its members.

You often need to know the size of an array. You can use one of two functions to determine the size: GetSize, and GetUpperBound. Both functions return an int, but there is a subtle difference between the values returned by these two functions. If your array contains five elements, GetSize will return 5, the actual number of elements in the array, but GetUpperBound will return 4, the index of the last element in the array. This is because arrays are indexed starting at 0, not 1.

It also is possible to remove elements from an array. You can remove one or more elements from a specific position with the RemoveAt function. The following statement will remove three elements from strArray, starting at position 4.

```
strArray.RemoveAt( 4, 3 );
```

If you do not provide a number of elements to remove (the second parameter), the RemoveAt function will remove one element. To remove the last element in an array, use RemoveAt with GetUpperBound, as follows:

```
strArray.RemoveAt( strArray.GetUpperBound() );
```

You haven't seen this type of syntax yet in this book. At first it might look confusing, but it is actually very simple and is very common in most C++ programs. When C++ evaluates this line of code, it first performs the GetUpperBound function for strArray. That call returns the index of the actual last element of strArray, which is then passed to the RemoveAt function. The preceding line is the equivalent of the following two lines:

```
int lastElement = strArray.GetUpperBound();
strArray.RemoveAt( lastElement );
```

Of course an array wouldn't be much use if you couldn't access its elements. CStringArray provides several ways to access elements in the array. Just as there are functions to SetAt and RemoveAt elements of the array, there also is a function to get an element. You have probably already guessed its name—GetAt. The GetAt function returns the element at a given position. The following two lines will return, respectively, the third element in an array and the last element.

```
strArray.GetAt( 3 );                        // third element
strArray.GetAt(strArray.GetUpperBound()); // last element
```

Finally, CStringArray has an overloaded operator that makes it possible to retrieve or set elements using the same syntax you would use with an ordinary C++ array—the [] operator. The paired opening and closing square brackets are considered an operator and therefore can be overloaded. You can access elements of a CStringArray using the same syntax as a regular C++ array. The following example uses the overloaded [] operator to step through all the elements of a CStringArray.

Example

1. This example is a rewrite of C35CSTR2, the second example you wrote using CString. The only differences are that a CStringArray is used instead of a regular C++ array, and you don't need to set a limit on how many names can be entered.

```
// Filename: C35CSAR.CPP
// Demonstrates CString Array

#include <iostream.h>
#include "c35mfcqw.h"  // Quickwin workaround file
#include <afxcoll.h>    // MFC Collection classes

#define MAXIN    80

void main()
{
    char inBuff[MAXIN + 1]; // input buffer
    CStringArray nameArray; // dynamic string array

    cout << "Enter a list of names.\n";
    cout << "End the list by entering a blank name.\n";
    while (TRUE)  // Loop forever
    {
        cout << "Enter Name ==>";
        cin.getline(inBuff,80);
        if ( strlen(inBuff) == 0 )  // empty name
            break;                  // quit the loop
        nameArray.Add(inBuff);  // add to end of array
    }

    cout << "\nYou entered " << nameArray.GetSize()
        << " names, and here they are.\n";
    cout << "No.\tLength\tName\n";
    for( int i = 0; i < nameArray.GetSize(); i++ )
    {
        cout << i+1 << "\t"
            << nameArray[i].GetLength() << "\t"
            << nameArray[i] << "\n" ;
    }
}
```

Notice that the syntax for looping through a CStringArray is the same as it is for a conventional C++ array. Instead of using the defined size of the C++ array, however, you are able to use the GetSize() function to control the loop.

What Is AFX?

Most class libraries adopt TLA's (Three Letter Acronyms) that relate to the name of the library. You often will see the Microsoft Foundation Classes referred to as MFC. So what is this AFX in the class header name? It is the name of the main MFC header file, and now it is part of the header file name for the collections. How do you get from MFC to AFX?

AFX is the internal name of the development group at Microsoft who developed the Foundation Class library. According to Microsoft, the name was given to the group by Bill Gates when he formed the group in 1989 with a mission to *Utilize the latest in object-oriented technology to provide tools and libraries for developers writing the most advanced GUI applications on the market.*

What does AFX mean? Is AFX really an acronym for something or just some letters strung together that sound high-tech? According to Microsoft, the AF stands for Application Framework, and the X doesn't stand for anything.

Lists

A *list*, or *linked list*, is similar to an array because items are kept in the order they are added. In a list, however, each item has a "link" to the next item in the list, and an item's position is determined by its relation to adjoining items. Some lists also maintain a link to the previous item in the list. These are called *doubly linked* lists.

A *list* has an advantage over an array when you need to insert items into the middle of the list. In an array, if you insert a new item into the middle of the array, all the elements past the new item must be shifted up in some manner. This usually involves copying each element to a new memory location, which can be time-consuming and inefficient for large arrays. In a list, all that is necessary to insert a new element is to change the links in the preceding and following items to point to the new item. Therefore, you can insert a new item into the list very quickly. (You don't have to know how to change the links—the list class does that for you when you insert an element.)

A list's strength also gives rise to its weakness. The only way to get to a given element in a list is to start at the beginning or end of the list and move from one element to the next until you have moved the desired number of elements or arrive at the one you want. Because of this design, you also would not want to navigate through a list by incrementing an index. Instead, you need a way to tell the list to give you the next (or previous) element from wherever you happen to be in the list.

Iteration is the process of going through a collection one element at a time.

The process of going through a collection one item at a time is called *iteration*. To iterate through an array, you increment or decrement an index value by one to move to the next, or previous element. To iterate through a list, you use the position. The list classes have member functions that return the element at a given position in the list. The functions also update a position variable to the position of the next, or previous, element from the one that was just returned.

To find the first element in a list, you use a function named `GetHeadPosition`. This function does not return an element of the list. Instead, it returns the position of the first element, the head element, in the list. The return value is a data type named `POSITION`. Be sure to use all uppercase letters for the data type. After you have the head position, you can then move through the list with a series of calls to `GetNext` or `GetPrev`. If you have a `POSITION`, you can get the element at that position with a call to `GetAt`.

Listing 35.2 illustrates how to iterate through a list. Lists are used a lot in the main Microsoft Foundation Classes, and you will see this sequence a lot. Whenever you see a sequence of code like this, it is very likely that a list is being processed.

Listing 35.2. Iterating through a *CStringList*. (*strList* is a *CStringList* variable that was built elsewhere.)

```
CString aStr;  // working variable
POSITION pos;  // position in list

pos = strList.GetHeadPosition; // get top of list
while ( pos != NULL )          // quit when pos is NULL
{
    aStr = strList.GetNext( pos );
    cout << aStr;
}
```

The tricky part of Listing 35.2 is the call to `GetNext(pos)`. It isn't apparent from the syntax exactly what happens there. `GetNext( pos )` actually does two things. First, it returns the `CString` element at the position (pos) that was passed to it. Second, pos is passed here by reference so that it can be updated to the position of the next element in the list. If there are no more elements, pos is updated to `NULL`, and the `while` loop terminates the next time control comes around to the `while` condition. The syntax is a bit awkward at first, mainly because the workings of `GetNext` aren't as intuitive as you might like, but once you understand `GetNext` (or `GetPrev`) this is a very easy and safe way to iterate through a collection.

Example

1. Here is the name collection program again, this time implemented as a
CStringList. After you have done this example, go back and study the
other two versions of this program and compare them for differences and
similarities. Which version you use in your own programs is up to you.
Each one has its own strengths and weaknesses, so there is no universal
best choice. As you gain experience you will find that you are able to
choose which collection to use for each individual problem.

```cpp
// Filename: C35CLST.CPP
// Demonstrates CString List

#include <iostream.h>
#include "c35mfcqw.h"  // Quickwin workaround file
#include <afxcoll.h>   // MFC Collections

void main()
{
    CStringList nameList;
    char inBuff[80];

    cout << "Enter a list of names.\n";
    cout << "End the list by entering a blank name.\n";
    while (TRUE)  // Loop forever
    {
        cout << "Enter Name ==>";
        cin.getline(inBuff,80);
        if ( strlen(inBuff) == 0 )
            break;      // break the loop
        nameList.AddTail(inBuff);  // add to end of list
    }

    cout << "\nYou entered " << nameList.GetCount()
         << " names, and here they are.\n";
    cout << "No.\tLength\tName\n";

    int i = 0;
    CString curName;
    POSITION pos = nameList.GetHeadPosition();
    while ( pos != NULL )
    {
        curName = nameList.GetNext( pos );
```

```
            cout << ++i << "\t"
                 << curName.GetLength() << "\t"
                 << curName << "\n" ;
    }
}
```

The output from this program should be the same as the other two examples of this problem.

Summary

You now have a good understanding of the key concepts of designing and using your own classes and of using class libraries provided with Visual C++. In other words, you have mastered the central skills of object-oriented programming.

In this chapter you saw that class libraries are just like function libraries, but that they also can be used to extend the C++ language itself. In the next chapter you will learn some of the theory behind object-oriented programming, and why so many experts think it is a major advance in programming languages.

Review Questions

Answers to Review Questions are in Appendix B.

1. What is a class library?

2. True or false: Because C++ does not have a built-in data type for character strings, the only way you can manipulate character strings in C++ is through character arrays.

3. Arrays and lists are types of _____.

4. What is iteration?

5. What is position?

Review Exercise

1. Write a function that will accept a reference to a CStringList, and a CString and insert the CString into the list in alphabetical order.

CHAPTER 36

Introduction to Object-Oriented Programming

You have written many programs in the preceeding chapters using C++, a language which supports object-oriented programming, but most of those programs were not object-oriented programs. In the last three chapters, you began to utilize the tools and techniques of true object-oriented programming—classes, inheritance, and polymorphism. You even started to use some class libraries.

This chapter covers the following topics:

♦ The basic ideas behind object-oriented programming

♦ The advantages of object-oriented programming

♦ Learning to think in terms of objects

This chapter will focus on the main ideas behind object-oriented programming and how it differs from conventional programming methods. You will learn how object-oriented programming helps you to start thinking about programming problems in terms of the things and ideas they represent, rather than the computer language representation of those things.

There aren't any example programs in this chapter. Instead, you will be learning about the concepts and ideas behind object-oriented programming.

What Is Object-Oriented Programming?

In Chapter 18, you learned that functions are a tool which can help you break a program into several smaller tasks. You learned to write programs that are a collection of functions in which each function does a part of the work. This type of programming is called *structured programming*. The structured programming approach has been used to write thousands of successful programs, many of them very complex. Microsoft Windows itself was written using structured programming methods. The method works because it allows you to break a complex problem down into a set of smaller, less complex problems.

Object-oriented programming does not replace structured programming; it builds on it. In structured programming, you learned to think of program designs in terms of functions. Each function helped solve a part of the problem at hand. A complete program was a collection of functions working together to solve the problem.

In object-oriented programming you break a problem down into objects instead of functions. An object-oriented program, then, is a collection of objects working together to solve the problem at hand. object-oriented programming is the programming method that utilizes objects as the primary means of dividing a programming problem into smaller, more manageable parts.

An object-oriented program is a collection of objects working together.

Note: Object-oriented programming is usually referred to as OOP, so we will use this abbreviation most of the time throughout the remainder of this book. Some other abbreviations you may encounter in the literature are OOA—object-oriented analysis, and OOD—object-oriented design.

What happened to functions? They are still there in OOP, but now they are contained within objects. Each object contains all the functions which are necessary to its role in the overall program.

What Is an Object?

An object is an instance of a class.

You know that object-oriented programming uses objects to divide a programming problem into smaller, easier to manage parts, but we still haven't defined an object. Simply put, an object is an instance of a class.

In the programs you have written so far, you have used many of the C++ data types. Variables defined for various types could be used to store values. You then used *operators* to manipulate the variables. Then, starting with Chapter 33, you began to work with classes. First, you would design a class and write its member functions. Then, you would declare a variable in a program whose type was that of a class. When you did this, you were creating an object.

Elements of Object-Oriented Programming

You have already seen some of the power of Classes, and the objects you can create from a class. There is a considerable literature of the theory of this approach that explains why this is a more powerful way to write programs. Usually two concepts are discussed: abstraction and encapsulation.

Understanding Abstraction

Abstraction lets you look at just the important facts.

Abstraction is a way of looking at a subject so that you ignore the unimportant details and concentrate instead on the details that are important to you or to your treatment of the subject. That was part of the point behind the paintings of abstract artists like Picasso. Abstract artists ignore unimportant details and paint only the details that are relevant to their subject. Some people become confused on this, remembering paintings that don't look anything like what they claim to be, and think that abstraction is something that makes it harder to see the main subject. Figure 36.1 shows three different abstract views of a cat.

Figure 36.1

Abstraction demonstrated by three different views of a cat.

Perhaps none of the views of the cat in figure 36.1 look exactly like a real cat, but all three views do emphasize an important feature of the cat from a certain viewpoint. These three views of the cat are three different "abstractions" of the total "subject" that comprises a cat.

Additionally, in OOP, abstraction is what lets you think about the problem in terms of the problem instead of in terms of the computer.

Early computer languages were very literal. To use them, you had to spend almost as much time thinking about how the computer would do something as you spent thinking about the problem you set out to solve. The earliest computers were programmed by setting switches or dials on the front panel. Even simple programs were very difficult to plan and enter into the computer because they were dealing with the problem totally in terms of the switches and lights on the front of the computer.

These early languages forced you to think about the problem in terms of the computer instead of in terms of the problem. The most important details, to the programmer, were the myriad of little details concerning the computer instruction set. No wonder early programs were so "user-unfriendly."

One of the first successful computer languages was FORTRAN I (FORTRAN stands for FORmula TRANslator.) FORTRAN was designed to help calculate the results of complex mathematical expressions. FORTRAN allowed programmers to solve math problems on a computer by writing the program in mathematical terms, not computer terms.

Later, COBOL (COmmon Business Oriented Language) allowed programmers to write programs in a language that used ordinary English for its actions, and allowed very long names for data and procedures. This was a big step toward allowing the programmer to think in terms of the problem.

You've already been using one kind of abstraction with functions. With a function, you can give a descriptive name to a complex process or idea, and thus improve your ability to "talk" about that idea in your program. In a similar way, structs let you define simple terms for complex data structures. Finally, in Chapter 33, you began using classes, which combine functional and data abstraction in a way that is much more than the sum of the parts.

Abstraction is a powerful principle that is often misunderstood. If you just remember that abstraction is the ability to concentrate on the important details while ignoring things that don't matter to your program, you will be on the right track.

Understanding Encapsulation

Encapsulation is the idea of hiding or protecting the details of a solution so that the solution itself is easier to understand. Users of the circle class in Chapter 33 didn't have to know how the circumference was being computed, they only had to know how to ask for the answer.

The real world is full of examples of encapsulation. Consider the cat in figure 36.2. It is really true that science still has not learned how a cat purrs, and it is equally true that the "interface" to this function is often extremely simple. A cat's purr is a perfectly encapsulated capability.

Figure 36.2

A cat's purr is very well encapsulated.

For another example of encapsulation, consider the gas pedal of your car. Suppose that when you wanted to speed up the car you had to: 1. Turn a knob to open the fuel flow valve a little more; 2. Turn another knob to speed up the fuel pump; 3. Adjust a lever to change the spark plug timing; and 4. Pull another lever to open an air flow valve. Then, to slow down, you had to reverse this process, while also adjusting several components of the brake system. It would be almost impossible to operate the car, wouldn't it? But instead, all this complexity is encapsulated in the gas and brake pedals.

As a problem becomes more complex, the need for encapsulation becomes greater. With procedural languages a solution to a complex problem will often be expressed as a collection of functions. Although the functions were usually all related to the same problem, often the relationship between the functions would not be readily apparent.

Procedural programming is in some ways analogous to the step-by-step approach to speeding up a car that was outlined above. A good example of the procedural approach is the collection of C++ functions that let a programmer deal with character arrays so that the arrays can be used as pseudo-strings. The string functions can all be recognized as related because they all share a similar naming pattern. The names even give good clues as to the purpose of each function. But sometimes even the most experienced programmer has to look up how to use a particular string function because the solution doesn't encapsulate the details enough.

For example, the line of code below uses the string compare function (strcmp) to test two strings for equality. What should you put in place of the question mark so that the if statement will be true when the two strings are equal?

```
if (strcmp(str1, str2) == ?)
```

Maybe you remember that strcmp returns a zero when the two strings are equal, and maybe you don't. And even if you do remember that fact about strcmp, there is a chance that the next time you come across this line, you may have forgotten the return values for strcmp. The same holds true for the next programmer who looks at the code.

But with the C++ cString class, you don't have to remember these details—they have been encapsulated in an overloaded operator. Now you can write code as follows:

```
if ( str1 == str2 )
```

Both lines of code (the strcmp version and the == version) do the same thing. Down somewhere inside of cString, a function very much like strcmp is probably doing the work of the comparison, but that work has now been encapsulated in the easy-to-use and easy-to-remember ==.

Encapsulation, in a sense, is a complement to abstraction. While abstraction helps you focus on the important details, encapsulation helps you hide the details of a complex implementation.

Reusing Code

One of the greatest benefits of object-oriented languages, and OOP, is that it encourages reusing your code. You don't have to keep resolving the same problem. Instead, you can reuse a previous solution to the same problem, and even customize that solution to fit the needs of your own special problem.

You have probably already been doing some simple code reuse. When you cut a code line or small block of code from one place in a program and paste it into another place in a program, you are reusing that code. This method is inefficient, especially if it is a piece of code that may need to be changed later, but in some instances it is all you need. Its use, however, is limited to extremely simple situations.

The next level of code reuse comes when you start to use functions, and function libraries. Now you can reuse any block of code easily, and if it needs to be changed later all it takes is changing the function, not every place it is used. Even if the function prototype is changed, it is a relatively easy thing to track down every place the old prototype is referenced and do the update.

Classes, with their ability to be refined, enhanced, or changed through inheritance bring the next big step in code reuse. Now you are truly reusing code. If the base class changes, all of the derived classes automatically gain access to the changed base class.

The final level of code reuse comes when you start to use large class libraries. Now you are reusing the solution to an entire, large programming problem. Certainly, there is a lot of time involved in becoming proficient with using one of these large solutions, but the time involved in learning to use the solution is far less than the time involved in solving the problem to begin with.

Learning to Think in Terms of Objects

Often, the hardest part of OOP is learning how to identify the objects (and therefore, the Classes) in any given problem. When you first start to look at a problem, some objects are apparent right away, while others only show up after you start work.

Suppose that you were designing a program to plan the weekly menus for your household. You want a program that will keep your recipes and let you easily retrieve the recipes to plan the meals you will prepare for a week. Just from the statement of the problem, several objects become apparent. First, you will need a recipe class. You will also need a meal class.

As you progress in the design of the program, other classes start to appear. You want to be able to print out a shopping list for the week's groceries, which takes you back to the recipe class—it now needs to know the ingredients in a recipe. An ingredient for a recipe also becomes a new class in your design. As you think about the ingredient class, you realize that you need to be able to scale a recipe to serve different numbers of people, which leads you to discover that if you want to be able to keep your ingredients in conventional cookbook notation, you will need to be able to do arithmetic on compound numbers (fractions) in order to easily scale a recipe. So now you need a compound number class with overloaded operators so that you can do the arithmetic in a natural way.

Notice that the problem you are defining, and the elements of the problem, aren't any different than they would be with ordinary procedural programming. But now you are expressing the problem in terms of the problem itself. You are able to talk about a recipe instead of a recipe database record.

As you gain experience with OOP, you will find yourself thinking more and more of objects when you start to analyze how to solve a particular programming problem.

Summary

This chapter has been more theory than code, but it is helpful to know some of the reasons why C++ and object-oriented programming is considered such an important advance.

Review Questions

1. What is an object-oriented program?

2. What is an object?

3. True or False. Abstraction helps you ignore unimportant details.

Part IX

The Microsoft Foundation Classes

CHAPTER 37

Introduction to the Microsoft Foundation Classes

When you first start studying the Microsoft Foundation Classes (MFC) you may feel like you have taken on the job of eating an elephant. And no wonder. There are well over 100 classes, and each class has several, and in some cases dozens, of public member functions.

But this elephant *can* be eaten—one bite at a time. This chapter will help you take the first couple of nibbles.

This chapter covers the following topics:

♦ Overview of the main components of MFC

♦ The Visual C++ utilities that support MFC

Like the previous chapter on object-oriented programming, this chapter does not contain any code samples. It is intended to help you see the overall picture of MFC, and how Visual C++ helps you work with classes to develop Windows applications.

Application Frameworks

The Microsoft Foundation Class Library (MFC) is an *application framework*. An application framework is a class library that encapsulates all of the functionality necessary to manage the user interface and overall architecture portions of a program. Modern graphical environments such as Microsoft Windows are extremely complex, and as such they are ideal candidates for abstraction and encapsulation by a carefully designed class library.

Components of the Microsoft Foundation Classes

The Microsoft Foundation Class library was designed to encapsulate the details of the Microsoft Windows API (Application Programming Interface). The Windows API is extremely complex. The documentation alone requires three large books. MFC classes can be divided into several broad categories, depending on what role they play in the application.

Almost all MFC classes are descended from a single parent class named CObject. CObject contains support for several useful features which you may want to use in your own classes, including serialization, debugging aids, and runtime class identification. *Serialization* is a method of saving an object to disk and restoring it later, which is also called *object persistence*.

Application Architecture Support

Every program must have a basic architecture that supports things like overall program layout and coordination, data handling, managing the display, routing commands, and so on. That is the function of this group of classes. Classes in this category include the following:

◆ CWinApp. Every MFC application must have one, and only one, CWinApp object. This class encapsulates all of the basics of the application. It contains the equivalent of the main() function you have become accustomed to using. Actually, a Windows application (as opposed to a DOS or Quickwin application) does not have a main() function. The main function of a Windows program is called winmain(). winmain() fulfills the same purpose for Windows applications as does main() in the programs you have been writing. But with MFC, you never need to write a winmain() because it has been encapsulated in the CWinApp class.

◆ CCmdTarget. Windows is a *message-driven* environment. Every action that the user takes generates a message that reflects what action was taken. A Windows program interacts with the user by receiving the messages and taking actions based on the message contents. Most of the messages an

MFC application receives are what are known as *command messages*, so the base class for all classes that need to receive and act on messages is named CCmdTarget—Class Command Target.

You will never use CCmdTarget directly in your programs. Instead, you will use one of the classes which have been derived from CCmdTarget. The two major application architecture classes which are derived from CCmdTarget are CDocument and CView. You will derive your own documents and views from these two classes.

♦ CDocument. Every application needs data, or it doesn't have a reason to exist. Most applications need a way to manage reading their data from a data source such as a disk file, and often, a way of writing data back to the disk or other medium. CDocument is intended to coordinate all data management tasks in an application. You do not use CDocument directly, but rather you derive your own specialized version from it to fit the needs of your application.

♦ CView. Most applications must have a way to show their data to the user, and accept input to change or otherwise interact with the data. CView is a base class you use to derive your own views of the data, and contains the necessary functionality to help you manage the interaction between the user and the application's data.

♦ CDocTemplate. This class is the base class for two derived classes named CSingleDocTemplate and CMultiDocTemplate. These template classes coordinate the creation of new documents and views. You will use CSingleDocTemplate if your application is a *Single Document Interface* (SDI) application, and CMultiDocTemplate if your application is a *Multiple Document Interface* application (MDI).

SDI applications have only one document open at a time, and only one main display window. The Windows Notepad application is an SDI application. MDI applications can have multiple documents and multiple views of their documents open in multiple windows, all at the same time. The Visual C++ Application Workbench is an example of an MDI application. Figure 37.2 shows Application Workbench with two open windows.

Windows Interface and Display Support

Windows is a highly visually oriented environment. As such, there are many types of objects to be displayed. Every type of display object in Windows must appear in a rectangular area called, appropriately enough, a window. MFC includes a very large selection of classes that support the display of all the native Windows visual objects, as well as classes for drawing on-screen or on another output device.

These are the classes you will use to display the actual windows, menus, toolbars, dialog boxes, and controls in your application. These classes also include the various objects such as pens, brushes, and device contexts used to draw the actual contents of a window.

Objects and Windows Objects

Windows 3.1 is not an object-oriented environment in the sense we have been talking about as object-oriented programming. Although you will sometimes see the standard Windows display items, such as buttons, list boxes, and so on described as "objects," this is only a convenient term. These objects do not fit the OOP definition of an object as "an instance of a class." When they have been encapsulated within an MFC class, however, instances of that MFC class are true objects, in the OOP sense.

Following is a summary of MFC's classes that support the various methods of creating visual output to a Windows program:

◆ CWnd is the main base class for all types of windows within MFC. There are a large number of classes derived from CWnd that cover a wide range of standard Windows display types, but you can also derive your own classes from CWnd if one of the predefined classes does not fit your needs. Since everything that appears on the display in a Windows application must appear in a window, this base class is second only to CObject in the number of classes derived from it.

All windows in Microsoft Windows consist of two parts—a frame and a display area. In Windows terminology, the frame is often called the *nonclient area*, while the display area is called the *client* area. Windows manages most of the user's interaction with the frame, which includes the border of the window, the title bar area, any menus, and any scroll bars. The programmer controls and manages the contents of the display area. MFC implements this architecture through its frame and view classes.

◆ CFrameWnd, CMDIFrameWnd, and CMDIChildWnd. All MFC applications use a frame window as the application's main window. CFrameWnd is a base class for an SDI application main window, while CMDIFrameWnd serves as the base for an MDI application's main window. In an MDI application, each view of the data is presented in a CMDIChildWnd, which is owned by the application's single CMDIFrameWnd. In an MDI application, therefore, the CMDIFrameWnd owns and manages one or more CMDIChildWnds.

Figure 37.1 shows a skeleton SDI application created with MFC, and points out some of the components of the application as they relate to the various MFC classes. Figure 37.2 does the same thing for a skeleton MDI application.

♦ CView. Frame windows do not actually display the application's data. They provide a means of controlling the display of the data through the next set of classes—the view classes. The view classes are intended to work in the client area within a CFrameWnd or CMDIChildWnd. All view classes are derived from CView. This is indeed the same CView that is considered a part of the application architecture. It is the bridge between the architecture of the application and the display of the data.

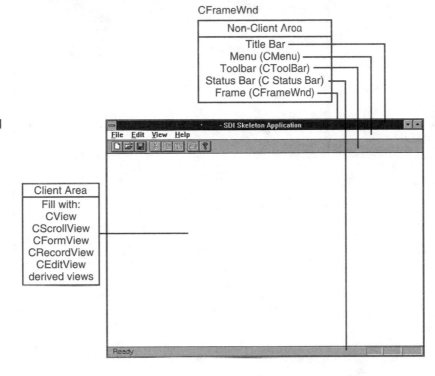

Figure 37.1

A skeleton SDI application.

Three view classes are derived from CView:

♦ CScrollView is a base class for any view that needs scrolling capabilities.

♦ CFormView is actually derived from CScrollView, so it also has scrolling capability. A CFormView's appearance can be designed like a dialog, so this view provides a way to design form-based views such as those frequently encountered in database applications.

♦ CEditView is a text-editing view. It includes scrolling capacity, along with the ability to mark, cut, paste, and replace its text contents.

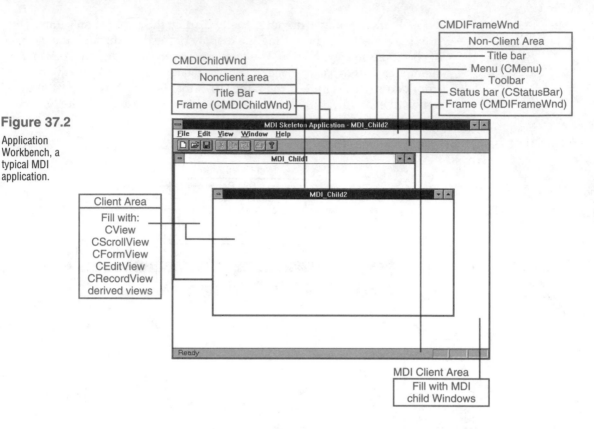

Figure 37.2

Application
Workbench, a
typical MDI
application.

Next to views and menus, the most common way a user interacts with a Windows application is through dialog boxes. The base class for all dialog boxes in MFC is CDialog. You can derive your own dialog box from CDialog, and then fill in the design using App Studio, or you can use one of the common dialog boxes supplied with Windows. The Common dialog boxes include dialogs for opening and saving files, for controlling printing, for searching and replacing, and for selecting fonts and colors. Figure 37.3 shows the File Open common dialog box.

Dialogs and form views both utilize Windows controls, and MFC includes classes for all standard Windows controls. These controls include the usual buttons, edit boxes, list and combo boxes, radio buttons, and checkboxes. In addition, MFC includes classes which help support custom controls such as bitmap buttons, control bars, and even controls for use with Windows for Pens. You should be familiar with most of these controls by now from working with dialogs in Visual C++, but just in case there are some you didn't notice, figure 37.4 shows a sample dialog with all of the standard controls.

Figure 37.3

The File Open
common dialog
box.

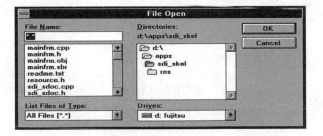

Figure 37.4

A sample dialog
illustrating
Windows controls.

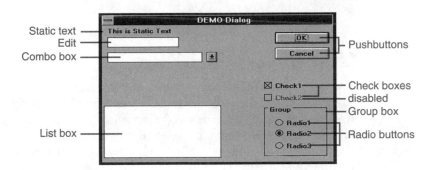

The final vital class in this category is the CMenu class. Although most of your work with menus will be handled through the App Studio, this class is useful when you need to dynamically manage your menus while your application is running.

General Purpose Classes

You have already used some of the general purpose classes. The general purpose classes are a set of classes that would be useful in any program, not just a Windows program. These classes include the following:

♦ *A group of what Microsoft calls general support classes.* CString is typical of this group of classes. Also included here are CTime and CTimeSpan, a pair of classes for storing and manipulating dates and times.

♦ *The collection classes.* You have already learned about these classes. To summarize, the collection classes provide a means of storing groups of related data. They are all able to dynamically size themselves. Three types of collections are supported: arrays, lists, and maps.

♦ CFile. A class that encapsulates C++ binary file input-output operations.

◆ *The diagnostic and error-handling classes.* Every application and every programmer, sooner or later, will encounter a bug or an unrecoverable error. Through the CException, CDumpContext, CMemoryState, and CRuntimeClass classes, you have a powerful set of tools to help you diagnose problems and bugs, and to provide a mechanism to help your program gracefully exit when the (hopefully) rare unrecoverable error occurs.

This has been a very superficial look at some of the classes included with MFC. You should now have a better idea of just how big an elephant there is here to be eaten. A detailed examination of these classes needs a book all to itself. One such book is Que's *Using Visual C++.*

Visual C++ Utilities

The Microsoft Foundation Classes alone are a very powerful tool for creating Windows applications; but Visual C++ includes several utilities which are carefully designed to assist you in developing applications with MFC so that you can easily take full advantage of the power of the framework. The combination of MFC and the utilities included with Visual C++, working together in a highly integrated manner, adds up to a capability that is considerably greater than just the sum of its parts.

AppWizard

AppWizard is a part of the Visual C++ workbench that will create the basic files for your application, based on your choices of what features you want your application to have. Every time you begin a new program, you need a basic set of modules. For most programs, this set of modules includes a main program file, a module to manage the program's data, a module to display the data, and a module to coordinate interactions between the user interface and the data management modules. A Microsoft Windows program also requires a resource file and a definition file. As you learned in Chapter 34, any program that consists of multiple smaller program files requires a project file.

You could set up a set of skeleton modules and use them as boilerplate by copying your skeleton files into a new directory for each new program and then changing various names to fit the name of your new program. This would work, and would certainly be faster than writing it all from scratch each time, but AppWizard provides a better way.

AppWizard will create all the basic files you need for each program for you. It also allows you to specify the basic characteristics of the program, characteristics that would require considerable hand customization of the boilerplate code used previously.

Figure 37.5 shows the main AppWizard screen. In the next chapter you learn how to use AppWizard to create the basic files for your first MFC application.

Figure 37.5

AppWizard main screen.

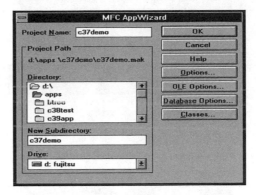

Note that you run AppWizard only one time for a given application. It is not intended to be a full code generator, but only a very efficient way to lay out the basic files that your program needs.

AppStudio

AppWizard generates only the basic application. You must add the menus, icons, dialogs, and other details that contribute to solving your application's problem. These items—the icons, menus, dialogs, and so on—are collectively known as *resources*. The Windows architecture allows these items to be defined in a separate file known as a *resource file*, which can be linked with the application as a separate part of the program.

Figure 37.6 shows AppStudio with the initial resource selection dialog open. The listbox on the left, labeled Type, shows the various types of resources you can create and modify using AppStudio. The list includes all defined types of Windows resources. Most of the names are self-explanatory, but a brief description will help bring things into focus.

Accelerator is a table of definitions of an application's accelerator keys. These are the special key combinations that allow the user to quickly access features without going through menus and dialog boxes.

Bitmap is a picture that is shown on a button face or in a dialog. The Visual C++ toolbar is a bitmap that was created in AppStudio. AppStudio includes a tool for drawing and editing bitmaps that has been specialized for Toolbar and Button faces.

Dialog is the layout of a dialog box, including all of its controls. AppStudio includes a very easy-to-use dialog editor to help you lay out your dialogs.

Figure 37.6

The initial screen of the AppStudio application.

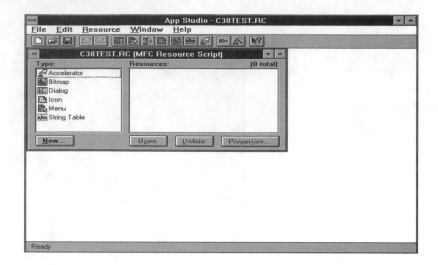

Icon. An icon is another type of bitmap, in this case one that is a specific size. AppStudio includes a tool for drawing and saving icons, or you can paste them in from other Windows applications.

Menu contains the application's menu resources. The menu tool lets you create menus as easily as you use them. You will use this tool in Chapter 40 to edit a sample application's menus.

In the past, the utility used to create and edit these resources has been called a *resource editor*, but Microsoft wanted to draw attention to the special nature of the Visual C++ resource editor, so they called it *AppStudio*. AppStudio is not the first resource editor to provide one-place editing for all of an application's resources. AppStudio is, however, the first resource editor to provide full integration with an application framework and development environment's project files. The key to AppStudio's integration with MFC and the rest of Visual C++ is the final utility covered in this chapter—ClassWizard.

ClassWizard

ClassWizard is perhaps the most unique tool in Visual C++. It is the glue that brings together your program code, AppStudio, the project, and the Microsoft Foundation Classes. One of the most tedious jobs faced by a Windows programmer is the task of tying the various menu, accelerator, and dialog resources created in a resource editor, or even AppStudio, to the appropriate parts of the program. ClassWizard provides a point-and-click method of doing this.

Other capabilities of ClassWizard are shown on the other three tabs. Figure 37.7 shows ClassWizard with the Message Maps tab selected. You will learn about all of ClassWizard's capabilities except OLE Automation in the next three chapters.

Figure 37.7

ClassWizard, with the Message Maps tab selected.

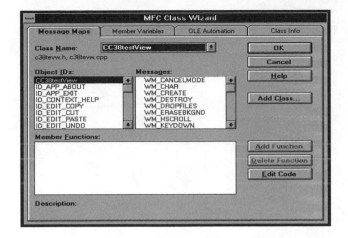

Summary

The Microsoft Foundation Classes, combined with the integrated tools in Visual C++, provide a powerful, feature-rich combination for developing Windows applications. That rich feature set brings with it a lot to learn before you can employ its full power, however. Like eating an elephant, though, you can do it if you approach it one "byte" at a time.

Review Questions

1. Of which MFC class will every MFC application have one and only one occurrence?

2. What are two terms for the technique of saving an object to a disk file and then restoring it later?

3. True or false: A CFrameWnd is the main window for an MDI application.

4. The Visual C++ tool you use to draw dialogs is named _____.

CHAPTER 38

Your First MFC Application

The first step in learning to create Windows applications with Visual C++ and the Microsoft Foundation Classes is to become familiar with how to create the basic skeleton of an application and the general layout of a typical application and its pieces. That is the subject of this chapter.

This chapter covers the following topics:

♦ Using App Wizard to create a skeleton application

♦ The capabilities of the skeleton application

♦ The App Wizard generated files

In this chapter you will create an MFC version of the traditional "Hello World" program and then examine its basic components to see how the application is put together.

App Wizard

You should start development of most of your MFC Windows applications with App Wizard. The next section walks you through the steps of using App Wizard to generate the initial files for your application. As was explained in the previous chapter, you only use App Wizard once for each application. After App Wizard has generated the skeleton files for your program, you use other Visual C++ tools to flesh out the details.

Using App Wizard

To use App Wizard, you must already be running Application Workbench. When Application Workbench is active, but before starting App Wizard, it is a good idea to close your current project, if one is open, and to also close all active windows in Application Workbench. To close the current project, pull down the **P**roject menu and select **C**lose. If you do not have a project active, the **C**lose menu item will be disabled. To close all active windows, pull down the **W**indow menu and select Close **A**ll.

Tip: If you follow the above sequence to close a project, close the Project before closing all active windows. The next time you open that project, all the project's active windows will also be opened because when you close a project, a list of the open windows is stored with the project.

To start App Wizard, pull down the **P**roject menu and choose App Wizard. Figure 38.1 shows the main App Wizard screen, filled in with information about a new project.

Figure 38.1

App Wizard main screen.

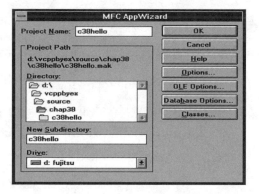

Keep each project in a separate directory.

Fill in the Project **N**ame field with the name you want your executable program to have when it is compiled. Figure 38.1 shows this field filled in with C38HELLO, so the compiled application's name will be C38HELLO.EXE. Underneath the Project **N**ame field is a group of controls that allow you to control the disk drive location and name of the directory where your project will be kept. You must keep each new project in a separate directory, because App Wizard-generated applications all have some file names in common, even though the files would have different contents on different projects.

When you are satisfied with the project name and location, you can move on to tell App Wizard what kind of application you want to create. You start this step by clicking on the **O**ptions button, which will open the Options dialog. The Options dialog is shown in figure 38.2 with App Wizard's default options checked.

Figure 38.2

App Wizard
Options dialog.

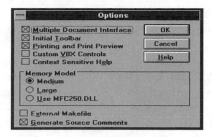

The sample application for this chapter will use App Wizard's default options, so you don't need to change anything in the main App Wizard Options dialog. The selected options will cause App Wizard to generate the skeleton of an MDI application, with a toolbar, and printing-with-print-preview capabilities. You will not be using any VBX controls or any help in this application.

> **Note:** VBX controls are custom controls developed for use in the Visual Basic environment. MFC supports the inclusion of VBX controls that are compatible with Visual Basic 1.0 in MFC applications. There is a wide variety of VBX controls available from both Microsoft and independent vendors.

You will not need to worry about changing memory models until you start working on large applications. The medium memory model is suitable for most Windows programs. MFC250.DLL is a special format DLL that contains most of the MFC library already compiled. If you need to distribute several separate executable files, you can save room by using this DLL because you only have to distribute one copy of most of the MFC functionality which can then be shared by all of the executables.

The final two options in the Options dialog are External Makefile and Generate Source Comments. External makefiles (project files) are useful if you want to work with extremely large projects because Application Workbench (as of Visual C++ Version 1.5) will compile a maximum of 128 files in one compilation run. The Generate Source Comments option causes App Wizard to add extensive comments to the source code files it generates. These comments make it much easier to follow what is being done in the files, and are good examples of professional commenting techniques. When you have finished choosing the main options for your application, click OK and the Options dialog will close and return you to the main App Wizard dialog box.

The next two buttons under the Options button open dialogs that let you select support for two advanced features of MFC. The first, OLE Options, enables you to easily add support for Object Linking and Embedding. The second, Database Options, enables you to add support for database operations through Microsoft's ODBC (Open DataBase Connectivity) libraries. Both of these options are beyond the scope of this book.

The last button is labeled **C**lasses. When you enter a name for you project in the main App Wizard dialog, App Wizard pre-assigns names to the classes and files that will form the skeleton of your application. For most simple projects, these names will work very well and you do not even need to use this button. If you expect to add additional views or documents to your application, however, you might want to change the name of the class, header, and implementation files to better fit your naming conventions. You can also use this dialog to change the initial view type from a CView to any of the other standard view types, such as CEditView or CFormView. Figure 38.3 shows the Classes dialog with the App Wizard generated view class selected in the New Application Classes list. The Base Class combo box is open to show the available choices. For the sample application in this chapter, use the default CView selection.

Figure 38.3

The Classes dialog in App Wizard.

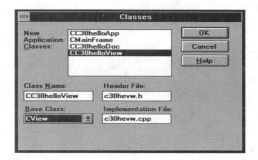

Building the Application

When you have finished making your selections from App Wizard's dialogs, you are ready to have App Wizard generate your skeleton application. There isn't a button labeled "Generate Application" in App Wizard. Instead, you just click the OK button. App Wizard displays the New Application Information dialog, shown in figure 38.4. This dialog gives you a chance to review the choices you have made all in one place. If you see something that isn't what you wanted, click the Cancel button to return to App Wizard so that you can change the options. If you are satisfied with the specifications, click the **C**reate button to have App Wizard generate your skeleton files.

It has long been a tradition among C and C++ programmers that the first program you should write in any new version of a language should print the words *Hello, World* on its output screen. It would be a shame not to do this with your new MFC application, so here is how you can have this application print "Hello MFC World" on its output screen. If you used the name C38HELLO as suggested above, there will be a file in your project named C38HEVW.CPP. Open this file in Application Workbench and locate the function named CC38helloView::OnDraw. Add the two lines of code shown in listing 38.1 immediately following the comment that begins with // TO DO:.

Listing 38.1. Code to add to *OnDraw*.

```
CString hello = "Hello MFC World";
pDC->TextOut( 10, 10, hello);
```

These two lines create a CString named `hello`, which holds the phrase you want to output. The second line causes the CString to be written on the view's client area beginning at location 10, 10 from the upper left corner of the client area. `pDC` is a pointer to an instance of an MFC class named `CDC`, which encapsulates a Windows *device context*. A *device context* is how you write output in Microsoft Windows applications. The one you are using here is passed to the `OnDraw` function by the application framework when it calls the `OnDraw` function. This is all handled for you by MFC.

Figure 38.4

The App Wizard
New Application
Information dialog.

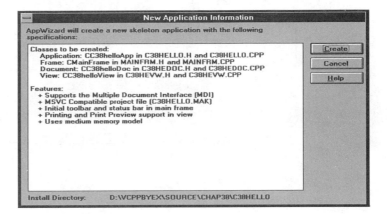

Now all you need to do is compile your program. This step is much the same as what you have been doing all along in the book. However, the compile will take longer, because App Wizard generated several program files, and there are other files to be included, such as the application's *resource file*. The resource file will be discussed in more detail in following chapters. For now, just be aware that it contains your application's menus, icons, dialogs, and other visual elements. To compile your program, you do what you've been doing all along—pull down the Application Workbench **P**roject menu and choose **B**uild C38HELLO.EXE.

Capabilities of the App Wizard Application

When the application finishes compiling, run the completed application. At first glance, your MFC application doesn't appear very much different from the Quickwin applications you have been writing. Perhaps the biggest difference is not immediately noticeable, but it is a huge one—this application is a true Windows application. It has full access to all the capabilities and services of Microsoft Windows.

Figure 38.5 shows the C38HELLO application the way it will look when you first start it. One difference between this MFC application and a Quickwin application is immediately apparent just below the menu—the toolbar. This kind of sophisticated user interface option is beyond the capability of Quickwin. Try out the various menu options to get a feel for what the basic application can do.

Figure 38.5

The C38HELLO application.

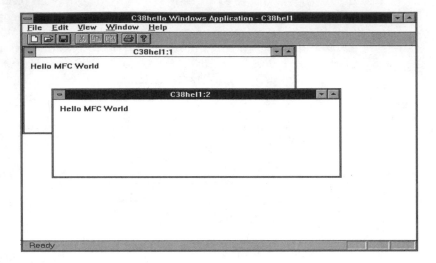

Work through the other menus. Use the arrow keys to cycle through the various menu options and notice what happens on the status bar at the bottom of the window. Each menu option displays a prompt which gives a brief description of what that option does. When you add your own enhancements to the menus, it is just a matter of typing the phrase you want displayed to add similar prompts to your own menu items.

Try out all of the options on all of the menus to see what they do. Be sure to experiment with the items on the File menu. Several of these, including New, Open, Save, Save As, Print, and Print Setup items utilize the Windows common dialog boxes. Of course you can't actually open or save any files with the program yet because you haven't implemented any code to actually do the work. Be sure to try out both Print and Print Preview.

Try using the New option on the Window menu to create several new windows, minimize some of the windows and see how they display an icon. Try out the Cascade and Tile options. All of this functionality is built in to the application framework.

Finally, pull down the Help menu and choose the About option. Even though you didn't specify Help, there is a dialog that you can easily customize to give information about your application.

As you add your own data and views to the application, the capabilities of this basic application are all in your own application. You can concentrate on the details of your particular application, and leave the Windows management to MFC. Certainly, there is still a lot you need to learn before you will be able to write complex applications, but while you are learning you will still be able to create full featured Windows programs.

The App Wizard Generated Files

The C38HELLO application which was generated by App Wizard consists of 16 files in the main C38HELLO directory and 4 additional files in a subdirectory named RES. One of these files, README.TXT, contains a brief description of each of these 20 files. Twelve of the 20 files are usually maintained by Visual C++ utilities such as ClassWizard and AppStudio. The other eight files are the ones you will modify to add your own application's functionality. The remainder of this chapter takes a closer look at these eight files. The eight files are actually four sets of header (.H) and implementation (.CPP) files which relate to the four main parts of your application.

As you read through this section, it will be helpful if you open each source file as it is discussed. The discussions that follow do not cover every line of the files, but focus on small portions of each file. The lines of code that are being discussed will be shown in the text, but it will be helpful if you are able to see the overall location in the file.

The Main Application Object

In the previous chapter, you learned that each MFC program must contain one, and only one, object derived from CWinApp. The files C38HELLO.H and C38HELLO.CPP contain the implementation of the CWinApp—derived class for this application. The main application object is responsible for overall management of the application. It maintains a list of the active documents in the application, and is the central "dispatcher" that routes commands to other parts of the application.

Because this may be your first time to look at actual production C++ code, we will look at some of the code in these files that is typical of the kind of code used by professional programmers to make compiling and debugging their programs easier. The first such code appears almost immediately at the beginning of C38HELLO.H, with the following three lines:

```
#ifndef __AFXWIN_H__
    #error include 'stdafx.h' before including this file...
#endif
```

These lines are a preprocessor directive in the form of a test to be sure that the main MFC include file, stdafx.h, has been included in the application. The #ifndef test on the first of these lines refers to a preprocessor definition that is set within the stdafx.h file when it is included in the compile. If the preprocessor constant AFXWIN_H has not been defined, stdafx.h has not yet been included in the compile and an error is displayed. The reason for trying to detect this kind of condition is that often the compiler errors that result from leaving out an include file do not directly implicate the omission and it can sometimes be very time consuming trying to determine which header has been left out. This message removes that doubt. You are probably wondering by now where stdafx.h was included. It is the first include file listed at the beginning of C38HELLO.CPP.

The remainder of C38HELLO.H is devoted to the class definition of the main application class, which is named CC38helloApp and is derived from CWinApp. The last part of the class definition contains a section of code you will become very familiar with—the message map. This part of the header file contains the prototypes of message processing functions. It begins with

```
//{{AFX_MSG(CC38helloApp)
```

and ends with

```
//}}AFX_MSG
DECLARE_MESSAGE_MAP()
```

Windows uses messages to communicate user actions to your application.

The beginning and ending comments are in a special format which is used by ClassWizard to locate the place to insert its message map function prototypes. The final line is a preprocessor macro that inserts appropriate message map handling function prototypes into the header file. Messages are how Windows and MFC communicate user actions to your application, so the message map is critical to its proper operation. You do not need to modify this code—indeed, you should not modify it but leave it in place as-is for ClassWizard to maintain.

Now open the implementation file, C38HELLO.CPP. This file begins with #include statements just as you are accustomed to seeing, followed by some additional preprocessor directives that are related to debugging, and then the message map itself. This section serves a different purpose than the function prototypes in the header file. This section will cause an actual main message processing function to be generated for this part of the application. You will learn a little more about message processing in the final chapter of this book. Listing 38.2 shows the message map part of C39HELLO.CPP. You will see similar constructs in nearly all App Wizard and ClassWizard generated class header and implementation files. In the next chapter, you will learn how to add your own message handler to a message map.

Listing 38.2. The Message Map section of C38HELLO.APP.

```
BEGIN_MESSAGE_MAP(CC38helloApp, CWinApp)
    //{{AFX_MSG_MAP(CC38helloApp)
    ON_COMMAND(ID_APP_ABOUT, OnAppAbout)
        // NOTE - the ClassWizard will add and remove. . .
        //    DO NOT EDIT what you see in these blocks . . .
    //}}AFX_MSG_MAP
    // Standard file based document commands
    ON_COMMAND(ID_FILE_NEW, CWinApp::OnFileNew)
    ON_COMMAND(ID_FILE_OPEN, CWinApp::OnFileOpen)
    // Standard print setup command
    ON_COMMAND(ID_FILE_PRINT_SETUP, CWinApp::OnFilePrintSetup)
END_MESSAGE_MAP()
```

Following the message map there is an empty constructor function for your derived `CWinApp` class. You rarely need to add anything here because the actual construction of the application takes place later in `InitInstance`.

The last thing before the `InitInstance` function definition is a line that declares the one and only instance of your application object:

```
CC38helloApp NEAR theApp;
```

Because this declaration is located outside of any functions, your application object, named `theApp`, is a global variable that is constructed before the program begins executing.

Finally, there is the `InitInstance()` function. This is where the work of building the application's main window and first views is done. The ClassWizard generated code is well commented to help you understand what each section is doing, but there are some parts that you might find a little confusing. The first of these is shown in listing 38.3.

Listing 38.3. *CMultiDocTemplate* construction in *InitInstance()*.

```
CMultiDocTemplate* pDocTemplate;
pDocTemplate = new CMultiDocTemplate(
    IDR_C38HELTYPE,
    RUNTIME_CLASS(CC38helloDoc),
    RUNTIME_CLASS(CMDIChildWnd),
    RUNTIME_CLASS(CC38helloView));
AddDocTemplate(pDocTemplate);
```

Listing 38.3 contains only three statements. The first declares a variable that is a pointer to a `CMultiDocTemplate` variable. The next statement, which actually occupies five lines, constructs a `CMultiDocTemplate` object and assigns it to the pointer variable. We will come back to that statement in a moment. Finally, the pointer variable is passed to a function named `AddDocTemplate`. The `AddDocTemplate` function is a member of `CWinApp` that will add the pointer to a `CPtrList` member of `CWinApp`. (`CPtrList` is one of the collection classes.) This list is used internally by `CWinApp` whenever a new document needs to be opened.

The new operator allocates memory for a variable on the heap.

The five lines in listing 38.3 that construct the actual `CMultiDocTemplate` object contain an operator that you haven't learned about yet—the `new` operator. `new` is a memory allocation operator. So far all the variables you have used have been destroyed when they go out of scope. In a real application, however, you often need to allocate a variable that will not go out of scope so that it will be available for use later. The `new` operator lets you create such a variable. In technical terms, it causes the memory to be allocated in an area known as the *heap*. Variables that are allocated on the heap do not go out of scope when you exit the block of code where you allocated them. Instead, they remain allocated until you specifically deallocate them. To deallocate a variable which was allocated on the heap using the `new` operator, call the `delete` operator with the variable you want to deallocate. Here is an example for the variable created in listing 38.3:

```
delete pDocTemplate;
```

Actually, you do not need to delete this particular variable because `CWinApp` automatically deletes all members of the template list when the application ends.

Listing 38.4 shows the code that creates the main frame window for C38HELLO. The process is similar to the creation of the template above. First a pointer variable is declared and initialized with a `CMainFrame` pointer to an object which has been allocated on the heap using the `new` operator. Next, the `CMainFrame` member function `LoadFrame` is called to initialize the frame window. If `LoadFrame` fails, it will return `False`, which in turn causes the application's initialization to fail by returning `False` from `InitInstance`.

Listing 38.4. Creation of the application's main frame window.

```
// create main MDI Frame window
CMainFrame* pMainFrame = new CMainFrame;
if (!pMainFrame->LoadFrame(IDR_MAINFRAME))
    return FALSE;
m_pMainWnd = pMainFrame;
```

The rest of `InitInstance` creates and initializes the main frame window for the application, opens a new, empty file, and then causes the main window to be shown and updated. Your application will "appear" on-screen when the `ShowWindow` function is called near the end of `InitInstance`.

The remainder of C38HELLO.CPP contains the class definition and implementation for the application's About dialog. You will learn about dialogs in the final chapter.

Where Is *WinMain( )*?

In Chapter 37 you learned that Windows applications have a function named `WinMain` instead of the `main` function you had been using up to that point, and that your `CWinApp` object would have your program's `WinMain` function. Now, you have just finished going through your first `CWinApp` derived program, and there is still no sign of `WinMain`. Where is it?

When you include the main MFC header file, stdafx.h, it contains the necessary directives to include a `WinMain` function in your application. Because it is included by the preprocessor, you normally won't see the code, but it is there in your compiled application.

The order of events when your application starts is as follows:

1. Your global `CWinApp` object is constructed. (C++ Global objects are constructed before the main program begins.)

2. `WinMain` begins executing.

3. `WinMain` calls your `CWinApp InitInstance()` function, which constructs the application's main windows and causes them to be displayed. `InitInstance()` then returns control to `WinMain`.

4. `WinMain` then calls the `CWinApp Run()` member function, which controls the remainder of your application's execution.

The Main Frame Window

The frame window manages the menus, toolbar, status bar, and active view.

In addition to a CWinApp derived object, every MFC application will also have a main frame window object. The frame window for each application generated by App Wizard is implemented in the files MAINFRM.H and MAINFRM.CPP. The frame window assists the main application object by managing the application's menus, toolbar, status bar, and the current active view.

Because C38HELLO is an MDI application, its main frame class is derived from `CMDIFrameWnd`. The class prototype is defined in MAINFRM.H, and the class is named `CMainFrame`. App Wizard generates the same main frame class name for both SDI and MDI applications, even though the classes are derived from different base classes because there is no need to differentiate this particular class name.

The first statement in C38HELLO.H after the class name declaration reads:

```
DECLARE_DYNAMIC(CMainFrame)
```

There is a matching statement near the beginning of MAINFRM.CPP:

```
IMPLEMENT_DYNAMIC(CMainFrame, CMDFrameWnd)
```

What are these statements? The clue comes from the fact that there is no semicolon on the end of the statements. These are preprocessor macros which are very similar to other preprocessor substitutions you learned about in Chapter 7. This particular substitution adds function prototypes to the CMainFrame class header, and then adds the function definitions to the class implementation, which will allow you access run time information about the class of an object.

Look at the code that begins on about line 31 of MAINFRM.CPP. Listing 38.5 shows part of this code.

Listing 38.5. The toolbar and status bar control arrays.

```
// toolbar buttons - IDs are command buttons
static UINT BASED_CODE buttons[] =
{
    // same order as in the bitmap 'toolbar.bmp'
    ID_FILE_NEW,
    ID_FILE_OPEN,
    ID_FILE_SAVE,
        ID_SEPARATOR,.
.

.
static UINT BASED_CODE indicators[] =
{
    ID_SEPARATOR,              // status line indicator
    ID_INDICATOR_CAPS,
.

.
```

This section of code contains two arrays that will be used to control construction of the toolbar and the status bar. The names in the arrays, ID_FILE_NEW, ID_INDICATOR_CAPS, and so on, are defined in one of the MFC include files, named AFXRES.H, which is included in your application when you include stdafx.h. The values refer to standard MFC menu and status bar resources which are available to all applications. You will learn how to use AppStudio to design your own resources in the last chapter of this book.

The final part of the CMainFrame class we will examine is the OnCreate member function, which is shown in listing 38.6. OnCreate is called as part of the processing that is initiated by the LoadFrame function call in InitInstance in the main application. The call to LoadFrame is shown in listing 38.4. OnCreate receives one parameter, a structure known as a Create Structure, which contains information about what kind of window is being created.

Listing 38.6. *The OnCreate* function of *CMainFrame*.

```
int CMainFrame::OnCreate(LPCREATESTRUCT lpCreateStruct)
{
    if (CMDIFrameWnd::OnCreate(lpCreateStruct) == -1)
        return -1;


    if (!m_wndToolBar.Create(this) ||
        !m_wndToolBar.LoadBitmap(IDR_MAINFRAME) ||
        !m_wndToolBar.SetButtons(buttons,
          sizeof(buttons)/sizeof(UINT)))
    {
        TRACE("Failed to create toolbar\n");
        return -1;        // fail to create
    }


    if (!m_wndStatusBar.Create(this) ||
        !m_wndStatusBar.SetIndicators(indicators,
          sizeof(indicators)/sizeof(UINT)))
    {
        TRACE("Failed to create status bar\n");
        return -1;         // fail to create
    }


    return 0;
}
```

OnCreate does three things. First, it calls the base class OnCreate function, passing the create structure along. Next, it constructs the application's toolbar. The member variable, m_winToolBar, is declared in MAINFRM.H as a member of CMainFrame. The toolbar is constructed using the buttons array shown in listing 38.5. Finally, the status bar is constructed, following a similar pattern to the construction of the toolbar.

An MFC Naming Convention

By now you may have noticed a pattern in the naming of member variables in the MFC classes. In case you haven't, look back through the listings and program files you have been studying in this chapter for variables whose names begin with m_. You should find several, including m_wndStatusBar and m_wndToolBar in MAINFRM.H, and m_pMainWnd, which is found in C38HELLO.CPP and is shown in use in listing 38.4.

These variables are all member variables of classes. MFC uses the m_ prefix to identify variables that are members of classes. This is only a naming convention, it has no meaning to the compiler, but is intended as a convenience when you are reading the code to help you separate class member variables from local variables by their names. Many MFC programmers follow this convention in their own source code.

The final section of code in MAINFRM.CPP begins right after the comment— // CMainFrame diagnostics—and includes two functions named AssertValid and Dump. You can add code to these functions to test whether the main frame variable has been properly initialized and then call AssertValid to determine if the variable is valid. Similarly, you can add code to the Dump function to list out its member variables to a file or debugging display window. The #ifdef __DEBUG, #endif preprocessor directives mean that these functions are only defined when you are creating a Debug version of your program, so any place where you call them should also be included in a similar #ifdef __DEBUG, #endif construct, or one of the predefined debugging macros that make use of these functions. Note that there is a double underscore preceding DEBUG.

Debug and Release Versions

The Project Options dialog box contains a radio button selection labeled Build Mode which offers two choices: Debug or Release.

Typically, a Debug version of a program contains many debugging aids, special displays, internal validity tests, and so on, that make the code slower and larger than will be needed once the program is completed.

A Release version, on the other hand, has all the debugging aids removed, and is frequently compiled with special compiler switches that optimize the code for either speed of small executable size. The optimization can noticeably improve a program's performance, but causes longer compile times, so programmers typically turn of the optimization switches during program development so that they can have the fastest possible compiles. When you choose Release, Application Workbench will automatically optimize your code for smallest executable size.

The Document

The document manages the application's data.

When you start adding your own data to an application, you will very likely work with the CDocument object to manage, store, and load that data. For C38HELLO, the CDocument class is defined in C38HEDOC.H and C38HEDOC.CPP, and is named CC38helloDoc.

One of the most important functions in the CDocument class is the Serialize function. This function is called by the framework to save data to a disk file when you choose **S**ave or Save **A**s from the **F**ile menu, or to load it back when you choose **O**pen. This process is called *serialization*. Listing 38.7 shows the skeleton Serialize function generated by ClassWizard.

Listing 38.7. The *Serialize* function.

```
void CC38helloDoc::Serialize(CArchive& ar)
{
    if (ar.IsStoring())
    {
        // TODO: add storing code here
    }
    else
    {
        // TODO: add loading code here
    }
}
```

The parameter passed to Serialize is a special type of file known as a CArchive. The archive object has overloaded operators that simplify reading or writing information contained in MFC CObject derived objects to and from disk. The CArchive member function IsStoring returns a True or False, depending on whether the archive is writing objects to disk or reading them back in from disk. Objects that can be saved to and restored from disk are often referred to as *persistent objects*. You will learn how to use the Serialize function in the next chapter.

You will learn more about the CDocument class and serialization in the next chapter.

The View

The view displays data and controls interaction with the user.

The last major component of C38HELLO is the view class, which is defined in C38HEVW.H and implemented in C38HEVW.CPP. The view class for C38hello is named CC38helloView, and is derived from CView. The view is responsible for displaying its document's data to the user, and for accepting the user's input through mouse and keyboard.

You have already worked with one part of CC38helloView, the OnDraw member function. OnDraw is called by the framework whenever a view needs to be drawn, or redrawn. Listing 38.8 shows the whole OnDraw function, including the text drawing code you added earlier.

Listing 38.8. The *OnDraw* function in CC38helloView.

```
void CC38helloView::OnDraw(CDC* pDC)
{
    CC38helloDoc* pDoc = GetDocument();
    ASSERT_VALID(pDoc);

    // TODO: add draw code for native data here
    CString hello = "Hello MFC World";
    pDC->TextOut( 10, 10, hello);
}
```

You learned earlier about the actual text drawing and the device context, so we only need to examine the first two lines of this function. The first line gets a pointer to the document to which this view is attached. Most of the time in this function you will use the pDoc pointer to retrieve the data you want to display from the document.

The second line is another preprocessor macro, one that generates a call to the document's AssertValid function. The purpose of this call is to ensure that during debugging the document has been properly initialized with valid data. If the document's AssertValid function returns False, the ASSERT_VALID macro will cause a message to pop up telling you that a problem has occurred, and the module name and line of code where the problem occurred. This can be very valuable when you are debugging an application. Later, when you build a release version of the application and __DEBUG is not defined, the ASSERT_VALID macro will generate a blank line instead of the function call. This is a built-in feature of the framework, so you do not need to use preprocessor #ifdef __DEBUG, #endif statements.

The last functon this chapter discusses in the view class is the GetDocument function. The GetDocument function is actually defined two times, once in the header file, and a second time in the implementation file. Listings 38.9 and 38.10 show the two versions of this function.

Listing 38.9. The release version of the *GetDocument* function as defined in C38HEVW.H.

```
#ifndef _DEBUG  // debug version in c38hevw.cpp
inline CC38helloDoc* CC38helloView::GetDocument()
    { return (CC38helloDoc*)m_pDocument; }
#endif
```

Listing 38.10. The debug version of the *GetDocument* function as defined in C38HEVW.CPP.

```
#ifdef __DEBUG
.
.
CC38helloDoc* CC38helloView::GetDocument() // debug version
{
    ASSERT(m_pDocument->IsKindOf(RUNTIME_CLASS(CC38helloDoc)));
    return (CC38helloDoc*)m_pDocument;
}
#endif //_DEBUG
```

The two listings of GetDocument are complementary. The DEBUG version is included in an #ifdef __DEBUG, #endif pair, while the release version is included when __DEBUG is not defined. (#inndef). There are two differences in these versions. The first difference is that the release version is declared to be inline. This is an instruction to the compiler that wherever a call to GetDocument is encountered in the source code, it should instead just insert the instructions contained in the function in the source code. Since the function in question only contains one line of code, this does not add any size to the application, but results in improved efficiency by saving a call to a function.

The other difference is found on the first line of the debug version of the function, the line that begins with ASSERT. ASSERT is another macro, similar to ASSERT_VALID, but different in that ASSERT will evaluate any expression inside its parentheses for TRUE or FALSE, and if the expression is false it will display a message. ASSERT is much more general than ASSERT_VALID, and it can be one of your best friends when you start debugging your own code. You use ASSERT to test that any assumptions about function parameters, return values, and so on, are true before allowing your code to continue. Bugs are easiest to fix when they are detected early in program execution.

> **Caution:** Do not initialize or assign values to variables in ASSERT statements. ASSERT code is present only in the debug version of your program and if you use ASSERT to initialize or assign values to variables, those assignments will no longer be made in the release version of your program. ASSERT is intended only as a debugging aid, not a part of your actual code.

One final thing to notice before we leave the view class and the GetDocument function is the remainder of the ASSERT statement—the part that reads:

```
m_pDocument->IsKindOf(RUNTIME_CLASS(CC38helloDoc))
```

This fragment of code verifies that the document pointer actually points to a document of the correct class. This is the kind of runtime class type checking that is enabled by the DECLARE_DYNAMIC, DECLARE_DYNCREATE, IMPLEMENT_DYNAMIC, and IMPLEMENT_DYNCREATE macros you have been seeing in all of the listings.

Summary

You have seen how App Wizard lets you define the basic nature of your application, and then generates a set of skeleton program files that can be compiled into a working application. The App Wizard generated application includes a main application object, a frame window object, a document, and a view.

The App Wizard skeleton application is a working program, but you still need to add your own application's special features. In the next two chapters you will work through the process of adding some common custom features to the skeleton application.

Review Questions

Answers to the Review Questions are in Appendix B.

1. Why should you keep each project in a separate directory?

2. In which object and function is the toolbar created?

3. What is new? What is its opposite?

4. What part of the skeleton application interacts with the user?

5. What happens to an ASSERT statement when you compile a release version of an application?

Review Exercise

1. Modify C38HELLO so that the "Hello World" string is stored in the document instead of being created when needed in the view, then change the view to retrieve the "Hello World" string from the document for display.

CHAPTER 39

Documents and Views

Most non-trivial applications require a common pair of closely related capabilities: the capability to manage their data, and the capability to show that data to the user and allow the user to interact with the data. The Microsoft Foundation Classes provide these capabilities through documents for the data and views to show the data.

This chapter will introduce the following topics:

♦ How to create a serializable class.

♦ How the document retrieves and saves serializable data.

♦ How to show data from the document in a view.

When you complete this chapter you will have a basic understanding of how to set up your documents to read and write their data, and how to display that data in a view.

The Document/View Architecture

The mechanism that manages the document and the view is often called the *document/view architecture*. Some programmers, when first confronted with the document/view architecture, think that documents are only suited to applications like word processors, spreadsheets, or drawing programs. This no doubt comes from the word "document" and its association with those products.

However, if you think of a document in MFC terms—as a place to manage your application's data—the power of the architecture becomes more apparent. An MFC document can store any kind of data you might need. This chapter uses a document to store a simple collection of objects. When you become more familiar with documents, you will see that many kinds of data can be managed, including word processor documents, simple collections, complex collections, files created by other applications (such as bitmaps), some database implementations, and even data from a modem or other external device.

The view concept is easier to understand. It displays the data by retrieving it from the document and painting it on-screen by using any of several specialized classes, depending on the type of data and how you want it to appear. MFC views can display all of the document's data, or only selected portions. A view can display graphics, text, Windows controls, or combinations of all these. It also can be laid out like a form.

The advantage of this architecture becomes even more apparent when you think of the event-driven nature of the Windows environment compared to older process-oriented DOS programs. In a Windows program, the user is able to move from one task to another, often suspending one task without completing it and then making a change elsewhere that affects the suspended task's data. By separating the data management function from the data display function, MFC is able to deal with complexities such as these.

Enhancing MFC Applications

When you start adding functionality to an MFC application, you must often add several data members and functions to multiple classes within the program before any results can be seen in the compiled application. In this chapter, you will be creating a document and a view, but you cannot display the document's data until you code the view, and the view will not have anything to display until the document has some data. The program cannot do anything useful until both the document and the view are ready.

Because of these factors, this chapter and the next one depart somewhat from the discussion-example pattern you have followed through most of this book. In these chapters, the examples represent separate steps you follow as you create the application and add code to implement the various features. Instead of compiling the program after every example, you type in the code for each example in order. After all the various pieces are finished, you compile and run the application one time.

The *Cellar* Application

For this chapter and the next one you will be working with an application named Cellar, which is a very simple list of the wines kept in stock by a restaurant for sale on its wine list. In this chapter, you develop the basic document and view for the application. In the next chapter, you add several ways for the user to interact with and modify the data.

Example

1. Begin the `Cellar` program by using App Wizard to create a skeleton application. This application will not be an MDI application like the `Hello` program in the last chapter, but otherwise uses the same options. On the main App Wizard screen, fill in the Project Name field with `Cellar`. You can accept the subdirectory name suggested by App Wizard, or change it to whatever is convenient. If you are using the source code disk, the first version of the `Cellar` application is in the CHAP39 directory, in a subdirectory named C39CELL1.

   You need to make changes to two of the App Wizard defaults. The first change is in the App Wizard Options dialog. Open the Options dialog by clicking on the Options button and remove the checkmark from the Multiple Document Interface checkbox. Now close the Options dialog by clicking the Close button. The second change is in the Classes dialog, so open the Classes dialog by clicking on the Classes button. In the Classes dialog, click on the document class name (`CCellarDoc`) in the New Application Classes list. When you click on the document name, two additional fields will be displayed at the bottom of the Classes dialog—File Extension and Doc Type Name. Fill in the File Extension with the three character filename extension that will be used for document files created by this application. This application will use **CEL** for its filename extension, so type that in now. Do not use a leading period. These are the only changes you need to make to the App Wizard defaults.

   Figure 39.1 shows the New Application Information screen for the `Cellar` application. This is the last time you will use App Wizard in this book.

Figure 39.1

New Application Information for the *Cellar* application.

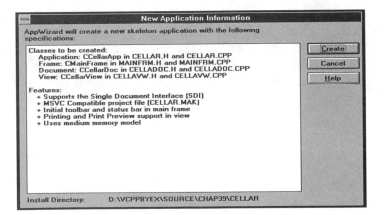

The Document and Your Data

The document class is intended to manage your application's data. Although the default version of the document is based on the serialization model, as you become more familiar with the document and how it interacts with the rest of the framework, you will quickly learn how to override it to fit many other types of data.

A Serializable Data Class

In the last chapter, you learned that it is possible to save and restore objects to and from a disk file through a process called serialization. The CDocument class generated by App Wizard contains an empty function named Serialize to support serialization. Serialized data is the easiest type of data to use with MFC because almost all of the required functionality is built into the framework and is handled automatically in many cases.

Before the document can serialize anything, however, there has to be something to serialize, so the first step of developing the Cellar application is to create a serializable class that stores information about the wines on a restaurant's wine list. Each instance of the class will store information about one wine. You will see later how the document will maintain a collection of all the individual wines.

The following examples walk you through the steps to create a serializable class named CWine and add it to the Cellar project. Before you begin, make sure that the Cellar project is open in Application Workbench.

Examples

1. The first step in creating a serializable class is to create the class definition in a separate header (.H) file. The class must be derived from CObject or another class that was derived from CObject. Additionally, the class definition must include the DECLARE_SERIAL macro and a prototype for the Serialize function.

The DECLARE_SERIAL macro is an extension of the DECLARE_DYNCREATE macro which provides additional information necessary for dynamic creation of objects as they are read in from a disk file. There is a matching IMPLEMENT_SERIAL macro that you include in the class implementation. These macros are necessary to support runtime creation or saving of C++ internal information about the class.

Because the Serialize function is declared virtual in the CObject parent class, you should include the virtual keyword with the Serialize function prototype in any derived classes as well.

Following is the CWine class definition. If you are working along with the text, type it in as shown here and save it in the Cellar project directory WINE.H.

```
// Filename: wine.h
// Interface of the CWine class

class CWine : public CObject
{
protected: // for create from serialization
    CWine() {};     // don't miss the {}, or it won't link
    DECLARE_SERIAL(CWine)

public:
    CWine( CString name, int yr, CString type,int qty );

    CString     m_sName;
    int         m_nYear;
    CString     m_sType;
    int         m_nOnHand;

    virtual     void Serialize(CArchive& ar);
};
```

CWine is a very simple class. Normally you would include AssertValid and Dump functions for debugging, and you would define a constructor for creating a copy of the object. For this example, however, we only want to focus on the serialization feature, and this is the minimum class which will support serialization. Notice that the DECLARE_SERIAL macro is included in the class definition, along with a prototype for the Serialize function.

2. Now create the CWine class implementation in a .CPP file. The implementation file must include both the main MFC header file, stdafx.h, as well as the class header. You must include the IMPLEMENT_SERIAL macro in this file.

Type in the implementation of the CWine class as shown below and save it as WINE.CPP, then read the explanation below.

```
// Filename: wine.cpp
// Implementation of the Serializable Wine class

#include "stdafx.h"
#include "wine.h"

IMPLEMENT_SERIAL(CWine, CObject, 0)

// constructor with parameters for new instances
CWine::CWine( CString name, int yr,
```

```
              CString type, int qty )
{
    m_sName = name;
    m_nYear = yr;
    m_sType = type;
    m_nOnHand = qty;
}

// CWine serialization function
void CWine::Serialize(CArchive& ar)
{
    CObject::Serialize(ar);  // serialize base class first

    if (ar.IsStoring())
    {
        ar << m_sName;
        ar << (WORD)m_nYear;  // allow for portability
        ar << m_sType;
        ar << (WORD)m_nOnHand;
    }
    else
    {
        WORD innum;              // to convert numbers
        ar >> m_sName;
        ar >> innum;
        m_nYear = innum;
        ar >> m_sType;
        ar >> innum;
        m_nOnHand = innum;
    }
};
```

The third parameter in the IMPLEMENT_SERIAL macro is called the schema number. The schema number is used by the serialization process to verify versions of objects. It must be equal to or greater than zero. Later, if you change CWine's data members and want to ensure that you are reading the correct version, you can change the schema number. If you try to read a wrong version, the framework displays an error message.

The Serialize function is typical of what you need to write for a simple class. The << and >> operators have roughly the same meaning here, for the CArchive object, as they have in iostream operations—they are used to insert objects into the archive, or to extract them from the archive. The arrows point toward the target of the operation. This function will be called by the document (actually, by the collection of objects in the document) for each CWine object that is to be saved or restored.

Serialized data must be read in the same order it was written.

One very important thing to remember while writing the Serialize function is that the data members must be read in the same order they are written.

Notice the CArchive parameter that is passed to the Serialize function. This object is created by the framework in response to user commands to open or close a file. The CArchive object is responsible for doing the actual reading and writing, and knows which purpose it was created to fulfill.

> **Note:** CArchive has defined extraction and insertion operators for all of the built in types, and for some of the general purpose classes such as CString so that those types do not need to be derived from CObject. However, Microsoft has not defined CArchive operators for some common data types such as int. This is because the size of an int can change as you move from one machine type to another, which would make it impossible to properly read an object on one machine that had been written on another machine where the size of an int is different. However, the WORD type will be defined on different machines so that it is the same length, so by casting an int to a WORD when it is saved, and then converting the WORD back to an int when it is read back in, you are assured that all machines will be able to share this archive. This type of compatibility must be considered more and more as the PC industry moves toward increased interoperability between various hardware platforms.

3. Finally, add the CWine class implementation file, WINE.CPP, to the Cellar project. To add WINE.CPP to the project, pull down the **P**roject menu and choose **E**dit to open the project edit dialog. In the project edit dialog, choose WINE.CPP from the File Name list, and click on the Add button. You do not need to add WINE.H. (These instructions assume that you have the Cellar project open in Application Workbench.)

Adding Data to the Document

You now have a serializable CWine class. But CWine does not exist in a vacuum. Something has to create instances of CWine, and then call the class Serialize function. That will be done by the document.

The Cellar application will keep a collection of CWine objects in the document. You have already learned about the MFC collection classes, and that is what we will use to store CWine objects in the document. This chapter uses a CObArray because it simplifies some operations you will need to perform in the view.

The following discussion assumes that you created the Cellar application in App Wizard as was described at the beginning of this chapter. The App Wizard generated document class is named CCellarDoc, and it is implemented in CELLADOC.H and CELLADOC.CPP.

You will be adding the following functionality to the generated document:

1. Add a collection of CWine objects to the document.

2. Implement serialization for the collection of objects so that Cellar's data can be saved to and restored from disk.

3. Add the ability to create new collections when the user chooses **F**ile **N**ew from the application menu.

Example

1. CCellarDoc will use a CObArray, one of the MFC collection classes to store the CWine objects. To add a CObArray of CWine objects to CCellaDoc, all you need to do is add a public CObArray member variable to the class definition.

Open the document header file—CELLADOC.H. You will make two changes to this file.

First, add the CObArray member to the class. It needs to be public so that the view can interact with it. A convenient place to add the array member is in the public section which immediately follows the DECLARE_DYNCREATE macro. Following is how the beginning of that section looks, with the CObArray member added.

```
// Attributes
public:
    CObArray m_cWineColl;  // our data
```

The second change to CELLADOC.H is a function prototype for a DeleteContents function. The reason for this function will be explained in the third example. For now, a good place to add the DeleteContents prototype is just before the prototype of OnNewDocument. The OnNewDocument prototype is found just before the message map comments. Here is how that code should look (the OnNewDocument prototype was generated by App Wizard):

```
protected:
    virtual VOID DeleteContents();
    virtual BOOL OnNewDocument();

// Generated message map functions
```

The preceding sample includes some lines from before and after the added prototype to help you locate the place in the file. Note that DeleteContents is also a virtual function. It is called automatically by the framework when it is needed.

These are the only changes to the CCellarDoc class header. You should save your changes to CELLADOC.H now.

There is one more thing you need to do to finish preparing the document to store CWine objects—you need to add the WINE.H header file to the document's implementation. Open CELLADOC.CPP and modify the beginning of the file to look like this:

```
// celladoc.cpp : implementation of the CCellarDoc class
//
#include "stdafx.h"
#include "cellar.h"

#include "wine.h"   // the CWine class definition
#include "celladoc.h"
```

2. Next you will implement serialization for the CObArray that will hold the CWine objects. This is even easier than it was for your CWine class because CObArray already has a Serialize function defined that will automatically call the Serialize function for all objects stored in the array. This is a direct benefit of having derived the CWine class from CObject. All you need to do is add a call to m_cWineColl.Serialize in the document's Serialize function, and the rest works just like the polymorphic collection of pets in Chapter 34.

Here is the App Wizard-generated Serialize function from CELLADOC.CPP, with the call to the collection's Serialize function added:

```
void CCellarDoc::Serialize(CArchive& ar)
{
    if (ar.IsStoring())
    {
        // TODO: add storing code here
    }
    else
    {
        // TODO: add loading code here
    }
    m_cWineColl.Serialize(ar);  // serialize the collection
}
```

Yes, it really is only one line of code. You don't have to code separate calls for storing and loading because you are passing the CArchive object to the collection's Serialize function, and the CArchive object knows which action is being performed.

You could delete the if statement and its branches for this application, but it does no harm to leave it there in case you need to use it later. You would use that part of the Serialize function if you added some other data to the document that was not part of the CObArray.

You do not need to add a call to the document's Serialize function because it is automatically called by the framework as part of the file open and close processing.

3. The final functionality you need to add to the document is the capability to create new documents. As with serialization, most of the processing is handled by the framework and you only need to add the specific code needed by your data. For this example, you will add code to the OnNewDocument function generated by App Wizard, and you will implement the DeleteContents function which you prototyped in the class header.

For the version of Cellar that will be implemented in this chapter, the code you add to the default OnNewDocument() function will create a few sample CWine objects so that you can test the view's display capabilities. In the next chapter you will remove these hard coded samples and provide a way for the user to add wines to the collection.

Here is the complete OnNewDocument function with code to add three wines to the collection. You should add at least three, but may put in more if you want. The syntax for adding wines is very similar to what you saw in Chapter 38 where a CMultiDocTemplate object was created with the new keyword and then added to a collection.

```cpp
BOOL CCellarDoc::OnNewDocument()
{
    if (!CDocument::OnNewDocument())
        return FALSE;

    // TODO: add reinitialization code here
    // (SDI documents will reuse this document)
    m_cWineColl.Add( new CWine
            ( "Chateau Lafite", 1985, "Red", 2));
    m_cWineColl.Add( new CWine
            ( "Lovers Leap Chardonnay", 1991, "White", 4));
    m_cWineColl.Add( new CWine
            ( "La Turk", 1985, "Red", 96));
```

```
        SetModifiedFlag( TRUE );

        return TRUE;
    }
```

The line immediately after the last wine is added is a call to a `CDocument` function named `SetModifiedFlag`. This function maintains a flag that indicates whether or not the document has been modified. If the flag is `True`, when the user tries to close the file, open a new file, or exit the application, MFC will automatically bring up a dialog that prompts them to save the file.

In an SDI application, MFC does not create a totally new instance of the `CDocument` class whenever a new document is opened. Instead, the existing document is "recycled," so there needs to be a way to clear out the document. Also, because you are allocating objects using the `new` operator whenever they are added to the document's collection, their memory must be freed with a call to `delete`. These actions are carried out in the `DeleteContents` function.

Here is the `DeleteContents` function for `Cellar`. You should type in this entire function, as shown, into the CELLADOC.CPP document implementation file.

```
VOID CCellarDoc::DeleteContents()
{
    int i;

    for (i = 0; i <= m_cWineColl.GetUpperBound(); i++ )
    {
        delete m_cWineColl[i];
    }
    m_cWineColl.RemoveAll();
}
```

The `DeleteContents` function steps through the contents of the `CObArray` and calls the `delete` operator for each object stored in the array. This frees the memory allocated for the objects by the `new` operator. However, the `delete` operator does not remove the pointer to the object from the array, so it is necessary to call the array's `RemoveAll` function, which, as its name implies, removes all entries from the array.

The `DeleteContents` function is called automatically by MFC whenever a document is closed, either because the user is opening a new document or exiting the application.

This completes the changes to CELLADOC.CPP. You can save the file now, and if you want to verify the syntax of your changes you can compile the application. Because the view doesn't have any code to display the data, however, you won't see much evidence of your work when you run the application except a request to save your data when you close the application. That will occur because you are setting the document's modified flag in OnNewDocument.

The View Displays Your Data

Now that the Cellar document has some data it is time to look at how that data can be displayed. If you did the exercise at the end of the previous chapter, you already have a good idea of how to get the data from the document for display, and the Cellar view is not much more complex than the view in C38Hello.

Implementing the View's Drawing Functions

The Cellar view will list the contents of the document's wine list in rows, with the various data items lined up in columns. You could implement this entirely in the view's OnDraw function, but most programmers would not do so. Instead, you will see how to implement a function that knows how to draw one row, and then call that function repeatedly from the OnDraw function, one time for each row.

You are already familiar with the OnDraw function from the previous chapter. This function is called automatically by the framework whenever the view needs to draw the data. The function to draw a row will be named OnDrawRow.

The preceding chapter's output was a simple, single line. Now, however, you need to draw several lines, each one properly spaced, and you need to arrange output on those lines into regular columns. Although the output is more complex, the means of creating the output is the same—a device context object that is passed to the OnDraw function by MFC.

All output to visual output devices in Windows is handled by a device context. The "context" part comes from the fact that each device context is slightly different depending on the "context" in which the output is being created. If the output is to a color display, the context is appropriate for the type and resolution of the display that is in use on the computer. If the output is for a printer, then the device context is appropriate for the model of printer currently selected for print output.

An MFC device context object encapsulates a Windows device context, and provides all of the functionality you will need for drawing on MFC views or creating printed output. In the last chapter, and in this one, you will be working with text output. The device context includes numerous member functions for formatting and outputting text. However, a device context is not limited to text output, and your control is not limited to simple row and column positioning. The device context has member functions that allow you to change all the aspects of the text output font, including typeface, orientation, size, and even the color of the text. In addition to text, the device context can be used to output graphics, lines, shapes, and even bitmaps. There are also member functions in the device context to fill areas with solid colors, or with patterns. Finally, the device context can even be used to output bitmaps.

The device context is not limited to drawing on views on the output screen, but is also the means of creating output for printers, plotters, or any other visual output device that may be attached to the computer. In most cases, once you can create output on-screen, you can create the same output on the printer by simply creating a device context for the printer—which is exactly how MFC handles the Print option in an MFC application. When you choose the Print option from an MFC application's File menu, MFC creates a device context that will send its output to the printer instead of the screen, then calls the same OnDraw function in the view as is used for screen output, but passes the printer device context. This is one of the advantages of the Windows environment. The mechanism of providing your OnDraw function with an appropriate device context is managed by MFC and Windows. You, the programmer, can concentrate on designing your output. If a different output device is substituted for the one you were using when you wrote the program, perhaps a larger output screen, or a new printer model, your OnDraw function does not have to be changed.

The following examples implement the view's drawing functions and supporting definitions.

Examples

1. You will begin adding the drawing capabilities to the view the same way you started to add capabilities to the document—by modifying the view class definition in the header file. The header file for Cellar's view is named CELLAVW.H. Open that file now in Application Workbench.

   The first thing you will add to the header file is the code that defines the columns for displaying the CWine member variables. The values to be used in the OnDrawRow function to control how a row is drawn.

   Add these lines to the beginning of CELLAVW.H, after the #include statements, but before the beginning of the CCellarView class definition:

   ```
   #define WINE_COL    1
   #define WINE_LEN    24
   #define YEAR_COL    (WINE_COL + WINE_LEN + 1)
   #define YEAR_LEN     4
   #define TYPE_COL    (YEAR_COL + YEAR_LEN + 1)
   #define TYPE_LEN    16
   ```

```
#define NUMB_COL    (TYPE_COL + TYPE_LEN + 1)
#define NUMB_LEN    3

class CWine;
```

Notice how each successive column location is based on the previous column, plus the width of the variable to display. This makes it very easy to change the width of a column.

Be sure to add the last line in the above code, the one that begins class. This statement simply informs the Visual C++ compiler that CWine is a class that will be defined later. This statement will save you from adding WINE.H to other parts of Cellar, such as the main application file, which include CELLAVW.H. The definition of CWine is needed because it will be a parameter in the OnDrawRow function prototype that is the next thing you will add to the header. Don't miss the semicolon (;) at the end of the line, or you may set a record for errors in one compile.

The last change to CELLAVW.H is shown below. Add the OnDrawRow prototype immediately following the OnDraw prototype, as shown here:

```
virtual void OnDraw(CDC* pDC);  // draw this view
virtual void OnDrawRow(CDC* pDC, int nRow, CWine* pWine);
```

OnDrawRow will be called by OnDraw. When you have finished adding the preceding lines, save CELLAVW.H.

2. Now you will begin implementing the actual view drawing. Open the view implementation file, CELLAVW.CPP. The first thing to do is make sure that WINE.H is included in the view. Standard practice is to add it as shown here:

```
// cellavw.cpp : implementation of the CCellarView class
//
#include "stdafx.h"
#include "cellar.h"

#include "wine.h"          // CWine definition
#include "celladoc.h"
#include "cellavw.h"
```

3. Now it is time to define the OnDraw function. Unlike the OnDraw in C38HELLO, this version will not actually draw anything on the view. Instead, it will just retrieve each CWine object from the document and pass them to the OnDrawRow function to do the actual drawing. This separation of functions will make it much easier to maintain and enhance the program later.

App Wizard created a skeleton OnDraw function. Modify that skeleton so that it looks like the code below:

```
void CCellarView::OnDraw(CDC* pDC)
{
     CCellarDoc* pDoc = GetDocument();
     ASSERT_VALID(pDoc);   // make sure we got a valid
Document

     // TODO: add draw code for native data here
     int nRowNumb = 0;      // current row in view
     int nWine = 0;         // current array index
     int lastWine;          // last array index
     CWine* curWine;        // for passing to OnDrawRow

     lastWine = pDoc->m_cWineColl.GetUpperBound();
     for (nWine = 0; nWine <= lastWine; nWine++)
     {
          curWine = (CWine*)pDoc->m_cWineColl[nWine];
          OnDrawRow(pDC, ++nRowNumb, curWine);
     }
}
```

In this example, all of the code is added after the // TODO: comment. The processing is very similar to some of the small programs you have already written. The first statement after the variable declarations is typical of how you go about getting information from the document:

```
lastWine = pDoc->m_cWineColl.GetUpperBound();
```

This statement uses the pointer to the document, pDoc, that was initialized at the beginning of the function to access the m_cWineColl member of the document. Recall that m_cWineColl is a CObArray. GetUpperBound is a member function of CObArray. Finally, the return value from GetUpperBound is stored in lastWine, which will be used to control the end of the for loop in the next statement. That is a lot of code for one statement, but this kind of statement is common in MFC programming. Many programmers would not have bothered with the intermediate lastWine variable and simply inserted the code you see to the right of the equal sign in the terminating condition of the for loop.

The inside of the for loop consists of a statement to retrieve the current CWine object from the array, and then pass it to OnDrawRow. The only unusual code in these statements is the cast of the return from the array to a CWine*, which is necessary because the array access operators all return CObject pointers and we need a CWine. The cast is safe because we will control what goes into the array.

4. The final function you need to define is `OnDrawRow`. The code is shown below. Type it in, and then read the discussion that follows:

```
void CCellarView::OnDrawRow(CDC* pDC, int nRow, CWine*
pWine)
{
    TEXTMETRIC tm;     // information about current font
    int nTxtHeight;    // height of a row using current font
    int nTW;           // avg char width of current font
    int vPos = 0;      // current vertical output position
    char cNum[10];     // buffer for formatting numbers


    // grab some stuff about the text
    pDC->GetTextMetrics(&tm);
    nTxtHeight = tm.tmHeight;          // text height
    nTW        = tm.tmAveCharWidth;    // average text width


    // Draw the row
    vPos = nTxtHeight * nRow;  // calc. vertical postion
    pDC->TextOut( WINE_COL*nTW, vPos, pWine->m_sName );
    wsprintf(cNum, "%u", pWine->m_nYear);
    pDC->TextOut( YEAR_COL*nTW, vPos, cNum, strlen(cNum));
    pDC->TextOut( TYPE_COL*nTW, vPos, pWine->m_sType );
    wsprintf(cNum, "%u", pWine->m_nOnHand);
    pDC->TextOut( NUMB_COL*nTW, vPos, cNum, strlen(cNum));
}
```

The key to understanding the `OnDrawRow` function lies in the first variable defined in the function, the `TEXTMETRIC tm` variable, along with the `GetTextMetrics` function immediately after the variable definitions, and how these factors relate to the device context (`CDC`) that is passed as the first parameter.

You will use the device context that was passed to the `OnDraw` function for all drawing on the view. It will already "know" which font will be used to draw on the view. This is called the *currently selected font*. You can never be certain what font has been passed in the device context because Windows allows the user to redefine the default fonts. Therefore, you cannot make any assumptions about how wide a character is, or how high a row of characters will be. `TEXTMETRICS` is a `struct` that contains all of the information about the currently selected font in the device context, including the character height and average width.

Before you can properly space your characters and rows, you need to know how high a row will be, and how wide each character will be. To get that information, create a TEXTMETRICS structure and pass it to the GetTextMetrics function, which will fill the structure with information about the current font. Finally you access the information you need from the TEXTMETRICS structure. The OnDrawRow function above uses the height and average character width of the font. These dimensions are in screen units, which vary according to the current screen resolution and drawing mode. For text drawing, the default units and drawing mode can be used without any manipulation.

Once you have the character height and average width from the TEXTMETRICS structure, you can easily calculate the position of any given row, or the width of a character string. OnDrawRow maintains the vertical position of a row in the VPos variable, which is calculated by multiplying the row number by the row height. Horizontal positioning is calculated by multiplying the number of characters, or spaces, by the average character width.

Now that you know how to space your characters and rows, you can draw a row. The first step is to find out the vertical location of the row, which is done here by multiplying the row number passed from OnDraw by the text height retrieved from the TEXTMETRICS structure.

Actual drawing is done by a series of calls to the device context TextOut function. TextOut takes four parameters, which are the horizontal position where output will start, the vertical position of the output, a character array or a CString to be written to the screen, and the size of the character array. (You do not need the fourth parameter if you pass a CString as the third parameter.) In the TextOut calls used here, the first parameter is calculated in place, using the column locations you defined in CELLAVW.H and the average character width.

The final thing to notice is how the numbers are formatted into strings using a function named wsprintf. This function is a formatted string output function that is similar to some of the output functions you used earlier in the book, but this function, instead of outputting to the screen, puts its result in a character array that is passed as the first parameter. A discussion of this function is beyond the scope of this book, but you can learn more about it from the on-line help files that come with Visual C++.

That completes the changes to CELLAVW.CPP. You are now ready to build the full application.

Figure 39.2

The *Cellar*
application.

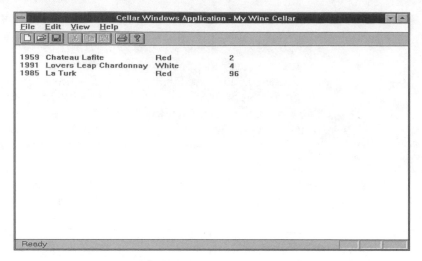

5. You are finally ready to build and run the application. When the build has finished, run the application. Figure 39.2 shows an output screen.

Experiment with the application a little. Because this is an SDI application, you can only have one window open instead of several. Try the **F**ile **S**ave option, and then open the file you just saved. Notice that whenever you have created a new file, you are prompted to save the changes before the framework will open another file. This is because the document is setting its changed flag in `OnNewDocument`. In the next chapter, you will see how you can control that flag when changes are made to an open file.

Summary

You have now learned how to create a serializable data class, how to modify a document to save and restore a collection of objects, and how to display those objects in a view. You did all of this with very few lines of code, considering the capabilities of the completed program.

The next chapter is the final chapter of the book. In that chapter you will enhance `Cellar` to allow the user to add wines to the list. In the process, you will learn about messages, menus, and dialogs.

Review Questions

1. True or false. An MFC document is only intended to store word-processor types of data.

2. List three ways a view can display data.

3. What function will MFC automatically call to save or restore a document's data?

4. Why does the document in an SDI application need a DeleteContents function?

5. What kind of information is stored in a TEXTMETRICS structure? How do you fill the structure with that information?

Review Exercises

1. The restaurant that is using Cellar wants to keep track of the cost of the wine in its wine list and then be able to print a wine list that shows its selling price beside the wine's name. The selling price will be determined by multiplying the cost of the wine by a fixed markup factor which it may want to change from time to time. Add the necessary member variables to the CWine class and the document, then change the OnDrawRow function to display the selling price instead of the quantity on hand. (*Hint:* Store the markup factor as a separate variable in the document and serialize it in the if statement you left in the document's Serialize function.)

CHAPTER 40

Menus and Dialogs

Two of the most common ways a user interacts with a Windows application are through the application's menus, and through a special type of window called a dialog. You have already been using both of these methods while you work in Visual C++. In this chapter, you learn how to add them to your applications.

This chapter covers the following topics:

♦ Laying out a dialog by using App Studio

♦ Adding a dialog to your project by using Class Wizard

♦ Adding menus to your application by using App Studio

♦ Binding a menu item to your application by using Class Wizard

You will not write very much code in this chapter. In fact, you will only write code in the last example in the chapter. Most of the code that will be added to the application will be added by Class Wizard.

Adding a Dialog to Your Application

By this time you are probably familiar with the appearance and behavior of Windows dialogs from using so many of them. Almost every Windows application utilizes several dialogs, and some of the more complex applications may have dozens of dialogs.

Something that is used as often as a dialog should be easy to add to your application, and with Visual C++, it is. Almost all of the work is done in two of the Visual C++ tools that were discussed in Chapter 37—App Studio and Class Wizard. You use App Studio to lay out the basic design of the dialog box and set the basic properties of the controls; then you use Class Wizard to create a new class definition and implementation, add the class to your application, and provide a way to invoke the dialog. Class Wizard even automatically creates a skeleton function to process the dialog.

The next sections of the chapter walk you through the basic process of designing the dialog in App Studio and adding a class to the application using Class Wizard.

Preparing for This Chapter

The examples in this chapter continue developing the `Cellar` application that you wrote in the last chapter. You don't start a new application, but you modify the final program from Chapter 39. If you want to make a copy of that program, be sure to copy the entire project, including any subdirectories, into a new directory.

Using App Studio to Design a Dialog

The dialog you add to the `Cellar` application allows the user to add wines to the wine list. The first step in creating any dialog is to lay out the dialog and its controls using App Studio.

If Visual C++ is not started, start it now and open the `Cellar` project from the previous chapter as the active project.

Windows Resources

In a Windows program, all of the menus, dialog boxes, icons, bitmaps, and even the cursor and mouse pointer, are called *resources*.

A Windows program's resources are defined in a special type of file called a resource file, (also sometimes called a resource script) whose file name extension is .RC. Just as you use a text editor to create and modify your program code, you use a special type of editor called a resource editor to create and modify your program's resource file. In Visual C++, the resource editor is called App Studio, and it has separate specialized editors for each type of resource—a dialog editor for dialogs, a Menu Editor for menus, and so on. You used the String Table editor in the last chapter.

When you build your application, one of the steps is to compile the resource file, and then a separate step merges the resource file into the final application in a process called "binding" the resources.

This system of maintaining the program's visual elements separately from the code has some advantages. For example, you can change the appearance or layout of a program's resources without recompiling the whole program. In fact, you don't even need access to the program's source code. This means that you can easily build multiple versions of a program when, for example, the program will be sold in a different country and the various text in the program needs to be in a different language.

Now, start App Studio. Select **T**ools from the Application Workbench main menu, and then click on **A**pp Studio. When App Studio has finished loading you will the Resource Script window, which is shown in figure 40.1.

Figure 40.1

The Resource Script Window.

The Resource Script window shows all of the resources in your application, organized by type. The box on the left, labeled Type, lists all of the resource types that are in your application. When you select one of the resource types by clicking it, a list of all of the resources of that type is shown in the right-hand window. Figure 40.1 shows the Dialog resource type selected in the left box. The right-hand box shows that there is only one dialog defined in the application so far—IDD_ABOUTBOX.

Click on Dialog in the left-hand box to select the dialog resource type, and then click on the New button underneath the list of resource types. This will start the part of App Studio that is called the Dialog Editor. Figure 40.2 shows the Dialog Editor the way it looks when you first ask it to start a new dialog.

Figure 40.2

The initial layout of a new dialog in App Studio's Dialog Editor.

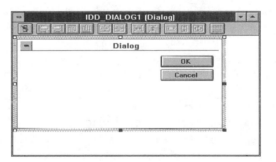

The new dialog in figure 40.2 contains two push buttons labeled OK and Cancel. Probably a majority of all dialogs contain these two buttons, which are always used to either accept the data in the dialog (OK), or to reject the data or any actions (Cancel), so a majority of the time you will just leave the buttons there. MFC's dialog class already knows how to process these buttons, so you do not need to write any code to use them in your dialog. If you don't want to use either, or both, of the initial buttons, you can delete them with no problem.

App Studio's dialog editor has two windows that you can keep active while you are designing a dialog—the Control palette, and the Properties window. Figure 40.3 shows the Control palette. The Control palette consists of a set of buttons, one for each type of Windows control that you can add to a dialog in the Dialog Editor.

Figure 40.3

The Control palette.

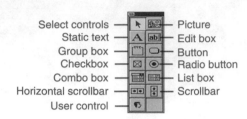

Select controls — Picture
Static text — Edit box
Group box — Button
Checkbox — Radio button
Combo box — List box
Horizontal scrollbar — Scrollbar
User control

To make the Control palette visible, choose Show **C**ontrol palette from the **W**indow menu. You use the set of buttons on the Control Palette to choose what kinds of controls you want to add to your dialog. For most of the buttons, the type of control represented is pretty obvious from the picture on the button, but if you aren't sure what kind of control a particular button will create, you can click the button and read a description of that button's particular control on the status bar at the bottom of the App Studio window. The buttons are labeled in Figure 40.3 to show you what kind of control is created by each button on the Control palette.

To add a control to a dialog, move the mouse cursor over the Tool Palette button for the kind of control you want, click the mouse button and hold it down, and while still holding down the mouse button, drag the mouse pointer over to the dialog. Notice that when you start to move the mouse, the cursor changes to a small representation of the control you clicked, and when the mouse cursor enters the dialog, a dotted rectangle appears which indicates the size and location of the control that will be added to the dialog. Continue dragging the control with the mouse until the control is where you want it and then release the mouse button to add the control to the dialog.

When you first add a control to a dialog, it will be surrounded by six small boxes, called *sizing handles*. Figure 40.4 shows the control you just dropped on the dialog with the sizing handles present. When sizing handles appear on a control, it is called the *selected* control. This is just an indicator for your convenience while you are designing the dialog; the sizing handles do not appear in the dialog when you compile your application. You can change the selected control by moving the mouse pointer over another control in the dialog and clicking the left mouse button, or you can select the dialog by clicking anywhere inside the dialog (except on a control).

Now move the cursor slowly across one of the sizing handles. As you pass over the small square, the cursor will change shape to a double-ended arrow. When the double-ended arrow appears, you can resize the control by clicking and holding the left mouse button, then continue moving the mouse in one of the directions pointed to by the double-ended arrow to adjust the size of the control.

Figure 40.4

A selected control with sizing handles.

Sizing handles —

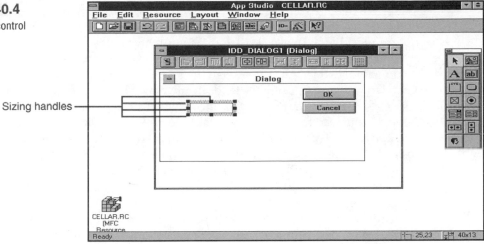

To reposition a selected control to a new location in the dialog, move the mouse pointer inside the selected control until the mouse pointer changes to a four-way arrow. Press and hold the left mouse button, and then drag the control to its new location.

You use the Properties window, as its name implies, to set various properties for each resource you add to your application. Figure 40.5 shows the Properties window displaying the properties of the default OK button.

Figure 40.5

The Properties window.

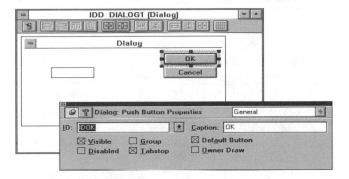

One thing to notice about the Properties window is the button in the upper left corner, just to the left of the button with the question mark. This is a picture of a tack, or pushpin, like one that you would use to pin a piece of paper to a bulletin board. In figure 40.5, the pin looks like it is pushed into the bulletin board to hold something in place, which is exactly what it is doing—it is holding the Dialog Properties box on your workspace. If you click this button, the pushpin changes to a picture of the pin from the side, waiting to be used for something, and as soon as you click anywhere outside the Dialog Properties box, the box disappears. When you are working with a new dialog, as you will be now, you may find it more convenient to keep the Dialog Item Properties box "pinned" to the work surface.

You navigate through the fields in the Properties window much the same way as you would move through the fields in any dialog box. The fields that show in the Properties window change depending on what kind of control is selected in the dialog. If you need help on a particular field, you can click the Help button for an explanation of all of the fields in that particular Properties box. (The Help button is the one in the upper left corner with a question mark on it.) You need to follow some guidelines when you fill in the textual information in fields like the **ID** and **C**aption fields shown in Figure 40.4. These guidelines will be explained as you work through the examples.

The following examples will walk you through the steps to lay out the controls on a dialog for `Cellar` that will allow the user to add a wine to the list and to set up the properties of those controls. You also will learn how to fill in the Properties window for the controls.

Examples

1. First, set the properties of the main dialog window. Click anywhere in the dialog except on one of the buttons placed there to start the dialog. Sizing handles will appear on the main border of the dialog. Now click on the Properties Window to activate it, and change the **ID** field of the dialog to `IDD_ADD_WINE`, and the **C**aption to `Add Wine`.

The ID field must be unique for every resource and control in your application. The name you type in the Properties window is actually just a preprocessor symbol which is used for the first argument in a preprocessor `#define` statement. The second argument in the preprocessor `#define` statement is an `unsigned int`, which contains the unique number that will be used internally by MFC and Windows to identify the resource. You can see the numeric values that have been assigned to your controls by opening resource.h in the Application Workbench editor, but ordinarily you will not be concerned with the actual numeric values assigned to the controls.

Note that the ID is in all capital letters. This is a universally followed convention, that all resource IDs are entered in all capital letters. Most MFC programmers also follow the convention that dialog IDs always begin with `IDD_`.

Notice that the `Add Wine` caption now appears in the title bar of the dialog in the Dialog Editor.

2. In this example, you will add a static text item to act as a label, and an edit box for the wine name field in the wine list.

Begin this example by dragging a Static Text control from the tool palette and dropping it on the dialog near the location shown in figure 40.6 for the text that reads Wine:. If you are unsure which button on the Tool Palette to use, refer to figure 40.3, or click each button until the status bar indicates you have chosen the button that will add a Static Text control.

When you have the Static Text control in place, you can change the text in the control from the default of Static to the label you want by just typing the text. For this control, type **Wine:**. Notice that when you start to type, the focus changes to the Properties window. When you press Enter, the focus changes back to the control.

Figure 40.6

The Wine Name edit box and static text label.

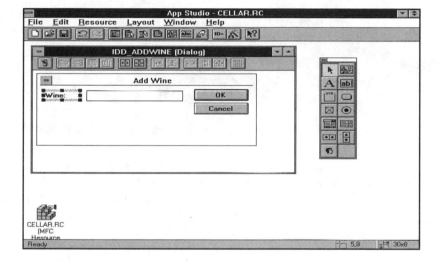

Next, drag an edit box control over to the dialog and position it as shown in figure 40.6. When you have it in position, move over to the sizing handle on the right-hand end and expand the width of the control to approximate figure 40.6. You do not have to be precise with the size.

That is the process of adding an edit box control with a static label to a dialog. Some dialog controls, such as checkboxes and radio buttons, have their own text labels and do not require you to add the label separately from the control the way an edit box does.

3. Now that you have an edit box and a matching static text label positioned on the dialog, you need to set the properties of the edit box.

The edit box should still be selected from the previous example. If it is not, click it to select it.

Fill in the Properties window to match the ID value shown in figure 40.7. This property is the only one you need to set on the edit boxes in this chapter.

Figure 40.7

The Properties window for the *Wine Name* edit box.

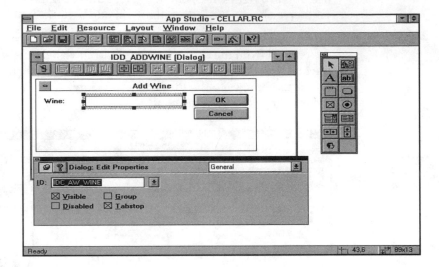

4. Now that you have seen how to add one edit box and Static Text pair, work through the rest of the fields for the dialog. You should add one control/label pair for each member variable of the CWine class from the Cellar application. The code below shows the four data members of the CWine class for reference while you work.

```
CString    m_sName;
int        m_nYear;
CString    m_sType;
int        m_nOnHand;
```

Figure 40.8 shows one way you might lay out the controls, although you are free to lay them out any way that makes sense to you.

Don't forget to set the properties for each control. Table 40.1 below lists the Static Text label, the ID you should use for each edit box, and the corresponding CWine member variable for each field in the dialog. The edit box controls are identified by the Static Text labels shown next to them in figure 40.8, which correspond to the member variables of the CWine class shown in the code fragment above.

Figure 40.8

The Add Wine dialog with all controls in place.

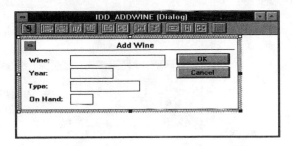

Table 40.1. Add Wine dialog edit control *ID*s.

Text Label	Control ID	CWine Member Variable
Wine Name:	IDC_AW_WINE	m_sWine
Year:	IDC_AW_YEAR	m_nYear
Type:	IDC_AW_TYPE	m_sType
On Hand:	IDC_AW_ONHAND	m_nOnHand

The OK and Cancel buttons placed in the dialog by default are the only other controls in this dialog. Their properties were set when App Studio added them to the dialog, so you have now finished laying out the dialog. Do not close the dialog editor window in App Studio, however. You will need to have it open with the dialog loaded for the next part of the chapter.

Using Class Wizard with a Dialog

When you have finished laying out a dialog in the Dialog Editor, the next step to add that dialog to your application is to create a new class in your project. Each dialog in your application will require that a class be defined to process that particular dialog. You may remember typing in the CWine class in the previous chapter, but that is not necessary to add a new dialog class—you can do it with Class Wizard.

The next two examples will show you how to use Class Wizard to create a new class for your application for the Add Wine dialog, and then add member variables to the dialog to allow you to capture the user's input to update your document.

Examples

1. Be sure you are still in App Studio, with the Add Wine dialog open in the Dialog Editor.

   Start Class Wizard. Pull down the **R**esource menu and click App Wizard, or you can use the accelerator key, Ctrl-W. Class Wizard starts and recognizes that a new dialog is present in the dialog editor. It automatically displays the Add Class dialog as shown in figure 40.9.

Figure 40.9
The Class Wizard
Add Class dialog.

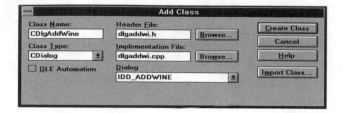

Fill in the fields in the Add Class dialog as shown in figure 40.9. Be careful to type the names exactly as shown in the figure because you will need to refer to them later in other exercises. You will not have to fill in a value for the **D**ialog field—it will have been filled in by Class Wizard from the value you entered in the ID field of the Properties window for the Add Wine dialog.

When you have finished filling in the Class **N**ame, Header **F**ile, and Implementation File fields, click the **C**reate Class button, and Class Wizard will create the header and implementation files for your dialog and add them to your project.

You will continue to work in Class Wizard in the next example, so do not close it at this time.

2. The Add Wine dialog has four data fields, represented by the four edit boxes. In order for your application to access the data the user types into the edit boxes, you must define member variables in the dialog class to hold the edit box data, and then connect each variable to the appropriate dialog box control.

You could define the variables and the associations with the edit boxes by editing the dialog's class header and implementation files in the Application Workbench editor, but this is very tedious and it is easy to make a mistake. This is one of the chores for which Class Wizard is designed, and instead of being tedious and error prone it becomes almost fun, as you are about to learn.

Class Wizard should still be open from the last example. If it is not, start Class Wizard following the steps you took to open it in the last example. Notice that there are four tabs across the top of the main Class Wizard window. Click the tab labeled Member Variables, which will display Class Wizard's member variable screen. This screen is shown in figure 40.10 as it will appear for the Add Wine dialog.

Figure 40.10

The Class Wizard
Member Variable
screen.

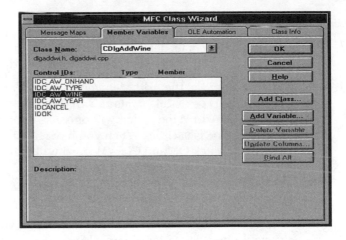

If the name shown in the Class Name field is not CDlgAddWine, click the arrow on the right end of the Class Name field and locate the name of the Add Wine dialog class that you created in the last example.

Just below the Class Name field is a large list box that shows all of the Control IDs defined in the dialog except those defined as IDC_STATIC. Static controls are controls that the user cannot change or otherwise interact with, so there is no need to define data members for them. To the right of the control IDs are columns that will show the type and name of any member variables you have assigned to the controls.

To create a member variable in the dialog class and assign it to a specific control, first click on the control ID in the Control ID's list box to highlight that row in the list box. Now click the button labeled Add Variable. This will open up the Add Member Variable dialog, which is shown in figure 40.11.

Figure 40.11

The Class Wizard
Add Member
Variable dialog.

The Add Member Variable dialog has three fields for you to fill in. The first is the Member Variable Name. This is the name that this variable will have in your code. Notice that Class Wizard has already provided the conventional m_ prefix for the variable name. The second field, labeled **P**roperty, should be left in its default setting of value unless you want to directly manipulate the properties (not values) of the dialog's controls.

The final field in the Add Member dialog is Variable **T**ype. Use this field to pick the type of data contained in the variable from the list of available types. The Add Wine dialog will only use CString and int. The default variable type is CString. When you have filled in all of the information for a variable, click OK and Class Wizard will create the variable and return you to the Member Variable screen where you can move on to the next variable.

Table 40.2 shows the Control IDs from the Add Wine dialog that should have member variables assigned to them, the variable type for each variable, and the variable name. Work through the list, creating member variables for each control shown in the table.

Table 40.2. Add Wine dialog member variables.

Control ID	Variable Type	Variable Name
IDC_AW_ONHAND	int	m_nOnHand
IDC_AW_TYPE	CString	m_sType
IDC_AW_WINE	CString	m_sWine
IDC_AW_YEAR	int	m_nYear

Note that the variable names used for dialog member variables are the same as the names of the CWine member variables. These are two different sets of variables, but because each set is in a different class, there is no conflict because of duplication of variable names. There is one nice advantage that comes from this naming, however: it is very easy to remember the names when you are copying data from the dialog to a CWine instance. You will see an example of this near the end of the chapter.

When you have finished entering all of the variable names, click OK in the Class Wizard Member Variable Screen. This closes Class Wizard and returns you to App Studio.

You can close App Studio now and return to Application Workbench for the next section of the chapter. Be sure to have App Studio save the modified resource file.

The Class Wizard Generated Code

It probably took you a lot longer to read through the above process for creating a dialog than it took to do the actual work. You may be wondering what is the end result of all of the various steps you just went through. At this point, you could compile your application, and the application would execute, but there wouldn't be any sign of the dialog you just designed in the running application.

Pause here for a moment and look at what Class Wizard just did for you. There is more here than meets the eye. First, if you inspect your project file, you will see that Class Wizard added the dialog's implementation file to your project automatically. That is an easy step to forget in all the detail of designing the dialog and creating the class.

Of course, there is the dialog class itself. Class Wizard generated two files for the dialog class—a header file, and a class implementation file. A detailed explanation of the internal workings of the dialog class is beyond the scope of this book, but you may want to open up the files in the editor and see what they look like. You might be surprised at how simple they are.

The key to the working of an MFC dialog is found in the function named DoDataExchange in DADDWINE.CPP. This function controls the transfer of data between the member variables you defined in Class Wizard and the windows text edit boxes you defined on the dialog layout.

Adding Menu Items

As mentioned previously, there still isn't a way to invoke the Add Wine dialog. That will be done through a menu item.

The process of adding a menu item to an application is very similar to the process of creating a dialog. First you use App Studio's Menu Editor to visually lay out the menu, then you use Class Wizard to create a connection between the menu and the application.

Using App Studio to Add a Menu Item

Start App Studio again. When the Resource Script window appears, click Menu. There will only be one menu listed in the Resource box, named IDR_MAINFRAME. Select IDR_MAINFRAME by clicking it, and then click the Open button to open the App Studio Menu Editor with the IDR_MAINFRAME menu.

The Menu Editor is shown in figure 40.12, with IDR_MAINFRAME open for editing. Editing a menu in the Menu Editor is very similar to the process of using a menu. When you click on any item on the main menu bar, two things happen: first, the pull-down menu for that top level menu appears, and second, the Properties Window is activated with the properties for that particular menu item.

Figure 40.12

The App Studio
Menu Editor.

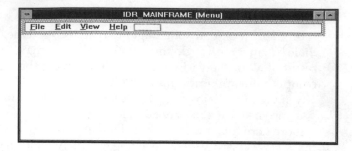

The small dotted box on the main menu bar, next to the **Help** menu, is called the New-item box. The New-item box indicates that the Menu Editor is ready to add a new menu item in that location. You can drag this box to a new location with the mouse, or just fill it in with the name of the menu where it is by typing the name of the menu. Cellar will not add any new top level menu items, so you can leave the top level New-item box as it is.

To add an item to one of the submenus, first click the top level item whose submenu you want to edit to display the submenu. The submenu will have its own New-item box, which you can drag the same way you can a top level item.

Examples

1. In this example, you will add one menu item to the Cellar application which will be used to invoke the Add Wine dialog. All references to menu items in this example refer to the menu items you are editing in the Menu Editor, not the menus of App Studio.

If you have not been working along with the text, open the Menu Editor now, with the IDR_MAINFRAME menu, following the steps outlined previously.

Now, click on the **Edit** menu item to pull down its drop-down menu as shown in figure 40.13. Notice that there is a New-item box at the bottom of the drop-down menu. As with the top level menu, you can drag the New-item box with the mouse if you want to add the item somewhere besides the bottom of the menu.

To create a new menu item, first select the New-item box, and drag it to its desired location. Next, just start typing in the name of the menu. When you start typing, the focus will automatically shift to the Properties window. If you want the user to be able to select the menu item by typing a single letter, put an ampersand (&) in front of the letter that represents the letter you want the user to be able to type for this menu item. Notice that this letter is underlined in the menu item.

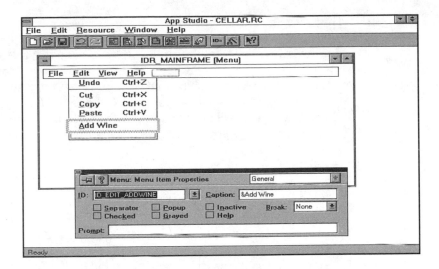

Figure 40.13

Editing a drop-down menu in the Menu Editor.

Figure 40.14 shows Cellar's Edit menu with a new menu item titled **Add** Wine added to the menu. The new item is located in the default location that was provided by the Menu Editor, and has the "A" of **Add** Wine set as its mnemonic key.

Now finish filling in the Properties window for this menu item. There is one other required entry, and a second optional, but desirable, one.

The required entry is an ID for the menu item. Figure 40.14 shows the ID filled in as ID_EDIT_ADDWINE. This is typical of the IDs that are usually used for menu items. A prefix of ID_ is always used, followed by the name of the top level menu item, followed by another underscore, and finally the name of the menu item. This makes it very easy when reading code that refers to menu items by their IDs to determine exactly what menu is being referenced in the code.

The optional entry is the field at the bottom of the Properties window, the one labeled Prompt. Any string you enter in this field will appear on your application's status bar when this menu item is selected.

That completes the steps to add an item to the menu for your application. Next you will complete the process by providing a way for the menu to communicate with the application. Do not close the Menu Editor yet.

Using Class Wizard to Bind a Menu Item

Now that a menu item exists, you need to tell your application how to respond when the user selects the item. You can do most of this work in Class Wizard.

The process of using Class Wizard to connect user interface objects such as menu items to code in your application is called *binding* the menu item. Note that this type of binding is different from the binding that occurs when the resource file is added to the application. You do this in Class Wizard's Message Maps dialog. Once you bind the menu item to a function in the program, the only thing you have left to do is write a few lines of code to actually process the dialog.

The following examples will walk you through the process of binding the **Add** Wine menu item to the application, and then writing the code to process the dialog.

Examples

1. To bind a menu item to your application, start with the menu in which the item appears active in the App Studio Menu Editor, which in this example is the IDR_MAINFRAME menu. Select the **A**dd Wine menu item you added to the IDR_MAINFRAME menu in the last example, and then start Class Wizard by choosing Class Wizard from the **R**esource menu. When Class Wizard starts, choose the Message Maps tab in the main Class Wizard screen, if it is not already selected.

The first step in binding a menu item to your application is to choose which class in the application will perform the menu item's processing. For this example you will be binding the Add Wine menu item, and because the Add Wine menu item will cause a change to the document, the document is the most logical place to process an Add Wine request.

The document class in the Cellar application is named CCellarDoc. To prepare Class Wizard to bind commands to CCellarDoc, look at the field named Class **N**ame in the Message Maps dialog. If the Class Name field does not show the class name you want to use for command binding, click the arrow on the right-hand end of the Class Name field, and choose the class name you want from the drop-down list that will appear—in this case, choose CCellarDoc.

Figure 40.14 shows the Class Wizard Message Map dialog, with CCellarDoc selected in the Class Name field.

The next step is to select the command you want to bind to CCellarDoc. You do this by choosing one of the items that appears in the Object IDs: list in the Message Maps dialog. The Object IDs: list shows all IDs in your application that can generate a command that can be processed by the class which is selected in the Class Name field. For this example, choose the ID of the Add Wine menu item. It is easy to find in the list because of the descriptive name you gave it in the previous example—ID_EDIT_ADDWINE. To select ID_EDIT_ADDWINE in the Object IDs: list, click it with the mouse. Class Wizard confirms your selection by highlighting ID_EDIT_ADDWINE.

Figure 40.14

The Class Wizard Message Maps dialog.

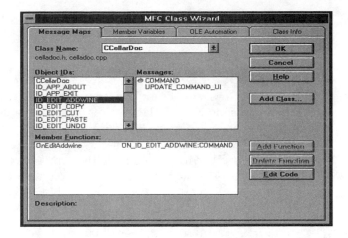

When you select an ID in the Object IDs: list, Class Wizard responds by displaying a list of all the messages that can be generated by that ID in the Messages box, just to the right of the Object IDs: list. Menu items all have a message named COMMAND, which is the message you need to bind to CCellarDoc. To bind the COMMAND message to CCellarDoc, select COMMAND in the Messages box (click on the COMMAND item) and then click the Add Function button. When you click the Add Function button, Class Wizard will display a small dialog called Add Member Function, which is shown in figure 40.15. The purpose of the Add Member Function dialog is to show you the function name Class Wizard has generated and to give you a chance to change the function name if you desire. To accept the function name displayed in the Add Member Function dialog, click the OK button. Class Wizard will add the function to the CCellarDoc class, add a function prototype to the class header, and update the class message map to recognize the new function. (Remember the message map? You looked at it briefly in the App Wizard generated code in Chapter 38. Now, finally, you get to see it put to use.)

Figure 40.15

The Add Member Function dialog.

The only remaining task is to write the actual code for the function generated by Class Wizard. You can go straight to the Class Wizard generated function by clicking the Edit Code button in the lower right corner of the Message Maps dialog. Click the Edit Code button now to go to the

OnEditAddWine function—Class Wizard will open the program file for CCellarDoc in Application Workbench, and position the cursor to a comment in the function that reads:

```
//TODO: Add your command handler code here.
```

Talk about service! Class Wizard put you closer to the place to add your code than the second place car rental agency puts you to your rental car. All you have to do now is type in a few lines of code. (Well, maybe more than a few for complex commands.) Here is the complete OnEditAddWine function, with code added to do the actual processing. Type in the code that appears below the //TODO:. . . comment.

```
void CCellarDoc::OnEditAddwine()
{
    // TODO: Add your command handler code here
    CDlgAddWine dlg;  // the dialog object
    int dlgRet;       // place to save return from dlg

    dlgRet = dlg.DoModal();  // display and process the
                             // dialog
    if (dlgRet == IDOK)      // if user clicked the OK
                             // button
    {
        m_cWineColl.Add( new CWine( dlg.m_sWine,
                                    dlg.m_nYear,
                                    dlg.m_sType,
                                    dlg.m_nOnHand));
        SetModifiedFlag( TRUE );
        UpdateAllViews( NULL );  // make the view redisplay
    }
}
```

The code in the OnEditAddwine function creates an instance of the CDlgAddWine class, invokes the dialog, turns control over to it, and then processes the result of the dialog. The instance of CDlgAddWine is named dlg. The dialog is invoked, and given control, on the line

```
dlgRet = dlg.DoModal();  // display and process the dialog
```

The DoModal() member function of the dialog controls all of the dialog processing. When the user ends the dialog, DoModal returns a value that corresponds to how the user ended the dialog, either by clicking OK, or by clicking Cancel. So, if the return value from the dialog is equal to the ID of the dialog's OK button (IDOK), the user wants to accept the contents of the dialog, and you need to add those results to the document's list of wines. The `if` statement tests the dialog's return value for `IDOK`, and if that is the return value, a new wine object is constructed from the dialog's member variables, the document's `modified` flag is set to true, (`SetModifiedFlag`), and the view is updated to reflect the changes (`UpdateAllViews`).

There are just a couple of small code details to complete before `Cellar` will be ready to compile, both of them in the document implementation file you are already editing.

The most important thing you must do is to add the #include file for the AddWine dialog to the beginning of CELLADOC.CPP. You are already editing CELLADOC.CPP, because that is the implementation of `CCellarDoc`, so just page up until you are at the top of the file and add the `include` file just before the `include` for `celladoc.h`. Here are those lines of code:

```
#include "wine.h"
#include "dlgaddwi.h"
#include "celladoc.h"
```

The other thing you might want to do is to remove the code from the document's `OnNewDocument` function that creates the wines in every new document. That code was useful to demonstrate that the document was working, but now that you have the ability to add any wines you want to add, it is no longer necessary. Locate the `OnNewDocument` function in CELLADOC.CPP, and delete these lines:

```
m_cWineColl.Add( new CWine
        ( "Chateau Lafite", 1985, "Red", 2));
m_cWineColl.Add( new CWine
        ( "Lovers Leap Chardonnay", 1991, "White", 4));
m_cWineColl.Add( new CWine
        ( "La Turk", 1985, "Red", 96));
SetModifiedFlag( TRUE );
```

You have now completed all of the steps necessary to invoke the Add Wine dialog in the `Cellar` application, and to use its results to update `Cellar`'s document and view with the user's input.

Rebuild and Test Your Application

You have done a lot of work in this chapter. Now it is time to see the payoff. If Class Wizard is still open, close it, and also close App Studio, if it is still open. Pull down the Application Workbench Project menu, and click Build CELLAR.EXE. When Cellar has completed building (of course there won't be any errors!), run the program.

In the Chapter 39 version of Cellar the application started with three wines listed in the view. If you deleted the code from OnNewDocument as suggested, the new version of Cellar will not show any wines initially—that is why you did so much work to create the Add Wine dialog.

It's time to see your work in action. Click on Cellar's Edit menu. The Add Wine item should appear at the bottom of the Edit pull-down menu. Click on the Add Wine selection. The Add Wine dialog should appear. Go ahead and add a few wines into the application. To add a wine to Cellar, fill in the four fields in the Add Wine dialog and click the OK button. When you click OK in the Add Wine dialog, the dialog should close, and the information on the wine you added should appear in Cellar's view.

Figure 40.16 shows Cellar running, with a few wines added to the list and the Add Wine dialog open with information filled in about another wine.

Figure 40.16

The Cellar Application, with its Add Wine dialog.

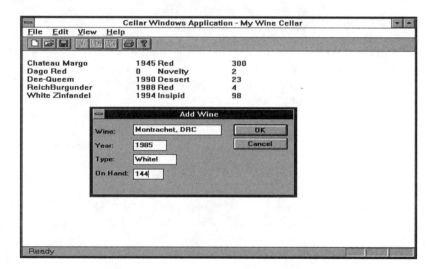

Congratulate yourself! You have completed a working Windows application.

Going Forward with MFC

MFC is an immensely rich and complex environment. So far, you have only looked at a few small parts of its capabilities. Even then, you have come a long way from your first C++ program. Look at the first programs you wrote at the beginning of this book. Now, look at the application you just completed.

You are well on your way to becoming an accomplished Windows programmer. You also have completed this book, and are ready for more advanced fare, such as Que's *Using Visual C++*, which will help you build on the skills you have learned here. But the best way to learn MFC is to write MFC programs. Pick out a simple subject that interests you, maybe a name and address book or a calendar, or maybe even a simple drawing program. The important thing is to choose a subject that isn't too complex and that interests you. As you work on an application of your own choosing, you will quickly learn how to add new features to an MFC program, and how to enhance the features of the program you developed here.

Summary

The process of creating a dialog and adding a menu item to invoke the dialog is actually much faster and simpler to do than it is to read (or write) about. Just remember the basic steps:

1. Design the dialog in App Studio.

2. Create a class for the dialog in Class Wizard.

3. Use App Studio to add a menu item to invoke the dialog.

4. Use Class Wizard to bind the menu item to a function to process the dialog.

5. Write the code to process the dialog.

You have done a lot in the last 40 chapters, but the process is just beginning. Good luck with your Visual C++ programming career!

Review Questions

1. How do you add a control to a dialog?

2. How can you tell which control is currently selected in the Dialog Editor?

3. How does Windows communicate user actions to your application?

4. What function do you call to cause a dialog to display itself, so that the user must complete the dialog before using other parts of the application?

Part X

Appendixes

Memory Addressing, Binary, and Hexadecimal Review

You do not have to understand the concepts in this appendix to become well-versed in C++. The only way you can master C++, however, is to spend some time learning about the "behind the scenes" roles played by binary numbers. The material presented here is not difficult, but many programmers do not take the time to study it. Hence, there are a handful of C++ masters who learn this material and understand how C++ works "under the hood," and there are those who will never be as expert in the language as they could be.

You should take the time to learn about addressing, binary numbers, and hexadecimal numbers. These fundamental principles are presented here for you to learn, and although a working knowledge of C++ is possible without understanding them, they will greatly enhance your C++ skills (and your skills in every other programming language).

After reading this appendix, you will better understand why different C++ data types hold different ranges of numbers. You also will see the importance of being able to represent hexadecimal numbers in C++, and you will better understand C++ array and pointer addressing.

Computer Memory

Each memory location inside your computer holds a single character called a *byte*. A byte is any character, whether it is a letter of the alphabet, a digit, or a special character such as a period, question mark, or even a space (a blank character). If your computer contains 640K of memory, it can hold a total of approximately 640,000 bytes of memory. This means that once you fill your computer's memory with 640K, there will be no room for an additional character unless you overwrite something else.

Before describing the physical layout of your computer's memory, it may be best to take a detour and explain what 640K means.

Memory and Disk Measurements

K means approximately 1,000 and exactly 1,024.

By appending the *K* (from the metric word *Kilo*) to memory measurements, the manufacturers of computers do not have to attach as many zeros to the end of numbers for disk and memory storage. The K stands for approximately 1,000 bytes. As you are about to see, almost everything inside your computer is based on a power of 2. Therefore, the K of computer memory measurements actually equals the power of 2 closest to 1,000, which is 2 to the 10th power, or 1,024. Because 1,024 is very close to 1,000, computerists often think of K as meaning 1,000, even though they know it equals *approximately* 1,000.

Think for a moment what 640K exactly equals. Practically speaking, 640K is about 640,000 bytes. To be exact, however, 640K equals 640 times 1,024, or 655,360. This explains why the PC DOS command CHKDSK returns 655,360 as your total memory (assuming that you have 640K of RAM) instead of 640,000.

M means approximately 1,000,000 and exactly 1,048,576.

Because extended memory and many disk drives can hold such a large amount of data (typically several million characters), there is an additional memory measurement shortcut used, called *M*, which stands for *Meg*, or *Megabytes*. The M is a shortcut for approximately one million bytes. Therefore, 20M is approximately 20,000,000 characters, or bytes, of storage. As with K, the M literally stands for 1,048,576 because that is the closest power of 2 (2 to the 20th power) to one million.

How many bytes of storage is 60 megabytes? It is approximately 60 million characters, or 62,914,560 characters to be exact.

Memory Addresses

Like each house in your town, each memory location in your computer has a unique *address*. A memory address is simply a sequential number, starting at 0, that labels each memory location. Figure A.1 shows a diagram of how your computer memory addresses are numbered if you have 640K of RAM.

Figure A.1

Memory
addresses for a
640K computer.

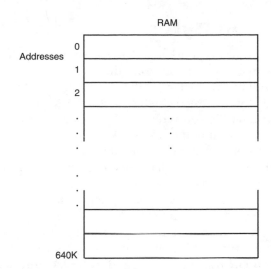

By using unique addresses, your computer can keep track of memory. When the computer stores a result of a calculation in memory, it finds an empty address, or one matching the data area where the result is to go, and stores the result at that address.

Your C++ programs and data share computer memory with DOS. DOS must always reside in memory while you operate your computer; otherwise, your programs would have no way to access disks, printers, the screen, or the keyboard. Figure A.2 shows computer memory being shared by DOS and a C++ program. The exact amount of memory taken by DOS and a C++ program is determined by the version of DOS you use, how many DOS extras (such as device drivers and buffers) your computer uses, and the size and needs of your C++ program and data.

Figure A.2

DOS, your C++
program, and your
program's data
share the same
memory.

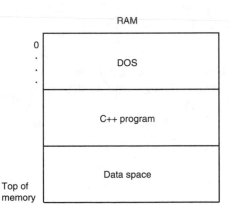

Bits and Bytes

You now know that a single address of memory might contain any character, called a byte. You know that your computer holds many bytes of information, but it does not store those characters in the same way that humans think of characters. For example, if you press the letter W on your keyboard while working in your C++ editor, you see the W on-screen, and you also know that the W is stored in a memory location at some unique address. Actually, your computer does not store the letter W; it stores electrical impulses that stand for the letter W.

Electricity, which is what runs through the components of your computer to make it understand and execute your programs, can exist in only two states: on and off. As with a light bulb, electricity is either flowing (it is on) or not flowing (it is off). Even though you can dim some lights, the electricity is still either on or off.

Today's modern digital computers use this on/off concept. Your computer is nothing more than millions of on and off switches. You may have heard about integrated circuits, transistors, and even vacuum tubes that computers over the years have contained. These electrical components are nothing more than switches that rapidly turn electrical impulses on and off.

The binary digits 1 and 0 (called bits) represent on and off states of electricity.

This two-state (on and off) mode of electricity is called a *binary* state of electricity. Computer people use a 1 to represent an on state (a switch in the computer that is on) and a 0 to represent an off state (a switch that is off). These numbers, 1 and 0, are called binary digits. The term *binary digits* is usually shortened to *bits*. A bit is either a 1 or a 0, representing an on or off state of electricity. Different combinations of bits represent different characters.

Several years ago, someone listed every single character that might be represented on a computer, including all uppercase letters, all lowercase letters, the digits 0 through 9, the many other characters (such as %, *, {, and +), and some special control characters. When you add up the total number of characters that a PC can represent, you get 256 of them. These are listed in Appendix C's ASCII (pronounced "ask-ee") table.

The order of the ASCII table's 256 characters is basically arbitrary, just as the radio's Morse code table is arbitrary. With Morse code, different sets of long and short beeps represent different letters of the alphabet. In the ASCII table, a different combination of bits (1s and 0s strung together) represents each of the 256 ASCII characters. The ASCII table is a standard table used by almost every PC in the world. Its letters form the acronym for *American Standard Code for Information Interchange*. (There is a similar table that some minicomputers and mainframes use, called the EBCDIC table.)

It turns out that if you take every different combination of eight 0s strung together all the way to eight 1s strung together (that is, from 00000000, 00000001, 00000010, and so on, until you get to 11111110, and last, 11111111), you will have a total of 256 of them! (256 is 2 to the 8th power.) Each memory location in your computer holds eight bits each. These bits can be any combination of eight 1s and 0s. This brings you to the following fundamental rule of computers:

Because it takes a combination of eight 1s and 0s to represent a character, and because each byte of computer memory can hold exactly one character, it holds true that eight bits equal one byte.

For a better perspective on this, consider that the bit pattern needed for the uppercase letter A is 01000001. No other character in the ASCII table "looks" like this to the computer because each of the 256 characters is assigned a unique bit pattern.

Suppose that you press the A key on your keyboard. Your keyboard does *not* send a letter A to the computer; instead, it looks in its ASCII table for the on and off states of electricity that represent the letter A. As figure A.3 shows, when you press the A key, the keyboard actually sends 01000001 (as on and off impulses) to the computer. Your computer simply stores this bit pattern for A in a memory location. Even though you can think of the memory location as holding an A, it really holds the byte 01000001.

Figure A.3

Your computer keeps track of characters by their bit patterns.

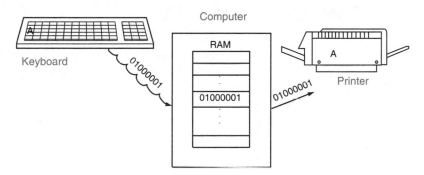

If you were to print that A, your computer does not send an A to the printer but sends the 01000001 bit pattern for an A. The printer receives that bit pattern, looks up the correct letter in the ASCII table, and prints an A.

From the time you press the A until the time you see it on the printer, it is *not* the letter A! It is the ASCII pattern of bits the computer uses to represent an A. Because a computer is electrical and electricity is easily turned on and off, this is a very nice way for the computer to manipulate and move characters, and it can do so very quickly. Actually, if it were up to the computer, you would enter everything by its bit pattern and look at all the results in their bit patterns! This would not be good, so devices such as the keyboard, screen, and printer work part of the time with letters as we know them. That is why the ASCII table is such as integral part of a computer.

There are times when your computer treats two bytes as a single value. Even though memory locations are typically eight bits wide, many CPUs access memory two bytes at a time. In that case, the two bytes are called a *word* of memory. On other computers (commonly mainframes), the word size may be four bytes (32 bits) or even eight bytes (64 bits).

739

A Summary of Bits and Bytes

A bit is either a 1 or a 0 that represents an on or off state of electricity.

Eight bits represent a byte.

A byte, or eight bits, represents one character.

Each memory location of your computer is eight bits (a single byte) wide. Therefore, each memory location can hold one character of data. A list of all possible characters can be found in the ASCII table in Appendix C.

If the CPU accesses memory two bytes at a time, those two bytes are called a word of memory.

The Order of Bits

To further understand memory, you should know how programmers refer to individual bits. Figure A.4 shows a byte and a two-byte word. Notice that the far right bit is called bit 0. From bit 0, keep counting by 1s as you move left. For a byte, the bits are numbered 0 to 7, from right to left. For a double byte (a 16-bit word), the bits are numbered from 0 to 15, from right to left.

Bit 0 is called the *least-significant bit*, or sometimes the *low-order bit*. Bit 7 (or bit 15 for a 2-byte word) is called the *most-significant bit*, or sometimes the *high-order bit*.

Figure A.4

The order of bits in a byte and a two-byte word.

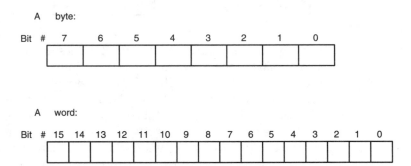

Binary Numbers

Because a computer works best with 1s and 0s, its internal numbering method is limited to a *base-2* (binary) numbering system. People work in a *base-10* numbering system in the real world. The base-10 numbering system is sometimes called the decimal numbering system. There are always as many different digits as the base in a numbering system. For example, in the base-10 system, there are 10 digits,

0 through 9. As soon as you count to 9 and run out of digits, you have to combine some that you already used. The number 10 is a representation of 10 values but combines the digits 1 and 0.

The same is true of base 2. There are only two digits, 0 and 1. As soon as you run out of digits, after the second one, you have to reuse digits. The first 7 binary numbers are

> 0   1   10   11   100   101   110

If you do not understand how these numbers were derived, that is okay; you will see how in a moment. For the time being, you should realize that no more than two digits, 0 and 1, can be used to represent any base-2 number, just as no more than 10 digits, 0 through 9, can be used to represent any base-10 number in the regular "real world" numbering system.

You should know that a base-10 number, such as 2,981, does not really mean anything by itself. You must assume what base it is. You get very used to working with base-10 numbers because that is what the world uses. However, the number 2,981 actually represents a quantity based on powers of 10. For example, figure A.5 shows what the number 2,981 represents. Notice that each digit in the number stands for a certain number of a power of 10.

Figure A.5

The base-10 breakdown of the number 2,981.

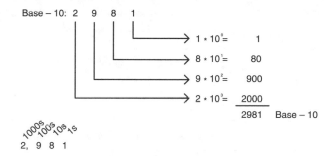

This same concept applies when you work in a base-2 numbering system. Your computer uses this numbering system, so the power of 2 is just as common to your computer as the power of 10 is to you. The only difference is that the digits in a base-2 number represent powers of 2 and not powers of 10. Figure A.6 shows what the binary numbers 10101 and 10011110 are in base-10. This is how you convert any binary number to its base-10 equivalent.

A binary number can contain only the digits 1 and 0.

A base-2 number contains only 1s and 0s. To convert any base-2 number to base-10, add each power of 2 everywhere a 1 appears in the number. The base-2 number 101 represents the base-10 number 5; there are two 1s in the number—one in the 2 to the 0th power (which equals 1), and one in the 2 to the 2nd power (which equals 4). Table A.1 shows the first 17 base-10 numbers, and their matching base-2 numbers.

Figure A.6

The base-2 breakdown of the numbers 10101 and 10011110.

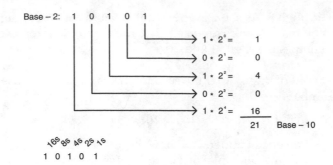

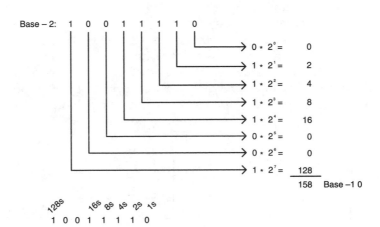

Table A.1. The first 17 base-10 (decimal) and base-2 (binary) numbers.

Base-10	Base-2	Base-10	Base-2
0	0	9	1001
1	1	10	1010
2	10	11	1011
3	11	12	1100
4	100	13	1101
5	101	14	1110
6	110	15	1111
7	111	16	10000
8	1000	17	10001

You do not have to memorize the preceding table; you should be able to figure the base-10 numbers from their matching binary numbers by adding the powers of 2 over each 1 (on bit). Many programmers do memorize the first several binary numbers, however, which can come in handy in advanced programming techniques.

What is the largest binary number a byte can hold? The answer is all 1s, or 11111111. If you add the first 8 powers of 2, you get 255.

A byte holds either a number or an ASCII character, depending on how it is accessed. For example, if you were to convert the base-2 number 01000001 to a base-10 number, you would get 65. However, this also happens to be the ASCII bit pattern for an uppercase letter A. Check out the ASCII table, and you will see that the A is ASCII code 65. Because the ASCII table is so closely linked with the bit patterns, the computer knows (by the context of how they are used) to work with a number 65, or a letter A.

Unlike an ASCII character, a binary number is not limited to a byte. Sixteen or 32 bits at a time can represent a binary number (and usually do). There are more powers of 2 to add when converting that number to a base-10 number, but the process is the same. You ought to be able to figure out by now (although it may take a little time to calculate) that 1010101010101010 is 43,690 in the base-10 decimal numbering system.

To convert from decimal to binary takes a little more effort. Luckily, you rarely need to convert in that direction. Converting from base-2 to base-10 is not covered here.

Binary Arithmetic

At their lowest level, computers can only add and convert binary numbers to their negative equivalents. Computers are not truly able to subtract, multiply, and divide, although they simulate these operations through judicious use of the addition and negative-conversion techniques.

If a computer were to add the numbers 7 and 6, it can do so (at the binary level). The result will be 13. If the computer is instructed to subtract 7 from 13, it cannot do so. However, it can take the negative value of 7 and add that to 13. Because –7 plus 13 equals 6, the result is a simulated subtraction.

To multiply, computers perform repeated addition. To multiply 6 by 7, the computer adds seven 6s together and gets a 42 as the answer. To divide 42 by 7, a computer keeps subtracting 7 from 42 repeatedly until it gets to a 0 answer (or less than 0 if there is a remainder), and then counts the number of times it took to reach 0.

All math is done at the binary level, so the following additions are possible in binary arithmetic:

$0 + 0 = 0$

$0 + 1 = 1$

$1 + 0 = 1$

$1 + 1 = 10$

Because these are binary numbers, the last result is not the number 10, but the binary number 2. (Just as the binary 10 means "no ones, and carry an additional power of two," the decimal number 10 means "no ones, carry a power of ten.") There is not a binary digit to represent a 2, so you have to combine the 1 and the 0 to form the new number.

Since binary addition is the foundation of all other math, you should learn how to add binary numbers. You will then understand how computers do the rest of their arithmetic.

Using the binary addition rules previously shown, consider the following binary calculation:

```
 01000001  (65 decimal)
+00101100  (44 decimal)
 01101101  (109 decimal)
```

The first number, 01000001, is 65 decimal. This also happens to be the bit pattern for the ASCII A, but if you add with it, the computer knows to interpret it as the number 65 instead of the character A.

The following binary addition requires a carry into bit 4 and bit 6:

```
 00101011  (43 decimal)
+00100111  (39 decimal)
 01010010  (82 decimal)
```

Typically, you have to ignore bits that carry past bit 7, or bit 15 for double-byte arithmetic. For example, both of the following binary additions produce incorrect positive results:

```
 10000000 (128 decimal)    1000000000000000 (65536 decimal)
+10000000 (128 decimal)   +1000000000000000 (65536 decimal)
 00000000 (0 decimal)      0000000000000000 (0 decimal!)
```

Because there is no 9th or 17th bit for the carry, both of these additions produce incorrect results. Because the byte and 16-bit word cannot hold the answers, the magnitude of both of these additions is not possible. The computer must be programmed, at the bit level, to perform *multiword arithmetic*, which is beyond the scope of this book.

Binary Negative Numbers

Negative binary numbers are stored in their 2's complement format.

Because subtracting requires understanding binary negative numbers, you need to learn how computers represent them. The computer uses *2's complement* to represent negative numbers in binary form. To convert a binary number to its 2's complement (to its negative) you must do the following:

1. Reverse the bits (the 1s to 0s, and the 0s to 1s).

2. Add 1.

This may seem a little strange at first, but it works very well for binary numbers. To represent a binary – 65, you need to take the binary 65 and convert it to its 2's complement, such as

01000001 (65 decimal)

10111110 (Reverse the bits)

_____+1 (Add 1)
10111111 (–65 binary)

By converting the 65 to its 2's complement, you produce –65 in binary. You might wonder what makes 10111111 mean the negative 65, but by the 2's complement definition, it means –65.

If you were told that 10111111 is a negative number, how would you know which binary number it is? You perform the 2's complement on it. Whatever number you produce is the positive of that negative number. Note the following example:

10111111 (–65 decimal)

01000000 (Reverse the bits)

_____+1 (Add 1)
01000001 (65 decimal)

Something might seem wrong at this point. You just saw that 10111111 is the binary –65, but isn't 10111111 *also* 191 decimal (adding the powers of 2 marked by the 1s in the number, as explained in a previous section)? It depends on whether the number is *signed* or *unsigned*. If a number is signed, the computer looks at the most-significant bit (the leftmost bit) called the *sign bit*. If the most-significant bit is a 1, the number is negative. If it is 0, the number is positive.

Most numbers are 16 bits in length. That is, two-byte words are used to store most integers. This is not always the case for all computers, but it is true for most PCs.

In the C++ programming language, you can designate numbers as either signed integers or unsigned integers (they are signed by default if you do not specify otherwise). If you designate a variable as a signed integer, the computer will interpret the high-order bit as a sign bit. If the high-order bit is on (1), the number is negative. If the high-order bit is off (0), the number is positive. If you designate a variable as an unsigned integer, however, the computer uses the high-order bit as just another power of 2. That is why the range of unsigned integer variables goes higher (generally from 0 to 65536, but it depends on the computer) than for signed integer variables (generally from –32768 to +32767).

After so much description, a little review is in order. Assume that the following 16-bit binary numbers are unsigned:

0011010110100101   1001100110101010   1000000000000000

These numbers are unsigned, so bit 15 is not the sign bit, but just another power of 2. You should practice converting these large 16-bit numbers to decimal. Following are the decimal equivalents:

13733   39338   32768

If these numbers are signed numbers, however, the high-order bit (bit 15) indicates the sign. If the sign bit is 0, the number is positive, and you convert the numbers to decimal in the usual manner. If the sign bit is 1, you must convert the numbers to their 2's complement in order to find what they equal. Following are their decimal equivalents:

+13733   –26197   –32768

To compute the last two binary numbers to their decimal equivalents, take their 2's complement and convert it to decimal. Put a minus sign in front of the result, and you find what the original number represents.

> **Tip:** To make sure that you convert a number to its 2's complement correctly, you can add the 2's complement to its original positive value. If the answer is 0 (ignoring the extra carry to the left), you know that the 2's complement number is correct. This is just like saying that decimal opposites, such as –72 + 72, add up to zero.

Hexadecimal Numbers

Hexadecimal numbers use 16 unique digits, 0 through F.

All those 1s and 0s get confusing to people. If it were up to your computer, you would enter *everything* as 1s and 0s! This is unacceptable because people don't like to keep track of all those 1s and 0s. Therefore, a *hexadecimal* numbering system (sometimes called *hex*) was devised. The hexadecimal numbering system is based on base-16 numbers. As with other bases, there are 16 unique digits in the base-16 numbering system. Here are the first 19 hexadecimal numbers:

0 1 2 3 4 5 6 7 8 9 A B C D E F 10 11 12

Because there are only 10 unique digits as we know them (0 through 9), we must use the letters A through F to represent the remaining six digits. (Anything could have been used, but the designers of the hexadecimal numbering system decided to use the first six letters of the alphabet.)

To understand base-16 numbers, you should know how to convert them to base-10, so that they represent numbers with which people are familiar. You perform the conversion to base-10 from base-16 in the same way that you did with base-2, but instead of representing powers of 2, each hexadecimal digit represents powers of 16. Figure A.7 shows how to convert the number 3C5 to decimal.

Figure A.7

Converting hexadecimal 3C5 to its decimal equivalent.

Base –16: 3 C 5

$5 * 16^0 = 5 * 1 = \quad 5$

$C * 16^1 = 12 * 16 = \quad 192$

$3 * 16^2 = 3 * 256 = \underline{768}$

965   Base –10

256s 16s 1s
3 C 5

Tip: There are calculators available for programmers to do conversions between numbers in base-16, base-10, and base-2, as well as perform base-2's complement arithmetic.

You ought to be able to convert 2B to its decimal 43 equivalent and convert E1 to decimal 225 in the same manner. Table A.2 shows the first 20 decimal, binary, and hexadecimal numbers.

Table A.2. The first 20 base-10 (decimal), base-2 (binary), and base-16 (hexadecimal) numbers.

Base-10	Base-2	Base-16	Base-10	Base-2	Base-16
1	1	1	11	1011	A
2	10	2	12	1100	B
3	11	3	13	1101	C
4	100	4	14	1110	D
5	101	5	15	1111	E
6	110	6	16	10000	F
7	111	7	17	10001	10
8	1000	8	18	10010	11
9	1001	9	19	10011	12
10	1010	A	20	10100	13

Why Learn Hexadecimal?

Hexadecimal notation is extremely efficient for describing memory locations and values because of its close association to the actual binary numbers your computer uses. It is much easier for you (and more important at this level, for your *computer*) to convert from base-16 to base-2 than from base-10 to base-2. Therefore, you sometimes want to represent data at the bit level, but using hexadecimal notation is easier (and requires less typing) than using binary numbers.

To convert from hexadecimal to binary, convert each hex digit to its 4-bit binary number. You can use Table A.2 as a guide for this. For example, the hexadecimal number

> 5B75

can be converted to binary by taking each digit and converting it to four binary numbers. If you need leading zeros to "pad" the four digits, use them. The number becomes

> 0101 1011 0111 0101

It turns out that the binary number 0101101101110101 is equal to the hexadecimal number 5B75. This was much easier than converting them both to decimal first.

To convert from binary to hexadecimal, reverse this process. If you are given the binary number

1101000011110111111010

you can convert it to hexadecimal by grouping the bits into groups of four, starting with the right bit. Since there is not an even number of groups of four, pad the leftmost one with 0s. You will then have the following:

0011 0100 0011 1101 1111 1010

Now you just have to convert each group of four binary digits into their hexadecimal number equivalents. You can refer to Table A.2 for help. You then get the following base-16 number:

343DFA

The C++ programming language also supports the base-8 *octal* representation of numbers. Because octal numbers are rarely used much in today's computers, they are not covered here.

How This Relates to C++

The material presented here may seem foreign to many programmers. The binary and 2's complement arithmetic resides deep in your computer and is shielded from most programmers (except assembly language programmers). Understanding this level of your computer, however, explains everything else you learn.

Many C++ programmers learn C++ before delving into binary and hexadecimal representation. For them, there is much about the C++ language that seems strange but could be explained very easily if they understood these basic concepts.

For example, a signed integer holds a different range of numbers from that of an unsigned integer. You now know the reason for this: The sign bit is used in two different ways, depending on whether the number is designated as signed or unsigned.

The ASCII table should make more sense to you after this discussion as well. The ASCII table is an integral part of your computer. Characters are not actually stored in memory and variables; instead, their ASCII bit patterns are. That is why C++ is able to move between characters and integers with ease. The following two C++ statements are allowed, although they probably would not be in another programming language:

```
char c = 65;     // Put the ASCII letter A in c
int ci = 'A';    // Put the number 65 in ci
```

The hexadecimal notation taught to a lot of C++ programmers also makes more sense when the programmers truly understand base-16 numbers. For example, if you saw the line

```
char a = '\x041';
```

you would be able to convert the hex 41 to decimal (65 decimal) if you wanted to know what was really being assigned. In addition, C++ systems programmers find that they can better interface with assembly language programs if they understand the concepts presented here.

If you gain only a cursory knowledge of this material at this point, you will be very much ahead of the game when you program in C++.

Answers to Review Questions

Chapter 1 Answers

1. Low-level languages express a problem and its solution in a language that is very close to the computer's native machine language. High-level languages allow you to express a problem and its solution in a language you can readily understand.

2. It has aspects of both.

3. C++ embodies some of the object-oriented models and allows the user to define data types not possible under C++.

4. It offers very close integration of all the tools required to produce a Windows program.

5. DOS and Windows

6. BIOS calls are faster. Operating system calls are more portable.

Chapter 2 Answers

1. False

2. The text window

3. Clicking means to press a mouse button once quickly. Double-clicking means to press a mouse button twice rapidly. Dragging means to press a mouse button and hold it down while you move the mouse.

4. No. The menus are there so that you don't have to memorize commands.

5. Click **Help**.

6. It means that the help screen you bring up is a response to whatever the cursor is on.

7. Pressing F1 or clicking the **Help** menu item.

8. You use the shortcut keys as an alternative to having to go through the levels of menus.

Chapter 3 Answers

1. A set of detailed instructions that tells the computer what to do

2. Buy one or write it yourself.

3. False

4. The program produces the output.

5. A program editor

6. .CPP

7. You must first plan the program by determining the steps you will take to produce the final program.

8. To get the errors out of your program

9. False. You must compile a program before linking it. Most compilers link the program automatically.

10. The menu cannot be customized and they cannot display dialog boxes or other custom Windows controls.

Chapter 4 Answers

1. /* before and */ after

2. A holding place for data that can be changed

3. A value that cannot be changed

4. False

5. +, -, *, and /

6. = (the assignment operator)

7. False. There can be floating-point, double floating-point, short integers, long integers, and many more variable data types.

8. cout

9. city must be a variable name because it is not enclosed in quotation marks.

10. All C++ statements must be in lowercase.

Chapter 5 Answers

1. my_name and sales_89

2. Characters: 'X' and '0'

   Strings: "2.0" and "X"

   Integer: 0 and -708

   Floating-point constants: -12.0 and 65.4

3. Seven variables are declared—3 integers, 3 characters, and 1 floating-point variable.

4. A null zero, also called a binary zero

5. True

6. 1

7. As a series of ASCII values, representing the characters and blanks in the string, ending in a binary 0

8. As a single binary 0

Chapter 6 Answers

1. `char my_name[ ] = "This is C++";`
2. 11
3. 12
4. Binary zero
5. Two character arrays are declared, each with 25 elements.
6. False. The keyword `char` must precede the variable name.
7. True. The binary zero terminates the string.
8. False. The characters do not represent a string because there is no terminating zero.

Chapter 7 Answers

1. False. You can define constants only with the `#define` preprocessor directive.
2. `#include`
3. `#define`
4. True
5. The preprocessor changes your source code before the compiler sees the source code.
6. Use angle brackets when the include files reside in the compiler's include subdirectory. Use quotation marks when the include file resides in the same subdirectory as the source program.
7. Defined constants are easier to change because you just have to change the line with `#define`, not several other lines in the program.
8. `iostream.h`
9. False. You cannot define constants enclosed in quotation marks (as `"MESSAGE"` is in the `cout` operator).
10. Amount is 4

Chapter 8 Answers

1. cout sends output to the screen, and cin gets input from the keyboard.

2. The prompt informs the user of what is expected.

3. Four values will be entered.

4. The cin function gets its value(s) from the keyboard, and the assignment statement gets its value from data in the program.

5. The backslash, "\" character is special

6. The following value prints (with one leading space): 123.456

Chapter 9 Answers

1. **a.** 5

    b. 6

    c. 5

2. **a.** 2

    b. 7

3. **a.** a = (3 + 3) / (4 + 4);

    b. x = (a - b) * ((a - c) * (a - c));

    c. f = (a1 / 2) / (b1 / 3);

    d. d = ((8 - x * x) / (x - 9)) - ((4 * 2 - 1) / (x * x * x));

4.
```
#include <iostream.h>

#define PI 3.14159
int  main(void)
    {
    cout << (PI * (4 * 4));
    return 0;
    }
```

5.
```
r = 100 % 4;

cout << r;
```

Chapter 10 Answers

1. ==

2. **a.** False

b. True

c. True

d. True

3. True

4. The `if` statement determines what code executes if the relational test is true. The `if-else` statement determines what happens for both the true and the false relational tests.

5. No

6. **a.** True

b. False

c. True

Chapter 11 Answers

1. &&, ¦¦, and !

2. **a.** False

b. False

c. True

d. True

3. **a.** True

b. 11

c. True

4. g is 25 and f was changed to 35

Chapter 12 Answers

1. The `if-else` statement

2. The conditional operator is the only C++ operator with three arguments.

3.
```
if (a == b)
    ans = c + 2;
else
    ans = c + 3;
```

4. True

5. The increment and decrement operators compile into single assembly instructions.

6. A comma (,) operator that forces a left-to-right execution of the statements on either side

7. The output cannot reliably be determined. Do not pass an increment operator as an argument.

8. The size of name is 20

Chapter 13 Answers

1. `!, &, ^, ¦, &=, ^=, ¦=, <<,` and `>>`

2. **a.** 1

   b. 1

   c. 0

   d. 0

3. True

4. The 2's complement converts a number to its negative; the 1's complement simply reverses the bit pattern.

Chapter 14 Answers

1. The `while` loop tests for a true condition at the top of the loop, and the `do-while` loop tests at the bottom.

2. A counter variable increments by one, and a total variable increments by the addition to the total you are performing.

3. `++`

4. True. The braces are not required if the body of the loop is a single statement, but the braces are always recommended.

5. There are no braces. The second `cout` will always execute no matter what the `while` loop's relational test results in.

6. `stdlib.h`

7. One time

8. By returning a value inside the `exit()` function's parentheses

9. `This is the outer loop`

   `This is the outer loop`

   `This is the outer loop`

   `This is the outer loop`

10. The program could have executed a divide by zero.

Chapter 15 Answers

1. A sequence of one or more instructions executed repeatedly

2. False

3. A loop within a loop

4. The expressions may be initialized elsewhere, such as before the loop or in the body of the loop.

5. The inside loop

6. `10`
   `7`
   `4`
   `1`

7. True

8. The body of the `for` loop stops repeating.

9. False, because of the semicolon after the first `for` loop

10. There is no output. The value of `start` is already less than `end` when the loop begins; therefore, the `for` loop's test is immediately false.

Chapter 16 Answers

1. To force a program to pause

2. Some computers are faster than others.

3. If the `continue` and `break` statements are unconditional, there would be little use for them.

4. There is no output because of the unconditional `continue` statement.

5. *****

6. A single variable rarely can hold a large enough value for the timer's count.

Chapter 17 Answers

1. The program does not execute sequentially, as it would without `goto`.

2. The `switch` statement

3. The `break` statement

4. False

5.
```
switch (num)
     {
     case 1:
          cout << "Alpha";
          break;
     case 2:
          cout << "Beta";
          break;
     case 3:
          cout << "Gamma";
          break;
     default:
          cout << "Other";
          break;
     }
```

6. do

```
        {
        cout << "What is your first name? ";
        cin >> name;
        }
    while ((name[ 0 ] < 'A') ¦¦ (name[ 0 ] > 'Z'));
```

Chapter 18 Answers

1. True

2. `main()`

3. Several smaller functions, so that each function performs a single task

4. Function names always end with a set of parentheses.

5. By putting separating comments between functions

6. The function `sq_25()` cannot be nested within `calc_it()`.

7. A function call

Chapter 19 Answers

1. True

2. A local variable is passed as an argument.

3. False

4. The variable data types

5. Static

6. You should never pass global variables; they do not need to be passed.

7. Three

Chapter 20 Answers

1. Arrays are always passed by address.

2. Nonarray variables are always passed by value (unless you override the default with & before each variable name).

3. True

4. No

5. Yes

6. The data types of variables x, y, and z are not declared in the receiving parameter list.

7. C

Chapter 21 Answers

1. By putting the return type to the left of the function name

2. One

3. To prototype library functions

4. `int`

5. False

6. Prototypes ensure that the correct number and type of parameters are being passed.

7. Global variables are known across functions already.

8. The return type is float. Three parameters are being passed—a character, an integer, and a floating-point variable.

Chapter 22 Answers

1. To achieve portability between different computers

2. False. The standard output can be redirected to any device through the operating system.

3. `get()` assumes `stdin` for the input device.

4. `cout`

5. `>` and `<`

6. `getche()`

7. False. The input from `get()` goes to a buffer as you type it.

8. Enter

9. True

Chapter 23 Answers

1. The character-testing functions do not change the characters passed to them.

2. `gets()` and `fgets()`

3. `floor()` rounds down, and `ceil()` rounds up.

4. False (the inner function returns 1)

5. `ParkerPeter`

6. `8 9`

7. True

8. `Prog` with a null zero at the end

9. True

Chapter 24 Answers

1. False

2. The array subscripts differentiate array elements from one another.

3. C++ does not initialize or zero out arrays for you.

4. `0`

5. Yes. All arrays are passed by address because an array name is nothing more than an address to that array.

6. C++ initializes all global variables (and every other static variable in your program) to zero or null zero.

Chapter 25 Answers

1. False

2. From the low numbers "floating" to the top of the array like bubbles

3. Ascending order

4. The name of an array is an address to the starting element of that array.

5. **a.** Eagles

   b. Rams

   c. les

   d. E

   e. E

   f. s

   g. g

Chapter 26 Answers

1. `int scores[ 5 ][ 6 ];`

2. `char initials[ 4 ][ 10 ][ 20 ]`

3. The first subscript represents rows, and the last subscript represents columns.

4. 30

5. **a.** 2

   b. 1

   c. 91

   d. 8

6. Nested for loops step through multidimensional tables very easily.

7. **a.** 78

   b. 100

   c. 90

Chapter 27 Answers

1. **a.** Integer pointer

   b. Character pointer

   c. Floating-point pointer

2. Address of

3. *

4. `pt_sal = &salary;`

5. False

6. Yes

7. **a.** 2313.54

   b. 2313.54

   c. Invalid

   d. Invalid

8. B

Chapter 28 Answers

1. Array names are pointer constants, not pointer variables.

2. Four

3. A, B, C, D, and E. (Parentheses are needed around `iptr + 4` to make F valid.)

4. You just have to move pointers, not entire strings.

5. A, B, and D

Chapter 29 Answers

1. Structures hold groups of more than one value, each of which can be a different data type.

2. Members

3. At declaration time and at runtime

4. Structures are passed by copy.

5. False. Memory is reserved only when structure variables are declared.

6. Globally

7. Locally

8. Four

Chapter 30 Answers

1. True

2. Arrays are easier to manage.

3. **a.** `inventory[32].price = 12.33;`

   b. `inventory[11].part_no[0] = 'X';`

   c. `inventory[96] = inventory[62];`

4. **a.** `item` is not a structure variable.

   b. `inventory` is an array and must have a subscript.

   c. `inventory` is an array and must have a subscript.

Chapter 31 Answers

1. Write, append, and read

2. Disks hold more data than can fit in memory.

3. You can access sequential files only in the order in which they were originally written.

4. An error condition occurs.

5. The old file is overwritten.

6. The file is created.

7. The `eof()` function returns true when an end-of-file condition is met.

Chapter 32 Answers

1. Records are stored in files, and structures are stored in memory.

2. False

3. The file stream continually updates to point to the next byte to read.

4. `write()` and `read()`

5. `rewind()` and `seekg(0, beg);`

6. `beg` (or 0), `cur` (or 1), and `end` (or 2)

7. No file name is specified.

Chapter 33 Answers

1. Data members and member functions
2. No
3. No
4. Private
5. Place the label `public:` before it in the class.

Chapter 34 Answers

1. A file that contains a set of instructions to automate the process of compiling and linking a multiple file program
2. As used in Chapter 34, an operator that helps tell the compiler to which class a function belongs
3. `class myComputer : Computer`
4. An access specifier that allows a derived class to access members, but denies access to the members to outside users of the class
5. False

Chapter 35 Answers

1. A collection of precompiled classes stored in a .LIB file
2. False
3. Collections
4. The process of going through a collection one element at a time
5. A data type that represents the location of an element in an MFC List Collection

Chapter 37 Answers

1. `CWinApp`
2. Serialization and persistence
3. False. The main window of an MDI application is a `CMDIFrameWnd`.
4. App Studio

Chapter 38 Answers

1. Because App Wizard uses the same name for some files in every project

2. `CMainFrame, OnCreate`

3. A memory allocation operator that allocates memory on the `heap`. `delete`

4. The view

5. It does not generate any code.

Chapter 39 Answers

1. False

2. Text, Graphics, laid out like a form

3. `Serialize()`

4. Because the document is reused in an SDI application when a new file is opened

5. Information about the currently selected font. Call the `GetTextMetrics()` function

Chapter 40 Answers

1. Drag a copy to the dialog from the Control Palette.

2. It will have sizing handles.

3. Through messages

4. `DoModal`

ASCII and Extended ASCII Codes

ASCII (American Standard Code for Information Interchange) is a widely used standard that defines numeric values for a common set of alphabetic characters. The first 32 characters are reserved for formatting and hardware control codes. Following these codes are 96 "printable" characters. IBM defined symbols for the final 128 ASCII values when it released the IBM PC, and referred to the additional characters as *Extended ASCII codes.* This entire set of 256 characters is often referred to as the PC-8 character set, or code page 437.

Dec X_{10}	Hex X_{16}	Binary X_2	ASCII Character	Ctrl	Key
000	00	0000 0000	null	NUL	^@
001	01	0000 0001	☺	SOH	^A
002	02	0000 0010	●	STX	^B
003	03	0000 0011	♥	ETX	^C
004	04	0000 0100	◆	EOT	^D
005	05	0000 0101	♣	ENQ	^E
006	06	0000 0110	♠	ACK	^F
007	07	0000 0111	●	BEL	^G
008	08	0000 1000	■	BS	^H
009	09	0000 1001	○	HT	^I

Dec X_{10}	Hex X_{16}	Binary X_2	ASCII Character	Ctrl	Key
010	0A	0000 1010	■	LF	^J
011	0B	0000 1011	♂	VT	^K
012	0C	0000 1100	♀	FF	^L
013	0D	0000 1101	♪	CR	^M
014	0E	0000 1110	♪♪	SO	^N
015	0F	0000 1111	☼	SI	^O
016	10	0001 0000	►	DLE	^P
017	11	0001 0001	◄	DC1	^Q
018	12	0001 0010	↕	DC2	^R
019	13	0001 0011	‼	DC3	^S
020	14	0001 0100	¶	DC4	^T
021	15	0001 0101	§	NAK	^U
022	16	0001 0110	–	SYN	^V
023	17	0001 0111	↨	ETB	^W
024	18	0001 1000	↑	CAN	^X
025	19	0001 1001	↓	EM	^Y
026	1A	0001 1010	→	SUB	^Z
027	1B	0001 1011	←	ESC	^[
028	1C	0001 1100	∟	FS	^\
029	1D	0001 1101	↔	GS	^]
030	1E	0001 1110	▲	RS	^^
031	1F	0001 1111	▼	US	^_
032	20	0010 0000	Space		
033	21	0010 0001	!		
034	22	0010 0010	"		
035	23	0010 0011	#		
036	24	0010 0100	$		
037	25	0010 0101	%		
038	26	0010 0110	&		
039	27	0010 0111	'		
040	28	0010 1000	(		
041	29	0010 1001	)		

Dec X_{10}	Hex X_{16}	Binary X_2	ASCII Character
042	2A	0010 1010	*
043	2B	0010 1011	+
044	2C	0010 1100	,
045	2D	0010 1101	-
046	2E	0010 1110	.
047	2F	0010 1111	/
048	30	0011 0000	0
049	31	0011 0001	1
050	32	0011 0010	2
051	33	0011 0011	3
052	34	0011 0100	4
053	35	0011 0101	5
054	36	0011 0110	6
055	37	0011 0111	7
056	38	0011 1000	8
057	39	0011 1001	9
058	3A	0011 1010	:
059	3B	0011 1011	;
060	3C	0011 1100	<
061	3D	0011 1101	=
062	3E	0011 1110	>
063	3F	0011 1111	?
064	40	0100 0000	@
065	41	0100 0001	A
066	42	0100 0010	B
067	43	0100 0011	C
068	44	0100 0100	D
069	45	0100 0101	E
070	46	0100 0110	F
071	47	0100 0111	G
072	48	0100 1000	H
073	49	0100 1001	I

Dec X_{10}	Hex X_{16}	Binary X_2	ASCII Character
074	4A	0100 1010	J
075	4B	0100 1011	K
076	4C	0100 1100	L
077	4D	0100 1101	M
078	4E	0100 1110	N
079	4F	0100 1111	O
080	50	0101 0000	P
081	51	0101 0001	Q
082	52	0101 0010	R
083	53	0101 0011	S
084	54	0101 0100	T
085	55	0101 0101	U
086	56	0101 0110	V
087	57	0101 0111	W
088	58	0101 1000	X
089	59	0101 1001	Y
090	5A	0101 1010	Z
091	5B	0101 1011	[
092	5C	0101 1100	\
093	5D	0101 1101	]
094	5E	0101 1110	^
095	5F	0101 1111	–
096	60	0110 0000	`
097	61	0110 0001	a
098	62	0110 0010	b
099	63	0110 0011	c
100	64	0110 0100	d
101	65	0110 0101	e
102	66	0110 0110	f
103	67	0110 0111	g
104	68	0110 1000	h
105	69	0110 1001	i

Dec X_{10}	Hex X_{16}	Binary X_2	ASCII Character
106	6A	0110 1010	j
107	6B	0110 1011	k
108	6C	0110 1100	l
109	6D	0110 1101	m
110	6E	0110 1110	n
111	6F	0110 1111	o
112	70	0111 0000	p
113	71	0111 0001	q
114	72	0111 0010	r
115	73	0111 0011	s
116	74	0111 0100	t
117	75	0111 0101	u
118	76	0111 0110	v
119	77	0111 0111	w
120	78	0111 1000	x
121	79	0111 1001	y
122	7A	0111 1010	z
123	7B	0111 1011	{
124	7C	0111 1100	¦
125	7D	0111 1101	}
126	7E	0111 1110	~
127	7F	0111 1111	Delete
128	80	1000 0000	Ç
129	81	1000 0001	ü
130	82	1000 0010	é
131	83	1000 0011	â
132	84	1000 0100	ä
133	85	1000 0101	à
134	86	1000 0110	å
135	87	1000 0111	ç
136	88	1000 1000	ê
137	89	1000 1001	ë

Dec X_{10}	Hex X_{16}	Binary X_2	ASCII Character
138	8A	1000 1010	è
139	8B	1000 1011	ï
140	8C	1000 1100	î
141	8D	1000 1101	ì
142	8E	1000 1110	Ä
143	8F	1000 1111	Å
144	90	1001 0000	É
145	91	1001 0001	æ
146	92	1001 0010	Æ
147	93	1001 0011	ô
148	94	1001 0100	ö
149	95	1001 0101	ò
150	96	1001 0110	û
151	97	1001 0111	ù
152	98	1001 1000	ÿ
153	99	1001 1001	Ö
154	9A	1001 1010	Ü
155	9B	1001 1011	¢
156	9C	1001 1100	£
157	9D	1001 1101	¥
158	9E	1001 1110	P$_t$
159	9F	1001 1111	ƒ
160	A0	1010 0000	á
161	A1	1010 0001	í
162	A2	1010 0010	ó
163	A3	1010 0011	ú
164	A4	1010 0100	ñ
165	A5	1010 0101	Ñ
166	A6	1010 0110	a̲
167	A7	1010 0111	o̲
168	A8	1010 1000	¿
169	A9	1010 1001	⌐

Dec X_{10}	Hex X_{16}	Binary X_2	ASCII Character
170	AA	1010 1010	⌐
171	AB	1010 1011	½
172	AC	1010 1100	¼
173	AD	1010 1101	¡
174	AE	1010 1110	«
175	AF	1010 1111	»
176	B0	1011 0000	▒
177	B1	1011 0001	▓
178	B2	1011 0010	█
179	B3	1011 0011	│
180	B4	1011 0100	┤
181	B5	1011 0101	╡
182	B6	1011 0110	╢
183	B7	1011 0111	╖
184	B8	1011 1000	╕
185	B9	1011 1001	╣
186	BA	1011 1010	║
187	BB	1011 1011	╗
188	BC	1011 1100	╝
189	BD	1011 1101	╜
190	BE	1011 1110	╛
191	BF	1011 1111	┐
192	C0	1100 0000	└
193	C1	1100 0001	┴
194	C2	1100 0010	┬
195	C3	1100 0011	├
196	C4	1100 0100	─
197	C5	1100 0101	┼
198	C6	1100 0110	╞
199	C7	1100 0111	╟
200	C8	1100 1000	╚
201	C9	1100 1001	╔

Dec X_{10}	Hex X_{16}	Binary X_2	ASCII Character
202	CA	1100 1010	⊥
203	CB	1100 1011	⊤
204	CC	1100 1100	⊩
205	CD	1100 1101	=
206	CE	1100 1110	╬
207	CF	1100 1111	⊥
208	D0	1101 0000	⊥
209	D1	1101 0001	⊤
210	D2	1101 0010	⊓
211	D3	1101 0011	⊔
212	D4	1101 0100	⊢
213	D5	1101 0101	⌐
214	D6	1101 0110	⊓
215	D7	1101 0111	╫
216	D8	1101 1000	╪
217	D9	1101 1001	⌐
218	DA	1101 1010	⌐
219	DB	1101 1011	█
220	DC	1101 1100	▄
221	DD	1101 1101	▌
222	DE	1101 1110	▐
223	DF	1101 1111	▀
224	E0	1110 0000	α
225	E1	1110 0001	β
226	E2	1110 0010	Γ
227	E3	1110 0011	π
228	E4	1110 0100	Σ
229	E5	1110 0101	σ
230	E6	1110 0110	μ

Dec X_{10}	Hex X_{16}	Binary X_2	ASCII Character
231	E7	1110 0111	τ
232	E8	1110 1000	Φ
233	E9	1110 1001	θ
234	EA	1110 1010	Ω
235	EB	1110 1011	δ
236	EC	1110 1100	∞
237	ED	1110 1101	ø
238	EE	1110 1110	∈
239	EF	1110 1111	∩
240	F0	1111 0000	≡
241	F1	1111 0001	±
242	F2	1111 0010	≥
243	F3	1111 0011	≤
244	F4	1111 0100	⌠
245	F5	1111 0101	⌡
246	F6	1111 0110	÷
247	F7	1111 0111	≈
248	F8	1111 1000	°
249	F9	1111 1001	•
250	FA	1111 1010	·
251	FB	1111 1011	√
252	FC	1111 1100	η
253	FD	1111 1101	²
254	FE	1111 1110	■
255	FF	1111 1111	

C++ Precedence Table

Precedence

Level	Symbol	Description	Associativity
1	++	Prefix increment	Left to right
	—	Prefix decrement	
	( )	Function call and subexpression	
	[ ]	Array subscript	
	->	Structure pointer	
	.	Structure member	
2	!	Logical negation	Right to left
	~	1's complement	
	-	Unary negation	
	+	Unary plus	
	(type)	Type cast	Type cast
	*	Pointer dereference	
	&	Address of	
	sizeof	Size of	Size of

continues

Precedence

Level	Symbol	Description	Associativity
3	*	Multiplication	Left to right
	/	Division	
	%	Modulus (int remainder)	
4	+	Addition	Left to right
	-	Subtraction	
5	<<	Bitwise left shift	Left to right
	>>	Bitwise right shift	
6	<	Less than	Left to right
	<=	Less than or equal to	
	>	Greater than	
	>=	Greater than or equal to	
7	==	Equal test	Left to right
	!=	Not equal test	
8	&	Bitwise AND	Left to right
9	^	Bitwise exclusive OR	Left to right
10	¦	Bitwise inclusive OR	Left to right
11	&&	Logical AND	Left to right
12	¦¦	Logical inclusive OR	Left to right
13	?:	Conditional test	Right to left
14	=	Assignment	Right to left
	+=	Compound add	
	-+	Compound subtract	
	*=	Compound multiply	
	/=	Compound divide	
	%=	Compound modulus	
	<<=	Compound bitwise left shift	
	>>=	Compound bitwise right shift	
	&=	Compound bitwise AND	
	^=	Compound bitwise exclusive OR	
	¦=	Compound bitwise inclusive OR	
15	,	Sequence point	Left to right
	++	Postfix increment	
	—	Postfix decrement	

Glossary

accelerator keys In Windows, a special key combination that invokes a menu action without having to select the menu.

access specifier A keyword used in a class definition that determines whether or not a member of the class is accessable by users of the class.

address Each memory (RAM) location (each byte) has a unique address. The first address in memory is 0, the second address is 1, and so on, until the last address (which comes thousands of bytes later).

argument The value sent *to* a function or procedure. This can be either a constant or a variable and is enclosed in parentheses.

array A list of variables, sometimes called a table of variables.

ASCII Acronym for *American Standard Code for Information Interchange.*

ASCII file A file containing characters that can be used by any program on most computers. Sometimes the file is called a text file or an ASCII text file.

AUTOEXEC.BAT A batch file in PCs that executes a series of commands whenever you start or reset the computer.

automatic variable A variable which is erased when the block in which it was declared ends. All local variables are automatic by default.

backup file A duplicate copy of a file that preserves your work in case you damage the original file. Files on a hard disk are commonly backed up onto floppy disks or tapes.

base class A class from which another class, or classes, have been derived. Sometimes known as the parent class.

binary A numbering system based on only two digits. The only valid digits in a binary system are 0 and 1. See also *bit*.

binary zero Another name for null zero.

bit Binary digit, the smallest unit of storage on a computer. Each bit can have a value of 0 or 1, indicating the absence or presence of an electrical signal. See also *binary*.

bitwise operators C++ operators that manipulate the binary representation of values.

block Two or more statements treated as though they are a single statement. A block is always enclosed in braces ({ }).

boot To start a computer with the operating system software in place. You must boot your computer before using it.

bubble sort A type of sorting routine.

bug An error in a program that prevents it from running correctly. Originated when a moth short-circuited a connection in one of the first computers, preventing the computer from working!

byte A basic unit of data storage and manipulation. A byte is equivalent to 8 bits and can contain a value ranging from 0 through 255.

called function A function controlled by, or called by, another function. A called function may also receive parameters from the function which called it.

calling function A function that calls to other functions. A calling function may also pass parameters to the functions it calls.

cathode ray tube (CRT) The television-like screen, also called the *monitor*. It is one place to which the output of the computer can be sent.

central processing unit (CPU) The controlling circuit responsible for operations within the computer. These operations generally include system timing, logical processing, and logical operations. The central processing unit controls every operation of the computer system. On PCs, the central processing unit is called a microprocessor and is stored on a single integrated circuit chip.

class A unit of related information and functions containing one or more members and functions that act on those members. See also *structure*.

class implementation The actual code for the member functions of a class.

class interface The definition of a class which specifies the member variable names, member function prototypes, access specifiers, and base class, if any.

client area In Windows, the art of a window where output is displayed to the user. See also, *non client area*.

code A set of instructions written in a programming language. See *source code*.

compile Process of translating a program written in a programming language such as C++ into machine code that your computer understands.

concatenation The process of attaching one string to the end of another or combining two or more strings into a longer string.

conditional loop A series of C++ instructions that occurs a fixed number of times.

constant Data that remains the same during a program run.

constructor The function executed when the program declares an instance of a class.

CPU See *central processing unit*.

CRT See *cathode ray tube*.

data Information stored in the computer as numbers, letters, and special symbols such as punctuation marks. Data also refers to the characters you input into your program so that it can produce meaningful information.

data member A data component of a class or structure.

data processing This is what computers really do. They take data and manipulate it into meaningful output, which is called *information*.

data validation The process of testing the values input into a program—for instance, testing for a negative number when you know the input cannot be negative, or ensuring that a number is within a certain range.

debug Process of locating an error (bug) in a program and removing it.

declaration A statement that declares the existence of a data object or function. A declaration reserves memory.

default A predefined action or command that the computer chooses unless you specify otherwise.

definition A statement that defines the format of a data object or function. A definition reserves no memory.

demodulate To convert an analog signal into a digital signal for use by a computer. See also *modulate*.

dereference The process of finding a value pointed to by a pointer variable.

derived class A class that has inherited all or part of its interface and functionality from another class. See also *base class*.

destructor The function called when a class instance goes out of scope.

digital computer A computer that operates on binary (on and off) digital impulses of electricity.

directory A list of files stored on a disk. Directories within existing directories are called subdirectories.

disk A round, flat magnetic storage medium. Floppy disks are made of flexible material enclosed in 5 1/4-inch or 3 1/2-inch protective cases. Hard disks consist of a stack of rigid disks housed in a single unit. A disk is sometimes called *external memory*. Disk storage is nonvolatile. When you turn off your computer, the disk's contents do not go away.

disk drive Device that reads and writes data to a floppy or hard disk.

diskette Another name for a removable floppy disk.

display A screen or monitor.

display adapter Located in the system unit, the display adapter determines the amount of *resolution* and the possible number of colors on the screen.

DOS Acronym for *Disk Operating System*.

dot-matrix printer One of the two most common PC printers. (The *laser* printer is the other.) A dot-matrix printer is inexpensive and fast; it uses a series of small dots to represent printed text and graphics.

element An individual variable in an array.

execute To run a program.

expanded memory RAM that is above and beyond the standard 640K. It is accessed with special software and can be copied in and out of memory below 1M. Expanded memory can be obtained through special hardware or through emulation by extended memory drives.

extended memory RAM that is above and beyond the standard 640K. It is accessed with special software and is found only on PCs with 80286, 80386, and 80486 microprocessors.

external modem A modem that sits in a box outside your computer. See also *internal modem*.

file A collection of data stored as a single unit on a floppy or hard disk. A file always has a filename that identifies it.

file extension Used by PCs and consists of a period followed by one to three characters. The file extension follows the filename.

filename A unique name that identifies a file. Filenames can contain up to eight characters and may have a period followed by an extension (usually three characters long).

fixed disk See *hard disk*.

fixed-length record Each of this record's fields takes the same amount of disk space, even if that field's data value does not fill the field.

floppy disk See *disk*.

format Process of creating on the disk a "map" that tells the operating system how the disk is structured. This is how the operating system keeps track of where files are stored.

function A self-contained coding segment designed to do a specific task. All C++ programs must have at least one function called `main()`. Some functions are library routines that manipulate numbers, strings, and output.

function keys The keys labeled F1 through F12 (some keyboards go to F10 only).

global variable A variable that can be seen from (and used by) every statement in the program.

hard copy The printout of a program (or its output); also a safe backup copy for a program in case the disk is erased.

hard disk Sometimes called a *fixed disk*, they hold much more data and are many times faster than floppy disks. See also *disk*.

hardware The physical parts of the machine. Hardware has been defined as "anything you can kick" and consists of the things you can see.

header file A text file which usually contains information about function prototypes, class definitions, or constant definitions used in a program. Header files are used by employing the `#include` preprocessor directive. By convention, header file names end with an extension of `.H`.

hexadecimal A numbering system based on 16 elements. Digits are numbered 0 through F (0, 1, 2, 3, 4, 5, 6, 7, 8, 9, A, B, C, D, E, and F).

hierarchy of operators See *order of operators*.

indeterminate loop Unlike the `for` loop, a loop whose number of cycles is not known in advance.

infinite loop The never-ending repetition of a block of C++ statements.

information The meaningful product from a program. Data goes *into* a program to produce meaningful output (information).

inline function A function that compiles as inline code each time the function is called.

input The entry of data into a computer through a device such as the keyboard.

input-process-output This model is the foundation of everything that happens in your computer. Data is input, it is then processed by your program in the computer, and finally information is output.

I/O Acronym for *Input/Output*.

instance In OOP, a variable, usually of a class type.

integer variable A variable that can hold an integer.

internal modem A modem that resides inside the system unit. See also *external modem*.

iteration The process of going through a collection in order, usually one element at a time.

kilobyte (K) A unit of measurement that is 1,024 bytes.

laser printer A type of printer that is generally faster than a dot-matrix printer. Laser printer output is much sharper than that of a dot-matrix printer because a laser beam actually burns toner ink into the paper. Laser printers are more expensive than dot-matrix printers.

least significant bit The rightmost bit of a byte. For example, a binary 00000111 would have a 1 as the least significant bit.

line printer Another name for your printer.

local variable A variable that can be seen from (and used by) only the block in which it is defined.

loop The repeated execution of one or more statements.

machine language The series of binary digits that a microprocessor executes to perform individual tasks. People seldom, if ever, program in machine language. Instead, they program in assembly language, and an assembler translates their instructions into machine language.

main module The first function of a modular program, called `main()`, which controls the execution of the other functions.

maintainability The computer industry's word for the ability to change and update programs that were written in a simple style.

manipulator A value used by a program to tell the stream to modify one of its modes.

math operator A symbol used for addition, subtraction, multiplication, division, or other calculations.

megabyte (M) A unit of measurement that is approximately a million bytes (1,048,576 bytes).

member A piece of a structure variable that holds a specific type of data, or a piece of a class variable that holds a specific type of data, or a class variable function acting on class data.

member function A function of a class. Sometimes called a *method*.

memory Storage area inside the computer, used to store data temporarily. The computer's memory is erased when the power is turned off.

menu A list of commands or instructions displayed on the screen. A menu organizes commands and makes a program easier to use.

menu-driven Describes a program that provides menus for choosing commands.

method See *member function*.

microchip A small wafer of silicon that holds computer components and occupies less space than a postage stamp.

microcomputer A small computer, such as a PC, that can fit on a desktop. The microchip is the heart of the microcomputer. Microcomputers are much less expensive than their larger counterparts.

microprocessor The chip that does the calculations for PCs. Sometimes this chip is called the central processing unit (CPU).

modem A piece of hardward that modulates and demodulates signals so that your computer can communicate with other computers over telephone lines. See also *external modem* and *internal modem*.

modular programming The process of writing your programs in several modules rather than as one long program. By breaking a program into several smaller program-like routines, you can isolate problems better, write correct programs faster, and produce programs that are easier to maintain.

modulate Before your computer can transmit data over a telephone line, the information to be sent must be converted (modulated) into analog signals. See also *demodulate*.

modulus The integer remainder of division.

monitor A television-like screen that lets the computer display information. The monotor is an output device.

mouse A hand-held device that you move across the desktop to move a corresponding indicator, called a mouse pointer, across the screen. Used instead of the keyboard to select and move items (such as text or graphics), execute commands, and perform other tasks.

MS-DOS An operating system for IBM and compatible PCs.

multidimensional array An array with more than one dimension. Two-dimensional arrays are sometimes called tables or matrices, which have rows and columns.

nested loop A loop within a loop.

non client area In Windows, the border of a window, including the title bar, system menu, and minimize and maximize buttons.

null string An empty string whose first character is the null zero and whose length is zero.

null zero The string-terminating character. All C++ string constants and strings stored in character arrays end in null zero. The ASCII value for the null zero is 0.

numeric functions Library routines that work with numbers.

object code A "halfway step" between source code and executable machine language. Object code consists mostly of machine language but is not directly executable by the computer. Such code must first be linked in order to resolve external references and address references.

operator An operator works on data and might perform math calculations or change data to other data types. Examples include +, -, and `sizeof()`.

operator overloading A feature of C++ that allows most operators to be redefined so that they work on different types of data than their original definitions, or perform a different operation than their original implementation.

order of operators Sometimes called the *hierarchy of operators* or the *precedence of operators*, this order determines exactly how C++ computes formulas.

output device The device where the results of a program are output, such as the screen, the printer, or a disk file.

parallel arrays Two arrays working side by side. Each element in each array corresponds to an element in the other array.

parallel port A connector used to plug a device, such as a printer, into the computer. Transferring data through a parallel port is much faster than through a serial port.

parameter A list of variables enclosed in parentheses that follow the name of a function or procedure. Parameters indicate the number and type of arguments that will be sent to the function or procedure.

parent class See *base class*.

passing by address Also called *passing by reference*. When an argument (a local variable) is passed by address, the variable's address in memory is sent to and assigned to the receiving function's parameter list. (If more than one variable is passed by address, each variable's address is sent to and assigned to the receiving function's parameters.) A change made to the parameter within the function will also change the value of the argument variable.

passing by copy Another name for *passing by value*.

Passing by reference Another name for *passing by address*.

passing by value By default, all C++ variable arguments are passed *by address*. When the value contained in a variable is passed to the parameter list of a receiving function, changes made to the parameter within the routine will *not* change the value of the argument variable. Also called *passing by copy*.

path The route that the computer "travels" from the root directory to any subdirectories when locating a file. The path refers also to the subdirectories that MS-DOS examines when you type a command that requires the operating system to find and access a file.

peripheral A device attached to the computer, such as a modem, disk drive, mouse, or printer.

persistent objects Objects which can be saved to and restored from disk or other permanent storage. See also, *serialization*.

personal computer A microcomputer that is sometimes called a PC, which stands for *p*ersonal *c*omputer.

pointer A variable that holds the address of another variable.

precedence of operators See *order of operators*.

preprocessor directive A command, preceded by a #, that you place in your source code to direct the compiler to modify the source code in some way. The two most common preprocessor directives are #define and #include.

printer A device that prints data from the computer to paper.

private class member A class member that is inaccessible except to the class's member functions.

program A group of instructions that tells the computer what to do.

programming language A set of rules for writing instructions for the computer. Popular programming languages include BASIC, C, Visual Basic, C, C++, and Pascal.

prototype The definition of a function. The prototype includes the function's name, return type, and parameter list.

public class member A class member that is accessible to any functions.

RAM Acronym for Random-Access Memory. See *random access memory*.

random-access file A file in which records can be accessed in any order you want.

random-access memory (RAM) What your computer uses to store data and programs temporarily. RAM is measured in kilobytes and megabytes. Generally, the more RAM a computer has, the more powerful programs it can run.

read-only memory (ROM) A permanent type of computer memory. It contains the BIOS (*Basic Input/Output System*), a special chip used to provide instructions to the computer when you turn it on.

real numbers Numbers that have decimal points and a fractional part to the right of the decimal.

record An individual row in a file.

relational operators Operators that compare data, telling how two variables or constants relate to each other. Relational operators can tell whether two variables are equal or not equal, or which variable is less than or more than the other.

ROM Acronym for Read-Only Memory. See *read-only memory*.

scientific notation A shortcut method of representing numbers of extreme values.

sectors A pattern of pie-shaped wedges on a disk. Formatting creates a pattern of tracks and sectors where your data and programs are stored.

sequential file A file that has to be accessed one record at a time, beginning with the first record.

serial port A connector used to plug in serial devices, such as a modem or mouse.

serialization A Microsoft foundation Class technique for saving and restoring objects to and from disk files.

single-dimensional array An array that has only one subscript. A single-dimensional array represents a list of values.

software The data and programs that interact with your hardware. The C++ language is an example of software.

sorting A method of putting data in a specific order (such as alphabetical or numerical order), even if that order is not the same order in which the elements were entered.

source code The C++ language instructions, written by humans, that the C++ compiler translates into object code.

spaghetti code Term used when there are too many gotos in a program. If a program branches all over the place, it is difficult to follow, and trying to follow the logic resembles a "bowl of spaghetti."

static variable A variable which is not erased, but which retains its value, when its block ends. All global variables are static by default. Local variables must be explicitly declared static.

stream A stream of characters, one following another, flowing between devices in the computer.

string constant One or more groups of characters that end in a null zero.

string literal Another name for a *string constant*.

structure A unit of related information containing one or more members, such as an employee number, employee name, employee address, employee pay rate, and so on. See also *class*.

subscript A number inside brackets that differentiates one element of an array from another element.

syntax error An error that is the result of an incorrect statement in the code.

system unit The large box component of the computer. The system unit houses the PC's microchip (the CPU).

TLA *Three Letter Acronym.*

tracks A pattern of paths on a disk. Formatting creates a pattern of tracks and sectors where your data and programs are stored.

truncation The fractional part of a number (the part of the number to the right of the decimal point) is taken off the number. No rounding is done.

two's complement A method your computer uses to take the negative of a number. This method, when used with addition, allows the computer to simulate subtraction.

unary operator The addition or subtraction operator used before a single variable or constant.

user-friendliness A program is user-friendly if it makes the user comfortable and simulates what the user is already familiar with.

variable Data that can change as the program runs.

variable-length records This record's fields take up no wasted space on the disk. As soon as a field's data value is saved to the file, the next field's data value is stored immediately after it. There is usually a special separating character between the fields so that your program knows where the fields begin and end.

variable scope Sometimes called the *visibility of variables*, this describes how variables are "seen" by your program. See also *global variable* and *local variable*.

visibility See *access specifier*.

volatile Temporary. For example, when you turn the computer off, all the RAM is erased.

word In PC usage, two consecutive bytes (16 bits) of data.

Index

E

early exit example program, 289
Edit command (Project menu), 697
Edit pull-down menu, 19
editing
  menus (Menu Editor), 723
  Properties window (Dialog
    Editor), 716
  resource files, 712
  schema number,
    IMPLEMENT_SERIAL macro,
    696
  view class definitions, header files,
    703-704
editors
  Dialog Editor, 712-713
  Menu Editor, 712, 723
  programming, 30
  resource editor, 712
elements in arrays, 80, 784
  CStringArray, 643
  initializing, 424-434
  inputting into structures, 536
  internal locations, 489
  multidimensional arrays, 461
  out-of-range, 423
  printing with cout function, 420
  referencing with subscript
    formulas, 421
  reserving for exemptions, 423
  subscripts, 81
  variable subscripts, 420
  zeroing-out, 425-426
ellipsis in dialog boxes, 22
else statements, 165-169
encapsulation in OOP, 653-655
#endif preprocessor directive, 686
endless loops (infinite loops), 292
enhancing MFC applications, 692
entering fields, Add Class dialog
  box, 720
environment variables, error-level,
  227

environments
  message-driven, Windows, 662
  QuickWin, 39
  Visual C++, 15
equal sign (=) assignment
  operator, 51, 63
equal to relational operator, ==
  (double equal sign), 154
erasing arrays, 352
error messages, #define statements, 104
error-handling classes, 668
error-level environment variable,
  227
errors
  checking with after open( )
    function, 558
  program code, 37
  syntax, 791
Esc key, removing displayed
  menus, 20
escape sequences characters
  \ (backslash), 74
  \t (tab), 76
evaluating relational results, 155
even/odd number printing
  program, 250
examples
  program in Visual C++, 34-36
  string constant lengths, 72
  variable values, 64-66
  variables, 59-60
exclusive bitwise OR operator, 201
EXE file extension, 34
executable statements, semicolons
  (;), 308
executing programs, 31, 784
exemptions, reserving elements for
  in arrays, 423
Exit command (File menu), 26
exit( ) function, 227-232

W

Order Your Program Disk Today!

You can save yourself hours of tedious, error-prone typing by ordering the companion disk to *Visual C++ 1.5 By Example*. This disk contains the source code for all the programs in the book.

Samples include all example code for testing all the Visual C++ material. You can see how to perform keyboard and screen control, file I/O, control construct statements, structures, pointers, and much more, giving you approximately 200 programs to help you master Visual C++. With the disk, you'll be able to concentrate better on the book's training. Each disk is only $15.00 (U.S. currency only). Foreign orders must enclose an extra $5 to cover additional postage and handling. Disks are only available in 3 1/2-inch format.

Just provide the following information with your check or postal money order to:

Greg Perry
Dept. VCBE
P.O. Box 35752
Tulsa, OK 74153-0752

Please **print** the following information:

Number of disks: _____ @ $15.00 (U.S. Dollars) = _____

Name: _____

Address: _____

City: _____ State: _____ ZIP: _____

Foreign orders should use a separate page if needed to give your exact address in the format required by your postal service.

Make checks and postal money orders payable to: **Greg Perry**. Sorry, but we cannot accept credit cards, checks drawn on a non-U.S. bank, phone orders, or purchase orders. Please do not staple your check to the order form.

(This offer is made by the author, not by Que Publishing.)